Endorsements for
A Theology of James, Peter, and Jude

A clear, thorough work from an eminent scholar of the General Epistles, *A Theology of James, Peter, and Jude* is sure to be a valuable resource for the classroom.

> Karen H. Jobes, Gerald F. Hawthorne Professor of New Testament Greek & Exegesis,
> Wheaton College and Graduate School

When Peter Davids writes a book, it gets my attention. *A Theology of James, Peter, and Jude* is no exception and represents Davids at his best. After devoting four decades to the study of the General Epistles, Peter Davids is uniquely qualified to write this volume. He engages the most recent scholarship and examines the texts in their Greco-Roman context and from an eschatological perspective. His clarity of thought and writing style combine to make this a valuable resource for professors, pastors, seminarians, and Bible teachers.

> R. Alan Streett, Senior Research Professor of Biblical Exegesis,
> W. A. Criswell Endowed Chair of Expository Preaching, Criswell College

With key commentaries on James, the two epistles of Peter, and Jude under his belt, there are few scholars in the arena better equipped than Peter Davids to tackle a theology of these central texts in the Catholic collection. Davids is clear, comprehensive, and cogent as he helps us hear the heartbeat of books often neglected in church and curriculum.

> Gene L. Green, Professor of New Testament,
> Wheaton College and Graduate School

While James, Jude, and Peter are often left standing in the hallway when the theology of the New Testament is being discussed, Peter Davids shows us how meaningful their voices can be when they are invited to fully participate in the dialogue. As he places these books within their original streams in early Christianity and the broader river of God's salvific work in Jesus Christ, Davids shows us how richly they contribute to our theological understanding. By freeing these books from the rigid scales of systematic theology, Davids allows them to have their own solos within the choir of biblical theology.

> Duane F. Watson, Professor of New Testament Studies,
> Malone University, Canton, Ohio

For forty years Peter Davids has labored lovingly over the Catholic Epistles; now he offers us the mature fruit of that labor. He delivers what the series promises: a rich theological reading of James, Peter, and Jude grounded in exegesis and well informed by the best in recent scholarship. If you want to know how to do biblical theology, look no further.

> David B. Capes, Thomas Nelson Research Professor,
> Houston Baptist University

Living in the Light of the Coming King

A THEOLOGY OF JAMES, PETER, AND JUDE

BIBLICAL THEOLOGY OF THE NEW TESTAMENT

PETER H. DAVIDS

ANDREAS J. KÖSTENBERGER, GENERAL EDITOR

ZONDERVAN

A Theology of James, Peter, and Jude
Copyright © 2014 by Peter H. Davids

This title is also available as a Zondervan ebook. Visit www.zondervan.com/ebooks.

Requests for information should be addressed to:

Zondervan, 3900 *Sparks Dr., Grand Rapids, Michigan 49546*

Library of Congress Cataloging-in-Publication Data

Davids, Peter H.
    A theology of James, Peter, and Jude / Peter H. Davids.
       pages cm. — (Biblical theology of the New Testament ; volume 6)
    Includes bibliographical references and index.
    ISBN 978-0-310-29147-3 (hardcover printed : alk. paper) 1. Bible. Catholic epistles — Theology. I. Title.
BS2777.D38 2014
227'.906 — dc23
                                                                 2014003049

Cover photography: Bridgeman Art Library
Interior design: Matthew Van Zomeren

Printed in the United States of America

16 17 18 19 20 /DCI/ 22 21 20 19 18 17 16 15 14 13 12 11 10 9 8 7 6 5 4 3 2

In memoriam Ralph P. Martin (1925–2013)

Careful Mentor, Beloved Colleague, Gracious Example

His contribution to the field of this work was significant (as the bibliography only shows in part), but his contribution to scholarship in general and to the lives of those who knew him was even more significant. May this work be a small, if inadequate, example of the type of contribution to God, to God's church, and to scholarship that flowed from him. It is sad that he did not live to see this, read it, and receive our gratitude in person.

Contents

Contents (Detailed)

CHAPTER 3

Series Preface

The Biblical Theology of the New Testament series consists of eight distinct volumes covering the entire New Testament. Each volume is devoted to an in-depth exploration of a given New Testament writing, or group of writings, within the context of the theology of the New Testament, and ultimately of the entire Bible. While each corpus requires an approach that is suitable for the writing(s) studied, all volumes include:

(1) a survey of recent scholarship and of the state of research
(2) a treatment of the relevant introductory issues
(3) a thematic commentary following the narrative flow of the document(s)
(4) a treatment of important individual themes
(5) discussions of the relationship between a particular writing and the rest of the New Testament and the Bible

While Biblical Theology is a relatively new academic discipline and one that has often been hindered by questionable presuppositions, doubtful methodology, and/or flawed execution, the field is one of the most promising avenues of biblical and theological research today. In essence, Biblical Theology engages in the study of the biblical texts while giving careful consideration to the historical setting in which a given piece of writing originated. It seeks to locate and relate the contributions of the respective biblical documents along the lines of the continuum of God's salvation-historical program centered in the coming and salvific work of Christ. It also endeavors to ground the theological exploration of a given document in a close reading of the respective text(s), whether narrative, discourse, or some other type of literature.

By providing in-depth studies of the diverse, yet complementary perspectives of the New Testament writings, the Biblical Theology of the New Testament series aims to make a significant contribution to the study of the major interrelated themes of Scripture in a holistic, context-sensitive, and spiritually nurturing manner. Each volume is written by a scholar who has written a major commentary or monograph on the corpus covered. The generous page allotment allows for an in-depth investigation. While coming from diverse academic backgrounds and institutional affiliations, the contributors share a commitment to an evangelical faith and a respect for the authority of Scripture. They also have in common a conviction that the canon of Scripture is ultimately unified, not contradictory.

In addition to contributing to the study of individual New Testament writings and to the study of the New Testament and ultimately of Scripture as a whole, the series also seeks to make a methodological contribution, showing how Biblical Theology ought to be conducted. In each case, the way in which the volume is conceived reflects careful consideration of the nature of a given piece or body of writings.

The complex interrelationships between the three so-called "Synoptic Gospels"; the two-volume nature of Luke-Acts; the relationship between John's gospel, letters, and the book of Revelation; the thirteen letters making up the Pauline corpus; and the theologies of Peter, James, and Jude, as well as Hebrews, each present unique challenges and opportunities.

In the end, it is hoped that the volumes will pay tribute to the multifaceted nature of divine revelation contained in Scripture. As G. B. Caird put it:

> The question we must ask is not whether these books all say the same thing, but whether they all bear witness to the same Jesus and through him to the many splendoured wisdom of the one God.... We shall neither attempt to press all our witnesses into a single mould nor captiously complain that one seems at some points deficient in comparison with another. What we shall do is rejoice that God has seen fit to establish His gospel at the mouth of so many independent witnesses. The music of the New Testament choir is not written to be sung in unison.[1]

In this spirit, the contributors offer their work as a humble aid to a greater appreciation of the magnificent scriptural symphony of God.

Andreas J. Köstenberger, series editor
Wake Forest, NC

---

1. G. B. Caird, *New Testament Theology*, compl. and ed. L. D. Hurst (Oxford: Clarendon, 1995), 24.

Author's Preface

I finished my first work on one of these General or Catholic Epistles in 1974, in my doctoral thesis on James, if one does not count a paper that I had written four years earlier for Dr. Richard Longenecker, which became the seed for that thesis (a seed that Dr. Longenecker encouraged and continued to encourage with a lifelong friendship, and which Ven. Dr. Stephen S. Smalley guided in its growth into a thesis). Since that time I have written two commentaries on each of the Catholic Epistles, although 2 Peter and Jude were always together in one volume. Some were longer and some were shorter. On top of that I have written numerous articles about these works for journals, books, or Bible dictionaries (one of which, the *Dictionary of the Later New Testament and Its Developments*, I coedited with Ralph P. Martin, an experience I deeply appreciated).

So one might wonder why I would accept the task of writing another work on these four letters. That thought crossed my mind as well when the request came in. But I quickly put it aside, realizing that (1) I had wanted to write a New Testament theology and so this opportunity put me in that field, and (2) I needed to pull together some of the insights I had gained from my work on these books. Furthermore, while I knew I would not be repeating the detailed exegesis that one can do in a commentary, I also realized that my first commentary on James came out in 1982 (having been sent to the publisher in 1980), so it was about thirty years old, and my work on 1 Peter was over twenty years old. My thinking had, I hoped, matured over the years. For instance, I no longer believe that 1 Pet 5:12 refers to the amanuensis of the letter, but rather to the letter carrier. There would also be something new to say by putting these works together with one another.

There are several reasons why these works have come to dominate my career. First, the letter of James draws heavily on the teaching of Jesus, and I am convinced that the teaching of Jesus is foundational for the church. In one sense, James shows us how the teaching of Jesus was used by the first-century movement that Jesus founded (and whose members believed he was still their leader).

Second, the names attached to these biblical works (we will discuss later whether the attributions are accurate) were the biggest leaders in the Jesus movement. Paul was a known but controversial figure in the first century, at least outside the communities he had founded. James was the core leader of the movement, leading the Jerusalem community. Peter ("Rock") was as much as anyone Jesus' designated "successor." Jude was part of Jesus' family in a world in which that counted for something. Even Paul calls two of these men "pillars" (Gal 2:9). So the fact that Paul has tended to dominate because more of his writings were preserved and because the war of 66–70 CE had significantly reduced the influence of the central Jerusalem community seemed to me "unfair," as was Martin Luther's disparaging of James and, to a lesser degree, 2 Peter and Jude. I believe the church, especially the Western church, will be more balanced and healthier if these other voices are given equal respect to Paul (and if both are subordinated to Jesus).

Third, I had the opportunity to write. I had finished my Greek handbook on 2 Peter and Jude (although there would be some further editing to do), I had taken a voluntary unpaid sabbatical from St. Stephen's University in New Brunswick, Canada, to help that school with their economic straights, and while I had church responsibilities as an interim pastor, the church was an hour's drive away (that included crossing the US – Canada border twice), so that participation was limited to Sundays. The first two-thirds of this work was finished in rough draft form during that sabbatical, most of it while living in the town of St. Stephen (in my study in a converted horse stall), the rest while living with my in-laws in Houston. I was able to finish the last third of that first draft during a summer break between terms at Houston Baptist University, using the lovely facilities of the Lanier Theological Library, which not only provided me with the best theological library in Houston, but also gave me (deliberately) something of the English ambiance of my country of doctoral study and of ethnic origin (and of one of my three citizenships). The support of Dr. Charles Mickey and the library staff has been invaluable.

Finally, there is the wider supporting context that allowed me to pull these threads together. The Anglican Parish of Campobello in New Brunswick, Canada, and then All Saints Episcopal Church in Stafford, Texas, gave me the ongoing ministry environment that is important in doing any type of biblical theology that will be useful to the wider church. My daughter and son-in-law, Gwenda and Brent Bilsky, and their three (now four) sons, as well as my wife, gave me the familial context that supported me emotionally and kept me grounded in reality. In St. Stephen we all lived in the same house; during the summer of writing in Houston my daughter was having her fourth son (and almost dying afterward), my wife being in St. Stephen helping and allowing me the freedom to keep writing.

Of course, I am also thankful to Dr. Andreas Köstenberger for inviting me to write this volume and for his editorial help, and to the folk at Zondervan for producing it so well (and for caring for me as a minor Zondervan author over these years — that encouragement is meaningful, if rarely acknowledged). Both have been in the background, but they have not therefore been any less important. Otherwise, I would have been limited to posting a much poorer book (one that I would likely not have dreamed up without Dr. Köstenberger) on my website for no one to read.

Peter H. Davids
Houston, The Feast of the Resurrection, 2013

ABBREVIATIONS

AB	Anchor Bible
ACCS	Ancient Christian Commentary on the Scriptures
ACNT	Augsburg Commentary on the New Testament
AJBI	*Annals of the Japanese Biblical Institute*
AnBib	Analecta biblica
ANTC	Abingdon New Testament Commentary
APOT	*The Apocrypha and Pseudepigrapha of the Old Testament*. Ed. R. H. Charles. 2 vols. Oxford, 1913
AUSS	Andrews University Seminary Studies
BBR	*Bulletin for Biblical Research*
BCBC	Believers Church Bible Commentary
BDAG	Danker, F. W., W. Bauer, W. F. Arndt, and F. W. Gingrich. *Greek-English Lexicon of the New Testament and Other Early Christian Literature*, 3rd ed.
BECNT	Baker Exegetical Commentary on the New Testament
BETL	Bibliotheca ephemeridum theologicarum lovaniensium
BFCT	Beiträge zur Förderung christlicher Theologie
BI	*Biblical Illustrator*
Bib	*Biblica*
BibInt	*Biblical Interpretation*
BibLeb	*Bibel und Leben*
BIS	Biblical Interpretation Series
BK	*Bibel und Kirche*
BNTC	Black's New Testament Commentary = HNTC
BSac	*Bibliotheca sacra*
BTN	Bibliotheca theologica Norvegica
BZ	*Biblische Zeitschrift*
BZNW	Beihefte zur Zeitschrift für die neutestamentliche Wissenschaft
CBQ	*Catholic Biblical Quarterly*
CBSC	Cambridge Bible for Schools and Colleges
CEB	Common English Bible
CEJL	Commentaries on Early Jewish Literature
CGTSC	Cambridge Greek Testament for Schools and Colleges
ConBNT	Coniectanea biblica: NT Series
CTJ	*Calvin Theological Journal*
DLNT	*Dictionary of the Later New Testament and Its Developments*. Ed. Ralph P. Martin and Peter H. Davids
EKKNT	Evangelisch-katholischer Kommentar zum Neuen Testament
ErbAuf	*Erbe und Auftrag*

ErfTSt	Erfurter theologische Studien
EstEcl	*Estudios eclesiásticos*
ESV	English Standard Version
ET	English translation
ETR	*Études théologiques et religieuses*
EvQ	*Evangelical Quarterly*
Exp	*Expositor*
ExpTim	*Expository Times*
GTJ	*Grace Theological Journal*
HNT	Handbuch zum Neuen Testament
HNTC	Harper's New Testament Commentary = BNTC
HTKNT	Herders theologischer Kommentar zum Neuen Testament
HTR	*Harvard Theological Review*
ICC	International Critical Commentary
Int	*Interpretation*
JBL	*Journal of Biblical Literature*
JETS	*Journal of the Evangelical Theological Society*
JNES	*Journal of Near Eastern Studies*
JSJ	*Journal for the Study of Judaism in the Persian, Hellenistic, and Roman Periods*
JSNT	*Journal for the Study of the New Testament*
JSNTSup	Supplements to the Journal for the Study of the New Testament
JSOT	*Journal for the Study of the Old Testament*
JTS	*Journal of Theological Studies*
KD	*Kerygma und Dogma*
KEK	Kritisch-exegetischer Kommentar über das Neue Testament (Meyer-Kommentar)
LNTS	Library of New Testament Studies
MHT	James H. Moulton, Wilbert F. Howard, and Nigel Turner, *A Grammar of New Testament Greek*
MNTC	Moffatt New Testament Commentary
MSGVK	Mitteilung der schlesischen Gesellschaft für Volkskunde
NAC	New American Commentary
NASB	New American Standard Bible
NCB	New Century Bible
Neot	*Neotestamentica*
NIBC	New International Biblical Commentary
NICNT	New International Commentary on the New Testament
NIDNTT	New International Dictionary of New Testament Theology
NIGTC	New International Greek Testament Commentary
NIV	New International Version
NovT	*Novum Testamentum*
NovTSup	Supplements to Novum Testamentum

NRSV	New Revised Standard Version
ns	new series
NSBT	New Studies in Biblical Theology
NTD	Das Neue Testament Deutsch
NTG	New Testament Guides
NTS	*New Testament Studies*
Pillar	Pillar New Testament Commentary
Proclamation	Proclamation Commentaries
PSTJ	*Perkins School of Theology Journal*
RB	*Revue biblique*
ResQ	*Restoration Quarterly*
RevExp	*Review and Expositor*
RivB	*Rivista biblica itialiana*
RSR	*Recherches de science religieuse*
RTP	*Revue de théologie et de philosophie*
SB	Sources bibliques
SBLDS	Society of Biblical Literature Dissertation Series
SBLMS	Society of Biblical Literature Monograph Series
SBLSCS	Society of Biblical Literature Septuagint and Cognate Studies
SBT	Studies in Biblical Theology
ScEccl	*Sciences ecclésiastiques*
Scr	*Scripture*
SD	Studies and Documents
ser	series
ST	*Studia theologica*
SVTP	Studia in Veteris Testamenti Pseudepigrapha
TBST	The Bible Speaks Today
TDNT	*Theological Dictionary of the New Testament.* Ed. G. Kittel and G. Friedrich. Trans. G. W. Bromiley. 10 vols. Grand Rapids, 1964–1976
Theol	*Theologica*
THKNT	Theologischer Handkommentar zum Neuen Testament
THNTC	Two Horizons New Testament Commentary
ThTo	*Theology Today*
TLZ	*Theologische Literaturzeitung*
TNTC	Tyndale New Testament Commentary
TynBul	*Tyndale Bulletin*
TZ	*Theologische Zeitschrift*
UUÅ	Uppsala Universitetsårsskrift
WBC	Word Biblical Commentary
WTJ	*Westminster Theological Journal*
WUNT	Wissenschaftliche Untersuchungen zum Neuen Testament
ZAW	*Zeitschrift für die alttestamentliche Wissenschaft*

ZECNT	Zondervan Exegetical Commentary on the New Testament
ZNW	*Zeitschrift für die neutestamentliche Wissenschaft und die Kunde der älteren Kirche*
ZWT	*Zeitschrift für wissenschaftliche Theologie*

Chapter 1

INTRODUCTION: COMMON
THEMES AND ISSUES

The letters of James, Peter, and Jude, or, to put them in what may be their historical order, James, Jude, and 1 and 2 Peter, form four of the seven works collectively known since the fourth century as the "Catholic Epistles," or, more recently in some Protestant circles, as the "General Epistles." This is because at least two of these seven (James and 1 Peter) and possibly all of them (except 2 and 3 John) were letters sent to multiple churches and thus were historically viewed as universal (i.e., "catholic") or general rather than problem-solving letters to specific Christian communities (such as Romans, 1 and 2 Thessalonians, or 1 and 2 Corinthians). In this present volume we will not discuss 1, 2, and 3 John, for in style, theology, and probably historical origin they fit better with the Fourth Gospel and thus are included in *The Theology of John's Gospel and Letters* in this series.

The remaining four letters are disparate enough to require every bit of the present volume to give them a hearing. And a good hearing is what they deserve, for their theological voices have often been neglected because of the dominance of Paul (whose work for centuries was believed to include Hebrews), particularly in Reformation and post-Reformation Protestantism, and the Synoptic Gospels (including the two-part Luke-Acts), and the Johannine writings in the New Testament. We do not for a moment wish to disparage the importance of these other works; yet we must emphasize that the four voices that constitute our present enquiry, while minor in size, were of great importance during the first century (perhaps of more importance than Paul before the fall of Jerusalem and the circulation of Paul's letters), and they must be allowed to balance and nuance the louder voices found in the present configuration of the New Testament.

The problem with these four works is in knowing how to handle them. When this present author along with Ralph P. Martin and Daniel Reid set about to organize what became the *Dictionary of the Later New Testament and Its Developments*,[1] the first discussion session was about what to name this project. Should it be (facetiously) "Dictionary of the Rest" or "The Leftovers" after the two previous dictionaries on Paul and the Gospels? There are few common themes that unite the works (which, to be fair to that dictionary, included Acts, Hebrews, and Revelation, as well as the Catholic Epistles), much less common authorship or (except for Jude and 2 Peter)

---

1. Ralph P. Martin and Peter H. Davids, eds., *Dictionary of the Later New Testament and Its Developments* (Downers Grove, IL: InterVarsity Press, 1997).

literary dependence. The term "Later" was chosen because most of the works come toward the end of printed Bibles and some of them may well be the latest works in the New Testament ("and Its Developments" indicated that the work also included articles on the Apostolic Fathers and some other second-century works).

This present volume faces a similar problem of diversity, so we propose to proceed as follows: an initial chapter will cover common themes and issues; then a chapter will be devoted to each of the works, in each case (1) surveying recent scholarship and research; (2) treating relevant introductory issues; (3) producing a thematic commentary; and (4) treating important individual themes that arise out of the commentary. None of this can or will be totally comprehensive, for, as the present author has shown, one can easily write a full commentary on each of these works and then continue writing articles about them.[2] Nor can any of this be totally final because this author, at least, is constantly growing in his understanding of these works and is also aware that he is writing about literature from a culture in which neither he nor any person has lived for at least 1,700 years. That, of course, is why new discovery is possible and why there are arguments about the meaning of these works: one can never know with full certainty what these ancient authors were intending to communicate (just as one can never know with full certainty what a contemporary person, perhaps even one's spouse, is intending to communicate, although in that case one can get feedback from that person to indicate whether one has understood sufficiently). Yet we can grow in our understanding, although we are limited to questioning the text and understanding its context rather than directly questioning the ancient author. It is toward that goal that this present work is dedicated.

As we try to come to clearer understandings, this author will use his own translations of biblical texts (unless otherwise indicated). These translations will often avoid terms that he believes have become misleading. Often the traditional term will be included as an alternative translation, but it is alternative only if one understands it as meaning the same as the author's preferred term. For instance, "faith" will often be translated as "commitment," for when it (or its corresponding verb, "believe") has a personal object expressed or implied, it means "trust," "commitment," or the like; it only means "belief" when the object is impersonal and mental (e.g., in James this is true about the clause "believe that God is one"). Likewise some terms, such as "Christ" and "apostle," are really transliterations rather than translations, and we believe that these and similar terms were understood by initiates in the Jesus movement. Thus we will tend to translate them "the Anointed One" (often putting "Messiah" as an alternative) and "official delegate" respectively.

Other terms have taken on additional meanings by association over the years (e.g., "church"), so we will tend to say "Jesus movement" or "community" rather

2. Peter H. Davids, *The Epistle of James* (NIGTC; Grand Rapids: Eerdmans, 1982); idem, *The Epistle of 1 Peter* (NICNT; Grand Rapids: Eerdmans, 1990); and idem, *The Letters of 2 Peter and Jude* (Pillar; Grand Rapids: Eerdmans, 2006). These works will be referred to so that the present study need not repeat the detailed exegetical argument found in the commentaries.

than "church" because in our view the "early church" was more movemental and less structured than terms such as "church" tend to connote in our cultural context. This author has been committed to translating the Scriptures so that they speak to contemporary people,[3] and the translations and other language used in the theological reading of these works will reflect that commitment.

This author is also convinced that words only have meaning in context; in our case that means the social context of the writers of these works. This means referring to the theology of the Jewish Scriptures when it is believed that an author is picking up on that theology (i.e., is demonstrating intertextuality), to the social structures of the Greco-Roman world when they are reflected in the text, and to rhetorical devices when the texts reflect the tools of ancient rhetoric. So while this book is primarily a theological reading of the texts, it is a theological reading informed by a social-rhetorical understanding of the texts—that is, what the texts meant in the context of their original cultural settings, as best this can be determined.

1 THEMES AND ISSUES

While at first blush it looks as if there are few common themes and issues in these works, a closer look identifies a number of them. All of the works share a background in the Greco-Roman world, even if perhaps in different segments of it. All of the works share a similar theology, Christology, view of the source of sin, and eschatology, even if it is at times stated in compressed form. All of the works ostensibly come from authors identified with the Palestinian Jewish followers of Jesus of Nazareth. But all of the works are also thought by many scholars to be pseudonymous. Let us look at those themes in that order.

1.1 Greco-Roman Background

Each of these works is written within the Greco-Roman world, and all four are written by relatively educated authors. Each of the authors has at least completed the *progymnasmata* level of education,[4] and some at least were likely educated to a higher level, although they do not seem to have achieved the highest levels of education. This is evident from their writing style. For example, 1 Peter has some of the best-quality Greek in the New Testament, but James and 2 Peter are not far behind. It is true that there are Semitisms in the works—for instance, the notorious "doers of the word" in Jas 1:22–25, which contemporary readers find understandable in context as an expression drawn from Semitic constructions for one who does what "the word" instructs him or her to do, but which in "normal" Greek should mean

---

3. He has, for example, been on the translation committees of the *New Living Translation*, the *Common English Bible*, and *The Voice*, among others.

4. Examples of this education can be seen in Craig A. Gibson, trans. and ed., *Libanius's "Progymnasmata": Model Exercises in Greek*

Prose Composition and Rhetoric (Writings from the Greco-Roman World 27; Atlanta: Society of Biblical Literature, 2008) or George A. Kennedy, trans. and ed., *"Progymnasmata": Greek Textbooks of Prose Composition and Rhetoric* (Writings from the Greco-Roman World 10; Atlanta: Society of Biblical Literature, 2003).

one who writes words, such as a poet. But these "Semitisms" are not especially numerous and could be the result of the reading of Semitic literature in church, that is, the reading of the Greek translation of the Hebrew Scriptures, which we know of through the Septuagint. This would take place in that age much as King James language has crept into the written and, at times, spoken language of this author when he was a youth (much to the consternation of his high school teachers), for that was the language read, sung, and, at times, spoken in his church.

But this reference to Greek style shows another thing that these works have in common, the use of a Greek translation of the Scriptures; for it is difficult, although not impossible on a limited basis,[5] to argue that any of these authors had direct knowledge of the Hebrew Scriptures. (We will say more about this as we work through the individual letters.) What we have, then, are four works composed within a Greco-Roman context, some perhaps in the Palestinian end of the Greco-Roman world, but still rooted in that world and its language. There are, of course, differences in the parts of that world that they address, but these specific points of view will be covered as we encounter them.

1.2 Theology

These works also share a common theology in that they all agree that there is only one God, who is to be identified with the God of the Hebrew Scriptures. James 2:19 is explicit about the belief that "God is one" (and while this is an insufficient belief, James indicates that it is a starting point, "You do well"), but each of the other works refers to the narratives of the Hebrew Scriptures and thereby identifies the God in whom each author believes. He is the God of creation (Jas 1:17; 1 Pet 4:19; 2 Pet 3:5), the God of Noah (1 Pet 3:20; 2 Pet 2:5), the God of Abraham (Jas 2:23), and God the Father (Jas 1:27; 3:9; 1 Pet 1:2; 2 Pet 1:17; Jude 1).

There are many other things that one can say about this God, such as that he is a God of grace (Jas 4:6; 1 Pet 5:10; Jude 4), but enough has been said to indicate that each of these writers lives within the same narrative, namely, that of the one creator God whose story is found in the Hebrew Scriptures (whether read in translation or in Second Temple retellings) and who revealed himself through the (Hebrew/Jewish) prophets. They may emphasize different aspects of this God, but unless one understands their common assumptions, one will have large gaps in one's understanding of what they are intending to communicate.

1.3 Christology

By noting that God is God the Father, we pass into the realm of Christology, for God is primarily "the Father" of "our Lord Jesus Christ" (1 Pet 1:3). While only

---

5. Richard Bauckham, *Jude, 2 Peter* (WBC 50; Waco, TX: Word, 1983), 88, argues that Jude 13 depends on a knowledge of the Hebrew text of Isa 57:20, but, while possible, this is not an argument that has convinced most scholars. See the discussion in Peter H. Davids, "The Use of Second Temple Traditions in 1 and 2 Peter and Jude," in *The Catholic Epistles and the Tradition* (ed. Jacques Schlosser; BETL 176; Leuven: Peeters/Leuven University Press, 2004), 420–21.

1 Peter says this explicitly, the title "Father" is used in 2 Pet 1:17 and Jude 1 as part of differentiating "the Father" from Jesus Christ. Only James is not clear about this point (Jas 1:27 may be referring to God as the Father of orphans and Jas 3:9 is probably referring to the creator God as "Lord and Father"), but then James has much less to say about Christology than any of the other three. Yet it is clear that he agrees with the others (and with Paul) on the core concept of the "good news" that Jesus is Lord (Jas 1:1; 1 Pet 1:3; 2 Pet 1:2; Jude 4, 17); that he is presently exalted (Jas 2:1; 1 Pet 3:22; 2 Pet 1:11 [if viewed as presently reigning in the light of 2 Pet 1:17]; possibly Jude 1); and that he is to return, in the words of the (much later) Apostles' Creed, to "judge the living and the dead" (Jas 5:7–9; 1 Pet 1:7 [he is to be revealed from heaven]; 2 Pet 1:16; Jude 21).

All of these authors also agree that Jesus is the "Anointed One" (usually translated "Messiah" or transliterated "Christ"); that fact places him as well within the Second Temple Jewish narrative that in a number of its forms expected God to designate or "anoint" a ruler for his people, usually thought of as a descendant of David on the basis of 2 Sam 7:12–13. These works may differ in their application of sacrificial metaphors to Jesus (more prominent in 1 Peter) or their use of the title "Savior" (used only in 2 Peter [5x] and Jude), but their particular christological emphases are built on a common foundation.

1.4 View of the Source of Sin

Another feature of these letters is that all of them view sin or human evil as rooted in desire (*epithymia*). In fact, a quarter of the uses of this term in the New Testament occur in these four relatively short letters. Whether it be Jas 1:14–15 or 1 Pet 2:11 or 2 Pet 1:4 or by implication Jude 18, desire is the source of testing or that which fights against virtue or the source of corruption in the world. The term is often mistranslated "lust," for "lust" implies something illicit, usually sexual, while the Greek term simply means "desire" or "drive" (in the psychological sense). These "passions" are tied to the body, and when they control a person, they lead that one into evil.

One can illustrate this from Matt 4:2–4 (although *epithymia* does not appear in this passage). Jesus has fasted for forty days and is hungry; that is, he has a desire for food, a legitimate need that is necessary for survival. But God has told him to fast, since the forty-day fast is Spirit-directed. Thus it is a test of his obedience to God when the devil suggests Jesus use his powers to create food. But Jesus submits to God's word rather than to his own desire. This narrative reveals the nature of desire: when it is one's motivation, unconstrained by divine direction, it leads one into evil. It is not *specific* desires that are evil, but *any* desire in control of one's behavior. It is, so to speak, the question of Eden: Will I follow what is good (or avoid what is evil) in my eyes, or will I submit to the divine direction and let God decide what is good or evil?

The four works we are examining share the perspective that desire, when in control, is the source of evil. They express this in Greek, of course, and some forms of Greek philosophy, especially Stoicism, would nod in agreement. Likewise a number of strains of Jewish thought (including later rabbinic writings) would agree, using the term *yēṣer* for desire. Where the Jesus followers differed from these others was in the solution. The Greek thought generally considered the solution as a form of rationality, and Jewish thought as a form of Torah obedience, but our works will suggest the solution is a gift from God — that is, divine wisdom (James), or knowledge of God (2 Peter), or the will of God/spiritual milk (1 Peter). Paul would say, the Holy Spirit. Our works differ when it comes to expressing the solution, but they agree in that it is some gift or favor that finds its source in God.

1.5 Eschatology

All of these works have a similar eschatology, although they differ in the details presented. They agree that a day is coming — coming quickly for James (it is "near," Jas 5:8, or "at the doors," 5:9) and delayed for 2 Peter (2 Pet 3:9) — in which God or Jesus will judge the living and the dead. For James this includes the "coming of the Lord" and thus his presence on earth (Jas 5:7); Jude 14–15 uses the prophecy of *1 En.* 1:9 to describe this "coming" of the Lord to execute judgment. Thus there are some differences in the images used[6] (even within a single book such as 1 Peter) as to whether God or Jesus is going to come/be revealed as judge, and whether the judgment is the result of his coming to earth (James, 1 Peter, Jude) or of his exposing to his sight what is happening on earth (2 Peter), but all would agree with Heb 6:2 that "the resurrection of the dead and eternal judgment" are part of the essence of Christian belief.

1.6 Implied Authorship

All four of these works have an implied author identified with the early community of the followers of Jesus in Jerusalem. As we will argue, James is attributed to James, brother of Jesus, the leader of the Jerusalem community from at least 44 CE to 61 CE. First and 2 Peter are attributed to Simon Peter, who left Jerusalem by the end of 44 CE, perhaps never to return, though Paul describes him as having been, along with James, a brother of the Lord, and John son of Zebedee, a "pillar" of the Jerusalem community (Gal 2:9). What is more, Peter is described by Paul as being entrusted with "the gospel for the circumcised" (Gal 2:7), which would also identify him as a leader among Jewish followers of Jesus, as James also was.

The author of Jude describes himself as "brother of James" and so presumably one of the youngest two brothers of Jesus (the order of the listing of the final two brothers differs; cf. Matt 13:55 and Mark 6:3). The identification with James suggests that Jude is part of the same general community, even after the death of his older brother and the destruction of Jerusalem. His citation of or allusion to Second Temple Literature (*1 Enoch* and the *Testament of Moses*, among others) would seem to confirm that he at least lived within a Jewish community. It may be no accident that the two "pillars" James and Peter were bound together with the words that many

---

6. All theological language is to some degree metaphorical, given the limitations of human experience and language, but eschatology is especially so, since it deals with things that no one can have experienced and that often transcend the limitations of the present age. Thus we would expect variety in images/metaphors.

have attributed to the third pillar, John, although the letters of John themselves simply refer to the author as "the elder," in an early collection of the "Seven." They had a similar implied authorial background, they fit onto a single scroll, and they formed a balance of sorts to the Pauline collection.

1.7 Pseudonymity

All four of these works are in one of two senses pseudonymous. In one of these two senses, many modern scholars view the works as fully pseudonymous, perhaps inspired by the memory of or perhaps only trading on the authority of the author to whom they are attributed. While, as we will see in the introduction to each document, this is to some degree reasonable, given the difficulty of attributing the rhetoric of these works to their respective ascribed authors as well as the differences in perspective and style between 1 and 2 Peter, the fully pseudonymous perspective is likewise problematic, especially in the case of Jude. Even in the case of the other works, it goes far beyond our evidence. But, be that as it may, the claim is there, a claim not made about any of the main Pauline works (Romans, 1 and 2 Corinthians, Galatians) and not as universally made about the other Pauline works, with the possible exception of the Pastoral Epistles.[7]

But in another sense, virtually all scholars argue for some degree of pseudonymity or, better, anonymity for these works, even if it is not stated in so many words. That is, scholars who argue that James, Peter, and Jude did stand behind the letters almost always admit that none of these men was capable of writing the quality of Greek of these letters (although they often point out that they undoubtedly knew Greek), and so they attribute the grammar and vocabulary (i.e., the writing style) to a secretary or amanuensis who had significant freedom in the composition of the final document. Since this surely amounts to coauthorship and since the coauthor is never named (we will later argue that 1 Pet 5:12 is referring to letter carrier, not the amanuensis), one has at least partial anonymity that can lead to the impression of pseudonymity insofar as the contribution of this coauthor/amanuensis is hidden behind the simple attribution of the letter to the implied author.[8] This differs significantly from Paul, who often names a coauthor (who we assume made a significant contribution to the letter in question, e.g., 1 Cor 1:1; 2 Cor 1:1), and whose letters

---

7. And even in the case of the Pastoral Epistles it is far from universal. Eckhard J. Schnabel, "Paul, Timothy, and Titus: The Assumption of a Pseudonymous Author and of Pseudonymous Recipients in the Light of Literary, Theological, and Historical Evidence," in *Do Historical Matters Matter to Faith? A Critical Appraisal of Modern and Postmodern Approaches to Scripture* (ed. James K. Hoffmeier and Dennis R. Magary; Wheaton, IL: Crossway, 2012), 383–403, is a recent and articulate example of a defense of Pauline authorship of these works. But given the number of institutions of the type that Schnabel represents, as well as numerous Roman Catholic and Orthodox scholars who take a similar stance, one can argue that those holding Schnabel's conclusions are numerically more than those who argue for the pseudonymous authorship of these works.

8. This practice is not unknown even today: an executive may instruct an administrative assistant to write a letter that says thus and so, leaving the wording and tone to the discretion of the assistant. It certainly was common in the first century, as any literature on ancient letter writing and amanuenses would show; see the respective sections in E. Randolph Richards, *Paul and First-Century Letter Writing: Secretaries, Composition and Collection* (Downers Gove, IL: InterVarsity Press, 2004). The readers no more thought of such a composition as pseudonymous than those of us now would think of such a letter as "not from" the bank manager or executive who signs it, even if one knows the person well enough to realize that he or she uses a significantly different style of vocabulary, rhetoric, etc.

seem more likely to have been dictated (as evidenced in some of the grammatical breaks in the letters), limiting the contribution of any secretary/scribe/amanuensis.[9]

There is also another authorship commonality among these works in contrast with three types of other works in the New Testament. First, unlike the four Gospels, Acts, Hebrews, and 1 John, they are not anonymous. While one might cherish the later traditions about the authorship of these just-mentioned works, there is no claim of authorship within them. They cannot be called pseudonymous, for they are anonymous. That is not true of our four works, since each one clearly identifies a known individual as in some sense the author (however much an amanuensis or ghostwriter may have assisted).

Second, as already noted, unlike 2 and 3 John and Revelation, the authors so identified are known individuals. While "the elder" of 2 and 3 John was known to the recipients, there is nothing in the text that requires one to put a specific name to that individual. This is not true of our works, for while there have been various individuals named "James" or "Jacob" to whom James has been attributed, scholarship overwhelmingly agrees that the letter is attributed to the leader of the Jerusalem church known as Jesus' brother, who was martyred in 61 or 62 CE. The same can be said for the other three letters. One can argue whether the "John" of Revelation was John the son of Zebedee or "John the elder" or some other John, but that is of no consequence in terms of the authorship claim of the text, so long as one agrees that it was some person named "John." As a result, one does not find a lot of discussion about pseudepigraphy in Revelation. That is not true about our letters. Either they are in some sense by the authors indicated[10] or they are pseudepigraphal. They may be transparent pseudepigraphal works (i.e., with no deception involved for the original recipients) or deceptive ones (i.e., with the intention to deceive about who the author was in order to claim the authority of someone who in no sense authored the work), but either perspective makes them pseudepigraphal.

Third, unlike the Pauline letters and to some degree the Johannine literature, there is no accepted body of literature with which to compare these works in order to determine authorship. With Paul there are the *Hauptbriefe*, his main letters that virtually every scholar agrees he wrote. It is comparisons with those works that make up a significant part of Eckhard Schnabel's chapter referred to in footnote 7. While the Johannine works are, strictly speaking, anonymous (or at best attributed to "the elder"), we do have the gospel with which to compare the letters to help determine whether they are one body of literature or not. When it comes to James and Jude,

---

9. Hebrews, of course, is anonymous, while Revelation is usually accepted as being by someone named John, whose idiosyncratic grammar would seem to make scribal contributions to style unlikely. The four Gospels and Acts are all anonymous, without relying on later tradition to supply any putative author. It is true that at least the content of the last half of the Fourth Gospel is attributed to the so-called "beloved disciple," but he and the disciple who is "known to the high priest" (who may be one and the same) come without names, so in that sense they are anonymous (and probably intentionally so). Thus the comparison with Paul is the most relevant.

10. We say "in some sense," for that "sense" could vary in antiquity from word-for-word dictation, to the author giving the general sense of what he wanted to say, which was then filled out on the basis of the briefest of instructions, to a posthumous collection of the author's teaching. What we want to point out is that in antiquity, as now, the author did not need to write or dictate every word for it to be their work.

we have only the one letter each. And when it comes to 1 and 2 Peter, we do have two letters, but with a very different handling of the Hebrew Scriptures and a different Greek style. The only other literature attributed to these individuals is either a speech in Acts, which in that case is probably filtered through the author of Acts (there are stylistic similarities among the speeches, and the speeches themselves were surely much longer than the versions we have) or perhaps Mark's gospel itself, which many hold to be the preaching of Peter,[11] although in that case edited and written down by Mark. Furthermore, while the letters themselves are not long in comparison with Paul's letters, they are long in comparison with the speeches attributed to James and Peter in Acts. This is not intended to disparage such comparisons, but to point out that one is in a much different situation than with the Pauline literature. In these three aspects of the authorship discussion these four General or Catholic letters have a commonality.

1.8 Ecclesiological Stance

At least two of these four also have another commonality: James and 1 Peter portray a type of patriarchate in that these letters are probably written to communities that the authors have not planted and perhaps not visited. Paul, with the notable exception of Romans, limits himself to writing to communities that he or his colleagues have established. In other words, the authors of James and 1 Peter are functioning like patriarchs. Now, before one jumps to premature conclusions and says, "Aha! They are functioning like Clement of Rome in *1 Clement* and thus must be dated to that period," one should observe that, as will be pointed out in the introduction to James, the "Diaspora letter" form in which the central authorities in Jerusalem write to Jewish communities in the Diaspora predates *1 Clement*. One might better say that James is viewed in the letter that bears his name as the Jerusalem "patriarch" writing to Diaspora communities, even if the work itself reflects situations in Jerusalem.

This portrayal of James agrees with the picture of James in Acts, in which he presides at the "council" in Acts 15 (one must be careful not to picture it anachronistically like later church councils, such as the Council of Nicea) and is the person to whom Paul reports to in Acts 21 (as well as the one whom Paul says in Gal. 1 he specifically visited and who is one of the three "pillars" in Gal. 2). In other words, the followers of Jesus, viewing themselves as the renewed Israel, took over the organization of Judaism, and James reflects this.

However, it is also true that 1 Peter likewise reflects this type of structure, namely, that of a revered central authority writing to outlying communities. But in this case the communities are largely composed of former Gentiles, and at least some of the areas in which they exist were evangelized by Paul and his colleagues. Furthermore, the "patriarch" is now in Rome (if the identification made in the

---

11. See, e.g., Martin Hengel, *Saint Peter: The Underestimated Apostle* (Grand Rapids: Eerdmans, 2010). In fact, for Hengel Mark is the only access to the preaching or teaching of Peter, since he rejects the Petrine authorship of the letters.

commentary on 1 Peter of "Babylon" with Rome is correct), not Jerusalem. While in the interpretation of this work Jude and 2 Peter appear to be addressed to more localized groups, perhaps even groups that the respective authors had a hand in founding, if these works are read as addressed to a more general group of communities (as would be the case for 2 Peter with those interpreters who identify the "first letter" of 2 Pet 3:1 with 1 Peter), then 2 Peter and perhaps Jude would also be part of this phenomenon.[12]

Thus, there is some commonality among these works, a commonality that justifies including them together in this one book and in many courses in theological institutions. But, as we will see, this commonality does not justify homogenizing them so that we do not grasp their individual voices. It is to these individual voices that we now turn.

---

12. We have used the term "patriarch" because, if not taken in the later developed sense that it received in the Orthodox Church, it best describes how James and the central Jewish authorities appear to have operated. Naturally, when transferred into the Roman world, it would shift toward Roman organizational forms and language. But in our view Clement of Rome is inheriting and expressing a position of influence that ultimately comes from Jerusalem through the person of Peter rather than being either a retrojection of a later episcopal structure or a totally new development. Nor do we believe that this type of organization would take long to develop; we have personally watched it develop within a decade or so in a North American movement that became a denomination, even though during much of that time period the movement was anti-structure. Of course, that contemporary movement had precedents, but so did James. Any movement has to develop structure, formal or informal, as it grows, or else it disintegrates, and the faster the movement grows, the faster it develops structure. One should not be surprised by "developed ecclesiastical structures" found in, for example, the Pastoral Epistles and implied to some degree in 1 Peter and James. Rather, one should be surprised, assuming traditional dating, that the structures are not more developed given the rapid spread of the Jesus movement.

Chapter 2

JAMES

J ames is the first of the General Epistles in the traditional collection of the seven. While it has been loved by parts of the church since it came into general circulation in the mid-third century and by the church as a whole since its final acceptance in the sixth century, in the period after the Reformation it has been the most controversial work in the New Testament because of one section, Jas 2:14–26. Yet this controversy often means that the teaching of James, not only in the controversial passage, but also in the other nine-tenths of the book, has been ignored, despite being a rich trove of biblical theology.

BIBLIOGRAPHY

Allison, Dale C., Jr. *James: A Critical and Exegetical Commentary.* ICC. New York and London: Bloomsbury T&T Clark, 2013. **Bauckham, Richard**. *James: Wisdom of James, Disciple of Jesus the Sage.* New Testament Readings. London/New York: Routledge, 1999. **Blomberg, Craig L., and Mariam J. Kamell**. *James.* ZECNT. Grand Rapids: Zondervan, 2008. **Chilton, Bruce, and Craig A. Evans**, eds. *James the Just and Christian Origins.* NovTSup 98. Leiden: Brill, 1999. Idem. *The Missions of James, Peter, and Paul: Tensions in Early Christianity.* NovTSup 115. Leiden: Brill, 2005. **Chilton, Bruce, and Jacob Neusner**, eds. *The Brother of Jesus: James the Just and His Mission.* Louisville: Westminster John Knox, 2001. **Davids, Peter H.** *The Epistle of James.* NIGTC. Grand Rapids: Eerdmans, 1982. Idem. "The Meaning of Ἀπείραστος in James i.13." *NTS* 24 (1978): 386–92. Idem. "The Meaning of Ἀπείραστος Revisited." Pp. 225–40 in *New Testament Greek and Exegesis: Essays in Honor of Gerald F. Hawthorne.* Ed. Timothy Sailors and Amy Donaldson. Grand Rapids: Eerdmans, 2003. Idem. *Themes in the Epistle of James That Are Judaistic in Character.* Unpublished PhD thesis, University of Manchester, 1974. **Deppe, Dean B.** *The Sayings of Jesus in the Epistle of James.* Chelsea, MI: Bookcrafters, 1989. **deSilva, David**. *The Jewish Teachers of Jesus, James, and Jude: What Earliest Christianity Learned from the Apocrypha and Pseudepigrapha.* Oxford/New York: Oxford University Press, 2012. **Dibelius, Martin**. *Der Brief des Jakobus.* KEK. Göttingen: Vandenhoeck & Ruprecht, 1921, 1964. ET: Martin Dibelius and Heinrich Greeven. *James: A Commentary on the Epistle of James.* Hermeneia. Philadelphia: Fortress, 1976. **Frankemölle, Hubert**. *Der Brief des Jakobus.* Kapitel 1/Kapitel 2–5. Ökumenischer Taschenbuch-Kommentar zum Neuen Testament 17/1–2. Gütersloh/Würzburg: Gütersloher Verlaghaus/Echter, 1994. **Haaker, Klaus**. "Justification, salut et foi: Étude sur les rapports entre Paul, Jacques et Pierre." *ETR* 73 (1998):

177–88. **Hartin, Patrick J.** *James and the Q Sayings of Jesus.* JSNTSup 47. Sheffield, JSOT, 1991. Idem. *James of Jerusalem: Heir to Jesus of Nazareth.* Interfaces. Collegeville, MN: Liturgical, 2004. **Hort, F. J. A.** *The Epistle of St. James.* London: Macmillan & Co., 1909. **Johnson, Luke Timothy.** *Brother of Jesus, Friend of God: Studies in the Letter of James.* Grand Rapids: Eerdmans, 2004. Idem. *The Letter of James.* AB 37A. New York: Doubleday, 1995. **Kirk, J. A.** "The Meaning of Wisdom in James." *NTS* 16 (1969): 24–38. **Kloppenborg. John S.** "Reception and Emulation of the Jesus Tradition in James." Pages 121–50 in *Reading James with New Eyes: Methodological Reassessments of the Letter of James.* Ed. Robert L. Webb and John S. Kloppenborg. LNTS 342. London/New York: T&T Clark, 2007. **Knox, W. L.** "The Epistle of St. James." *JTS* 46 (1945): 10–17. **Laws, Sophie.** *The Epistle of James.* HNTC. New York: Harper and Row, 1980. **Martin, Ralph P.** *James.* WBC 48. Waco, TX: Word, 1988. **Mayor, Joseph P.** *The Epistle of St. James: The Greek Text with Introduction, Notes and Comments, and Further Studies in the Epistle of St. James.* London: Macmillan, 1913. **McCartney, Dan G.** *James.* BECNT. Grand Rapids: Baker Academic, 2009. **McKnight, Scot.** *The Letter of James.* NICNT. Grand Rapids: Eerdmans, 2011. **Meyer, Arnold.** *Das Rätsel des Jakobusbriefes.* Giessen: Arnold Meyer, 1930. **Mussner, Franz.** *Der Jakobusbrief.* HTKNT. Freiberg: Herder, 1964, 1967. **Niebuhr, Karl-Wilhelm.** "Der Jakobusbrief im Licht frühjüdischer Diasporabriefe." *NTS* 44 (1998): 420–24. **Niebuhr, Karl Wilhelm, and Robert W. Wall**, eds. *The Catholic Epistles and Apostolic Tradition: A New Perspective on James to Jude.* Waco, TX: Baylor University Press, 2009. **Nienhuis, David R.** *Not by Paul Alone: The Formation of the Catholic Epistle Collection and the Christian Canon.* Waco, TX: Baylor University Press, 2007. **Painter, John.** *Just James: The Brother of Jesus in History and Tradition.* Minneapolis: Fortress, 1999. **Painter, John, and David A. deSilva.** *James and Jude.* Paideia. Grand Rapids: Baker Academic, 2012. **Popkes, Wiard.** *Der Brief des Jakobus.* THKNT 14. Leipzig: Evangelische Verlagsanstalt, 2001. **Reicke, Bo Ivar.** *The Epistles of James, Peter and Jude.* AB. Garden City, NY: Doubleday, 1964. Idem. *Diakonie, Festfreude und Zelos.* UUÅ. Uppsala: Lundequistska, 1951. **Ropes, James Hardy.** *A Critical and Exegetical Commentary on the Epistle of St. James.* ICC. New York: C. Scribner's Sons, 1916. **Schlatter, Adolf.** *Der Brief des Jakobus.* Stuttgart: Calwer, 1932. **Seitz, O. J. F.** "Two Spirits in Man: An Essay in Biblical Exegesis." *NTS* 6 (1959): 82–95. **Smit, Peter-Ben.** "A Symposiastic Background to James?" *NTS* 58 (2012): 105–22. **Spitta, F.** *Der Brief des Jakobus untersucht.* Göttingen: Vandenhoeck & Ruprecht, 1896. Idem. "Das Testaments Hiobs und das Neue Testament." Pp. 139–206 in *Zur Geschichte und Literatur des Urchristentums.* Göttingen: Vandenhoeck & Ruprecht, 1907, III/2. **Thomas, J.** "Anfechtung und Vorfreude." *KD* 14 (1968): 183–206. **Wall, Robert W.** *Community of the Wise: The Letter of James.* The New Testament in Context. Valley Forge, PA: Trinity Press International, 1997. **Wall, Robert W., and David R. Nienhuis.** *Reading the Epistles of James, Peter, John, and Jude as Scripture.* Grand Rapids: Eerdmans, 2013. **Ward, Roy Bowen.** "Partiality in the Assembly: James

2:2–4." *HTR* 62 (1969): 87–97. Idem. "The Works of Abraham: James 2:14–26." *HTR* 61 (1968): 283–90. **Webb, Robert L., and John S. Kloppenborg**, eds. *Reading James with New Eyes: Methodological Reassessments of the Letter of James.* LNTS. London/New York: T&T Clark International, 2007. **Wessel, W. W.** "An Inquiry into the Origin, Literary Character, Historical and Religious Significance of the Epistle of James." Ph.D. diss., Edinburgh, 1953.

2.1 RECENT SCHOLARSHIP

For a long period of time James languished in the scholarly world, as witnessed to by the fact that J. P. Mayor and J. H. Ropes were the most-cited commentaries in the English-speaking world up through at least the 1960s.[1] The German-speaking world was hardly better served, for the standard there was the work of Martin Dibelius, which was heavily influenced by form criticism, and even in its later editions did not move on to redaction criticism.[2] For Dibelius James was a collection of New Testament paraenesis, or strung together ethical teachings, that reflect a common theological background but do not present a unified argument. While there were commentaries published between these early twentieth-century works and the late twentieth century, none were major works. James was too dominated by Luther's apparent rejection of the letter to be of theological interest.

This started to change with the work of Sophie Laws[3] in English and Franz Mussner[4] in German. Both took more of a theological interest in James, as in Mussner's case the series title (Herders *theologischer* Kommentar …) implied. It helped, perhaps, that both the commentators lived in the world of redaction criticism that expected ancient literature, whatever sources they used, to come up with something of a unified theology. It was in this context that this author's own early writing on James was published, work that explicitly viewed James as a theological document.[5] It was also at this time that Jack T. Sanders[6] used James as an independent theological-ethical voice to relativize the voice of Paul. One does not need to agree with Sanders to appreciate the fact that James was finally being viewed as a theologically significant work in its own right rather than substandard Paul.

Since roughly 1990 there have been a plethora of serious studies and commentaries

---

1. Joseph P. Mayor, *The Epistle of St. James: The Greek Text with Introduction, Notes and Comments, and Further Studies in the Epistle of St. James* (London: Macmillan, 1913); James Hardy Ropes, *A Critical and Exegetical Commentary on the Epistle of St. James.* (ICC; New York: C. Scribner's Sons, 1916).

2. Martin Dibelius, *Der Brief des Jakobus* (KEK; Göttingen: Vandenhoeck & Ruprecht, 1921, 1964[11]). The English version of this still-important work is Martin Dibelius and Heinrich Greeven, *James: A Commentary on the Epistle of James* (Hermeneia; Philadelphia: Fortress, 1976).

3. *The Epistle of James* (HNTC; New York: Harper and Row, 1980).

4. *Der Jakobusbrief* (HTKNT; Freiberg: Herder, 1964, 1967). Significantly, Mussner is Catholic, and the Catholic tradition has never lost its appreciation for James in the way the Protestant tradition did.

5. Peter H. Davids, "Themes in the Epistle of James That Are Judaistic in Character" (unpublished PhD thesis, University of Manchester, 1974), is consciously redaction-critical, looking for the new theological insights that come from the joining of largely Jewish theological themes. Peter H. Davids, *The Epistle of James* (NIGTC; Grand Rapids: Eerdmans, 1982) expands these insights into full commentary coverage.

6. Jack T. Sanders, *Ethics in the New Testament* (Philadelphia: Fortress, 1975).

on James, which together give James a much clearer voice than it has had in decades, perhaps centuries (at least in the Western Protestant world). First, there have been a series of biographical studies on James son of Joseph, the man—studies that invariably also discuss the letter, whether or not they believe that James actually wrote the letter. Two of these come from a four-year seminar on James and his letter sponsored by Bard College under the direction of Bruce Chilton and Jacob Neusner, namely, *James the Just and Christian Origins*,[7] and the more popular *The Brother of Jesus*.[8] John Painter, a member of that seminar, wrote his own work on James, *Just James*.[9] Finally, Patrick J. Hartin, whose doctoral dissertation, *James and the Q Sayings of Jesus*,[10] indicated some of the direction in which his later work would go, has written *James of Jerusalem*.[11]

These works are studies of developing tradition, often starting with studies about the family of Jesus, moving through the portrayal of James in Paul and Acts, examining the picture of James in the letter of James, and continuing with the tradition about James included in Eusebius and other second- through fourth-century writings. The issues they seek to address are: (1) Was James as anti-Pauline as some readings of Galatians suggest, or was he conciliatory towards Paul, as Acts 21 suggests? (2) Was James capable, both in terms of his knowledge of Greek and of his leadership beyond Jerusalem, of writing the letter attributed to him? (3) Did later traditions about James either distort scholarship's perception of him (e.g., make him more of a superpious Jew than he was) or give a reason for a pseudepigrapher to write the letter (i.e., make him enough of a respected leader long after the fall of Jerusalem that someone might write in his name)?

A somewhat different tack is taken in the more theological and canon-critical readings of James. These began with the brief work of Chester and Martin in 1994[12] and continue with the works of Luke Timothy Johnson and Richard Bauckham.[13] Notable in these works are the sections on canonical reception and canonical interpretation. Canonical context is also stressed by Robert W. Wall in his *Community of the Wise*, and even more so by his colleague David R. Nienhuis in his *Not by Paul Alone*.[14] It is important to note that, although Nienhuis does not have James in either

---

7. Bruce Chilton and Craig A. Evans, eds., *James the Just and Christian Origins* (NovTSup 98; Leiden: Brill, 1999).

8. Bruce Chilton and Jacob Neusner, eds., *The Brother of Jesus: James the Just and His Mission* (Louisville: Westminster John Knox, 2001).

9. John Painter, *Just James: The Brother of Jesus in History and Tradition* (Minneapolis: Fortress, 1999).

10. Partick J. Hartin, *James and the Q Sayings of Jesus* (JSNTSup 47; Sheffield: JSOT, 1991).

11. Patrick J. Hartin, *James of Jerusalem: Heir to Jesus of Nazareth* (Interfaces; Collegeville, MN: Liturgical, 2004).

12. Andrew Chester and Ralph P. Martin, *The Theology of the Letters of James, Peter, and Jude* (New Testament Theology; Cambridge: Cambridge University Press, 1994). In some ways this builds on the work of F. F. Bruce, *Peter, Stephen, James, and John: Studies in Non-Pauline Christianity* (Grand Rapids: Eerdmans, 1979).

13. Luke Timothy Johnson, *Brother of Jesus, Friend of God: Stud-*

ies in the Letter of James (Grand Rapids: Eerdmans, 2004). He had already written *The Letter of James* (AB 37A; New York: Doubleday, 1995), so he is building on earlier work. Richard Bauckham, *James: Wisdom of James, Disciple of Jesus the Sage* (New Testament Readings; London/New York: Routledge, 1999).

14. Robert W. Wall, *Community of the Wise: The Letter of James* (The New Testament in Context; Valley Forge, PA: Trinity Press International, 1997); David R. Nienhuis, *Not by Paul Alone: The Formation of the Catholic Epistle Collection and the Christian Canon* (Waco, TX: Baylor University Press, 2007). Karl Wilhelm Niebuhr and Robert W. Wall, eds., *The Catholic Epistles and Apostolic Tradition: A New Perspective on James to Jude* (Waco, TX: Baylor University Press, 2009), is largely a continuation of this discussion, for eight of its sixteen articles are on James, with James playing a significant role in at least three others. The discussion is summed up for all our literature in Robert W. Wall and David R. Nienhuis, *Reading the Epistles of James, Peter, John, and Jude as Scripture* (Grand Rapids: Eerdmans, 2013).

the title or the subtitle of his work, James is a major focus, for he believes that James was written about 180 CE to introduce the Catholic Epistles collection and thus picks up themes from the other works in the collection in a deliberate contrast to Paul. This carries Wall's concern with reading James in the context of canon formation to its full conclusion. Yet, while this raises date and context issues, not to mention the issue of purpose, the reading of James in such a canon-conscious context is not surprising, given a commentary such as Gerald Bray's that reads James through the eyes of later (patristic) interpreters rather than limiting itself to seeking a meaning in a putative original context.[15] There is also a recent concern with the hermeneutic of James, as seen in Webb and Kloppenborg's collection, *Reading James with New Eyes*.[16]

Many of the works cited above are not commentaries, but there is certainly also a relatively large body of commentary literature presently available, which is an immense contrast from when this writer first began his work in James. One cannot mention all of the works available, but, to cite a few (and we will only mention the larger ones that have not already been cited), there is the especially valuable work of Ralph P. Martin in the Word series, the massive work of Hubert Frankemölle in the Ökumenischer Taschenbuch-Kommentar zum Neuen Testament series, that of the late Wiard Popkes, Ben Witherington III's *Letters and Homilies for Jewish Christians*, and Scot McKnight's *The Letter of James*.[17] In the conservative evangelical world one has the work of Craig L. Blomberg and Mariam J. Kamell and that of Dan G. McCartney.[18] Taken together, these works give a range of dates for James, with Martin, Witherington, Blomberg/Kamell, and McCartney dating it into the lifetime of James, and Popkes and Frankemölle dating it later. For this study it is not the date itself that is important, but the influence that the date has on exegetical and theological understandings. The earlier the date, the less likely that James is directly interacting with Paul's letters, and the later the date the more likely that that is the case.

2.2 INTRODUCTORY ISSUES

The literature cited above and other works that will be cited later all show that, unlike, say, Romans or Revelation, two works that are generally agreed to be by the implied authors (although in the case of Revelation who that John was is disputed)

15. Gerald Bray, *James, 1–2 Peter, 1–3 John, Jude* (ACCS–NT 11; Downers Grove, IL: InterVarsity Press, 2000). See also the discussion on the reception of James in Dale C. Allison Jr., *James: A Critical and Exegetical Commentary* (ICC; New York and London: Bloomsbury T&T Clark, 2013).

16. Robert L. Webb and John S. Kloppenborg, eds., *Reading James with New Eyes: Methodological Reassessments of the Letter of James* (LNTS; London/New York: T&T Clark International, 2007), which is the product of the Society of Biblical Literature's The Letters of James, Peter, and Jude Section.

17. Ralph P. Martin, *James* (WBC 48; Waco, TX: Word, 1988); Wiard Popkes, *Der Brief des Jakobus* (THKNT 14; Leipzig: Evan-

gelische Verlaghausanstalt, 2001); Hubert Frankemölle, *Der Brief des Jakobus Kapitel 1/Kapitel 2–5* (Ökumenischer Taschenbuch-Kommentar zum Neuen Testament 17/1–2; Gütersloh/Würzburg: Gütersloher Verlaghaus/Echter, 1994); Ben Witherington III, *Letters and Homilies for Jewish Christians: A Socio-Rhetorical Commentary on Hebrews, James and Jude* (Downers Grove, IL: IVP Academic, 2007); Scot McKnight, *The Letter of James* (NICNT; Grand Rapids: Eerdmans, 2011).

18. Craig L. Blomberg and Mariam J. Kamell, *James* (ZECNT; Grand Rapids: Zondervan, 2008); Dan G. McCartney, *James* (BECNT; Grand Rapids: Baker Academic, 2009).

and to have been written at a given date, there is a lot of dispute about James. For our purposes it is necessary to look at two issues: (1) the date (and therefore the authorship) of the work, for that indicates the historical and cultural context, without which one cannot establish a probable or possible original meaning; (2) the nature of the work, for that also has a significant impact on meaning.

2.2.1 Date, Authorship, and Historical Context

It is clear that the stated author of James is, despite the cryptic self-designation "slave of God and of the Lord Jesus the Anointed One/Messiah" (Jas 1:1), James son of Joseph ben Heli (if we follow Luke 3:23, or ben Jacob according to Matt 1:16), a construction worker who originally lived in Nazareth in Galilee.[19] He is always named next after Jesus in lists of Jesus' brothers, so he was presumably considered to be Jesus' next younger brother (or the eldest of Jesus' cousins, if one follows Jerome's interpretation that *adelphos*, ἀδελφός, means "cousin," the children of Mary wife of Clopas, also identified as "the mother of James and Joses").[20] Only this James had prominence among the communities of the followers of Jesus living in Palestine in the first century, enough prominence that Paul names him, along with Cephas (Peter) and John, an acknowledged "pillar" of the Jerusalem community (Gal 2:9); emissaries from that community are designated by Paul as "from James" (Gal 2:12).

The author of Acts agrees with this assessment in that James is the only one whom Peter wanted informed about his (divinely orchestrated) release from prison (Acts 12:17). James chaired the so-called Jerusalem Council (15:13–21),[21] and Paul visited him and took advice from him on his final visit to Jerusalem (21:18). There is no other figure from that early period who could be identified with such a designation. On this virtually the whole tradition of literature on this work is agreed.[22]

What is not agreed on is whether that person did indeed write this particular work or whether the work is simply attributed to him. This issue involves several questions. (1) Would a person with James's background be capable of the quality of Greek and the rhetorical sophistication that is found in this letter? (2) Does James show a knowledge of Paul's letters and, if so, would James have been alive long enough to have written such a letter? (3) Was James prominent enough after his martyrdom and the fall of Jerusalem in 70 CE that a later writer or community might have used his name to give authority to a letter that they composed? (4) Finally, if

---

19. There were others named James (the Greek form of Jacob, *Iakōbos*) among the early followers of Jesus, such as James son of Zebedee, James "the little," and James son of Alphaeus (these latter two are sometimes considered the same person). While a few scholars have championed one or the other of these in the past, contemporary scholarship virtually unanimously agrees that James son of Joseph is the implied writer, for, as will be pointed out, only he was a significant enough leader of the first-century Jesus movement to have been able to be identified by the simple description we find in this letter.

20. This is the standard Roman Catholic and Orthodox view.

21. While many scholars do not view the "Jerusalem Council" as historical and there are also problems in fitting the chronology of

Acts with that of Galatians, it is nonetheless true that the author of Acts presents James in cultural terms as the senior leader present at that gathering in that he speaks last, and when he speaks, he refers to his decision about the matter as if his decision is the final word.

22. The minor exceptions include Martin Luther, who attributed the work to "some good pious man who had taken some sayings from the apostles' disciples" (*Sämmtl. Werke*, Erlangen ed., vol. 63, p. 157, as cited in James H. Ropes, *A Critical and Exegetical Commentary on the Epistle of James* [ICC; Edinburgh: T&T Clark, 1916], 45, and Arnold Meyer (*Das Rätsel des Jakobusbriefes* [Giessen: Arnold Meyer, 1930]), who, following F. Spitta, believed that the designation referred to the patriarch Jacob.

James, the Lord's brother, did write the letter, why is the letter so poorly attested until the period of Origen?

(1) That a person with James's background would have spoken some Greek is relatively certain. Even in Jerusalem Greek culture and Greek education were widespread,[23] and Greek was commonly used as the language of commerce in Galilee, with its mixture of Gentile and Jewish towns and cities. Tiberius, for instance, was Gentile-founded, and Sepphoris (Zippori) was a Gentile (and so Hellenistic) town being built within walking distance of Nazareth during the period when Jesus and James were growing up. While as Galilean Jews they may (or may not) have spoken Aramaic at home, they needed to be able to communicate in Greek with those overseeing the construction (since Jesus and James appear to have followed Joseph in his vocation), with soldiers and other officials, with traders, and with fellow Jews from the Diaspora who were passing through on their way to Jerusalem.[24]

The issue is not whether James would have been able to communicate in Greek, but whether he would have commanded the quality of Greek needed to write this letter. While one may dismiss opinions like that of F. C. Burkitt, who, influenced too much from later legends concerning James's Jewish piety, viewed James as an "unshaven devotee who haunted the Temple Colonnades" and was thus incapable of and perhaps not inclined to write Greek of the literary quality of James,[25] it is questionable whether a person such as James (ostensibly the second brother in an artisan family with at least seven children) would have had access to sufficient Greek education to have composed some of the better Greek in the New Testament and sufficient rhetorical education to demonstrate the skill found in this work.[26]

The usual solution is to appeal to the use of an amanuensis, who would be responsible for putting James's ideas into good Greek. That is possible, and it is true that an amanuensis, necessary for the process of writing in any case, was sometimes given a lot of liberty in the composition of a letter.[27] But at what point does an amanuensis become a coauthor or even the main author of a work? If he is responsible for the style and wording, is he not at least a coauthor? How would one recognize what is from the implied author and what is from the "secretary" if one does not have works that are undisputedly in the wording and thought forms of the author? This present writer does not know how one can resolve such an issue, nor is it necessarily theologically significant.

First, if the implied author approved the sending of the work, one would consider it "his work" even if the language and rhetoric of the work were not his. We

---

23. E.g., the evidence cited in J. N. Sevenster, *Do You Know Greek?* (NovTSup 19; Leiden: Brill, 1968), 190–91.

24. MHT I,8.

25. F. C. Burkitt, *Christian Beginnings* (London: London University Press, 1924), 66.

26. At the same time, one must not overestimate the quality of the Greek. There are some Semitisms, as will be noted, whether they originated in the author's own idiom or in his being influenced by the LXX. And the Greek and rhetoric, while showing the influ-

ence of a solid education (through the level of the *progymnasmata*) as described by Craig Gibson or George Kennedy, is not of such a literary quality as to indicate higher education (*gymnasium*, roughly equivalent to university education).

27. E. Randolph Richards, *Paul and First-Century Letter Writing: Secretaries, Composition and Collection* (Downers Grove, IL: InterVarsity Press, 2004), 57–80, discusses the use of secretaries in some detail.

do this all the time today when we say, "I received a letter from my senator," when in all likelihood the senator had told an aid to write a letter saying thus and so to anyone who questioned this or that stance of his. We also do the same when a work is ghostwritten. Second, while the probabilities are that James did not have a good education, perhaps no education at all,[28] given surprising turns of fate in life and the lack of knowledge about James's biography, one cannot *know* that he did not have an education.[29] It is true that James's speeches in Acts are certainly in Lucan style (as are all other speeches in Acts) and interpretation, and references to James outside the New Testament are coated with legendary material; thus, we have no other evidence than the letter that would indicate his education, style, and manner of thought. We know even less about a purported amanuensis and James's relationship to this person and thus the degree to which he would have been capable of or entrusted with the composition of this letter. Thus without having a detailed biography of James's youth,[30] we will remain agnostic on this question of how educated he might have been, while acknowledging that historical probability would attribute what we see in the letter to an amanuensis of some type.[31]

(2) The second question, as to whether James knew and used Pauline letters, is more significant, for it refers to intertextuality and not to one's knowledge or lack thereof of the educational background and relationships of an ancient figure. The key passage here is Jas 2:14–26, in which James argues that faith without works is "dead" (Jas 2:17, 26)—that is, that it cannot save anyone (Jas 2:14). Three aspects of this passage remind one of Paul: (a) the expression "faith without works" and its various permutations; (b) the citation of Abraham and specifically the citation of Gen 15:6 in Jas 2:23 (also cited in Rom 4:3 and Gal 3:6); and (c) the linking of "justification" to "works" as opposed to "faith alone" (Jas 2:24). If these three aspects are in fact borrowed from Pauline letters, then James must be later than Romans and Galatians, for Rom 3:28 and Gal 2:16 are the key passages in which Paul asserts that one is justified by faith and apart from "works of the law," which would be the statements James is opposing.

While Galatians is variously dated (as early as 49 CE or as late as toward the end of Paul's life), Romans dates itself toward the end of Paul's final stay in Corinth (ca. 56 CE). Since Romans was sent west to Rome, not east to Palestine, since it would take time for it to become known and influential, and since it would have had to be influential and have had a copy sent to Palestine (a copy costing perhaps $2,000 in current money, since it is the longest of Paul's letters) before James could react

28. One would expect a laborer like James to be uneducated and illiterate, as Acts 4:13 describes Simon Peter and John son of Zebedee as being. Only 10 to 20 percent of the population would have been literate, and most of those would have been in the upper classes or, perhaps, slaves educated by the upper classes to be their scribes.

29. He could have, for example, somehow impressed a patron who then paid for his education. Education was available in Galilee. The issue was that most peasants had neither the money nor leisure to invest in it, and if they did, it would normally be the oldest child

who received an education.

30. We say "in his youth," for one doubts that after the Jesus movement began to expand after the resurrection of Jesus, any of its leaders had the leisure for literary education.

31. Yet theologically one cannot discount miracle in that those church fathers who comment on the topic of the authorship of the Catholic Epistles view the quality of the Greek that came from, in their estimate, uneducated men, as being evidence of the miraculous power of God.

to it, it is unlikely that the historical James, who was martyred by 62 CE, could be responding to Romans. However, as we will argue below in the thematic commentary, what often goes unnoticed in Romans and Galatians is that the subject is "the works of the law," which are not concerns of James (James's works are works of love or charity); that James's use of "justify" means "to declare one to be just or in the right on the basis of evidence or observation" (a verdict), which may well be Paul's meaning as well, although traditionally Paul has been thought to mean "to make someone who is not just to be just or righteous"; and that Abraham was a favorite topic of both Jewish and Christian discourse, appearing in some seventy-one verses of the New Testament.

Furthermore, James's focus is on the binding of Isaac (Gen 22) as seen in Jas 2:21, which he reads as fulfilling the earlier Gen 15 passage (probably with reference to the justifying statement in Gen 22:12, "Now I know …"). In other words, if the author of James knew Romans, he has seriously misread it, which is why Klaus Haaker argued that to such a theoretical author we must say, as in the children's song, "Frère Jacques, dormez-vous?" (Brother James, are you sleeping?).[32] So we conclude that if James is reacting to Pauline ideas, he must be writing before Romans and Galatians became available to him, for he does not seem so ignorant as to have completely misunderstood those letters if he had had them.

(3) The third question, whether James the brother of Jesus was prominent enough that a later pseudepigrapher would use the name, is a bit more difficult to answer, for it depends on knowing whom Christians would have pointed to as influential figures in the period before 230 CE (i.e., the time of Origen). David R. Nienhuis has argued that he was indeed that influential, believing that James was written about 180 CE and placed as the first of the "book of the seven" (the collection of the seven Catholic Epistles) as part of a literary strategy that put a brother of Jesus at the beginning and end of the collection, a collection that included all three "pillars" that Paul names in Gal 2:9.[33] James certainly did have some continuing importance in that Josephus mentions his death (*Ant.* 20.200–201), as does Hegesippus (according to Eusebius, *Hist. eccl.* 2.23). The *Protevangelium of James* (mid- to late second century CE) claims to have been written by him. He is mentioned, according to Jerome (*De viris illustribus* 211–213) in the *Gospel of the Hebrews*, and apparently also by Clement of Alexandria (again according to Eusebius, *Hist. eccl.* 2.1.3–4), as well as a number of Gnostic or semi-Gnostic works (*Apocryphon of James*, *First Apocalypse of James*, *Gospel of Thomas*, *Pseudo-Clementine Recognitions*).

However, most of these works are late second century or third century (some are fourth century). Anything written after the mid-third century would be after our letter of James was circulating in the church. Most of these works were looking for an anti-Paul figure, and James fit the bill because he was not well known and yet had prominence as a brother of Jesus and as a figure in Acts and Galatians. Our

---

32. Klaus Haaker, "Justification, salut et foi: Étude sur les rapports entre Paul, Jacques et Pierre," *ETR* 73/2 (1998): 177–88.

33. Nienhuis, *Not by Paul Alone.*

letter is definitely not Gnostic (it has nothing to say about knowledge, mysteries, or secret revelation, for instance, although it does refer to knowing this or that), nor is it interested in the martyrdom of James or of anyone else (other than the obscure reference in Jas 5:6), for that matter. In other words, it does not fit the pattern of interest found in the references to and use of James in post-first-century works. In fact, its interests (including its lack of interest in Christology) are those of the first century, not of the second.

(4) The final question as to why the letter would be so poorly attested until the time of Origen[34] if it was a genuine letter of James the brother of Jesus, or even from his community after his death, has in part been answered in the answer to the previous question. First, James originated in a part of the world that was thrown into turmoil five or so years after his death. He was reportedly the leader of the Jerusalem community of the followers of Jesus, who, tradition claims, fled to Pella before the Romans reached Jerusalem and whose city was, therefore, destroyed after they left. In other words, both his community and his natural constituency, ethnic Jewish followers of Jesus, were in disarray after 66–70 CE, a tragedy that was compounded by later Jewish uprisings elsewhere in the Roman world and the second Jewish war of 133–135 CE.

Second, it is not surprising that as James became used by Gnostic and other groups,[35] there would be some, such as Origen, who would want to capture him for what became known as the orthodox stream of Christianity.[36] Origen, living in Palestine, was well placed to make use of a document valued (at least in some circles) there.

Third, James was not useful in the doctrinal controversies of the second and following centuries, for the letter has little to say about Jesus, at least not with respect to what was being debated about him during those centuries, or about ecclesiology, so it is not surprising that this letter was neglected. This, of course, also makes it unlikely to have been composed in the second century, unless the writer was skillfully and purposely able to avoid current issues in the attempt to create a verisimilitude of an earlier period,[37] which this present author does not believe to be likely.

---

34. Origen is the first to cite it by name. James shares terminology he may have created, that is, the word δίψυχος (dipsychos, "double-minded") with the *Shepherd of Hermas* (written around the end of the first century), and James may have been known by *1 Clement*—these and other possible echoes are laid out by J. B. Mayor, *The Epistle of St. James*, in an appendix that has never been duplicated and so is part of the continuing value of the commentary. But there are never enough words and constructions in common to prove that the author must have known James, and such arguments can be turned on their head, as Nienhuis, *Not By Paul Alone*, does, arguing that James reveals knowledge of these late first and early second century works. But if James was known by *Hermas* and *1 Clement*, then it was known in Rome by the end of the first century. This, however, has led to theories that James was written in Rome about the end of the first century (see, e.g., the works of Bo Reicke and Sophie Laws). Thus we have chosen to work with the first unambiguous citation of James rather than with possible

indications of knowing James, for that choice limits speculation.

35. That such groups used James is no surprise, for there seems to have been a tendency to attribute works to known figures among the Twelve or the early Jesus movement, as one sees in the *Gospel of Thomas*, the *Gospel of Philip*, and the *Gospel of Mary* [Magdalene]. James is more prominent in the New Testament than any of these figures.

36. Origen, of course, does not claim to have discovered James, but rather comments that he is among the books being read in churches and that not all accept it. He also cites James a number of times, indicating that he accepted the letter. So we know that it was being used in some places in Palestine, but do not know how widely it was being used outside of Palestine, although clearly it was not being used enough or not being used in the right contexts to be cited in the works of the early church fathers.

37. This is what Nienhuis, *Not by Paul Alone*, claims.

It is therefore our conclusion that the best explanation of the data is that the letter of James was written shortly after the death of James, the brother of Jesus, making use of sermons and sayings stemming from James (and/or Jesus).[38] First, it fits the historical context in which there was discrimination in the Judean region against followers of Jesus, but before the later Roman persecution of either them or Jews in general.[39]

Second, it shows signs of being an edited work with its catchword transitions and shifts in vocabulary for the same topic (for example, the use of ὑπομονή (*hypomonē*) in 1:2–4 and μακροθυμία (*makrothymia*) and its verbal cognate in the thematic reprise in 5:7–11 (both terms indicating endurance, although traditionally translated "patient endurance" and "longsuffering," respectively).[40]

Third, at the least its language (rather good Koine Greek) is the product of an amanuensis, for, as noted above, it is unlikely that the historical James had a Greek education, even though he could almost certainly speak and possibly read Greek, and this makes the amanuensis in effect the ghostwriter, although using the oral or written literary remains of the revered James.[41]

Finally, the death of James gave a good reason for the production of such a letter, made up as it is of diverse materials, for the community would want to preserve the teaching of the now-deceased leader in the absence of his living voice (as tradition tells us that the community in Rome did in asking Mark to write down the teaching of Peter after the latter's martyrdom).

Still, it would be presumptuous to argue that the work could not have been produced during the lifetime of James or that James would never have put his own sermons and sayings together. Thus, Scot McKnight, for one, eloquently argues that James himself (with help) wrote the work in the 50s.[42] This author is inclined to think that, given the (in McKnight's view, oral) influence of Pauline thought, 60 or 61 might be a better date; yet we agree that McKnight's date is possible if one does not believe that the evidence for the editing together of preexisting material is strong enough to make a posthumous collection of James's sayings more likely.[43]

---

38. Davids, *James* (NIGTC), 9–12.

39. Of course, it was slander and discrimination that was experienced by the followers of Jesus in Asia Minor to which 1 Peter was written, as will be pointed out below. Our point is that this "low-grade" persecution (in comparison with second-century Roman persecution, not in the eyes of those experiencing it) is consistent with the period leading up to the first Jewish war in Palestine. The Neronic persecution was violent, but it was limited and localized.

40. There is also the evidence that Jas 2:1–13 and 2:14–26 each follow a Jewish sermonic format and so were probably originally separate sermons.

41. Some of his teaching may have been written down, but surely many in the Jerusalem community could have repeated his sayings and sermons, especially those who were in close contact with him. This is similar to what we believe happened in the case of Jesus, about whom more was remembered, and with good reason, but with respect to whom a similar dynamic was at work—limited

or no writing by him, but people close to him passing on his words and deeds.

42. McKnight, *James*, 28, although the whole argument runs from 13–38.

43. Posthumous editing together of an author's work does not make him or her less of an author. This present author has Edwin H. Friedman's *Failure of Nerve: Leadership in the Age of the Quick Fix* (New York: Seabury, 1999, 2007). Now Friedman died in 1996, so it is clear that the book is a posthumous work. He had intended to publish it, but had not finished it, and apparently he had left partially finished materials and, at least to some degree, unordered materials. The editors had their work cut out for them. Yet anyone who has read Friedman's other works, as this author has, recognizes that this is his material, his voice. He is the author, even if the editors played a significant role in getting his message to the public that he intended to read it. The publisher is right to feature Friedman's name as author (with the editors' names, as well as lots of other publishing information, in smaller print).

2.2.2 The Literary Form

2.2.2.1 Overall Literary Form

James is very much a letter, even if it is a general or catholic letter; as is typical in letters, its rhetorical form is mixed. Thus, while we can speak of rhetorical elements within in, it cannot be labeled epideictic, deliberative, or judicial rhetoric as a whole.

While there are almost as many analyses of James's structure as there are commentaries on James, what follows is, in our mind, the best way to outline it.[44] It starts with a typical letter salutation (1:1), but it has no thanksgiving before plunging into the body opening (1:2–18). The body middle (1:19–4:10) and body closing (4:11–5:6) are followed by a letter closing (5:7–5:20). The letter closing does not end with personal greetings and a final blessing or doxology in the author's hand, as Paul's letters usually do, for this is a general letter and most likely posthumous. Instead, it follows another typical letter convention of the period by ending with a summary (5:7–11), oath (or, in James's case, a non-oath, 5:12), health wish (in James's case, a healing prayer, 5:13–18), and purpose statement (5:19–20). It is this overall form that gives context and thus a particular meaning to the individual units.

2.2.2.2 Sources

James, like all New Testament authors, uses sources. He clearly has two major sources: (1) the teaching of Jesus, and (2) a Greek version of the Jewish Scriptures (all of James's quotations conform to the LXX). (1) A saying of Jesus appears clearly in 5:12 (parallel to Matt 5:33–37); since its source is not cited (our author probably believed that followers of Jesus would recognize his teaching), that should alert us to the probability of other allusions to and citations of the teachings of Jesus. In fact, James is relatively close to the Matthean version of the "Q" tradition of Jesus' teaching, and in particular to the Sermon on the Mount,[45] even if, in his woes on the rich, he at times seems a bit like Luke. There is no New Testament work outside of the Gospels that is as deeply influenced by the teaching of Jesus as James. He seems to expect that his readers know that teaching and will recognize his reconfiguration of it in his letter.

It is even possible that the letter includes a number of agrapha (sayings of Jesus not recorded in the Gospels), although, because James does not attribute any of his allusions or references to the teaching of Jesus, we cannot know for sure.[46] This is precisely what one would expect in James, for if the author is educated to the pro-

---

44. It should be noted that this differs in significant respects from Davids, *James*, 25–28, for, while he is still convinced of the basic unitary argument of the work, the development of rhetorical and discourse analytical studies of James have pushed this author to change his mind in some respects.

45. For parallels see Davids, *James*, 47–49; Franz Mussner, *Jako-*

busbrief, 48–50; Dean B. Deppe, *The Sayings of Jesus in the Epistle of James* (Chelsea, MI: Bookcrafters, 1989); and Hartin, *James and the Q Sayings of Jesus*.

46. See Davids, *James*, 16, 50, 97. Origen, for example, believed that Jas 1:22 was an agraphon. Others have cited Jas 3:18 as another possibility.

gymnastic level, he has learned the rhetorical technique of *aemulatio*. That is, he has learned to take the words of a well-known author and reconfigure them to fit into different contexts. One was to do this in such a way that educated (in our case, those who knew the Jesus tradition) listeners (to an oration) or readers (of a document) would recognize the source of the material and also recognize the skill with which it had been adapted to the present context. Once one recognizes the ubiquity of this rhetorical technique in the ancient world and its presence in James, its similarity to the teaching of Jesus without clear direct quotations, let alone attributed quotations, becomes clear.[47] In other words, there is a high degree of intertextuality between James and the Matthean form of the teaching of Jesus, and in particular, the Sermon on the Mount, which form was probably current in the eastern Mediterranean world well before the gospel of Matthew was written.

(2) Examples of quotations of the Jewish Scriptures occur in Jas 2:8 (Lev 19:18); Jas 2:11 (Exod 20:13–14; Deut 5:17–18); Jas 2:23 (Gen 15:6); and Jas 4:6 (Prov 3:34), as well as in James's allusions to theological concepts and his citation of ancient narratives, such as Jas 2:21 (Gen 22) and Jas 2:25 (Josh 2; 6:17, 22–23, 25).

When it comes to the citing of narratives as opposed to didactic passages of the Hebrew Scriptures, James also reveals an awareness of and dependence on Second Temple Jewish literature. For instance, the Job of Jas 5:11 is not the Job of the Jewish Scriptures, who is never said to have exhibited patient endurance and in fact complains quite a lot, but the Job of the *Testament of Job*—a work that depends on and uses phrases from canonical Job, but revolves around the idea of patient endurance (ὑπομονή, *hypomonē*, the very word used in James). Another example is James's citation of the binding of Isaac (Gen 22), which James seems to read through the lens of such works as *Jubilees* (*Jub.* 17–19) or the War Scroll from Qumran (1QM 16–17), both of which interpret Gen 22:1 through the lens of Job and attribute the test to Satan and not to God; this allows James to say what he does in Jas 1:13.

Clearly, then, James was much a part of his culture, having either listened to (in oral form) or read the interpretations of the narratives of the Jewish Scriptures found in works such as these. In fact, when it comes to narratives, there is no evidence that he had actually read or checked the original Scriptures in either Greek or Hebrew form.[48]

---

47. See further John S. Kloppenborg, "Reception and Emulation of the Jesus Tradition in James," in *Reading James with New Eyes: Methodological Reassessments of the Letter of James* (ed. Robert L. Webb and John S. Kloppenborg; LNTS 342; New York: T&T Clark, 2007), 121–50.

48. See further David A. deSilva, *The Jewish Teachers of Jesus, James, and Jude: What Earliest Christianity Learned from the Apocrypha and Pseudepigrapha* (Oxford/New York: Oxford University Press, 2012). We do not know that the historical James could understand Hebrew. Among Jews it was the liturgical language of his day, but as anyone knows who has had experience with people exposed to the use of archaic English in liturgy today, the fact that one might listen to a liturgical language and might even repeat creeds or prayers in it does not mean that one can understand, much less speak it.

We also know relatively little about the first-century synagogue. But assuming that James had gone there regularly, he would have heard the Torah (including Gen 22) read in Hebrew and possibly the other narratives he cites as well. However, as is often the case now, the more contemporary literary renditions of the text are the versions he apparently remembers. For instance, how many contemporary believers are aware that "the ox and the ass" do not appear in Jesus' birth narratives? Moreover, while Luke says there was a "manger" in the place where Jesus was born (Luke 2:7) and while we know farm families often brought the animals into the house at night, there is no mention of animals being present. Yet these are fixed parts of nativity art, plays, and sermons.

2.2.2.3 Literary Structures and Language

Within this overall structure, the letter is made up of short discourses, sayings, proverbs, and the like, often joined by catchwords. For instance, 1:4 is joined to 1:5 by the catchword pair λειπόμενοι (*leipomenoi*, "lacking") — λείπεται (*leipetai*, "lacks"). Within the paragraph 1:5–8 internal unity is created by the use of complementary terms (αἰτείτω, *aiteitō*, "ask," and λήμψεται, *lēmpsetai*, "receive"). The saying in 1:8 sums up and ends the paragraph before a new subject is introduced in 1:9. The testing or trials of 1:2 is picked up again in 1:12 through the use of three different terms from the earlier passage.[49] With the thematic unity established, the paragraph goes on to discuss why one might fail the test. In other words, James is skillful in using rhetorical devices such as catchwords, complementary terms, and repeated use of the same root to maintain the flow and unity of what seems on the surface to be (and probably originally was) a collection of disparate units.

New major sections of the argument are often introduced with "my siblings" or "my beloved siblings" (traditionally translated "my brothers" or "my brothers and sisters"), as in 1:19 and 2:1, 14. Of course, changes in subject can also be used to mark out paragraphs and other sections of the argument, although they are rarely used to mark out major sections.

Generally, the language of James is good Koine Greek, among the better examples of Greek in the New Testament. But sometimes one finds the intrusion of Semitisms, especially in 1:22–25, where "doer of the word" is understandable English, and good Hebrew or Aramaic, but in Greek should mean a poet or perhaps a writer ("one who makes words"), although the context makes the Semitic idiom understandable, if awkward, even in Greek.[50] But it is only such expressions that show Semitic influence on the style, for even within this paragraph most of the grammatical structures are very much Greek. James is not translation Greek (except where the Greek version of the Jewish Scriptures is quoted). Ironically, the section starting with the paragraph referred to above follows a verse in which we have a phrase that probably originated in Orphic wisdom and is found in Stoic philosophy ("the implanted word," τὸν ἔμφυτον λόγον, *ton emphyton logon*).[51]

In other words, James has picked up expressions from more than one source, just as various expressions and idioms creep into contemporary language.[52] James can also use unusual terms, some of which he may have created himself. For instance, δίψυχος (*dipsychos*, "double-minded") in Jas 1:8 may well be a neologism, for the next time it appears in Greek is in the *Shepherd of Hermas* (where it appears multiple times;

49. This symmetry is often obscured when the term translated "trials" or "tests" in Jas 1:2, or its verbal equivalent is translated "temptation" or "tempt" in 1:12–13.

50. The author is reminded of what his students at Bibelschule Wiedenest said during his first year of teaching in German: "We like Mr. Davids because he says things, so … so differently." In other words, English idioms and images were understandable from context, but clearly were not how a native German would have said it.

51. The exact phrase is attributed to Epictetus, although it is not in his *Discourses*, but the general idea can also be found in Philo. What Epictetus actually says using "implanted" is found in *Diatr.* 2.11.3: ἔμφυτον ἔννοιαν.

52. This author grew up in a church community using the King James Version for Bible reading and equally archaic language in hymns. This language sometimes appeared in his high school essays, especially if there was a religious theme or allusion to the Bible or the hymns, only to be flagged as wrong by his teacher (for the language was incorrect grammar in the then-contemporary English).

this is dated around 96 CE);[53] and ἀπείραστος (*apeirastos*, "ought not to be tested" or "unable to be tested") in 1:13 next appears in Greek literature long after James.[54]

There are some larger literary structures in James. For example, Jas 2:1–13 and 2:14–28 are units structured similarly to one form of the later synagogue sermon (we have no surviving first-century sermons for comparison, so we must rely on second-century sermons).[55] Each of them starts with a statement of the issue, continues with a short narrative example (in both cases overdrawn for effect), then adds a theological argument and two biblical passages before concluding with a summary saying. That these units contribute to the whole theme of the book should not make one forget that they are in themselves complete arguments in a known literary form.

2.2.2.4 Outline

While the purpose of James is to "turn a sinner from the error of their ways" and thus to save that person from death (5:20), how James does that and what the errors are appear in the structure. As indicated above, there have been a lot of attempts to outline James, but this is how it looks to this author:

A. Letter Salutation and Greeting (1:1)
B. Letter Body Opening: Testing (in Speech and Deed) and God (1:2–18)
  1. The value in testing (1:2–4)
  2. God's provision in the test (1:5–8)
  3. The irony of wealth (1:9–11)
  4. Why one fails a test (1:12–15)
  5. God's contrasting goodness (1:16–18)
C. Letter Body Middle (1:19–4:10)
  1. Controlling speech (1:19–27)
  2. About favoritism based on economic status (2:1–13)
  3. Doing good is part of the essence of faith, not an option (2:14–26)
  4. The danger of conflict (3:1–4:10)
D. Letter Body Closing (4:11–5:6)
  1. Do not judge (4:11–12)
  2. Trust God rather than money (4:13–17)
  3. The condemnation of the rich (5:1–6)
E. Letter Conclusion (5:7–20)
  1. Summary/conclusion (5:7–11)
  2. The non-oath (5:12)
  3. Praying for healing (5:13–18)
  4. Purpose statement (5:19–20)

---

53. There are verbal forms of δίψυχος that may be earlier, depending on how one dates the various Apostolic Fathers. For instance, the verbal form appears in *Did.* 4.4, as well as in *Barnabas* 19.5; *1 Clem.* 11.2; 23.2–3; *2 Clem.* 11.2, 5; 19.2. For further information on this issue, including the relative dating, see Carolyn Osiek, *The Shepherd of Hermas: A Commentary* (Hermeneia; Minneapolis: Fortress, 1999), 30, n. 232.

54. See Peter H. Davids, "The Meaning of Ἀπείραστος Revisited," in *New Testament Greek and Exegesis: Essays in Honor of Gerald F. Hawthorne* (ed. Timothy Sailors and Amy Donaldson; Grand Rapids: Eerdmans, 2003), 225–40.

55. See W. W. Wessel, "An Inquiry into the Origin, Literary Character, Historical and Religious Significance of the Epistle of James" (PhD diss., Edinburgh, 1953), 71–112.

2.3 A LITERARY-THEOLOGICAL
READING OF JAMES

As we turn to the letter itself, we will observe both the development of various theological themes and the skillful way in which the author uses his language to link and structure those themes. While theology will "come together" in the biblical theological section that follows, this section will see how the teaching is presented within the rhetorical structure of the letter.

2.3.1 Letter Salutation and Greeting (1:1)

The salutation is in standard Greek form, identifying the author and the recipients and concluding with the usual Greek greeting χαίρειν (*chairein*, "greetings," the only New Testament letter to use this standard form; cf. two letters embedded in Acts: Acts 15:23; 23:26).

Theologically, the greeting identifies God and Jesus the Anointed One (or Messiah) as co-owners of James, the slave. The slave had no social status on his or her own, but took their status from the master whom he or she represented. Thus, in the Hebrew Scriptures in Exod 4:10 Moses, speaking to God, refers to himself as "your slave"; in Exod 14:31 the narrator says that "the people trusted in YHWH and in his slave Moses" (the order being significant); and in Num 12:7–8 YHWH twice honors Moses, referring to him as "my slave Moses" (one who took his authority and status from his relationship to YHWH in contrast to prophets, who have a more clouded relationship).

Just as significant is the use of such language in the Greco-Roman world, where Caesar's slave was indeed a social zero in and of himself or herself, but because Caesar was the master, the slave, when on official business, had virtually the authority of Caesar himself. In our text the "government" is that of God and Jesus the Anointed One (since James only uses titles of authority for Jesus in the rare instances when he mentions him, we believe that he is fully aware of the significance of Χριστοῦ [*christou*, "Christ," "Messiah," "Anointed One"]; thus, transliterating it as if it were Jesus' surname is misleading). James does not explain how he sees the two of them linked in government (i.e., what the role of the "Anointed One" is in relationship to God), but he does see them linked, with James as the slave of both—one might say "family slave" but James is not using family language for God or for Jesus; rather, he is using governmental language.[56]

James writes, "To the twelve tribes in the Dispersion." While in a Jewish Diaspora letter this phrase would refer to ethnic Jews living outside of Palestine, it is clear to virtually all commentators from James's self-identification that James is

---

56. James will call God the "Father of lights" in Jas 1:17 (a creational reference) and portrays him as a mother giving birth in 1:18. God is referred to as "God, the Father" in 1:27 and as "Lord and Father" in 3:9, but they are in a worship context (true religious practice and the action of "blessing" a ruler or deity). So family language is muted at best in James, other than in the one reference to God's giving "us" birth.

writing to followers of Jesus.[57] Thus, the question is whether this address is a limiting reference ("to Jewish followers of Jesus scattered outside of Palestine, who are the true Israel") or an inclusive reference ("to all the scattered followers of Jesus, Jews as well as Gentiles, all of whom are viewed as Israel"). James does not seem conscious of a Jew-Gentile division among the followers of Jesus; so, although the work is written with ethnic Jewish assumptions (e.g., we will later see that "the law" is not an issue for James, but is a term that he uses unselfconsciously as applicable to his implied readers), it appears that the inclusive meaning is intended. But this meaning is not intended as a developed theological statement (such as one finds in Paul, e.g., Gal 6:16 ["the Israel of God"], or 1 Peter, e.g., 1 Pet 2:9, discussed later in this volume); rather, it is an unselfconscious inclusion of all followers of Jesus in the "Twelve Tribes."

They are "in the Dispersion" (or "Diaspora"), which is not a statement about their being scattered from their "heavenly home" (i.e., a spiritualization of "Dispersion"), but rather an indication that they are outside of Palestine, and that this letter is in the style of so-called "Diaspora letters," letters written from Jewish leaders in Jerusalem to the scattered Jewish communities outside of the land.[58] Thus this appears primarily as a sociological rather than a theological designation, although without any indication that would or could think of any follower of Jesus as being outside of Israel.[59]

2.3.2 Letter Body Opening: Testing and God (1:2–18)

While Greek letters often began with a thanksgiving to the gods for the recipients (which Paul expands in monotheistic form, often making it into a major theological statement), James omits this and plunges directly into the opening to the body of the letter, in which opening he wishes to establish the major themes of the letter. Thus in this body opening we will discover three major themes: testing (its positive aspects and why one may fail), God's role with respect to testing, and a theological perspective on wealth and poverty, which will later appear as significant with respect to testing. Because these themes are so significant in the rest of the letter, each of the five paragraphs deserves significant treatment.

2.3.2.1 The Value in Testing (1:2–4)

The first paragraph of the letter body opening sets the topic as "testing" (πειρασμός, *peirasmos*) and, in common with 1 Pet 1:6–7 (and, with a lesser degree of verbal agreement, with Rom 5:2b–5), speaks about joy in such testing or trials. James

---

57. A few commentators, starting with F. Spitta, *Der Brief des Jakobus untersucht* (Göttingen: Vandenhoeck & Ruprecht, 1896), have argued that James was originally a Jewish work written to ethnic Jews and that the references to Jesus are later interpolations. This position has had little influence in the history of interpretation of the letter.

58. Karl-Wilhelm Niebuhr, "Der Jakobusbrief im Licht frühjü-

discher Diasporabriefe," *NTS* 44 (1998): 420–24.

59. If one were to date James late and assume that he knew the Pauline letters, one would have to read this as a clear statement that the "twelve tribes" are now the church rather than, as we believe, a simple inclusion of Gentile believers with Jews in the "twelve tribes," which are that part of ethnic Jews who recognize Jesus as the Messiah.

uses an imperative, "consider it total joy." Thus two theological concepts are introduced, the first one being that of testing and the second being that of eschatological anticipated joy.

The first theological concept starts in the Hebrew Scriptures in Gen 22:1, "After these things God tested Abraham" (using the verbal form of the same word found in James), and its outcome is found in 22:12 ("now I know that you fear God") and the blessing of 22:17–18 (which confirms the previous promises to Abraham in 12:1–3; 15:5–6; 17:1–6 [i.e., all the promises other than the promise of land] on the basis of Abraham's having passed the test). It is significant that the Gen 22 narrative is important to James (see below on Jas 2:14–26), and the Gen 15:6 promise is cited within the context of the reference to the Gen 22 narrative, just as in 22:17–18.

The testing theme continues in the Pentateuch with YHWH testing Israel in Exod 15:25 and 20:20. It is also found in Josh 3:1, 4; Ps 11:5; and 26:2 ("Prove me, O LORD, and try me; test my heart and mind," NRSV). In all of these passages it is stated or assumed that God is doing the testing.[60] Judith 8:25–26 has God testing Israel (and refers explicitly to Gen 22) and Wis 3:5 and 11:10 refer to God's testing the righteous (although in both cases paralleling it to a parent's discipline, so mitigating it). First Maccabees 2:52 parallels the suffering of the Maccabean period (169–166 BCE) to the testing of Abraham in Gen 22. But in Sir 2:1 ("My child, when you come to serve the Lord, prepare yourself for testing," NRSV), the testing appears not to come from God, for in the following verses God is cited as the one to cling to in the test or the one who helps one in the test. In Matt 4:1 and its parallels it is the devil who tests Jesus, as he does followers of Jesus in Rev 2:10. In 1 Cor 10:13 God appears to allow and limit testing, but is not said to cause it. That may be the meaning of the line in the Lord's Prayer, "do not bring us to the test" (Matt 6:13). The point is that James had ample reason to believe (1) that followers of Jesus/God would have their commitment to God/Jesus tested; and (2) that successful navigation of these trials would lead to divine approval.

The idea of divine approval lies behind the second theological concept, that of eschatological anticipated joy.[61] James is not a masochist who believes that testing, which often involves some type of suffering, is pleasant, but he does believe that one can reframe testing in the light of its eventual consequences and thus view it as a reason for joy. After mentioning joy in testing James goes on to refer to "the process or means of determining the genuineness of"[62] their commitment (or faith) — notice that it is biased toward a positive outcome — which will produce the virtue of patient endurance. This is the virtue that brackets James, appearing here, again in the inclusio in 1:12, and finally in the summary of the work in 5:11. It is also the virtue that

60. As the concept of Satan (under one name or another) developed, testing tended to shift from God's agency in testing to Satan's, just as 1 Chr 21:1 does to God's inciting David in 2 Sam 24:1. Thus in Job, where the concept but not the language of testing appears, it is Satan who does the testing. This will become important later, as we look at Jas 1:13.

61. This expression is a translation of the German *eschatologische Vorfreude,* first used in relationship to this passage by J. Thomas, "Anfechtung und Vorfreude," *KD* 14 (1968): 183–206, esp. 183–85.

62. BDAG, 256, δοκίμιον, def. 1.

the Matthean Jesus says is necessary for salvation in the context of persecution, "The one who endures to the end will be saved" (Matt 10:22; 24:13 NRSV).

If one gains this virtue, one will be "mature" or "perfect" (again a virtue that Jesus commanded, Matt 5:48, and Noah had, Gen 6:9 LXX), lacking "nothing," that is, no virtue. In this light one can have joy in testing, for, if endured, testing will show one's commitment (or faith) is genuine and results in virtues that are necessary to salvation. This end result (which is eschatologically anticipated) is something in which one can rejoice now, right in the middle of the painful test, just as one might rejoice in a surgery that will preserve or vastly improve one's life or as an athlete might during a punishing practice that holds out the promise of victory in the coming game.

This teaching, of course, needs to be read in the light of the purpose statement of the whole letter found in Jas 5:19–20, that the letter is intended to save a person (or "soul") from death. It will be clear later that James is concerned that some are not passing the test, but are verbally attacking one another, are showing favoritism to the wealthy, and/or are failing to demonstrate care of the poor—the results of a community under economic and social pressure. In our passage we have his anticipatory positive teaching: we should rejoice in this undoubted pressure, for if it shows our commitment as genuine, it will produce the saving virtue of endurance, which will bring one through to "the end."

2.3.2.2 God's Provision in the Test (1:5–8)

As will become clear in this letter, not everyone is proving one's commitment (to God and to Jesus) to be genuine and thus advancing in virtue. Some need help. Using a catchword link ("lacking"–"lack"), James suggests that what is lacking is "wisdom," that divine agent known from Prov 8, and especially from Wisdom of Solomon and Sirach. Whereas Paul or John would have referred to the Holy Spirit as the divine agent helping human beings, James, who never mentions the Spirit[63] (and in that sense is binitarian, assuming that he thought of Jesus as divine), but is steeped in the wisdom tradition, refers to wisdom, which will receive extended treatment in 3:13–18.

The point of this present passage is that this wisdom is a divine gift, and so those feeling a need should request wisdom from "the giving God." That is, God is presented as the ideal patron (patron-client relationships were fundamental to the Mediterranean world, and so the concept would not be foreign):[64] generous with his resources and not someone who reproaches or reprimands[65] the supplicant (who would often come to his patron for his daily needs).

The client (the one feeling a need for Lady Wisdom), however, needs to make his or her request from the position of single-minded commitment to the patron

---

63. Jas 2:26 and 4:5, the only references to πνεῦμα (pneuma, "spirit") in the letter, both refer to the human spirit.

64. David A. deSilva, *Honor, Patronage, Kinship and Purity:*

Unlocking New Testament Culture (Downers Grove, IL: InterVarsity Press, 2000), 95–156.

65. BDAG, 710, ὀνειδίζω, meaning 2.

(the giving God). It is important that this commitment to the patron does not waver (which is a better translation than "doubting").[66] Unfortunately, too often in past interpretation it has been forgotten that πίστις (*pistis*, "commitment," "trust," "faith") is a commitment word when it is related to a personal object, not a term indicating what one mentally thinks or believes (which is a meaning that it can have when related to facts or data, and which its verbal form does have in such a context in Jas 2:19). It has also often been forgotten that διακρινόμενος (*diakrinomenos*, traditionally translated "doubting" and thus related to a mental state, but here translated "wavering") must be interpreted here as a wavering in allegiance[67] or commitment.

This meaning is seen not only in the illustrations James uses, e.g., the waves washing back and forth, but especially in the reference to instability in 1:8 and in the possible neologism[68] usually translated "double-minded" (δίψυχος, *dipsychos*, lit., "double-souled"). This latter term picks up the concept in the Hebrew Scriptures in which the double-hearted person (e.g., Ps 12:1–2) is reviled and the one who is not double-hearted (e.g., 1 Chr 12:33) is praised. That is, the person who lacks loyalty (thus flatters the king, but their loyalty is elsewhere) is contrasted to the one who is loyal, who has a single heart (e.g., Deut 6:5).

This same contrast is found in the later wisdom tradition (e.g., Sir 1:28–29; 2:12–14; and frequently in the Dead Sea Scrolls). So James is saying that the one who is sincerely loyal to his or her patron (God) will receive wisdom generously, but the one who wavers in their loyalty or allegiance will not. The patron (God) is not fooled. He knows that a person with divided loyalties is unstable in every aspect of their life. They are approaching him now, but will just as easily approach some other "patron" (in James the alternative is not personal, but wealth or "the world"); they will therefore receive nothing from God. This theme will be picked up again in the extreme in Jas 4:1–5.

2.3.2.3 The Irony of Wealth (1:9–11)

James appears to turn to another issue, wealth, devoting a single paragraph to it. Here it appears unrelated to what precedes, but, as we will see, it is the major symbol of "the world," the alternative "patron." James begins as in 1:2 with a seemingly paradoxical statement, in this case that the "lowly" or "poor" community member (the Greek term caries both meanings, just as the corresponding Hebrew term does in the Hebrew Scriptures) is to "boast" in their being exalted. But the paradox is the paradox of two worldviews. While the society around them has labeled the person "poor" or "lowly," James's audience boasts because they have committed to the Jesus of the Sermon on the Mount (who said about the poor, "theirs is the kingdom," Matt 5:3) and are therefore "heirs of the kingdom" (Jas 2:5). Their this-age out-

---

66. BDAG, 231, διακρίνω.

67. This is how Ropes, *James*, does indeed translate it in commenting on the verse.

68. The word does not appear earlier in Greek literature unless

one dates James later than the *Shepherd of Hermas*, as Nienhuis, *Not by Paul Alone*, does. Thus it is possible that James or someone in his community coined the term.

ward circumstances are still limited and their this-age social standing low, but once they "see" with "eschatological eyes," they understand that they are royalty, soon to inherit it all. Such "boasting" is a confession of faith.

On the other hand, the rich[69] are told, with biting irony, to "boast" in their "humiliation." The irony is only caught when one realizes that "humiliation" and "lowly"/"poor" are forms of the same root. In other words, when viewed with "eschatological eyes," the rich are precisely where society thinks that the "lowly" community member is. Actually, James goes on to say, they are in a worse place, for as happens when the Mediterranean sun burns down on the flowers of the field, they wither and die without warning, that is, right in the middle of their busy lives.

Thus we have two worldviews. The one values people, including themselves, from God's eschatological point of view, while the other values them according to conventional marks of wealth and social status. The issue for James will be whether or not the communities he is addressing, which claim to be committed to God, are in fact living according to the kingdom/eschatological perspective.

2.3.2.4 Why One Fails a Test[70] (1:12–15)

Using an inclusio that summarizes and resumes the argument of Jas 1:2–4, our author states that the person who patiently endures testing is "blessed" or "happy" or "fortunate."[71] Then, adding to what was said in 1:2–4,[72] James says that when such a person has been "approved" or has been found to be "genuine," that person will receive "the crown that is life itself," which God has promised to those who love him (an idea also mentioned in Rev 2:10). James does not say much about loving God, but this is one text in which he does.[73] While "crown" is an image from the trophy (a circlet of laurel) that was awarded to the victors of games and significant military battles, that idea that God promises life to those who love him (i.e., serve

---

69. "The rich" in James are not believers. When wealthier believers are mentioned, the term "rich" is not used, but rather a description that lets one know that they have means. When "the rich" is used elsewhere in James, it is clear that they are viewed as persecutors (Jas 2:6; 5:1–6). Thus it is our argument that here James deliberately does not call "the rich" members of the community of the followers of Jesus as he does "the lowly" (i.e., he can say ὁ ἀδελφὸς ὁ ταπεινός, the *tapeinos adelphos*, the "lowly community member," but never says *plousios adelphos*, but rather just πλούσιος, *plousios*, "rich") because they are not members of the believing community. It was Jesus, of course, who said that it was impossible for "the rich" to be saved (Mark 10:25 and parallels). Luke, after quoting this in Luke 18:25, goes on to show an example of God's miracle in saving a rich man in 19:1–10, but the evidence of this salvation is that the rich man gives up a significant portion of his wealth.

70. Many translations shift from "trials" or "tests" to "temptation" at this point. It is true that the Greek *peirasmos* covers all those semantic fields, but (1) testing is the basic concept, for a temptation is a test that the tester hopes the one being tested will fail; and (2) there is no semantic signal in James that he is shifting to a significantly different meaning of the word group. Thus, in order to

understand the flow of ideas in James, it is important not to shift to a different English translation.

71. BDAG, 610–11; the Greek term *makarios* means all of these things, depending on context; it is not a specifically religious term, so "blessed" can be misleading. Here it picks up on the idea of "considering it total joy" of 1:2.

72. The first clause of 1:12 picks up no less than three Greek terms from 1:2–4, making it an admirable summary, but the second clause no longer has any references to 1:2–4, showing that it is introducing a new idea.

73. In biblical literature "love" is more volitional than emotional; it is the choice or disposition to do good to someone, while "hate" is the choice or disposition to do ill to them. Thus loving God, serving God, and obeying God are essentially synonymous, although "love" focuses on the disposition to serve and obey (when the object is God), a disposition that is meaningless if there is no "follow through" in actual service/obedience. The point for the Western reader is that "love" does not necessarily have any emotion connected to it, certainly not passion, although it is often read in from Western culture.

him) is found throughout the New Testament. Here that life is the reward for proving one's love and commitment by enduring testing.

But James's concern in this passage is not primarily with those who pass the test, but with those who fail. The first step in failure is to blame God. This picks up another theme of the Hebrew Scriptures, which is that of testing God or putting God to the test. Just as passing the test starts with Abraham, failing the test starts with the Israelites in the wilderness, who repeatedly blame Moses or God for the tests and trials of life in that location (e.g., Exod 17:2, 7; Num 14:22; Deut 6:16). There is no trust, allegiance, or commitment in the Israelite cry, "Back to Egypt!"

Unlike the Hebrew Scriptures, James says that this testing of God is wrong, not just because it is a failure of allegiance (which he would surely agree with, given his previous negative reference to being "double-minded"), but also a failure to realize that God does not test anyone. How can James say that in the light of Gen 22:1, "After these events, God tested Abraham"[74] (and similar passages)? He can do so because he is reading Gen 22:1 through the lens of some Second Temple tradition like that in *Jub.* 17–19, which retells Gen 22:1 using Job 1–2 as its template. Now, Satan is the tester, not God.[75] Moreover, James implies that to accuse God of being the source of testing is to put God to the test (just as Israel did in the wilderness), for he says, "God ought not to be tested by evil people."[76] So for James God is *not* the one who puts people to the test, and to accuse him of doing so ("Why did God send this test/trial?") is to fall into the sin of Israel, that of testing God.

We would now expect James to state, along with *Jubilees* and similar literature, that Satan is the cause of human testing, but, while he in some sense believes that Satan is involved (as we can see the call to repentance in Jas 4:7 or the description of pseudo-wisdom in 3:13–15), he instead pins the blame directly on human weakness: desire. Already in Genesis there are references to defects in the human heart (Gen 6:5; 8:21, the one giving the reason for the deluge and the other giving the same reason for why there will never again be such a deluge); the Jews developed this into the concept of an uncontrolled impulse in humanity, referred to in Hebrew as the *yēṣer,* an idea not dissimilar to the Freudian *id* or what contemporary psychology would refer to as the human drives (the issue in this early period being, not that it was evil per se, but that it lacked boundaries and so would eventually lead to evil).

James, who may or may not know the Hebrew term, uses the standard Greek term "desire" (ἐπιθυμία, *epithymia*), for Greek philosophers were just as distrustful of the human drives as the Jews, especially because such drives were changeable unlike reason. For the Greeks the answer was self-control, sometimes in the form of

---

74. The translation is from the CEB. James uses not only the same subject, God, as Gen 22:1, but also the same verb, repeating the verb (in various forms) four times in two verses.

75. In the Dead Sea Scroll 1QM 16–17 Satan is also presented as the active tester of God's people.

76. This author has defended the translation of this clause in Jas 1:13 in two articles, "The Meaning of Ἀπείραστος in James i.13," *NTS* 24 (1978): 386–92; and "The Meaning of Ἀπείραστος Revisited." Other translations of this verse, such as "God cannot be tempted by evil and he himself tempts no one" (NRSV), end up with a non sequitur, for why should God's not being tempted or tested imply that he does not himself test or tempt? This is especially problematic in Greek, where the same word for "test" is used in 1:2, 12, and 13.

philosophical detachment, while for the developing Jewish theology the answer was meditation on the Torah. While having a different solution to the problem, James agrees with both Greek and Jewish cultures that it is our desires, our emotional drives — not any drive in particular, but drives in general — that are the source of human failure in the various tests of life.

James pictures desire first as the bait in a trap and then as a seductress (the fact that *epithymia* is grammatically feminine in Greek, as is wisdom, which is God's gift to assist us in the test, makes this image easier), who gets pregnant (it does not say by whom), gives birth to sin (also grammatically feminine), which in turn gives birth to death, the same death that it is the purpose of the book to deliver a person from (Jas 5:19–20). This chain of desire–sin–death, then, starts within the person. Thus, for James, human beings can rightly say, "We have followed too much the devices and desires of our own hearts, we have offended against thy holy laws, we have left undone those things which we ought to have done, and we have done those things which we ought not to have done."[77] The devil did *not* "make me do it," nor did the test come from God.

2.3.2.5 God's Contrasting Goodness (1:16–18)

If God is not behind the test, where is God? James has already told us (1:5). God, at our request, sends his good lady Wisdom to help us should we not be perfect or mature in virtue. James resumes this statement of 1:5 by saying that "every good gift and every perfect act of giving" come from God. It is clear that James thinks of God as "Father" in this first of three times that he uses that title for him (see also 1:27; 3:9). But he adds "of lights" and so here he means "Father" in the sense of "the Creator of the heavenly bodies." Creation is probably being thought of as at least one of the good gifts God has given. However, the title also enables James to play on the characteristics of heavenly bodies and to point out that, unlike them,[78] God never changes (with regard to his character). The moon may wax and wane, the sun may rise and set, but God gives good and only good. He does not give good one day and evil the next; he does not give wisdom one day and testing the next.

James has an example of the goodness of the "Father of lights," one that parallels the negative chain of desire–sin–death above. God willingly (i.e., not accidentally, but by deliberate choice) birthed us. This is a startling metaphor, for the verb is the verb "to give birth" and is normally applied only to feminine agents (as in 1:15). Yet continuing with the metaphor, James not only says that God gives birth, but that the "sperm" is "the word/saying of truth" or "the true word/saying,"[79] which surely means the good news of Jesus as the Anointed King and the coming-and-already-

77. "Confession of sin in Penitential Order I," The Episcopal Church, *The Book of Common Prayer* (New York: Seabury, 1979), 320–21.

78. While many scholars think that the phases of the moon best fit this description of "variation" and "shadow due to change," the truth is that while we know perfectly well what James means by his metaphor, we do not know the particular astronomical phenom-

enon to which he is referring. Many astronomical bodies appear to change, but God does not, despite having created them.

79. The Greek *logos* can mean a word, but it also means a saying or utterance, a speech-act. Here, of course, more than a single word is intended, so we need at least to think of "word" as a whole utterance.

come kingdom. And, in contrast to sin giving birth to death as in 1:15, God's birthing is to be the best of life, resulting in "a type of firstfruit of those things that he created," that is, the best or apex of creation.

But what creation is this? Since it is through "the true word," not through physical birth, James must be thinking of the new order of the world, the new creation, which fits with his earlier insistence that his readers need to "put on eschatological glasses" so as to see the world from God's point of view. The coming age has already come to birth in them, and this is a prime (probably for James, *the* prime) example of God's unchanging goodness.

This leaves human beings with a choice of following their desires or single-mindedly seeking God and seeking wisdom from him, found first of all in the wisdom of "the true word." The problem with failing in the test is found squarely in their choice, not in whether they pray per se, but in whether they seek God with their total commitment and allegiance, or whether they seek God verbally but then also give allegiance to something else, such as money or another of "the world's" manifestations. This would split their allegiance by giving in to desire. This "two ways" teaching, God's way or desire's way, is what James will expand in the main part of the body of the letter.

2.3.3 Letter Body Middle: The Great Tests: The Tongue and the Wallet (1:19–4:10)

In pursuing his goal of "bringing a sinner back from wandering" (Jas 5:20) James has introduced his readers to the issue of the tests encountered in life, the good results of withstanding the tests, the internal reason why one fails in the test, God's role in relation to the tests, and an eschatological view of wealth and poverty. In this middle part of the letter James expands on the particular issues that he believes his readers are facing, namely, the problem of controlling their tongues (speech-ethics) and the problem of their perspective on wealth. When a group is under economic pressure, there is a tendency to become less generous and to take the view of economic status held by their oppressors. James will use biblical and theological tools to oppose both of these tendencies. There is also a tendency for groups under pressure to develop internal conflicts and lose their solidarity. James brackets his discussion of economic perspectives with a discussion of speech. The theological and ethical rubber is meeting the practical road.

2.3.3.1 Controlling Speech (1:19–27)

As in the wisdom tradition (Prov 29:20; Eccl 7:9; Sir 1:22; 4:29; 5:11; 6:35), controlling anger was an important theme of the Greco-Roman world, and particularly important to the Stoics.[80] Whatever one's philosophical orientation, it is important

---

80. William V. Harris, *Restraining Rage: The Ideology of Anger Control in Classical Antiquity* (Cambridge, MA: Harvard University Press, 2001).

in community maintenance. James commands that one should be quick to hear (i.e., to listen to the content of speech, not just to hear the sounds), slow to speak, and slow to anger. James condemns anger because it will not produce God's type of justice or righteousness (he would not "buy" the myth of righteous indignation). Later he will tell us that the coming of the Judge will produce this type of justice (Jas 5:7), but at this point, without mentioning the future, James is clear that anger is out. One needs to understand that what James is talking about is angry actions — either the obvious ones of violent attack or angry speech or the more subtle ones of judging/criticizing others in the community. He is not talking about angry feelings (just as the love is not about warm feelings, but about caring actions). Such angry actions are incompatible with divine justice, period.

In contrast to anger, James calls for (1) conversion: repentance, or the removal of "moral uncleanness" (a Greek term used especially for greediness) and abundant malice (i.e., a form of anger);[81] (2) commitment, or the Christian virtue of meekness (i.e., the refusal to defend oneself because one trusts in God); and (3) a reception of, or a commitment to act on, the "implanted word" (i.e., that good news about God's rule that has been implanted by God in a person, as Jas 1:18 can be read as implying).[82] This implanted word, if acted on or received, is able to save one's person or life (i.e., not one's physical life necessarily, but one's essential life). In James's world one can give a call to conversion, not just to those outside the Christian community, but also to members of Christian communities who demonstrate vice, especially anger or greediness.

James reinforces this call to conversion by underlining which type of hearing or receiving he has been intending. He contrasts the one who simply hears the spoken word and perhaps recognizes themselves in it (the analogy of the mirror suggests some immediate recognition of their state) and then fails to act on it, with the person who hears and puts into practice the word of the good news. The one says (anachronistically), "Good sermon; it spoke to me," but deceives themselves, according to James, for no change in their life has taken place. The other "looks into and remains in the perfect law that brings freedom" (1:25; in our view, the "perfect law" includes the good news, but could be best described as the Mosaic Torah as reinterpreted by Jesus [cf. the Sermon on the Mount, esp. Matt 5]), and receives the blessing entailed in it (e.g., see the Beatitudes) because he or she puts it into practice.[83]

In 1:26–27 James summarizes the teaching of the previous couple of paragraphs and at the same time creates a transition to the following two units that focus on economic righteousness. (1) If someone considers themselves a worshiper[84] of God

---

81. On the meaning of the terms see Davids, *James*, 93–94.

82. As noted earlier in this chapter, this phrase appears to come from Orphic wisdom, and a version of it appears in the Stoic teacher Epictetus. But for the Stoic λόγος (*logos*) was "reason" or "rationality," while for an early follower of Jesus it means "word," especially the proclaimed message of Jesus as Lord. *Logos* was a term with a wide semantic field, so context is important in interpreting it.

83. The first half of the Beatitudes bless those followers of Jesus

who are poor or oppressed in some way, but the second half bless those followers of Jesus who act in a godly manner, that is, who show mercy, act as peacemakers, act from pure motivation, etc.

84. BDAG, 437, see *thrēskos*. Being religious, that is, one involved in cultic worship or one involved in piety, is always viewed positively in the New Testament. This particular term occurs only here and indicates cultic or ritual worship.

the Father and of Jesus his Anointed One, but also has outbursts of anger (i.e., fails to "controls their tongue" from angry outbursts), and then persuades themselves that this is allowable, to James, such a one "deceives their own heart"; their worship, however pious and "uplifting," is useless. (2) If someone wants to know the type of worship that God the Father considers excellent, it is worship that offers to God ("pure and blameless" are cultic terms associated with offerings) care for widows and orphans and remains free from allegiances to the values of this age (see James 4). In other words, worship, which is an expression of submission to the deity, is just empty, self-deluding words if it does not lead to actual obedience (e.g., avoiding angry language and supplying the needs of widows and orphans). With this summary, which serves as a type of hinge, James is ready to shift to the next subject, which is related to the second part of this verse, caring for orphans and widows.

2.3.3.2 About Favoritism Based on Economic Status (2:1–13)

Both this section and the next follow a sermonic format that can be found in one form of later synagogue sermons, although like all good rhetoric, both sections also fit within the canons of the Greco-Roman rhetorical handbooks. The Greco-Roman categories will be used to distinguish the sections of the argument.

Propositio. The thesis statement for this section is clear: commitment to[85] "our glorious Lord Jesus the Anointed One" is not compatible with favoritism. Depending on how one reads the sentence,[86] it implies that one does not really have a commitment to Jesus if one shows favoritism. Perhaps James is thinking that God shows no favoritism (e.g., Rom 2:11; Eph 6:9; Col 3:25; in the latter two the favoritism is toward the slave-owning class), although as the passage develops, it becomes clear that to the extent God has favoritism it is to the poor.

Narratio. An exemplary story is told about a community gathering, either about a community judicial gathering[87] or a community worship gathering, which in those days was a meal,[88] into which two persons come. One is a poor person, described as

---

85. We read the genitive as an objective genitive; that is, faith in or, because the object is personal, commitment to "our glorious Lord Jesus the Anointed One."

86. Because James often starts a section with an imperative, the sentence is usually read as "Do not hold a commitment to our glorious Lord Jesus the Anointed one with favoritism." The rest of the argument shows that to do so puts one on the side of the enemies of this Lord rather than on the Lord's side. This seems awkward. But the verb is identical in the indicative and the imperative, so it can be read as a question implying a negative answer, as in the NRSV: "My brothers and sisters, do you with your acts of favoritism really believe in our glorious Lord Jesus Christ?" In that case this sentence alone implies that they do not really believe in or demonstrate a commitment to Jesus if they show favoritism. This is a smoother reading.

87. It is unlikely that in a synagogue-like worship or teaching situation, places were assigned and postures differed; thus, R. B. Ward, "Partiality in the Assembly: James 2:2–4," *HTR* 62 (1969): 87–97, could be correct that this is a judicial assembly, where the

difference in postures and clothing indicates a presumptive favoritism and therefore injustice on the part of those deciding between the two plaintiffs.

88. This was first argued by Daniel Streett in the "Letters of James, Peter, and Jude Section" of the Society of Biblical Literature's annual meeting in San Francisco in 2011, but the argument was first published by Peter-Ben Smit, "A Symposiastic Background to James?" *NTS* 58 (2012): 105–22. In a Greco-Roman banquet (*symposium*), the various couches (one actually lay on one's left side, although the place could be referred to as a "seat") were viewed as indicating one's status, starting with the place next to the host. Nonparticipant observers stood or perhaps sat on the floor (the latter had the advantage of being able to compete with the dogs for scraps of food that fell from the table). The host (in the case of the Christian community, the one hosting the church in their house) had the prerogative of indicating where participants' places were, although "regulars" probably needed little direction.

poor and in filthy clothing. From James's language one can almost smell him. The other is obviously wealthy and upper class (but because he is a community member the term "rich" is not used), described as wearing a gold ring and impressive clothing (lit., "shining"). The wealthy one is given a seat[89] and the poor one is told to "stand" or sit on the floor by the footstool of one of those in authority (indicating subordination). The narrator concludes with a rhetorical question indicating that the church leaders have made distinctions within the community (clearly based on values extrinsic to the community, those of "the world"), and they have therefore become unjust judges ("judges characterized by evil thoughts," 2:4). Now he needs to prove this assertion.

Confirmatio (in three parts). There are three proofs of their favoritism (both in the extreme case above and in lesser instances that James probably assumes were more common in his intended reader's lives), the first being based on the character of God and the others being based on two passages of Scripture.

First, God has chosen the poor. One could refer this to the major theme of God's concern for the poor in the Hebrew Scriptures, but the rest of the passage tells us that this is probably based on the "Q" tradition[90] behind Matt 5:3 and Luke 6:20: [91] the poor followers of Jesus are declared blessed because "yours" is the "kingdom of God." Both of these passages are addressed to followers of Jesus, one in the third person and the other in the second person, so they are apprentices (otherwise translated "disciples") and therefore people with enough commitment (faith) to follow Jesus. So, says James with deliberate irony, God has chosen the poor (from "the world's" point of view) to be rich, rich in commitment to him and heirs of the kingdom (thus very rich from James's and God's perspective) that God has promised "those who love him."

But these Christians have dishonored the very ones whom God has honored, which means that they have insulted their great patron, God. Thus, in honoring the wealthy person they have sided with "the rich," those who oppress them, those who use the courts against them, and, most important, those who slander "the excellent name" (surely the name of Jesus, especially if this letter has anything to do with Judea, where those oppressing the followers of Jesus would certainly not slander the name of God), which was "called over" or "invoked over" (NRSV) them at the time of their baptism. Those who favor the rich in contrast to the poor are siding with those slandering Jesus and against God, who has chosen the poor.

Second, one should follow the "royal law," which is "according to the Scripture" (i.e., one acts virtuously or "does well" in following this "royal law"). If this were merely a reference to the Torah (Lev 19:18), it would be unclear why this law was

---

89. Given that leaders, rulers, and judges tended to be the ones with seats, this may indicate authority, if one takes the judicial interpretation; but if one takes the meal interpretation, then he is given one of the best places, perhaps on the head couch.

90. By "Q" this author means the tradition shared by Matthew and Luke, but not found in Mark, whether it be an oral-mnemonic tradition or a written one.

91. While the "Q" form of the Beatitude probably read just "poor," as in Luke 6:20 and *Gospel of Thomas* 54 (so James M. Robinson, Paul Hoffmann, and John S. Kloppenborg, *The Critical Edition of Q* [Leuven: Peeters, 2000], 46–47, on Q 6:20), Robert A. Guelich, *The Sermon on the Mount: A Foundation for Understanding* (Waco, TX: Word, 1982), 97, has pointed out that the "in spirit" in Matthew is a linking of the Beatitude to Isa 61:1 and the theology of the ʿānāwîm (one of the crucial words for "poor" or "oppressed" in the Hebrew Scriptures).

"royal" and why it was necessary to add "according to the Scripture." However, it is likely that the prominent citation of this law in the teaching of Jesus (Matt 19:19; 22:39; Mark 12:31; also in Paul, Gal 5:14) is what made it "royal" (since Jesus is "Lord" and "the Anointed One," both royal titles); in that case the "according to the Scripture" indicates that Jesus is endorsing a law found in the Hebrew Scriptures (and specifically the Torah) rather than speaking on his own. In other words, for a community for which those Scriptures were already an authority, this gave that law a double authority. Favoritism, however, stands in contrast to this law. Thus if one shows favoritism, one is a lawbreaker, which James clearly does not view as positive.

James then brings in a second Scripture to argue that one is a criminal, or lawbreaker, if even a single law is broken. This time he cites Exod 20:13–14 in reverse order, making the point that, for example, a Mafia hit man is a criminal even though he may be absolutely faithful to his wife and a good family man. He cannot claim that he has only broken one law, that is, that against murder. Likewise, someone who has not loved their neighbor as themselves cannot excuse themselves by saying that they have only broken one little law.

Peroratio. The "law of liberty" (as in Jas 1:25) will be the standard for the final judgment,[92] so the community members should speak and act with this in mind. This warning about final judgment is underlined by a saying that may be James's, may be his rephrasing of Jesus, or may be an agraphon of Jesus: show no mercy in your judgment and you will receive none in the final judgment (cf. Matt 7:2 for a saying close to this one).[93] That mercy triumphs over judgment is clear in the teaching of Jesus: "Blessed are the merciful, for they will receive mercy" (Matt 5:7). So for James life is to be lived in the light of the coming final judgment. The standard will be "the law of liberty," and the mercy that human beings have shown during the life of this age will be a determinant in whether judgment is strict or merciful.

2.3.3.3 Doing Good Is Part of the Essence of Faith, Not an Option (2:14–26)

The first sermon has argued that those who show favoritism based on a person's economic status will face a final judgment characterized by strict justice and will do so in company with "the rich," their king's enemies. This second sermon will argue that the type of commitment to that king (i.e., "faith") that does not share economically is no commitment at all—it is totally useless.

Propositio. Someone claims to have a commitment (faith) and assumes that on this basis they will be saved or delivered in the final judgment (which is the context for judgment throughout James). If this person does not have works of charity and other forms of obedience to God (as the sermon will go on to make clear), they are

---

92. This is another indication that James's community had no problem with speaking of the Torah or law as the standard of behavior and judgment, albeit the Torah as interpreted by Jesus.

93. This concept is one with which the Jewish wisdom tradition

agreed (Sir 27:30–28:7; Tob 4:9–11; cf. *T. Zeb.* 8:3; *b. Šabb.* 151b: "Rabbi Barabbi said, 'To him who is merciful to the created, Heaven is merciful, but to him who is unmerciful to the created, Heaven is also unmerciful.'"

deceived. Commitment or faith in itself cannot save or deliver them.[94] James has made a profound theological statement, especially when read within the context of the whole of the New Testament.

Narratio. The exemplary story is clear enough. A fellow community member is obviously in need ("naked," "lacking daily bread").[95] The community member who has been approached is assumed to have the means of alleviating the need, but instead turns them away ("Go in peace"), expressing what appears to be a pious conviction ("be warmed, be filled").[96] Far from being an example of great faith, James's evaluation is that this does not help the person at all ("What's the use of that?"). Thus, commitment or conviction or faith that does not result in appropriate deeds is "dead."

Confirmatio/Confutatio. In this brief homily the argument supporting James's position is more of a response to a series of stated or implied objections rather than an exposition of the position that James holds.

First, the implied objector questions, could not faith and works be separate gifts? No, for without the appropriate actions flowing from it, faith or commitment cannot be demonstrated. It "exists" like the "elephant" in the argument that there is a large, silent, invisible elephant in the room, which, due to the vibrations of its atoms cannot be felt or smelled, nor do its steps make impressions on the floor or anything else that it stands on. Not only is there no way to prove that said elephant exists, but there is also no difference between its being present and there being no elephant at all. James is in this regard an empiricist. He will demonstrate his commitment to God and Jesus by means of his deeds.

Second, the objector may protest, this disregards the sincere confession of the faith.[97] "I do believe!" The reference to what is believed is indeed to the basic confession of Judaism, the *Shema,* so-named from the first Hebrew word of Deut 6:4 with which it begins. That is good, says James, for the unity of God is fundamental to the Jewish religion, but the demons have gotten farther than this in that they both believe this truth and respond to this belief appropriately — that is, they "shudder," presumably in anticipation of judgment. The demons do something that shows that this confession is more than theory to them.

Third, moving on from objections to his position, James argues that a commitment without appropriate deeds is worthless by bringing in two biblical narratives. The first narrative is that of the Aqedah, or the binding of Isaac, in Genesis 22.[98] In

---

94. The form of the question, "Can faith save you?" expects a negative answer in Greek.

95. While sounding like Matt 6:11 and Luke 11:3, the Greek terms used here for "daily bread" are different.

96. This is probably thought of as a prayer, a faith-filled prayer, for "Go in peace" could be a polite dismissal, but probably picks up Jesus' tone in sending people away when he heals at a distance, e.g., Matt 8:11; Mark 7:29; John 4:50; with the content of the prayer being "be warmed, be filled," a prayer of command.

97. In this case "faith" or "conviction" or "belief" is the correct translation of the Greek *pisteuō,* for it is followed by content, "that," rather than by a personal object.

98. Jewish tradition refers to this as the "binding" because in the end Isaac was not sacrificed, while Christian tradition tends to refer to it as the "sacrifice of Isaac," probably because it is often read as a foreshadowing of Jesus, who did die even though Isaac did not. James says that Abraham "placed his son Isaac upon the altar." Roy Bowen Ward, "The Works of Abraham: James 2:14–26," *HTR* 61 (1968): 283–90, argued that the fact that Abraham was ultimately spared from offering Isaac was a reward for his previous works of charity and hospitality, which is certainly true in various Jewish traditions and may be implied by the context of James, with the *narratio* focused on charity and the following Rahab narrative focused on hospitality.

Genesis 22 Abraham is declared to be "in the right" or "justified" by God (although the term "justified" per se is not used in the LXX) after it is clear from Abraham's actions that his commitment to God is such that he has obeyed God's command to offer his one and only son on an altar and is about to complete that act. It is then that God says, "Now I know" (22:12), and God therefore reaffirms the earlier promises of progeny and blessing on the basis of Abraham's current obedience (22:15–18). James relates this to 15:6, "Abraham believed God and it was reckoned to him as righteousness (or, as an act of righteousness)," which Scripture, he states, was "fulfilled." To James, Gen 15:6 was proleptic insofar as Abraham was only declared to be righteous, or justified, *after* the deed of Genesis 22, for that is when God makes the declaration that "he knows."

The result of Abraham's act and God's declaration is that Abraham was considered a special client of the divine patron, a friend, the most honored level of client. While the phrase "friend of God" is not found in the Hebrew Scriptures, the idea is referred to twice (2 Chr 20:7; Isa 41:8) and was used in Second Temple Judaism (*Jub.* 19.9; 30.20; Philo *Abr.* 273, who attributes it to Abraham's action of faith), as well as later in the Christian writing *1 Clem.* 10.1. The conclusion, argues James, is that "a person is justified by works, not by faith alone" (Jas 2:24).

The second narrative, that of Rahab, is discussed more briefly. As in Heb 11:31, she is identified as "Rahab the prostitute," which fits with the description in Josh 2:1, so this is probably not intended to have a theological meaning (e.g., that even a prostitute was justified). The point is that she was declared just on the basis of her deeds in that she hid the messengers and directed them how to remain safe when they left. Of the three factors mentioned in James, two must be inferred from knowledge of the Hebrew Scriptures or Second Temple traditions about Rahab. While the narrator of the Hebrew Scriptures never says that she had a commitment to or faith in God, Rahab's speech in Joshua 2 certainly shows that she is convinced that Israel's God is able to deliver Jericho into Israel's hands. Her being declared just in James is a reflection of her deliverance in the Hebrew text (6:22–25) and the connection that was made between that deliverance and her deeds in Joshua 2.

The point James is making is that all of her conviction that the God of Israel was about to give Jericho into the hands of the Israelites and that YHWH was "God in heaven above and on earth below" (Josh 2:11) would have counted for nothing had she not saved the lives of the messengers and followed through on their instructions. Her faith would have been empty without action based on it.

Peroratio. James ends with a pithy analogy that sums up his point. He accepts that the human being is body and breath/spirit; when the spirit departs, one has a corpse, a decomposing body. So also when deeds are separated from faith or commitment, one has, not just something that is defective, but something that is dead.

2.3.3.4 The Danger of Conflict (3:1–4:10)

Both of the previous sections have dealt with economic issues, one with acting on a bias against the poor and the other with a failure of charity. In each case James has argued that the actions were unjustified and entailed negative consequences (no mercy at the final judgment or a dead "faith" that cannot save one—i.e., that the people involved will not be justified). Now he returns to the other issue that concerns him, that of conflict in the community, which he will develop using material drawn from the Jewish wisdom tradition. He will then bring both themes together in the first part of chapter 4.

Teaching is something that happens via speaking and therefore exposes one to a harsher sentence at the final judgment. This is so because, while everyone in general "trips up"[99] with relative frequency, people are especially vulnerable to verbal "trip-ups"; thus, teachers are more vulnerable than most. In fact, the person who has control of their speech so that they do not "trip up" is perfect (in the sense found in Jas 1:4) or mature and thereby also has control of their whole body, as analogies from horses and ships show. The tongue may be small, but it is powerful. It is no wonder that in 1:19 James recommended that one be slow to speak and that many later monastic traditions incorporate this advice into their rule of life.

In the illustrations James uses, the bridle and bit on a horse's tongue or the (tongue-shaped) rudder of an ancient sailing ship controlled the whole of the animal or ship, presumably for good. Yet from looking experientially at speech, the "tongue" is often used negatively, like a ship on a deliberate collision course, so to speak. So James shifts his metaphor to use the image of fire: a small flame setting a forest on fire, a flame that enflames the "cycle of nature"[100] and that is itself enflamed by Gehenna (probably meaning that it is influenced by evil or demonic forces).[101] Using another image James says that it pollutes (stains) our whole body and that it is "a world of iniquity." It is uncontrollable. It is full of poison, as if it were a snake. It is "a restless evil" and therefore possibly demonic, since restlessness is a characteristic of demons, while peace is what God and his agents grant. With all of these images James indicates that at the least speech is the seat of the yēṣer or desire (ἐπιθυμία, epithymia) (Jas 1:14) and possibly that the power behind desire is demonic.[102]

From James's point of view, this denunciation of speech comes to a head in the fact that the same people who are worshiping (blessing) "the Lord and Father" (which form a hendiadys, two titles for the one being) are verbally attacking their fellow human beings, who are made in God's image. But everyone in that age knew that to

---

99. James chooses not to use the usual words for sin or transgression; instead, he uses a term (πταίω, ptaiō) that means either "to lose one's footing, stumble, trip," or "to experience disaster, be ruined, lost" (BDAG, 894). In this passage the first meaning seems to be in view, for it would be strange to say that one is often "lost" (many scholars believe the latter meaning is found in 2 Pet 1:10).

100. This expression is drawn from Orphic literature, where it means the "cycle of becoming" but appears to have later become an idiom meaning something like "the whole course of life" (see Davids, James, 143).

101. The problem with this image is that Gehenna is everywhere else in the New Testament used as a place for the *destruction* of evil

(e.g., Matt 5:22, 29, 30; its only other uses in the New Testament are in the Synoptic Gospels), not the source of evil. It is possible that Rev 9:1–11; 20:7–8 point to a tradition that evil could also emanate from Gehenna, although in neither case is the term "Gehenna" used, and rightly so, for Gehenna is not a prison from which something could be allowed out or possibly escape, but a place of destruction (like an incinerator). Perhaps it is used as a type of metonymy, the destination of evil being used for the evil it will consume.

102. The problem comes in knowing how literally to take James's language, whether he is piling up images for rhetorical effect or whether he intends each image to be taken with utmost seriousness.

insult or deface the image of a king was to insult or assault the king himself (with pre-dictable consequences). This is an inconsistency so horrible that it is against nature. Since nature does not produce two different kinds of output from the same source, there is probably the suggestion that the source of speech has become corrupted, that the insult of the image of God is the accurate depiction of their hearts, and, unbe-known to the implied readers, that therefore their worship of God is itself far from pure. This implication fits well with the purpose statement of the letter (5:19–20).

James has already stated that God's gift of wisdom is what is needed when one is being tested. However, not all that is claimed as wisdom is really wisdom. That is, some of the criticism or "cursing" of others referred to in the previous paragraph could have been being attributed to divine wisdom; that is, rather than being evil, it demonstrated divine insight. James therefore goes on to lay out the characteristics of wisdom and its counterfeit (3:13–18).

Wisdom, says James, is characterized by a good or virtuous lifestyle (as in 2:14–26). Deeds inspired by wisdom are characterized by gentleness or meekness rather than aggressive speech. Doing rather speaking is the watchword.

Pseudo-wisdom[103] is anything but gentle or meek; rather, it is characterized by the vices of envy, selfish ambition (or party-spirit), and boastfulness—to call this "wisdom" is a denial of the truth. The source of such vices is not "above" but below: this earth, the natural human life, rather than the spirit, the demonic. Moreover, it leads to disorder or restlessness (a characteristic of the demonic) and other types of evil deeds. In other words, while there is a lot of speech in this pseudo-wisdom, its actions demonstrate its real source. It is community-destroying.

Genuine wisdom is in fact community-building: pure, peaceable, gentle, prepared to be persuaded, full of mercy, full of good deeds (fruits), without partiality, and with-out hypocrisy. While rhetorically arranged in alliterative groups (in Greek), the cata-logue is clear in any language, expanding as it does on the initial description of wisdom.

James closes with a proverb that some consider an agraphon of Jesus, a proverb that stresses the peaceableness of this wisdom and its reward. Those who create peace are sowing in peace and will reap "a harvest of righteousness," presumably at the final judgment (since that seems to be what James is waiting for).

In 4:1–10 James is ready to sum up this core section of his letter. He drops some of his metaphors and shifts into a more denunciatory mood. The source of com-munity strife[104] is "pleasures" (ἡδοναί, hēdonai, a synonym for "desires" or "drives," the term used earlier in James and the verbal form of which appears in 4:2), which cause internal conflict within the individual.[105] Frustrated desire leads to character

---

103. James never calls what comes from below "wisdom," but simply "not the wisdom from above." Wisdom, for him, is God's gift, and any claim otherwise is simply not wisdom at all. Thus in this work we are using "pseudo-wisdom" rather than suggesting that there is any real wisdom (in James's sense) "from below."

104. Not all metaphor is dropped in that James refers to "wars and battles," but since these are "in you" they are unlikely to be

literal, but rather verbal and other types of conflict within the com-munity.

105. The "pleasures" are "waging war" "in your members," which could indicate the members of the community viewed as a body. However, James does not use the body metaphor for the commu-nity elsewhere, so the location for the strife is probably within the individual.

assassination (it is unlikely that James is talking about literal murder) and conflict. The problem is that the addressees are thinking on the horizontal plane, on the level of this age, and so struggling to establish their own position when they should be praying. The protest comes back, "But we did pray!" "Yes," returns James, "but you asked evilly; you asked God to feed the demands of your desires, and therefore you did not receive." One hears here another echo of Jas 1:6–8.

This is spiritual adultery. While many translations fail us in that they use the masculine or a neutral form ("adulterers," NRSV, NET; "you adulterous people," ESV, NIV 1984), James uses the feminine form "adulteresses" (NASB), which is a deliberate paralleling of this community with adulterous Israel (e.g., Ezekiel 16). They think that they can have both the world and God as their patron (or, to continue the metaphor, husband/lover). Instead, their pursuit of this age has turned God into their enemy. James has already repeatedly pointed out this irony. Seeking or living for the values of this age is not simply a distraction from seeking or living for God, but ends with one at cross-purposes with God.

For example, James has pointed this out in 2:1–13, where viewing people from the economic standards of this age (perhaps for the sake of "honor by association," perhaps for the sake of larger offerings) ends with the community siding against those whom God has chosen and with those who definitively reject God. Here, having accused them of being God's unfaithful spouse and therefore his enemies, James then cites an unknown "Scripture"[106] (4:5) and points out that God has put the spirit in the human being and he is jealous over this spirit (which explanation is the least problematic way of understanding this difficult clause and fits with the reference to "adulteresses" in the previous verse).

Given what happened when God was jealous over Israel (e.g., in Hosea), it might be easy for the reader (or community of readers) to think, "I've had it. The final judgment will come and that will be it for me." But James has already argued that God is not critical of those who come to him and that he gives only good (1:5, 17), so he hurries on to note that God is prepared to "give yet greater favor." The divine patron may not be happy, but he has not utterly rejected them and will again show them his favor. This assertion is supported by Prov 3:34, which focuses on God's giving his favor to the humble (the same person he exalts in Jas 1:9).

How does one get into this position of being counted the humble and receiving God's favor? One does this by repentance, that is, by submitting to God and resisting (the opposite of submitting to) the devil, who now appears as the force behind the world and/or desire and who will flee if appropriately resisted. This establishes which patron will be a person's one and only patron. Then, using a cultic metaphor, James pictures them as coming close to God as if they were entering a sanctuary,

---

106. Some have tried to link this to Exod 20:5 in some unknown version or argued that it is not a quotation at all, and so James does not intend to cite Scripture. However, the "Scripture says" formula elsewhere in the New Testament always introduces a quotation, not a vague allusion. Thus the only satisfying conclusion is that James is quoting some Scripture that his community valued but which we do not have, another indication that James is writing before there was a definitive canon. See further Davids, *James*, 162.

as ritually washing their hands. This was an appropriate activity for those who had become impure through some error or another, as was going through a rite of purification for their hearts. As a result, they would no longer be "double-minded" but solely trusting in and committed to God (as the other use of the term in 1:8 indicates is needed if God is to respond to their prayer).

Repentance includes contrition as well as confession and amendment of life, and James describes appropriate contrition similar to that described in Joel 2:12–14 (although with more assurance of a favorable divine response than Joel gives) or Zech 12:10–12, as it comes home to the addressees what a dangerous condition they are in. This mourning, however, is not about something that cannot be changed, for their making themselves low in the presence of "the Lord"[107] will produce a result consistent with who he is: "he will lift you up" (again we have a play on Jas 1:9).

2.3.4 Letter Body Closing (4:11–5:6)

The main argument is finished, but James needs to clean up three points before he gets to his conclusion. One has to do with speech, and two have to do with money or finance.

2.3.4.1 Do Not Judge (4:11–12)

First, James summarizes the bottom line for the issue of speech: do not speak evil of/slander one another and do not judge one another. In one sense these two are the same, for one must form a judgment before one can speak evil of another, although this is true only in the case of a negative judgment. It is clear that slander is critiqued in both the Hebrew Scriptures and later Judaism, including the New Testament (e.g., Num 21:5, 7; Pss 50:20; 101:5; Prov 20:13; Wis 1:11; *T. Iss.* 3.4; *T. Gad* 3.3; and the vice lists in Rom 1:30; 2 Cor 12:20; 1 Pet 2:1),[108] for community unity was important in all of those settings.

The sanction is different from that found in other New Testament settings. For instance, in Matt 7:1–2 one is not to judge so that they will not be judged, for those who do will receive the same judgment they give (similar to Jas 2:13, which revolves around mercy rather than judgment). But in Jas 4:11–12 a different reason is given, namely, that the one who does this is implicitly criticizing the law (whether the Hebrew Scriptures in general or the Torah as interpreted by Jesus—this text is not clear), which sets the person above the law as a judge and not under the law as an obedient doer. But there is already One who is above the law in the sense of being both Lawgiver and Judge, and he is also able to enforce his judgments, unlike human critics. If people take that One's place by critiquing others, they are usurping the role of divinity. It may not be accidental, then, that the last thing James says about this

---

107. Often in James "Lord" means "Jesus," who is the coming judge. However, given that the divine being referred to in the earlier part of this section is God and that Lord (κύριος, *kyrios*) is at times used for God, it is possible that James is referring to God here.

108. In each of the texts from the Hebrew Scriptures the LXX uses the same Greek word used here. Thus one Torah text, Lev 19:16, was not cited, since James's Bible, the LXX, does not translate it using this term, although the idea appears to be similar.

Judge is that he is able to destroy (4:12). Thus the first basis for condemning slander is that one is not obeying the Scriptures, but instead is implicitly critiquing it; the second basis is that in critiquing Scripture and in judging other human beings one is taking a role reserved for God alone. James will return to this topic once more—in the final summary of the letter.

2.3.4.2 Trust God Rather than Money (4:13–17)

Second, James returns to the question of finances and the control finance may or may not have over an individual. At first blush, he seems to be critiquing normal business plans. Planning for travel, investment, and return on investment is hardly strange in the world of business.[109] One plans and conducts business based on a reasonable projection into the future. But James points out that the future is not under human control, and, in particular, one's length of life is not under human control. Human mortality, of course, is a significant theme of biblical literature (e.g., Ps 90:3–10), so it does not surprise us that James picks up on this theme. However, his response to human mortality is neither resignation nor despair: James instructs his readers to consult God on their plans, whether this consultation is to be considered submission to the Lord and his values or whether it is a request that the Lord reveal his wishes to his follower.

At any rate, in the context of James it is clear that the phrase "if the Lord wills" or "if the Lord wishes" is not a formula, but is an expression of submission to the divine will. This is seen in James's considering normal planning to be boasting and arrogance, which, of course, is evil. He calls normal planning (without consulting God) evil and not ignorance or stupidity. It would be ignorant if someone simply forgot that life is ephemeral, but in James's view what happens in such planning is that the Lord's wishes and values are not the overarching umbrella under which one makes plans. James explains this further: the sin is not just in doing what is wrong, but it is also in failing to do what one knows to be right.[110] While 4:17 may be another possible agraphon of Jesus, it makes James's point well. It is not that the planning per se was evil, but that it was not done as a slave of the Lord should do it.

2.3.4.3 The Condemnation of the Rich (5:1–6)

Third, James comes the final part of the body of his letter, and this part is a type of prophetic lamentation over the rich. They have surplus, and it is going to waste, and that very waste will witness against them at the last judgment. There is corrosion

---

109. Notice that James does not call this person "rich," but simply describes his or her activities. The activities mean that such a person is not poor—they have the means to travel and to do business—although the activities do not necessarily mean that the persons are wealthy, for we do not know on what scale the trade is being carried on. However, it is clear that they are members of the community, for they know to do good, that is, to at least submit their ideas to "the

Lord," so they are by definition not "the rich."

110. It is possible in the light of Jas 2:14–26 that the good one knows to do is to give one's surplus money to the poor. That would certainly be doing "good" in the James's eyes. However, he does not say explicitly that that is what he means, so we have chosen to go with the minimum that he must mean.

on their coins, and as that corrosion seemed to eat the coins, so in the judgment it will be evidence of their unused surplus and will, as it were, eat their flesh like the fire of Gehenna. They have indeed laid up treasure, but it is the last days,[111] and judgment is upon them.

These "rich" are farmers,[112] and they have cheated their laborers by withholding their wages at the end of the day. Surely, this is not the evaluation that James thinks that "the rich" put on their actions. They have some means of justifying their actions (although, if they were Jews, it might be difficult in the light of Lev 19:13 and Deut 24:14); they might argue that the workers had done a less than perfect job or that withholding part of the pay was necessary to guarantee that enough workers would show up the next day—but James views it as wrong because the laborers who lived hand to mouth needed their daily wage to purchase food. So, using the image of the money crying out for justice (like the blood of Abel in Gen 4:10), which is perhaps an indication of the poor praying to God (which prayer James's beloved wisdom tradition taught would be heard quickly, Sir 7:20; 31:4), James indicates that "the Lord Sabaoth" (traditionally translated "the Lord of Hosts") has heard.

This term for YHWH is a particular favorite of Isaiah, often used in the context of God's judgment (e.g., Isa 2:12). It summons an image of the majesty and sovereignty of YHWH, and this exalted executor of justice is the One who has listened to the injustice done to the poor laborer. In contrast to the situation of the laborer, "the rich" have lived luxuriously (as the rich man did in Luke 16:19–31) and have "fattened your hearts in a day of slaughter." This expression is another wordplay, for if one slaughtered an animal, one ate one's fill of fresh meat (since there was no refrigeration and what was left had to be dried or otherwise preserved, or else destroyed), but the "day of slaughter" is also an allusion to the frequent image in the Prophets of God's judging as if he were making a great sacrifice (see Isa 34:5–8; Jer 46:10 as two examples). "The rich" are having their feast on their "day of slaughter," but they should be mourning, for unbeknown to them God's "day of slaughter" has arrived.

The summary saying in 5:6 is like the summary sayings that have ended many units in James. It states, "You [the rich] have condemned, have murdered the righteous." There is more than one way of reading this. It could refer to Jesus (as in Acts 3:14), or to James himself (according to Hegesippus as quoted by Eusebius, *Hist. eccl.* 2.23.4, 7, 16), or to the righteous in general (for, after all, "the rich" have just been pilloried for cheating their laborers, which could lead to their starvation being viewed as murder, and "the rich" were earlier charged with dragging followers of Jesus into court, Jas 2:6). The question with Hegesippus is whether his tradition is early enough, for there are a number of unlikely, legendary elements in

---

111. There may well be a play on words here in that one does lay up treasure in the light of one's own last days, either to support oneself in the end of life or to pass on as an inheritance to one's heirs. But these "rich" do not know what time it is, for they are doing this, not just in their own last days, but in the last days of the age.

112. If we are to imagine the letter of James as being set in Jerusalem before the war with Rome, these would be absentee landlords, living in Jerusalem, but having estates in Galilee and elsewhere in Palestine, as was often the case with the upper classes. They might indeed go to their estates at harvest time, checking out their return on investment.

his account.[113] Generally, the decision is between Jesus and the generic righteous person (presumably the type who were members of James's community). Since "the rich," that is, wealthy (possibly absentee) landowners, are not those identified in the Gospels as those who had Jesus executed (some of the Sanhedrin[114] were surely wealthy, but wealth was hardly the defining qualification for membership in that body), James is more likely to be thinking of the generic righteous person.

But the last clause can also be read two ways: "Does he not resist you?" or "He does not resist you." Since the person is viewed as dead, but the clause is present tense, it is likely the question that is intended (in a form that implies an answer of "Yes, he does"). While there may well have been no resistance when killed, especially if one is imagining death by starvation or malnutrition, James pictures the righteous person as still active after death and, like the "souls under the altar" of Rev 6:9–11, engaged in active resistance; that is, they are crying out to God for justice. The implication is that God will surely hear that call for justice.

2.3.5 Letter Conclusion (5:7–20)

Having finished the letter body, it is time for James to draw the letter together. He will do so following a typical Greek letter form with the various parts expressing his own theological convictions.

2.3.5.1 Summary/Conclusion (5:7–11)

As in the letter body opening, the call is to patient endurance, not as a strategy to change the persecutor, but because of "the parousia[115] of the Lord." The farmer planting the crop and then waiting for the early rain to get it to sprout and the latter rain to ripen it is an example of patient waiting in the light of an expected event, but is the event James is calling his addressees to wait for distant or proximal? The readers are to be patient, says James; they are to "confirm" their "hearts," or fix their commitment and keep it from wavering. And they are to do this in the light of the fact that "the parousia of the Lord is near."

If this Lord is coming, then one had best be found doing what that Lord wishes. In particular James writes, "Do not complain about one another," not just because complaining would weaken the solidarity of the community, but so that one will not be judged for it. The Judge (Jesus) is right at the door! Here again behavior is predicated on the imminent parousia, although in this case the implication of the parousia is expressed in the shift of the title from Lord to Judge.

---

113. He flourished in the mid-to late second century, so only the latest dates for James would allow for his description itself to lie behind this text.

114. To the extent that James follows the traditions found in the Gospels, and he certainly seems familiar with at least the teaching of Jesus in the form that was later inscribed in the gospels, the Sanhedrin, rather than the Romans, was responsible for Jesus' death: they plot to kill Jesus beforehand, they condemn him after his arrest,

and they manipulate Pilate into executing him. This is the tradition James appears to know; its historical reliability is a matter for gospel scholars to discuss.

115. Parousia is a transliteration, and it is better than "coming" in that it had a technical sense in which it indicated the coming of a divinity or, especially, the formal visit of a ruler or person of high rank. In the latter case, rewards and punishments were associated with the person's arrival. See further BDAG, 780–81.

The final paragraph of the summary again picks up on the patient endurance theme, noting the suffering (for only when one is suffering does one need patience) and endurance of the prophets, who are defined as those who "spoke in the name of the Lord." Jewish literature, especially Second Temple Jewish literature (including the wisdom tradition), celebrated the prophets, sometimes with stories of postmortem reward, but often by simply praising them. Honor was the highest good in a Mediterranean society, so they were indeed "considered blessed" (a term that also reminds one of the Beatitudes, in which Jesus names certain types of people "blessed" or "fortunate"). Then, alluding to the *Testament of Job*[116] (which, unlike Job of the Hebrew Scriptures, revolves around the concept of patient endurance), James states that his readers "have heard" of Job's patient endurance and "have seen" the conclusion that the Lord made in that narrative. That is, in the *Testament*, Job, about to die in a ripe old age surrounded by children and grandchildren, attributes all of his present felicity to God's response to his patient endurance when he was tested by the devil.

The conclusion is indeed that "the Lord is compassionate and concerned" (the two words are synonyms). Naturally, if God never changes his character, the implication is that James's implied readers will experience this compassion, assuming that they likewise patiently endure.

2.3.5.2 The Non-oath (5:13)

With the summary completed, the letter form expected an oath at this point, such as "I swear by the gods that what I have written is true." James follows the form, but instead of an oath, he has a version of the teaching of Jesus (e.g., Matt 5:33–37): do not use oaths of any type, for all that you say should be true. So just affirm ("yes") or deny ("no"). If you creates two levels of speech (one that is affirmed with an oath and one that is not), then you are liable to "fall under judgment" or "fall under condemnation," presumably in the final judgment when the Judge is present, for at the least the tendency is to be less honest in speech that is not supported with an oath,[117] and at the most you will be condemned for ignoring a teaching of Jesus. Again the concern for godly speech is underlined.

2.3.5.3 Praying for Healing (5:14–18)

The next part of the Greek letter form was a health wish, often in a form such as, "I pray to the gods that you may be in good health and prosper." James includes his own type of health wish, but he does so in accord with the themes of the letter.

---

116. While picked up by many later authors, the relationship of this Second Temple work to James was first pointed out by F. Spitta, "Das Testaments Hiobs und das Neue Testament," in *Zur Geschichte und Literature des Urchristentums* (Göttingen: Vandenhoeck & Ruprecht, 1907), III/2, 139–206.

117. This concern is also reflected in Paul in 2 Cor 1–2, where Paul defends his change of plans. In 1 Cor 16 he had announced his plan to visit Corinth both before and after his trip to Macedonia, but, after a quick trip to Corinth at the end of which he withdrew or was forced out of the Corinthian church, he changed his plan. Paul felt he had to defend himself against the charge of vacillation. Thus, he argues that *they* had changed, so to be consistent with his good intentions he *had* to change as well. In his whole discussion of the issue, especially in his references to saying "yes" and "no," one can hear Jesus' teaching echoed.

First, James again refers to the idea of "suffering," first brought up in 1:2. Suffering in the New Testament includes persecution and oppression, whether because one is a believer or because one is a member of some other oppressed or persecuted group (a day laborer in 5:4, the poor in 2:1–13, and, often in the ancient world, an ethnic Jew). Suffering can also include the privations that one incurs for serving Jesus, such as the hardship of Paul's travel. But it does not include sickness, which is never called "suffering" in the New Testament.[118] James's response to suffering is prayer, presumably prayer for wisdom (as in 1:5), so that one can endure and arrive at the good end.

Second, if one is "cheerful" (so neither suffering nor sick), they are to sing songs of praise. In other words, being in a good state is not to be taken for granted, but rather God is to be thanked appropriately. This also seems to indicate that for James prayer is more petition than anything else, such as praise.

Third, if someone is sick, that person should seek prayer. While it has sometimes been argued that this refers to spiritual sickness or weakness,[119] the variety of vocabulary used in this passage (5:14, 15, and 16 use a variety of terms for both sickness and healing) indicates that a physical dysfunction of some type (to use our terminology) is in view. In James's view the gathering of the followers of Jesus (or "church"; this is the only time the term ἐκκλησία, ekklēsia, is used in James) appears to be led by elders. They are to be called (so presumably James is thinking of a situation in which the person cannot go to the elders or attend the gatherings). They are to pray over that person and anoint him or her with oil.

This oil is hardly medicinal, for the ancient world knew of a variety of medicines (as a reading of works of Galen or Hippocrates would quickly show), and if such were intended, the possible range would be indicated. Even the unprepared "good Samaritan" used both oil and wine. Rather, this appears to be a sacramental action in that oil was often used in the Hebrew Scriptures for anointing when the presence of God was expected to empower a person (usually for an office); Mark claims that it was used by the Twelve in carrying out the healing mission of Jesus (Mark 6:13), so it must have had some such meaning for them. Jesus was not present, but through the oil the person would experience a type of sacramental presence of Jesus, under whose authority they were healed. In James, neither Jesus nor God is present, but the oil is a physical mediation of such presence, which indicates that James (or whatever precedent he is following) takes both the physical world and the physical human body seriously. The healing is attributed to "the prayer of trust" or "the prayer of commitment," the prayer-while-anointing combination that is done out of trust in God or Jesus.

But this action is not magic. It has no power in itself, for it is "the Lord"—an ambiguous term in James, for, as we have seen, it can refer to either God or Jesus,

118. See the long discussion "Excursus: Suffering in 1 Peter and the New Testament," in Peter H. Davids, *1 Peter* (NICNT; Grand Rapids: Eerdmans, 1990), 30–44.

119. In Roman Catholic teaching this has often been applied to spiritual healing in the light of impending death, that is, last rites. But while prayer at the time of death is appropriate, the natural reading of "God will raise them up" is that the person is healed, not that they die and go to heaven.

who has been called upon and will "raise them up." The great patron responds to the petition. And not only that, if the sickness is related to any sin, it will be forgiven (the sentence is conditional; so sin is not necessarily the case, yet "if" it be the cause, then it will be forgiven). Since we will see in the purpose statement that James is trying to turn people from sin, this "if" is clearly important for James.

Then James generalizes. No longer is it "the elders," but "one another." Everyone is involved. Sins need to be confessed to another human being, to "one another." And prayer should be made for "one another." This prayer could have to do with the sins confessed, but since the result is healing, it probably refers to prayer for healing. This is a description of what takes place within the gathering, not of someone confined to their home calling the elders. James appears to be saying that one should deal with sin and sickness while one is still able to attend the community gathering before the problem escalates; he is at least saying that while the elders may be the best at it, everyone in the community gets to participate in these activities.

Will such prayer "work"? James argues in the affirmative, citing the example of Elijah. While the Elijah of the Hebrew Scriptures is not specifically said to have prayed until he was fleeing for his life (1 Kgs 17:20–22),[120] in later Jewish tradition Elijah (often merged with Elisha) was viewed as a man of prayer (e.g., 2 Esd 7:109; *m. Ta'an.* 2.4 E). Likewise the length of time that it did not rain comes from Jewish legend, for it is not found in the Kings account. This number seems to refer to a period of judgment, half of seven, as in Dan 7:25; 12:7. James's point is that the man Elijah was not an angelic visitor or other type of super being, but a human being "with similar feelings (or circumstances) to us." He prayed and things happened: the rain itself stopped and the rain itself started again with the predictable result of a fruitful earth. So surely the readers could pray effectively in the lesser circumstances of human sickness.

2.3.5.4 Purpose Statement (5:19–20)

Since the summary, oath, health wish, and purpose statement were set parts of a letter ending, James shifts without transition from the health wish (or healing prayer command) to the purpose statement of the letter, expressed in a sort of syllogism.

The major premise is that someone in the community ("someone among you") has wandered away from the truth. James has pointed out some of the ways that one can wander—for example, by not controlling one's speech or by trusting in "the world" rather than solely in God, such as by showing favoritism. The minor premise is that "someone turns the person back." This is what the letter has been trying to do, and James apparently hopes that the community will continue to do this. The conclusion is that this person has "saved [a] life from death" and "covered a multitude of sins."

The question is: Whose life is saved, and what is the meaning of "death"? While there is precedent in the Hebrew Scriptures for arguing that one who fails to rebuke

---

120. Elijah does "cry out to the LORD" in 1 Kings 17:19–24, but this is related to a dead boy, not the presence or absence of rain. His posture in 18:41–42 is not a normal prayer posture; it may be a posture of waiting.

the sinner incurs guilt (Ezek 3:16–21), both the grammar of the sentence and the focus of the book argue for interpreting this as saving the life of the "sinner" from death. It is true that physical death can be the result of sin (1 Cor 11:30), and James has made a possible connection between sin and sickness (Jas 5:15–16). But the clearest connection of sin to death is in 1:13–15, and there he equally clearly contrasts it to the life that God gives. Furthermore, his focus throughout the letter has been on the final judgment. Thus what James is saying is that the one who brings an erring brother or sister to repentance delivers them from total death—the total death that would happen at the final judgment if they did not repent. Naturally, as a concomitant result, this covers a multitude of sins. The person will not have to do penance to pay for them (although appropriate penance is a sign of true repentance); rather, they are, as Jas 4:6, 10 indicates, covered by God's grace.

2.4 IMPORTANT THEOLOGICAL THEMES

Having read through the letter from a rhetorical and narrative viewpoint and having noted James's theology as it develops, it is now possible to synthesize the theological contributions into an organized collection. In doing this one must exercise care in that this is the only document that we have from this author (no matter who one thinks the author was). Although, as a Diaspora letter, it has a relatively general audience, it also addresses a rather limited situation, one that existed inside and outside of the community committed to following Jesus as God's exalted ruler at the time of the writing.[121] Thus we have only a limited selection of the author's theology, although a carefully selected one.[122] One dare not overgeneralize and say that because this letter has such and such a theological position, the author *could not* have had a broader position. But we can say that this, at least, is what our author gives evidence that he believed.

2.4.1 The Nature of God

James is a monotheist; he believes in one God, affirming the creed of Israel (Jas 2:19, which probably alludes to Deut 6:4, the Shema). This one God is the Creator, the "Father of lights" (Jas 1:17), which means the creator of the heavenly lights. But since this is most likely a reference to the first creation story (i.e., Gen 1:14–19, the filling of the dome/expanse/structure that was formed in Gen 1:6), it indicates a belief, not just in God's creation of the heavenly bodies, but also of the whole creation. This one God is also the one who made humanity in his own image (Jas 3:9; cf. Gen

---

121. We have argued that James could well be an edited collection of sermons and sayings of James put together after James's demise, but this still means that the work as we have it is addressing the situation at the time of the editing, for we do not have the context of the individual parts when they were originally created.

122. Of course, the same is true of Paul, whose letters are directed to specific situations in specific communities, or the John of Revelation, who addresses seven specific communities. Likewise, 1–3 John address specific situations in at least two communities. However, in the case of Paul we have more letters, although this does not mean that, given his focus on certain subjects in multiple letters, we *necessarily* have a fuller expression of his theology.

1:26–27). In other words, wherever we can check, James affirms the tenets of Jewish monotheism and the theology of the Genesis creation account.

James also refers to God as "Lord and Father" in 3:9, which is one of three references in James to God as Father (the other two are 1:17, just mentioned, and 1:27). While 1:17 is clearly a creational reference and 3:9 could be argued to be a creational reference,[123] 1:27 is not. Rather, "God, the Father," is presented as the one whom his community worships. It is true there are occasions in the Hebrew Scriptures in which God is called "Father" (Pss 68:5; 89:26), but this is relatively rare. It was Jesus who frequently used "Father" as an appropriate address of God (at least fifteen times in the Sermon on the Mount alone), and who taught his followers to do so (e.g., Matt 6:9). Thus James reflects what one might call a "Jesus-shaped" understanding of God in which God is presented as head of a large family.

While we need to be careful not to read the modern Western family into the ancient family, as Joachim Jeremias tended to do,[124] there is a sense of belonging expressed in this designation of God. God is not an "impersonal force" behind the universe; rather, he is the Father, whose family includes the followers of Jesus,[125] even if the father in a Mediterranean culture was known more for being the source of identity, authority, and provision than for intimacy (with either his wife or his children). James underlines the authority of this Father by using the term "God" or "Lord" with the term "Father." It is clear that this Father is very much head of the family and Lord of the universe.

This "God, the Father" may be pictured as the exalted family head and ruler of the universe, but he is also pictured as a generous and ungrudging (or noncritical) patron. So if one has single-minded commitment toward him, one goes to him and asks with confidence for what is needed (see Jas 1:5 in context); the chief need in James's eyes is wisdom in the situation of testing. He will not complain about how one failed to use his generosity well last time, nor will he hold back like a miser, trying to keep "his stuff" for his own use. He is a generous patron, which encourages one to approach him freely.

This is, then, a picture of a God who gives good and perfect gifts and who does not send anything else (Jas 1:17), for unlike the heavenly bodies he created, he does not change (the topic of discussion here is character). Thus he is not the source of testing or trials (Jas 1:13), for while they may lead to a good end (if one endures and thus is justified in the end, as Abraham was), tests and trials are not in themselves

123. It could also be argued to be a reference to divine rule in the light of creation; that is, he is presently ruler (Lord) and *paterfamilias* of at least the believing community, having created humanity in his image.

124. Joachim Jeremias, "Abba," in *The Prayers of Jesus* (SBT 2.6; London: SCM, 1967), 11–65, documents Jesus' use of *Abba* or Father and argues that it indicates a unique familial relationship between Jesus and God. However, he goes too far when he states that this is a young child's term for a father, for, as James Barr has pointed out ("Abba Isn't 'Daddy,'" *JTS* ns 39 [1988] : 28–47,

and "'Abba, Father' and the Familiarity of Jesus' speech," *Theol* 91 [1988]: 173–79), the term was used to address a father by adult children as much as by younger children.

125. James does not indicate that God is "Father" to those who are not followers of Jesus, although he does not deny it either. One might suggest that since James clearly believes that human beings are made in the divine image, he also believes that in some sense all human beings are God's "children." This is possible, but James does not express this belief, even if it is the logical implication of what he does say.

good. Rather, quite to the contrary, God is the source of what counteracts the trials; at least he counteracts them for those committed to him. The proof of this is that he has given birth to every follower of Jesus, making them into the firstfruit (i.e., the earliest example and also the best)[126] of the creation that he is renewing. The means of God's giving birth (i.e., the male function,[127] since in this case God is taking the female role of giving birth) is "the word of truth," one of several terms that James uses for the good news. So God is indeed good, the giver of life in contrast to death.

That this is a true description of God is also seen in two other statements about God. First, God's goodness is seen in his choice of the poor (in the eyes of the present age). They are the ones he has made "rich in commitment" and, more significantly for this topic, "heirs of the kingdom." So this God is the good God of the Beatitudes (Matt 5:3//Luke 6:20), who promises the "kingdom" to the poor. Second, while God can be hostile to those whose commitment is a both–and commitment to God and the world (Jas 4:4), and while he "jealously desires" the human spirit (4:5, probably meaning he wants the spirit to be purely devoted to him), because he is indeed good and ungrudging, he is also a forgiving God toward those who repent and return to him (this response of God to the repentant is the only basis given for the forgiveness offered in Jas 4:6–10). That offer of forgiveness to the repentant is a confidence that permeates James, for bringing "sinners" to repentance is the key aim of God's work. God is indeed good, and with this description James banishes the image of an angry and punitive God of the Hebrew Scriptures (whether or not it really exists except as a caricature in the modern imagination), for in James, despite the darker colors of 4:5–7, it is not God who is connected to judgment.

2.4.2 The Nature of Jesus

James rarely mentions Jesus. The only passages in which Jesus is certainly mentioned are Jas 1:1 ("Lord Jesus, the Anointed One") and 2:1 ("our glorious Lord, Jesus the Anointed One"). There are passages that probably refer to Jesus, such as 5:9 ("the Judge is at the door") and 5:8 ("the coming of the Lord"), and still others that are at least somewhat indeterminate: Who has promised "the crown of life" in 1:12? Who raises up the sick in 5:15? In whose name are the sick anointed in 5:14? What is clear is that all of these passages present Jesus as a ruler (Lord) and thus the counterruler to Caesar or any other earthly or heavenly sovereign. They present Jesus as God's ruler

---

126. "Firstfruit" (ἀπαρχή, aparchē) originally meant the beginning of the sacrificial ritual, the first thing sacrificed, but in the LXX it refers to God's portion, the holy portion of the harvest or other forms of fertility, which was also viewed as the best and chronologically the first part of the harvest. BDAG, ἀπαρχή, 1.b.α, p. 98, suggests that the emphasis here and in Rev 14:4 is less on chronological priority and more on quality, although at least one early Christian thinker (Paul in Rom 8:19–23, which is, like James, in a suffering context) sees a temporal priority of believers' renewal by the Spirit before the full renewal of creation at the time of the resurrection of the dead. This is not seen in the use of aparchē, which

Paul applies temporally to the believer's experience of the Spirit in contrast to receiving the fullness of redemption in the resurrection of the dead, but in his contrast of the present experience of the Spirit by believers to the eventual redemption of creation. Yet whether or not BDAG is correct about Jas 1:18, the term contains both temporal and qualitative aspects, regardless of which one might be the emphasis in a given context.

127. In 1 Pet 1:23 Peter will refer to God's word as imperishable sperm, versus the temporality of the human sperm of natural birth. That is the type of image we have here, this time with God as the one giving birth.

("the Anointed One" or "Messiah"). Is Jesus more than God's anointed and exalted (glorious) ruler who is coming? James does not say. God is Father, but he is never called Jesus' Father, nor is Jesus ever called "the Son." So while Jesus is clearly God's agent for ruling the world, we do not discover in James whether he has any closer affinity to God than that.[128]

Interestingly enough, James never even mentions the death of Jesus. Jesus is "our glorious Lord," but nothing is said about his humiliation. God forgives those who are repentant, but nothing is said in that context (or any other context in James) about the death of or blood of Jesus or its having anything to do with forgiveness. It is difficult to imagine any follower of Jesus in the first century or two of our era not knowing about Jesus' crucifixion, but, as with the topic of the relationship of Jesus to God the Father, it is clear that James did not feel a need to bring it up or even allude to the subject of Jesus' death in relation to any of the topics that he discusses. Christian life may be cruciform (i.e., involve suffering and humiliation), but that does not mean that a first-century believer felt a need to mention the cross.[129]

Because Jesus is Lord, the teaching of Jesus is important for James, even if he alludes to it or adapts it more than cites it. This probably means that he expects his readers to recognize the source of the teaching and to accept the liberty that he takes in transforming the tradition, as was normal and expected in that culture.[130] There are some more distant adaptations of the teaching of Jesus: for example, the reversal-of-fortunes teaching found in Jas 1:9–11 and the parable of the rich man and Lazarus (Luke 16:19–31); the theme of endurance found throughout James and in the teaching of Jesus (Matt 10:22; Matt 13:21//Mark 4:17//Luke 8:14–15; Matt 24:13; Luke 21:19); the teaching on anger in the Sermon on the Mount (Matt 5:21–23) and Jas 1:19–21; being doers of the word (Jas 1:22–25) and the parable in Matt 7:21–27. There are also closer connections, such as the choosing of the poor to be heirs of the kingdom (Jas 2:5) and Matt 5:3//Luke 6:20; the reference to the "royal law" (Jas 2:8) as being Lev 19:18 and its use in the Jesus tradition in Mark 12:31//Matt 22:39, and in Matt 19:19;[131] and the rejection of judging (Jas 4:11–12,

---

128. Did James believe in the divinity of Jesus? We do not know. Some works that could be as early as James appear to affirm this (e.g., Phil 2:6, 10–11; Col 1:15, 17, 19, although some scholars, such as J. D. G. Dunn, do not believe these are references to divinity); the later one dates James, the more likely that he at least knew the idea, which appears in our literature in 2 Pet 1:1 (if taken at face value) and also in John 1:1 and Heb 1:3. Yet James himself gives us no evidence that he believed Jesus was divine. His titles for Jesus could just as well have been applied to, say, David, had David been raised from the dead by God and taken to heaven (or even without resurrection, as Luke 16:22–31 pictures Abraham in a type of executive function for God, as also Enoch of *1 Enoch*). But since James does not discuss the topic, we have no reason for saying that he did not believe in it. We only know that the relationship between Jesus and God was not important enough in the context of this letter and the situation it addresses that James felt a need to bring it up.

129. 1 Peter does mention the cross, as we will see, but it is not mentioned in either 2 Peter or Jude, other than the reference to "the Master who bought them" in 2 Pet 2:1.

130. John S. Kloppenborg, "Reception and Emulation of the Jesus Tradition in James," 121–50, documents both James's use of the Jesus tradition and also the source of the methodology, pointing out that "that verbatim repetition of predecessor texts" was neither expected nor desirable in that day (p. 130); what was expected was the creative transformation and paraphrasing of texts, a technique known in rhetorical texts as *aemulatio*. Kloppenborg concludes the text of his article with a five-page table laying out the use of "Q" in James.

131. In the same context in James he refers to the commands against murder and adultery, which are also the two Decalogue commands first taken up in the Sermon on the Mount (Matt 5:21–32).

among other places in James, and Matt 7:1 – 2). And of course there is the parallel to Matt 5:33 – 37 in Jas 5:12, which appears to be a virtual citation of a saying of Jesus without any citation formula (e.g., "Jesus said"). James breathes the ethical authority of Jesus, which is another way of saying that Jesus' lordship permeates the letter.

Because Jesus is Lord, Caesar (or any other earthly or heavenly authority) is not. The Judge whom one fears is not Caesar, but the one who is "at the door" (Jas 5:9). The "glorious Lord" is not a Roman official, but Jesus. God's agent in the world is not Caesar (the person viewed as so much an agent of the gods that he would in most cases eventually be deified), but Jesus "the Anointed One." And given that James is against divided loyalties ("double-minded" is not a good term for him, nor is any other both–and loyalty), it is unlikely that he would have tolerated divided loyalties. One cannot read James in the context of the Greco-Roman world without realizing the political import of both his statements and his attitude.[132]

Finally, as alluded to above, Jesus is not just the exalted, "glorious Lord," but also the coming one. James can refer to "the coming of the Lord" (Jas 5:7) and then say that "the Judge is at the door" (5:9). The imminence of divine judgment through this Lord is an important part of his description of Jesus. In fact, Jesus is the only one to whom the judging function is explicitly attributed, not the Father, and certainly not the Holy Spirit (which is not even mentioned). Put Renan's simple Galilean peasant aside along with popular notions of Jesus as "meek and mild" (often portrayed in art as effeminate and virtually anemic) or as a "loving buddy"; the Jesus of James would leave one slack-jawed from awe, if not face down in obeisance, and perhaps weak-kneed if one thought of him as Judge, even if one expected to be on the positive side of that judgment.

2.4.3 The Nature of Wisdom

James also talks about wisdom, but, as noted above, he never mentions the Holy Spirit. Thus, unless wisdom is a stand-in for the Holy Spirit, James's theology as presented in this letter is at most binitarian rather than trinitarian.[133] But is wisdom such a stand-in? Certainly, some have argued that it is.[134] James mentions wisdom twice, once as a gift of God that enables one to endure testing or trials (1:5) and once as "the wisdom from above" that produces certain virtues in the followers of Jesus (3:13 – 18). In both cases wisdom seems to have an effect on individuals, but in neither case is wisdom said to "act" in even a semipersonal manner. Thus, while James like Proverbs has an association of wisdom with virtue, he does not personify wisdom as Proverbs 8 does, nor divinize it as Wis 7:22 – 8:1 does. For

---

132. If one reads James as written just before or early in the Jewish war with Rome, this attitude should become doubly clear, for while it may not have been clear to Palestinian Jews who the Jewish leader was (the high priest? a Pharisaic leader? the head of the council in Qumran? Herod Agrippa II?), it was equally clear that Caesar was not a candidate.

133. We say "at most" because since James never relates Jesus to God other than as "the Anointed One," he also gives us no evidence that he thought of Jesus as divine or "Son of God," although he may have. If he did not, then he was a nontrinitarian monotheist like traditional Judaism.

134. E.g., J. A. Kirk, "The Meaning of Wisdom in James," *NTS* 16 (1969): 24 – 38.

James, wisdom is a gift, and wisdom brings virtue, but wisdom is not personal. In this sense it is more like a gift of the Spirit than the Spirit himself; yet, as noted, James never mentions the Spirit specifically. Wisdom is not a gift of the Spirit, but a gift of the Father.

Nevertheless, James does drink deeply from the wisdom tradition, as indicated by the numerous parallels with Proverbs, Sirach, and Wisdom, noted above in the rhetorical and narrative reading of the letter. And wisdom is for James that gift of God that enables one to live a virtuous life. Furthermore, the virtues of wisdom are similar to the fruit of the Spirit in Gal 5:22–23, or the characteristics of the law/spirit (both terms are used) in the Rule of the Community from the Dead Sea (1QS 4).

James 3	1QS 4	Matthew 5	Galatians 5
πραΰτητι σοφίας wisdom's meekness	humility	πραεῖς meek, humble	πραΰτης meekness
ἁγνή pure	admirable purity	καθαροὶ τῇ καρδίᾳ pure with respect to their heart	
εἰρηνική peaceful		εἰρηνοποιοί peacemakers	εἰρήνη peace
ἐπιεικής easily entreated	patience		μακροθυμία long-suffering
εὐπειθής willing to yield	discernment		χρηστότης kindness
μεστὴ ἐλέους full of mercy	abundant charity	ἐλεήμονες merciful	
καὶ καρπῶν ἀγαθῶν and of the fruit of good deeds	unending goodness		ἀγαθωσύνη goodness
ἀδιάκριτος without partiality	steadfastness of heart	πεινῶντες … δικαιοσύνην hungering … for righteousness	
ἀνυπόκριτος without hypocrisy			
			ἀγάπη love
			χαρά joy
			ἐγκράτεια self-control

Table 1: A Comparison of Virtues

In other words, while James does not personalize wisdom nor give her divine characteristics, she functions similarly to the Holy Spirit in that she is a divine gift that enables one to live the virtuous life. The focus remains on God, for he is the one who gives wisdom. Wisdom is not called on apart from a calling on God to grant it.

God is the source of all wisdom. In the passage on the true versus the counterfeit (Jas 3:13–18), the wisdom "from above" always produces virtue. The other influences that may claim to be wisdom James does not call wisdom, but rather "not the wisdom from above." They are earthly/demonic, and thus by definition are not wisdom, since the only source of wisdom is God. The fact that these influences produce vice is a mark that indicates that they are not the genuine item at all. Wisdom *always* produces virtue, for it is a gift from God.

2.4.4 The Nature and Situation of Humanity

Wisdom is given to human beings, but what is a human being? The human being, according to James, consists of a body and spirit.[135] Thus in Jas 2:26 James makes the observation that "the body without the spirit is dead." Both elements are needed to have a functioning person. Later on he states that God has caused this spirit to "dwell in" human beings,[136] a creative reference. That James accepts the first creation narrative in Gen 1 is clear enough in his comment that human beings "have come into being according to the likeness of God" (3:9). That this likeness still exists in human beings is clear in the argument that because of this fact, cursing human beings while blessing God is contradictory, much like honoring a patron or ruler to their face while defacing their image that stands in the courtyard of their house or in the town square. James takes the human being existing in the image of God seriously.

But there is another side to human existence. The human being is often controlled by "one's own desire" (Jas 1:14), which lures one away from the path of virtue. The "battles and conflicts" within the community are due to desires (a different term than in 1:14, but used synonymously) "fighting in your members" (4:1).[137] Following Seitz,[138] I have argued[139] that this is an expression of Second Temple

---

135. James does use the word "soul" (ψυχή, *psychē*) twice (1:21; 5:20). In neither case does it seem to be a part of the human being, soul as opposed to body. In 1:21 the "implanted word" is able to "save your souls," and in 5:20 the one who turns a sinner from error "saves a soul from death." In both cases either BDAG's (1098–99) meaning 1b, "life itself," or 3, "an entity with personhood, person," fit the context well. One saves a life or a person from death; the implanted word will save one's life or whole person. This is the whole of who one is, not a part, much less an immortal part versus a mortal body.

136. While what is said about the spirit is controversial, it is relatively certain that the text is saying that God caused it to dwell "in us." The spirit is unlikely to "cause itself to dwell," so God is the probable subject, as is clear in a parallel construction in *Herm. Mand.* 3.1, which may be dependent on this text (cf. a similar statement in *Herm. Sim.* 5.6.5, although in this case Hermas is talking about the Holy Spirit).

137. While Adolf Schlatter, *Der Brief des Jakobus* (Stuttgart: Calwer, 1932), 240–41, believed that these were conflicts within the Jewish community; and B. I. Reicke, *Diakonie, Festfreude und Zelos* (WÅ; Uppsala: Lundequistska, 1951), 341–44, argued that these were revolutionary movements among Roman Jews, neither has been followed by recent scholars, who agree that the "battles and conflicts" are within the community ("among you") and metaphorical, not physical "wars and fighting" (which would be a nonmetaphorical reading of the text).

138. O. J. F. Seitz, "Two Spirits in Man: An Essay in Biblical Exegesis," *NTS* 6 (1959): 82–95.

139. Davids, *James*, 83–85.

Jewish *yēṣer* theology, namely, that there is an impulse in the human being that, if not controlled, will lead the human being to evil because, like the Freudian *id*, it lacks boundaries. It is separate from the human *ego*, which leaves the human being with a choice, although without assistance (which in later Jewish literature came through the law, and which in James comes through God's gift of wisdom), the struggle against this impulse is often lost. Given *yēṣer*'s nature, the Jewish works indicate a belief that it was part of the human being *as created*; the problem was not the existence of desire/*yēṣer*, for without such drives one would not care for one's legitimate needs. The problem was the disorder, namely, that without some external force—for the Jews, the law—the *yēṣer* would cross the boundary into sin.

James has expressed this as a good Greek would, using *desire(s)*, for Stoic philosophers in particular were suspicious of desire (the human drives and emotions) for the same reason as Jews distrusted *yēṣer*. Desire was changeable (as the human limbic system is by nature) and thus disturbed human self-control and tranquility.[140] The Stoics, like James, thought that the solution would be found in wisdom, although Stoic wisdom was not primarily a gift of the gods, but rather the gift of philosophy, thinking rightly about nature and one's situation in nature.

If unrestrained desire (*yēṣer*) is the main problem in humanity, assuming that that desire is what makes one double-minded (trying to trust both the world and God), speech is the way that human beings most easily express this problem. Some of the rabbis would later locate the *yēṣer* in the kidneys, but James locates it in the tongue (in the sense that the tongue most easily expresses it). Speech is viewed as powerful enough to control the direction of the body, but it is also untamable and influenced by Gehenna.

This figure of speech is interesting, for in the New Testament Gehenna is always pictured as a place of punishment, not as a place from which evil emanates.[141] It appears, then, that James is using a type of ironic metonymy in which the evil that will eventually be punished in Gehenna (along with the whole person embodying that evil) is replaced with the place of punishment itself. James, of course, will go on to suggest the antidote, wisdom and, if one is not already single-mindedly committed to God, repentance. This choice appears to be within the ability of the individual, at least of the individual who already has committed to the good news.[142]

2.4.5 The Nature and Content of the Good News

The main part of Paul's definition of the good news (Rom 10:9–10) that James witnesses to is that Jesus is Lord, since his two clear references to Jesus both use

---

140. See, e.g., Epictetus, *Diatr.* 2.1.36–44; 2.20.15–20.

141. See, e.g., H. Bietenhard, "γέεννα," in *NIDNTT*, 2:207–8.

142. In Jas 3:1–4:10 it is clearly within the range of human choice, for while no one can tame the tongue, once one realizes that one's "wisdom" is "not the wisdom from above" and heeds the call to repentance, God's favor (grace) is granted. In this passage it comes after repentance, not before. But James can also speak of the "implanted word" in 1:21 that, while it needs to be "received" or "welcomed," appears to imply an agency outside the individual, although this is not entirely clear. James 1:18 is clearer in that God is the one who "gives birth to us" willingly, so the process there appears to be within God's control, or at least within his volition.

the title "Lord." There needs to be commitment to this Lord, as James indicates in the rhetorical question of Jas 2:1. But James is writing to people who are already members of the community of the followers of Jesus as Lord, so he often refers to the good news (a term that he never uses) by means of a simple phrase that is rather more oblique than we might like.

In the metaphor of 1:18 we learn that God "gave birth to us" by means of the "word of truth." This new life (the result of birth) leads to our being "a type of" firstfruit of that which (the plural things) he has created or is creating. Since this is something that has happened during our lives, it is less likely that this refers to the creation we were already in than to creation that he will make in the future, the eschatological creation.[143] Thus, while James does not say "new birth" as 1 Pet 1:3 does, he appears to have a similar concept in mind, and in both cases God the Father is the active agent of the birth.[144] In James the more passive agent of this birth is "the word of truth," which, given the context, is the good news. Thus, God takes the female role of giving birth with the "sperm" as "the word of truth"; thus, God ends up with an eschatological person, so to speak, either in terms of human beings as the first temporally of God's eschatological re-creation, or, more likely, the human beings as the fulfillment of God's creative purpose as his representative rulers within and yet over creation (as in Gen 1:27–28; Ps 8:6–7). How much James is conscious of this theology or how much he has used images that imply more than he is conscious of, we cannot tell, since he does not give us that information; but, if taken as a conscious expression of his theology, that would be what the images imply.

In 1:21 James changes his image from birth by means of the word and refers to "the implanted word" that is able to save one's life.[145] Some have argued that this word is "inborn" or "innate" rather than "implanted."[146] While it is true that this word can have this meaning (cf. its only other biblical appearance, in Wis 12:10, of "wickedness inborn"), this meaning does not fit well with "receive," for how can one receive something that is "innate" or "inborn"? Thus, the general scholarly view is that this word is something implanted by God.[147] This "word," presumably the good news, needs to be "received" as opposed to "rejected," and this reception is done in "meekness," which is the virtue of Matt 5:5 and which Dibelius argues is

---

143. Since the word "firstfruit" is a noun, it has no tense. But it is part of a purpose clause, so implies a goal subsequent to his "giving birth to us."

144. This differs in tone from John 3 in that "born again" in John 3 is a misunderstanding on the part of Nicodemus with "born from above," which is Jesus' meaning, as he makes clear in explaining it as birth "from/out of water and Spirit." The only active agent mentioned is Spirit rather than the Father. On the other hand, the contrast of "flesh" and "Spirit" births implies that the "Spirit" birth is subsequent to the "flesh" birth and so fits with "born again" language in 1 Peter (where "born again" is not a misunderstanding), and this birth that is not natural birth in James.

145. We have argued above that *psychē* means "life" in the sense of "self" or "person." We have avoided the translation "soul," for often "soul" is opposed to "body," a part rather than the whole. The

New Testament narrative always includes the resurrection of the dead, the final judgment (referred to frequently in James), and the co-rule of the righteous with Jesus as its culmination, so the salvation of the whole of the individual is in view, not just that of a part.

146. For instance, W. L. Knox, "The Epistle of St. James," *JTS* 46 (1945): 14–15, who argues that this is the Stoic concept of inborn reason, which would fit well with the word *logos,* which does often mean "reason" in Greek literature. F. J. A. Hort, *The Epistle of St. James* (London: Macmillan & Co., 1909), argued less plausibly (since the text says that the word is "inborn" or "implanted," not that an ability to receive it was) that it was an inborn ability to receive revelation.

147. This is true even for Dibelius and Greeven, *James,* 113, who are generally disposed to see more Hellenistic meanings in James. See further Davids, *James,* 95.

the main point of the verse.[148] This is the opposite of anger, which does not produce God's type of justice or righteousness (Jas 1:20), whereas this attitude does receive the word and thus does presumably produce God's righteousness. What is clear is that even after the divine action of implantation, the human being must "receive" the word for it to become effective.

Having identified two elements of the good news—namely, the conviction that Jesus is Lord and a message that needs to be received in order to save a person, one needs to ask what other elements of the good news, the foundational message of the life of a follower of Jesus, are found in James. If one goes through the list in Heb 6:1–2 ("the basic teaching about Christ," NRSV),[149] James does discuss repentance (Jas 4:6–10), commitment or faith (in his rejection of being double-minded and in his discussion of the topic in 2:14–22), and eternal judgment (as will be seen below), but not baptism(s)—although it may well be alluded to in Jas 2:7, as will be discussed below—or laying on of hands. But, then, James is addressing communities of followers of Jesus, so presumably all are baptized, and James never discusses the Spirit, so it is not surprising that he does not mention laying on of hands (one might expect this in 5:14–15, but he only mentions oil and prayer). What he has are the basic elements useful in calling a person who claims to follow Jesus back to a sincere commitment. He is not addressing the naïve or proclaiming the good news to those outside the community. Instead, he is proclaiming it to the initiate.

2.4.6 Opposition to Human Welfare and God's Plan

It is not that God's good news is the only force affecting the human being. Besides unbridled desire (which is, after all, part of the individual), there are other forces affecting a person. When James says that God does not put anyone to the test (Jas 1:13), it is a little surprising that he follows this up with accusing desire within of doing it rather than Satan, as in Job and in the reconfiguration of Genesis 22 in, for example, *Jubilees* 18. There "the prince Mastêmâ" is in some type of honor contest with God, as Satan is in Job, and is put to shame as a result of Abraham's faithfulness. Does James have a role for the devil and the demonic?

There is a hint that he does in Jas 3:15, where pseudo-wisdom that leads one into vice is described as "earthly" and "soulish" or "merely naturally human" (which are what would be expected if traced to desire within) and then "demonic" (δαιμονιώδης, *daimoniōdēs*), which goes beyond the other two. Thus James believes that such pseudo-wisdom has a source in the "lower" spiritual world, but we are not informed as to the degree to which this is true or as to how the demonic world is involved with desire.[150]

---

148. Dibelius and Greeven, *James*, 112.

149. We have tried to focus on explicit statements of the good news in letters to communities of followers of Jesus, rather than look at the Gospels or at reconstructions of the good news from statements in letters that the author does not identify as the good news, remembering that all New Testament letter writers are writing to self-identified followers of Jesus.

150. We have discussed Gehenna (Jas 3:6) above and noted that at this period Gehenna was not viewed as the abode of the devil or demonic (as hell would be in the Middle Ages), but as the place of punishment of evil/evil beings. Thus, the ultimate punishment of evil has been substituted for the evil itself, without revealing whether this is the evil within or external, perhaps demonic evil.

In 4:7, however, having accused his readers of "friendship with the world" and thus "enmity with God," James starts his call to repentance with, "Submit yourselves therefore to God, and resist the devil and he will flee from you." Since it was "the world" that readers were involved in (4:4), the devil appears to be viewed as standing behind the world. The resisting of the devil is also called for in 1 Pet 5:8–9, again with no discussion of how the devil relates to the persecution that the church is undergoing. Thus we can conclude that while James wants to keep "desire" and "the world" in the forefront of his argument, he believes that in the shadows behind these more conscious influences lurks the devil. He, or at least demons, are the source of pseudo-wisdom that would lead one astray. He is apparently the spiritual force behind "the world." Since so little is said, James apparently believes that he shares with his readers an understanding of the role of these forces and their relationship to God, but it remains unstated precisely because our author views it as shared information.

2.4.7 The Role and Function of the Law

The main influence that James cites as helping the followers of Jesus is wisdom, but there is also another positive force in their world, and that is "the law." James never refers to the law without qualifying it, so it is unlikely that he means by it the Torah plain and simple. The law James is talking about is "the perfect law," which he immediately calls "the law of freedom" (Jas 1:25). This law, if not just read but put into practice, will make the person "blessed" in their actions. It is clear that Jews could speak of the law as perfect (Ps 19:7 and frequently in Psalm 119), but what is unusual is the term "freedom." Stoics spoke of the freedom that comes from following the law of nature (Epictetus, *Diatr.* 4.1.158; Seneca, *Vit. beat.* 15.7), and this was applied to the Mosaic Torah by Philo (*Prob.*43–48). So also here in James as in Philo, we appear to have a law-abiding community, or at least a community that has no tension with the Mosaic Torah, that reads that instruction through lenses originally crafted by Stoicism. Yet given the heavy dependence of James on the teaching of Jesus, and in particular on the teaching we have preserved in the Sermon on the Mount, when James thinks of the Torah, he is probably interpreting the law according to the teaching of Jesus.

This suspicion becomes stronger when one examines the next term James applies to the Torah, "the royal law," or "the king's law according to the Scripture" (Jas 2:8). While Dibelius cites 4 Macc 14:2, where reason is called royal,[151] and Mussner suggests that this refers to the royal rank of the command,[152] the fact that the reference here is to the law as a whole (*nomos*) not a command (*entolē*) and that Maccabees applies the epithet to reason, not the law, makes these interpretations unlikely. However, we must remember that Jesus is viewed as "the Anointed One" and thus "Lord," that repeatedly in the Matthean tradition he gave his authority

151. Dibelius, *James*, 143.   152. Mussner, *Jakobusbrief*, 124.

to the Torah as he interpreted it (Matt 5:17–20; 23:3, 23), and that this particular passage cited in James was reportedly endorsed by Jesus as a summary of that Torah (Mark 12:31//Matt 22:39; Matt 19:19). Hence, it is likely that James considers the law "royal" or "belonging to the king" because it was endorsed and interpreted by the one who was king, namely, Jesus (cf. Jesus' references to the kingdom of God).

Whether or not this is the correct understanding of "royal," it is clear that for James the law, which he also calls "the law of liberty" (Jas 2:12), is the standard for final judgment. Those who have not shown mercy in their treatment of others will experience, in its full force ("without mercy"), judgment according to the law. For James, freedom in no way meant freedom *from* the law, but rather that in following the law as interpreted by Jesus one became indeed free.

2.4.8 The Nature of the Community

The concept of Torah implies a community that keeps the law, just as the concept of something being royal implies that there is a kingdom in which a group of people is living under that royal authority. It is therefore appropriate to examine James's view of the community of the followers of Jesus that he believes that he is addressing.

Since James is addressing a community and thus people who have already entered the community, he does not discuss the means of entrance in detail. However, there is an allusion to this entrance in his mentioning "the good [or honorable] name that was called upon you" (2:7). Since "to call a name upon" or "to be called by a name" is a Septuagintalism that is most often used to indicate relationship to God (Deut 28:10; 2 Chr 7:14; Isa 43:7; Jer 14:9; Amos 9:12; *Pss. Sol.* 19:18), for followers of Jesus it was Jesus' name that was "called upon" them, first and foremost in baptism (e.g., Acts 2:38; 8:16; 10:48; *Herm. Sim.* 9.16.3),[153] which is why baptism was not just the "door to the church," but also the door to the type of persecution to which Jas 2:7 refers.

James makes three references to this community. First, it is a representative of the "twelve tribes" that are "in the Diaspora" (1:1). This views these communities of followers of Jesus as elements of the renewed Israel, each representing the whole in their locality. Probably these communities were ethnically Jewish, but that is not the point. In writing to followers of Jesus but not to other Jews (cf. the fact that Jesus' being Lord and Anointed One is stated rather than argued), James is saying that these are the remnant of Israel, the true twelve tribes.

Moving to the local gathering per se, James speaks in 2:2 of people coming "into your gathering" (συναγωγή, *synagōgē*). In this expression it is at least clear that James does not shy away from using the standard terminology of a Jewish gathering (in fact, all of the other fifty-five times that the word occurs in the New Testament

---

153. The analogy can be made to traditional marriage customs in the English-speaking world, in which the surname of the husband is first used and taken by the wife in the marriage ceremony, which is precisely why more egalitarian forms are commonly practiced today. But since Jesus is Lord, and since there is no way in which his followers claim equality with him, there is no such issue with the "calling upon" his name in baptism.

are in reference to a Jewish synagogue, even if the references are negative, as in Rev 2:9 and 3:9). So one way of referring to a gathering of the Jesus community was as a "synagogue," even if the gathering envisioned in 2:2–4 is judicial, as argued above (the other possibility is that it is a gathering for a meal, i.e., the Lord's Supper or Eucharist). In a similar context, 1 Cor 6:4, Paul uses "church" (ἐκκλησία, ekklēsia), which indicates that the concept of "church" can be connected with judicial proceedings by a letter writer. Thus, James had no reason he must use synagōgē if he is indeed referring to a judicial gathering. James simply does not find "synagogue" problematic to use when describing a gathering of the Christian community.

James can also refer to the community as a "community gathering" or "church," for he uses the term ekklēsia in 5:14, which indicates that he shares the common terminology of the rest of the New Testament for the community of Jesus' followers. This community has "elders," who are presumably the leaders, representatives, or at least the most experienced members of the community. They are the ones called to pray for healing (James gives no theology that lets us know which meaning he has in view). Judging from known Jewish communities, one would expect these people to at least be the community leaders.

Since we find these elders being called to a sick individual, it is clear that one of their functions is to pray for those seriously ill. They follow the example of the Twelve (Mark 6:13) and anoint with oil in "the name of the Lord" as they pray. In neither passage are we informed about the meaning of the oil, but since only oil is involved in every case, it is clearly not medicinal. Thus its function must be sacramental, a physical acting out of the prayer or a physical acting out of God's action in touching the person.[154] That the action is done "in the name of the Lord" connects the action to the authority of Jesus. Of the twenty-seven times that the phrase occurs in the New Testament, only in John does it refer to the Father, and in those cases it is Jesus talking about his authority. In all the other cases, and particularly in all passages about healing, the action is clearly in the name of Jesus. Thus the elders' act, including their prayer, is done under the authority of Jesus.

There is significant confidence in James that the action of the elders will be effective, that the person will be healed, but along with this confidence in healing is his confidence that sin will be forgiven. Thus, James believes that in some but not all cases (cf. "if"), sin is connected to sickness (cf. 1 Cor 11:29–30 for the Pauline version, where Paul connects certain sickness and death to disciplinary judgment by "the Lord"). Confession of any such sin (implicit in Jas 5:14–15, but explicit in 5:16) to an individual clears the way for healing prayer.

While the elders of the community are the ones to "call," they are not the only ones who can pray effectively. All of the members of the community can pray for one another, for they presumably fall into the category of being righteous persons (5:16b). Thus, while James ascribes a certain prominence to community leadership,

---

154. If this were Paul, he would say, "an acting out of the action of the Spirit," but since James never mentions the Spirit and does mention "the Lord," we have been cautious about putting words such as "Spirit" into his mouth.

he does not give them exclusive rights to healing prayer, but rather expects the whole community to participate. We do not know if in James's mind there are other functions of the elders to which they do have exclusive rights, for healing prayer is the only function he describes.

2.4.9 The Nature of Eschatology

While James may agree with Paul that sickness can be a proximate judgment of God (1 Cor 11:31–32), it is certainly something he does not stress, for his focus is on God's ultimate judgment. The threat of judgment is pervasive in the letter, whether it be the comment to teachers ("We will receive a greater judgment," Jas 3:1), a reference to a faith that cannot save (2:14), or a statement that his readers "are to be judged according to the standard of the law of liberty" (2:12). In fact, the minute that one starts to ask various passages, "When does this (being saved, being blessed, etc.) happen?" the answer is usually, "At the final judgment."

This judgment is marked by "the coming of the Lord," which is "near" or "at hand" (the term in Jas 5:7–8 carries either meaning). Thus one gets a progression: "until the parousia ['arrival' or 'coming'] of the Lord" (5:7), "the parousia of the Lord is near/at hand" (5:8), and "Look! The Judge is standing at the doors" (5:9). The term "parousia" is normally connected to Jesus (or "the Son of Man"),[155] so it is most probable that here "the Lord" and "the Judge" are Jesus. James, then, believes that Jesus' "coming" will be the initiation of final judgment, that Jesus will be "the Judge," and that the coming of this judge is imminent.

While the standard at this judgment will be "the law of liberty," there are both gradients in judgment and mitigating factors. Teachers, presumably because they are expected to embody what they teach, will be judged more harshly or strictly (lit., "greater judgment," the term [κρίμα, *krima*] referring both to the process and to the verdict and punishment).[156] The verdict, however, is not always negative (perhaps for the group addressed even rarely negative), for it is after enduring (a term connected to the final judgment in Jas 5:7) that one is declared "blessed" and receives "the crown of life" or "crown that is life."

The mitigating factor mentioned with respect to judgment is that "mercy triumphs over judgment" (Jas 2:13), so by the mercy that one shows in this age, one chooses the standard of judgment when that day comes. While this is stated as a general principle, it is not clear whether James intends it as a parallel to his following discussion of the proper type of commitment to Jesus as Lord (i.e., one that produces charitable action), that such commitment will save one in that day. If the latter is indeed the case, then mercy does indeed have a significant effect.

If some are saved, this implies that others are not. Indeed, James argues (2:13–26) that some who have "faith" (what we might call orthodox doctrinal commitments)

---

155. There are noneschatological uses of *parousia* in 1 Cor 16:17; 2 Cor 7:6–7; 10:10; Phil 2:12; and a negative eschatological *parousia* in 2 Thess 2:9, but of the remaining sixteen uses in the New Testament outside of our passage, only 2 Pet 3:12 does not refer to a "com-

ing" or "arrival" of Jesus. There the "coming" is not a coming of God, but a coming of "the day of God," for it is referring to astronomical phenomena associated with the event, not to the person coming.

156. BDAG, 567, *krima*, esp. meanings 3 and 4.

will not be saved, for their faith is "dead" or "useless." This implies that some who view themselves as followers of Jesus will be among those whom God "destroys" (4:12). While this may not be a comfortable observation, it fits with James's concern to save people from death (5:19–20), which implies that denying that there are people, including people in the orthodox community, who are in danger is a living in denial, which is neither helpful nor ultimately effective.

2.5 JAMES'S CANONICAL CONTRIBUTION

James has, of course, been involved in a significant amount of controversy about its place in the canon; but when taken on its own terms, it makes as significant a contribution to that canon as any other work in the collection. We see that contribution as taking place in five general areas: (1) the role of Jesus; (2) the theology of suffering; (3) the theology of healing; (4) the meaning of commitment to Jesus (faith); and (5) the ethical importance of speech and money. Just because the body of literature called James consists of one letter with five chapters does not mean it is less important theologically than, say, Paul's multiple letters, many of which revolve around the same topic.

2.5.1 The Role of Jesus

It is clear that telling the foundation story about Jesus was important to the early Jesus movement. This resulted in the four canonical Gospels, which also demonstrate that one could tell the story in different ways shaped by the needs of various communities. It is also clear that the teaching of Jesus was important enough for this same early Jesus movement that there was a common teaching tradition found in, for example, Matthew and Luke (which we refer to as "Q"). Without entering into the debate as to whether this tradition was oral or written, its mere existence is enough to show that the teaching of Jesus was important to the community that claimed to follow him.

Yet when one turns to the Pauline literature, there appears to be little reference to this Jesus teaching tradition. Naturally, one would not expect Paul to cite the Gospels, since he was probably martyred before at least three and quite possibly all four existed as formal writings. But was Paul aware of the oral Jesus tradition? Paul frequently refers to Jesus as Lord, most notably in Rom 10:9–10, but is this lordship simply cosmic (as one might think if one had only Col 1:15–20 as a sample of his thought), or is there a connection between this lordship and the teaching of the earthly Jesus? Now, even though Paul is generally discussing topics about which there is no record that the earthly Jesus spoke and is speaking to committed followers of Jesus who already knew and accepted the foundation narrative, there are occasional hints that Paul did value the teaching of Jesus. For instance, while 1 Cor 6:1–8 resonates with ideas in the teaching of Jesus, 6:7–8 could well reflect teaching like that in Matt 5:38–42. Likewise, 1 Cor 7:10–11 most likely reflects the teaching of Jesus about divorce (cf. also 11:23–25). The teaching of Jesus seems to have played some role in Paul's ethical thinking, but this pales in comparison with James.

As noted repeatedly above, (1) James's only references to Jesus are as exalted Lord and coming Judge. But (2) the role that Jesus as Lord plays in James's community is expressed through frequent allusions to the teaching of Jesus, or, perhaps more accurately put, the reprocessing of this teaching into James's words. This is true whether one thinks of the closest reference that we have to a gospel in James (Jas 5:12//Matt 5:33 – 37), or whether we think of the words and phrases that crop up in James, such as Jas 2:5/Matt 5:3 (and such examples could be multiplied). Whether the topic is wealth and poverty, speech and anger, or persecution, in James the teaching of Jesus appears to be foundational to James's thinking.

James, then, is showing how the teaching of Jesus presently found in the Gospels functioned in the movement that acclaimed Jesus as Lord. This teaching was foundational—not that it was quoted verbatim all of the time, but that it was authoritative when a leader taught on a subject covered in the teaching. Thus it is not only the teaching content of James that is a contribution to the canon, but also his theological methodology of referring to the teaching of Jesus. For James, if Jesus is Lord, then following the teaching of Jesus shows that someone is truly his follower.

2.5.2 The Theology of Suffering

When it comes to a theology of suffering, James joins Jesus and virtually every other author of the New Testament in contributing to the total theological picture. James's particular stress is on suffering as a test of commitment to Jesus and therefore as something that needs to be endured. While he is close to the conception of suffering in the Matthean testing-of-Jesus narrative (Matt 4:1 – 11),[157] James looks more closely than Matthew does at failure in the test and connects this to "desire" within the human being. As is typical of his Jewish background, James does not attribute the problem with desire to a fall, but rather views it as something that is a problem only when it starts to control the agenda. While there is the presence of "the devil" lurking behind the scenes, James's argument that what is needed to stand in the test is divine wisdom and renunciation of "the world" and its values is a significant contribution to New Testament theology.

2.5.3 The Theology of Healing

In speaking of suffering, James distinguishes it from sickness. For suffering he prescribes prayer for endurance until the Lord comes and sets the world to right. For sickness he prescribes prayer for healing. While it is clear in the Gospels that Jesus healed and that he authorized the Twelve (and in Luke also the Seventy) to heal in his name, and while it is clear in Acts that the major leaders of the Jesus movement did heal people similarly to how Jesus healed them, there is little instruction on this topic outside of James. Paul does indeed talk about "gifts of healing" (1 Cor 12:11, 30), which indicates that there was some experience of healing ministry in

---

157. On which see Birger Gerhardsson, *The Testing of God's Son (Matt 4:1 – 11 & Par): An Analysis of an Early Christian Midrash* (ConBNT 2:1; Lund: CWK Gleerup, 1966).

his churches, but the theology that he is interested in is that of the *variety* of gifts rather than the practice of healing in particular.

Thus, when it comes to healing, one either extrapolates from the teaching and example of Jesus (remembering that the Gospels were written, not as historical artifacts, but to instruct the church),[158] or else one must turn to James. While historically the bias of the church against the body has meant that James has been interpreted as limited to spiritual healing, such as extreme unction (i.e., anointing before death) in the Roman Catholic tradition, the language in James resists that interpretation.[159] What one has in James is a discussion of a practice that must have been assumed to have been part of the community's teaching) note its position as one of the topics touched on in a typical Greek letter ending. This teaching mentions the "who," "when," "how," and, by implication, "where" of the practice, relating healing prayer to trust, anointing, and sin. It is probably as extensive as it is in James because of the link to sin, for it is clear in James that the author believes that those whom he addresses need to deal with sin. The extended segment on healing may suggest that it is precisely because of sin that healing is needed to the extent that it is. Yet whatever the situation, clearly James gives us the most explicit teaching about healing in the New Testament.

2.5.4 The Meaning of Commitment to Jesus

Healing, however, is related by James to commitment to or trust in Jesus and his Father. It is this topic that raises the most canonical controversy in James because of the apparent conflict between James and Paul, particularly between James and Galatians and Romans. It is therefore necessary to look at it more closely. The critical terms are all found in these verses:

Galatians/Romans	James	Shared Terms
… we know that a person is justified not by the **works of the law** but through **faith in Jesus Christ**. And we have come to believe in Christ Jesus, so that we might be **justified by faith** in Christ, and **not by doing the works of the law**, because **no one will be justified by the works of the law**. (Gal 2:16, NRSV)	[14]What good is it, my brothers and sisters, if you say you have **faith but do not have works**? **Can faith save you**? … [17]So **faith by itself, if it has no works, is dead**. (Jas 2:14, 17, NRSV)	Faith Works of the law Works Justified

(Continued on the next page)

---

158. E.g., Ken Blue, *Authority to Heal* (Downers Grove, IL: Inter-Varsity Press, 1987), a responsible and theologically thoughtful discussion of the topic, roots his argument in the kingdom of God theology of the four Gospels.

159. See the discussion in Davids, *James*, 191–97.

Galatians/Romans	James	Shared Terms
[28]For we hold that a person is justified by faith apart from works prescribed by the law. (Rom 3:28, NRSV)	[24]You see that a person is justified by works and not by faith alone. (Jas 2:24, NRSV)	Justified Faith apart from works Works not faith alone
[2]For if **Abraham was justified by works**, he has something to boast about, but not before God. [3]For what does the scripture say? "Abraham believed God, and it was reckoned to him as righteousness." [4]Now to one who works, wages are not reckoned as a gift but as something due. [5]But to one who **without works trusts him who justifies** the ungodly, such **faith is reckoned as righteousness**. (Rom 4:2–5, NRSV)	[20]Do you want to be shown, you senseless person, that **faith apart from works is barren**? [21]Was not our ancestor **Abraham justified by works** when he offered his son Isaac on the altar? [22]You see that **faith was active along with his works, and faith was brought to completion by the works**. [23]Thus the scripture was fulfilled that says, "Abraham believed God, and it was reckoned to him as righteousness" (Jas 2:20–23, NRSV)	Abraham Justified by works Faith apart from works Faith active with works Faith brought to completion by works Without works trusts (= has faith in) him who justifies Faith is reckoned as righteousness Gen 15:6 quoted
[30]What then are we to say? Gentiles, who did not strive for righteousness, have attained it, that is, righteousness through faith; [31]but Israel, who did strive for the righteousness that is based on the law, did not succeed in fulfilling that law. [32]Why not? Because they did not strive for it on **the basis of faith**, but as if it were **based on works**. (Rom 9:30–32, NRSV)	[25]Likewise, was not Rahab the prostitute also **justified by works** when she welcomed the messengers and sent them out by another road? [26]For just as the body without the spirit is dead, so **faith without works is also dead**. (Jas 2:25–26, NRSV)	Basis of faith versus basis of works Justified by works Faith without works is also dead

Table 2: James and Paul Comparison

The table above, of course, could also make cross comparisons, and to some degree the listing of terms is intended to do that, picking out key terms that are found in more than one of the passages.

When one first examines these comparisons, it looks like James (since James is probably written after Romans and Galatians) is intentionally contradicting Paul, or at least his understanding of Paul.[160] "No, it is not faith alone, it is faith completed by works. This is what results in justification." One notices not just the overlap of the three critical terms, "faith," "works," and "justified" (the verb δικαιόω, *dikaioō*), but the overlapping use of the example of Abraham and the mutual quotation of Gen 15:6 (LXX). If these observations are accurate, we have two equal voices in the New Testament contradicting each other and we must choose which voice to apply to which situation.[161]

Yet such a conclusion tends to overlook the linguistic differences between James and Paul. Paul in the contexts in which he discusses faith and works always refers to "works of the law," either in the sentence itself or earlier in the same paragraph. James never uses this phrase, and while there is evidence that James's community was law observant (see sec. 2.4.7, "The Role and Function of the Law"), the role of the law does not seem to be an issue for him. Instead, in the critical Jas 2:14–26 passage, James specifically refers to charitable deeds, obedient sacrificial actions (which may be honored by the Jesus community, but were not expected to be repeated by its members), and acts of hospitality under threat.[162] When Paul wants to illustrate the works of the law he opposes, he uses the example of circumcision and, to a lesser extent, Sabbath and purity regulations. These are the works against which he argues in Romans and Galatians (as well as in other letters), but where Paul does speak of hospitality and other charitable works, he commends them (e.g., Rom 12:13). It looks as if the conceptions of "works" in the two bodies of literature are different.

There is also a difference in the presentation of "faith" in that Paul normally relates "faith" or "commitment" to "Jesus the Messiah" (three times in Gal 2:16 alone). James *in this passage* gives only one example of "faith," and it is of the "faith that" or "belief that" type. What is believed is "God is one," the foundational statement of Jewish belief. The rest of the passage leaves "faith" undefined, so one wonders if James is not thinking of "faith" as "doctrine," although that would only be true for this passage.[163]

Then there is a difference in the use of Abraham as an example. In Paul the point is that Abraham's "work" of circumcision (Gen 17) came after he had trusted God and God had already declared him righteous, that is, after 15:6. James never mentions circumcision—it does not appear to be an issue for him—but he does mention Abraham's attempted offering of Isaac (Gen 22), at the end of which there is an explicit justification of Abraham, "Now I know that you fear God." It is only after this that James cites 15:6, apparently viewing it more as a promise of justification than as a declaration of justification, a promise that was not fulfilled until the

160. E.g., John Painter, "The Power of Words: Rhetoric in James and Paul," in *The Missions of James, Peter, and Paul* (ed. Bruce Chilton and Craig A. Evans; NovTSup 115; Leiden: Brill, 2005), 268–72.

161. This is the conclusion of Sanders, *Ethics in the New Testament*, 101–6, 129–30.

162. It is also possible that the Abraham reference has a hospital-ity and thus charitable allusion with the binding of Isaac being the culmination of Abraham's deeds. See Ward, "The Works of Abraham: James 2:14–26," 283–90.

163. This is one place where the idea that James is an edited work has significance, for it explains how one can have more than one usage of "faith" within the same work.

actual declaration of justification comes after the binding of Isaac in Gen 22. In other words, both James and Paul appeal to the example of Abraham (an example cited relatively frequently in Second Temple Jewish literature as well as by later rabbis), but James and Paul appeal to different aspects of that example, although they overlap in their use of a single verse, even if they use the verse quite differently.[164]

Thus, what we have in the linguistic overlap of James and Paul are two writers of the first-century Jesus movement addressing themes that were common in Jewish teaching. Indeed, if James had read Romans or Galatians and is intending to reply to them, it is clear that he has misunderstood them, as Klaus Haaker has pointed out.[165] It is possible that echoes of Paul have reached James, which could account for some of the similar phrases, which at the same time leave out key words (such as "of the law" with "works"). If so, this was an already distorted version of Paul that James heard, a distortion not unlike Luther's understanding of Paul that in turn led to his condemnation of James.[166]

It is appropriate to argue that, far from being weighed against Paul and found wanting, James gives us a canonical perspective from which we can ask if we are reading Paul appropriately. Perhaps if we read James and Paul as being in conflict rather than being two voices in a presystematic period of the church, we are reading Paul's teaching on faith, works, and especially justification incorrectly.[167]

2.5.5 The Ethical Importance of Speech and Money

One of the characteristics of James is the ethical focus on speech and money (or wealth in general). While dealing with anger is a theme of the teaching of Jesus in "Q" (e.g., Matt 5:21–26//Luke 12:57–59), and it is also a theme in Paul (2 Cor 12:20; Gal 5:20; Eph 4:26, 31; Col 3:8), it receives more emphasis in James in relationship to the size of the body of literature than it does in either the Gospels or the Pauline corpus. Likewise, judging or criticizing fellow community members is an issue in the teaching of Jesus (e.g., Matt 7:1–2//Luke 6:37; Matt 12:36) and Paul (e.g., Rom 2:1; 14:3–4, 10, 13; 1 Cor 4:5), but the topic comes up repeatedly in James. What is more, unlike Paul and to a lesser degree the teaching of Jesus, James never mentions sexual ethics, so the focus on speech ethics stands out in stronger relief.

The same similarity with the other parts of the New Testament and yet highlighted in James because of his lack of mention of sexual ethics is true of James's discussion of money. His emphasis on the poor and his rejection of "the rich" (recall that these are the wealthy outside of the community, for he uses circumlocutions to refer to the wealthier members of the community) is similar to the teaching of Jesus in general and the theological position of Luke–Acts in particular (e.g., Luke

164. See the discussion in Johnson, *The Letter of James*, 245–50, esp. 250.

165. Haaker, "Justification, salut et foi," 177–88.

166. See Krister Stendahl, *Paul among Jews and Gentiles* (Philadelphia: Fortress, 1976), for a discussion of the lens through which Luther read Paul and its concomitant result in the rejection of James.

167. Justification, of course, has become a major item of discussion. See N. T. Wright, *Justification: God's Plan and Paul's Vision* (Downers Grove, IL: IVP Academic, 2009), for a perspective that fits that of James.

6:20–26; 12:13–21; 16:19–31; 18:25).[168] The poor in the community are rich because the kingdom has been promised to them (Jas 2:5; cf. Luke 6:20//Matt 5:3). The rich should realize that they are in a sad position; in fact, James raises a lament over them. The danger for the community is that they will favor the wealthier members because they are controlled by desire for what "the world" might provide. James accuses his readers of adultery, because "friendship with the world constitutes one God's enemy," while Jesus says, "You cannot serve God and Mammon." In effect, their teaching is the same.

But it would be a mistake to think that what James has to say does not find its echoes in Paul and elsewhere. It is clear that 1 John would add his "amen" to James in that he says, "Love not the world, neither the things in the world" and then he goes on to say, "The love of the Father is not in those who love the world" (1 John 2:15). Likewise, 1 John 3:17 and Jas 2:14–16 agree that generosity is an essential mark of commitment to Jesus (in 1 John this is expressed as "God's love" being in one). Paul, however, can devote two chapters to the need to be generous (2 Corinthians 8–9), arguing that there should be an economic "equality" among the followers of Jesus in communities spread around the Mediterranean. Then there is in the Pauline corpus the teaching about contentment with what one has coupled with the danger of wishing to be wealthy and the command to the rich to be generous (1 Tim 6:6–10, 17–19).[169]

The difference between John and James is that James speaks of commitment (or faith) and 1 John speaks of love (God's love or the Father's love being in one). Because of the love emphasis, 1 John only briefly mentions the Spirit and never mentions wisdom. Likewise, the chief difference between James and Paul is that Paul focuses on the role of the Spirit in producing generosity (and in 2 Cor 8:5 the role of commitment, for the Macedonians first "gave themselves to the Lord") and avoids any reference to law (which is marked in that he never uses the tithe of the Hebrew Scriptures even as an example, much less as a rule). In contrast to Paul's persuasive rhetoric (using pathos, ethos, and a number of other persuasive methodologies), James is more of a prophetic denunciation. When it comes to the ability to avoid the test that possessions can cause, he would appeal to divine wisdom rather than the Spirit.

2.5.6 Summary of Canonical Contribution

James has a unique place in the canon. On the one hand, the work shows how the traditions enshrined in the Gospels were used and applied among some first-century

---

168. This is not the place to discuss the teaching of Luke–Acts on wealth and poverty; suffice it to say that (1) there are parallels to a significant amount of the Lucan teaching in Matthew and some to Mark as well, so there is no intention to draw an absolute distinction between Luke–Acts and Matthew (or Mark). (2) Luke has additional sayings and parables to those found in Matthew, and where there are parallels, the Lucan redaction often makes the teaching stronger. (3) In the New Testament only Luke and James have woes on the rich. (4) Acts applies the Lucan theology in that communities of the Jesus movement are described in detail as characterized by ongoing generosity (based on the underlying attitude that they were all one extended family and empowered by the presence of the Spirit).

169. Whether one takes the Pastoral Epistles as Pauline or post-Pauline, they are part of the canonical Pauline collection and on this topic clearly fit with undisputed Pauline teaching.

followers of Jesus, thus linking the putative teaching of Jesus to the later community that accepted him as exalted Lord and coming Judge. On the other hand, he shows some of the differences within that later community. In his perspective on ethics and wisdom, it is more a difference of stress, highlighting themes that do also appear elsewhere in the New Testament. In his take on the relationship of commitment or faith and works and their relationship to justification, depending on how one reads Paul, James may be a distinct voice. This writer is not convinced that James is the first of the Catholic Epistles collection for theological reasons[170] (it seems to him that the collection of seven was more a convenient way to collect and bind seven letters that did not fit with Paul, but only collectively were long enough for their own codex). Yet in retrospect. it is fitting that a collection that gives voice to some parts of the first-century group of followers of Jesus who sounded and still sound quite different than Paul begins with the letter of James.

170. Contra Nienhuis.

Chapter 3

FIRST PETER

Firirst Peter is the best known and liked of the General Epistles, arguably because it is the one most like the Pauline writings. It is, however, far more than "Paul lite," for it is a work with its own voice, as we will see, a voice that give us distinctive teaching lacking elsewhere in the New Testament, including in Paul.

BIBLIOGRAPHY

Achtemeier, Paul J. *1 Peter*. Hermeneia. Minneapolis: Fortress, 1996. **Balch, D. L.** *Let Wives Be Submissive: The Domestic Code in 1 Peter*. SBLMS 26. Ed. J. Crenshaw. Chico, CA: Scholars Press, 1981. **Bauer, J. B.** "Der erste Petrusbrief und die Verfolgung unter Domitian." Pp. 513–27 in *Die Kirche des Anfangs: Festschrift für H. Schürmann*. Ed. R. Schnackenburg. ErfTSt 38. Leipzig: St. Benno, 1978. **Beare, Francis Wright**. *The First Epistle of Peter*. Oxford: Basil Blackwell, 1970. **Best, Ernst**. *1 Peter*. NCB. Grand Rapids: Eerdmans, 1971, 1982. **Blazen, I. T.** "Suffering and Cessation from Sin according to 1 Peter 4:1." *AUSS* 21 (1983): 27–50. **Boismard, M.-É.** *Quatres hymnes baptismales dans la première épître de Pierre*. Lectio Divina 30. Paris: Editions du Cerf, 1961. **Bornemann, W.** "Der erste Petrusbrief: eine Taufrede des Silvanus?" *ZNW* 19 (1919/1920): 143–65. **Brown, J. P.** "Synoptic Parallels in the Epistles and Form-History." *NTS* 10 (1963–1964): 27–48. **Brown, R. E., K. P. Donfried, and J. Reumann**, eds. *Peter in the New Testament*. Minneapolis: Augsburg, 1973. **Brox, N.** *Der erste Petrusbrief*. 2nd ed. EKKNT 21. Zürich: Benziger, 1986. Idem. *Zeuge und Märtyrer: Untersuchungen zur frühchristlichen Zeugnis-Terminologie*. Munich: Kösel, 1961. **Burridge, Richard A.** "The Gospels and Acts." Pp. 512–13 in *Handbook of Classical Rhetoric in the Hellenistic Period 330 B.C.– A. D. 400*. Ed. Stanley E. Porter. Boston/Leiden: Brill, 2001. **Burtness, J. H.** "Sharing the Suffering of God in the Life of the World." *Int* 23 (1969): 277–88. **Campbell, Barth L.** *Honor, Shame, and the Rhetoric of 1 Peter*. SBLDS 160. Atlanta: Scholars Press, 1998. **Campbell, J. B.** "Domitian." Pp. 237–38 in *The Oxford Companion to Classical Civilization*. Ed. Simone Hornblower and Anthony Spawforth. Oxford/New York: Oxford University Press, 2004. **Chevallier, M. A.** "Condition et vocation des chrétiens en diaspora: remarques exégétiques sur la 1re Épître de Pierre." *RSR* 48 (1974): 387–400. **Clemen, C.** "The First Epistle of St. Peter and the Book of Enoch." *Expositor* 6/4 (1902): 316–20. **Cross, F. L.** *1 Peter: A Paschal Liturgy*. London: Mowbray, 1954. **Cullmann, O.** *Petrus: Jünger-Apostel-Märtyrer*. 2nd ed. Zürich: Zwingli, 1960; ET by F. V. Filson: *Peter: Disciple, Apostle, Martyr*. Philadelphia: Westminster, 1962. **Dalton, W. J.** *Christ's Proclamation to the Spirits: A Study of 1 Peter 3:18–4:6*.

AnBib 23. Rome: Pontifical Biblical Institute, 1965. **Danker, F. W.** "1 Peter 1:24–2:17: A Consolatory Pericope." *ZNW* 58 (1967): 93–102. **Davids, Peter H.** "A Silent Witness in Marriage: 1 Pet 3:1–7." Pp. 224–38 in *Discovering Biblical Equality: Complementarity Without Hierarchy*. Ed. Ronald W. Pierce and Rebecca Merrill Groothuis. Downers Grove, IL: InterVarsity Press, 2004. Idem. *The Epistle of 1 Peter*. NICNT. Grand Rapids: Eerdmans, 1990. Idem. "What Glasses Are You Wearing? Reading Hebrew Narratives through Second Temple Lenses." *JETS* 55 (2012): 763–71. **Elliott, J. H.** *The Elect and the Holy: An Exegetical Examination of 1 Peter 2:4–10 and the Phrase βασίλειον ἱεράτευμα*. NovTSup 12. Leiden: Brill, 1966. Idem. *1 Peter: A New Translation with Introduction and Commentary*. AB 37. New York: Doubleday, 2000. Idem. *1 Peter: Estrangement and Community*. Chicago: Franciscan Herald, 1979. Idem. *A Home for the Homeless: A Sociological Exegesis of 1 Peter, Its Situation and Strategy*. Philadelphia: Fortress, 1981. Idem. "The Rehabilitation of an Exegetical Stepchild: 1 Peter in Recent Research." *JBL* 95 (1976): 243–54. Reprinted in *Perspectives on First Peter*. Ed. C. H. Talbert. Macon, GA: Mercer University Press, 1986, 3–16. **Filson, F. V.** "Partakers with Christ: Suffering in First Peter." *Int* 9 (1955): 400–412. **Furnish, V. P.** "Elect Sojourners in Christ: An Approach to the Theology of 1 Peter." *PSTJ* 28 (1975): 1–11. **Goldstein, H.** "Die politischen Paraenesen in 1 Petr. 2 und Röm. 13." *BibLeb* 14 (1973): 88–104. **Goppelt, L.** *Der erste Petrusbrief*. KEK 12. Ed. F. Hahn. Göttingen: Vandenhoeck & Ruprecht, 1978. **Green, Joel B.** *1 Peter*. THNTC. Grand Rapids: Eerdmans, 2007. **Gross, Carl D.** "Are the Wives of 1 Pet 3:7 Christian?" *JSNT* 35 (1989): 89–96. **Grudem, Wayne**. *1 Peter*. TNTC; Grand Rapids: Eerdmans, 1988. **Gundry, R. H.** "Further 'Verba' on 'Verba Christi' in First Peter." *Bib* 55 (1974): 211–32. Idem. "'Verba Christi,' in I Peter: Their Implications concerning the Authorship of I Peter and the Authenticity of the Gospel Tradition." *NTS* 13 (1966–1967): 336–50. **Helyer, Larry R.** *The Life and Witness of Peter*. Downers Grove, IL: IVP Academic, 2012. **Hengel, Martin**. *Der unterschätzte Petrus: Zwei Studien*. Tübingen: Mohr-Siebeck, 2006. ET: *Saint Peter: The Underestimated Apostle*. Grand Rapids: Eerdmans, 2010. **Hill, D.** "On Suffering and Baptism in 1 Peter." *NovT* 18 (1976): 181–89. **Holdsworth, J.** "The Sufferings in 1 Peter and 'Missionary Apocalyptic.'" Pp. 225–32 in *Studia Biblica* 3. Ed. E. A. Livingstone. Sheffield: JSOT, 1980. **Holtzmann, O.** *Die Petrusbrief*. In *Das Neue Testament nach dem Stuttgarter griechischen Text übersetzt und erklärt* 2. Giessen: Töpelmann, 1926. **Horrell, David G.** *1 Peter*. New Testament Guides. London/New York: T&T Clark, 2008. **Huther, J. E.** *Kritisch-exegetisches Handbuch über den 1. Brief des Petrus, den Brief des Judas und den 2. Brief des Petrus*. 4th ed. KEK 12. Göttingen: Vandenhoeck & Ruprecht, 1877. ET by D. B. Croom and P. J. Gloab: *Critical and Exegetical Handbook to the General Epistles of Peter and Jude*. Edinburgh: T&T Clark, 1881. **Jobes, Karen H.** *1 Peter*. BECNT. Grand Rapids: Baker Academic, 2005. Idem. "The Syntax of 1 Peter: Just How Good Is the Greek?" *BBR* 13 (2003): 159–73. **Jonsen, A. R.** "The Moral Teaching of the First Epistle of St. Peter." *ScEc* 16 (1964): 93–105. **Lapham, F.** *Peter: The Myth, the Man and the Writings: A Study of Early Petrine Text and Tradition*. JSNTSup 239. Sheffield: Sheffield Academic,

2003. **Lohmeyer, E.** "Probleme paulinischer Theologie: I. Briefliche Grussüber-schriften." *ZNW* 26 (1927): 158–73. **Martin, Troy W.** *Metaphor and Composition in 1 Peter.* SBLDS 131. Atlanta: Scholars Press, 1992. Idem. "The *TestAbr* and the Background of 1 Pet 3:6." *ZAW* 90 (1999): 139–46. **Michaels, J. Ramsey.** "1 Peter." *DLNT* 914–23. Idem. "Eschatology in I Peter III.17." *NTS* 13 (1966–1967): 394–401. Idem. *1 Peter.* WBC 49. Waco, TX: Word, 1988. Idem. "Jewish and Chris-tian Apocalyptic Letters: 1 Peter, Revelation, and 2 Baruch 78–87." *SBL Seminar Papers* 26 (Atlanta: Scholars Press, 1987), 268–75. **Millauer, H**. *Leiden als Gnade: Eine traditionsgeschichtliche Untersuchung zur Leidenstheologie des ersten Petrusbriefes.* Bern: H. Lang, 1976. **Nauck, W.** "Freude im Leiden: zum Problem einer urchristli-chen Verfolgungstradition." *ZNW* 46 (1955): 68–80. **Perkins, Pheme**. *Peter: Apostle for the Whole Church.* Minneapolis: Fortress, 2000. **Piper, John**. "Hope as the Moti-vation of Love: 1 Peter 3:9–12." *NTS* 26 (1980): 212–31. **Richards, E. Randolph**. *Paul and First-Century Letter Writing: Secretaries, Composition and Collection.* Down-ers Grove, IL: InterVarsity Press, 2004. Idem. "Silvanus Was Not Peter's Secretary: Theological Bias in Interpreting διὰ Σιλουανοῦ ἔγραψα in 1 Pet 5:12." *JETS* 43 (2000): 417–32. **Richardson, R. L., Jr.** "From 'Subjection to Authority' to 'Mutual Submission': The Ethic of Subordination in 1 Peter." *Faith & Mission* 4 (1987): 70–80. **Schattenmann, J.** "The Little Apocalypse of the Synoptics and the First Epistle of Peter." *ThTo* 11 (1954–1955): 193–98. **Schelkle, K. H.** "Das Leiden des Gottesknechtes als Form christlichen Lebens (nach dem 1. Petrusbrief)." *BK* 16 (1961): 14–16. **Schrage, W.** "Zur Ethik der neutestamentlichen Haustafeln." *NTS* 21 (1974–1975): 1–22. **Schutter, W. L.** *Hermeneutic and Composition in First Peter.* WUNT 2/30. Tübingen: Mohr-Siebeck, 1989. **Schwank, B.** "Wir Freie—aber als Sklaven Gottes (1 Petr. 2:16): Das Verhältnis der Christen zur Staatsmacht nach dem ersten Petrusbrief." *ErbAuf* 36 (1960): 5–12. **Selwyn, Edward Gordon**. *The First Epistle of St. Peter.* New York: Macmillan, 1946, 1969. Idem. "The Persecutions in I Peter." *Bulletin of the Society for New Testament Studies* 1 (1950): 39–50. **Senior, D.** "The Conduct of Christians in the World (1 Pet. 2:11–3:12)." *RevExp* 79 (1982): 427–38. **Sleeper, C. F.** "Political Responsibility according to 1 Peter." *NovT* 10 (1968): 270–86. **Sly, Dorothy I.** "I Peter 3:6b in the Light of Philo and Josephus." *JBL* 110 (1991): 126–29. **Spicq, C.** *Les Épîtres de Saint Pierre.* La Sainte Bible. Paris: Gabalda, 1966. **Steuernagel, V.** "An Exiled Community as a Mission Community: A Study Based on 1 Peter 2:9, 10." *Evangelical Review of Theology* 10 (1986): 8–18. **Sylva, D.** "The Critical Exploration of 1 Peter." Pp. 17–36 in *Perspectives on First Peter.* Ed. C. H. Talbert. Macon, GA: Mercer University Press, 1986. **Talbert, C. H.**, ed. *Perspectives on First Peter.* Macon, GA: Mercer University Press, 1986. **Thomas, J.** "Anfechtung und Vorfreude: Ein biblisches Thema nach Jakobus 1:2–18, im Zusammenhang mit Ps 126, Röm 5:3–5 und 1 Petr 1:5–7, formkritisch unter-sucht und parakletisch ausgelegt." *KD* 14 (1968): 183–206. **Thompson, J. W.** "'Be Submissive to your Masters': A Study of 1 Pt 2:18–25." *ResQ* 9/2 (1966): 66–78. **Thurén, Lauri**. *Argument and Theology in 1 Peter: The Origins of Christian Paraene-sis.* SBLDS 114. Atlanta: Scholars Press, 1995. Idem. "The General New Testament

Writings." Pp. 596–99 in *Handbook of Classical Rhetoric in the Hellenistic Period 330 B.C.–A.D. 400*. Ed. Stanley E. Porter. Leiden: Brill, 2001. Idem. *The Rhetorical Strategy of 1 Peter*. Åbo: Åbo Academy Press, 1990. **Unnik, W. C. van**. "The Teaching of Good Works in I Peter." *NTS* 1 (1954–1955): 92–110. **Utley, Bob**. *The Gospel according to Peter: Mark and I and II Peter*. Study Guide Commentary Series, NT 2. Marshall, TX: Bible Lessons International, 2000. **Villiers, J. L. de**. "Joy in Suffering in 1 Peter." *NeoT* 9 (1975): 64–86. **Volkmar, G.** "Über die katholischen Briefe und Henoch." *ZWT* 4 (1961): 422–36. **Watson, Duane Frederick, and Terrance Callan**. *First and Second Peter*. Paideia. Grand Rapids: Baker Academic, 2012. **Webb, R. L.** "The Apocalyptic Perspective of First Peter." Unpublished ThM thesis, Regent College, Vancouver, BC, Canada, 1986. **Webb, Robert L., and Betsy Bauman-Martin**, eds. *Reading First Peter with New Eyes: Methodological Reassessments of the Letter of First Peter*. LNTS 364. London/New York: T&T Clark, 2007. **Witherington, Ben, III**. "Not So Idle Thoughts about *eidōlothyton*." *TynBul* 44 (1993): 237–54. **Workman, Herbert B.** *Persecution in the Early Church*. Oxford/New York: Oxford University Press, 1980.

3.1 RECENT SCHOLARSHIP

Modern English scholarship on 1 Peter begins in the period after the Second World War.[1] The foundational commentary on the Greek text was that of E. G. Selwyn,[2] which is still useful for its detailed interaction with the text and its significant appended essays; this work was followed by those of F. W. Beare and Ernst Best, who commented on the English text.[3] Selwyn is the great proponent of the so-called Silvanus hypothesis in defense of Petrine authorship (i.e., that the Greek of 1 Peter is to be attributed to Silvanus/Silas, who was the amanuensis), while Beare and Best both opt for pseudonymity.

Within the period in which these foundational English commentaries were produced, two different hypotheses about the nature of 1 Peter also developed: the first, from M.-É. Boismard,[4] who viewed 1 Peter as a baptismal liturgy, and the second, from F. L. Cross,[5] who viewed it as a paschal liturgy. These were too late for Selwyn to interact with them, although in his second edition he does mention the help he

---

1. There were some significant works in German from the late nineteenth century and early twentieth century that continued to be influential, such as J. E. Huther, *Kritisch-exegetisches Handbuch über den 1. Brief des Petrus, den Brief des Judas und den 2. Brief des Petrus* (4th ed.; KEK 12; Göttingen: Vandenhoeck & Ruprecht, 1877; ET by D. B. Croom and P. J. Gloab, *Critical and Exegetical Handbook to the General Epistles of Peter and Jude*. [Edinburgh: T&T Clark, 1881]); and O. Holtzmann, *Die Petrusbrief*, in *Das Neue Testament nach dem Stuttgarter griechischen Text übersetzt und erklärt* 2 (Giessen: Töpelmann, 1926), but in general the modern study is a postwar phenomenon. A summary of the more contemporary material on 1 Peter can be found in David G. Horrell, *1 Peter* (NTG; London/New York: T&T Clark, 2008).

2. Edward Gordon Selwyn, *The First Epistle of St. Peter* (London: Macmillan, 1946, 1969).

3. Francis Wright Beare, *The First Epistle of Peter* (Oxford: Basil Blackwell, 1970); Ernst Best, *1 Peter* (Grand Rapids: Eerdmans, 1982; orig. pub. London: Oliphants, 1971).

4. M.-É. Boismard, *Quatres hymnes baptismales dans la première épître de Pierre*, (Lectio Divina 30; Paris: Editions du Cerf, 1961). This followed on a series of articles during the previous five years in *Revue Biblique*. Boismard may have been influenced by W. Bornemann, "Der erste Petrusbrief: eine Taufrede des Silvanus?" *ZNW* 19 (1919/1920): 143–65.

5. F. L. Cross, *1 Peter: A Paschal Liturgy* (London: Mowbray, 1954).

received from Cross, but they are discussed in most subsequent works on 1 Peter. While the theories themselves have not been widely accepted by later scholarship, they do point to the foundational level of the teaching contained in 1 Peter, which does call for explanation. Also from this period comes the basic work on the life of Peter by Oscar Cullmann,[6] which would lead to a number of later studies.[7]

The relevant issues in these studies of Simeon (Peter) bar Jonah for this present work are (1) the nature of Peter's background and likely ability in Greek; (2) the degree to which Peter is to be identified with Torah-observant Jewish Christianity; (3) the degree to which Peter's mission focused throughout his life on the evangelism of Jews (versus shifting to a focus on Gentiles later in his life); (4) the degree to which Peter and Paul were reconciled after their falling out in Antioch; and (5) the historicity of the tradition that Peter traveled to Rome and was martyred there. The problem is that there are great holes in our knowledge of Peter, especially since, unlike Paul, for much of his career there is no author of Acts taking a focal interest in him.

The first burst of post-WWII Petrine scholarship tended to keep 1 Peter in the shadow of Paul, for there are a number of similarities in their perspectives, as will be seen below in the discussion of the place of 1 Peter in the canon. This first burst did include some brief theologies of 1 Peter, such as F. F. Bruce's *Peter, Stephen, James and John*,[8] which attempted to give a voice, albeit a brief one, to these lesser-known authors. At the same time and overlapping with these now-classic commentaries and monographs, there was the start of several series of studies that would give 1 Peter more of a distinctive voice in that they investigated several of the most important themes of the letter: (1) who are the resident aliens and foreigners in the Diaspora to whom the letter is addressed; (2) what does it mean to be a witness in the context of 1 Peter; (3) what contribution does 1 Peter make to New Testament ethics, particularly to church-state relations; (4) what background does Second Temple Jewish literature, particularly apocalyptic literature, provide for 2 Peter; and (5) what does 1 Peter have to say about suffering?

The first theme shows up in the work of M. A. Chevallier,[9] and theologically in that of V. P. Furnish,[10] but the scholar best known for his contribution in this area is John H. Elliott, particularly his *A Home for the Homeless*,[11] with its thesis that

6. Oscar Cullmann, *Petrus. Jünger-Apostel-Märtyrer* (2nd ed. Zürich: Zwingli, 1960); Eng. trans. by F. V. Filson as *Peter: Disciple, Apostle, Martyr* (Philadelphia: Westminster, 1962).

7. For example, R. E. Brown, K. P. Donfried, and J. Reumann, eds., *Peter in the New Testament* (Minneapolis: Augsburg, 1973), Pheme Perkins, *Peter: Apostle for the Whole Church* (Minneapolis: Fortress, 2000); and, F. Lapham, *Peter: The Myth, the Man and the Writings: A Study of Early Petrine Text and Tradition* (JSNTSup 239; Sheffield: Sheffield Academic, 2003). A late-in-life work of Martin Hengel also fits into this category: Martin Hengel, *Der unterschätzte Petrus* (Tübingen: Mohr-Siebeck, 2006), translated as *Saint Peter: The Underestimated Apostle* (Grand Rapids: Eerdmans, 2010).

8. F. F. Bruce, *Peter, Stephen, James and John* (Grand Rapids: Eerdmans, 1979).

9. M. A. Chevallier, "Condition et vocation des chrétiens en diaspora: remarques exégétiques sur la 1re Épître de Pierre," *RSR* 48 (1974): 387–400.

10. V. P. Furnish, "Elect Sojourners in Christ: An Approach to the Theology of 1 Peter," *PSTJ* 28 (1975): 1–11.

11. J. H. Elliott, *A Home for the Homeless: A Sociological Exegesis of 1 Peter, Its Situation and Strategy* (Philadelphia: Fortress, 1981). While this is his most-quoted work in this regard, Elliott's investigations started much earlier: see, e.g., *The Elect and the Holy: An Exegetical Examination of 1 Peter 2:4–10 and the Phrase βασίλειον ἱεράτευμα* (NovTSup 12. Leiden: Brill, 1966); and *1 Peter: Estrangement and Community* (Chicago: Franciscan Herald, 1979).

1 Peter addresses, not a group of metaphorical resident aliens (resident aliens in this world because their true home is in heaven), but a literal group of resident aliens. Contemporary work on 1 Peter takes Elliott as the starting place in this discussion, although not necessarily agreeing with him.[12]

The second theme shows up in the work of Norbert Brox, culminating in his commentary on 1 Peter.[13] The third theme concerning the ethics of 1 Peter is found in the early part of the modern period,[14] but comes to the fore in studies of the ethical lists, or *Haustafeln*,[15] in 1 Peter. E. Kamlah produced a general work on such lists,[16] building on the work of Wibbing,[17] but there are a number of studies of specific ethical themes[18] or specific parts of the *Haustafeln*[19] in 1 Peter, that give a clear picture of 1 Peter as an ethical book, if not always agreement on what that ethic is.

The fourth important theme, 1 Peter's use of Second Temple Jewish literature (esp. *1 Enoch*) and his apocalyptic eschatology, was brought to the fore by W. J. Dalton, particularly in his *Christ's Proclamation to the Spirits*,[20] but it was discussed as early as 1902 by Clemen.[21] This has continued to be a theme of study into the contemporary period.[22]

The fifth theme (suffering) would seem to be the most obvious one in 1 Peter, and it has received some significant attention, starting with Selwyn's study in 1950[23]

---

12. E.g., V. Steuernagel, "An Exiled Community as a Mission Community: A Study Based on 1 Peter 2:9, 10," *Evangelical Review of Theology* 10 (1986): 8–18.

13. Norbert Brox, *Der erste Petrusbrief* (EKKNT 21; Zürich: Benziger, 1986²). Brox's series of monographs and articles begin as early as *Zeuge und Märtyrer: Untersuchungen zur frühchristlichen Zeugnis-Terminologie* (Munich: Kösel, 1961).

14. E.g., A. R. Jonsen, "The Moral Teaching of the First Epistle of St. Peter," *ScEcc* 16 (1964): 93–105.

15. Haustafeln means literally "house tablets," i.e., codes of behavior for those in a household. As such they are specialized ethical lists, instructing the household in virtue.

16. E. Kamlah, *Die Form der katalogischen Paränese im Neuen Testament* (Tübingen: Mohr, 1964).

17. S. Wibbing, *Die Tugend- und Lasterkataloge im Neuen Testament* (BZNW 25; Berlin: Töpelmann, 1959).

18. An early general work is that of W. C. van Unnik, "The Teaching of Good Works in I Peter," *NTS* 1 (1954–1955): 92–110.

19. E.g., general studies of the *Haustafeln*, D. Senior, "The Conduct of Christians in the World (1 Pet. 2:11–3:12)," *RevExp* 79 (1982): 427–38; W. Schrage, "Zur Ethik der neutestamentlichen Haustafeln," *NTS* 21 (1974–75): 1–22; R. L. Richardson Jr., "From 'Subjection to Authority' to 'Mutual Submission': The Ethic of Subordination in 1 Peter," *Faith & Mission* 4 (1987): 70–80; studies of the state, H. Goldstein, "Die politischen Paränesen in 1 Petr. 2 und Röm. 13," *BibLeb* 14 (1973): 88–104; C. F. Sleeper, "Political Responsibility according to 1 Peter," *NovT* 10 (1968): 270–86; B. Schwank, "Wir Freie—aber als Sklaven Gottes (1 Petr. 2:16): Das Verhältnis der Christen zur Staatsmacht nach dem ersten Petrusbrief," *ErbAuf* 36 (1960): 5–12; a study of slavery, J. W. Thompson, " 'Be Submissive to your Masters': A Study of 1 Pt 2:18–25," *ResQ* 9/2 (1966): 66–78; a study of wives, D. L. Balch, *Let Wives Be Submissive: The Domestic Code in 1 Peter* (SBLMS 26; Chico, CA: Scholars Press, 1981).

20. W. J. Dalton, *Christ's Proclamation to the Spirits: A Study of 1 Peter 3:18–4:6* (AnBib 23; Rome: Pontifical Biblical Institute, 1965). While Dalton published at least three articles summarizing this research, the monograph is the most complete version. See further Peter H. Davids, *The Epistle of 1 Peter* (NICNT; Grand Rapids: Eerdmans, 1990), 214.

21. C. Clemen, "The First Epistle of St. Peter and the Book of Enoch," *Exp* 6/4 (1902): 316–20. This builds on an article in German published two years earlier.

22. E.g., J. R. Michaels, "Eschatology in I Peter III.17," *NTS* 13 (1966–1967): 394–401, followed twenty years later by his "Jewish and Christian Apocalyptic Letters: 1 Peter, Revelation, and 2 Baruch 78–87," *SBL Seminar Papers* 26 (Atlanta: Scholars Press, 1987), 268–75. He would later publish *1 Peter* (WBC 49; Waco, TX: Word, 1988). See also G. Volkmar, "Über die katholischen Briefe und Henoch," *ZWT* 4 (1961): 422–36; and the 300+-page thesis of R. L. Webb, "The Apocalyptic Perspective of First Peter" (unpublished ThM thesis, Regent College, Vancouver, BC, 1986). There are, of course, quite a number of studies of the "descent into hell" in 1 Peter, but that was a specific focus of the later 1800s up through the first half of the 1900s, when it tended to get subsumed under the broader studies of eschatology and apocalyptic, since 1 Pet 3:19 does not use a term for "hell" nor speak about a "descent" but rather refers to a "going" to "the spirits in prison."

23. E. G. Selwyn, "The Persecutions in I Peter," *Bulletin of the Society for New Testament Studies* 1 (1950): 39–50. This, of course, shows that there were two types of interest in the theme of suffering, the first identifying the source of and reasons for persecution, and the second examining the teaching on suffering itself.

and Filson's article in 1955.[24] Like Filson, others noted the connection of the suffering of believers with the suffering of Jesus.[25] Thomas gave language to the similarity of the response to suffering in 1 Peter to that in James, "eschatological anticipated joy."[26] The most extensive work from this period is that of Millauer,[27] while others focused on single aspects of suffering.[28] A long excursus in Davids's commentary defines what the New Testament means by suffering and sets suffering in 1 Peter into this context, carrying the discussion forward into the following centuries of church history.[29] Yet the commentaries from this period most aware of the ongoing study of 1 Peter were those of L. Goppelt in the German-speaking world and R. Michaels in the English-speaking world,[30] both later built on by Davids. Many of the themes mentioned above were also gathered together in the essays edited by Charles Talbert.[31]

The last two decades of work in 1 Peter have been marked by a series of developments. The first is the extension to 1 Peter of social-rhetorical analysis, under which general rubric we will also consider genre analysis. Two significant studies in this regard are those of Troy W. Martin[32] (who has put to rest once for all the baptismal homily and liturgical theories and instead opts for the paraenetic letter as the basic genre of the work) and Barth L. Campbell,[33] whose social-rhetorical study of 1 Peter brought to light the sociology of the letter. This would be followed up by socio-rhetorical commentaries, such as the one by Ben Witherington III.[34]

The second development has picked up on earlier discussions about the relationship between 1 Peter and the Synoptic Gospels[35] and developed the material into a

---

24. F. V. Filson, "Partakers with Christ: Suffering in First Peter," *Int* 9 (1955): 400–412.

25. E.g., K. H. Schelkle, "Das Leiden des Gottesknechtes als Form christlichen Lebens (nach dem 1. Petrusbrief)," *BK* 16 (1961): 14–16; and J. H. Burtness, "Sharing the Suffering of God in the Life of the World," *Int* 23 (1969): 277–88.

26. Thomas, J. "Anfechtung und Vorfreude: Ein biblisches Thema nach Jakobus 1:2–18, im Zusammenhang mit Ps 126, Röm 5:3–5 und 1 Petr 1:5–7, formkritisch untersucht und parakletish ausgelegt," *KD* 14 (1968): 183–206. See also the later work of J. L. de Villiers, "Joy in Suffering in 1 Peter," *Neot* 9 (1975): 64–86. Both build on the more general work of W. Nauck, "Freude im Leiden: zum Problem einer urchristlichen Verfolgungstradition," *ZNW* 46 (1955): 68–80.

27. H. Millauer, *Leiden als Gnade: Eine traditionsgeschichtliche Untersuchung zur Leidenstheologie des ersten Petrusbriefes* (Bern: H. Lang, 1976).

28. E.g., on the connection of suffering to apocalyptic, see J. Holdsworth, "The Sufferings in 1 Peter and 'Missionary Apocalyptic,'" in *Studia Biblica* 3 (ed. E. A. Livingstone; Sheffield: JSOT, 1980), 225–32; on the connection of suffering to baptism, see D. Hill, "On Suffering and Baptism in 1 Peter," *NovT* 18 (1976): 181–89; on suffering and the concept of witness/martyr, see Brox, *Zeuge und Märtyrer*; and, as a representative of those interested in the specific connection between suffering and ceasing from sin, see I. T. Blazen, "Suffering and Cessation from Sin according to 1 Peter

4:1," *AUSS* 21 (1983): 27–50.

29. Davids, *1 Peter*, 30–33.

30. L. Goppelt, *Der erste Petrusbrief* (KEK 12; Göttingen: Vandenhoeck & Ruprecht, 1978). The major work in French was that of C. Spicq, *Les Épîtres de Saint Pierre* (La Sainte Bible; Paris: Gabalda, 1966); Michaels, *1 Peter* (WBC).

31. C. H. Talbert, ed., *Perspectives on First Peter* (Macon, GA: Mercer University Press, 1986). Among these essays, that of D. Sylva, "The Critical Exploration of 1 Peter" (pp. 17–36), is significant for being a bibliographical essay.

32. Troy W. Martin, *Metaphor and Composition in 1 Peter* (SBLDS 131; Atlanta: Scholars Press, 1992).

33. Barth L. Campbell, *Honor, Shame, and the Rhetoric of 1 Peter* (SBLDS 160; Atlanta: Scholars Press, 1998).

34. Ben Witherington III, *Letters and Homilies for Hellenized Christians II: A Socio-Rhetorical Commentary on 1–2 Peter* (Downers Grove, IL: InterVarsity Press, 2007).

35. J. P. Brown, "Synoptic Parallels in the Epistles and Form-History," *NTS* 10 (1963–1964): 27–48; R. H. Gundry, "Further 'Verba' on 'Verba Christi' in First Peter," *Bib* 55 (1974): 211–32; idem, "'Verba Christi,' in I Peter: Their Implications concerning the Authorship of I Peter and the Authenticity of the Gospel Tradition," *NTS* 13 (1966–1967): 336–50; J. Schattenmann, "The Little Apocalypse of the Synoptics and the First Epistle of Peter," *ThTo* 11 (1954–1955): 193–98.

careful examination of intertextuality as well as a study of the theology of 1 Peter (particularly eschatology).[36] Another direction has been taken by those focusing on the theological interpretation of 1 Peter, ancient[37] and modern.[38] Much of this material has been summed up in the works of Karen Jobes[39] and Reinhard Feldmeier,[40] the former best on the linguistic side and the latter excelling both in making theological connections and in cultural background; his discussion of the persecution of Christians in the Roman Empire deserves wider recognition than it is likely to get as part of the introduction to a commentary. The two largest scholarly commentaries in English are those of Achtemeier[41] and Elliott.[42]

The study of 1 Peter continues with new methodologies being added. Like the work of Talbert mentioned above, a new group of scholars is now applying narrative criticism, rhetorical criticism, and postcolonial criticism to 1 Peter,[43] all of which are contemporary indeed, as well as effective in a work that is set in a context of some form of persecution, perhaps connected to Jewish nationality (postcolonial criticism), that revolves around an implied narrative, and that is built on Greco-Roman rhetoric.

In 1976 J. H. Elliott, who has been more responsible than anyone else for changing the situation he describes, wrote an article describing 1 Peter as an "exegetical stepchild" in need of "rehabilitation."[44] It is clear more than a quarter century later that that rehabilitation has to a large extent been successful.

3.2 INTRODUCTORY ISSUES

What, then, is this work that we call 1 Peter? With its salutation (1 Pet 1:1 – 2) and closing (5:12 – 14) the document indicates it belongs to the letter genre, but what can one say beyond that?

3.2.1 Author, Implied and Actual

The letter begins with "Peter, an official delegate of Jesus the Anointed One." This structure is almost identical to several Pauline letter salutations (2 Corinthi-

36. Rainer Metzner, *Die Rezeption des Matthäusevangeliums im 1. Petrusbrief* (WUNT 2/74; Tübingen: Mohr, 1995). The most controversial part of Metzner's thesis is that he believes that 1 Peter is dependent on Matthew, not "Q" or other traditions underlying Matthew.

37. Gerald Bray, ed., *James, 1 – 2 Peter, 1 – 3 John, Jude* (ACCS 11; Downers Grove, IL: InterVarsity Press, 2000), 65 – 127.

38. Pheme Perkins, *First and Second Peter, James, and Jude* (Interpretation; Louisville: John Knox, 1995); Joel B. Green, *1 Peter* (THNTC; Grand Rapids: Eerdmans, 2007), the latter being the more self-consciously hermeneutical.

39. Karen H. Jobes, *1 Peter* (BECNT; Grand Rapids: Baker Academic, 2005).

40. Reinhard Feldmeier, *Der erste Brief des Petrus* (THKNT 15; Leipzig: Evangelische Verlagsanstalt, 2005), ET by Reinhard Feld-

meier, *The First Letter of Peter* (Waco, TX: Baylor University Press, 2008).

41. Paul J. Achtemeier, *1 Peter* (Hermeneia; Minneapolis: Fortress, 1996).

42. John H. Elliott, *1 Peter: A New Translation with Introduction and Commentary* (AB 37; New York: Doubleday, 2000). As the bibliography will show, Elliott has been writing on 1 Peter for years, and this absolutely massive work gathers up that knowledge and adds to it.

43. Robert L. Webb and Betsy Bauman-Martin, eds., *Reading First Peter with New Eyes: Methodological Reassessments of the Letter of First Peter* (LNTS 364; London/New York: T&T Clark, 2007).

44. J. H. Elliott, "The Rehabilitation of an Exegetical Stepchild: 1 Peter in Recent Research," *JBL* 95 (1976): 243 – 54. Reprinted in *Perspectives on First Peter* (ed. C. H. Talbert; Macon, GA: Mercer University Press, 1986), 3 – 16.

ans, Ephesians, Colossians, and 1 and 2 Timothy are identical except for using "Paul" instead of "Peter"; several others are similar).[45] There is no serious debate about whom this designation indicates, Simon (or Simeon as in 2 Pet 1:1) Peter bar Jonah, a fisherman from northern Galilee (Matt 4:13, 18; Mark 1:21, 29//Luke 4:31, 38 locate Peter's home in Capernaum, while John 1:44 says that he was from Bethsaida, both towns located on the north shore of Lake Galilee). He became an apprentice of Jesus, who nicknamed him "Rock" (*Petros* in Greek and *Kēpa'* in Aramaic, transliterated into Greek as *Kēphas*), and was appointed by Jesus as one of the twelve official delegates who appear to be so designated as the core of the renewed Israel.

After Easter Peter continues as a leader of the Jesus movement, as Paul indicates in Gal 2:9 and with which Acts agrees; Luke describes Peter's initial leadership in Jerusalem and then his having a traveling ministry in Judea and the bordering provinces. Acts 12 reports that sometime between 41 and 44 CE he was arrested by Herod Agrippa I and, after his release, attributed to divine intervention, he is only once more described as being in Jerusalem (Acts 15:7). Paul confirms that before Galatians was written Peter had left the Judean area and traveled as far north as Syrian Antioch (Gal 2:11), although he makes it clear that while there Peter was unduly influenced by "those from James" and, when push came to shove, feared "those from the circumcision party."

After Gal 2:11–14 or Acts 15[46] we lose track of Peter. There is a possible hint that he had been in Corinth in the presence of the "Cephas party" there (1 Cor 1:12) and in the Corinthians' apparent knowledge that Peter traveled with his wife (9:5—neither she nor the wife of any other of the twelve is ever named), although there are plenty of explanations of the existence of such knowledge without necessitating Peter's personal presence. Peter is referred to in *1 Clem.* 5:2–4 as one who "[after having] given his testimony went to his appointed place of glory," which is certainly a reference to his death and conceivably to his martyrdom. There are definitely third-century traditions that he was martyred in Rome by Nero (presumably between 64 and 68 CE, that is, between the great fire in Rome and Nero's suicide).[47] But there are no reliable traditions of what Peter did in the last fifteen to twenty years of his life (depending on when one dates the events of Galatians 2 and Acts 15), if we assume that the traditions about his time, place, and manner of death are accurate.[48]

---

45. E. Lohmeyer pointed this out close to ninety years ago; see his "Probleme paulinischer Theologie: I. Briefliche Grussüberschriften," *ZNW* 26 (1927): 158–73. For him, this indicated that 1 Peter was, broadly speaking, part of the Pauline literature.

46. Scholars have debated whether the council described in Acts 15 or the event Paul describes in Gal 2:11–14 came first, with some doubting that the so-called "Jerusalem council" took place at all, viewing it instead as an idealized presentation by Luke. For the purposes of this volume those issues do not matter.

47. John 21:18–19 also appears to allude to such a martyrdom,

which, of course, raises the possibility that it, not solid historical tradition, is the source of the third-century traditions of Peter's martyrdom.

48. Despite the gap between the event and the traditions, scholars seem inclined to accept the traditions as reasonably accurate, for they fit the period and fit with what we know about Nero and Roman execution. And there are no countertraditions to challenge them. However, even if they are accurate, we do not know why Peter was in Rome. Nero's arrests were within the vicinity of Rome, so Peter would have had to have already been there.

The reason that this information is important is that while the implied authorship of 1 Peter is clear, the actual authorship has been questioned. A series of issues have been raised that suggest to many scholars that Simon Peter did not write 1 Peter. (1) Paul claims that Peter was sent to the "circumcision" (i.e., Jews, Gal 2:7), while this letter seems to indicate a ministry to a largely Gentile church (see 3.2.2). (2) Peter was a fisherman (a class of people not known for their education either then or now). But since he lived in Galilee, he could certainly get along in Greek, just as the less-educated Hispanic people living in our area can usually get along in English. Acts claims that he was illiterate and uneducated (Acts 4:13), and yet the Greek of this letter is excellent and its rhetoric skillful. (3) Paul had an altercation with Peter (Gal 2:11–14), but this letter is addressed to churches in Paul's sphere of influence and has numerous similarities to Pauline thought. (4) Peter probably died before 68 CE, and there is no evidence of Roman persecution in Asia Minor or even in Greece that early—the letter seems to fit a later period, perhaps, like Revelation, fitting into the rule of Domitian (81–96 CE, the latter part of this period being when he persecuted followers of Jesus).[49] We will take up these issues below and only at the end return to draw those conclusions that may be drawn about authorship.

3.2.2 Addressees

It is clear that 1 Peter is addressed to "those resident aliens whom [God] has chosen of the Diaspora in Pontus, Galatia, Cappadocia, Asia, and Bithynia" (1 Pet 1:1). One immediately notices that this is a circular letter, that the locations are arranged in a rough circle, as if the messenger were to start at a Black Sea port in Pontus (Amisus? Sinope?) and circle around to leave from a port in Bithynia (Nicomedia?), and that the provinces are mostly places where Paul had been active. Galatians refers to Paul's ministry in Galatia, of course, and Colossians and Philemon to his ministry in Asia. Acts 16:7 says that Paul wanted to go into Bithynia but was not allowed; that same context indicates that he also wanted to go into Asia, but was also not allowed, yet his letters indicate that he did eventually go to Asia. Cappadocia (which lacked large cities) would have been on Paul's itinerary as he traveled from Tarsus through the mountains via the Cilician Gates towards Derbe, Lystra, and Pisidian Antioch. All of these provinces were clearly in Paul's arc of ministry described in Rom 15:19.

While there were Jews in all of these areas (e.g., Acts 18:2 describes Paul's colleague Aquila as a "native of Pontus"), it is also clear that the majority of the implied readers are not described as if they were Jews. Note these verses from 1 Peter:

---

49. See, e.g., J. B. Bauer, "Der erste Petrusbrief und die Verfolgung unter Domitian," in *Die Kirche des Anfangs: Festschrift für H. Schürmann* (ed. R. Schnackenburg; ErfTSt 38; Leipzig: St. Benno, 1978), 513–27.

Reference	Text (NRSV)
1:14	the desires that you formerly had in ignorance
1:18	You were ransomed from the futile ways inherited from your ancestors.
2:9–10	But you are a chosen race, a royal priesthood, a holy nation, God's own people … him who called you out of darkness into his marvelous light. Once you were not a people, but now you are God's people.
2:25	You were going astray like sheep, but now you have returned.
3:6	You have become [Sarah's] daughters.
4:3–4	You have already spent enough time in doing what the Gentiles like to do, living in licentiousness, passions, drunkenness, revels, carousing, and lawless idolatry. They are surprised that you no longer join them in the same excesses of dissipation.

Table 3: References to the Addressees of 1 Peter

While there are scholars who try to explain how these passages are consistent with a largely Jewish implied readership,[50] especially the first three and the final passage imply that at least a significant portion of these readers are from a Gentile background. A Jew might be apostate and need to "return," but they could hardly claim ignorance if they were in fact returning. Nor could they claim that the ways inherited from their "ancestors" were "futile," even if their manner of keeping them may have been. Paul goes to great length in Romans to argue that the Torah, the basic "way" of Jewish life, whatever the Jewish group one belonged to, was good and holy, so one could hardly call such a way of life "futile." Furthermore, the Jews cited Exodus 19 (referred to in 1 Pet 2:9) to show that they were indeed God's people, so how could one say to Jewish followers of Jesus that "once you were not a people"?

Finally, Diaspora Jews were largely characterized by their differences from the Gentiles, and particularly by their aversion to idolatry. Jews who did what "the Gentiles like to do" were considered apostate, having abandoned the traditions of their forefathers. But these readers, with no implication that they had ever left the traditions of their ancestors, had been fully a part of pagan culture until they became adherents of the Jesus movement. These addressees are, it appears, largely from a pagan background, although, as in the Pauline churches that we know from Paul's letters, there were surely ethnic Jewish believers in Jesus among them.

This means that our author is addressing a group that he views as largely coming from a pagan background. Despite this background he views them as God's true Israel in dispersion. Could this be the Peter we know of from Galatians, the one

50. Witherington, *Hellenized Christians*, 28–33. His argument about Jewish membership in trade guilds is invalidated by his inclusion of Paul (and Aquila) as examples, given that Paul describes himself as having been a rigorously observant Jew who even as a follower of Jesus refuses to agree to participation in sacrificial meals in pagan temples (cf. Ben Witherington III, "Not So Idle Thoughts about *eidōlothyton*," *TynBul* 44 [1993]: 237–54). In other words, idolatry was not necessarily characteristic of Jews involved in trades.

whose mission was to the "circumcision," to Jews? Those who posit a fixed polar relationship between Peter and Paul would argue that this cannot be the case, that the author of 1 Peter must be a Paulinist writing in the name of Peter, especially since he is writing to an area of Pauline influence and thus trespassing on Paul's "territory."

But it is difficult to sustain this view. First, while Paul reacts strongly to those who try to transform his churches either by attacking his leadership or by bringing in what he considers "another gospel" (see 2 Corinthians and Galatians respectively), he shows no concern about leaders whom he perceives as more or less in agreement with him who enter the sphere of his churches, even if others promote them as rivals. His reference to Apollos in 1 Cor 16:12 (cf. 1:12) is a prime example of this Pauline nondefensiveness. While it is incorrect to call 1 Peter "Pauline" (as will be argued below), since it has different interests, it is close enough to Paul's thought that some have considered it "Pauline," and there is no contradiction between it and Paul on theological topics that Paul considered critical. There is no reason why Paul would be concerned about this author, especially since there are no plans announced to travel to the locations of these churches or evidence that the author has ever visited them (he only speaks in general about their situation, and he does not send any personal greetings in 1 Pet 5:13).

Second, Paul may already have died by the time this letter was written, although, assuming that both Peter and Paul were executed by Nero and that the traditions about their deaths come from considerably later, it would be idle speculation to insist on who must have been executed first. Of course, Paul would have certainly been dead if 1 Peter was written after Nero's suicide and Nero had executed Paul.[51]

Third, and perhaps most important, the mission that one has at one point in one's career can shift as the years go on and the situations change. That James may always have focused on ethnic Jewish followers of Jesus is reasonable, since the evidence is that he lived in Jerusalem right up until his martyrdom (even if Hegesippus's account of his Jewish piety is probably overblown). If Peter moved from Palestine in the direction of Rome, it is not unreasonable to suppose that he may have refocused his ministry. This is, of course, speculation informed by contemporary experience of how ministries change, but it is not unreasonable speculation. Nor is it unreasonable to view Peter as more of a shepherd of established churches and Paul as more of a church planter, since Paul's expressed desire was not to remain in Rome or to return to his previous churches, but to continue westward to evangelize Spain (Rom 15:20, 23–24).

We have, however, not fully explained who these addressees are. Elliott argues that at least some of them are literal resident aliens or immigrants (a status above that of freed-persons and slaves, but below that of citizens, the Greek term indicat-

---

51. It is quite possible that Paul was executed first, for he was the one who, according to Acts, came to Rome as a prisoner who had appealed to Nero. He made an obvious target, assuming the tradition is correct that Nero blamed the Christians for the great fire in Rome. One would not be surprised if, under those circumstances, Peter, who was a key leader, did not "go underground" (even if eventually caught and executed himself) and yet continue to "shepherd" communities of believers in the Roman empire via letters.

ing a person from another province or district who had settled in a new locale for over thirty days) who had joined what for them was a Jewish messianic sect open to Gentiles. These believing immigrants had found, however, that rather than simply becoming part of a more supportive form of community to which they now related, they now experienced heightened rejection from the local population (in an area characterized more by rural villages than by urban centers).[52]

Achtemeier, however, points to the *second* occurrence of "resident aliens" (in 1 Pet 2:11) and notes the term "as" (*hōs*, ὡς), which, he argues, indicates that the term is metaphorical. His picture of the believing community is one that is mixed (Jews, Gentiles, all classes of society), but with a preponderance of Gentiles, who had at one time been fully accepted in their society.[53] Achtemeier makes a significant point about 2:11 when he notes that these followers of Jesus seem to be surprised by their new status (or nonstatus, 4:12), just as their neighbors are surprised by the changes in the new believers' behavior (4:4). Jews would never have felt acceptance in the pagan world,[54] and it is difficult to see how immigrants/resident aliens would expect to find security in a Jewish messianic sect. Neither in the case of their being Jews nor in that of their being literal Gentile resident aliens do we have a change in status that is surprising.

It seems most reasonable, then, to view the recipients as largely Gentile citizens of the various small cities and villages in the provinces indicated in the address, mixed indeed with Jews and actual immigrants, although without these "already-outsiders" forming a majority, a picture not unlike that of the Pauline mission except that, as Elliott rightly points out,[55] no major centers are named, so the communities of believers do not appear to have been concentrated in or centered on urban locations.[56]

Whether or not they were evangelized, as Elliott suggests, by Jews returning from Jerusalem after the first Pentecost,[57] in which case the oldest groups of believers would be at least thirty years old, they had clearly been initiated into the narrative of Israel and the reading of the Hebrew Scriptures (in Greek translation), or at least our author assumes that that is the case. We know of no communities of the Jesus movement that did not use a Greek translation of the Hebrew Scriptures or the members of which (whatever their background), upon joining the group, were not initiated into this use (i.e., into listening to these Scriptures being read and under-

---

52. Elliott, *1 Peter* (AB), 94–103. This, of course, summarizes his position in *A Home for the Homeless*. Note that Roman citizens from other provinces, Jews, traders, and similar groups would have all been lumped together under this designation. Elliott assumes that the varied images in the group are aimed at different groups within the scattered community of followers of Jesus.

53. Achtemeier, *1 Peter*, 55–57. Also, unlike Elliott, he believes that the sect composed of followers of Jesus had started in the urban centers and then expanded into the rural bulk of the provinces.

54. Even if aspects of Judaism were admired by individual pagans, Jews in general were despised and often persecuted, espe-

cially on the local level.

55. Elliott, *1 Peter* (AB), 87–88.

56. First Peter is one of six New Testament letters (2 Timothy, Titus, 2 Peter, 2 John, and Jude being the others, all significantly shorter than 1 Peter) that do not use *ekklēsia* (translated "church" in most English translations), despite referring to the community of believers more than once (e.g., 1 Pet 5:1–2). Is this because *ekklēsia* was an urban term for a civic assembly and did not fit as well in the more rural village situation, or is it a coincidence?

57. Elliott, *1 Peter* (AB), 89.

standing them, for the vast majority were unable to read), as the many references to those Scriptures in the various New Testament documents indicate.

We do not know how Simon Peter could have had contact with these communities of believers. They are on the edges of the *Pauline* mission, not in territory where Peter is said to have traveled according to any early traditions, including those of the second century. But this would also be a problem if we were talking about a later follower or admirer of Peter being the author.[58] No reference is made to any form of personal contact between Peter and the addressees — no greetings are exchanged. In fact, the general nature of the teaching in the letter that has led some to consider it a baptismal homily or liturgy is because the author does *not* know these communities and so has to write using material that he assumes all followers of Jesus everywhere would know and accept.[59]

3.2.3 Greek Style and Rhetoric

First Peter is written in good Greek. Our author has had a decent education, both grammatically and rhetorically. Witherington[60] argues that the letter is written in the milder form of the Asiatic style of Greek, while Selwyn[61] points to the Classical Greek parallels to 1 Peter's style, which would make it more Attic. First Peter is characterized by a proper use of the definite article, a lack of vulgarisms, a careful use of the optative mood (1:2; 3:14, 17), and careful attention to tense. Naturally, the letter does quote the Greek translation of the Hebrew Scriptures, which means that it includes translation Greek and contains Hebraisms. But passages such as 1:3–12, for example, are a delight to anyone schooled in Classical Greek. All this points to this writer's being a man with education, at least that of the *progymnasmata*, a level of education similar to Paul's.[62]

First Peter is also rhetorically sophisticated. Thurén[63] states, "The use of stylistic devices mostly reflects good conventional rhetoric." He notes devices such as *antithesis* and decorative devices such as *alliteratio*. Thurén concludes, "The technique of reasoning is sophisticated." Naturally, there is the usual problem with letters in that they do not necessarily contain a single type of rhetoric. Thus one can read the rhetoric of 1 Peter as deliberative (i.e., calling on the readers to decide to follow the instructions of the author) or epideictic (i.e., persuading the readers that the way of Jesus is honorable and that of the world around them ultimately dishonorable). In fact, it is most realistic to argue that 1 Peter contains elements of both forms of rhetoric, even if epideictic tends to predominate, for the author tries to persuade the

---

58. Why would such a person place Peter in relationship to groups with which Peter is never depicted as having contact?

59. Of course, if one were the remaining major leader of the Jesus movement living in Rome, given Rome's central role in the empire, it would be natural for one to care for the movement throughout the empire, especially as news tended to flow toward Rome and as Judea (and with it Jerusalem) moved toward the conflict with Rome that would lead to its destruction (i.e., the 66–70 CE war, although tensions were rising well before 66).

60. Witherington, *Hellenized Christians*, 42–43.

61. Selwyn, *First Epistle of St. Peter*, 499–501.

62. The Greek of 2 Peter is different, not in that it is grammatically problematic, but in that it is clearly the more bombastic type of the Asiatic style.

63. Lauri Thurén, "The General New Testament Writings," in *Handbook of Classical Rhetoric in the Hellenistic Period 330 B.C.–A.D. 400* (ed. Stanley E. Porter; Boston/Leiden: Brill, 2001), 596–97.

readers that the way of Jesus is honorable and thus the means of *their* ultimate honor despite their presently being held in disrepute by their neighbors. The author must argue this in order to persuade the addressees to continue without compromise in the way of Jesus. More will be noted about the rhetoric of 1 Peter in the commentary portion below, particularly his reframing of the situation in which the readers find themselves (which Thurén terms "the status of redefinition").

All this, of course, raises the issue of whether a Galilean fisherman could have written such a grammatically and rhetorically sophisticated letter (even if it is not of an educational level that we might term "university"). As already noted, it is probable that a fisherman from Galilee (and likely also tradespeople from Judea) would have been able to communicate in Greek, since there were Hellenistic towns and cities in the area (e.g., Sepphoris/Zippori, Tiberias) and Greek was generally used in first-century Palestine. But it is one thing to get along in Greek in the marketplace (or even the workplace, if one were a tradesman like Jesus) and quite another to compose speeches in Greek.[64]

As noted above, Acts 4:13 refers to Peter and John as "uneducated" or "illiterate" (the latter is the basic meaning of the first Greek term) and "relatively unskilled or inexperienced in some activity or field of knowledge."[65] This at least refers to their reputation at the beginning of their post-Easter ministry in the circles of the author of Acts.[66] Naturally, thirty years of preaching could improve one's rhetorical skill, and living outside of Palestine for perhaps half of that time would surely improve one's Greek (and, in Italy, perhaps, Latin, although some ancient writers claimed that one was more likely to hear Greek than Latin in Rome). But is there any reason to think that he would have opportunities for education and rhetorical training?

Mark, for example, is reputed by tradition to have come from the Petrine circle,[67] and his gospel is clearly written for a Gentile, perhaps Roman, context, but "Mark's Greek style is rather primitive, full of Aramaisms and Matthew and Luke tend to 'improve' his Greek," and the same is true rhetorically.[68] In other words, Mark is a published document attributed (rightly or wrongly) to the Petrine circle but shows no evidence in that circle of the level of grammatical education or rhetorical

---

64. For instance, this author and his wife functioned reasonably comfortably in German in Innsbruck, Austria, for several years, but his wife, who could counsel in German, never felt comfortable enough in the language to preach, and the author, while he did teach and preach in German, realized that although he communicated, everyone immediately knew, both from his accent and his grammatical and vocabulary mistakes, that he was a foreigner. Anything he published in German was (and is) first corrected by an educated native speaker. The same is true of most of Hispanic and Oriental students in his present classes, even though they were born and brought up in Texas.

65. BDAG, 468.

66. If Acts stems from Rome during the last third of the first century, which is not an unreasonable date and provenance, then the fact that this statement is never contradicted could be read as

representing Peter's reputation in Rome during the period when Acts was written.

67. The tradition is that John Mark wrote the gospel based on what Peter had taught at the request of the Roman community of believers, either just before or just after the death of Peter. See Eusebius, *Eccl. hist.* 3.39.15 (referring to Papias); Irenaeus, *Haer.* 3.1.2; the *Anti-Marcionite Prologue* to Mark, and the *Muratorian Fragment*. This tradition is strong enough that Bob Utley could entitle his work, *The Gospel according to Peter: Mark and I and II Peter* (Study Guide Commentary Series, NT 2; Marshall, TX: Bible Lessons International, 2000).

68. Richard A. Burridge, "The Gospels and Acts," in *Handbook of Classical Rhetoric in the Hellenistic Period 330 B.C.–A.D. 400* (ed. Stanley E. Porter; Boston/Leiden: Brill, 2001), 512–13.

sophistication that one finds in 1 Peter. Nevertheless, there is evidence in the syntax of 1 Peter that the author's first language may have been Aramaic and not Greek.[69]

The frequent response to this problem is the introduction of an amanuensis,[70] who is often assumed to be Silvanus (Silas) on the basis of 1 Pet 5:12. Here is the person responsible for the grammatical and rhetorical quality, and, what is more, this person was a coworker of Paul (and thus, perhaps, the Pauline-sounding language).[71] It is clear that virtually any first-century author would have used an amanuensis, since maintaining and using ink, stylus, and papyrus or parchment took training, and the maintaining of these materials was most easily done by people who used them on a daily basis.[72] Furthermore, even people who could read well were not necessarily skilled in the physical act of writing.[73]

However, in a careful investigation in the corpus of Greek literature (Thesaurus Linguae Graecae) of the formula used by 1 Peter ("through Silvanus," that is, διά, followed by a personal name), Richards discovered that this formula is not used of the amanuensis but of the letter carrier.[74] This stands to reason, for no one (other than the author himself) cared who the amanuensis was, especially if the author finished the letter in his own handwriting, indicating that he approved the work. But people did care who the letter carrier was, for the letter carrier was more than a postal worker. He or she (Phoebe, in the case of Romans) was expected not only to bring the letter to the destination, but also to read (or perform, since the reading was done for an audience and should be appropriately expressive) the letter and answer questions about the letter and the author. One wanted to know that the author trusted the letter carrier (thus Silvanus is labeled "a faithful brother, in my estimation"), which is why the letter carriers are sometimes mentioned in letter endings.[75] This does not mean that Silvanus could not have been the amanuensis, but it means that the letter does not provide any direct evidence that he was.

First, we do not know whether Silvanus (or Timothy or others associated with Paul in the salutations of his letters) had the appropriate training,[76] or even how lit-

---

69. Jobes, *1 Peter*, 325–38. She sees evidence of Aramaic syntactic interference in the Greek, indicating that Aramaic was the author's first language. This present author finds this evidence suggestive, but wishes that it were more controlled for the presence of Septuagintalisms.

70. E.g., Green, *1 Peter*, 7.

71. So Witherington, *Hellenized Christians*, 49–51.

72. See E. Randolph Richards, *Paul and First-Century Letter Writing: Secretaries, Composition and Collection* (Downers Grove, IL: InterVarsity Press, 2004), 47–55, who also suggests (pp. 60–64) that it was common to go down to the market and hire an amanuensis if one wished to write something.

73. Paul's reference to his "large letters" in Gal 6:11 does not necessarily indicate disability. It was customary for a letter writer to take the stylus for the last few lines of a letter, and the change in handwriting from the neat handwriting of the scribe to the much larger and cruder writing of the author is clearly visible on many Greco-Roman letters. The authors, although literate people, were

not practiced in the skill of writing. The crude writing served as something of a signature.

74. E. Randolph Richards, "Silvanus Was Not Peter's Secretary: Theological Bias in Reading Bias in Interpreting διὰ Σιλουανοῦ . . . ἔγραψα in 1 Pet 5:12," *JETS* 43 (2000): 417–32.

75. In the one New Testament document in which the scribe is mentioned (Rom 16:22), it is the scribe himself who speaks, sending his greetings, not the author who mentions the scribe. It appears that the scribe knew people in the destination community; so sending his personal greetings was appropriate. At any rate, the amanuensis's greeting is only one of a series of greetings from individuals in the Corinthian community to those in Rome.

76. This Silvanus is probably Silas, Paul's coworker; we do not know whether, like Paul, he was unskilled in the actual act of writing, and so would have himself needed an amanuensis, or whether that perhaps was his training, similar to Paul's training as a leatherworker or tentmaker. There just is no evidence about Silas's possible trade.

erate he was (although being literate and having a secretary's skills are two different things; all secretaries/scribes/amanuenses were literate, but, as noted, most literate people did not have the skills necessary to make ink, maintain papyrus, and write in a good hand). Silvanus was certainly literate enough to read the letter, but some of the "reading" could come from memory of a text read rather laboriously.

Second, given that Paul treated Silvanus (and we are assuming that Paul's Silvanus/Silas and 1 Peter's are references to the same person, which is probably the case) as a coworker, it would be surprising to find him used as an amanuensis without including him as a coauthor, for surely in such a case the amanuensis would have had significant content input as well, especially if some of these communities addressed were communities he had helped Paul evangelize.

Yet even if Silvanus was not the amanuensis, there surely was one. However, unless Peter somewhere managed to obtain a significant education, we are talking about an amanuensis responsible not just for the physical writing, but also for the grammar, style, and rhetoric of this letter—that is, the parts that involved education. This means that we basically hear the style of the amanuensis in, perhaps, the content of Peter. Furthermore, we do not know if and how well Peter could read (while Luke says that Jesus could read Hebrew, Luke 4:16–17, and Paul could surely read, there is no evidence one way or another as to whether anyone else in Jesus' band of followers could read; cf. again Acts 4:13). Nor do we know whether Peter depended on the accuracy of the amanuensis in reading the letter back to him (if Peter could write, he probably wrote 1 Pet 5:12–14 in his own hand, but we are not told that this is the case—but, then, Paul only rarely mentions that he followed this common practice).

An amanuensis could simply take dictation, but in the case of 1 Peter we are talking about something more than that, closer to the role that Richards calls "composer," which was at the other end of the spectrum of the degree to which amanuenses might be involved.[77] We are talking about something closer to an anonymous ghostwriter.[78] With our lack of a detailed biography of Peter and especially of the impression he made on educated people during his later ministry, we cannot prove or disprove that Peter could have written this work with the help of some type of amanuensis. The degree to which Peter was or was not involved becomes, then, a matter of faith[79] that is either supported or not supported by the historical context of the letter; as we will discuss later, it is supported if the historical context of the letter could have taken place in Peter's lifetime.

---

77. Richards, *Paul and First-Century Letter Writing*, 59–80. One could dictate a letter without being fully literate, for one could compose in one's head, but in this case it is the quality of the Greek and the rhetoric that is the issue.

78. If one wishes to imagine scenarios, one could imagine Peter in prison, wishing to write those in Asia Minor, and asking someone to write, or to have someone else write, in his name along this or that line. In that case Peter's contribution would be small indeed.

79. That is, a matter of trust in the authorial attribution in 1 Pet 1:1. Of course, there has been no discussion of the assertion of some church fathers that Peter could not have written this letter but was miraculously enabled to do so, for such an assertion, while theologically possible, is not historically investigable. But let us be clear that even if something has not left historical traces, this situation does not mean that it did not happen.

3.2.4 Pauline Influence

One part of the historical context is the relationship of 1 Peter to Pauline literature. It is clear that there is significant overlap in form, vocabulary, and intertextuality. In form, both use the Greek letter form with similar modifications. For instance, as noted above, (1) the author of 1 Peter identifies himself similarly to the way Paul identifies himself in some of his letters; (2) both authors address communities of believers within the Pauline sphere (e.g., Galatians, Colossians, and Ephesians all address believers within the areas to which 1 Peter was written); (3) both use the "grace and peace" greeting rather than "greetings" (as in Jas 1:1), the standard Greek greeting in a letter; and (4) both tend to use an extended thanksgiving (although it is absent in Galatians) rather than the brief thanksgiving to a god or gods common in Greek letters. Of course, with our limited supply of letters from leaders of the Jesus movement in the first century, we cannot be sure that these idiosyncrasies were not common over a wide range of leaders. First John does not use them, nor does Hebrews (which is more a sermon with a letter ending than a letter), and James and Jude are limited in their overlap, but 2 John, 2 Peter, and the letter opening of Rev 1:4–6 are similar.

More interesting is the overlap in ideas and terminology, especially between 1 Peter and Romans and Ephesians, but to some degree also between 1 Peter and some of the other Pauline letters. Most striking are the facts that only 1 Peter and Paul use the *en Christō* (ἐν χριστῷ, "in Christ") formula (1 Pet 3:16; 5:10, 14, and 164 times in Paul) and that only these two refer to *charismata* (χαρίσματα, "gifts," 1 Pet 4:10 and 16 times in Paul, esp. 1 Cor 12 and Rom 12). There are numerous other vocabulary overlaps,[80] but these other terms are neither as theologically significant nor as exclusive to 1 Peter and the Pauline corpus.

Along with vocabulary, there are similar structures used, like the *Haustafeln* (household management lists) in 1 Pet 2:18–3:7, which are most similar to those in Eph 5:22–6:9 and Col 3:18–4:1. There is also a similar use of some of the same passages from the Hebrew Scriptures—for instance, the use of Isa 8:14 and 28:16 in combination with Hos 2:1, 25 (23 in Eng.) in 1 Pet 2:4–10 and Rom 9:25–33. The similar combinations of prophetic texts also mean that 1 Peter and Romans are methodologically similar in their use of such texts.

These and other such similarities have led a number of scholars, particularly German scholars and especially those from the second half of the nineteenth century through the first half of the twentieth century, to view 1 Peter as a less substantial presentation of Pauline themes, which contributed to the neglect of 1 Peter during that period. Yet there are also scholars from the second half of the twentieth century who believe that 1 Peter is dependent on Paul. Beare, for example, states: "The book is strongly marked by the impress of Pauline theological ideas, and in language the dependence on St. Paul is undeniably great. All through the Epistle,

80. See the list in Elliott, *1 Peter* (AB), 22–23.

we have the impression that we are reading the work of a man who is steeped in the Pauline letters."[81]

But is that so? We have noted above two items of vocabulary that are exclusive to 1 Peter and the Pauline corpus, but they are the only ones. All other themes share a wider base in early Christian discourse. Goppelt, for instance, lists the following parallels between 1 Peter and Romans and Ephesians:

1 Peter	Romans	1 Peter	Ephesians
1:14	12:2	1:3–4	1:3, 14
1:22	12:9	1:14–18; 4:2–3	4:17–18; 5:8
2:(2) 5	12:1	2:1	4:25, 31
2:4–10	9:25, 32–33	2:4–6	2:20–22
2:13–17	13:1, 3–4, 7	3:1	5:22
3:9	12:17	3:22	1:20–21
4:1	6:7	5:8–9	6:11–13
4:10–11	12:6		
4:13; 5:1	8:17		

Goppelt then comments that other than the common use of material from the Hebrew Scriptures, none of the parallels are verbally identical; nine of the parallels with Romans are in paraenetic sections, which contain common themes for the early followers of Jesus, not specifically Pauline themes; and of the seven parallels with Ephesians four refer to common paraenetic expressions and three to a common image for the believing community. Thus Goppelt concludes, "so there can be no mention of any literary dependence."[82]

Furthermore, many of the major Pauline themes are missing from 1 Peter. Faith, justification, and works are not an issue for 1 Peter, much less specific "works of the law" such as circumcision and Jewish festivals, which are so important for Paul. First Peter does not use the term ekklēsia (ἐκκλησία, "church"), which is also important for Paul. While both Paul and 1 Peter discuss election, the discussion in 1 Pet 2:4–10 is much different than that in Rom 11:26–29, nor does Paul ever cite Exod 19:6, which is central to 1 Peter's discussion. When Paul talks about gifts, he associates them with the Spirit, but Peter makes no mention of the Spirit in his discussion about gifts. Finally, the list of terms and ideas that are important to 1 Peter and not found in Paul or important to Paul and not found in 1 Peter is significant.[83]

It is, of course, possible that our author did know one or more of the Pauline letters. If 1 Peter were written in Rome, it would be surprising if he did not know Romans, which on any acceptable dating of 1 Peter should have arrived in Rome

81. Beare, *First Epistle of Peter*, 44. While first written in 1958, the third edition, from which the quotation is taken, is dated 1970.

82. Goppelt, *Der erste Petrusbrief*, 49. The wider discussion of the

relationship to Paul is on pp. 48–51.

83. Elliott, *1 Peter* (AB), 38–39.

at least five years previously. In fact, it is more surprising that one cannot prove that our author *did* know Romans than it would be if we could prove knowledge of Romans, if we accept the (reasonable) tradition that Peter lived in Rome for a number of years before his death. The fact is that one cannot prove the case either way; it is a "perhaps, perhaps not" situation. Thus Elliott is surely correct when he writes that the data "constitute incontestable evidence that, while one or more of the Pauline letters may have been known to the author of 1 Peter, the Petrine author constructed, on the basis of the same tradition known to Paul, a distinctive pastoral message and spoke with a distinctive voice."[84]

This information, then, does not help us in evaluating the authorship issue, for while indisputable evidence for 1 Peter's dependence on several of Paul's works (certainly the Pastoral Epistles, and, depending on dating, the Prison Epistles) would argue for a date of writing after these letters were collected, which was probably after both Paul's and Nero's deaths (and so after Simon Peter's death), its lack of clear dependence on Romans fails to tie the letter to Paul at all.

Likewise, there is no evidence one way or the other with respect to authorship that 1 Peter always quotes a Greek translation of the Hebrew Scriptures rather than the Hebrew Scriptures themselves (which Paul seems to do on occasion, although not often). If Simon Peter was not literate, as Luke claims, then while he may well have spoken Aramaic and perhaps (but not definitely) understood Hebrew,[85] he would not have read it. Even if he did, once he left the eastern end of the Mediterranean Sea, the language of Scripture reading was Greek (based on the evidence we have from the communities committed to Jesus). Even James, which whatever one says about authorship (see the discussion of James above) is usually located in the eastern end of the Mediterranean, agrees with the Greek translation of the Hebrew Scriptures wherever Scripture is quoted. As a result, this aspect of 1 Peter is not surprising, although it does have implications for what constituted the canon of Scripture for the followers of Jesus.

3.2.5 Persecution

It is clear that 1 Peter is written to followers of Jesus who are facing some type of persecution, so perhaps an examination of the cultural and religious situation in the Roman empire will help us in setting the context of our letter.

In the Greco-Roman world the gods were omnipresent. There were statues and sometimes altars or shrines along the streets and temples in the towns and cities. Most meat sold in the markets came from sacrifices made in those temples. In the pagan world as in the Jewish world, only certain parts of the animals were used in most sacrifices. In the Jewish world the blood and fat were normally used; the priest received a portion of the rest, and the worshiper ended up with the bulk of the meat.

---

84. Ibid., 40.

85. One could have been in a synagogue where Hebrew was read and have understood some of it from Aramaic, but it would have been no more necessary for a Galilean Jew to know Hebrew than it was for traditional Catholics to know Latin when the Mass was said in Latin.

In the pagan world various parts of the animal were used, depending on the cult, but in general the meat was either the property of the priests/temple or of the worshiper, who might consume it or sell it in the marketplace. That, of course, created a problem for those who were strict monotheists and wanted to keep separate from polytheistic religions (see discussion in 1 Cor 8–10). But this same type of problem extended to the whole of society, not just the butcher shop.

In the household there would be a shrine, perhaps to Vesta, the Roman goddess of the hearth, perhaps to some other god, perhaps to a combination of deities. The mistress of the house was responsible for putting the appropriate offerings before the god or goddess every day—perhaps some wine and a bit of bread or grain or flowers, perhaps lighting a lamp, sometimes a pinch of incense. Slaves would assist in this duty.

The extended family would celebrate various special occasions, such as births, birthdays, marriages, deaths, or building a new house. In the ancient world these celebrations included offerings to the appropriate god or goddess (depending on the occasion and/or the patron deity of the family or clan); if large enough, the celebration would take place in part in the dining hall of the temple of that god or goddess.

If the family were an artisan family, they would belong to a trade guild, which in essence regulated the practice of that trade in the city or town. The trade guild also had meetings and celebrations, often in the dining hall of the temple of the god or goddess that was the patron deity of the guild.

All civic celebrations had a similar religious component to them, whether the dutiful worship of the patron deity of the town or city or the worship of the genius of the emperor.[86] This was especially true of Asia Minor, for it was in this area that the cult of the emperor (including temples built for various deified emperors) was the strongest.[87] The Romans were also serious about the religious duties of the emperor. Starting with Julius Caesar, every emperor was also high priest (often before he became emperor, as a type of precondition). He presided at major ceremonies that related to the whole state and ensured that the rites of the various deities related to the state were properly carried out.[88]

So one could say that in the Greco-Roman world there was a hierarchy. The family was the foundation of the society, and the society culminated in the state (in essence the Roman Empire was a huge city-state, which was one reason for its eventual collapse). But the foundation of the family was its deities, and various deities related to each level of society right up to the state. That meant that the appropriate worship of these deities was important, for if the family gods were offended, the

---

86. This would be similar to patriotic ceremonies today, such as flag rituals (and songs) dutifully carried out at civic celebrations in the USA, including at sports events, the modern equivalent of gladiatorial events that would grace the Circus Maximus and other arenas in the Roman world.

87. Emperor worship was slower to take root in Italy, perhaps because residents of Italy and esp. Rome knew the various emperors all too well. In the first century, those emperors who claimed divine

honors for themselves while alive were eventually assassinated, and not all emperors received divine honors after their deaths.

88. Again, this is not unlike the Queen of England, who is the titular head of the Church of England (and has "Defender of the Faith" as one of her titles); the President of the United States is severely criticized if he does not attend national prayer breakfasts and similar religious rituals.

family would collapse, with ramifications for the city and state. The same was true of all the gods.

An example of how seriously this was taken comes from the Peloponnesian War (the fifth- and fourth-century BCE war between Athens and its allies and Sparta and its allies). Before the fleet sailed in the Athenian attack on Syracuse (415 BCE), it was discovered that during the night a number of religious images known as *herms* had been vandalized. Now these statues (a pillar with a head representing the god Hermes with an erect phallus on the front of the pillar, symbolizing Hermes's fertility) were everywhere: in streets, squares, and highways, and in front of temples and private houses. The Athenians were both outraged and fearful, for it was clear to them that someone was trying to deprive the city of divine protection. This outrage was used by one faction in Athens to implicate Alcibiades, one of three Athenian generals involved in the attack on Syracuse. Had he been tried, he would have been condemned and executed, or so he feared, so he fled to Sparta, and the Athenian attack on Syracuse failed.[89] The point of this excursus into Greek history is that sacrilege was taken seriously enough that it created the type of fear and outrage that could result in execution, even at the cost of a leading general important to the Athenian cause. However important a person was, the gods and their propitiation were more important. The same was true of Rome both before and after it became the dominant power in the Mediterranean world.

Into this polytheistic society enter the Jews. They were monotheists and would not participate in the various religious rites of the pagan communities around them.[90] This meant that, while they participated in trade and commerce (fewer were farmers, since Jews had come to Asia Minor either because of forced relocation resulting from war, including as slaves sold as booty of war, or as traders and traveling artisans), they could not fully participate in the trade guilds nor civic affairs, even though by the first century they had lived in the pagan areas for generations. But even then there were some sticky issues, for statues and shrines were everywhere.

A story from the Mishnah, a dialogue between a pagan and a rabbi, illustrates the problem of a Jew in a pagan environment:

A Peroqlos b. Pelosepos asked Rabban Gamaliel in Akko, when he was washing in Aphrodite's bathhouse, saying to him, "It is written in your Torah, *And there shall cleave nothing of a devoted thing to your hand* (Dt. 13:18). How is it that you're taking a bath in Aphrodite's bathhouse?"

B He said to him, "They do not give answers in a bathhouse."

C When he went out, he said to him, "I never came into her domain. She came into mine. They don't say, 'Let's make a bathhouse as an ornament for Aphrodite.' But they say, 'Let's make Aphrodite as an ornament for the bathhouse.'

---

89. For a fuller description of this event, see William E. Dunstan, *Ancient Greece* (Fort Worth, TX: Harcourt, 2000), 218–19.

90. Israel and Judah did have problems of involvement with polytheism between the conquest of Canaan and their respective exiles,

but the literature from the Second Temple period (when they were called Judeans or Jews, whatever their tribal origins) may show an issue with intermarriage (solved differently in Ezra-Nehemiah and Ruth or Esther), but it does not reveal an issue with polytheism per se.

D "Another matter: Even if someone gave you a lot of money, you would never walk into your temple of idolatry naked or suffering a flux, nor would you piss in its presence.

E "Yet this thing is standing there at the head of the gutter and everybody pisses right in front of her."

F It is said only, " ... *their gods*" (Dt. 12:3) — that which one treats as a god is prohibited, but that which one treats not as a god is permitted.[91]

This quotation illustrates how Jews were always having to decide what compromises they could live with and where they had to draw the line. But unless they were leaving their faith (which, of course, some did), it was difficult for them to eat with a pagan or actively participate in much of pagan society, for so much of it was entwined with pagan religion. And, of course, they particularly could not remain faithful to YHWH and engage in the pagan religion, even in marginal ways.

This naturally led to suspicion of the Jews. They were considered foreigners (even if they had lived in the city for generations), and they were clearly atheists (they had no images, so they obviously had no deities); they practiced genital mutilation on their sons (this is how Greco-Romans viewed circumcision), as one could see if one met a Jewish man in the bathhouse.

Jews did, however, have a protected legal status in the Roman Empire. They had had a treaty with Rome going back to the period of the Maccabean Wars (i.e., 186 BCE). Those living outside of Palestine often enough served as auxiliaries in the Roman army (and some received Roman citizenship for it).[92] Despite the Jewish refusal to burn incense to the genius of the emperor or to the chief Roman deities,[93] Judaism (in its various forms, for it was not a single religion before 70 CE) was permitted as a *religio licita* (legal religion), under the proviso that a sacrifice was offered daily in the Jerusalem temple for (rather than to) the emperor. This exception was justified by the Romans on the basis of the Jewish relationship with Rome and the fact that all forms of Judaism traced their history back to Moses, making Judaism in general an ancient religion in a world that valued ancient traditions.

The official Roman acceptance did not mean that the local populace or the local government was equally tolerant. Sometimes Jews were able to live peacefully as "the nation of the Jews" in this or that city. That is, they were a considered a foreign people, citizens of a nation located in Palestine — colonies, so to speak, immigrants or resident aliens; they were not "one of us." They were separate and allowed to live under their own traditions and practices, so long as they did not break local law or offend local sensitivities (Acts 18:13–16 illustrates this attitude). But they were "other," and so they often experienced discrimination of various types. Sometimes

91. 'Abodah Zarah 3.4 in Jacob Neusner, *The Mishnah: A New Translation* (New Haven, CT: Yale University Press, 1988), 665.

92. It has been suggested that Paul's father may have gained citizenship in this manner, for Luke reports Paul saying that he was born a citizen (Acts 22:26–28).

93. Note that in the Seleucid context this refusal of patriotism was a significant part of the causes of the persecution of Jews under the Seleucid ruler Antiochus IV Epiphanes and thus a cause of the Maccabean War.

this underlying suspicion boiled over into anti-Jewish violence of various sorts, perhaps triggered by something that a particular Jew had done (as Acts 16:20–22 illustrates) or perhaps triggered by the need of a scapegoat.

Philo of Alexandria's *Legatio ad Gaium* is an example of a Jewish leader in the 40s CE going to Rome to appeal to Emperor Gaius to stop anti-Jewish attacks in Alexandria, attacks that the Roman officials in the city were not stopping and perhaps were even encouraging. This situation on a much more limited scale was the periodic experience of Jewish residents in Asia Minor and elsewhere in the empire. Sometimes they were tolerated, sometimes pagans even admired their monotheism, and some of these even attended the synagogue; but often the Jews faced suspicion and discrimination and sometimes were violently persecuted. After all, what else does one do to a group refusing to worship the civic gods and thus undermining the welfare of the town or city?

When followers of Jesus entered this mix, they were (at least during much of the first century) considered just another sect of Jews and took pains to claim that status for themselves (e.g., Rom 2:29; Phil 3:3; Col 2:11, where Paul claims that followers of Jesus are spiritually "circumcised," the mark of the Jew; he also claims that they are descendants of Abraham, the ancestor of all Jews). That meant that they could both claim the acceptance offered the Jewish religion and experience the popular suspicion and distrust that Jews experienced. To the outside world there was no difference between followers of Jesus and other Jews, as long as the followers of Jesus were ethnically Jewish.[94]

But it was a different matter when a Gentile member of the town or city became a follower of Jesus. In Greco-Roman eyes this person had no ancient right to live like a Jew. The person was rejecting the gods of the community and undermining the welfare of the city, and he had become antisocial ("a hater of humanity") and atheistic. The person was sometimes tolerated (just as Jews were sometimes tolerated) but also was often treated according to the local perception of their having become antisocial and thus a threat to the welfare of the community.

During the first century CE and well into the second there was no widespread *official* Roman persecution of Christians. It is true that Nero did persecute followers of Jesus, but (1) the numbers were probably relatively small; (2) the persecution was limited to Rome and its vicinity; and (3) the reason was suspicion of arson in the great fire of Rome (64 CE). In other words, the followers of Jesus were scapegoats. Partly this may have been to divert popular suspicion from Nero himself, but partly this was because it made sense. Here was (in the popular view) an odious group — especially odious because they were bringing Romans into their "superstition" and inducing them to abandon the proper worship of the Roman gods. Now look what happened! Rome had burned. The gods were angry and no longer protecting her. It's the fault of those apostate followers of that "Christ."

---

94. Thus, when the Emperor Claudius expelled Jews from Rome (Acts 18:2; Suetonius, *Divus Claudius* 25.4), apparently due to inner community turmoil over the followers of Jesus, Suetonius viewed it as a riot instigated by a certain Chrestus (*Chrestus* and *Christos* would have been pronounced identically). Thus it made sense to expel all Jews.

Tradition says that some Jewish leaders of the group (e.g., Simon Peter and Paul of Tarsus) were executed as part of this attack on the followers of Jesus, for of course a persecutor first wants to remove the leaders of the sect they are suppressing, hoping to thereby scatter the general membership. Perhaps some Jews who were innocent of being followers of Jesus were killed as well—that would be no issue for Nero, and this would be especially true after the Jews in Palestine revolted in 66 CE. We do not know how well Nero could or did differentiate Jews from Christians. But the easiest target would have been those Gentile Romans who had become followers of Jesus.

There was another mostly local, sporadic persecution under Emperor Domitian toward the end of the first century. Domitian is known for a number of reforms, one of which was his reform of and devotion to traditional Roman religion. As a result and coupled with his conflict with the Roman Senate, some followers of Jesus (or sympathizers of the followers of Jesus) who had significant positions in the Roman aristocracy were executed or banished. There is also evidence that Domitian wanted divine honors during his life, and naturally followers of Jesus would not offer these. Furthermore, Domitian was somewhat paranoid, and anyone or any group who aroused his suspicion became a target.[95] Individuals or an entire group who would not participate in the Roman religion would be suspect, especially if those individuals were highly enough placed that they came to Domitian's attention. We do not know how many died in this persecution, but it was mostly localized and appears to have focused on leaders who did come to Domitian's attention.[96]

It is clear that two emperors later, there was still no explicit policy concerning Christians, although insofar as the Christian movement was known by officials, it was viewed negatively. Pliny the Younger, governor of Bythinia-Pontus in northwest Asia Minor, had some Christians indicted before him, possibly by trades dependent on temple sacrifices that, because of the growing Christian movement, were no longer being made in the same numbers. Pliny had executed Christians who would not sacrifice to the emperor because of their "stubbornness," but he then consulted the emperor to see if he was handling the affair correctly. Trajan tells his governor how to deal with those Christians who were accused before him of this or that crime, but he also tells Pliny not to seek Christians out or hunt them down. There is no official policy on Christians that either Trajan or Pliny could cite. Being a Christian in and of itself was not something to cause them to be hunted, so they were relatively safe unless someone else was bothered enough to denounce them to the magistrate.[97]

It is into this setting that one must place 1 Peter. If one reads 1 Pet 4:12 ("fiery ordeal") as referring to official persecution, one must look for instances of state persecution widespread enough to include the provinces addressed in the letter (5:9 claims

---

95. His paranoia was to a degree justified, since he was eventually assassinated by a conspiracy within his household, having survived a number of other rebellions and conspiracies.

96. See further J. B. Campbell, "Domitian," in *The Oxford Companion to Classical Civilization* (ed. Simone Hornblower and Anthony Spawforth; Oxford/New York: Oxford University Press, 2004), 237–38.

97. Herbert B. Workman, *Persecution in the Early Church* (Oxford/New York: Oxford University Press, 1980), 84–86.

the suffering is taking place "in the whole world"). Nero's persecution clearly would not qualify, since it was local, which fact has led some scholars to date the letter in the period of Domitian.[98] The problem is that there is no evidence that the persecution under Domitian reached into Asia Minor, nor that the specific charges had to do with "the name of Christ" (1 Pet 4:14, NRSV; cf. 4:16). The events that Pliny refers to did take place in a province to which 1 Peter is addressed, but it is clear that even then state persecution was a sporadic affair. First Peter's view of the Roman government is of an emperor who sends governors "to punish those who do wrong and to praise those who do right" (2:14, NRSV). There is not a word of criticism of the Roman state. Thus, (1) trying to date the letter by a specific Roman persecution is futile, for 1 Peter does not refer to an official state persecution; and (2) the persecution that is referred to by 1 Peter appears to be local, without official sanction, but based on pagan prejudice against followers of Jesus. This analysis of the historical situation of the letter appears to be the consensus of contemporary scholarly opinion.[99]

3.2.6 Conclusions about the Historical Situation

It is clear that 1 Peter is written to a group of believers who were suffering, for the letter uses the terms for "suffer" or "suffering" more frequently in relation to its length than any other work in the New Testament. It is not clear that the author himself was feeling any particular threat or danger, for he never refers to his own suffering, arrest, or threat of arrest, or possible personal danger, other than in generalizations that include all the followers of Jesus in the world. If the author is Peter in Rome in the time of Nero, he does not reveal any sense of threat from Nero, which could mean one of three things: (1) it was written before Nero started to scapegoat Christians, (2) it was written after the death of Nero, or (3) Peter did not feel particularly threatened by Nero at first or, if he did feel threatened, he is unlike Paul in that he chooses to focus on the recipients rather than to share his own situation.[100]

Asia Minor, however, was particularly patriotic in the first century CE. The previous two centuries had seen a lot of turmoil: struggles among the various kingdoms, invasions from the east, conflicts among Roman generals and other leaders who fought it out on the soil of Asia Minor, and exploitation by all sides involved in the various conflicts. The ascension of Augustus had changed everything, bringing relative peace and orderly government to the whole area. It is no wonder that the Asians in particular embraced the cult of Augustus. Furthermore, although there were ups and downs over the succeeding decades, in general this situation remained the case throughout the first century (e.g., Domitian reformed problematic situations in Asia Minor and ruled it well) and beyond.

The new group, followers of a certain Jesus of Nazareth, a group soon nick-

---

98. E.g., Bauer, "Der erste Petrusbrief und die Verfolgung unter Domitian," 513–27.

99. See the longer discussions in both Feldmeier, *First Letter of Peter*, 2–13; and Elliott, *1 Peter* (AB), 97–103.

100. One does occasionally run across a scholar who thinks that the persecution under Nero was a Christian fiction, but this author does not believe that the position is widespread enough to warrant discussion.

named "Christians" because they followed a "Christ" (i.e., an Anointed One),[101] threatened this relative well-being. It was bad enough having a foreign nation (i.e., Jews) in their midst—a "nation" who had strange customs, were not sociable (thus were "haters of humanity"), and refused to be involved in the all-important service of the deities.[102] Then this Jewish splinter group arose (or, more likely, came into town), which proceeded to welcome some of their fellow citizens, and even actively recruited them. These fellow citizens joined this group more readily because it did not demand the genital mutilation that the other Jews demanded. After these fellow citizens joined this Jewish splinter group, they then began to act like Jews themselves, withdrawing from civic and social events, refusing the worship of the family and civic deities, and claiming that there was an unseen King, one Jesus of Nazareth or Christ, a revolutionary whom Rome had executed but whom, so they claimed, the one and only deity had appointed to rule the world.

The societal response to this Jewish splinter group that followed Jesus of Nazareth and recruited Gentiles varied with time and place. Often the adherents of this new group were accused of various evil practices. Certainly, in the eyes of their Gentile neighbors, they were "haters of humanity," and they were "atheists," which meant they were undermining the stability of society. To the extent that they were viewed as different as Jews (which certainly happened when the majority of the group was Gentile, as appears to be the case in the communities 1 Peter addresses), they were viewed, not as part of an officially tolerated (if unofficially despised and persecuted) *religio licita*, but as a *collegia*, a social club.

Such social clubs, unless explicitly permitted by the government, were illegal societies (since they were potential sources of instability), although the government only sometimes cracked down on them. This group of "Christians" (as they were called) greeted one another with a kiss as if they were family, despite not being related or even being from the same ethnic group. This reality spawned rumors of improper sexual intimacy at their meetings, even without knowing that they sometimes referred to them as "love feasts." Such prejudice would give rise to slander. Any problem in the town or city might be blamed on them (either blamed directly on them or blamed indirectly on them because this or that god was obviously angry). This rejection and slander would clearly be a shock to those individuals who were now followers of Jesus but who had grown up in the locality, whose families had

101. If one were an ethnic Jew from a Jewish group that believed in the coming of a Messiah or if one were any Jew or Gentile initiated into the Jesus movement, one would know the meaning of the title "Christos"; that is, one would know that it indicated the royal status of Jesus and his function in God's plan. But if one were a Gentile with little knowledge of the real teachings of the followers of Jesus, then "Christ" was a nonsense title (since in the Greco-Roman world anointing was used only for medicinal or cosmetic reasons, not to designate people as divinely appointed) or a proper name and thus "Christian" (those belonging to Christ or in the Christ party) formed a developing nickname for the group. First Peter uses it only as a name that outsiders use in slandering the movement, but in so using it he reframes it as a name that can be a source of honor rather than shame (as pagans using it intended).

102. Provincial Jews themselves rarely went to Jerusalem. Most probably never went or, if they did, it was a once-in-a-lifetime pilgrimage. Some made this pilgrimage close to their deaths so as to die in Jerusalem, which would mean they never returned. Thus even the Jews themselves would, for the most part, be only theoretically aware of the sacrificial system. One wonders if the Gentiles among whom they lived were even dimly aware of it, much less aware that there was a daily sacrifice for the emperor.

deep roots there, who had played with their accusers as children, and who were related to them by descent or marriage.

Furthermore, for all those in both the believing community and pagan society, honor was the highest good and social shame the greatest evil, being more important than wealth and poverty.[103] Yet whereas those who had grown up locally had once had some honor in their society (unless they were slaves, who by definition had no honor), they were now being spoken of only in terms of shame, and that by people whom they had known perhaps all their lives. The changed situation would be shocking and disturbing to these formerly pagan followers of Jesus.

This cultural-historical setting, of course, means that official Roman persecutions[104] are irrelevant for dating the letter. More relevant would be knowing the percentage of followers of Jesus in the populations of a given area, for the higher the concentration, the greater the perceived threat. But this data must have varied widely from place to place, and it is difficult to estimate.

So where are we in determining the date, authorship, and provenance of 1 Peter? First, while it does not appear that the author has used a Pauline letter, the terminology found in Romans and Ephesians does appear in 1 Peter, so at least some Pauline terminology is "in the air." One would think that this would date the letter at least a year or two after 60 CE, after the letter to the Romans had been around long enough that one might use its terminology without directly quoting it. Second, the author's positive view of the Roman government is quite different than the negative view of Rome found in Revelation (e.g., Rev 17), which probably dates from the last tumultuous year or so of Domitian's reign.

Furthermore, it appears that the author of *1 Clement* knew 1 Peter,[105] which means that it was in circulation before 96 CE. To this we can add that it was probably written in Rome (which is the way the majority of scholars interpret "Babylon" in 1 Pet 5:13).[106] Since the author does not refer to any ongoing persecution in his area or to a chaotic government situation, the letter probably does not come from the period when Nero was persecuting the followers of Jesus or the following "year of the four emperors." That would mean that either the letter was written in the pre-persecution years of Nero's reign or else in the relatively calm Flavian period before the end period of Domitian's reign (70–94 or 95 CE).

Earlier in this introduction we noted the problem of the style and rhetoric of

---

103. See David A. deSilva, *Honor, Patronage, Kinship and Purity: Unlocking New Testament Culture* (Downers Grove, IL: InterVarsity Press, 2000), 41–93.

104. The first official empire-wide persecution of Christians was that of Decius in 250 CE (Esusebius, *Hist. eccl.* 6.39.1–6.42.6; 7.1; *Sib. Or.* 13:81–88).

105. This is the conclusion of Elliott, *1 Peter* (AB), 138–40; there is no explicit citation, but there is significant overlap in the use of rare vocabulary and expressions. Elliott provides the data.

106. This is supported by the later church traditions that place Simon Peter, Silvanus, and John Mark in Rome. As for the New Tes-

tament data, Col 4:10 and Phlm 24 associate Mark with Paul later in Paul's ministry, although neither letter may stem from a Roman imprisonment of Paul; many scholars believe they come from an Ephesian imprisonment. Second Timothy 4:11 would associate Mark with a Roman imprisonment if 2 Timothy is by Paul and if Mark actually went to Rome as Paul requested. Silvanus/Silas is associated with an earlier part of Paul's life and always in combination with Timothy (2 Cor 1:19; 1 Thess 1:1), which fits well with Acts, for Acts mentions Silas only in Acts 15–18, and also often couples him with Timothy.

the letter, that unless Simon Peter had some education, which no one in the New Testament or in later traditions concerning him knows about, barring a miracle (which was the preference of the church fathers), someone else is responsible for the Greek style and rhetoric. While Silvanus is proposed as this amanuensis who had essentially ghostwritten the letter, we pointed out that there is no evidence that requires this; that 1 Pet 5:12 points to Silvanus as the letter carrier, not the letter writer; and that unlike in 1 and 2 Thessalonians, Silvanus is not included by 1 Peter as a cowriter of the letter. Since an amanuensis was not normally mentioned in a letter, this does *not* mean that Silvanus *could not* have been the amanuensis, but we also have no reason to believe that he had the appropriate training.[107] Furthermore, if he had been responsible for the letter in the form that we read it, one would think that he would have been included as coauthor.

So one is left with two options: (1) accepting the implied author, Simon Peter, as the actual author on the basis of 1 Pet 1:1, realizing that we are not hearing his exact voice,[108] but that of an amanuensis serving as what we would call a ghostwriter (i.e., we are hearing his *ipsissima vox*, not his *ipsissima verba*), and dating the letter to the pre-persecution part of Nero's reign;[109] or (2) dating the letter in the Flavian period and realizing that Simon Peter has inspired the letter in one form or another, but that those who valued him or his memory are the ones who have written it.[110] There is nothing in the work that demands it was written in the Flavian period (i.e., references to historical situations that only occurred then); one's decision is a matter of theological conviction and a historical weighing of the material laid out above.

3.3 OUTLINE

During the time when 1 Peter was viewed primarily as a liturgy or baptismal homily, there were a variety of attempts to argue that it was a composite work and that therefore the letter structure was secondary. Such positions are rarely argued in

---

107. Serving as an amanuensis was skilled work; it was not something that every schoolboy could have done even in an age in which only a small proportion of the population went to school. One would make one's own ink, prepare reeds to be proper styluses, and keep papyrus in writable condition. Often one needed to know a type of shorthand so as to be able to keep up with dictation. And of course one needed a clear, even, small handwriting, which even educated people often lacked. Nowhere does the New Testament indicate that Silas/Silvanus had such training, although neither does it indicate that he had a different training.

108. While some point to the shepherd imagery of 2:25 and 5:2 as pointing to Peter, or the use the Hebrew Scriptures (in which the author is clearly steeped), or similar data, such arguments, while showing that the content is not inconsistent with what is known about Simon Peter, are not strong enough to prove that he did write it. And they can cut both ways, for, in 5:1 the author refers to himself, not as an apostle (as in 1:1), but as an elder; furthermore, the author does not quote or allude to the teaching of Jesus, unlike, for

example, James. Nor is Simon Peter said by the New Testament to have been steeped in the Hebrew Scriptures, as Paul is said to have been because his study in Jerusalem. And of course shepherd imagery is connected with Simon Peter in John, which is probably a late first-century work and which has its own historical debates raging around it. So one can use the content data to distance the letter from Simon Peter as much as to argue that it fits with Simon Peter.

109. It is important to again assert that such a practice was as common and acceptable then as it is now. Indeed now, even though a higher percentage of the population is literate, even quite literate but busy individuals, such as John Michael Talbot, use ghostwriters to write at least significant parts of some of their works.

110. In that case it would bear the same relationship to Peter that Mark is said to bear, and one could even posit that Silvanus was the one who wrote it (through an amanuensis) in Peter's name. But that would just be another version of the type of theory that conveniently gives one closure using the names mentioned in the letter.

contemporary scholarship, for the stress today is on the unitary theology and thematic unity of the letter, even if it may draw from all sorts of preexisting traditions and material. Thus, the structure of 1 Peter is viewed as relatively clear, at least on the micro level,[111] although on the macro level there are debates as to whether 1 Pet 2:11–4:11 is a separate section from 4:12–5:11 or whether they are two major subsections of a single unit.[112]

It is clear that 1 Pet 1:1–2 and 5:12–14 form the letter salutation and ending respectively, structured like Pauline salutations and endings. The letter body opening is formed by the extended thanksgiving, 1:3–12, the implications of which are taken up in 1:13–2:3 and 2:4–10, which together make up the first major section of the letter. While 2:11–5:11 forms the second major section, it subdivides into 2:11–4:11, which in turn has three parts (2:11–3:12; 3:13–4:6; and 4:7–11), and 4:12–5:11, which also breaks into three parts (4:12–19; 5:1–5; and 5:6–11 [the latter functioning as the letter body closing]). The outline, then, looks something like this:[113]

A. Salutation to God's Chosen People, Who Are Foreigners (1:1–2)
B. Their Situation as God's Chosen People, but Foreigners (1:3–2:10)
   1. Thanksgiving to God for rebirth and secure position (1:3–12)
   2. Hope and holy lifestyle (1:13–21)
   3. Rebirth into a new family through the good news (1:22–25)
   4. Growth as children (2:1–3)
   5. Election as God's people and household (2:4–10)
C. Living as Foreigners in a Hostile Society (2:11–5:11)
   1. God's people suffering for living honorably (2:11–4:11)
      a. The maintenance of honorable conduct within the structures of this age (2:11–3:12)
         i. Introduction: Resident aliens and foreigners are to maintain honorable conduct (2:11–12)
         ii. Honorable conduct in the civic realm (2:13–17)
         iii. Honorable conduct in the household realm: slaves (2:18–25)
         iv. Honorable conduct in the household realm: wives and husbands (3:1–7)
         v. Concluding exhortation on honorable conduct (3:8–12)
      b. Responding to hostility (3:13–4:6)
         i. Doing right despite suffering (3:13–17)

---

111. Elliott, *1 Peter* (AB), 68–80, has an exhaustive list of rhetorical and discourse features that mark out the smaller units of the letter.

112. Feldmeier, *First Letter of Peter*, 17–23, argues cogently for the unity of 1 Pet 2:11–5:11, with two major subunits, which this author has come to prefer to his own outline (Davids, *1 Peter*, 28–29).

113. This outline has been influenced by Elliott, *1 Peter* (AB), 82–83, who has done an excellent job of identifying the discourse units and the sociological logic, and Feldmeier, *First Letter of Peter*, 17–23, and especially p. 22, who brings out the macro structure and the underlying theological argument. It is a step forward in detail from Davids, *1 Peter*, 28–29.

   ii. Example of the Anointed One's suffering and vindication
       (3:18–22)
   iii. Following the example of the Anointed One (4:1–6)
  c. Community solidarity in troubled times (4:7–11)
 2. Responding to and reframing suffering (4:12–5:11)
   a. Reframing suffering positively (4:12–19)
   b. Community unity in the face of suffering (5:1–5)
   c. Summary on the response to and reframing of suffering (5:6–11)
D. Letter Ending (5:12–14)

3.4 THEMATIC AND RHETORICAL COMMENTARY

If the structure is as presented above, what is being communicated with that structure? What is the flow of the argument in 1 Peter? There are three aspects to this:
the flow of the argument itself within its social context, the rhetorical structures
used to communicate the content, and the theology being communicated through
the argument. We will address all three in this section, although we will draw the
theological material together in the next section.

At the outset we should note that 1 Peter is a paraenetic letter in that it is trying
to communicate to the addressees how to behave in the context in which they find
themselves. Thus we will find a number of ethical lists and exhortations. To that
extent it is deliberative rhetoric, calling for a decision. But 1 Peter is more than that,
for our author needs to reframe the situation in which the readers find themselves
so that the readers view it as honorable even though the culture around them calls
it shameful. To that extent it is epideictic rhetoric, demonstrating what is honorable
and good. Both of these features will be important as we move through the letter.

3.4.1 Salutation to God's Chosen People, Who Are Foreigners (1:1–2)

The letter begins with the identification of the author just as Paul identifies himself
in 2 Corinthians, Ephesians, Colossians, and 1 and 2 Timothy: "Peter, an official
delegate of Jesus the Anointed One." The readers are familiar enough with this Peter
to recognize the writer by his nickname (Peter) and title. He does not expand on the
title, for at no place in this letter is he defending himself or his ministry.[114] The letter
will focus on Peter's message to the implied readers, not the person of Peter himself.

The implied readers are described as "resident aliens of the Diaspora" living in five
Roman provinces in Asia Minor that our author names. This was the literal situation of the Jewish Diaspora after the Assyrian and Babylonian armies forced the exile

---

114. As, for example, Paul sometimes does. In 2 Corinthians Paul
strongly defends himself, but as there is a lot of relief in the first
part of the letter concerning what had been a tense situation with
the Corinthian church, he does not do so in the first verse, as he

sometimes does in other letters (Rom 1:1; Gal 1:1; or even 1 Cor 1:1).
He also does so in chapters 10–13, which may have been written
after further news came from Corinth or may be a second letter. The
tone of this defensive section is quite different from chapters 1–9.

of Israelites from Palestine: they were exiled from their native land where they were citizens and forced to live as immigrants or resident aliens in foreign lands. But in the New Testament this term is used only in 1 Peter (here and 2:11) and Heb 11:13, where it is clearly used metaphorically. In the LXX it appears in a literal sense for Abraham in Gen 23:4 and in a metaphorical sense in Ps 38:13 (which may borrow from Gen 23:4; Eng. Ps 39:12). Thus here in 1 Peter the imagery of the resident aliens of the exile of Israel seems called upon to picture one conscious aspect of the situation of these readers.

This is confirmed when we jump to the end of the letter, where the author identifies his location by means of this greeting: "she who is co-elect with you in Babylon"; this probably refers to a church, although one cannot rule out the possibility of "she" being Peter's wife.[115] Greetings come from those around the author, and the location is Babylon, which, as in Revelation (e.g., chapters 17 and 18), is almost certainly a term for Rome. Rome, like Babylon, is the capital of an empire that opposes and oppresses "Israel," and it is there that the author is a resident alien, an exile, just as the readers feel that their status has become in the provinces in which they live. Thus we have a concept that rhetorically brackets the letter: a people who do not belong, a people living in exile.

There is a second part to the salutation's description of the implied readers. They are "chosen" or "elect" (just as "she" in 5:13 is "co-elect"). This is a term of privilege, depending on who has chosen one for what. Our author surely reads the term in the light of God's choosing Abraham and Israel, as is clear in 2:9, where he again uses the term to introduce the language of Exod 19:6. That the choosing is divine is stated in 1:2, where all three members of what would later be called the Trinity are mentioned: this choosing is according to God the Father's foreknowledge or determination (the word has both meanings); it is in the Spirit's sanctification (holiness will be a major theme of the letter); it is for obedience to Jesus the Anointed One, since he is the king. Although Jesus may be the reigning king now, he is the king who has purified or set the implied readers apart with his death (sprinkled blood was the blood of a sacrificial victim used either to set something apart as holy [Exod 29:21; Lev 8:11; Num 19:4] or to purify something that has become defiled [Lev 4:6, 17; 5:9; 14:27, 51; 16:14–15, 19]; the former is more likely).[116] We already get intimations of the fact that this king has suffered and that these people have benefitted from that suffering.

It is these people—who are not at home where they live and thus feel like Israel in exile, and who are nevertheless privileged, chosen, set apart as holy by the triune God—who are addressed with the greeting used by Paul and other followers of Jesus: "grace" and "peace." The rest of the letter will unpack the tension and the privilege implied in these first two verses.

---

115. See the discussion in Davids, *1 Peter*, 201–2.

116. The only other New Testament book using the image is Hebrews, where blood is sprinkled in a covenant-making process in 9:19, 21, which appears to be more in the "setting apart as holy" meaning, so also perhaps the Passover reference in Heb 11:28 and 12:24, the latter being explicitly covenantal. But both meanings of the term do appear in Hebrews, for 9:18 speaks of covenantal inauguration, while 9:22 interprets the actions as "forgiveness of sins" and purification.

3.4.2 Their Situation as God's Chosen People, but Foreigners (1:3 – 2:10)

Before the readers can respond to their situation, they first need to recognize it, and part of this recognition is understanding their theological and particularly their eschatological standing. This section positions the readers within the divine narrative, starting not at the point of creation, which is assumed, but at the point of the choice of Israel and continuing up until the reign of Jesus the Anointed One on earth. The narrative is assumed more than told, and the readers are related to its various parts in a rhetorical rather than a chronological order.

3.4.2.1 Thanksgiving to God for Rebirth and Secure Position (1:3 – 12)

God is blessed for his favorable actions toward the readers as the divine patron.[117] The divinity who is blessed is identified as "the God and Father of our Lord Jesus the Anointed One." This identifies the readers as those who, like the writer, recognize Jesus of Nazareth as Lord and, in continuity with the hopes of some Jews for a ruling Messiah (Anointed King), recognize Jesus as God's Anointed One. God is conversely identified as that God who was Jesus' God and whom Jesus referred to as Father. The two are bound closely together in a reciprocal relationship.

This God is most favorable toward the readers, seen especially in their new birth, which is, of course, why they are now resident aliens in the lands in which they were originally citizens, for they have now been born into a new race and family. As birth is normally hopeful, this one is as well, but the hope is founded not just in the fact that *they* are alive (which would be true of birth in general), but in the fact that Jesus the Anointed One is alive, having been raised from the dead. This hope is not just hope in hope or hope in birth, but hope in an "inheritance" — not in the sense of something that would belong to them when the owner died, but in the sense of inheritance as a part in the family business or farm (which picks up on the family inheritance that Israel was promised and received), which a son or daughter received upon reaching adulthood.

This inheritance metaphor explains the delay in receiving the blessings they expected from their submission to God's rule in Jesus. Unlike their inheritances in this age, which they might well be in danger of losing, this inheritance will always be there in unspoiled[118] condition (the three terms are alliterative, *aphtharton* and *amianton* and *amaranton*, rare words in the New Testament). This, of course, is the nature of God's sphere (i.e., heaven), where the inheritance is being kept as one might keep something safe in a bank. This description could mean, of course,

---

117. A thanksgiving to a god or the gods was a normal part of a Greek letter, but in the Pauline letters in general, and here in 1 Peter, the thanksgiving has been lengthened considerably, forming the body opening of the letter and introducing a number of its major themes.

118. The term *amiantos* (ἀμίαντος) has two meanings, "undefiled" and "pure" in the religious and moral sense (BDAG, 54). The this-age inheritance could be both defiled religiously and morally impure, but not the inheritance in the coming age.

that they would need to leave this world and enter God's sphere to enjoy their inheritance, but our author makes it clear that this is not the case. This heavenly protection of their inheritance is matched by an earthly protection of the addressees themselves.[119]

The instrument of their protection is God's "power," the means is their commitment or faithfulness, and the goal is a future salvation or deliverance (in their present state, they live under threat, and thus they are in need of such a salvation or deliverance). It is not that this deliverance has no shape or plan. After all, the ruler who is to set the world to rights has already been mentioned. So this salvation is already prepared, "waiting to be unveiled in the last time." This means that the implied readers may be experiencing being immigrants/resident aliens under threat, but they are in fact God's favored ones, having enormous wealth and honor status. The only problem remaining is that their reality has yet to be unveiled before the wider world.

While the addressees are being protected in the present and thus are experiencing situations from which they need protection, they can already rejoice in the coming age. This was a common theme of the first-century Jesus movement, found in three New Testament books:

Romans 5	1 Peter 1	James 1
[3]And not only that, but we also boast in our sufferings, knowing that suffering produces endurance, and endurance produces character, and character produces hope, [5]and hope does not disappoint us, because God's love has been poured into our hearts through the Holy Spirit that has been given to us. (NRSV)	[6]In this you rejoice, even if now for a little while you have had to suffer *various trials*, [7]so that *the genuineness of your faith* — being more precious than gold that, though perishable, is tested by fire — may be found to result in praise and glory and honor when Jesus Christ is revealed. (NRSV)	[2]My brothers and sisters, whenever you face *trials of any kind*, consider it nothing but joy, [3]because you know that *the testing of your faith* produces endurance; [4]and let endurance have its full effect, so that you may be mature and complete, lacking in nothing. (NRSV)

Table 4: Joy in Suffering

It is clear that 1 Peter is closer to James than to Romans (two expressions in James and 1 Peter that are identical in Greek are in italics above), although the basic underlying thought in all three is the same, even if each has a different application.

---

119. While the author of 1 Peter may have thought of heaven and earth in terms of up and down and described the universe as an expanse of some type in which were suspended the heavenly bodies (with God above that expanse), in contemporary speech we should think of "heaven" and "earth" language in terms of God's sphere or dimension and that of the world or universe as we know it. See N. T. Wright, *Simply Christian* (New York: HarperOne, 2006), 58–66.

Our author talks about rejoicing even if one is "made sorrowful" or "grieved" by trials. The reason for rejoicing is that trials show that one's commitment is genuine (just as gold was in that period determined to be genuine by being melted) and will result in the believer's receiving the highest goods of the first-century world, that is, praise, glory, and honor, when Jesus the Anointed One is revealed to the world. Thus there is enlightened self-interest, so to speak, in enduring suffering (i.e., persecution), and if the readers take this perspective, they will rejoice, even while they recognize that the trials are painful (there is no masochism or denial in 1 Peter, nor anywhere in the New Testament).

Our author then expands on the idea of the revelation of Jesus. In the New Testament in general, Jesus not only already exists, but also already rules, for he is "seated at the right hand of the Father." Thus his position or rule needs to be "revealed," not established. The addressees have never laid eyes on Jesus—yet they love him (a term that indicates positive action more than emotive feeling) and are committed to him (1:8). They also rejoice, for they view themselves as already in the process of receiving the end result of their commitment to Jesus, namely, the deliverance or salvation of their selves (1:9).[120]

The first-century followers of Jesus had to contend with the charge that theirs was a new religion; our author immediately sets the expectation of salvation or deliverance into an ancient context, that of the ancient Hebrew prophets (1:10–12). We do not know what prophecies of national deliverance or salvation our author may be thinking about, but whatever those prophecies were, they have turned out to be about the divine favor that has been showed to these addressees. In the second of four references to a divine Spirit, he asserts that it was the "Spirit of the Anointed One" or "the Spirit of the Messiah" that was in the prophets, testifying to "the sufferings of the Anointed One and his subsequent glories (or honor)," that is, the death and resurrection of Jesus, referred to earlier in this chapter.

The prophets, naturally, wanted to know the time and context of the fulfillment of their prophecies. What was revealed to them was that they were not prophesying about their own period, but were rather serving others, whom 1 Peter identifies (with hindsight) as "you." The "you" is the implied readers, of course, but they are further identified as those who had received the announcement of "these things" by means of those who had announced the good news to them. Thus the prophetic vision of deliverance is now identified with the "good news" of the present. Furthermore, this proclamation of the good news was accomplished by means of the Holy Spirit sent from heaven, from God's sphere. This action of the Spirit is contrasted with the situation of the divine messengers or angels, who presumably live in God's

120. Many translations have "salvation of your souls," but the word translated "soul," ψυχή, psychē, is not being contrasted with the body in this passage, especially since the passage began with a reference to the resurrection of Jesus the Anointed One. Nor are these addressees being threatened with imminent physical death. The salvation or rescue is tied to the "revelation" of Jesus, and so it is tied to the consummation of the about-to-dawn new age. "Lives" would be an appropriate translation, although that might be limited for some readers to physical life, so "selves," the continuing existence of the embodied person, including the resurrection of the embodied person, seems to fit best. See BDAG, 1098–99, for the range of meanings in this word.

sphere and who desire to look into "these things." It is implied, however, that they do not receive that insight, but by virtue of the divinely inspired announcement the addressees have received it.

In one fell swoop, then, Peter has accomplished a number of tasks. First, by identifying the contemporary message of the good news with the ancient prophets of Israel, he has given an ancient pedigree to the present commitment of the readers. This is not a new religion, but the consummation of an ancient one. He also makes Israel's story into their story, the narrative of which will continue in the following chapter.

Second, by referring to the "Spirit of the Anointed One" as inspiring the prophets, he both avoids anachronizing the Holy Spirit as if the prophets were *conscious* of that Spirit as being the "Spirit of the Anointed One" and identifies him with the Spirit inspiring the prophets.

Third, he points out that God was working out a plan in history, for these prophetic references to the Messiah or Anointed One (whichever prophecies they were) include both the suffering and the glorification of that royal person, who in the person of Jesus of Nazareth was relatively contemporary with respect to the addressees.[121]

Fourth, this implies a pattern of suffering and then glory as part of the divine plan, which gives meaning to present suffering.

Finally, this information makes the addressees more privileged than the prophets (after all, they now know the time and circumstances, which the prophets did not, and the prophets served them, not some other people). They are also more privileged than the angels—that is, these addressees have received the good news from messengers empowered by the Holy Spirit himself, while angels only get to wish they could look into "these things." So these suffering people have become an unbelievably privileged people, both in terms of the deliverance they expect to receive at "the revelation" of Jesus and in terms of the message that they have already received of the good news about this deliverance. This is a massive reframing of the existential situation of these readers.

3.4.2.2 Hope and Holy Lifestyle (1:13–21)

Privilege, however, implies responsibility. Using a live metaphor drawn from a man or woman wearing a long garment (e.g., the Greek *himation,* ἱμάτιον) and catching it up in their belt so as to leave the legs free for activity, our author calls for a mental version of such preparation, which will make one sober-minded or self-controlled, that is, mentally disciplined. This discipline is so that one sets one's total expectation, or hope, on the coming eschaton, or, as 1:13 puts it, on the favor that Jesus the Anointed One will bring to them when he is revealed. That is the goal. Eschatology is to determine present behavior, but it takes discipline to live this out in practice.

---

121. Even if one dates 1 Peter at 90 CE, any individual in the community over, roughly, sixty would have been alive during Jesus' ministry in contrast to the prophets who lived and died centuries before Jesus. Of course, if one dates 1 Peter closer to 70 CE, then the same would be true of people in the community who were forty.

What does this discipline look like? They have been reborn into a new family; thus, as "obedient children" they are to conform to that family's values (i.e., those of the *paterfamilias*), not to the values of their pre-rebirth pagan life, which are characterized as "desires." Pagan life, then, is described as a life lived under the control of the human limbic system — that is, desires, drives, and emotions. Reborn life or life in God's family is described as life lived under the control of the human cerebral cortex, so long as that cortex is informed by a vision of the future in which Jesus is revealed as God's reigning king. That would mean that present life would be "holy," a life set apart for the divinity. The nature of that holiness is defined by the character of the divinity to which one is so dedicated — in this case, the God who spoke to Israel in Lev 19:2, which is directly applied to the predominantly Gentile congregations whom 1 Peter addresses.

The author describes the reborn children as addressing God as "Father" (the same God who is also Father of Jesus the Anointed One). But "father" in the ancient world was not so much the one who had emotional contact with the children as the one who was the authority figure in the family, providing identity (one took on his honor status) and provision as well. This Father is indeed an authority, for he "impartially judges [people] according to each one's deeds." Therefore one's way of life during this period of sojourning away from home should be marked by "fear"; this fear is not abject terror, but the fear that a well-disciplined child expressed when he or she says, "I would not dare to ... for Dad would find out." In 1 Peter's world, behavior has consequences — consequences that may or may not be evident during this time of sojourning, but which will certainly become evident when Jesus is "revealed." When one grasps this reality, one uses it to discipline one's life.

Peter again refers to the change from their previous life, but this time rather than use the metaphor of rebirth and family, he uses the metaphor of ransom, such as one might pay for a captive or hostage. Their previous way of life was "empty" or "useless" (1:18, as are the gods of the Gentiles in Lev 17:7; Jer 8:19; 10:15 in the LXX), but it is not as if these addressees had started out right and turned aside into such a way of life: they had *inherited* this way of life from their ancestors, which is one of the indications that this book is addressed primarily to an audience composed of former Gentiles. In tune with the general New Testament teaching about wealth, silver and gold are not viewed as something lasting, but as something subject to decay. Such useless things were not the means of "ransom." Instead, these commodities are contrasted with something valuable, the "blood of the Anointed One," which is mentioned without any defensiveness about the Anointed One's dying; the intended audience accepts Jesus' death and resurrection as an article of their faith.[122]

The image of the blood of a ruler could indicate a ruler who died in battle to gain the release of these people, but that is not our author's intention here, for he

---

122. Achtemeier, *1 Peter*, 126, points out that the grammar is the same as Paul often uses "to indicate an elementary Christian belief in which the author can presume the readers have been instructed."

uses a sacrificial metaphor from the Hebrew Scriptures, that of an unblemished lamb without defect.[123] Our author's main point, however, is not the sacrificial metaphor, but the idea that this sacrifice was part of a divine plan, "known (or chosen) before this age began (i.e., before the world was founded) and revealed at the end of time for your sake." This statement parallels what was said earlier about the prophets, although now we go back before the prophets to before the beginning of the world as we know it. God had a plan, but the open revelation and outworking of that plan were recent, "at the end of time," and for the benefit of the addressees. Again 1 Peter reframes his readers' situation as one that is privileged. He further defines his addressees as those who trust in or are committed to that God who has raised the Anointed One from the dead and has given him glory (honor). The sacrifice was not the last word, just as we will later learn that their suffering is not the last word. The last word is resurrection and honor, and as a result the addressees' trust or commitment and hope are fixed on that God who has already done this for Jesus.

3.4.2.3 Rebirth into a New Family through the Good News (1:22–25)

As a paraenetic letter 1 Peter does not discuss doctrine for its own sake, but in order to make a point relevant to the lives of his readers. They have purified their selves[124] by their obedience to "the truth" (1:22), which is our author's term in this passage for the good news. The good news is the announcement that Jesus is Lord, and so a call to submit to him, to be obedient, goes forth. "Obedience" is a favorite term in 1 Peter, for God foreknew or destined his chosen for obedience (1:2); they are to be obedient children (1:14), and now their lives have been cleansed by obedience to the truth. This obedience has resulted in a purification, which is what one would expect to be the result of a sacrifice. Yet this purification in turn results, not in individual purity, but in community, that is, genuine (unhypocritical) love of one's siblings.

Love of one's siblings was a family virtue in the ancient world, but now it is love for one's siblings in the family of the "reborn." They have been born into a new family, a new people, so they ought to genuinely love these new "natural" (in the sense that they are reborn into the same family) brothers and sisters. The resultant command is to do it, to love one another fervently or constantly from pure hearts (i.e., purified, unhypocritical).

123. Contrary to scholars such as Beare, *First Epistle of Peter*, 106, and Spic, *Les Épitres de Saint Pierre*, 66, this is not a reference to the Passover lamb of Exodus, for the power of God rather than that lamb is what is said to have redeemed Israel from Egypt, and that lamb is never said to be unblemished. Likewise, the lamb of Isaiah 53 is unlikely to be alluded to, since there "lamb" is the only term this passage in 1 Peter has in common with that passage. Where "*unblemished* lamb" is found in the general sacrificial cult of the Hebrew Scriptures, e.g., Exod 29:1; Lev 22:17–25; Num 28–29. The term for "without defect" is not found in the Hebrew Scriptures, but is used in our literature and that related to it (1 Tim 6:14; Jas 1:27; 2 Pet 3:14, where it is also paired with "without blemish").

124. As noted above, the term *psychē* is often translated "soul," but in a passage like this, where there is no contrast with the body stated or implied, it means "self" or "life," the whole of the person.

This reference to the new family again brings up the basis for their presence in that family, with 1 Peter giving the cause as their having been born anew. Their original birth was from perishable sperm[125] (*spora*, σπορά; just as gold and silver are perishable commodities in the previous paragraph), but their new birth is from imperishable sperm — that is, by means of the good news, God's living, life-giving, and enduring word.[126] This is supported by a quotation of Isa 40:6b–8 from the Greek version of the Hebrew Scriptures; the emphasis in the use of this quotation[127] is on human perishability versus the enduring nature of the divine word. This reference to the enduring good news is part of the author's overall strategy — the addressees have the valuable, enduring word, while their persecutors and society in general are among those who are perishable.

3.4.2.4 Growth as Children (2:1–3)

The paraenetic point of loving one another is repeated negatively: they have gotten rid of[128] community-destroying vices, all types of evil, all types of deceit or underhandedness, insincerity, envy, and all types of slander. These are all vices that make the community a place where one cannot trust the intentions and words of other members, and so they are repeatedly critiqued in the New Testament. First Peter itself refers to deceit no less than three times (2:1, 22; 3:10). The point is that these vices are part of the former way of life — the "old birth," to coin a phrase. These addressees are reborn, so like newborn babies, they are to "long for" pure[129] metaphorical[130] milk.

The goal of this "milk" is, as that of literal milk with babies, growth, but here the growth is "unto salvation" in keeping with 1 Peter's frequent emphasis on salvation or deliverance as future, as something that will happen when Jesus is revealed, not as something present (which the suffering of the addressees would make clear was not the case). Our author gives a reason for his imperative about desiring metaphorical milk with an allusion to Ps 34:8, introduced by "since." The tasting metaphor in the psalm is the link. They have tasted (in their conversion) that the Lord is good, so they should desire more.

---

125. The Greek term is "seed," for in the ancient world reproduction was viewed as a process in which the man sowed "seed" in the woman's "field," thus the resultant child continued the father's line. There was no concept that the woman contributed an egg, or half the genes, to the resultant fetus. However, given that "seed" is archaic in contemporary English when one means semen, and that our term for the active part of semen is "sperm," this is an appropriate translation in contemporary English.

126. Notice that this differs from the Johannine use of "word" for the preincarnate existence of Jesus (John never calls him "the word" after "the word" "becomes flesh" in John 1:14). Here the word is not Jesus, but the word God speaks, the good news.

127. The use of the passage varies, for "in the Isaianic context it refers to the destruction of Israel under the judgment of God as contrasted to the word of redemption God is now speaking" (Davids, *1 Peter*, 79), while in Jas 1:10–11 it is used to stress the transitory

nature of the wealthy. Here the general perishability of humanity is contrasted with "the Lord's word." That this quotation basically conforms to the LXX and differs from the Masoretic Text is evidence that our author is reading the Hebrew Scriptures in Greek.

128. We are reading the participle, not as imperative, but as circumstantial, preceding the imperative that is the main verb. See the discussion in Davids, *1 Peter*, 79–80.

129. There is a play on words here, for *dolos*, δόλος, "deceit," has been given up and in its place is milk that is *adolos*, ἄδολος, "pure," "without adulteration."

130. This term (*logikos*, λογικός) is often translated "spiritual," and in some contexts could be translated "reasonable," but here it is spiritual as opposed to literal, not spiritual in the sense of "of the spirit" (*pneumatikos*, πνευματικός), so our normal term would be "metaphorical," as BDAG, 598, points out.

3.4.2.5 Election as God's People and Household (2:4–10)

Our author shifts the image from family to temple. The main concept of the meta-phor will be *God's people* being built into a temple, but first he sets up the situation. He has mentioned that the Lord is gracious or good, and it is to this good Lord that they are coming in their conversion, and this is like coming to the site of the build-ing of God's temple (as will become clear later). Jesus is the living stone that human beings rejected, but who in God's view is chosen (as these addressees are chosen) and precious. The parallel with the situation of the readers is obvious.

The image shifts from coming to a temple to becoming part of the temple. They are also themselves as living stones (because they have come to *the* living stone, their status coming from his), as it were, being built[131] into a "spiritual house," a new or renewed temple.[132] But then there is another shift in the imag-ery, for they become "a holy priesthood" offering spiritual sacrifices (rather than animal sacrifices or incense) by means of Jesus the Anointed One (rather than on their own) to God, which sacrifices are acceptable (a sacrificial term also found in Rom 15:16).

Our author then wants to support these assertions from the Hebrew Scrip-tures, using a catena of Scriptures that appear to have been commonly used *testi-monia* in the early Jesus movement: Isa 28:16 (also in Rom 9:33 and alluded to in Eph 2:20), Ps 118:22–23 (also in Matt 21:42; Acts 4:11), and Isa 8:14–15 (also in Rom 9:33).

Hebrew Scriptures	1 Peter	Romans	Others uses
Isa 28:16 therefore thus says the Lord GOD, See, I am laying in Zion a founda-tion stone, a tested stone, a precious cornerstone, a sure foundation: "One who trusts will not panic."	2:6 For it stands in scripture: "See, I am laying in Zion a stone, a cornerstone chosen and pre-cious; and whoever believes in him will not be put to shame."	9:33 as it is written, *"See, I am laying in Zion a stone* that will make people stumble, a rock that will make them fall, and whoever believes in him will not be put to shame."	Eph 2:20 built upon the foundation of the apostles and prophets, with Christ Jesus himself as *the cornerstone*.

131. The main verb can be read as either indicative ("you are being built") or imperative ("let yourselves be built," NRSV). Lauri Thurén (*The Rhetorical Strategy of 1 Peter* [Åbo: Åbo Academy Press, 1990], 21) argues that there is deliberate ambiguity as part of 1 Peter's rhetorical strategy. While Thurén's assertion is possible, it is a bit more likely that the indicative is intended. See Jobes, *1 Peter*, 156, who lays out the options and the literature favoring each one.

132. While the language could indicate "a spiritual household [*oikos*]," the fact that the New Testament thinks of the community of Jesus' followers as a new temple (e.g., in the teaching of Jesus in Mark 14:58; 15:29; in Paul, 1 Cor 3:16–17; 2 Cor 6:16; and esp. Eph 2:19–22; see also Rev 3:12; 11:1), as did the writers of the Dead Sea Scrolls (4QFlor 1.1–7; 1QS 5.5–7; 8.4–10), points to *oikos* meaning "temple" in this context. Note also that as well in the LXX, the verb found here when followed by "house" always refers to the building of the temple,

Psalm 118:22 The stone that the builders rejected has become the chief cornerstone. ²³ This is the LORD's doing; it is marvelous in our eyes.	2:7 To you then who believe, he is precious; but for those who do not believe, "The stone that the builders rejected has become the very head of the corner,"		Matt 21:42 Jesus said to them, "Have you never read in the scriptures: 'The stone that the builders rejected has become the cornerstone; this was the Lord's doing, and it is amazing in our eyes'?
Isa 8:14 He will become a sanctuary, *a stone one strikes against*; for both houses of Israel he will become *a rock one stumbles over* — a trap and a snare for the inhabitants of Jerusalem. ¹⁵And many among them shall stumble; they shall fall and be broken; they shall be snared and taken.	2:8 and "A stone that makes them stumble, and a rock that makes them fall." They stumble because they disobey the word, as they were destined to do.	9:33 as it is written, "See, I am laying in Zion a stone that will make people stumble, a rock that will make them fall, and whoever believes in him will not be put to shame."	

Table 5: Cornerstone *Testimonia* (all quotations NRSV)

It appears that the Isaiah quotations come from a *testimonia* source that had already merged and edited them, a source that our author and Paul had in common,[133] while the Psalm 118 quotation is identical to what we know from the LXX, although given that it is shared with Matthew and Acts, this may also have been a *testamonium*.

The key point for both Paul and 1 Peter in their use of Isa 28 is that God is refounding Zion on a "stone" that they identify as Jesus and that those committing to or trusting in this stone will not suffer shame. The second part of this prophecy

---

133. The Isa 28 citation agrees with an edited version of the LXX and differs from the Hebrew, while the Isa 8 passage appears closer to the Hebrew, but the citation only uses a few words from the passage. Since they are combined in Romans, it is likely that both authors shared a common Greek source that had already mined the passages.

is still future for 1 Peter, for his addressees are presently suffering shame, although he has argued that ultimately they will experience honor.

First Peter uses the Psalm 118 passage to give prophetic backing to the idea that Jesus was rejected before he was exalted, an experience that parallels what our author says will be the experience of his readers. The Isa 28 passage explains why Jesus was rejected, that he was, so to speak, that type of a rock for some people. Our author explains that those who "stumbled" over Jesus refused to obey the word (again, the good news is something to be obeyed, for it commands submission to Jesus as Lord). Then he adds that this was not an unexpected event, for "they were also destined" or "they were also appointed" to do this. This is not an unusual idea in the New Testament (cf. 2 Pet 2:9, 12, 17; as well as Rom 9:14–24). It does not explain who has destined or appointed them to do this, of course, although we could (probably accurately) guess that this must be God. And it does not tell us why God so destined them, whether it was his own inscrutable decision or whether it was due to something that he anticipated (since it is enshrined in prophecy) in their lives. But such issues are not our author's interest.

The structure of this passage is A B A B in that it starts with stone/temple imagery, with both Jesus and the implied readers being "living stones," and then shifts to priests offering sacrifices in the temple. Then come the Scriptures that have to do with stones, and now Scriptures that have to do with priesthood. These reborn readers, Gentile as well as Jew, are the fulfillment of prophecies given to Israel:

Exodus 19:5–6	1 Peter 2:9	Isaiah 43:20–21
"And now … you will be my own people more than any other nation; for the whole earth is mine, but you will be my *royal priesthood* and *holy nation.*" These are the words you will say to the children of Israel.	But you are a <u>chosen race</u>, a *royal priesthood*, a *holy nation*, <u>God's own people,</u> in order <u>that you may proclaim the mighty acts</u> of him who called you out of darkness into his marvelous light. (NRSV)	And the beasts of the field will bless me … because I have given water in the wilderness and rivers in the desert to give drink to my <u>chosen people, my people whom I have taken as my own that they might recount my glorious deeds.</u>

Table 6: The Sources of 1 Peter 2:9

The underlining shows how our author has skillfully woven the passages from the Greek version of the Hebrew Scriptures together, first with an expression from Isa 43, then with two expressions from Exodus 19, then with two phrases from Isa 43.[134] The point is that the reborn people are the chosen people, heirs of the promises

---

134. The verbal closeness of the expressions becomes much clearer in Greek: for instance, in the rare word used in 1 Peter (*peripoiēsin* περιποίησιν, translated as "God's own") that is found in its verbal form in Isa 43 (translated as "whom I have taken as my own"). The grammar of the quotations has been adapted to the new grammatical context in 1 Peter.

and purposes of God that he spoke to Israel through Moses and Isaiah. What our author adds is the designation of God as "the one who has called you out of darkness into his wonderful light." That is the experience of the reborn people: they were once in pagan darkness and now are experiencing God's light. But it is also their calling, for they are to proclaim, not so much what has happened to them, but the virtues of this God.

Our author closes this first part of the letter with allusions to Hosea 1. Hosea 1:6–7 and 9–10 refer respectively to the kingdom of Israel as those not receiving mercy and the kingdom of Judah as those who will, and to Israel as not being God's people and then to God's future calling them his people. But the topic in 1 Peter is not ancient Israel. Phrases from the Greek translation of Hosea 1 are woven in here to describe the experience of the letter's addressees: they were once (as Greco-Roman polytheists) no people of God, but now (having committed themselves to Jesus) they are; they once received no mercy from God, but now they do. Their life may be socially painful in terms of the society around them, but they are in fact in a happy condition when viewed from our author's perspective.

3.4.3 Living as Foreigners in a Hostile Society (2:11 – 5:11)

This once–now contrast raises the question as to how they are to get on with the society around them. How can they minimize the inevitable conflict? How can they deal with the conflict when it comes? These questions dominate the second half of this letter's body, which structurally falls into two parts: the first, longer part (2:11–4:11) deals with the issue of suffering and its minimization; the second, shorter part (4:12–5:11) is a more direct reframing of the suffering, serving as something of a letter body ending and a rhetorical *peroratio*.

3.4.3.1 God's People Suffering for Living Honorably (2:11 – 4:11)

The problem the addressees are facing is that despite living upright lives as the people of God (which he has just discussed) and indeed because of it, they are facing slander and other forms of persecution. Therefore it is necessary for him to deal with some of the practical problems involved and help his readers to come to terms with the situation. This is handled in two different discussions: (1) how to deal with the structures of this age, and (2) how to deal with suffering itself.

3.4.3.1.1 The Maintenance of Honorable Conduct within the Structures of This Age (2:11 – 3:12)

If one has been reborn and is now a member of God's people, a people unlike the society in which they live, since they "march to the tune of a different Drummer," there are bound to be tensions, which is precisely what the addressees have been experiencing. However, these tensions do not need to be exacerbated by the behavior of the addressees. The New Testament in general and 1 Peter in particular do not advocate rebellion against the structures of this age. They do, however, advocate uncompromising living as members of God's people. Our author argues that one can do that in a way that reduces tensions to a minimum.

3.4.3.1.1.1 Introduction: Resident Aliens and Foreigners Are to Maintain Honorable Conduct (2:11–12)

With two verses that serve as a type of transition, picking up the themes of the previous section and introducing some of the themes of the present section, our author begins his paraenetic appeal with a typical noun of address, "Beloved" (which will also appear in 4:12 and thus marks off 2:11–4:11 as a section of the letter).[135] He again refers to his addressees as "foreigners and immigrants," as he did in 1:1. However, now he is not going to write about the cause of their being resident aliens/immigrants in the place where most of them were born, but about their behavior as resident aliens in a country that is not yet their own:[136] they are to avoid or keep away from "physical desires" (or "fleshly desires"), because these make war against their selves or lives. As in Jas 1:13–15 and as will be discussed in 2 Pet 1:4, the human drives are constantly threatening to take over the individual and control their lives, thereby destroying it.

The problem, of course, is that since these drives are within, being natural drives built into the human brain, in one sense they cannot be avoided.[137] One more avoids their control and domination than their existence. Furthermore, in 1 Peter as in James (1:13–15 paired with 4:7), it seems that the internal desires are in one way or another influenced by the external power of evil, for this whole larger section of 1 Peter is bracketed by the war of desire against the individual, on the one hand, and the devil seeking to devour (1 Pet 5:8), on the other.

The positive side of avoiding or keeping away from desire is for one to conduct oneself honorably among the various peoples within whom one lives. Honor, the result of honorable conduct, was highly prized in the Mediterranean world; it was worth more than money or life itself. But who defines honorable conduct? First Peter admits that the people among whom they live are maligning them, calling them evildoers for that very conduct. But that is the first word, not the last word, for when the people around them see their honorable deeds (honorable in the sight of God, not in their sight), they will glorify or give honor to God when he comes to judge (i.e., in "the day of visitation"), an allusion to Isa 10:3 and elsewhere in the LXX

---

135. It will also appear with this function four times in 2 Peter 3 (and twice with other functions in 2 Peter), making one of the few commonalities between 1 and 2 Peter.

136. We say "not yet," for while the immigrants of this world may remain in their liminal situation for generations and never expect to "take over" from the native population, 1 Peter has already told us in chapter 1 that there is a king, the leader of this immigrant people, who is going to be revealed to all and then his people will reign with him. The Christian hope is not to be removed from this world, but to take it over under the reign of Jesus when he comes to

renew it and set up right government. Thus their situation is a "not yet" but not "never."

137. The Talmud would later make this clear, for while the hunger drive, for example, can be behind overeating (the classical sin of gluttony), stealing food from others, hoarding, and similar vices, it is also the force that is behind planting a field (and other forms of agriculture), preparing a healthy meal, and eating appropriately to sustain one's life. In that sense these desires can even be called "good," according to the rabbis.

where that the expression is used.[138] The focus of the passage is on the honor that accrues to God, not that these suffering readers will be justified and appropriately rewarded,[139] although that is an implication of the passage in its wider context.[140]

The chief characteristic of their good deeds will be living out their appropriate roles in society, i.e., not rebelling against them, expressed in the term "accept the authority of" or "submit to" (hypotassō, ὑποτάσσω), which carries the sense of taking one's appropriate role in society by living within its authority structures.

3.4.3.1.1.2 Honorable Conduct in the Civic Realm (2:13–17)

One is to accept the authority of "every human governance system."[141] All systems of governance of this age, democratic or autocratic,[142] are human, not divine, so there certainly could be a question about the degree to which those who are resident aliens/immigrants in this age and acknowledge someone as Lord, as the Anointed One, their ruler, should accept the authority of or in any way be subject to those non-Jesus systems of governance. One should be a loyal subject (to the extent consistent with loyalty to Jesus as Lord), not because they have intrinsic authority, but "on account of the Lord," that is, because it is the will of the real government to whom one owes one's ultimate allegiance.[143]

It is the true Lord's will that one accept the authority of the "king." Since none of the provinces to which our author was writing had a king at this time and since our author sees himself as living "in Babylon," "king" (basileus, βασιλεύς) probably refers to the reigning Roman emperor, whoever he was.[144] He is described as "being in authority,"[145] since every other official in the Roman empire held authority under the emperor or the senate (which in practice was not distinguished from the emperor by non-Romans). It is also the Lord's will that one accept the authority of governors (in the Roman system, legates, proconsuls, propraetors, procurators, etc.) who were sent by the emperor and/or the senate to maintain the good order of the empire.

---

138. In the New Testament the expression occurs only in Luke 19:44, with a related expression appearing in Luke 1:68. In the LXX similar expressions appear not only in Isa 10:3, but also in Gen 50:24; Job 10:12; Jer 11:23; and Wis 3:7.

139. While "judgment" tends to be negative in modern speech, in the ancient world when a ruler held a "visitation" (i.e., sat in judgment upon a visit), he both punished those deserving such (often corrupt officials and their lackeys) and rewarded his faithful citizens. Only the first group would look ahead to this visitation in fear; the second group would be excited about it.

140. While the rule of God benefits the loyal subject (i.e., believer), it is not about the subjects, but about the king. Here 1 Peter keeps his focus on the king.

141. Or "every human creation"; the Greek word for "creation" (ktisis, κτίσις) sometimes means "system of established authority that is the result of some founding action" (BDAG, 573.3).

142. At this point in time the Roman Empire was technically a republic, the Senate of which had elected the emperor. Even if in reality the emperor and the army (especially the Praetorian Guard) had the ultimate power, the Senate as a whole and certain Senators in particular continued to enjoy significant power. In the provinces where the addressees lived, the governor would be either an imperial or a senatorial appointee, although there would often be local assemblies, councils, and magistrates who served under (or perhaps virtually alongside) the governor. Thus local officials, some of them elected, had a voice, often an influential voice, especially in local affairs, even if it was not the ultimate voice.

143. Thus the fact that in a context where the patriotic affirmation "Caesar is lord" was an indication of one's loyalty to the Roman Empire, to use the term "Lord" only for Jesus and to refer to the emperor as a "king" (who were often clients under the Roman emperor) is a political statement.

144. Depending on one's dating of the letter, this would have been either Nero, the last of Julio-Claudian emperors, or one of the three Flavian emperors who succeeded the Julio-Claudian line.

145. Paul uses this term in combination with the term for "authorities" as a term for "governing authorities" in Rom 13:1, the Pauline parallel to this passage.

Of particular interest to both Paul in Rom 13:3 and Peter here in 1 Peter are the functions of meting out justice on those doing evil and praising those doing good — the two sides of judgment that any good ruler practiced. But it is not because they have intrinsic authority over the believer that he or she is to accept such praise (from 1 Peter's point of view any blame a follower of Jesus receives should be undeserved, as will become clear), but because it is God's will that by doing good the believer may silence the ignorance of foolish people who accuse the followers of Jesus of all sorts of unjust things.[146] Followers of Jesus are in fact free, a concept Paul uses to describe the freedom they have from the rules embodied in the Torah and specifically the boundary markers of Judaism such as circumcision (Gal 5:1, 13 – 15).

Here our author uses the freedom of believers to describe the relationship of followers of Jesus to the states (and presumably other social structures that he will mention) of this age. Believers are free, and only accept the authority of those structures because it is the will of their Lord. Yet, argues 1 Peter, they are not to use this freedom as a stratagem for concealing evil. Instead, they must realize that while free from the structures of this age, they are still God's slaves, which could mean either that they are to follow his will, which is to accept the authority of human government (so long as it does not conflict with his instructions), or that they are his representatives, much as the emperor's slaves were his representatives and thus should represent him well. After all, much of what we call evil is defined similarly by both God and human governments (e.g., murder, theft, and similar vices).

Our author sums up his teaching so far. How does one minimize conflict with the ruler? Show respect (or honor) to everyone, high and low, citizen or foreigner, follower of Jesus or not. Love the family of believers.[147] This means to show loyalty and support to fellow citizens of the people of God, fellow members of God's family. One is to fear (*phobeō*) God (i.e., "have a profound measure of respect for, with special reference to fear of offending").[148] He is the true ruler with ultimate authority. And, naturally, one should show respect to the emperor. He is, of course, one of "everyone."

---

146. Often these were half truths, such as the accusation recorded about Paul that he taught that there was another king than the emperor (Acts 17:7) or that he was slandering the gods (Acts 19:26 – 27). Judging from Paul's (and the church's) claim that Jesus is Lord (e.g., Rom 10:9 – 10) and his frequent statement that Jesus was the Anointed One, Paul did indeed teach that there was another king, and Rom 13 shows that he believes that the emperor was more or less a hired servant of God and his Lord, Jesus the Anointed One. But Paul did not call for rebellion against the emperor; in fact, he argued for paying taxes to him, for Paul was willing to wait until Jesus returned for the issue of the Roman Empire to be dealt with, and believers follow the way of the cross, not the way of violence. Likewise Paul did teach that the various deities of the Roman Empire were "nothing" or even "demons" (see 1 Cor 8 – 10), but he

did not bother to engage in slandering the various deities, much less attacking their cults (Acts 19:37). Rather, his strategy was to bring all people into obedience to Jesus, which would weaken their cults, but through a defection of members rather than direct attack. In these examples in Acts one sees both the pagan misunderstanding of Paul (according to Luke), and in the comparison with Paul's teaching the reality that a writer like 1 Peter hopes will eventually become clear even to pagans.

147. The Greek term *adelphotēs* (ἀδελφότης) is traditionally translated "brotherhood," but it means "a group of fellow-believers, a fellowship," BDAG, 19.1. See also Elliott, *Home for the Homeless*, 195, where the social significance of this term is discussed.

148. BDAG, 1061, meaning 2.

3.2.3.1.1.3 Honorable Conduct in the Household Realm: Slaves (2:18–25)

A second difficult area of interface with the society was in the household itself, and 1 Peter begins by addressing household slaves,[149] of whom a number had become followers of Jesus, as the letter to Philemon illustrates. Because the topic is the interface of followers of Jesus with an unbelieving society, there is no reference to slave owners, for generally when the head of a household committed to Jesus, his (or her, in some cases) slaves and other household members did as well.[150]

Just as all believers are to accept the authority of the government (i.e., the Roman Empire), so all household slaves are to accept the authority of their masters "with all reverential fear [of God]."[151] As a general statement in a society in which slaves did not have much choice (they were not "persons" in the eyes of society, so they had no rights and could be and were beaten and punished for failing to show proper respect and deference; if they ran away, they might well be killed), this is not surprising. Our author, however, argues that submission and respect should not only be shown to the good and kind (or tolerant) masters, but also to those who are unjust (or harsh).[152]

It is clearly the latter type of master whom the author has primarily in mind, for he adds, "This is that which brings [God's] favor:[153] if someone, because of their conscience before God, submits to (or endures) affliction, suffering unjustly." It is not that submission is their fate in life, part of their station, and it is not that submission is a wise course of action, for resistance is futile. It is that God sees and rewards such behavior, for it is done out of respect for God, not because of one's recognition of the rights of the master. The whole situation has been reframed. Injustice is called injustice,[154] and presumably God will deal with that too "on the day he comes to judge." But now injustice has a meaning beyond teeth-gritting silent

---

149. Household slaves were generally the best-off class of slaves, although they were still slaves and so without honor status or rights in society. Italy also had slaves who worked on the agricultural estates, slaves who worked in the mines, and slaves who manned the galleys, all of whom, and especially the latter two classes, were far worse off. It is possible that Asia Minor was more like Greece and lacked the large slave-worked agricultural estates found in Italy. And it is doubtful that slaves who worked in the mines or the galleys could gather outside of work and thus be part of a Christian community. But even relatively modest households had at least one household slave.

150. It was a societal assumption that the head of a household (usually the *paterfamilias*) determined the religion of their household. Thus if that person became a follower of Jesus, the whole household was programmed by society also to become followers of Jesus. One of the offensive things about the Jesus movement was that it invited individuals to follow Jesus *regardless* of whether the head of the household approved or not. Thus the movement was viewed as family hostile in a society in which the family was viewed as the basis of the society. It is this sort of situation that sets up the social conflict 1 Peter is addressing.

151. Or "with due respect [of the master]," for, as noted above, fear (*phobos, φόβος*) has multiple connotations. While one might indeed argue that 1 Peter is teaching that one should treat all masters with socially proper deference and respect, the use of "fear" in 1 Peter and particularly in the immediately preceding context argues for this being "fear of God," much as "conscience of God" appears in the following verse. See further Achtemeier, *1 Peter*, 195.

152. The word itself means "crooked," "bent," or "twisted" and so in a moral sense can mean "dishonest," "unscrupulous," or perhaps even "morally perverse." In this context it means the opposite of "good" and "kind." See *skolios* in BADG, 930.

153. Literally, "this is grace" or "this is favor," but "by metonymy [*charis* means] *that which brings someone* (God's) *favor* or *wins a favorable response* from God" (BDAG, 1079, meaning 2.c). This term also appears in Luke 6:32–34.

154. That a slave might suffer injustice is not something lightly said by 1 Peter. Aristotle, for instance, argued that injustice could never be done to a slave since a slave is not a person but mere property (*Eth. nic.* 5.10.8). Stoics, however, did admit that injustice could be done to a slave, so there were other voices in antiquity as well.

suffering, for what James would have called "patient endurance" of that injustice will receive God's favor.[155]

First Peter goes on to clarify that not all patient endurance is praiseworthy: "What fame (or 'glory') is there if one endures patiently when one makes a mistake and is beaten? But if one endures patiently when they have done good and suffers—this brings God's favor." It is enduring injustice, enduring suffering, not as a result of unintentional or intentional errors, but of actually doing something that is good (whether good in the eyes of God or good according to societal standards is not explained)—this is what brings God's favor (presumably on the day of judgment, for clearly the one suffering is not experiencing favor from anyone in the present).

But why does this bring God's favor? Because this is part of their calling itself. In 1:1 we learn that the letter is addressed to a people who are called or elected, and that is repeated in 1:15 as a reason for holy living; it comes up again in 2:9, where we discover that they are the elect/chosen people of God. Now we find that calling or election is the reason for patient endurance under suffering (the idea of calling will appear again in 3:9 and 5:10). And why is it true that the calling of a follower of Jesus is to endure unjust suffering patiently? Because that is what the Anointed One did. In a five-word series of alliterations beginning with ὑ-, 1 Peter points out in 2:21 that this Anointed One's suffering was on their behalf (he does not yet spell out what he means by that), and he thereby left an example[156] to his followers "in order that you might follow his footprints." In other words, as Jesus is reported to have said in Mark 8:34 and parallels, at least with respect to suffering it was expected that his followers would truly become his apprentices: his pattern of life would be their pattern of life.

But what is that pattern? Using Isa 53:9b from the LXX (with the one exception of changing "lawlessness"[157] to "sin" or "mistake" to conform it to the language of the chapter in 1 Peter), our author explains: Jesus did not do anything wrong, nor did he say anything deceitful. When Jesus was verbally abused, he did not return in kind, and when he suffered, he did not threaten. That does not mean that he considered the suffering okay, but rather that he could hand the situation over "to the one judging justly." That One has indeed vindicated Jesus, as we will learn in chapter 3, but that is not the point here, where only the pattern of patient endurance of suffering is being considered.

Our author continues, citing Isa 53:4: Jesus was lifted up, not for his sins or mistakes, but ours; then he adds the explanation that this was in his own body on the post. First Peter does not use the word for "cross," but uses a word that refers to a "tree" or "piece of wood" or "wooden post," which was a less direct way to refer to a cross (as in Acts 5:30; 10:39; Gal 3:13). The word "cross" itself was shameful

---

155. The two uses of "favor" (*charis*, χάρις) in vv. 19 and 20 form an *inclusio*, bracketing the complex rhetorical pattern of the passage.

156. The term for "example," used only here in the New Testament, is a word used earlier for a pattern of the letters of the alphabet, often a series of words containing all of the letters of the Greek

alphabet, for children to trace over and so learn to write.

157. Unlike Paul or James, 1 Peter never uses any term derived from the Greek stem *nom-*, νομ-, from which the word for "law" comes. Thus one would not expect him to use "lawless" or "lawlessness."

enough that it was thought vulgar to speak it, although that did not stop Paul (e.g., 1 Cor 1:18).[158] The purpose was so that "we" might live for justice or righteousness, since we no longer have any part in[159] sins. In 1 Peter's words, sins were part of the pre-reborn life, while justice or righteousness is part of the reborn life. Our author sums up this aspect of his thought with another reference to Isa 53:5, "by his stripes you were healed."

The author has now reframed the unjust suffering of the slaves. It is wrong. It is unjust. But by patiently enduring it, they follow the footsteps of their master. The results of his suffering were what gave these slaves the life and community they now enjoy. By weaving together Isa 53 and his own comments, our author has given dignity to the suffering of the slaves. They are identifying with the Anointed One himself. Yet having gone so far with Isa 53, our author cannot avoid one further comment, yet another reference to Isa 53:6. "You were 'like straying sheep,' but now you have returned to the shepherd and overseer of your lives." This is a beautiful weaving together of the metaphor of the "lost sheep" from the teaching of Jesus (e.g., Luke 15:2–7 = Matt 18:12–14) and that of "God as shepherd of Israel" (e.g., Gen 48:15; Ps 23; Isa 40:11), which could at times take on messianic overtones (Jer 31:10; Ezek 37:24).

3.4.3.1.1.4 Honorable Conduct in the Household Realm: Wives and Husbands (3:1–7)

While the slaves were the lowest-status persons in a household in that they had no social status or honor and normally were considered property, the next-lowest adult person in the household was the wife, whose status was dependent on her husband, and who was not a full citizen of the Greek *polis* in that women did not have voting rights. Sometimes they were restricted in their movement outside of the house, and they often were vulnerable to abuse by their husbands.[160]

In the context of 1 Peter we must remember that one of the more important duties of women in the ancient Mediterranean world was the domestic religious routine, that is, the placing of offerings before and otherwise caring for the family deities, images of which were kept on a shelf or in a niche in the house. Naturally, believing women would no longer carry out this duty, which thus undermined the solidarity of the family, and the authority of the head of the family (one of whose prerogatives was the choice of the family religion), and endangered its well-being. That was how pagans tended to see such behavior. Furthermore, the attending of

---

158. It may be significant that Paul in writing to the Romans does not use either "cross" or "crucify" (in any literal sense) but always a more polite way of referring to how Jesus died, and 1 Peter, probably written from Rome, where such sensitivity was at its greatest, also does not use those terms, but rather a politer substitute.

159. Often this is translated "died to sins," but that comes, not from the word itself, which means "to be away from," "be far from," "have no part in," "separate oneself from," but from the contrast

with "live," the main verb of the clause. We think, however, that this unique New Testament expression is deliberately chosen to underline the separation from sin, rather than to express the Pauline dead-to-sin-and-alive-to-God contrast.

160. We do not know about all of the areas to which 1 Peter is addressed, especially the inland areas, but the coastal fringe of both the Aegean and Black Seas had been settled by Greeks and thus reflected Greek culture and civic structure.

secret clubs (which is what the communities of the followers of Jesus were considered) was questionable, if not scandalous. Wives were expected to follow the religion of their husbands,[161] so this independent religious choice was viewed as domestic and/or societal rebellion.

In this fraught context, wives are told to "accept the authority of" their husbands "in the same way" as slaves accept the authority of their masters and every follower of Jesus is to accept the authority of the state. This was what Hellenistic society expected, and it was a stance that the Jesus movement could endorse, at least within the framework of prior submission to Jesus as Lord.[162] Some women would find this less problematic because they had believing husbands, but this section focuses on husbands who do not "obey the word," where there was a conflict of values. The hope was that these husbands would be won over (cf. 1 Cor 9:19–22) without any word spoken by their wives—that is, simply by their wives' lifestyles, and particularly insofar as this lifestyle was characterized by purity (valued in everyone in the New Testament, Phil 4:8; 1 Tim 5:22; Jas 3:17; 1 John 3:3, where it replaces the cultic purity of the Hebrew Scriptures, and valued as chastity in women, but often not in men, in the Greco-Roman culture).

But our author adds that this purity is "in fear," a phrase that in 1 Peter refers to the fear of God (cf. 2:18, above). In other words, these married women are to be pure, but not primarily because of their society or their husbands, but because of God. Thus chastity or purity has been raised to a different level, and their culturally expected behavior has been reframed as behavior before God.

This purity should be observed in these wives living up to the highest values of pagan virtue;[163] that is, they should avoid the forms of outward adornment that symbolized their attempts to attract male interest and their acceptance of society's objectification of them (at times encouraged by husbands who enjoyed others thinking that they *had* a desirable wife). Of course, this means that 1 Peter, at least in theory, contemplates higher-class women as part of the church, for while lower-class women may have harbored such desires, they did not have the opportunity or the finances for striking dress. Furthermore, while pagan philosophers shared this value, the statement also critiques a society that did not embody the best of pagan ethics.

Yet our author is not so much concerned with what the women did *not* do as with what they are to do; his strategy is to contrast the outward with the inward, a contrast also found in the words of Jesus (e.g., Matt 15:8, 18) and the teaching of

---

161. See, e.g., Plutarch, *Praec. Conj.* 19.

162. Since the whole Jesus movement was modeled on the life of Jesus, in which, rather than asserting his authority by force, he accepted the various authority structures and served to the point of death, while at the same time maintaining his sense of person, authority, and mission, the idea of accepting the authority of other various human social structures, an acceptance limited by a prior acceptance of Jesus as Lord, was "natural" (to the degree that anything they did out of obedience to Jesus could be said to be "natural") to the followers of Jesus.

163. This avoiding of fancier coiffures, jewelry, and clothing was clearly an ideal pagan virtue, as Plutarch (*Mor.* 1 and 141), Epictetus (*Ench.* 40), and Seneca (*Ben.* 7.9) show, but *T. Reu.* 5.5 and Philo *Virt.* 39 show the same critique within Second Temple Judaism, and 1 Tim 2:9 shows that 1 Peter is not alone on this topic within the New Testament.

Paul (e.g., 2 Cor 4:16). The inward "spirit"[164] is to be "gentle and peaceful," which type of virtue Plutarch states was valued in women (*Praec. Conj.* 45; *Consol.* 2), but which followers of Jesus valued in everyone (e.g., Gal 6:1, 3).[165] The idea of "gentleness" indicates a person who, when wronged, does not attack back, for they know that in the end God will judge righteously and so they can endure evil without bitterness, while the idea of "peacefulness" is that of being calm and tranquil as opposed to restless and rebellious. There is a rhetorical twist in calling these virtues "precious" or "valuable," for the clothing and jewelry that he has rejected were valuable to human beings, while 1 Peter refers to what is valuable to God, thus taking an eschatological perspective.

These wives, and in particular the believing wives of pagan husbands, need not feel alone in practicing such virtue, for our author attributes it to unnamed "holy women"[166] of Jewish tradition who practiced such virtues and accepted the authority of their husbands, which, given the nature of these virtues, would indicate some experience of oppression. No text is cited for this, so we cannot be sure what incidents our author is thinking about or whether he is simply generalizing from Sarah, whom he does cite as having called Abraham "lord." There is at best tenuous support in the Hebrew Scriptures[167] for Sarah's having referred to Abraham as "lord," and a lot of first-century Jewish embarrassment in the presentations of her strong initiative in those same Hebrew Scriptures.[168]

First Peter is, therefore, almost certainly referring to either the *Testament of Abraham* or the traditions incorporated into it, where, rewriting Sarah into the ideal Hellenistic woman, she does indeed consistently refer to Abraham as "my lord Abraham" (as does Isaac, as a dutiful son, who also refers to Sarah as "my lady").[169] In other words, our author cites the Sarah of contemporary cultural adaptation as an illustration of an ideal wife in that cultural situation.[170] The women addressed have

---

164. While K. H. Schelkle, *Die Petrusbriefe; der Judasbrief* (HTKNT; Freiberg: Herder, 1961), 89–90, argues that this is the Holy Spirit, that is unlikely, for that is not the normal use of "spirit" in 1 Peter and the idea that the Holy Spirit would be "very precious to God" would be too obvious to need stating.

165. The pair itself occurs together in *1 Clem.* 13.4 and *Barn.* 19.4, apparently influenced by a Greek version of Isa 66.

166. It is quite unusual for anyone other than God to be called "holy" in the Hebrew Scriptures, including in New Testament references to the Hebrew Scriptures, although in the New Testament Jesus joins God as holy and followers of Jesus collectively are sometimes referred to as "holy ones" (traditionally translated "saints").

167. It is true that although she laughs at the divine messengers, Sarah does appear to naturally refer to Abraham as "my husband" (*wa'dōnî,* a term that in nonmarital contexts might mean "my lord"), which is translated in the LXX as "ὁ δὲ κύριός μου" (*ho de kyrios mou*); this expression could be translated "and my lord," if one was unaware of the Hebrew idiom. Still, this is one reference, and it depends on the LXX, so it is tenuous evidence for a habit of speech, since we never hear Sarah saying that in addressing Abraham.

168. See Dorothy Sly, "I Peter 3:6b in the Light of Philo and Josephus," *JBL* 110 (1991): 126–29.

169. As noted above, the only passage in the Hebrew Scriptures that has Sarah referring to Abraham as "lord" (if taken literally and not idiomatically) is Gen 18:12, in which she is laughing at the divine messengers and not speaking to Abraham directly. But, as Troy W. Martin, "The *TestAbr* and the Background of 1 Pet 3:6," *ZAW* 90 (1999): 139–46, has shown, the impression of Sarah as a "feisty" woman in Genesis has been corrected into the image of an ideal Hellenistic woman in the *Testament of Abraham*. See also Peter H. Davids, "A Silent Witness in Marriage: 1 Pet 3:1–7," in *Discovering Biblical Equality: Complementarity without Hierarchy* (ed. Ronald W. Pierce and Rebecca Merrill Groothuis; Downers Grove, IL: InterVarsity Press, 2004), 224–38.

170. We do not suggest that this is a conscious, culturally aware use of Sarah, but rather a use of the then-current presentation of Sarah in his community, perhaps without an awareness that this differs from the presentation of Sarah in the Hebrew Scriptures (although Philo is aware of his culture's dissonance with the Hebrew Scriptures and apologetically defends Abraham).

become her daughters[171] as they do what is right (i.e., practice appropriate virtue, both theologically and culturally) and "do not fear any intimidation" (i.e., from their husbands; there may be an allusion to Prov 3:25 LXX).

Thus in addressing wives, as in addressing slaves, our author encourages culturally appropriate behavior to the extent that it is consonant with the values encouraged in the Jesus movement. And yet it is clear that neither the master's authority nor that of the husband is in any sense ultimate: God is the only one who is to be "feared." These other relationships are temporary ones that endure only until Jesus is "revealed." During this period of "exile" the job of the wife or slave is to behave honorably (at least in God's eyes, since the culture around them may be blinded to their honorable behavior due to their loyalty to Jesus) and thus give a good reputation to the good news (even if that may only be admitted at the final judgment).

When 1 Peter turns to men, primarily husbands, but including all males in the household, our author speaks differently. The husband had the cultural right to determine the religion of the family, so should he become a follower of Jesus, the rest of the household would likely do the same. Thus there is no reference to the possibility that the husbands have pagan wives.[172] And yet marriage is still one of the "human institutions" (2:13) and a context in which one is to "live an honorable lifestyle among the nations" (2:12), which continue as the overarching themes of this section; thus, husbands are also to "submit to" or "accept the authority of," although the object is never named.[173] Are they to submit to the marital situation, or is it to their wives? Perhaps the radical nature of either of these implications is the reason that the object remains unexpressed, having to be filled in from context.

The wife and other women in the household are "the weaker female vessel," for both men and women are vessels (otherwise one would not be the comparatively weaker one), but women are in some way weaker. In what way is this true? While both Jews and Greco-Romans called women mentally and morally weaker than men,[174] it is difficult to believe that our author is doing that, for his strategy has

---

171. The idea that they have *become* her daughters is another indication that they were not her daughters by birth, that is, were not ethnic Jews, and merely need to live as her daughters. This author was born a citizen of the United States and of the United Kingdom, but he *became* a Canadian citizen in 1989; one might urge him to live appropriately due to his being a citizen of the USA or the UK, but one cannot say that he ever should or had become such a citizen, since those citizenships were his by birth.

172. Since no wives are explicitly mentioned, but rather "weaker female vessel," this makes the argument of Carl D. Gross, "Are the Wives of 1 Pet 3:7 Christian?" *JSNT* 35 (1989): 89–96, unlikely. See Achtemeier, *1 Peter*, 217.

173. While it is clear that 1 Pet 3:7 is a separate sentence, it contains no finite verb, just a series of participles and then an infinitive at the end. However, the "likewise" implies a parallel with the two previous sentences addressing slaves and wives respectively. Thus it is quite appropriate to supply an implied "accept the authority of" or "submit to" and then ask whether its omission is just stylistic

(i.e., the avoidance of too much repetition) or rhetorical (i.e., by not stating it explicitly, 1 Peter avoids being offensively "in your face").

The Pattern of 2:13–3:7	
2:13	"accept the authority of" ὑποτάσσω *hypotassō*
2:18	"accept the authority of" ὑποτάσσω *hypotassō*
3:1	"likewise" … "accept the authority of" ὁμοίως … ὑποτάσσω *homoiōs … hypotasso*
3:7	"likewise" [no main verb expressed] ὁμοίως *homoiōs*

174. E.g., Plato, *Laws* 6.781; *Republic* 5.455, 457; *Let. Arist.* 250 ("the female sex is bold, positively active for something which it desires, easily liable to change its mind because of poor reasoning powers, and of naturally weak constitution"); Tacitus *Ann.* 3.34. See the many more references in Achtemeier, *1 Peter*, 206, although he also notes that some of the same ancient writers could speak of "exceptions," such as women who were not "womanish."

been to address slaves and wives, not as morally or mentally deficient, but as fully capable moral agents whose necessary conformity he is dignifying by giving it a deeper meaning. Rather, it is more likely that he realizes that women are generally physically weaker than men[175] and were certainly socially weaker.[176] The man is to live considerately with the woman, recognizing that he and not she has the power, and to show her honor, which is precisely what she did not have in Greek society, where a woman had shame rather than honor.

The man, then, is to be countercultural and treat his wife with honor; that is, he is to give her equal status, for she is his "co-heir" of "the (divine) favor that leads to (eternal life)." And what if he does not do this, but slips back into or remains in conformity to the culturally accepted treatment of women? God will notice, and his prayers will be "hindered," for he is failing to accept God's view of his wife and the other women in the household, so that his relationship with God will be disturbed. One hardly wants to be in the middle of an urgent prayer and realize that it is not getting higher than the ceiling.

3.4.3.1.1.5 Concluding Exhortation on Honorable Conduct (3:8–12)

Our author concludes his exhortation with a summary. Internally, honorable conduct is characterized by communal unity, a refusal to let the hostility of the wider society influence inner-community relationships: "like-minded," "sympathetic" (both terms unique in the biblical literature, but common in Greek ethical discussion), "loving" those in the family of believers, "tenderhearted," and "humble-minded." Externally (with "humble-minded" forming a transition from the internal to the external) honorable conduct is characterized by a refusal to retaliate—indeed, the repaying of evil with blessing. And why should they do this? In words that may echo the Beatitudes and certainly reflects Jesus' teaching in Matt 5:44//Luke 6:27–28, 1 Peter states that the addressees' calling or election (cf. 1:1) was so that they would "inherit" a blessing that they can pass on to others. They respond to others as God in Jesus has responded to them.

This teaching is supported by a citation of Ps 34:12–16a.[177] In the context of 1 Peter the quotation argues that the one who desires the life of the coming age[178] must refrain from all evil speech and action (cf. 2:11, which began this section) and instead do good, in particular pursue peace (cf. Matt 5:9). Why? Because the Lord's eyes are on the righteous and his ears open to their prayers (cf. 3:7), but he is against

---

175. Until the 1600s women on average lived shorter lives than men, for the loss of nutrients through pregnancy and lactation left them weaker and more susceptible to disease.

176. So Achtemeier, *1 Peter*, 217; Davids, *1 Peter*, 122–23.

177. The psalm conforms to the vocabulary of the LXX, but differs grammatically, principally in the shift from second to third person. Is this the result of following a different Greek text, of quoting from memory, or of deliberate theological adaptation? Note John Piper, "Hope as the Motivation of Love: 1 Peter 3:9–12," *NTS* 26

(1980): 212–31, who argues that the shift in person was to make it a summary rather than command.

178. Achemeier, *1 Peter*, 226, points out that while the reference in 3:7 to eschatological life sets the immediate context, the reference to present life in 2:24 and the return to present life in 3:13–16 mean that one cannot rule out a reference to present life, which is the thought of the psalm. Even so, eschatological life is the near context and must predominate.

those doing evil. It is a neat summary and could be translated into the context of
the letter thus: in all of the situations in which the addressees find themselves,
whether as sidelined citizens, slaves, or wives of pagan husbands, they are to watch
their speech and actions in ways that are most likely to promote peace. In this way
they will receive God's blessing, whether it be eschatological or, in a more limited
manner, within the present age.

3.4.3.1.2 Responding to Hostility (3:13–4:6)

The paraenesis of 2:11–3:12 has given one response to the addressees' situation,
namely, that of minimizing the hostility of others by doing good; this new section
advances from that response to the "what if" of their doing good not being enough.
What if they are persecuted precisely because they did good?

3.4.3.1.2.1 Doing Right despite Suffering (3:13–17)

Who is going to do evil to one if one is zealous for good? Certainly not God, for the
psalm quoted has just indicated that much, and in most cases, not people either (assuming that they can recognize the good as good). But should one suffer because of one's
righteousness,[179] precisely then one is blessed (an idea that echoes Matt 5:10, the eighth
beatitude of the Sermon on the Mount). The situation of suffering, then, has been dra-
matically reframed, so that now the one suffering is pronounced "blessed" or "happy."

This new perspective is underlined by citing Isa 8:12–13 (from a version agreeing with the LXX): "Do not be intimidated by them!" But rather than fearing and
setting apart as holy "the Lord" (as in the LXX; the Hebrew is *YHWH ṣĕbāʾôt*,
"YHWH of armies"), 1 Peter instructs the addressees to "set apart in your hearts
the Anointed One as Lord." Theology has become Christology. Yet this is not just
an inward spirituality, something that one keeps hidden in their heart, for despite
the obvious risk, one is also to be prepared to explain the reason for one's hope to
anyone who asks. It is true that one is to do this "with meekness" rather than as an
"in your face" type of boast ("Of course I am hopeful, for when my Lord is revealed
I will get my reward, and you will get yours. Then we shall see who is laughing").
Moreover, it is done in fear of God (or Jesus the Anointed One, since he is referred
to in the context) and with a good conscience before him, for it is he and not human
beings who will judge in the only judgment that matters.

---

179. The optative mood (*paschoite*, πάσχοιτε) along with "even
if" (*ei kai*, εἰ καί) on the face of it should suggest that this outcome
is improbable. However, the letter suggests elsewhere (e.g., 4:13–19)
that precisely this outcome is being experienced and the "if" picks
up on 1:6 and 2:19–20, and will be picked up (with optative) in
3:17. F. W. Danker, "1 Peter 1:24–2:17: A Consolatory Pericope,"
ZNW 58 (1967): 100, argues that this optative indicates the desir-
ability rather than potentiality of suffering for righteousness, which
conclusion Elliott, *1 Peter* (AB), 622, accepts. Achtemeier, *1 Peter*,
230–31, however, argues that while the optative, rather than
indicating remote potentiality, "may reflect the author's indirect

approach to the topic of suffering," "it seems more likely to intend
to express the fact that while Christians are not undergoing continuous suffering, they do live in an environment charged with suspicion
and hostility, which has erupted and can erupt into violence and
persecution at any time." While various commentators line up with
each of these views, what is clear is that the once fashionable idea
that 1 Pet 4:12–5:11 was a separate letter reflecting a later time
than 3:13–4:11 (i.e., a time when the persecution that was a remote
possibility in the earlier passage has now become an actuality) is no
longer seriously suggested, for the evidence for the literary unity of
the letter is too strong.

It is in that setting that those who now vilify the "good conduct that flows out of [the addressees'] union with the Anointed One" (a characteristically Pauline phrase)[180] will receive shame on account of their slander. The summary statement of 3:17 is a masterful understatement: if God should so will (the optative again, which therefore brackets this segment, beginning and ending it with an optative), it is better to suffer when one is doing good than when one is doing evil. The implication is that the God who so wills is the God who will judge and thus reward; all of life is lived in the light of the coming Judge and his anticipated judgment.

3.4.3.1.2.2 Example of the Anointed One's Suffering and Vindication (3:18–22)

An example is in order, and no better example can be given than the example of the Anointed One himself, which 1 Peter presents from what looks like a quotation from a catechetical or creedal piece of literature. Even he once suffered[181] with respect to sins, but the sins were not his own, for he was righteous, and he suffered on behalf of the unrighteous for the purpose of bringing the addressees to God. Again the readers are described as privileged, since Jesus has done this for their benefit.

The Anointed One himself was indeed executed in the human sphere, the sphere of the "flesh," but he was made alive in the divine sphere, the sphere of the "spirit,"[182] so the divine verdict became clear in the resurrection. And if this were not so, it became clear in his going in that same spiritual/divine sphere or power to the "spirits in prison" and making a proclamation to them. Who these spirits were is reasonably clear, for, referring to the legends recorded in *1 Enoch* that are in turn built on Gen 6:1–4, our author notes that these spirits (called "Watchers" in *1 Enoch* and "children of God" in Genesis 6)[183] once were "disobedient" in Noah's time, when God waited patiently; this clearly parallels the present time of the addressees when God is also being patient with those human beings who are "disobedient," even if not disobedient in the same way (the issue in *1 Enoch* is the crossing of the species

180. On the meaning of their behavior being "in the Anointed One" cf. G. E. Ladd, *A Theology of the New Testament* (rev. ed.; Grand Rapids: Eerdmans, 1974, 1993), 530–31; Herman Ridderbos, *Paul: An Outline of His Theology* (Grand Rapids: Eerdmans, 1975), 57–64.

181. A number of manuscripts read "died" instead of "suffered," but (1) the evidence for "suffered" has a slight edge in the manuscript evidence; (2) "died" (*apethanen*, ἀπέθανεν) and "suffered" (*epathen*, ἔπαθεν) look similar in Greek; (3) there are more frequent references in the New Testament to Jesus' dying than to his suffering, so there would be a tendency to shift the less familiar word to the similar more familiar word; and (4) "suffered" makes our author's point better than "died," since his addressees may have suffered, but certainly have not died.

182. One could also read this as his being put to death by flesh (human being) or in flesh (i.e., physically) and made alive by Spirit or in spirit. The point is the contrast of the human verdict and the divine verdict, which will be paralleled to the addressees' situation

in the following chapter.

183. While there are those who view these as human beings, that is, human spirits (e.g., Reinhard Feldmeier, *First Letter of Peter*, 202–6), the majority of scholars follow Dalton, *Christ's Proclamation to the Spirits*, who argued that they were the Watchers of *1 Enoch*, pointing out as part of the evidence that "spirit" standing alone never indicates a human spirit in biblical literature. Feldmeier counters that God's waiting in the days of Noah better fits the people alive during the building of the ark than the Watchers who rebel and thereby trigger God's decision to send the deluge and thus the building of the ark. However, human beings are never said to be in "prison" postmortem, while that is precisely the state of the Watchers in *1 Enoch*. The connection to *1 Enoch*, not only here but elsewhere in 1 Peter, has been more thoroughly investigated and established by Robert L. Webb in his 290-page "The Apocalyptic Perspective of First Peter." See the longer discussion in Davids, *1 Peter*, 138–42.

barrier by having sexual relationships with human women). It is also clear that this journey and proclamation are post-resurrection activities in that this action in or by the spirit contrasts with the Anointed One's being executed.

But what type of proclamation did Jesus make? On the one hand, if one takes the term to mean what it normally does in the New Testament, then Jesus proclaimed the good news, a post-imprisonment opportunity to hear and respond to the message about Jesus.[184] On the other hand, it is difficult to see how any such proclamation would in any way advance the argument of 1 Peter. But if one takes the term for proclamation (*ekēryxen*, ἐκήρυξεν) in its generic meaning of any type of formal proclamation (Luke 12:3; Rom 2:21; Rev 5:2), including (and perhaps especially) the proclamation of victory (by a king or general), it is clear how it makes sense: at the time of his resurrection, Jesus proclaimed his victory to the imprisoned spirits, thereby sealing their doom (as also happens in *1 Enoch* 16:3).[185]

In Noah's time, with violence going on around him in the earth, God waited patiently while Noah built an ark, in which only eight people were rescued "through water," from the whole population of the earth. Now 1 Peter's addressees also experience themselves as a small minority in their communities, and our author lets them know that in the ancient narrative he sees a picture of or precedent for their situation (more exactly, he sees the present situation as an antitype of the ancient situation): eight were rescued "through water," and now baptism, the central part of initiation into the believing community, saves or rescues the addressees, so they are also rescued by passing through water.

Our author quickly explains this remark: it is not that baptism removes dirt or pollution from the body ("the flesh"), but that in it there is an answer to God from a good conscience.[186] That is, in the rite of baptism one was formally asked to pledge oneself to Jesus in response to the questions of the one doing the baptizing, much as in the rite of a wedding one makes a formal pledge to one's spouse. Thus, baptism is the point in time and manner of salvation as a wedding is the point in time and manner of marriage.

Then 1 Peter adds the real point of his narrative, that this rescue or salvation comes through the resurrection of Jesus (which parallels the resurrection of his followers, a point Paul also makes in 1 Cor 15), and that this Jesus the Anointed One has now entered the divine sphere or dimension (i.e., heaven) and has taken up his rule ("at the right hand of God") with all sorts of spiritual beings ("angels, authori-

---

184. This is precisely how Reinhard Feldmeier, *First Letter of Peter*, 202–6, interprets the proclamation. It is clear that this takes place post-resurrection and in the "prison" (which we use deliberately, because it is what the text uses and parallels what *1 Enoch* refers to, which is not the final punishment of the Watchers, but a temporary place of custody as they await final judgment; "hell" would be a misleading term to use in this context).

185. This would make even more sense if the "prison" were in the second heaven, which is where *2 Enoch* locates it, although *1 Enoch* and other Second Temple literature locate it "on earth" or "in the

West" or under the earth. We do not know where 1 Peter thinks of the prison as being located.

186. The translation "answer/pledge to God from a good conscience" or "the pledge of a good conscience toward God" (NIV) is more satisfactory than "an appeal to God for a good conscience" (NRSV, ESV, NASV), for it takes the genitive "of a good conscience" more naturally and fits known cultural situations, whereas there seems to have been less concern in the early Jesus community about obtaining a good conscience.

ties, and powers") subjected to his authority. This phrase implies that any earthly beings are certainly under his authority, even if his rule is not yet open, even if it has yet to be revealed (1 Pet 1:7).

3.4.3.1.2.3 Following the Example of the Anointed One (4:1–6)

The argument has been about suffering, that it is better to suffer for doing good (should that be God's will) than for doing evil (so 3:17), with the good result of the Anointed One's suffering (i.e., his vindication and exaltation) being the example. Building on this example, our author argues that since the Anointed One (their leader and ruler) suffered in the human sphere ("in the flesh"),[187] the addressees should "arm themselves" with the same mind-set; that is, they should be prepared to "suffer in the flesh," expecting divine reward. The principle is that whoever carries through with this mind-set has broken off their life of sin, for otherwise they would not be suffering, since they would be doing what everyone else was doing and getting along just fine.[188]

However, the purpose of breaking with a sinful lifestyle is not just negative. It also means that one is no longer living the rest of one's time in the human sphere (i.e., "in the flesh") for those human desires or drives that previously controlled one. By contrast, one is living this time for God's will. Previously they had lived lives controlled by human drives just as other pagans did: they had lived in self-abandonment (often translated "licentiousness"); they had lived by their desires (or what we might call the limbic system), as seen in drunkenness, excessive feasting, drinking parties, and disgusting idolatry. The point is not that this was abnormal for pagan society; rather, it was normal behavior then as now, even if at times it got out of hand.

But their former pagan friends now think it is strange, absolutely weird, that the believers no longer are involved with them in this outpouring of debauchery, and they slander 1 Peter's addressees because of it. These followers of Jesus are no longer living as normal human beings, but have become "haters of humanity" (a typical charge against them). Ah yes, but there is another side to this situation. These who slander the believers now will have to answer to "the One who is prepared to judge the living and the dead." The issue is not *if* they will answer to this One, but *when* they will answer to him, for he is already prepared. "He who laughs last, laughs best," or so 1 Peter implies.

Now in the present the believers are being shamed for not doing that which from the perspective of the Jesus movement (and many Jews as well) was shameful, but *then* the Anointed One will show what is truly shameful and those doing it will have to answer for it. For this reason, says our author, the good news was proclaimed to

---

187. It is important to continually stress that "in the flesh" does not mean "in the body" versus "in a disembodied state," but "in the world as controlled by the natural human state" versus "in the time when Jesus appears as judge and those humans who have followed him live lives animated by God, by the spirit."

188. As James shows, especially in Jas 5:13–14, suffering in both

James and 1 Peter is that which one endures because of their commitment to Jesus as Lord. Old age and sickness, which all human beings, followers of Jesus and followers of the principalities and powers of this age, endure alike, are not the suffering as that term is used in these letters.

those who are now dead,[189] in order that even if they have been condemned in the human sphere ("in the flesh") from the human point of view,[190] they will then live in the divine sphere; or empowered by the Spirit, they will live according to God's judgment on their behavior. In other words, their lives will parallel the life of Jesus.

3.4.3.1.3 Community Solidarity in Troubled Times (4:7–11)

It is not, our author states, as if he is speaking about the distant future, as if one might weigh a long present life in debauchery over against a promised future life that would come in some distant time. No, "the end of all things is near." This age is winding up, nearing its conclusion. Therefore, the only thing that makes sense is a life of virtue and communal solidarity in the light of the coming judgment.

Think seriously, he instructs, instead of being personally or communally intoxicated (which could include being intoxicated by possessions or "isms," not just alcohol). Live a well-balanced or self-controlled life that results in prayer. But this is not an individualistic life of withdrawal into prayer, a sort of withdrawal into a monastic cell away from other people (although spiritual leaders have found limited times of retreat and prayer helpful). Rather, it is above all characterized by earnestly maintained love (love defined as caring action) toward those in the community of the followers of Jesus (see 1:22). This teaching is reinforced by the citation of Prov 10:12, which was also used in Jas 5:20 and was apparently commonly used in the Jesus movement, indicating that love will pass over the errors ("sin") of others.[191] What about traveling followers of Jesus? Be hospitable toward them ("one another") without grumbling about the cost and inconvenience.[192]

The summary our author adds is that whatever good or ability one has, it is a gift of God, an example of his favor that comes in many forms. One should treat that

---

189. Feldmeier, *First Letter of Peter*, 215–16, argues that this is a reference to 3:19 and thus a postmortem preaching of the good news to those who died in the deluge, that this is the most "unforced" way of reading the text, and that therefore theologically there is the possibility, even the probability, of hearing the good news and repentance after death. However, in our view and that of other scholars who read 3:19 as Jesus' proclamation of victory, 4:6 refers to an entirely different situation, a parallel to Jesus not a parallel to the "spirits in prison." Some now-deceased believers heard and welcomed the good news while alive, but what good has it done them since they died without vindication? The answer is that just as Jesus was vindicated in resurrection life, so these believers will be when Jesus returns to judge the living and the dead. Much as Paul argues in 1 Thess 4:13–18 and 1 Cor 15, Jesus' resurrection means the resurrection of his followers, and therefore at Jesus' parousia death will not disadvantage those who have died while following Jesus.

190. This condemnation could be read as execution, as in fact was in the case of Jesus. Or it could be read as human judgment on their lives (i.e., shaming) when they die of natural causes, "He/she missed the best parts of life and rejected human society, and they got nothing for it—they did not get that kingdom that they talked about but just died; he/she is simply a loser." Given that slander

seems to be what the communities addressed are currently suffering and physically more severe penalties are only potential, this latter is the most likely interpretation.

191. There are three interpretations of this use of the proverb. The one adopted here is that of the proverb in its context; other scholars view acts of love as covering one's own sins as in *2 Clem.* 16:4. Still others view the citation as being used as a general truism, God's love covers our sins, so our love covers (i.e., overlooks, forgives) the sins of others, as in Matt 6:14–15. For a discussion of the options and the reasoning behind the choice here, see Davids, *1 Peter*, 157–58.

192. While "traveling Christians" is the most natural reading of *philoxenoi* (φιλόξενοι, hospitality), it is also true that if some in the community were being tossed out of house and/or livelihood (one could easily imagine wives or adult children being ejected from their homes because of their commitment to Jesus), they would certainly be in need of such hospitality. However, there is no other evidence that ejection from one's family was common at this point in time, while traveling believers (including those who left their home area because of persecution) are a well-known phenomenon of the period. One could also understand how extended hospitality could lead to grumbling.

gift as something entrusted to one, as something that might be given to a trusted household slave to use for their Master's purposes. First Peter (as Acts 6:2 and Rom 12:7) divides these abilities into two categories. (1) The first is that of speaking. One should speak "as the words of God." Presumably this means speaking what God would have spoken in a manner in which he would have it spoken. Paul illustrates some of the uses and abuses of speech in 1 Corinthians 12–14, although it sounds as if 1 Peter is focused on prophecy more than on teaching or glossolalia.

(2) The second category is that of serving. "It probably covers all those deeds one Christian does to or for another: administration, care for the poor and sick (including contributing funds, distributing funds, and physical care), healing, and similar acts that express God's love and mercy in concrete form."[193] One does this, not according to one's own zeal or ideas of what should be done, but "according to the strength that God supplies," whether that "strength" is expressed in terms of materials or energy (the term can cover both). This leaves one without excuse when God nudges one to do something and should prevent one from exhaustion and burnout when, for whatever reason, one has gone beyond the strength that God has supplied.

The point is that whether in speech or service, what one does should bring honor to God through Jesus the Anointed One. It is God's words and God's strength at work, so it is an administration of what God has given. This should honor him, an honor that is often expressed through commitment to and honoring of his appointed ruler, Jesus the Anointed One. Having mentioned the honoring of God through Jesus, our author does it himself, closing the section with a doxology:[194] "To him [grammatically Jesus is the closer antecedent, but the author could also mean God] belong honor and strength unto the ages of ages. Amen." Indeed.

3.4.3.2 Responding to and Reframing Suffering (4:12–5:11)

The final section of the letter body reprises the topic of unjust suffering, helping the addressees reframe it appropriately and respond to it as a community. Together the reframing and response make this for many readers the most practical section of the letter with respect to suffering, for the previous responses were to specific life situations within a specific culture and were aimed more at minimizing suffering than at responding to it.

3.4.3.2.1 Reframing Suffering Positively (4:12–19)

Addressing his intended readers again as "beloved," our author indicates with this noun of address that he is starting a new major section, a new line of thought. While the "fiery ordeal" is indeed painful[195] and has occurred to test them (which always implies the possibility of failure), they are not to think of it as if something foreign is happening to them. No, they are to consider it part and parcel of sharing

---

193. Davids, *1 Peter*, 161.

194. The doxology is both an appropriate exclamation in context and a way of signaling that a major section is coming to an end, thus

breaking 2:11–5:11 into two major portions, 2:11–4:11 and 4:12–5:11.

195. I.e., "an intense degree of some painful occurrence or experience, *burning ordeal*," BDAG, πύρωσις, 900 (meaning 2).

the Anointed One's sufferings, and this reframing means rejoicing now so that they will also be glad, shouting for joy, when his glory or honor is revealed. As they have shared his suffering, so also they will share his honor.

The particular type of suffering they are experiencing or are likely to experience is that of being demeaned or insulted or otherwise verbally shamed "in the name of the Anointed One" or (since "the Anointed One" in Greek is *Christos*) "because you are considered a Christian" (see 4:16, where it is expressed precisely in this manner). If this is what they are experiencing, then they are blessed or happy (an idea that occurred in a similar context in 3:14 and finds its basis in the Jesus teaching tradition, e.g., Matt 5:11–12). This is an experience of the Spirit, that is, the Spirit of glory and of God,[196] perhaps parallel to what is promised in Matt 10:19–20, but here strongly influenced by Isa 11:2 (LXX). This age is shaming them, but precisely in that experience the Spirit rests on them, which indicates that God is honoring them. Naturally, any experience of the Spirit is an experience of God himself, but, as this text shows, experiences of the Spirit are not all joyous gifts and graces.

This blessedness does not apply to those of the community who might suffer as a murderer, thief, or criminal—or as a mischief maker, i.e., *one who meddles in things that do not concern the person, a busybody.*[197] Is it possible that then, as now, followers of Jesus were sometimes tempted to set the world to rights rather than sticking to living before the world an example of living rightly? Could this not be the real point of the verse, that while it was unlikely that a follower of Jesus would be accused of the first three charges (although manufactured evidence and trumped up charges are not unknown), the final charge is indeed a real possibility? Whatever the case, suffering under such charges (if true) is no blessing, but suffering as "one who belongs to Christ" or "to the Anointed One"[198] is a blessed state, and such a one should not be ashamed (should not accept the judgment of others that their behavior is shameful) but should rather proudly honor or glorify God in this name. The very charge becomes a badge of honor.

There is a wider purpose to this suffering, namely, that the time of judgment is beginning now in God's household. Our author does not indicate whether he thinks of the suffering/time of judgment as disciplining the household or purifying it or simply revealing its genuine members for who they are—all of these are functions of judgment in the New Testament. The point is that it has started *now* in God's own household, among those in his service and favor, as 1 Peter has said so eloquently in

196. That this is the proper reading of this grammatically and textually difficult phrase is argued in Davids, *1 Peter*, 167–68, esp. note 10.

197. Italics and meaning from BDAG, 47 *allotriepiskopos* (ἀλλοτριεπίσκοπος). Since the term is not found elsewhere in Greek literature, this meaning is developed from the word's etymology (always a risky practice, but sometimes necessary) and some expressions used about Cynic preachers. However, as the BDAG entry mentions, other scholars, feeling that this is not serious enough, have suggested "concealer of stolen goods," "spy, informer," or "revolutionist." We think that we can make sense of the passage without resorting to these later meanings.

198. While it is probable that followers of Jesus would know the meaning of the title *Christos* as "Messiah" or "Anointed One," it is not so clear that the pagans accusing them of being *Christianos* (Χριστιανός), "one who belongs to Christ," would know the meaning of the term; thus, leaving it untranslated here may best communicate the meaning. This is not necessarily an official judicial charge, which would not be used until the time of Trajan, 110 CE, but a pejorative identification that Acts claims was used by 50 CE and also apparently in Nero's persecution of 64 CE.

the first section of the letter body. But, if it starts first with "us," who have obeyed the good news, what will the result look like for those who are disobedient to God's good news? This is reinforced by a citation of Prov 11:31 (LXX; the Hebrew text differs). The righteous are being rescued by the skin of their teeth, so to speak, or at least that is what it feels like, so what will happen to the ungodly and the sinner? The implications are clear enough.

Our author concludes this section of his argument: those suffering according to God's will, that is, for being faithful followers of Jesus, should "entrust their selves to a faithful Creator" by doing good. The whole argument is there in a nutshell: there are those who are suffering, not because of their evil, but because of God's will—indeed, precisely because of their commitment to follow God. They should entrust themselves to this faithful Creator, for the Creator is also the one renewing creation. And they should do this by doing good (as defined by that Creator). The very act of doing good is an act of obedience and thus an act of trust.

3.4.3.2.2 Community Unity in the Face of Suffering (5:1–5)

Up until now 1 Peter has been addressing the relationship between the community of the followers of Jesus and the culture around them, answering the question as to where God might be in that picture of tensions and suffering. Now he turns to addressing the situation within the community that is under pressure from the culture around them.

The community is led by elders,[199] as most communities in the Mediterranean world were. Familial communities in particular were normally headed by the senior male (in the Roman world, the *paterfamilias*), who led the extended family in conjunction with the other adult males in good standing, or at least the most senior of them. Our author addresses these elders of this "family" (the followers of Jesus being considered a large family, as 5:14 will show) on a threefold basis: (1) he is himself an "elder," a senior male among the followers of Jesus, with the responsibilities and risks that that brings with it; (2) he is a witness of the Anointed One's sufferings[200] and so of the suffering of the leader of them all; and (3) he is one who shares with them the glory or honorable status that is "about to be revealed." The package appears to go together: eldership, testimony to the deep irony that the One anointed to rule has suffered, and sharing in the coming "revelation" of that rule and concomitant honor.

---

199. Achtemeier, *1 Peter*, 323, supported by a number of other scholars, argues that the absence of the article with "elders" and the expression "among you" indicate, "The term may therefore refer here not so much to a fixed group of leaders as to any people who functioned in a leadership capacity, with the assumption that such a group may well have varied in membership from time to time."

200. Both the terms "witness" (*martys*, μάρτυς) and "sufferings" (*pathēmata*, παθήματα) could have more than one meaning. At first reading they would seem to mean "eyewitness" of the personal "suffering" of Jesus, and especially the cross. If so, this is the only tradition that would make Simon Peter an eyewitness of the cross, since he

and the rest of the Twelve are missing from the trial and crucifixion scenes of the Gospels. But "witness" became a term for one who testified to their commitment (e.g., Rev 2:13) or who died due to their testimony (e.g., 17:6), and so the "suffering" of Jesus could indicate his suffering during his ministry or his suffering in the suffering of his community (e.g., Acts 9:4–5) rather than his specific crucifixion. Given that our author has apparently coined the term "fellow elder" and makes a point of his sharing (is there an implied "with you"?—he at least holds the possibility open) of the coming honor, one would think that "witness to the sufferings of the Anointed One" is also something with which they could hopefully identify.

These elders have a threefold duty: (1) shepherding "God's flock" (an image drawn from Israel, e.g., Pss 95:7; 100:3), exercising appropriate oversight willingly (as God would wish) rather than because they have to; (2) shepherding it freely or willingly rather than greedily or "in fondness for dishonest gain";[201] and (3) shepherding it by becoming an example to the flock rather than dominating those in their charge.[202] The promise is that if these duties are faithfully carried out, when the "chief shepherd" appears, these elders will receive an "unfading crown" consisting of glory or honor. Given that an honorable status was the chief good of the ancient Mediterranean world, an eternal honorable status (i.e., not one that faded like the laurel wreaths often used to honor victors in athletic events or to honor various officials) would be a reward indeed, compensation for the effort and risk of their duties (given that then, as now, persecutors often targeted leaders first and most severely).

As in 3:1 and 7 there is a "likewise," in this case for those who are "younger," who as in the case of chapter 2 are to "accept the authority of" others, in this case the "elders." The community is thus divided into "elders" and "younger,"[203] but the leadership of the latter, which has already been said to be by example, is not absolute in that all of them, elder and younger, are to clothe themselves with humility. This idea is reinforced by the citation of Prov 3:34 (LXX), which states that God himself opposes the proud but gives his favor to the humble. This citation, on the one hand, sums up appropriate behavior within the community, and, on the other, transitions into the final segment of the letter body.

3.4.3.2.3 Summary on the Response to and Reframing of Suffering (5:6–11)

The reference to humility has provided a segue for our author, and he uses it to transition from humility toward one another to humility toward God. If the persecution that the believers are suffering is in some way from God, if it is the final judgment beginning in God's own house or household, as 4:17 has argued, then the appropriate response is humble submission to "the mighty hand of God," even if God's "hand" is being experienced through the prejudicial actions of unbelievers. The implied result of this submission, or what James would have called "patient endurance," is passing the test in that one's[204] commitment is shown to be genuine (1 Pet 1:6–7).

In this conclusion of the letter body the ultimate result of this commitment is what is explicitly mentioned, i.e., that "in the time" of the final judgment "he will exalt you." The judgment that is now going on within the present age is anticipatory of the final judgment at the end of the age, which 1 Peter has indicated is just around the corner, and in that judgment the one who has humbly endured will

---

201. BDAG, 29, *aischrokerdōs*, αἰσχροκερδῶς; see also *aischrokerdēs*, αἰσχροκερδής.

202. This complex command is marked off by the term for "flock" appearing early in verse 2 and as the last word of verse 3, a lovely rhetorical turn (an *inclusio*).

203. On possible meanings of "younger" see Davids, *1 Peter*, 184–85.

204. All of the "you's" in this passage, whether in the verb or as a separate pronoun, are plural, and to that extent the use of "one" is inaccurate, for the address is to the community, to "y'all" rather than to individuals. There is a sense in 1 Peter that a community stands and falls together.

receive commendation and honor. So for the present his readers must throw their concerns on God because God is concerned about them. A person can endure suffering (i.e., persecution) because they recognize that God is sovereign, that he is concerned about them, and that his ultimate result will be their exaltation. That is one side of the situation.

The other side of the situation is that there is an adversary, and their success under testing is not assured. "Keep alert! Be on your guard!" is not the language of security. Rather, it is a warning, and it points to the fact that their "opponent, the devil" is walking around "as a roaring lion" (an image probably drawn from Ps 22:13), seeking someone[205] to gulp down. The image is a complex one, for "opponent" and "devil" (i.e., one who slanders) bring up the image of a law court, while "roaring lion" and "gulp down" is from another arena altogether. However, mixed though the metaphor is, the open mouth of the lion is a metaphor for the open mouth of the one slandering or opposing them in court, which shows the danger of the legal process. This one is to be resisted, and the manner of resistance is described as "steadfast" or "firm" with respect to "the faith" or with respect to "the commitment."

The one thing that the community is not to give up is their firm commitment to Jesus as Lord. They maintain this, knowing at the same time, not that God has *rescued* their fellow believers in other parts of the Mediterranean world and will therefore rescue them, but that they are *in solidarity* with their suffering brothers and sisters in the world, who are undergoing "the same sufferings." By putting the situation into a larger context, our author apparently seeks to strengthen their resolve.

Finally, it is time to shift back to God's side. He is "the God of all favor" and the God "who called you in the Anointed One Jesus into his eternal glory," so his ultimate purposes are obviously good. (This also picks up on the idea of their being called or elect, which appears in 1:1.) This very God, "after you suffer a little while," will himself restore them (meaning either restore to a former condition or put into proper condition, put to rights), confirm them (or strengthen them), make them strong, and establish them. These verbs have overlapping meanings, so they build up a composite picture rather than describing individual aspects of God's final restoration brought about by his final judgment.

The response to this description, and the closing of the letter body, is a doxology (the second in the letter): "to him be the power unto the ages!" It is followed by the communal response, "Amen!"

3.4.4 Letter Ending (5:12 – 14)

Now the tone of the letter totally changes. The letter shifts from the grand purposes of God and the struggle with the devil to the practical matters of a letter ending. The letter will be carried by Silvanus, probably the same Silvanus (Silas) known as Paul's coworker and co-author (2 Cor 1:19; 1 Thess 1:1; 2 Thess 1:1). The addressees

---

205. In this case the "someone" is indeed singular, an individual from the flock, so to speak. The community has to be alert and on guard and the community has to resist so that an individual does not get "devoured."

need to know that the author considers him "a faithful brother," for the letter carrier would not only deliver the letter, but usually read it aloud, explain it, and answer questions about it and the author; thus such carriers were often commended.[206]

The letter is described as short ("through a few [words]"), for it was polite to write and speak briefly, even if the end result was not brief. It was also appropriate to note the purpose of the letter at the end, and here it is described as (1) encouraging them, and (2) attesting to the fact that "this" (what is described in the letter) is "God's true favor." In one sense, the two purposes work together, for if the suffering that they are experiencing is in fact God's favor, designed to show their true commitment and so enhance their honorable status in the soon-arriving revelation of Jesus the Anointed One, that would surely be encouraging. What they need to do as a result of this encouragement is to "stand in it." That is, they are to stand firm, not giving up their commitment.

A letter ending also often contained greetings; in this case they come from "the fellow-elect one [feminine] in Babylon" and "Mark my son." While it is possible that these refer to the author's wife and blood son (and one cannot rule this out — Paul tells us in 1 Cor 9:5 that Peter had a wife who travelled with him, and if he had a wife, he likely had one or more children), most scholars are convinced that the reference is to the community of believers (*ekklēsia*, ἐκκλησία, or "church," which is feminine) in Rome, viewed as the place of exile and persecution. In other words, Babylon is an image for Rome (also taken up in Rev 17 – 18 with respect to the same city), and his younger colleague Mark had also been Paul's colleague (mentioned four times in Acts and then in Col 4:10; 2 Tim 4:11; Phlm 24). Since the letter is addressed to at least two areas where Paul had been active, it is not surprising to find Silvanus used as the trusted letter carrier and Mark mentioned in the greeting, for both had been colleagues of Paul.

There is apparently no one else around who would be known by the addressees, so our author simply adds, "Greet one another with the kiss of love." The kiss was a greeting normally only exchanged within a blood family or with friends that were as close as family. The kiss expressed in symbol that by "born again," the believers were all related, all part of one family, (so also Rom 16:16; 1 Cor 16:20; 2 Cor 13:12; 1 Thess 5:26, although Paul uses "holy kiss" rather than "kiss of love").

The author *may* have written the whole letter ending starting at 5:12 with his own hand, but he certainly writes the final blessing himself: "Peace to you all, to those in the Anointed One." The situation of the addressees was troubled, so the wish is for peace, perhaps even the wholeness of *šālôm* that the Hebrew word influencing this greeting (and the salutation in 1:1) suggests. The wish is for peace on the

---

206. We noted in 3.2.3 above that while it is possible that Silvanus functioned as Peter's amanuensis, the letter does not claim that he is a co-author, nor is he listed as such. We also noted that Richards, "Silvanus Was Not Peter's Secretary," has shown that the expression "through x I have written" is used elsewhere in Greek literature for the letter carrier, not for the amanuensis. The fact that the amanuensis did not need to be named or commended for their work was presumably checkable by the author before the letter was sent, while the letter carrier would read (or, better, perform) the work and then explain it as needed; thus, the addressees needed to know that the author trusted that person.

whole community, or, rather, communities, since the letter has been addressed to groups in multiple provinces of the empire. The author reminds them that they are "in the Anointed One," that there is a true emperor, that they belong to him, and, given the context of the whole letter, that he is about to be revealed.[207]

3.5 IMPORTANT THEOLOGICAL THEMES

While the goal of 1 Peter is pastoral (neither Paul nor any other New Testament letter writer set out to write a theological treatise, but rather to meet a pastoral need), it is also relatively theologically dense, not only in its own theological contributions, but in its use of earlier catechetical, hymnic, or poetic material, as well as in its intertextual relationship with the Greek translation (LXX) of the Hebrew Scriptures. Our goal is to unpack that theological density without distorting it by imposing the categories of later centuries of theological reflection, even if these sometimes need to be mentioned in order to point up the contribution of this work.

Yet while this work is theologically dense, it is also theologically difficult in that the intertextual relationships are not such that one can always go to the original text and find the meaning that 1 Peter intends. Furthermore, much of the teaching in the text is couched in metaphor ("shepherd," "Father," "children," "milk," etc.), which, on the one hand, carries with it a lot of cultural understandings, and, on the other, cannot be explained without losing some of its metaphorical richness, that is, its ability to speak directly to the feelings. It is also difficult to know when a metaphor (such as "family" or "sacrifice") is being viewed as more literal than metaphorical (certainly, e.g., "reborn" and "family" at least form a rather consistent metaphorical complex— does our author consider them a spiritual reality or are they still metaphorical?). Finally, metaphors are fluid, and an author can shift from one to another; he or she can mix metaphors and do so without any sense of impropriety. When one wishes to analyze theology, however, one is constantly trying to unmix and explain, which is risky if one wishes to preserve the author's thought. Nevertheless, we must attempt it.

3.5.1 The Nature of God

It is clear that the core category in 1 Peter is God, for all of the teaching in the letter is related to God in one way or another. In fact, the core problem of the letter—that is, the suffering of the followers of Jesus—is due to their perceived obedience to God in Jesus. Thus it is appropriate to begin this theological analysis with the doctrin of God, which, while we will structure it according to the triune categories of Father, Son, and Spirit, is at a significant distance from the more developed triune thought of some parts of the New Testament, especially the Fourth Gospel. Nevertheless, Father, Son, and Spirit all do appear in this letter, as we will see.

---

207. The letter ends with that simple blessing, but some manuscripts add "Jesus" to "the Anointed One" or, not content with the simple ending, add, "Amen," which was surely an appropriate and pious response, even if it is unlikely that it was penned by the author.

3.5.1.1 God the Father

The term "God" (*theos,* θεός) is reserved for "God the Father" or "Father God" (1:2, the second translation is probably the more accurate). The term "God" appears thirty-nine times in the letter, arguably always for "God the Father" (which designation, as noted, is not an anachronism, since the title appears in 1 Peter). While there are a number of times that the Hebrew Scriptures are cited (in translation), it is interesting that neither in the citations nor in the rest of the text is God declared to be creator, with the exception of an oblique reference in 4:19. Belief in "God the Father Almighty" (to use the language of the later Apostles' Creed) is axiomatic, but the idea in the second phrase of the Creed, "Creator of heaven and earth," is only alluded to once (4:19) — and that only in relation to that Creator's willing that the addressees suffer. Creation is assumed in this letter, but it is not discussed: the focus is elsewhere.

God is cited as the one who controls history, or at least significant aspects of history. It is "according to his foreknowledge" that the addressees have been chosen (1:1 – 2); it is his word that has led to their "rebirth" (1:23); it is by his power that they are being protected (1:5); it is his will that appears to determine whether they suffer for doing good (3:17; 4:19; cf. "the mighty hand of God," 5:6); it is his grace or favor that is expressed through their ministry (4:10); and it is he who will strengthen and establish them after they have suffered for a while (5:10). Furthermore, the timing of the deluge was determined by his long-suffering (3:20), and even now he is resisting the proud and giving his favor to the humble (5:5).

This is hardly enough data to argue that in 1 Peter God is in absolute control of history (there is no statement to that effect, and theologians arguing for it must go elsewhere in the New Testament for their evidence), but the data is sufficient to say that he controls *at least* these aspects of history, intervening where he wishes. Furthermore, in the statement that Jesus is sitting at the right hand of God (i.e., ruling beside and yet subject to God) and that "angels, authorities, and powers" are subject to Jesus, there is by implication the concept that such spiritual powers are also subject to God.

God is also the one who determines the standards for appropriate behavior (which, of course, is related to his coming judgment since it will be according to his standards). His will is the ethical standard for the life of the believer (2:15; 4:2), and the important issue in their "sacrifices" is that they be acceptable to him (2:5). The believer's behavior is or should be controlled by one's "conscience of [before] God" (2:19); some of their behavior in particular receives his favor (2:20) or is valued by him (3:4). Indeed, the purpose of the whole letter is to show the addressees that what they are experiencing, even though it is painful, is the true favor of God (5:10) and therefore not his punishment or disfavor. In short, God is to be feared (2:17); that is, a person must show him reverential submission and awe. Indeed, he is the only being, institution, or situation that is to be feared. Even Jesus is never said to be feared in this letter.

God is the Father of the believing community, which is a natural implication of the idea that he has chosen them and especially of the idea that he has (re)birthed them. This choosing is expressed in a number of ways, notably through the use of images from the Hebrew Scriptures, such as "people of God" (2:10) or "flock of God" (5:2), which present the followers of Jesus in the present as the continuation of God's people of the Hebrew Scriptures.

Shifting the metaphor from father as causing birth to father as head of the household, *paterfamilias*, the author describes the community as God's slaves (2:16) or household (4:17; a household of that time, of course, included slaves). People enter this household because Jesus has led them to God (3:18), and they are baptized before God (3:21; whether this verse means the answer from a good conscience to God or the request to God for a good conscience, the act is still related to God and, interestingly enough, not to Jesus). Like a good head of a household, God provides for his household, giving variegated favor to the community (4:10), which it experiences as his providing the various members with the words to speak and the strength for service (4:11). The family is to show the appropriate response to the head of the household by bringing honor to him (4:11, 16) and submitting to his will, even if his will is that of suffering (5:6).

God is the judge and goal of the consummation of the age. This was anticipated by his raising Jesus from the dead, with the result that our faith and hope are in God (1:21; hoping in God is also in 3:5 as a pre-Jesus virtue) — that is, in his raising all believers from the dead and giving them the appropriate honor before him. This is not just a postmortem hope (i.e., the hope that God will receive and honor them immediately after death); rather, it is a hope focused on a final judgment that includes resurrection. God will be glorified or honored in "the day of visitation" (2:12), and God will reverse the judgment of human beings on his followers and make those deceased followers alive (4:6).

3.5.1.2 Jesus the Anointed One

Our author talks a lot about Jesus the Anointed One, but how he does so forms a distinct pattern. First, Jesus is referred to as "Lord," clearly in a titular sense in 1:3 ("Lord Jesus the Anointed One") and 3:15 ("Lord the Anointed One"). In 2:3 Jesus is referred to simply as "the Lord" in a phrase taken from Ps 34:8.[208] This usage announces loud and clear in the Roman world that Jesus is the ruler in a way

---

208. There are eight occurrences of "lord" (*kyrios*, κύριος) in 1 Peter. First Peter 3:6 is not relevant in that it is Sarah calling Abraham "lord." The two in 1 Pet 3:12 contextually should refer to the Father both in Ps 34:12–16a, from which they are taken, and in the context in 1 Peter, but given that another phrase from Ps 34 has already been shifted to Jesus, our author might be referring to Jesus in this quotation as well, especially since this psalm is interpreted christologically in other New Testament and early Christian works. A similar argument can be constructed for the use of Isa 40:6b–8 in 1:25, although in this case the shift of language from "our God" of the LXX to "our Lord" in 1 Peter suggests that a christological interpretation was intended. This means that the expression "for the Lord's sake" in 2:13 may also refer to Jesus, even though there are later references to God in the same passage. In other words, there are three clear instances where "Lord" refers to Jesus, one in which it refers to a human being, and none of the remaining four where it *must* refer to God, although this would mean that 1 Peter, like contemporary Christian writers, can shift from God to Jesus and back again in some contexts. This is not surprising considering how closely God and Jesus are aligned.

that Caesar claimed to be. Thus, Jesus' lordship is a political challenge as well as a theological challenge. It probably reflects the basic confession of Jesus' followers that "Jesus is Lord" (Rom 10:9–10).

Second, our author refers to Jesus most frequently as "the Anointed One" (*Christos*, Χριστός), a title used twenty-two times in this letter. The name Jesus is used ten times, but never without the addition of this title, so that twelve instances of "the Anointed One" appear without "Jesus." The title "the Anointed One" is used alone with remarkable consistency when referring to the suffering and death of Jesus (1:11; 1:19 [along with "lamb"]; 2:21; 3:18; 4:1; 4:13; 5:1). In fact, it never appears alone as a title except in these expressions, in references to the suffering of believers (4:14), and in the stylized "in Christ"/"in the Anointed One" expression (3:16; 5:14).

This title, of course, is a political one in that it points to the divinely appointed ruler, or Messiah (to use the transliterated Hebrew form that 1 Peter does not use but which *Christos* was used to translate), of God's people. Therefore, when his authority is most emphasized, the combination "the Anointed One as Lord" is used (3:15). However, in his frequent use of this *Christos*/Messiah title, our author seems to be stressing the paradox of God's appointed ruler suffering, just as that paradox is pictured in Revelation when the lion turns out to be a slaughtered lamb (Rev 5:5–6). Perhaps the idea of a man, Jesus, suffering was not that surprising, especially if he had in some way threatened the human ruling powers; but the idea of *God's* ruler, the one about whom God had promised and who should be under God's protection, suffering was paradigm-changing, which appears to be the reframing that 1 Peter is about. This is done consistently enough so that when our author refers to the Spirit predicting the suffering of the Anointed One, the Spirit is called "the Spirit of the Anointed One" (1:11).

Third, Jesus is referred to as "Jesus the Anointed One" or "Lord Jesus the Anointed One" in references to his resurrection from the dead, his present rule, his future "revelation," and his being honored or his bringing honor to the Father. Does this mean that in 1 Peter's eyes there is a presently resurrected and exalted human being closely associated with the Father, or is this just a chance pattern[209] that appears in the text? Without more text in 1 Peter, this is an impossible question to answer, but the pattern is suggestive (and the idea is clearly stated in Hebrews and by Paul). At any rate, it is *this* Jesus[210] whose official delegate Peter is (1:1), who will be revealed (1:7, 13), who is the access for human beings to God and/or to honoring God (2:5; 3:21; 4:11), and in whom the believer is called (5:10). In other words, Jesus is clearly active in the present, even if his visible activity is through his delegate, and part of his activity is what might be called mediatorial in that human beings access God the Father through him. But he will not always exercise his rule in the "behind the scenes" manner that he presently does (e.g., through delegates), for he will eventually be revealed to the world.

209. The one exception to the pattern is in 1:2, where at first glance "sprinkling of the blood of Jesus the Anointed One" does not fit, but then one notices that the full expression is "unto obedience and sprinkling of the blood of Jesus the Anointed One," so obedience to this

Jesus is included in the expression, not just the sprinkling of his blood.
210. Given that "Jesus" was the Greek form of "Joshua" (as Heb 4:8 shows), there were many Jewish men called "Jesus," so it is appropriate to refer to a particular Jesus as the one our author is referring to.

Fourth, what is also clear in 1 Peter is that while Jesus is clearly exalted and ruling over angels and principalities and powers (3:22), he is never said to be divine (as, for example, in John 1:1–2 and possibly in 2 Peter, as we will see) and is always subordinated to God. Thus in 1:3 it is "the God and Father of our Lord Jesus the Anointed One" who is blessed (the single article in Greek suggesting that "God and Father" are to be thought of as one), and in 4:11 it is God who is glorified "through Jesus the Anointed One," and it is probably God to whom the doxology of the passage is offered (as also in 5:10–11). Jesus is great, Jesus is resurrected, Jesus is exalted to the right hand of God, and so he is presently ruling as some type of vice-regent; Jesus is apparently the agent of the coming judgment and the future ruler of the world (for the time of judgment and the coming of the new age are described as Jesus' "revelation"). Yet Jesus is kept subordinate to God the Father. In that sense 1 Peter has a "lower" Christology than Paul's Prison Epistles and certainly than John, Hebrews, and Revelation.[211] In fact, 1 Peter does call God "Father," but he never calls Jesus "Son." Is this because the topic of the letter calls for a particular shaping of his Christology, or is 1 Peter less comfortable than some of the rest of the New Testament with "Son" language? Again, because we only have this one relatively short letter, we cannot answer this question.

3.5.1.3 The Holy Spirit

The term "spirit" occurs eight times in 1 Peter, but such a count is misleading, for once (3:4) it refers to a human being's "spirit" (what might now be thought of as "personality"), once (3:19) it refers to "the spirits in prison," and twice (3:18; 4:6) it appears in the flesh-spirit pair, probably referring to a sphere of existence (sphere of the flesh versus sphere of the spirit; fleshly word versus spiritual world). However, in 1 Pet 1:2 the Holy Spirit is the agent of sanctification, as Jesus is the agent of God's rule and purification. The Spirit has worked through the prophets to indicate the suffering of the Anointed One, and in such a capacity the Spirit is called "the Spirit of the Anointed One" (1:11).[212] This "Holy Spirit sent from heaven" (1:12) is the agent behind the announcing of the good news in the present.

---

211. First Peter probably believes in the pre-existence of "the Anointed One," although not as definitely as Achtemeier, *1 Peter*, 109–10, argues. That idea that the Anointed One was "foreknown" from the beginning of the age is consistent with Acts 2:23, the only other place in the New Testament that the Greek term is used. That the Anointed One was "revealed" or "made manifest" is consistent with Jewish apocalyptic writings (as Elliott, *1 Peter* (AB), 377, makes clear). But it is not clear whether this is in the same sense as the "mystery of salvation" that Pauline letters indicate was "made manifest" in Jesus (Rom 16:25–26; 1 Cor 2:7–13; Eph 3:4–6, 9–10; Col 1:26; 2 Tim 1:9–10; Titus 1:2–3) or in the sense of personal preexistence. The latter is quite possible, but perhaps due to 1 Peter's consistent stress on all actions from the dawn of time having been done by God the Father he does not make clear whether or not he is thinking of the Anointed One as personally preexistent.

Feldmeier, *First Letter of Peter*, 119, is careful in his expression and avoids speculation in that he focuses on what 1 Peter focuses on, the divine plan and the divine action in the manifestation of Jesus.

212. While some (e.g., Thomas R. Schreiner, *1, 2 Peter, Jude* [NAC; Nashville: Broadman & Holman, 2003], 73; Achtemeier, *1 Peter*, 109–10) look on this as a possible reference to the preincarnate Jesus, this seems to us to read too much into the text. In 1 Peter the Spirit changes his name according to his function (Spirit of the Anointed One, Holy Spirit, Spirit of God), and it is consistent with this naming-according-to-function that when the Spirit reveals the suffering of the Anointed One, he would be called "the Spirit of the Anointed One" within the prophets. Thus we are reading the genitive as descriptive ("the Spirit characterized by 'the Anointed One'") rather than possessive ("the Spirit belonging to the Anointed One") or appositive ("the Spirit, i.e., the Anointed One").

This Spirit (designated "the Spirit of glory and of God," 4:14) rests on those who are being reviled "in the name of the Anointed One." In other words, the Holy Spirit is presented as mediating God's presence to human beings. When he is mediating information about the suffering of the Anointed One, he is "the Spirit of the Anointed One," and when he is mediating the presence of God (the Father) to those undergoing persecution, he is "the Spirit of God." In the presentation of the good news, he is "the Holy Spirit sent from heaven," presumably indicating the origin of the good news. When it comes to sanctification, he is active, and here there is no need to call him the "Holy Spirit" for the idea of "holy" (*hagios*, ἅγιος) is implied in the activity of sanctification (*hagiasmos*, ἁγιασμός).

First Peter does not develop the Spirit in any personal sense, but then he only refers to the Spirit four times, always in the context of revelation or sanctification (which is where we are grouping 4:14). Interestingly enough, when it comes to spiritual gifts (also discussed in 1 Peter 4), the Spirit is not mentioned at all. Instead, they are traced to the favor of the Father. So 1 Peter has a pneumatology, but it is a muted pneumatology, with a limited function for the Spirit in situations where the direct intervention of God is not experienced. This is quite different than Pauline pneumatology, where the presence of the Spirit is very much experiential.

3.5.2 Other Spiritual Beings

While, strictly speaking, God is in a unique category and cannot be compared with any other being, and while Jesus in 1 Peter is virtually always explicitly viewed as a human agent of God, whether suffering or resurrected, it is convenient at this point to note spiritual beings other than God that populate 1 Peter's universe. However, if 1 Peter has yet to develop full trinitarian theology (or, at least has yet to express it), the author *certainly* does not develop his thought about any of these other beings.

Along with many Jewish groups of the first century, 1 Peter believes in the existence of divine agents whom the author refers to as messengers (i.e., angels). The text makes it clear that these agents do not have the level of divine revelation that 1 Peter's addressees have, for they wanted to look into the matter of the suffering of the Anointed One and his being honored (after what had been revealed to the prophets, 1:12). This verse implies that the understanding of such revelation had not been allowed to the angels, but was now revealed to the addressees, since the prophets had been serving them. So angels are not all-knowing by any means; in fact, they may not receive the revelations that some human beings do.

That is not the only limitation of the angels, for they are subject to a resurrected human being, Jesus the Anointed One, who is now ruling at the right hand of God. This puts the angels in a relatively subordinate position vis-à-vis Jesus, and it is through Jesus (not through angels) that the addressees of 1 Peter relate to God.

Interestingly enough, 1 Peter does not use the term "messenger" (i.e., "angel") to refer to rebellious beings, for in 3:19 the author refers to "the spirits in prison" rather than to "angels in prison." As noted above, it is likely that 1 Peter is dependent on the traditions we know from *1 Enoch*, a writing that does not use separate terminology for the rebellious and the obedient beings in the divine court; they are both "angels" (and both have names ending in the theophoric *'el*), but unlike *1 Enoch* 1 Peter does use "spirits in prison"[213] for the rebellious beings. There is, however, little else about the divine messengers that can be discerned in the text.

Even less can be said about the "authorities and powers" of 1 Pet 3:22. Since they are grouped with angels, they are apparently spiritual beings, and since they are subject to Jesus, they are apparently viewed as superior to human beings. The terms that describe them indicate that they have influence in the universe.[214] Beyond that one can only note that 1 Peter's universe has such beings, perhaps as part of God's court. It is not an unpopulated spiritual universe.

Likewise there is little to say about the devil. As in Jas 4:7, the devil (*diabolos*, διάβολος, "slanderer") appears only once in this letter (1 Pet 5:8). He is introduced as the "enemy" or "opponent" of the addressees. While this is not explained in detail, it would appear that he and not the human opposition is the real opponent of believers (an idea that appears at least in part in the Pauline corpus in Eph 6:12). He is pictured as a "roaring lion" and thus with a metaphorical open mouth, ready to "gulp down" anyone he can. As in Jas 4:7 the author instructs believers to "resist" this being. In 1 Peter this instruction is expanded to being "firm" or "steadfast" with respect to the faith or the commitment. An unwavering commitment to Jesus the Anointed One, even in the face of threatened or actual suffering, defeats the devil. This, for 1 Peter, is "spiritual warfare."

Other than that, we learn nothing about the devil. We do not learn about his origins (which is no surprise since other biblical works also do not talk about his origin) or about his ultimate fate (which Rev 20:10 does mention). We do not learn about any assistants or agents he may have, although presumably those who bring suffering to the believers are at least his unwitting agents. In 1 Peter demonology is thin, for the focus is on God and Jesus. This may also say something about 1 Peter's theological perspective and perhaps about how he would advise the contemporary church.

3.5.3 The Nature of Revelation

In 1 Peter it is clear that the Christ-event is not a change in the divine plan. There were unnamed prophets who prophesied about it. Their revelation was from "the Spirit of the Anointed One," which we have argued is the Holy Spirit as he "testifies

213. These rebellious beings are presently "in prison," which also fits the picture of *1 Enoch*, in which the rebellious angels are in a prison in which they experience torment of various types. But, as the author of 1 Peter suggests in his choice of words, this "prison" is not their ultimate fate, for in *1 Enoch* they request clemency but receive back the proclamation that they will instead be judged and receive punishment. This parallels what Jude 6 and 2 Pet 2:4 (where they are called "angels who sinned" and where the prison is named "Tartarus") state, namely, that such beings are imprisoned but still face final judgment. Such statements show an acceptance of this Enochian tradition in the early Jesus movement. It is also clear that for none of these authors are these "fallen angels" presently active

in the world (i.e., they are not "demons"), nor are they ruled by the devil or Satan, who *is* presently active in the world.

214. Eph 1:21; 2:2; 3:10; and 6:12, as well as Col 1:16; 2:10; and 2:15 refer to such "principalities and powers." In some contexts they could be under God's authority, but in Eph 2:2 they or at least some of them are said to be under the control of the "ruler of the power of the air," who is at work among disobedient human beings; and in Eph 6:12 followers of Jesus are said to be in a fight against such beings. In neither context are they benign, and in the one context they are under a powerful spirit-being, who is probably Satan. But 1 Peter does not get this explicit about them.

beforehand" about the Anointed One. What he revealed to the prophets was the sufferings of the Anointed One and his subsequent honor (the exact nature of that honor is not stated). But the prophets did not have all the information they desired, for they were investigating the timing of the event ("time and circumstances," NIV) or possibly the person and event ("the person or time," NRSV, ESV).[215]

So there was information that the prophets had, such as the Anointed One's suffering and subsequent honor, and also information that they did not have. Prophetic methodology allowed for investigating this mystery, although the methods of this investigation are not stated. But that clearly means that for 1 Peter prophetic revelation was not entirely passive. In this case their investigation resulted in the revelation that the original prophetic insight did not concern them and their situation, but rather the people to whom 1 Peter is addressed. However, it is likely that our author wants to indicate by this that the prophets only knew that the prophecy was for some future generation, not that they could identify the specific people and time (scattered groups in Asia Minor in what is known to us as the first century). The stress on their "serving you" is more information about the privilege of the addressees than about prophetic insight.

So for 1 Peter the prophets did receive advance information through the Spirit, which is another way of speaking about divine sovereignty in that God can plan and execute; since that is so, God can announce beforehand what he is going to do (since 1 Peter cites Isaiah, our author is surely aware that Isa 40–44 repeatedly contrasts YHWH with idols in that YHWH can declare the future since he can produce the future, in contrast to idols, which cannot do anything). But the information revealed is partial, although it can be investigated; through investigation, by whatever means the prophets used, at least some more information can be discovered (in this case that the prophecy did not concern them but people in a later era). That insight about prophecy is probably how our author would describe each of the prophetic passages (and for our author anything that he quotes is prophetic) that he cites.

3.5.4 The Nature of Salvation

There are two ways in which 1 Peter describes the change from being Greco-Roman pagans to being followers of Jesus. The first is through sacrificial metaphors; the second, through birth metaphors.

3.5.4.1 Sacrificial Metaphors

It is clear that for 1 Peter the sufferings of the Anointed One include his death and that his death has positively affected the addressees. Our author does not explain exactly

---

215. The Greek is ambiguous as to whether *tina* (τίνα) is an interrogative adjective modifying *kairon* (καιρὸν, "time"; i.e., "what or what type of time") or an interrogative pronoun (i.e., "what person or what type of time"). Davids, *1 Peter*, 61–62; Feldmeier, *First Letter of Peter*, 92–94; and Achtemeier, *1 Peter*, 109–10, all opt for the former understanding, but as Achtemeier shows in his detailed discussion, Elliott, *1 Peter* (AB), 345–46, definitely has some basis for opting for the latter understanding, even if he hardly defends his choice. This ambiguity accounts for the disagreement in the published translations.

how this death affected them; rather, he presents it by using a series of metaphors or images. Moreover, while the fact of Jesus' suffering is important (and suffering includes, but is not to be limited to, his death), it is his exaltation and future revelation that the author stresses more than his death. Still, the metaphors used for the effect of the death of the Anointed One are important, so we must examine them in detail.

First, when it comes to the relationship of the believers to Jesus, they are not just obedient to him (a present relationship), but have also been "sprinkled" with his blood (1:2), an image taken from dedicatory and/or purificatory rituals, such as the Sinai covenant ratification ceremony (Exod 24:8; Lev 8:30). It is not clear whether a specific ritual is in mind or just the general sense of covenant ratification or purification. But the image speaks emotionally about the inclusion and/or purification of the addressees, especially if they had been initiated into and immersed in the content of the Greek translation of the Torah, as seems to have been the case in the typical first-century Jesus community.

Another image or metaphor used for the effects of the Anointed One's sufferings is "ransom," which is not per se an image taken from the Hebrew Scriptures, since they do not contain a clear connection between ransom and death/blood. However, 1 Peter specifies that what has effected the ransom is "the precious blood of the Anointed One," which he compares to that of "a lamb without defect or blemish."[216] Here is a mixed metaphor, in that by saying that the ransom is not through money but through the "precious blood of the Anointed One, as the blood of an unblemished lamb," he combines the metaphor of ransom, which normally was through money or goods and then brings in one of the Torah's sacrificial pictures (e.g., the *tāmîd* of Exod 29:38; cf. Num 28:3; the purification offering of Lev 14:10; the Pentecost lambs of Lev 23:18; Nazirite offering of Num 6:14; the Sabbath offering of Num 28:9), in which both a lamb (Greek *amnos* [ἀμνός], in most cases multiple lambs) and "unblemished" are mentioned. Or perhaps this is Passover imagery, viewed through a New Testament lens (although the term for "lamb" is not used in Exod 12:5 LXX, a passage that also clearly states it could be either a lamb or a kid).

Despite the lack of clear verbal overlap in the original texts, it is probably this latter metaphor that is involved, for Passover was the time of release from Egypt, thus comparable to being "ransomed" from slavery, which also could be roughly compared to release from "the empty way of life of your ancestors." Of course, that means that it is the metaphorical sense that our author is using rather than the details of the Exodus narrative. Here again the stress is on (1) that though the destined suffering of the Anointed One was planned "before the foundation of the world," the addressees are the privileged ones for whose sake it has been "revealed"; and (2) that the addressees trust in the God who has raised the Anointed One from the dead.

---

216. While the first term, "unblemished" or "without defect" (Greek *amōmos*), is found in the LXX, the second term, "spotless" or "unblemished" (Greek *aspilos*), is not found in the LXX, but occurs in the New Testament, but only here for Jesus or an animal (see also 1 Tim 6:14; Jas 1:27 ["keep oneself unspotted"]; 2 Pet 3:14).

Yet another image that our author uses is drawn from Isa 53, when in 1 Pet 2:22–25 he quotes or alludes to Isa 53: 9, 4 [12], 5, and 6 (in that order), probably using a preformed tradition of the community, perhaps a creedal formula. The first part of the section presents the Anointed One as an innocent sufferer who does not retaliate but rather commits his cause to the judgment of God. That much is an example for the addressees who are slaves. But then the text states, "he himself carried our sins in his body on the wood/wooden post, in order that we may live for righteousness/ justice, having been freed from sins. You are healed by his welt/ wound [the word is singular]." The final verse refers to their having been like sheep going astray, but having now returned.

One can look at this on several levels. On the one level one notes the style of 1 Peter, that he uses a euphemism for the word "cross" rather than the word itself, which substitution was polite in the Greco-Roman world. Likewise, we note the shift from the first person ("we") to the second person ("you"); the former is often used in creedal formulae while the latter shows a focus back on the addressees. But most important is the theological reading of Isaiah according to which the Anointed One carried the sins of the believers "in his body" during the crucifixion, which resulted in the removal of those sins, summed up in the pithy phrase, "By his wound you are healed."[217] Our author does not explain how this worked, how this carrying of the sins of others in his dying removed sin, or even how one can carry the sins of others; but he does make clear that for the believers the effect of the physical death of Jesus was the removal of their sin.

Then in 1 Pet 3:18 our author returns to this topic: "the Anointed One suffered once on behalf of sin, the just on behalf of the unjust, in order that he might bring you to God." Again we have an expression of substitution that is also probably drawn from a creed or hymn. And we also have a picture of substitution, "the just on behalf of the unjust." The suffering (which is the language that 1 Peter prefers over the word "death," perhaps because it is the language with which living believers could identify) likely has to do with sin, this time using the type of formula found in the sin offering (e.g., Lev 5:7; 6:30 [LXX 6:23]; Ps 40:6 (LXX 39:7]).[218] This presentation differs from Isa 53:5 in that different prepositions are used. One has, then, a sin offering metaphor explaining one effect of the Anointed One's suffering, with "in order than he might bring you to God" being the ultimate effect.[219] Then, of course, 1 Peter goes on to talk about the resurrection, for the

---

217. One wonders about the singular "wound" or "welt," but while 1 Peter does not mention it, Isa 53:5 does have the same Greek word for "wound" ("bruises" in the NRSV), and it is singular. Furthermore, Isa 53:7 refers to "a lamb that is led to the slaughter," and it was common to slaughter sheep with a single slash across the throat. In either way Isa 53 may have influenced 1 Peter's presentation.

218. The image is there, although if one examines the sin offering in the Hebrew Scriptures one will note that it only has to do with inadvertent errors; there was no offering in Torah for known

or deliberate transgression, that is, "sin with a high hand," although there was always the possibility of the mercy of God. To the extent to which the "concerning sin" of 1 Peter includes known or deliberate sin, 1 Peter is using the ancient image for a new purpose.

219. This is also a metaphor from the sin offering in that after one had offered the sin offering and was thus purified, one was in a position to "draw near" to the deity and offer the peace or fellowship offering, that is, to worship, eating a meal in the presence of the deity.

Anointed One was put to death in the human sphere, but was made alive in the divine sphere.[220]

For our author, while these sufferings are unique — or at least unique for the Anointed One in that he suffered once[221] — that does not mean that these sufferings cannot be shared by his followers when they suffer as a result of their obedience to or identification with him (4:13, 16). First Peter does not explain how this sharing relates to the ultimate sin-bearing function of the Anointed One's suffering. His interest is in reframing the suffering of his addressees so that they view their suffering in a positive context, as "suffering according to God's will" (4:19) or "shar(ing) the sufferings of the Anointed One."

3.5.4.2 New Birth Metaphors

First Peter is the only New Testament document[222] to use clear "born again" language; it uses *anagennaō* (ἀναγεννάω, "beget again" or "cause to be born again")[223] in two different passages (1:3, 23). The first passage connects this rebirth to "the God and Father of our Lord, Jesus the Anointed One"; that is, it connects it to a Father. The means of this rebirth is through the resurrection of Jesus the Anointed One from the death. Since there is birth into a new family, there is also an inheritance connected with that family. "Father" has not been used lightly.

The second passage starts with reference to the addressees invoking an impartial judge as "Father" (1:17) and contrasts the way of life of the new family with that "inherited from [their] ancestors (or fathers)" (1:18). Then, after using a sacrificial, purification metaphor, the teaching is summed up with a call to virtue "since you have been born anew, not from (*ek*, ἐκ) 'seed' that is subject to decay, but from that which is not subject to decay, by means of God's living and remaining word." The picture is that of a male "sowing" his "seed" in a woman, where it grows in the fertile "soil" of her uterus, so in our culture one might say, "since you were born anew, not from sperm/semen that is subject to decay, but from that which is not subject to decay."[224]

It is unclear whether the "by means of" (*dia*, διὰ) is intended to give the way that this new birth happens (i.e., the "seed" is "God's word"), or whether "God's

---

220. Even if this author has been in numerous communion services that had the tone of a funeral and seemed to focus on the death of Jesus, so that one could be forgiven for not realizing that he had risen from the dead, the New Testament, while very cognizant and very appreciative of the death of Jesus, rarely mentions his death without his resurrection. It usually ends with a focus on his present reign and exaltation. In that regard, Phil 2:6–11 is somewhat paradigmatic.

221. The "once" is what carries the uniqueness, for "suffered" is aorist, which, while compatible with a unique event at a point in time, in itself is of undefined aspect, although it is true that unlike the present and imperfect its aspect is not continuous.

222. In John 3 "born again" is Nicodemus's misunderstanding of an ambiguous word (*anōthen*), while Jesus' meaning "born

from above" is clear in context; Titus 3:5 may refer to rebirth using *palingenesia* (παλιγγενεσία), but the term can mean "renewal" or "becoming again" — it is not specifically a birth metaphor. See BDAG, 752, *palingenesia*, παλιγγενεσία.

223. BDAG, 59, *anagennaō*, ἀναγεννάω.

224. In fact, in this author's translation for the CEB, he put, "Do this because you have not been reborn from the type of sperm that is subject to decay, but from that which is not subject to decay, i.e., through God's life-giving and enduring word," although "sperm" was changed to "seed" in the process of producing the final version, even though in 1 John 3:9 the same Greek word is translated as "DNA" (with "genetic character" in the footnote). There still seems to be some squeamishness in Bible translations about sexual terminology.

word" is the means by which the "seed" is implanted, although the fact that "God's word" is described as "living and remaining/enduring"[225] makes one suspect that it is indeed the "seed." There is no mystery about what this word is. It is not some decree or command of God spoken in heaven unheard by human ears, but "the word that was proclaimed to you as good news"—that is, that which they heard when they were evangelized.[226]

The main point for our author is that this rebirth has real effects. First, as noted above, it puts one in a new family, which has a Father under whose authority one lives and from whose inheritance one expects to receive, even if the reception of this inheritance is more like coming into a trust fund or becoming a partner in the family business at a given age than receiving the estate after a parent's death. Second, new birth means that one is no longer a native-born son or daughter of one's physical city or nation. One is indeed a "foreigner" and "resident alien" or "immigrant," for one is now born of a new family and part of a different people under a different sovereign. The tensions felt by the addressees in 1 Peter are thus natural tensions, not unnatural ones, for one really no longer belongs.

The *Haustafeln* in 1 Peter (1 Pet 2:11–3:7) attempt to negotiate this tension by indicating where compromises can be made with the now-foreign-to-them majority in their towns and villages (some of whom are their "former" relatives, masters, and husbands), as well as where they have to be careful to remain true to their new sovereign and their new God and Father. Finally, it means that they are "newborn babies" (since they have been born again into a new family) and thus need "pure spiritual milk"—i.e., instruction and training in the values and lifestyle of the new family (2:1–3).[227] This is, of course, a metaphor, but it is a metaphor flowing from the rebirth metaphor and expressing its logical consequence.

3.5.4.3 Other Aspects of Salvation

First Peter also discusses the timing of this "new birth," at least the official timing. In the context of his reference to Noah and the deluge (3:20), triggered by Jesus' announcement in his resurrection/ascension of his triumph to the rebellious angels (Gen 6 mediated through *1 Enoch*), our author discusses salvation or deliverance. In the case of Noah, "a few … were rescued through water." Then our author adds (3:21) the enigmatic "in correspondence to which water baptism now rescues (or delivers or saves) you."[228] So in some manner corresponding to that of Noah's res-

---

225. This is backed up by a quotation of Isa 40:6b, 8 LXX.

226. While "word" in 1:23 is the Greek term *logos*, λόγος, and "word" in the last clause of 1:25 is the Greek term *rhēma*, ῥῆμα, our author is not making a distinction, but rather is picking up on the terminology of Isa 40:8 LXX, which is the previous clause. For 1 Peter at least the two terms can be used synonymously.

227. Since this paragraph flows from the previous one, connected by "therefore" and ends with an to Ps 34:8 LXX, "Taste and see that the Lord is good," it is probable that our author is thinking of the "milk" as the instruction that came with the good news; it is part

of "the word of God."

228. The Greek term *antitypos* (ἀντίτυπος) means here "pertaining to that which corresponds to something else," not Plato's theory of "copy, antitype, representation" as in Heb 9:24. See BDAG, 90–91 *antitypos*. A literal translation of this verse would read, "Which (water) also by way of correspondence [accusative of respect] now delivers you, baptism." For a detailed discussion of the various textual and grammatical possibilities in this text, see Elliott, *1 Peter* (AB), 666–76.

cue—namely, in that it is through the means of water—baptism rescues or saves in the present.

This idea is then clarified by noting that it is not the physical cleansing ("not the putting off of the flesh's dirt") but some action of a good conscience toward God that effects the rescue. What this action is, is disputed. The Greek term *eperōtēma* (ἐπερώτημα) can mean a "question," a meaning does not fit the context here, or a "formal request" or "appeal" or "pledge."[229] All three of these are possible, but there is evidence in the papyri and parallels in the Dead Sea Scrolls that argue for the third meaning, that of a pledge (expressed in Latin in the term *sacramentum*, originally the soldier's oath of allegiance).[230] It is this meaning that fits with what is known of later baptismal practice and also with the logic of the text (including the "unto God"), if we assume that the genitive "good conscience" is a subjective genitive with a meaning similar to what it has in 1 Pet 3:16. What this passage means, then, is that what saves or rescues a person in baptism is not the act of washing in water per se, but the pledge that one makes to God, a pledge that comes from a good conscience and hence is sincere and unfeigned.

Baptism, then, is that point in time that one makes one's official pledge to God, very much as at a wedding, when one makes one's official pledge to one's spouse. Later in church history it is clear that this pledge was made in response to a series of questions placed by the one baptizing; whether that was the case this early or whether the situation was that of a simple oath or pledge to God in Jesus (the "confess with your mouth 'Jesus is Lord'" of Rom 10:9), one cannot tell. However, it is clear that the power behind this rescue is not some magic in the words, but the fact that they connect one to the resurrected Jesus. In other words, this confession in baptism saves or delivers "through the resurrection of Jesus the Anointed One," who is presently at God's right hand and is therefore ruling.

As for Paul in 1 Cor 15:14, 17–18, the resurrection is the critical event in salvation. Of course, also like Paul in 1 Corinthians, 1 Peter has already mentioned the death of Jesus using a number of metaphors, although the letter never discusses it in detail. The history is not the issue for him.[231] For the individual person, however, it is baptism (and specifically the pledge of allegiance to God and/or Jesus taken during the baptismal act), empowered by the resurrection of Jesus that is the point of salvation to the extent that salvation can be spoken of as present.

As intimated above, while rescue or salvation can be spoken of as present, this is not often the case in 1 Peter. While 1 Pet 3:21 can say that "baptism now saves (or

---

229. BDAG, 362, *eperōtēma*. Feldmeier, *First Letter of Peter*, 207–8, clearly argues for this second meaning, "a request to God for a good conscience."

230. So Elliott, *1 Peter* (AB), 679–82.

231. Until Gnosticism arose, which would deny the appropriateness of a true incarnation, there was no questioning of the fact that Jesus was crucified. Even Gnostics usually agreed that someone was crucified, just not the *logos* or Christ-spirit. Who would be so stupid as to claim that their leader died such a dishonorable death, if that death had not happened? In fact, as Paul notes in 1 Cor 1–2, the

very fact that followers of Jesus confessed allegiance to a crucified person made them look foolish. It is the resurrection of Jesus that is argued for in the New Testament, although it is more witnessed to than argued for. In 1 Cor 15, for example, it is asserted as a fact and then argued from that viewpoint. Paul's main point is not that Jesus rose from the dead, but that because he did, deceased believers will also rise from the dead. Likewise, in 1 Peter our author does not argue for the resurrection of Jesus but asserts it, and then points out that because of it those pledged to this Lord Jesus are in a good situation.

'is now saving') you," which is about as "present" as Greek can express, frequently in 1 Peter salvation is referred to as future rather than present. Each of the times that our author refers to the noun "salvation" (or "deliverance"; i.e., 1:5, 9–10;[232] 2:2), it is spoken of as something that is "to be revealed in the last day"/ something that they will "receive" as "the goal of your commitment"/ something that they "grow into." And while 3:21 uses the verb "save" for something in the present, in 4:18 the verb is a prophetic reference to something both present and future: it is a prophecy of the righteous being saved with difficulty in the future in a context that indicates that this final judgment is taking place in the believing community in the present.

So the future judgment is on the addressees now in the persecution that they are experiencing. Is this to be understood as something gnomic in that every situation of persecution can be viewed as judgment "in God's household," in which those who remain faithful during and throughout the persecution are considered to be being "saved"? However one reads this, for 1 Peter one can hardly feel "saved" or "rescued" until Jesus finally rescues one from the suffering they are experiencing. At the same time, this does not deny the reality of a new birth experience and connecting to the rescuing Lord, which began "officially" at the point of one's baptism.

3.5.5 The Nature of the Believing Community

Who, then, are these who are being "saved," whether in the present act of baptism or in the future event of the final judgment? We immediately notice that these people are always plural, a group, a community. While baptism was certainly done one by one, the individuals are only spoken to as part of a group. This community is described in a number of ways.

First, they are a "chosen" or "elect" people (the Greek *eklektos*, ἐκλεκτός, can be translated either way). This idea brackets the whole letter, for it appears in 1:1 and 5:13, both times addressing the people as a group.[233] This picks up the theme of Israel in the Hebrew Scriptures, who were also a chosen people. Indeed the very language once used for Israel in Exod 19:6 is now applied to these addressees: "you are a chosen race, a royal priesthood, a holy nation [Greek *ethnos*, ἔθνος], a people for [God's own] possession" (2:9). Thus this people, this community, continue the status of Israel as the chosen people, who are God's royal priesthood.

As a result, they live under God's favor (or "grace," Greek *charis*, χάρις, mentioned ten times in the letter),[234] for this characterizes God, who is "the God of all grace" (5:10). This favor (or salvation in the context of 1:10) is what the prophets prophesied about, and ultimately this favor is what Jesus will bring when he is

---

232. First Peter 1:10 speaks of the prophets' interest in this salvation, but the term refers back to the salvation of 1:9 that is still future.

233. There is a way that *eklektos* is used in this letter as a singular, namely, when it is used for the elect or chosen stone (2:4, 6), which is Jesus, who is, of course, singular, one of a kind. In this context the people are joined to *this* chosen stone, which indicates how they came into their chosen status.

234. Divine favor or grace is a second concept (alongside that of being chosen or elect) that brackets the book, for it occurs in the formal greeting of 1:2 as a wish for the addressees, where it is a part of the traditional Christian greeting. But this concept occurs just a few verses later, and then at the end the letter closing the author expresses that "this is God's true favor: stand firm in it."

revealed (1:13). This favor is something that both men and women share equally (3:7); for 1 Peter this should be an important factor in how men treat their wives.

But favor is not just something given by God; it is also something human beings receive in response to their deeds—in particular, in response to suffering unrighteously or patiently enduring suffering for doing good (2:19–20). Favor is especially received by the humble (5:5). It is also seen in the variegated gifts that God gives, so in this sense it is individualized (4:10), although the gifts are in the context of the community and its needs. Here again God's favor is viewed as something that is for the most part collective because it is connected to their being chosen as God's people. It is the favor of the divine patron who has selected them as his clients.

Yet as in any group of clients, some can deserve or earn more favor with their patron than others, particularly those who suffer patiently for his honor and those who are humble. And while God's favor is seen collectively in his gifting the community, that does not mean that he gifts each individual alike. This theology of grace is not Luther's theology of grace, for there is the possibility of merit, but it is a theology of grace that does portray God as a great patron of a client people (or Father of a great family).

Second, the chosen people of God and thus recipients of his favor are also described as the (new or true) Temple. First Peter can smoothly segue from infant imagery (2:2) to temple imagery (2:4) by means of "the Lord" (= Jesus), who was the rejected stone (as they are also now rejected by human beings) but chosen by God (as they are also chosen). But the stone imagery allows our author to describe them as "living stones" in the (presumably new)[235] temple. This is a spiritual "house" (just as Jesus now lives in the sphere of the Spirit). But "house" can also mean "household," so it is only a slight shift to refer to them as a priesthood offering spiritual sacrifices (for if the temple is in the sphere of the Spirit, so are the sacrifices offered in it). And of course, such sacrifices would be acceptable to God (probably implying that sacrifices in the realm of the flesh are not)[236] because they are "through Jesus the Anointed One."

With that our author has come full circle from "the Lord" back to "Jesus." This, of course, leads to an interlude in which he cites the Hebrew Scriptures as supporting the rejection and subsequent exaltation of Jesus as a "cornerstone," and so indicates that the Hebrew Scriptures support the whole logic of the passage. It is in this context that he then applies Exod 19:6 to these people, for this is *the* passage where Israel then (and now the addressees) are called "a royal priesthood," which is just what he has asserted four verses earlier (2:9). In case the readers miss the point

---

235. If Simon Peter is the actual author of the letter, then the Second Temple is still standing, although it would have been under threat by the end of Nero's reign. For followers of Jesus, however, the Second Temple was irrelevant, since Jesus was the true temple.

236. Here is another place where the dating of 1 Peter has at least some significance, for if one dates it to the lifetime or a year or two after the likely death of Simon Peter, that is, late in the reign of

Nero, then sacrifices were still going on in Jerusalem; yet for 1 Peter the temple is now spiritual and the acceptable sacrifices are now offered by this new priesthood in the sphere of the Spirit. Of course, even after the destruction of the Second Temple in 70 CE there would be some sense of contrast as long as the hopes of rebuilding it remained alive.

of this application, 1 Peter cites "a poem based on Hos. 1:6, 9–10; 2:23, which are also cited independently in Rom. 9:25–26."[237] They once were not God's people, but now are.

Like Romans, 1 Peter is addressed to a largely Gentile community, but unlike Romans 1 Peter focuses on the implications of new birth (Paul prefers adoption language). As God's people, they are, like Israel, to proclaim "the excellence of character/miracles of the one calling you out of darkness into his marvelous light."[238] In other words, they have Israel's position as God's people, Israel's function as royal priests, and Israel's mission as proclaimers of God. All of this is through Jesus, Lord and Anointed One, i.e., the one who fulfills God's promise to Israel and the one whom they are "in" (e.g., 5:14).

Unfortunately, 1 Peter does not indicate whether this is a replacement theology in the sense that since the addressees are "in the Anointed One," they are the true Israel and thus heirs of Israel's promises; or in the sense that for him ethnic Israel is still in "the flesh" or natural human sphere in which the Anointed One was rejected and that God's true people are in "the spirit" or the divine sphere, the sphere in which Jesus the Anointed One is now exalted. He may have not made such distinctions. But it is clear for him who are now the people of God, the royal priesthood, the heirs of Exod 19:6.

Third, the community is a family, a household. In one sense this was already seen when "house" shifted to "household" in the sense of "holy priesthood" in 1 Pet 2:5. But a priesthood, while often a household in the sense of an extended family, is not necessarily related to the divinity, so that verse alone would leave one in doubt about the relationship of the priestly family to God. However, there are clearer passages in which our author makes his theology of family known.

The key passage around which all of the others revolve is 1:3: "according to his great mercy he has rebirthed us to a living hope through the resurrection of Jesus the Anointed One from the dead." The rebirthing or regenerating[239] one is God; insofar as the resurrection of Jesus is clearly the means, Jesus is not the rebirthing one. God is, therefore, the Father, as will be noted later. This rebirthing is by means of an "imperishable seed (or, in contemporary terms, 'sperm')," which is either transmitted by "the word of the living and abiding word of God" or is itself that word.[240]

---

237. Davids, *1 Peter*, 93.

238. The NRSV translates the term "mighty acts," which fits BDAG, 130 (meaning 2), *aretē*, ἀρετή, while "excellence of character" comes from BDAG, 130 (meaning 1), *aretē*, ἀρετή. Is 1 Peter making a distinction? Perhaps, if questioned, he would quickly admit that both "mighty deeds" and "excellence of character" are true, although, while Israel did focus a lot on God's wonders (exodus and conquest), 1 Peter rarely speaks of miracles and is more focused on virtue.

239. BDAG, 59, *anagennaō*, ἀναγεννάω, glosses the meaning as "beget again, cause to be born again," so "regenerate" in this sense would fit quite well, but since "regenerate" can be applied to a plant that regenerates from its root and thus to a natural process, and

since it has been used in a number of senses theologically, it is difficult to use without misunderstanding. Nor is "beget" (as in "beget again") contemporary English. "Cause to be born again" or "given us a new birth" is fine so long as the context indicates that God is the Father in the process, not, so to speak, the doctor overseeing a process external to him.

240. One is reborn from seed (*ek*, ἐκ) but through (*dia*, διά) the word of God. Is our author making a distinction? If he is, the word is the vehicle for the "seed" that is undefined in nature. That other option is that our author may in essence be using *ek* and *dia* synonymously, or rather using the *dia* phrase to explain the *ek* metaphor. In that he calls the word "living and remaining." This author tends to think that the latter is the case.

God, then, in this realistic language, is Father of the family into which these addressees have been reborn. This, of course, is a Mediterranean family, not a contemporary Western family. The Father is the *paterfamilias*, the authoritative leader from whom the family takes its honor status and receives its provision and whose direction the family follows. Thus, since Father is "holy," his children are to be "holy" (1:15), and the letter will in several places describe what "holy" means. Since the Father is an impartial judge, the children should live "in fear" (1:17); indeed, he is the only one that the children should fear, knowing that this Father will not play favorites, so only appropriate conduct will bring a favorable judgment in the final judgment.

Father's children are to be "obedient children" (1:14), which means a change of lifestyle to match the lifestyle of the new family, not their former birth family. At the same time, Father is providing them with what they need, with "spiritual milk" (2:2) that they are to desire. What this "milk" is remains undefined, although what they have already "tasted" is that "the Lord is benevolent" (2:3).[241] Given the reference to "the Lord," which in context means Jesus, the milk would either refer to him and his rule or to his offer in the good news to freely accept the allegiance of all who will turn to him. He will reward them with a place in his "kingdom," although this would apply more to what they have already "tasted" than to the "milk" that they are to desire, which would then have to be some extension of this.[242] The point is that ultimately this "milk" is a provision of the Father through "the Lord" for the children (who are never thought of as outgrowing this food, for they are always growing toward maturity). The Father sets the standard, but he is also providing the means of reaching the standard.

This family is also a structured family. There are elders in the family (5:1–3) who lead by example, caring for it as metaphorical shepherds, exercising appropriate oversight as the elder members of any family should.[243] There are younger members of the family (5:5), who are to accept the authority of the elder members, as younger members of any family are often called to accept the authority of their elder brothers and sisters. There is also apparently an "absent" eldest brother in the metaphor "chief shepherd," who will appear and (if the metaphor holds, on the Father's behalf) honor the elders who serve well (5:4).[244]

The Father also gives his favor (and thus his provision) to the family in the forms of "gifts" (4:10). Not every member gets the same gift, but each is equally responsible

---

241. The Greek term can mean "reputable," "kind," "loving," or "benevolent" when applied to persons. BDAG, 1090 (meaning 3), *chrēstos*, χρηστός.

242. It is not unusual for the "milk" to be viewed as scripture as in "milk of the word," as is pointed out in Witherington, *Hellenized Christians*, 112. But in this passage the focus is on Jesus and his benevolence; thus, BDAG, 598, *logikos*, λογικός, is correct in pointing out that only in etymology is *logikos* related to "word" (*logos*); in usage it means "thoughtful" or "reasonable" or "spiritual" (as in Rom 12:1) or, and this pertains particularly to our passage, "metaphorical" as opposed to "literal." Thus context rather than

logikos read etymologically needs to determine what "milk" is a metaphor for.

243. It is clear that there are dangers of abuse of power ("lording it over") and personal profit, that is, doing it for the money.

244. If the metaphor is being used consistently, then Jesus (who is consistently the one who is going to "appear" or, passively, "be revealed"), who is also probably the Shepherd of 2:25 (in context it is Jesus who is clearly the focus), is a shepherd just as the elders (and Peter) are shepherds, and so an elder of elders—or, to use the family imagery, the eldest brother. The "chief shepherd" metaphor does not separate him from the elders, but does make him their chief.

for the appropriate use of their gift(s), for through practicing these gifts the Father's provision apparently comes to the whole family. Some serve the others verbally and are to do so "as words of God" (presumably passing on the words that God has gifted them with). Others serve or minister in some physical sense and are to do so "as from the strength God supplies" (drawing on the skills and energy that God has gifted them with). The point is that in all of this the honor of the family Father is upheld in his evident provision for the family.

The family is an extended family in that there are gatherings of siblings "in the world" (5:9), a logical inference if they are all part of the same "ethnic group" of resident aliens/immigrants/foreigners. Each local group can receive an example from the experiences of other parts of the family. This, of course, has implications about how one thinks about and acts toward other groups and their members (whether they are the same as or radically different from one's own ethnicity and nationality). Our author, however, does not develop these implications, for they are not the focal issue for those whom he is addressing. Within the local group it is important to "love" the group (i.e., show care for the group); this is symbolized in the "kiss of love" that was apparently used in greeting one another (5:14). Since kisses were basically signs of family belonging in the ancient world and rarely used outside of the context of relatives by blood or marriage, this kiss would be a "sacrament" of sorts.[245]

As noted above, while fathers in the Mediterranean world were not necessarily emotionally intimate with their wives or children (and, in fact, did not take an active role in raising their children until the sons were able to join them in work and social activities), they were responsible for the protection of the family. That is also true of God as Father in 1 Peter. There is an implied level of protection in 1:1 in the choosing of the addressees, a choosing that is indeed protective if one reads *kata prognōsin theou patros* (κατὰ πρόγνωσιν θεοῦ πατρός) as "destined by God the Father" (1:2, NRSV), that is, according to his "omniscient wisdom and intention"[246] rather than "according to the foreknowledge of God the Father." There is less ambiguity in 3:12, for, although it is a quotation of the Hebrew Scriptures, our author is using it to make the point of the benevolent care that "the Lord" has for the righteous: his "eyes" are on them and his "ears" open to their prayer.

However, the protection that the divine Father gives does not mean that there

---

245. Interestingly enough, there is in 1 Peter no separation of male and female roles in the family. One has the generic masculine for elders and for younger. The scattered branches of the family or the family as a whole is termed the *adelphotēs* (ἀδελφότης), sometimes translated "brotherhood," but which clearly includes both brothers and sisters. Thus, unless we wish to gloss the Greek word with "family," BDAG, 19 (meaning 1), is certainly correct in giving "a group of fellow-believers, a fellowship" as the gloss, although this tends to drop the family image. It is an *adelphotēs*, for in this family only the siblings are present; the Father is involved, but absent. Only in 5:13 is feminine imagery used, and there the author's community (*ekklēsia*?—this would be grammatically feminine) is probably presented as a woman, the author's metaphorical wife, with his

coworker Markus as his "son" (unless this is literally the author's wife and son, which is not at all impossible). If the woman is the community, then the previous family metaphor has been dropped and a different metaphor taken up in which each community is feminine, "sisters chosen together," and in which community members can relate as metaphorical fathers to sons (and leaders relate as husbands to a community as a whole). Edwin Friedman, *From Generation to Generation* (New York: Guilford, 1985), who applies family emotional systems theory to church systems, would have loved this.

246. BDAG, 867 (meaning 2), *prognōsis* (πρόγνωσις). The following translation is according to BDAG, 866 (meaning 1), *prognōsis*.

will not be trials. Indeed, 1 Peter is very much about coming to terms with the trials that the addressees are facing. This situation is introduced in 1:6, where the addressees are said to be rejoicing in their future deliverance or salvation, although they are presently experiencing trials or tests. In these tests the fact that their commitment is genuine will be revealed, and that will bring them honor when Jesus the Anointed One is revealed. Thus trials result in increased honor, although in 1 Peter's use of this saying (in contrast to James's), one rejoices in the eschatological end, not in the intermediate trials.[247]

These tests of one's commitment are also something the divine Father may will. In 3:17 our author, who has previously suggested that good behavior will prevent suffering (3:13), now states that it is better to suffer for doing good than for doing evil, adding to the suffering for doing good "if God's will so wills" (usually translated with a phrase like the more idiomatic, "if God so wills"). The clause uses the Greek optative mood, which suggests that God might will such suffering, but it is not at all certain. Likewise in 4:19, which comes at the end of a discussion of suffering, 1 Peter uses the phrase "those suffering according to God's will," that is, for those suffering because of their commitment to the Anointed One (versus suffering for some criminal or evil behavior). This contrasts with Jas 1:13, where it is stated that God tests no one, so no one who is suffering should say that their trial comes from God. First Peter certainly does not emphasize God's willing trials or make such suffering a mark of spirituality, but he clearly states that it is a possibility.

There appear to be four reasons why God may will suffering as a result of righteous action. First, there is a blessing in suffering for doing good. This is stated clearly in 3:14, and then in 4:14 the situation is expanded from suffering to being "reviled" or "insulted" "in the name of the Anointed One" (i.e., because of one's commitment to Jesus). In that situation one is blessed (the same term used in the Beatitudes of the Sermon on the Mount for the blessedness or happiness of folk who suffer) because precisely in that situation "the Spirit of glory and of God"[248] is "resting" on one. In other words, one may not experience anything; one may not feel like one is blessed, but precisely in the situation of persecution one is objectively blessed and is in fact experiencing the presence of the Spirit. Otherwise said, God honors the persecuted with his presence in the Spirit. Thus, suffering for Jesus is not an unmitigated evil.

Second, the one who "suffers in the flesh has ceased from sin" (4:1). Although this statement is made in a context of Jesus' suffering, it probably is not a reference to martyrdom, since that does not appear to be the experience that 1 Peter is discussing (and it would be a rather obvious truism: if one has been martyred, one has stopped sinning). Rather, the core idea seems to be "arming" oneself with "the same mind-set" as "the Anointed One," which then flows into the comment that if

---

247. In 4:13 there is a note of *eschatologische Vorfreude* (eschatological anticipated joy) in 1 Peter as there is in Jas 1:2, the saying in James that parallels 1 Pet 1:6.

248. Some manuscripts add in "and of power," although that does not make a difference to the point being made here. See the discussion in the various commentaries.

one carries through with this mind-set and suffers, one has indeed broken with sin (which in 1 Peter is often identified with the pagan lifestyle). Our author goes on to stress that this break with sin "results in" living the rest of one's physical life "no longer for human desires" but for "God's will." Psychologically, the more it has cost one to take a stance, the less likely one is to change one's mind. Suffering, therefore, firms up one's commitment.

Third, this attitude toward suffering leads to a reframing of the suffering itself, for in 1 Peter to suffer in a test (*peirasmos*, πειρασμός) of one's commitment is to "share in the sufferings of the Anointed One" (4:12–13). This is an extension of 4:1, which reflects on the suffering of Jesus by which one adopts the same mind-set as Jesus had. Now our author declares that this suffering can be reframed not just as a shared mind-set but also as shared sufferings. One can rejoice in this sharing, for in doing so, one anticipates sharing in Jesus' exaltation upon the "revelation" of his most honorable status (i.e., glory). This statement is problematic to modern readers in that it raises the question of whether the suffering of these addressees (and, by extension, of followers of Jesus down through the ages) is in some sense redemptive. For 1 Peter that is an extraneous question, for his point is one of identification. After all, if one is "in the Anointed One" (5:14), has adopted his mind-set about suffering according to God's will, is part of God's family, and is born of divine "seed," it is hardly surprising that one is invited to reframe sufferings as a sharing in his sufferings. Suffering brings one closer to Jesus, as shared experiences do. Our author apparently feels no need to distinguish in this context between salvific and nonsalvific suffering.

Fourth, and the most problematic of the reasons, is that suffering may be God's will for the believing community and/or its members because judgment has begun, not in the world, but "in God's household" (4:17). The basis for this statement is the conviction that the community is living at the end of the ages (e.g., 1:20). Thus, God's judgment has already begun, not with God's "smiting the heathen," so to speak, but with his judging and presumably purifying his own "household." The passage clearly says that this is not anticipatory judgment or proleptic judgment; rather, the real judgment is beginning—it is the time (*kairos*, καιρός) of the event (the verb is an aorist infinitive) of judgment, not the starting of a process.[249]

This judgment is anticipated in Israelite, Jewish, and Christian literature (e.g., Jer 7:8–15; Amos 3:2; Zech 13:7–9; *1 En.* 1.7; 1QS 4.20–22; Matt 16:27; Rom 2:6; 1 Cor 3:12–15), although the idea of God's people being judged first is rare (Jer 32:29 LXX [Eng. 25:29]; Ezek 9:6 LXX; cf. Isa 10:11–12; Mal 3:1–6; 2 Macc 6:12–15; *T. Benj.* 10.6–11). Our author does not explain why this is the case, whether the suffering is purgative,[250] or whether by starting with God's people God is giving them less time to sin (both ideas are present in the ancient literature). But it is clear that it is better to suffer in this early judgment than in the later stages of

---

249. With Goppelt, *Die erste Petrusbrief*, 311; and Achtemeier, *1 Peter*, 315, we argue that the text does not present this as the messianic woes *before* the judgment, but as the judgment itself.

250. Feldmeier, *First Letter of Peter*, 228–29, does view it as purificatory, which may well be a correct conjecture.

the final judgment: if it is so with God's house,[251] "what will be the end of those disobeying God's good news?" The implication is that it will be far, far worse (see the author's use in 4:18 of Prov 11:31 [LXX]).

But 1 Peter's main concern is not in discussing final judgment, but in discussing present behavior. How does one deal with one's present suffering? What attitudes and lifestyle are appropriate for God's people during this period?

First, one should lead a life characterized by honorable conduct in the eyes of surrounding pagan society (2:11–12). Our author does not differentiate whether this conduct is also honorable in the eyes of God or the believing community or whether it is honorable in the eyes of pagan society and indifferent in the eyes of God. In the succeeding *Haustafel* (2:18–3:7), he mentions virtues that at least parts of both societies would value, but for different reasons and with different emphases. For instance, in discussing slave behavior, he notes that patient endurance of unjust suffering is virtuous, but while for Stoics (who, unlike many parts of society in the ancient world, believed slaves could act morally) this would be because they valued a tranquil spirit that rose above the vicissitudes of life and demonstrated *apatheia*, 1 Peter gives a different reason. For 1 Peter, it is virtuous because of identification with the Anointed One and in light of the final judgment (as one sees in "conscience before God" in 2:19 and "favor before God" in 2:20).

Thus, while the mere fact of recognizing Jesus as one's supreme leader and the refusal to worship other deities (be they household, guild, or civil) would mark one out at least as strange and probably as dishonorable or deviant, and while, when Jesus' values and those of pagan society came into conflict, it is clear that the former should trump those of pagan society, one stresses behavior that pagan society will consider honorable, even in situations where they may not live up to their own definition of honor. This is a type of pragmatic lifestyle.

Second, especially during this period of suffering, one is to stress community-preserving virtues and avoid community-destroying vices. Of course one rejects pagan vices (which, although they were accepted in pagan society, were also criticized by some pagan moral philosophers), such as "self-abandonment, drunkenness, excessive feasting, drinking parties, and disgusting idolatry" (4:3).[252] But one also rejects such human weaknesses as deceit or underhandedness, insincerity, envy, and all types of slander (2:1), which make the community an unsafe place. All of these are characterized as stemming from desire ("human desires" in 4:2; "desires of the body" in 2:11). Desires, or what we might characterize as the impulses of the human limbic system or one's psychological drives, are the flaw in humanity in 1 Peter (as in James) that "battles against the self" (2:11) or are contrasted with God's will (4:2).

251. The texts from the Hebrew Scriptures cited have judgment beginning in God's temple, and in the LXX "God's house" is his temple rather than his people. Yet while this may be the origin of the language, in 1 Peter "household" or "people of God" and "temple" (built of "living stones") are so intertwined, that while the spatial image of "temple" may be primary, the image of a father setting his house in order remains important. See Achtemeier, *1 Peter*, 315–16.

252. From the Greco-Roman point of view such behavior often *promoted* social connection and thus was acceptable. For a description of the purposes of and behavior at typical guest meals in the Greco-Roman world, see Hans Joachim Stein, *Frühchristliche Mahlfeiern* (WUNT 2/255; Tübingen: Mohr Siebeck, 2008), 28–64.

There is no discussion in 1 Peter as to the origin of such desire, although the way he words this may indicate that he, again like James, is influenced by the developing Jewish *yēṣer* theology in which the human being was viewed as created with a set of useful drives that are destructive if not controlled by a counterforce (in Jewish theology usually the law, while in James divine wisdom).[253] When the Hebrew term was translated with the term "desire" (usually *epithymia* ἐπιθυμία), it fit well within the Greco-Roman world, in which desire (including emotions in general) was viewed as problematic since it did not originate in reason and fluctuated rather than being steady. The question posed by 1 Peter, then, is whether human beings in the believing community will give in to desire, as they obviously did during their pagan life, or whether they will submit to God's will and thus express the life of his people. The proper lifestyle stresses avoiding community-destroying vices, that is, one's uncontrolled inner drives.

Third, there are virtues that express the new life as part of the people of God into which these followers of Jesus have been born. These internal virtues are, as we would expect from the vice lists, community-building virtues: like-minded, sympathetic, loving those in the family of believers, tenderhearted, humble-minded (3:8). All of these tend to minimize internal conflict in the community and build community unity. These are summed up in 4:9: "earnestly maintain love for one another" (love in the New Testament is not about feelings, but about caring deeds).

What is the implication of this love? "Love covers a multitude of sins" (Prov 10:12). In other words, love will seek resolution of hurt and conflict, leading to the passing over of small slights and sins against one and the working through to forgiveness of the more significant sins (as Paul also taught in 1 Cor 13:7).[254] This is primarily inward, within the community; when it comes to traveling believers, who might tax one's resources, love looks like "[Be] hospitable to one another without grumbling" (4:9). Love also means using one's gifts for the good of the community (4:10 – 11). A proper lifestyle, then, is characterized by communal love, by community-preserving virtues.

Finally, along with these virtues are those that will tend to calm the hostility of the surrounding world: repaying evil or abuse with a blessing rather than with more evil or abuse (3:9). In other words, in the situation of persecution one acts like Jesus. While appropriate rewards are promised for such behavior, it is not guaranteed to stop persecution. Persecution itself needs to be endured. Remaining firm in it — that is, not fearing what "they" fear (i.e., fearing only God) or being intimidated by external threats — is the bottom line. This is what it means to "resist the devil" (5:9) and so not to be "devoured" by him. The good news, of course, is that the persecution

---

253. See Peter H. Davids, *The Epistle of James* (NIGTC; Grand Rapids: Eerdmans, 1982), 83 – 84, and the literature cited there. This view of humanity is more normal in Jewish sources than reference to a fall of humanity as the source of human evil, although the latter does occur.

254. Some, based on a use of Prov 10:12 in *2 Clem.* 16.4 and a

similar saying in Sir 3:30 and also on Luke 7:47 ("Her sins, which are many, are forgiven, for she loved much"), argue that what love is covering is one's own sins, so that by acts of love we, so to speak, do penance. However, that is not the use of Prov 10:12 in Jas 5:20, nor does that meaning fit in the context of 1 Peter.

is only temporary (5:10). Jesus will be revealed, and then all will be well. But that moves us on to the next theological topic.

3.5.6 The Nature of Eschatology

It is clear that 1 Peter has a theology rooted in eschatology. Our author's basic conviction is that the Jesus-event took place "in the last of the ages" (*ep' eschatou tōn chronōn*, ἐπ' ἐσχάτου τῶν χρόνων, 1:20); therefore, the addressees are living in the end of the ages. It is no surprise, then, when he says later in the book that "the end of all things is near" (4:7, *to telos ēngiken*, τὸ τέλος ἤγγικεν). This age is moving toward its goal or culmination (*telos*), and that goal is "near" or "at hand."[255] This end expectation colors all that is written in the letter and is one reason that appeals to the "revelation" of Jesus the Anointed One have the type of force that they do. What, then, is 1 Peter expecting when "the end of all things" finally arrives?

The first and main thing that he is expecting is what he calls "the revelation" of Jesus the Anointed One. He mentions this three times in his letter: in 1:7 it is the time when the addressees will receive "praise, glory and honor"; in 1:13 they will receive favor (presumably from the divinely appointed ruler); and in 4:13 those who have shared in the Anointed One's sufferings will rejoice, for it will be the revelation of his "glory" or "honor."[256] For 1 Peter Jesus is already "Lord," but he is "our Lord" (1:3; cf. 3:15). A time is coming, which in the view of our author is "soon," when the honorable status of this Lord will be "revealed," which appears to be that he will rule openly, not just as "our Lord," but as Lord of the world.[257] God may be "Father," but he is a Father who never appears in the world (in 1 Peter); Jesus is the beloved Lord who is going to "be revealed" in this world. This is the same concept that Paul expresses using the term "parousia." That is the point of hope toward which history and the addressees are moving.

The second thing that our author is expecting is that with the revelation of the Lord a time of judgment will come. This final judgment has already begun in "God's house" (4:17), which is apparently another sign of the imminence of the end of the age, but it will continue to expand, so to speak, and include "those who do not obey the good news." First Peter does not have a lot to say about those who are not followers of Jesus. It is true that failure to obey God's announcement of the good news would sound ominous to anyone in the ancient world who was aware of what rulers did to rebellious subjects when the rulers "appeared." Likewise in 4:5 he notes that those pagans who slander the followers of Jesus because of the latter's refusal to join in their "dissipation" will "pay back an account" to "the one who is prepared to judge the living and the dead."

---

255. While 1 Peter does not set dates, it is clear from the descriptions of the end as imminent that the author, like the John who wrote Revelation (who repeatedly says, "the time is short" or "near"), would be astounded that history has continued for 1,900 years.

256. In 5:4 our author uses slightly different language, that of "the chief shepherd" "appearing" or "becoming manifest" rather than "being revealed," but while the metaphor of "shepherd" is dif-

ferent, the meaning of the event is the same.

257. This is not intended to deny Jesus' present universal sovereignty, for that appears to be implied in 3:22, at least in terms of the various spiritual powers. However, his universal sovereignty is not apparent on earth nor recognized by most of humanity. It is only his followers, believers, who recognize him as "Lord" and therefore consciously submit to his will.

Again, in the sense that he is already "prepared," there is a note of imminence, but more significantly, there is the sense that those who slander followers of Jesus are in deep trouble, as if they are school children getting into mischief and taunting the "good" children for not joining in, unaware that the teacher is coming down the hall. This teacher is noting from their voices who the problematic children are and is about to judge. Naturally, God's judgment is a far more serious affair than that of our illustration. Yet in 1 Peter our author knows that he is writing to believers, not to those who do not yet believe. Thus, although he alludes to the fate of those who are not obedient to God, he does not discuss it in detail.

The aspect of judgment he does discuss in detail is that of the followers of Jesus. They are not immune from this judgment. The fact that they "invoke God as Father" should make them live their lives in an appropriate fear of that coming judgment, for this Father "judges each according to their deeds without partiality" (1:17). He will not show favoritism to his "children." In that judgment, only living for him counts, not pious words about him. Yet for the most part 1 Peter is hopeful about the coming judgment. The fact that God will judge the living and the dead means that there will be a resurrection and those who have heard and obeyed the good news and have died will live according to God's verdict (4:6), just as Jesus did; in expectation of this judgment (as seen in his resurrection and exaltation), he could commit his present cause to God (2:23). The coming judgment is what makes the sacrifices of this age worth it.

It is worth it in the sense that it is at the time that their rescue comes, they will receive the goal of their commitment, namely, the deliverance of their selves or lives (1:9). As noted above when discussing salvation, in 1 Peter the focus is on salvation as future, for the addressees are clearly not thought of as experiencing rescue or deliverance in the present. Their time of rescue is when Jesus appears. With this will come their "inheritance" (1:4) or full role as adults in the family and possession of the family resources and status (since this inheritance is more a birthright that one receives when mature enough, than the type of inheritance one receives upon the death of the parent). This time of rescue is, so to speak, a "blessing," for in their calling there is the implicit promise of such blessing (2:9).

Another metaphor used is that of "praise and glory and honor" (1:7). When a ruler arrives in a city, he bestows such things on faithful subjects, and in an honor-shame society these were the most valuable commodities possible. Therefore this was surely a powerful metaphor in the context in which the letter was written. A final metaphor, one that is specifically applied to elders who are faithful, is their receiving a "crown of glory"; the analogy is to the wreath that was given to victors in the games and others whom a ruler wished to honor. This "crown" is "glory," or honor. In other words, they will be marked out for special honor. All of this expectation is summed up in a final metaphor, namely, that God has called the addressees in the Anointed One to his "eternal glory" (5:10). That is, those whom he has called (i.e., the addressees) will participate in or share in his "eternal honor."

Our author is apparently aware that negative reinforcement is relatively ineffective in changing behavior. Thus threats or warnings of punishment tend not to be effective. While he alludes to the possibility of such, our author does not major on the negative. Rather, he focuses on positive reinforcement, that is, promises of reward. All of the suffering that one may undergo in the present on account of loyalty to Jesus is worth it; to remain motivated one need only keep in mind the rewards that are coming and are coming soon. At the center of these rewards is the presence of Jesus.

3.6 CANONICAL CONTRIBUTION

First Peter is no true "stepchild" in the New Testament in any sense other than past neglect, for it makes a significant contribution to the canon, partially in what it says and does and partially in what it does not. The contribution is both forward looking and backward looking.

3.6.1 In Relationship to the Hebrew Scriptures

First, our letter is significant in its use of the Hebrew Scriptures. There are at least eighteen citations of the Hebrew Scriptures (usually clearly from the Greek translation, for our author's "Bible" was Greek), which Elliott groups into three categories according to the fullness of their introduction as a quotation.[258] Of these eighteen, three are from the Pentateuch, eight are from the Prophets (of which seven are from Isaiah), and seven are from the Writings, split evenly between Psalms and Proverbs, along with one citation of the Wisdom of Solomon. A similar pattern (including the dominance of Isaiah) appears in the author's allusions (of which Elliott lists thirteen with another eleven possible allusions). Naturally, some of the material came to our author in preprocessed form by means of exegetical traditions he takes up. Either way, it is clear that this writer is steeped in biblical material, either through his personal reading or through the use of the Hebrew Scriptures in the communities of which he was a part.[259]

More important for our purposes here is how our author uses this literature. For him it is his Jesus-following community that is heir to the Hebrew Scriptures, for they point to the experiences that his community is undergoing. Thus, since the addressees are followers of the Anointed One, passages that were read messianically

---

258. Elliott, *1 Peter* (AB), 13. His list of allusions and biblicisms and summary discussion continue to page 17. See also W. L. Schutter, *Hermeneutic and Composition in 1 Peter* (WUNT 2/30; Tübingen: Mohr Siebeck, 1989).

259. This is what makes it difficult to speak about "Semitisms" in 1 Peter as indicating the linguistic background of the author, as Jobes, *1 Peter*, 325–38, does. One needs to exclude not only quotations and allusions, for their syntax is likely that of the original author (or translator into Greek) rather than that of the author of the letter, but also biblicisms, for these are expressions that the author

has picked up from Scripture or his community. For a work like 1 Peter one suspects that up to half of the letter would need to be excluded from the analysis due to his use of preformed traditions, "biblical" allusions and citations, and language drawn from the usage of the communities of faith of which he has been a part. The reality of this unconscious influence dawned on this present author early, when his high school essays were criticized because biblical grammar he had picked up in his Plymouth Brethren community had crept into them.

are important (e.g., Ps 117 [LXX] and Isa 8 and 53). Since his addressees are experiencing "exile" from their communities, those texts addressed to exiled Israel are addressed to them (e.g., the experience of the patriarchs in Genesis, which was as "exiles" because of their obedience to YHWH [Ps 33; Isa 52; Jer 50–51]). Since they are the chosen people of God in continuity with Israel (although 1 Peter does not discuss, as Paul does, how this continuity comes about), passages such as Exod 19:6 or Lev 19:2 apply to them. First Peter is not a midrash on a specific text (as was once argued); rather, he uses numerous texts in midrashic fashion. "The letter employs a diversity of OT texts, motifs, and themes in order to illustrate the ancient heritage to which the Christian brotherhood is heir and to provide scriptural and hence authoritative substantiation for its message of affirmation and exhortation."[260]

What is clear, then, is that the biblical text — or at least those parts of it that can be read messianically or in terms of the experience of his community — is authoritative. Yet that does not mean the text cannot be altered. It is indeed altered in a number of ways, either by the author or by those from whom he received the results of the alteration. Texts can be "telescoped" or abbreviated or, perhaps more to the point, have the relevant parts pulled out of them so that the full context is not apparent (as is done in 2:10 to Hos 1–2 and in 2:22–25 to Isa 53). Texts can be joined together in catenae (as in 2:9–10) or conflated (as 1:19 does to Isa 53:7 and Exod 12:5, or 2:9 does to Exod 19:5–6 and Isa 43:20–21; 42:12; and Mal 3:17), and texts may be used with the presupposition of a wider exegetical tradition, as we will note below about 3:19–20 in its use of the transformation of Gen 6:1–4.[261] It is not the text in context that is authoritative; there is no attempt to limit the meaning of the intention of the original authors in part or in whole; there is no detailed exegesis. What is authoritative is the text as read and applied to the contemporary community in line with the hermeneutical traditions used by that community. Thus, 1 Peter is part of the reshaping of the meaning of the "canon"[262] of the Hebrew Scriptures within the first-century Jesus movement. In 1 Peter we are reading texts from several centuries BCE with first-century CE theological meanings.

Our author also reads texts through the lens of Second Temple literature. This is particularly true of narrative material. The primary piece of Second Temple literature, the one that it is most easily demonstrable that our author uses, is the LXX (or, to be more accurate, a version of the Greek translation of the Hebrew Scriptures that is similar to what later became known as the Septuagint). We do not have significant evidence that he read and consulted the Hebrew Scriptures themselves. And in that any manuscripts that we have of the LXX include what are known as the Apocrypha, our author appears to have been familiar with and to have used this literature; for

---

260. Elliott, *1 Peter* (AB), 17.

261. See further ibid., 16; Schutter, *Hermeneutic*, 43.

262. Strictly speaking, "canon" is applicable to the Hebrew Scriptures only after the first century, for it is only after the formation of Judaism as we know it in the post–135 CE era that the lists of books

were fixed, even if by the first century CE the Torah was authoritative for all known Jewish groups, as well as for Samaritans, and most seem to have accepted the Prophets as authoritative on some level, with a good number at least selectively reading the Writings.

example, one of his citations is a citation of Wis 12:13 in 5:7b. In this, of course, he is no different than the general usage of the Hellenistic synagogue.

But he also shows a familiarity with other Second Temple literature, particularly with *1 Enoch*. Unlike Jude, he never quotes *1 Enoch*, and unlike 2 Peter, he never discusses concepts in *1 Enoch* in detail (2 Peter does so in dependency on Jude), but it is clear that especially in 3:19 – 20 our author uses material from *1 Enoch* 6 – 36, although he also shows conceptual similarity to *1 Enoch* 65 – 67 and 106 – 8.[263] He also knows the exegetical tradition behind the *Testament of Abraham*, if not the *Testament* itself, as is seen in his presentation of Sarah in 3:6.[264]

This also brings up his similarity to Philo of Alexandria, whom he never quotes or alludes to, but with whom he shares a number of motifs.[265] The point is not that 1 Peter cites these works or even that he necessarily has read them, but that hermeneutically he is using the lenses we find in Second Temple literature, including the recasting of narratives from the Hebrew Scriptures, to read those Scriptures. In fact, there is little or no evidence that he has consulted the Hebrew Scriptures themselves for his narrative material (as opposed to poetic material).[266] He simply tells the stories as he knows them.[267] It is, so far as we can tell, a totally unconscious alteration on his part. He is fully acculturated in his Hellenistic world and shares the attitudes, concepts, and narratives of that world. Yet this cultural reading of the older narratives has in fact influenced how they have been read in Christian circles to this day.

3.6.2 In Relationship to Other New Testament Works

When it comes to New Testament literature, 1 Peter has a complicated relationship with Paul. On the one hand, it shares phrases with Paul: in particular, *en christō* ("in Christ" or "in the Anointed One"), which 1 Peter uses twice, and concepts (e.g., trusting or believing in God, who raised Jesus from the dead, in 1 Pet 1:21 and Rom 4:24; the use of Passover imagery for Jesus). Yet there are differences, ranging from more emphasis on creation theology in Paul and Paul's repeated use of the term "cross," which 1 Peter lacks, to the use of similar terms such as "justification" in different ways.

At one time scholars thought that 1 Peter knew some of the Pauline letters (especially Romans and Ephesians) and theologically was "Paul light." Thus 1 Peter was

---

263. See Dalton, *Christ's Proclamation to the Spirits*, 163 – 76; and Webb, "Apocalyptic Perspective of First Peter," for a discussion of the history of scholarly discussion of this issue and a presentation of the evidence of how more sections of 1 Peter fit with *1 Enoch*.

264. See Sly, "I Peter 3:6b in the Light of Philo and Josephus"; and Martin, "The *TestAbr* and the Background of 1 Pet 3:6." See also Davids, "Second Temple Traditions in 1 and 2 Peter and Jude," 412 – 13.

265. In addition to Sly, noted in the previous footnote, see Elliott, *1 Peter* (AB), 19. Eusebius (*Eccl. hist.* 2.17.1 – 2) claims, "It is also said that Philo in the reign of Claudius became acquainted at Rome with Peter, who was then preaching there. Nor is this indeed improbable, for the work of which we have spoken, and which was

composed by him some years later, clearly contains those rules of the Church which are even to this day observed among us." While scholars hold this claim to be highly improbable, it does show a recognition by Eusebius of conceptual similarities.

266. Many of his citations of poetic material (i.e., Psalms, Proverbs, and the Prophets) may well be from memory in that this material was in frequent use among the followers of Jesus as seen in its use in multiple New Testament documents, so for 1 Peter it was premined material.

267. See Peter H. Davids, "What Glasses Are You Wearing? Reading Hebrew Narratives through Second Temple Lenses." *JETS* 55 (2012): 763 – 71.

neglected in that if his theology were derived from Paul, it would be better to spend more time focusing on the source than on the derivative product. Now, however, it has become clear that it is unlikely that 1 Peter knew any of the Pauline letters; rather, more likely both 1 Peter and Paul used a similar stock of passages mined from the Hebrew Scriptures, a similar group of Second Temple Jewish theological concepts, and of course similar terminology developed in the Jesus movement, even if Paul and 1 Peter often use these common materials differently.[268]

Similarly, we have noted, both in our reading of 1 Peter and our theological analysis, that 1 Peter has a significant overlap with James. But while there may be more similarity between 1 Peter and James than between 1 Peter and Paul, this similarity seems to arise from (1) both works facing a similar situation of societal rejection and low-grade persecution; and (2) both works using the same stock of material from the early Jesus movement, including material (such as Prov 3:34) mined from the Hebrew Scriptures.

But again there are differences; for example, while James mentions the law (*nomos*) ten times, 1 Peter, although of similar length, never mentions it. Yet they do have a similar view of God (e.g., in both letters God has brought new birth with the word as the "seed," although the terminology for new birth is different) and a similarly "low" Christology that neither refers to Jesus as God's Son nor associates him with divine attributes, although both view him as God's appointed ruler (James, of course, hardly refers to Jesus at all).[269]

When it comes to the gospel tradition, and in particular Matthew, more of a relationship has been demonstrated. There is a lot of conceptual overlap between the "Q" tradition[270] and 1 Peter, and in particular between the Matthean form of the tradition and 1 Peter. This becomes clear if one reads Matt 5 and compares it with 1 Peter, but similarities also show up in eschatology and to some extent in Christology. However, Rainer Metzner goes too far in arguing that 1 Peter is dependent on Matthew's gospel,[271] for as with the other literature we have discussed, conceptual similarity does not become verbal similarity, except in the use of stock phrases and citations. So there is evidence of contact between 1 Peter and the Jesus tradition, in particular the "Q" tradition. It does look like the form of the tradition that 1 Peter uses is the form that eventually ended up in Matthew. But there is not enough evidence to argue that this means that 1 Peter is part of the reception history of Matthew.

In general, then, our author has a complementary relationship to the rest of the New Testament. He is from the same movement that produced the other books, so

268. See further K. Shimada, "Is I Peter Dependent on Ephesians? A Critique of C. L. Mitton," *AJBI* 17 (1999): 77–106; idem, "Is I Peter Dependent on Romans?" *AJBI* 19 (1993): 87–137; Elliott, *1 Peter* (AB), 22–23.

269. There is little overlap at all between 1 Peter and 2 Peter, Jude, Hebrews, or the Johannine literature. One aspect of this is discussed in the introduction to 2 Peter.

270. We are not taking a position on what the "Q" tradition was, only that there is material found in both Matthew and Luke, but not in Mark, that appears to have circulated among the early followers of Jesus.

271. Rainer Metzner, *Die Rezeption des Matthäusevangeliums im 1. Petrusbrief* (WUNT 2/74; Tübingen: Mohr-Siebeck, 1995).

he demonstrates a similar knowledge and use of the traditions of that movement, including its use of certain passages from the Hebrew Scriptures. His theology differs from other works of the New Testament; it is more similar to James than to any other work, but this differing is not a differing because of arguing with other positions found in the New Testament, but because of his being an independent and complementary voice dealing with different issues than, for example, Paul.

3.6.3 In Relationship to Canon Formation

Peter was an influential leader in the first-century Jesus movement, and no less than nine known works have him as a principal speaker, character, or writer.[272] Only two of these works, however, appear in any of the canon lists, and of the two 1 Peter is the only one to appear early and consistently.[273] There is good evidence, including mutual use of unique or rare vocabulary, that the author of *1 Clement* knew and used 1 Peter (to argue that he alluded to 1 Peter one would have to show that his use of the letter was conscious and that he expected his readers also to know the letter and thus to recognize the allusions), in which case 1 Peter was used in Rome by 96 CE. It is clear that Polycarp cites 1 Peter in his *Letter to the Philippians*, which means that the work was influential in western Asia Minor by 140 CE. Around 180 CE Irenaeus of Lyons explicitly cites 1 Peter by name, which demonstrates its use in Gaul in the late second century. From then on 1 Peter is repeatedly referred to by a variety of church fathers, such as Tertullian of Carthage, Cyprian of Carthage, Clement of Alexandria, and Origen of Alexandria. Eusebius (*Hist. eccl.*, 2.3.2; 3.3.4; 3.4.2; 3.25.2; 6.25.8) mentions that in the mid-fourth century CE the work was an acknowledged genuine work of Peter.

The fact is that although 1 Peter does not appear in the Muratorian Canon of the second or third century (which, however, is in mutilated condition), nor in Syriac until the Peshitta of the fifth century, it does appear in a papyrus of the Catholic Epistles ($\mathfrak{P}^{72}$) dated to the late third or early fourth century, as well as in later Greek papyri and uncial manuscripts. It appears in the canon list of Athanasius' *Festal Letter* of 367, as well as in other canon lists of the same period. More importantly, it is, along with 1 John, the only Catholic Epistle that was, so far as we know, never doubted or rejected, which, given its widespread use, is not surprising.

Nor is the reason for this acceptance surprising. First Peter provided a theology of suffering (i.e., persecution) for the developing church, which is precisely what the church was experiencing to a greater or lesser extent during the second, third, and first half of the fourth centuries. It also showed how to appropriate the exodus and exile traditions of Israel, which also fit the direction in which the church was going.

---

272. See F. Lapham, *Peter: The Myth, the Man and the Writings: A Study of Early Petrine Text and Tradition* (JSNTSup 239; Sheffield: Sheffield Academic Press, 2003). These works are: *The Gospel of Peter, The Acts of Peter, The Acts of Peter and the Twelve Apostles, The Pseudo-Clementines*, The First Epistle of Peter, The Second Epistle of Peter, *The Apocalypse of Peter*, and *The Coptic Apocalypse of Peter*. Many of the names are, of course, those given to the works by later writers.

273. For further detail on the following discussion, see Elliott, *1 Peter* (AB), 138–49.

To what extent 1 Peter drove these developments and to which extent it was simply used in them we will never know, for the writings of the early part of this period are fragmentary and allusive and the authors are unavailable for interviews. However, clearly 1 Peter influenced these developments, and perhaps it even originated them, although the metaphors and concepts were picked up because they also fit with the mentality of the later writers. In other words, although relatively neglected in biblical scholarship up through the middle of the last century, 1 Peter was, in fact, a formative influence in the first three or four centuries of the church, one that ranked next to the Gospels and Paul.

Chapter 4

SECOND PETER

BIBLIOGRAPHY

Adams, Edward. "Where Is the Promise of His Coming? The Complaint of the Scoffers in 2 Peter 3.4." *NTS* 51 (2005): 106–22. **Bauckham, Richard J.** "The Delay of the Parousia." *TynBul* 31 (1980): 3–36. Idem. *Jude, 2 Peter.* WBC 50. Waco, TX: Word, 1983. **Bonus, A.** "2 Peter III. 10." *ExpTim* 32 (1920–1921): 280–81. **Boobyer, G. H.** "The Indebtedness of 2 Peter to 1 Peter." Pp. 34–53 in *New Testament Essays: Studies in Memory of T. W. Manson.* Ed. A. J. B. Higgins. Manchester: University of Manchester Press, 1959. **Charles, J. Daryl**. *2 Peter, Jude.* In *1–2 Peter, Jude.* Believers Church Bible Commentary. Scottdale, PA: Herald, 1999. **Chilton, Bruce D.** "The Transfiguration: Dominical Assurance and Apostolic Vision." *NTS* 27 (1980–81): 120–21. **Conti, Martino**. "La Sophia di 2 Petr. 3.15." *RivB* 17 (1969): 121–38. **Danker, Frederick W.** "2 Peter: A Solemn Decree." *CBQ* 40 (1978): 64–82. Idem. "2 Peter." Pp. 84–93 in *The General Letters.* Ed. Gerhard Krodel. Proclamation. Minneapolis: Fortress, 1995. **Davids, Peter H.** *The Letters of 2 Peter and Jude.* Pillar. Grand Rapids: Eerdmans, 2006. **Elliott, John H.** *I–II Peter/Jude.* ACNT. Minneapolis: Augsburg, 1982. **Fitzmyer, Joseph A.** "The Name Simon." Pp. 105–12 in *Essays on the Semitic Background of the New Testament.* London: Geoffrey Chapman, 1971. **Gilmour, Michael J.** *The Significance of Parallels between 2 Peter and Other Early Christian Literature.* Academica Biblical 10. Atlanta: Society of Biblical Literature, 2002. **Green, E. M. B. (Michael)**. *2 Peter Reconsidered.* London: Tyndale, 1960. Idem. *The Second Epistle of Peter and the Epistle of Jude.* TNTC. Grand Rapids: Eerdmans, 1968. **Grundmann, Walter**. *Der Brief des Judas und der zweite Brief des Petrus.* Berlin: Evangelische Verlagsanstalt, 1974. **Haaker, Klaus, and P. Schäfer.** "Nachbiblische Traditionen vom Tod des Mose." Pp. 147–74 in *Josephus-Studien: Untersuchungen zu Josephus, dem antiken Judentum und dem Neuen Testament: Otto Michel zum 70. Geburtstag gewidmet.* Ed. O. Betz, K. Haaker, and M. Hengel. Göttingen: Vandenhoeck & Ruprecht, 1974. **James, M. R.** *The Second Epistle General of Peter and the Epistle of Jude.* CGTSC. Cambridge: Cambridge University Press, 1912. **Käsemann, Ernst**. "An Apologia for Primitive Christian Eschatology." Pp. 169–95 in *Essays on New Testament Themes.* Trans. W. J. Montague. SBT 41. London: SCM, 1964. = "Apologie der urchristlichen Eschatologie." Pages 135–57 in *Exegetische Versuche und Besinnungen I.* Göttingen: Vandenhoeck & Ruprecht, 1960. **Kee, Howard Clark**. "The Terminology of Mark's Exorcism Stories." *NTS* 14 (1968): 232–46. Idem. "The

Transfiguration in Mark: Epiphany or Apocalyptic Vision?" Pp. 137–52 in *Understanding the Sacred Text: Festschrift for M. S. Enslin.* Ed. John Reumann. Valley Forge, PA: Judson, 1972. **Kraftchick, Steven J.** *Jude, 2 Peter.* ANTC. Nashville: Abingdon, 2002. **Kraus, Thomas J.** *Sprache, Stil und historischer Ort des zweiten Petrusbriefes.* WUNT 2/136. Tübingen: Mohr-Siebeck, 2001. **Loewenstamm, Samuel E.** "The Death of Moses." Pp. 185–217 in *Studies on the Testament of Abraham.* Ed. G. W. E. Nickelsburg. SBLSCS 6. Missoula, MT: Scholars Press, 1976. **Lucas, Dick, and Christopher Green**. *The Message of 2 Peter and Jude: The Promise of His Coming.* TBST. Leicester, UK/Downers Grove, IL: Inter-Varsity Press, 1995. **Marín, F.** "Apostolicidad de los escritos neotestamentarios." *EstEcl* 50 (1975): 226. **Mayor, Joseph B.** *The Epistles of Jude and II Peter.* Grand Rapids: Baker, repr. 1979. **McNamara, Martin.** "The Unity of Second Peter: A Reconsideration." *Scr* 12 (1960): 13–19. **McRae, G. W.** "Why the Church Rejected Gnosticism." Pp. 128–30 in *Jewish and Christian Self-Definition*, vol. 1. Ed. E. P. Sanders. London: SCM, 1980. **Meier, Sam**. "2 Peter 3:3–7—An Early Jewish and Christian Response to Eschatological Scepticism." *BZ* 32 (1988): 255–57. **Milligan, G.** "2 Peter III. 10." *ExpTim* 32 (1920–1921): 331. **Molland, Einar**. "La thèse 'La prophétie n'est jamais venue de la volonté de l'homme' (2 Pierre I, 21) et les Pseudo-Clémentines." Pp. 64–77 in *Opuscula Patristica*. BTN 2. Oslo: Universitetsforlaget, 1970. = ST 9 (1955): 67–85. **Neyrey, Jerome H.** "The Form and Background of the Polemic in 2 Peter." Unpublished Ph.D. diss., Yale University, 1977. Idem. "The Apologetic Use of the Transfiguration in 2 Peter 1:16–21." *CBQ* 42 (1980): 504–19. Idem. "The Form and Background of the Polemic in 2 Peter." *JBL* 99 (1980): 407–31. Idem. *2 Peter, Jude.* AB 37C. New York: Doubleday, 1993. **Picirilli, Robert E.** "The Meaning of 'Epignosis.'" *EvQ* 47 (1975): 85–93. **Raphael, Lawrence W.** "The Teaching of Writing an Ethical Will." *Judaism* 48 (1999): 174–80. **Reimer, Andy M.** "In the Beginning … Lessons Learned in Teaching Genesis 1 to Evangelical College Students." *Canadian Evangelical Review* 29 (2005): 32–44. **Riemer, Jack, and Nathaniel Stampfer**. *Ethical Wills: A Modern Jewish Treasury.* New York: Schocken, 1983. **Riesner, Rainer**. "Der zweite Petrus-Brief und die Eschatologie." Pp. 124–43 in *Zukunftserwartung in biblischer Sicht: Beitrage zur Eschatologie.* Ed. Gerhard Maier. Wuppertal: R. Brockhaus, 1984. **Roberts, J. W.** "A Note on the Meaning of II Peter 3:10d." *ResQ* 6 (1962): 32–33. **Schlosser, Jacques**. "Les jours de Noé et de Lot: A propos de Luc, XVII, 26–30." *RB* 80 (1973): 13–36. **Schmithals, Walter**. "Zur Abfassung und ältesten Sammlung der paulinischen Hauptbriefe." *ZNW* 51 (1960): 225–45. **Schrage, Wolfgang**. *Der zweite Petrusbrief. Der Judasbrief.* In *Die "katholische" Briefe: Die Briefe des Jakobus, Petrus, Johannes und Judas, übersetzt und erklärt.* NTD 10. Göttingen: Vandenhoeck & Ruprecht, 1973. **Schrage, Wolfgang, and Horst Balz**. *Die "katholischen" Briefe: Die Briefe des Jakobus, Petrus, Johannes und Judas.* NTD 10. Göttingen: Vandenhoeck & Ruprecht, 1973. **Sibinga, J. Smit**. "Une citation du Cantique dans la Secunda Petri." *RB* 73 (1966): 107–18. **Sickenberger, Joseph**. "Engels- oder Teufelslästerer im Judasbrief (8–10) und im 2. Petrusbriefe (2, 10–12)?" Pp. 621–39 in *Festschrift zu*

Jahrhundertfeier der Universität zu Breslau. Ed. T. Siebs. MSGVK 13–14. 1911–1912. **Smith, Terence V.** *Petrine Controversies in Early Christianity: Attitudes towards Peter in Christian Writings of the First Two Centuries*. WUNT 2/15. Tübingen: J. C. B. Mohr, 1985. **Snyder, Graydon F.** "The *Tobspruch* in the New Testament." *NTS* 23 (1976–1977): 117–20. **Snyder, John I.** *The Promise of His Coming: The Eschatology of 2 Peter*. San Mateo, CA: Western Book, 1986. **Spitta, Friedrich**. *Die zweite Brief des Petrus und der Brief des Judas*. Halle a. S.: Verlag und Buchhandlung des Waisenhauses, 1885. **Strobel, August**. *Untersuchungen zum eschatologischen Verzögerungsproblem auf Grund der spätjudisch-urchristlichen Geschichte von Habakuk 2,2ff*. NovTSup 2. Leiden: Brill, 1961. **Taylor, Vincent**. "Does the New Testament Call Jesus 'God'?" Pp. 83–89 in *New Testament Essays*. London: Epworth, 1970. **Thiede, Carson Peter**. "A Pagan Reader of 2 Peter: Cosmis Conflagration in 2 Peter 3 and the *Octavius* of Minucius Felix." *JSNT* 26 (1986): 79–96. **Thurén, Lauri**. "The Relationship between 2 Peter and Jude: A Classical Problem Resolved?" Pp. 451–60 in *The Catholic Epistles and the Tradition*. Ed. Jacques Schlosser. BETL 176. Leuven: Peeters, 2004. **Townsend, Michael J.** "Exit the Agape?" *ExpTim* 90 (1978–1979): 356–71. **Vermes, Geza**. "The Targumic Versions of Gen 4:3–16." Pp. 96–100 in *Post-Biblical Jewish Studies*. Leiden: Brill, 1975. **Vögtle, Anton**. *Das neue Testament und die Zukunft des Kosmos*. Düsseldorf: Patmos-Verlag, 1970. Idem. *Der Judasbrief. Der Zweite Petrusbrief*. EKKNT 22. Solothurn and Düsseldorf/Neukirchen-Vluyn: Benzinger/Neukirchener, 1994. **von Allmen, Daniel**. "L'apocalyptique juive et le retard de la parousie en II Pierre 3:1–13." *RTP* 16 (1966): 255–74. **Watson, Duane Frederick**. *Invention, Arrangement, and Style: Rhetorical Criticism of Jude and 2 Peter*. SBLDS 104. Atlanta: Scholars Press, 1988. **Watson, Duane Frederick, and Terrance Callan**. *First and Second Peter*. Paideia. Grand Rapids: Baker Academic, 2012. **Wenham, David**. "Being 'Found' on the Last Day: New Light on 2 Peter 3.10 and 2 Corinthians 5.3." *NTS* 33 (1989): 477–79. **Werdermann, Hermann**. *Das Irrlehrer des Judas- und 2. Petrusbriefes*. BFCT 17/6. Gütersloh: C. Bertelsmann, 1913. **White, John L.** *The Form and Function of the Body of the Greek Letter*. Missoula, MT: Scholars Press, 1972. **Wilson, W. E.** "*Heurethesetai* in 2 Pet. iii. 10." *ExpTim* 32 (1920–1921): 44–45. **Wolters, Al**. " 'Partners of the Deity': A Covenantal Reading of 2 Peter 1:4." *CTJ* 25 (1990): 28–44. Idem. "Postscript to 'Partners of the Deity.' " *CTJ* 26 (1991): 418–20. Idem. "Worldview and Textual Criticism in 2 Peter 3:10." *WTJ* 49 (1987): 405–13. **Zahn, Theodor**. *Introduction to the New Testament*. New York: Scribners, 1909.

The short letter dubbed 2 Peter is, it is true, in many ways the "ugly stepchild" of the New Testament. The Hellenistic first chapter both delights and frustrates readers. The denunciations of the second chapter often repel readers in the twenty-first century. The discussion of the end of the age in the third chapter seems foreign and fantastic. And, finally, there is the question of authorship, since no part of the New Testament has been more questioned than 2 Peter.

These issues have often led to neglect or even rejection of the work, which is shunted to the end of courses that include all the General Epistles, which are often given short shrift as a whole. Yet 2 Peter is theologically significant, especially in its first and third chapters. What does it mean that corruption is in the world due to "desire"? What does it mean that God desires all to be rescued? What does it mean that the heavens will be dissolved, but that the earth will be "discovered"? These and more questions crop up in a study of this work. Furthermore, it is canonically significant, not just in the history of its canonization, but also in its own use of Jude and reference to Paul, the earliest references to both Jude and some form of a Pauline collection on record. It is with this in mind that we turn to the study of 2 Peter.

4.1 RECENT SCHOLARSHIP

While there have always been commentaries written on 2 Peter, it almost seems that the only reason was that no commentary set would be complete without such a work. Nor did one find a great number of such works. Focusing on British and American scholarship, Charles Bigg wrote the ICC volume at the start of the last century,[1] and it became a standard work that assumed that 2 Peter was written against Gnostics. Shortly afterward Joseph B. Mayor wrote *The Epistles of Jude and II Peter: Greek Text with Introduction, Notes, and Comments*.[2] Mayor agreed with Bigg in positing a late first-century date for the letter, although he disagreed with Bigg about the priority of Jude, which Mayor championed and is virtually universally accepted today.

The next significant commentary to appear in English was J. N. D. Kelly's *The Epistles of Peter and of Jude*,[3] which updated the language and bibliography on the book and thus became a standard work, but it was not in itself a significant move forward. The move forward started in the late 1970s with Karl Hermann Schelkle's *Die Petrusbriefe, Der Judasbrief* and continued with Anton Vögtle's *Der Judasbrief, Der Zweite Petrusbrief* and Richard J. Bauckham's *Jude, 2 Peter*.[4] All of these works viewed 2 Peter as a testament written long after Simon Peter's death. Bauckham argued that the testamental nature of the work was transparent to the original readers so there was no deception about the real author. Also, by the time of these commentaries eschatology had recovered from its rejection by biblical scholarship in the first half of the twentieth century, so these authors felt that 2 Peter made a theological contribution to the New Testament rather than being an embarrassment because it was so full of eschatology.

---

1. Charles Bigg, *A Critical and Exegetical Commentary on the Epistles of St. Peter and St. Jude* (ICC; Edinburgh: T&T Clark, 1901, 1902²).

2. New York: Macmillan & Co., 1907.

3. BNTC; London: A & C Black, 1969.

4. Karl Hermann Schelkle, *Die Petrusbriefe, Der Judasbrief* (HTKNT; Freiburg: Herder, 1976); Anton Vögtle, *Der Judasbrief,*

Der Zweite Petrusbrief (EKKNT; Düsseldorf/Neukirchen-Vluyn: Benziger/Neukirchener, 1994); Richard J. Bauckham, *Jude, 2 Peter* (WBC 50; Waco, TX: Word, 1983). What one observes is that the order of the two books that Schelkle has in the text of his commentary has become part of the title in the latter two works, which demonstrates the widespread acceptance of the priority of Jude.

Along with that breakthrough of 2 Peter into scholarly consciousness toward the end of the twentieth century, the study of 2 Peter has gone in three different directions. The first is rhetorical criticism, in which Duane Watson has written the preeminent work.[5] From this and related works we learn that the author of 2 Peter was reasonably well educated in Greco-Roman rhetoric and could use stylistic devices and a wide vocabulary effectively.

The second direction is Jerome Neyrey's *2 Peter, Jude* volume in the Anchor Bible series,[6] with its sociological analysis or social-rhetorical criticism. This is also the main strategy followed by J. Daryl Charles and Ben Witherington III.[7] Since these works it has been impossible to discuss 2 Peter without discussing the social location of the author and implied readers.[8]

The third direction of study has been looking at the theology of the book, as in the commentaries by Ruth Anne Reese in the Two Horizons series and Douglas Harink in the Brazos series.[9] Both of these explicitly interact with the theology of the letter, taking the author as a serious theological thinker. Neither of these works is massive, considering the ground that they cover, but they have been part of sparking a discussion that this present work, as well as this author's previous work,[10] continues. Most recently, there has been a new focus on the application of social, narrative, and rhetorical methodologies to 2 Peter, as seen in the work *Reading Second Peter with New Eyes.*[11]

4.2 INTRODUCTORY ISSUES

The introductory issues concerning 2 Peter are some of the most difficult in the New Testament. Unlike with most New Testament works, the discussion of authorship started in the third century (there is no mention of 2 Peter earlier than the third century), was restarted in the Reformation, and continues today. That makes it particularly difficult to identify social location of either author or addressees.

4.2.1 Date, Authorship, and Historical Context

One immediately notes that 2 Peter is different from 1 Peter, and this is true even if one takes the authorial self-identification at face value. Whereas the author of 1 Peter

---

5. Duane F. Watson, *Invention, Arrangement, and Style: Rhetorical Criticism of Jude and 2 Peter* (SBLDS 104; Atlanta: Scholars Press, 1988). Related to this, but more focused on linguistic analysis, is Thomas J. Kraus's *Sprache, Stil und historischer Ort des zweiten Petrusbriefes* (WUNT 2/136; Tübingen: Mohr-Siebeck, 2001).

6. Jerome H. Neyrey, *2 Peter, Jude: A New Translation with Introduction and Commentary* (AB 37C; New York: Doubleday, 1993).

7. J. Daryl Charles, *Virtue Amidst Vice: The Catalog of Virtues in 2 Peter 1* (JSNTSup 150; Sheffield: Sheffield Academic, 1997); and Ben Witherington III, *Letters and Homilies for Hellenized Christians: A Socio-Rhetorical Commentary on 1–2 Peter* (Downers Grove, IL: InterVarsity Press, 2007).

8. See, e.g., Gene L. Green, *Jude and 2 Peter* (BECNT; Grand

Rapids: Baker Academic, 2008).

9. Ruth Anne Reese, *2 Peter and Jude* (THNTC; Grand Rapids: Eerdmans, 2007); Douglas Harink, *1 and 2 Peter* (Brazos Theological Commentary on the Bible; Grand Rapids: Brazos, 2009). This is not to say that other contemporary commentaries are not theological, but these have a more explicit focus on theology.

10. Most notably, Peter H. Davids, *The Letters of 2 Peter and Jude* (Pillar; Grand Rapids: Eerdmans, 2006), which explicitly drew on Neyrey and Watson, but is also theologically aware as the volume was written for pastors as well as scholars.

11. Robert L. Webb and Duane F. Watson, eds., *Reading Second Peter with New Eyes* (LNTS; London/New York: T&T Clark, 2010).

identifies himself as Peter (*Petros*, Πέτρος) plus his titles, the author of 2 Peter identifies himself with his titles and Simeon Peter (*Symeōn Petros*, Συμεὼν Πέτρος); Simeon occurs six times in Luke-Acts (for both the Hebrew tribe and Peter) and once (for the tribe) in Rev 7:7. Meanwhile, the more common name, Simon (*Simōn*, Σίμων), occurs seventy-five times in the New Testament, including a number of times in Luke-Acts (where it is the name of both Peter and other individuals).[12]

4.2.1.1 Authorship

There is little scholarly doubt that by "Simeon Peter," especially along with the title "slave and official delegate [*apostolos*, ἀπόστολος] of Jesus the Anointed One," the one otherwise known as Simon bar Jonah, whom Jesus nicknamed "the Rock" (*Petros*, Πέτρος), is intended. One can take this claim at face value, accept the authority of the church fathers (or, as one might say today, the Tradition), as John Calvin did,[13] or one can examine it in terms of historical probability to see if it seems reasonable. However, any such critical examination is limited by the fact that we know little of Peter's biography; this lack of information is what makes the first two options reasonable.

We know that the Peter of the New Testament was a married fisherman in the northern Galilee area (both Capernaum and Bethsaida are named as his hometown), which means he lived in a border area of a province that itself contained both Jewish and Gentile towns. He was a follower of Jesus, selected to be a member of the twelve official delegates whom Jesus sent out. After Easter he was, according to Acts, the leader of the Jesus movement, but by the mid-40s had been eclipsed by James, perhaps because of his traveling, perhaps because of his being "on the run" as a man wanted by the Herodian family. We do not hear about him after the end of the 40s (unless one dates Galatians later than that), although the reference to him in 1 Cor 9:5 means that in the 50s, at least the Corinthian church knew that Peter traveled with his wife.[14]

---

12. In a 2013 presentation at the Society of Biblical Literature in Baltimore, Jermy F. Hultin, "What's in a Name? The Use of *Symeon Petras* in 2 Pet 1:1," argued convincingly that *Symeon* is not a variant of *Simon* but a different name altogether.

13. In his introduction to his commentary on 2 Peter, "The Argument," John Calvin, after discounting Eusebius's reference to the letter's being disputed, since Eusebius did not name who it was that disputed it, states, "What Jerome writes influences me somewhat more, that some, induced by a difference in the style, did not think that Peter was the author. For though some affinity may be traced, yet I confess that there is that manifest difference which distinguishes different writers. There are also other probable conjectures by which we may conclude that it was written by another rather than by Peter. At the same time, according to the consent of all, it has nothing unworthy of Peter, as it shews everywhere the power and the grace of an apostolic spirit. If it be received as canonical, we must allow Peter to be the author, since it has his name inscribed, and he also testifies that he had lived with Christ: and it would have been a fiction unworthy of a minister of Christ, to have personated another individual. So then I conclude, that if the Epistle be deemed worthy of credit, it must have proceeded from Peter; not that he himself wrote it, but that some one of his disciples set forth in writing, by his command, those things which the necessity of the times required.... Doubtless, as in every part of the Epistle the majesty of the Spirit of Christ appears, to repudiate it is what I dread, though I do not here recognise the language of Peter. But since it is not quite evident as to the author, I shall allow myself the liberty of using the word Peter or Apostle indiscriminately" (John Calvin, *Commentaries on the Catholic Epistles* [trans. John Owen; Bellingham, WA: Logos Bible Software, 2010], 363–64). In other words, the fact that it had been received as canonical and that the church fathers had acknowledged its value leads Calvin to the conclusion that for theological reasons it must be considered genuine.

14. This reference could indicate that Peter had visited Corinth. However, he is paired with "the rest of the official delegates" and "the brothers of the Lord," and most of the former and all of the latter almost certainly never visited Corinth. It is therefore unlikely that this reference indicates that Peter had ever been in the city.

The next clear references to Peter come from the second century, associating him with Corinth. Only after that do we discover a tradition about his martyrdom in Rome under Nero.[15] All this tells us little that interests us with respect to this letter. While from his area of origin and work one would assume that he was bilingual in Aramaic and Greek, we are not told whether he received any formal education. This contrasts with Paul, who not only indicates he was educated, but where he received his final education, or even with Jesus, who is reported in one gospel as being able to read (Luke 4:16–17)[16] and thus in that gospel's view had received at least a minimal education. If we believe that same author of Luke-Acts, however, Peter was uneducated and illiterate (Acts 4:13).[17]

Yet all this is brief and minimal information about Peter's education or lack thereof, and it does not include his last thirtysome years of life. The critical study of assertions about Peter's education and the authorship claim of the two Petrine letters is also limited by the fact that we have no literary work ascribed to Peter that is *not* disputed, unlike Paul, to whom most scholars of all stripes ascribe *at least* his *Hauptbriefe* (main letters): Romans, Galatians, 1–2 Corinthians, 1 Thessalonians, and Philemon—which give us a literary body to which we can compare the other letters. Consequently, we can never know for sure on historical-critical grounds whether Peter wrote 2 Peter or not. Since history does witness to unusual phenomena and individuals (e.g., Absalom Jones, an African-American slave who taught himself to read from the New Testament and later purchased his wife and himself from slavery and went on to become the first ordained African-American Episcopal minister), many unlikely events are possible (in a sense history is a record of the unique), but one can raise the issues that cause scholars to question Petrine authorship.

Two major issues appear: (1) Did the author of 1 Peter write 2 Peter; and (2) did Simon Peter bar Jonah write 2 Peter? The questions are related but not identical, for one could argue that Simon Peter wrote 2 Peter and not 1 Peter (or vice versa), and one could argue that the author of 1 Peter wrote 2 Peter, but that neither was written by Simon Peter.

In the previous chapter we discussed whether Simon Peter wrote 1 Peter. What was asserted there, from a critical point of view (although some take a different

15. *First Clement* 5 refers obliquely to Peter's and Paul's respective martyrdoms, which may well mean that Clement also associates them with Rome, and Peter in particular as the leader of the church there; Clement eventually became leader of the church in Rome. However, the references are oblique, indicating that they died, but not necessarily that they were martyred, and it does not say where they died. So it is possible that this is evidence from about 96 CE (although some have dated *1 Clement* as early as 70) associating the two men with Rome. But for explicit references, one has to go to later works.

16. Mark 6:3 places him in the category of a handworker (*tektōn*, τέκτων), which Josephus informs us were uneducated and expected to listen rather than to teach; Matthew softens this class identification in Matt 13:55 (he is the *son* of one in that class). As noted, Luke

not only has him reading, but also able to handle a scroll. He is scribally literate, and the people are not upset that he teaches, but only get upset about what he teachers. Moreover, John (John 7:53–8:11) has Jesus at least writing letters.

17. This is a comment of the narrator, not of the members of the Sanhedrin, so it is in the view of this author unlikely that this refers to some special type of education, such as rabbinic education, but rather to education in general. In other words, the two men were not behaving as Josephus says that members of the *tektōn* class should behave, i.e., deferentially toward their educated betters. However, some scholars grant the author of Acts knowledge of what the members of the Sanhedrin were thinking and thus limit this to a lack of knowledge of what would come to be called rabbinic education.

point of view), is that while 1 Peter shows a usage of the Hebrew Scriptures (in Greek translation) that would be consistent with an author with a Palestinian Jewish background, it is doubtful that Simon Peter would have had the education to write that letter. First Peter does contain Semitisms, but before we accept them as evidence of the author's Aramaic mother tongue, one needs to prove that they cannot be explained as Septuagintalisms or phrases from Jesus or the early Jesus movement that had become part of the religious language of any leader in the early Jesus movement. That means that if we are correct that Simon Peter was uneducated, 1 Peter is at least more or less ghostwritten (to use contemporary language) by an unknown amanuensis.[18]

It seems clear that 2 Peter is written in a very different style than 1 Peter, in an Asian style. This is not a poorer Greek, as has sometimes been thought, but a different Greek, as will be described below. Moreover, it is also written with a different use of the Hebrew Scriptures. Whereas 1 Peter often quotes the Hebrew Scriptures, as a quick scan of 1 Pet 2:1 – 10 illustrates, 2 Peter *never* does so. The author does cite narratives from the Hebrew Scriptures, but he does so in a form that is (1) dependent on Jude (as will be discussed below); and (2) dependent on how the narratives were being retold in Second Temple literature. One could even argue from the lack of evidence that the author of 2 Peter has never read the Hebrew Scriptures, although since they were used (in Greek) in the communities of the first-century Jesus movement, it is unlikely that he lacked exposure to them.[19]

Finally, the author of 2 Peter appears to be at home in the world of Hellenistic philosophy. One has only to look in 2 Peter 1 at the number of Hellenistic virtues found in the virtue list, the emphasis on knowledge as the way to freedom, or his focus on desire as the root of corruption and one can see this. One also notices that unlike 1 Peter, 2 Peter refers to the death of Jesus only once (2 Pet 2:1), and obliquely at that.[20] While some of this could be viewed as a matching of the philosophical thought of those he is criticizing or of his addressees, there is no indication in 2 Peter that the author is adopting a position that is not his own. All of this indicates that the one responsible for the style, the relationship to the Hebrew Scriptures, and the philosophical sophistication of 2 Peter is different from the one responsible for 1 Peter.

Consequently, the composers of the two letters appear to be different individuals. Furthermore, given his lack of education, it is unlikely that Simon Peter is responsible for the style of either letter. How does one explain this? One could

---

18. If, as tradition claims, Mark recorded the preaching of Peter posthumously, this observation would be even more true, for the style, diction, and rhetoric of Mark is nowhere near as good Greek style as that of 1 Peter, which is why Matthew and (especially) Luke worked so hard to improve the style of what they took from Mark. But to fully explore this issue would mean discussing the authorship of Mark.

19. See Peter H. Davids, "The Use of Second Temple Traditions in 1 and 2 Peter and Jude," in *The Catholic Epistles and the Tradition* (ed. Jacques Schlosser; BETL 176; Leuven: Peeters/Leuven University Press, 2004), 420 – 21, which documents these assertions.

20. See the phrase "the Master who bought them." Since all masters purchased their slaves that were not inherited, received as gifts, or born to another slave, and since the manner of purchase is not mentioned, this reference is oblique at best. Nor is there any other possible reference to the death of Jesus.

explain it as Peter giving general instructions to two different trusted colleagues, perhaps because he was in prison, perhaps at two significantly different times. Calvin says as much when he writes,

> not that [Peter] himself wrote it, but that some one of his disciples set forth in writing, by his command, those things which the necessity of the times required. For it is probable that he was now in extreme old age, for he says, that he was near his end. And it may have been that at the request of the godly, he allowed this testimony of his mind to be recorded shortly before his death, because it might have somewhat availed, when he was dead, to support the good, and to repress the wicked.[21]

One could thus explain the situation as Peter standing behind 1 Peter and as 2 Peter being written as a transparent (in the first century) Petrine testament after, perhaps long after, Peter's death; the letter would then be saying what he would or should have said in these particular circumstances.[22] Or, one could simply describe 2 Peter as pseudepigraphic in the sense that it is an attempt of a later writer to claim the authority of Peter, with or without thinking that he was writing in the spirit of Peter, and therefore as an attempt to deceive his potential readers into thinking that Simon Peter wrote it. This latter position is probably the majority position in the nonevangelical (although "evangelical" is itself a slippery word) scholarly world. Which position one takes will depend on one's reading strategy, influenced as it is by one's theological position, including previous decisions on the nature of Scripture and what God would or would not work through, and how one reads the evidence for the date of the work.

4.2.1.2 Addressees

Second Peter gives no explicit information about its addressees. This makes the comment in 2 Pet 3:1 that this is the second letter written to these addressees more significant than it otherwise would be, for it is often used to argue that 2 Peter was written to the same set of churches as are addressed in 1 Peter, namely, a group of churches in northern, northwestern, and western Asia Minor. However, other than this one reference, there is little evidence that this is the case. How so?

First, Paul shows us that it is possible to write multiple letters to more than one community (1 and 2 Corinthians, 1 and 2 Thessalonians, Colossians and Philemon).

Second, Paul also shows that it is possible to have one or more letters to a community become lost to later generations, since we have no record of at least two letters he wrote to the Corinthians.[23] Thus the reference to 2 Peter as a second letter

---

21. Calvin, *Commentaries on the Catholic Epistles*, 363–64.

22. Bauckham, *Jude, 2 Peter*, 131–35, 158–62, argues for this, dating 2 Peter in the 90s. It must be emphasized that Bauckham views this literary form as transparent in the first century, not as an attempt to deceive others as to the authorship of the letter.

23. Paul refers to a previous letter in 1 Cor 5:9, and in 2 Cor 2:3–4 he refers to the so-called "letter of tears" or "tearful letter" written between 1 and 2 Corinthians (which came after his painful visit, 2 Cor 2:1).

written to these addressees, if not itself being part of a pseudepigraphal persona (i.e., an attempt to build on 1 Peter),[24] is no evidence that 1 Peter is the first letter, unless supported by other parallel data.

Third, 1 and 2 Peter seem to presuppose different addressees. The addressees of 1 Peter are a clearly named group of communities that are experiencing persecution because of their following Jesus the Anointed One as Lord. They are Hellenistic in their location in Asia Minor, the customs mentioned, and their reading of some texts of the Hebrew Scriptures, but their Hellenism is, so to speak, general. Other than a concern they might again slip back to doing "the things that the nations do," the surrounding culture is a danger only in terms of persecution, for the Hellenistic culture, at least in its negative aspects, is "out there," not within the community.

The addressees of 2 Peter, by contrast, do not appear to be experiencing persecution; or if they are, it does not cross the author's radar. (This in itself raises doubts about a second-century date.) However, they are addressed in terms of Hellenistic virtues and in terms of salvation as knowledge, which indicate a far deeper immersion in Hellenistic thought, perhaps in Greek philosophy, than is evidenced in 1 Peter.[25] The threat to the community in 2 Peter is "false teachers," who seem to hold opinions similar to those the Epicureans held (see below). The obvious concern is that the community is vulnerable to these teachers, for otherwise there would be no reason to write the letter. Given the concern over the "false teachers," it is more likely that the addressees live in a single community or in communities in a limited area than in the widely scattered communities of 1 Peter, which cover a considerable geographic area.

Our conclusion, then, is that while it is possible that 1 and 2 Peter were written to the same communities, there is no significant evidence that they are. The Asiatic style of the letter is the style of the author (as style usually is), not an indication that the letter is written to a location in Asia Minor (unless one knew that the author did not normally use the Asiatic style and was able to deliberately shift style—only then would it be an indication of the addressees). We know only this about the implied readers of the letter, that in the author's estimation, they are a community characterized by Hellenistic thought in which it was possible for "false teachers" to arise, but we do not know where the community is located.

---

24. There are two different readings of the "second letter" reference: some conservative scholars (e.g., Reese, *2 Peter and Jude*, 122) view it as identifying the location of the addressees of the letter and linking the two letters, despite the great differences in content and style. Many mainline scholars, however, view it as a device used by the pseudepigrapher to connect his letter to 1 Peter, which he knows but did not write, which thus created more legitimacy for 2 Peter, since 1 Peter never (to our knowledge) lacked acceptance. Thus it is read as evidence for the letter's being pseudonymous. If the argument of this work is accepted, this evidence that 2 Peter is pseudepigraphical is a misreading of the text.

25. On the other hand, Reese, *2 Peter and Jude*, 121, points to Robert Wall, "The Canonical Function of 2 Peter," *BibInt* 9/1 (2001): 64–81, who notes some thematic continuities between 1 and 2 Peter, as if 2 Peter were complementing 1 Peter. For Reese this shows an underlying unity of thought, which is possible, although it is also possible that both reflect the thought forms of the first-century Jesus movement or that a pseudepigrapher created 2 Peter to fit/complete 1 Peter, which is probably more the point that Wall is making. Whatever the interpretation, one should not force a wedge between the two as if one contradicted the other. They just proceed differently from a similar basis.

4.2.1.3 Identity of the False Teachers

Second Peter 2:1 states, "there will be false teachers among you," which he compares to the "false prophets among the people" of Israel. Most of chapter 2 is devoted to denouncing these false teachers, which has led many scholars to view them as an actual threat, not a potential one, despite the future tense. That is, from the point of view of the letter they are future, but from the point of view of the community they are present.[26] Likewise, in 3:3 our author states, "in the last days mockers will come mocking." Again, it is not unusual for scholars to assume that this is something already happening in the community, which 2 Peter clearly locates "in the last days," and that these "mockers" are the "false teachers" of chapter 2 since the basic characteristic of the mockers ("living according to their own desires") fits a core characteristic of the "false teachers" (2:18). But who are these "mockers," these "false teachers"?

Three proposals have been made in answer to this question. (1) They are Gnostics; (2) they are an unknown out-group (from the perspective of the author); (3) they are Epicurean-influenced teachers. First, older commentators viewed these false teachers as Gnostics or incipient Gnostics.[27] Certainly there is an emphasis in 2 Peter on the knowledge of God, which could be mirror-read as countering a claim to knowledge by the "false teachers." Moreover, these teachers "deny the Master who bought them" (2:1), which could be read as indicating some type of different Christology. And there is the slandering of the "glorious ones," which could mean a rejection of angels as either the agents of creation or the agents of the giving of the Torah, although using this one reference to argue that these people believed that the creation or the Torah stemmed from a demiurge rather than God is like suspending a mountain of teaching from a hair of text (as Rabbi Akiba was said to be able to do). It is also clear that some type of antinomianism is the main point of the criticism that 2 Peter makes, and some Gnostics felt that the physical world was indifferent and thus that what one did with the body was also indifferent, and they were said to flaunt this liberty to prove their point.

But there are real questions as to (1) how early Gnosticism developed and (2) whether the few indications above are enough suggest a Gnostic connection. Is the denial of the Master a christological heresy (in the eyes of our author), or is it a rejection of "the Master's" authority as seen in their behavior? Is the slandering of the "glorious ones" a Gnostic separation of the creation from God or something different? And how is the rejection of the parousia and final judgment Gnostic? Is not an emphasis on knowledge found far more generally in Greek philosophy than just in Gnosticism? Because the text cannot answer these questions clearly, there is

26. This future tense is also sometimes read as a pseudepigraphical device; that is, the long-dead Peter is predicting what was then happening in the community receiving the letter. But one can also read it as an author writing, recognizing the time delay between writing a letter and sending it, with an awareness that the "false teachers" present in one part of the community he is addressing have not yet penetrated the whole community.

27. E.g., Kelly, *The Epistles of Peter and of Jude*, 230–31, who views the "others" of Jude and the "false teachers" of 2 Peter as identical.

at present a tendency for the Gnostic hypothesis to be out of favor, especially since 2 Peter does not have the type of christological discussion and anti-Gnostic rhetoric found in the second and third centuries.

Second, a number of scholars today are suspicious of reading any particulars out of the condemnation of the "false teachers" other than the fact that the author of 2 Peter wishes to roundly condemn them. Even Kelly, for example, refers to the condemnations as "stock condemnations"; that is, the condemnations were what was said about an opponent and did not necessarily describe their actual behavior, much like what one sees in political advertising today ("he is a socialist" or "she is a bigot"). Thus those whom our author opposes are accused of being "false teachers" parallel to the "false prophets" of Israel, of being impious and immoral and greedy, and of displaying shameful behavior, but all of this is said using language drawn from the condemnation of others by the various prophets of the Hebrew Scriptures. It does not tell us anything more than that the author did not like these teachers.

Others look for more specific clues as to who these folk are. Hans Joachim Stein,[28] for example, sees a clash of culture behind Jude (he includes 2 Peter with Jude) that comes out in more Hellenistic style meal behavior on the part of the "false teachers" (the basic Christian gathering in the first century was a meal)—behavior that is condemned by the author. We can agree that the language is stereotyped, that it does portray a parallel to the prophets criticized in the Hebrew Scriptures, without drawing the conclusion that it does not give us real information. For example, other than the slandering of the "glorious ones" (2 Pet 2:10–11), which could be viewed as theological, *all* of the charges leveled in 2 Peter 2 are moral, not doctrinal. Furthermore, the emphasis in 2 Peter 1 is on moral virtue and the rejection of desire. Only when we come to 2 Peter 3 do we discover a doctrinal issue that is discussed at any length, namely, whether there will be a parousia and a final judgment. This denial of final judgment appears to be more a rationalization of why the teachers' behavior is acceptable to them (i.e., it will never be judged) than the issue driving the letter as a whole. Thus, however stylized, it appears that behavior that deviates from the norm that our author and his community approve of is the central concern and thus the condemnations are relevant.[29]

Third, one can go further and ask the question of where in the Hellenistic world (which is clearly the thought world of 2 Peter) one finds a group whose ethical behavior might be characterized as giving in to desire and whose rationale for such behavior might include a denial of final judgment. Jerome Neyrey points to this combination in the Epicureans.[30] Their central goal in life was "pleasure," which was not unbridled desire, to be sure, but the "absence of trouble" or "freedom from

---

28. Hans Joachim Stein, *Frühchristliche Mahlfeiern: Ihre Gestalt und bedeutung nach der neutestamentliche Briefliteratur und der Johannesoffenbarung* (WUNT 2/255; Tübingen: Mohr Siebeck, 2008), 238.

29. See Peter H. Davids, "Are the Others Too Other? The Issue of 'Others' in Jude and 2 Peter," in *Reading 1–2 Peter and Jude* (ed. Eric Mason and Troy Martin; Atlanta: Society of Biblical Literature, 2014), 201–14.

30. Neyrey, *2 Peter, Jude*, 122–28, which section will be selectively paraphrased in the following argument.

pain and fear" (Diog. Laert. 10.128–32). Therefore, it follows that the deity cannot be troubled with punishing the evil and rewarding the righteous, for the deity must have an absolute "absence of trouble" (Diog. Laert. 10.139). Thus, over against the concept of a provident deity, they pointed to a world that was the result of the chance effects of atoms (Diog. Laert. 10.93–114), which one sees in the fact that fortune telling and divination are unreliable (or, in a context as Jewish as the Jesus movement, prophecy is unfulfilled), and they insisted that justice does not happen in this world. Indeed, if there were such a provident deity, there would be no human freedom (Diog. Laert, 10.133). Of course, if human beings are just atoms, then after death there is no afterlife, just nothing (Diog. Laert. 10.139). One should note, as Plutarch did, that divine providence, immortality of the soul, and postmortem judgment are logically connected (Plutarch, *Sera* 560F). An author might note one or two of these topoi and thereby imply the other(s).

This does not mean that in 2 Peter the author is countering full-blown Epicureanism. This type of thinking had a general influence as well as a specific philosophical expression. For instance, Josephus attributes it to the Sadducees (*J.W.* 2.164–65). For our purposes it does not matter whether his attribution is accurate or inaccurate, but from his perspective as a first-century Jew, this was an appropriate attribution for a first-century Palestinian Jewish group. Likewise, in *Targum Pseudo-Jonathan* on Gen 4:8 we discover Cain expressing similar sentiments about final judgment: "There is no judgment and no judge and no world hereafter; there is no good reward to be given to the righteous, nor any account to be taken of the wicked."[31] Here also we have the three elements of the Epicurean view in Jewish language: no divine providence, no final judgment, and no afterlife.[32] One should also remember that Cain was viewed in Jewish tradition as an immoral person (beyond his being a murderer). Thus it was possible in a Jewish context to view others as influenced by Epicurean thought. It is even possible that rabbinic Judaism developed a term for Jews holding Epicurean views, *Apikoros*.[33]

Thus, we conclude that while it may indeed be true that the condemnation of the "false teachers" is to some degree stylized and that we do not know the concrete behaviors that are being condemned, the description of them as licentious fits with the description of the scoffers as deniers of divine providence and final judgment, a charge backed up by reference to the delay of the parousia and the idea that the parousia is a myth (both are found in Epicurean arguments). This persuades us that the "false teachers" are under the influence of Epicurean thought, although they surely expressed it in a manner consistent with the language of the Jesus movement, just as Cain in the *Targum* expresses it in a manner consistent with Judaism.

---

31. Taken from John Bowker, *The Targums and Rabbinic Literature: An Introduction to Jewish Interpretations of Scripture* (Cambridge: Cambridge University Press, 1969), 132–33. Bowker also notes (p. 135) that the *Fragmentary Targum* has a similar dispute. While Pseudo-Jonathan in its final form is later than the seventh century, it also preserves traditions from a much earlier period.

32. So Henry Fischel, *Rabbinic Literature and Greco-Roman Philosophy* (Leiden: E. J. Brill, 1973), 35–50.

33. Neyrey, *2 Peter, Jude*, 127–28, admits that this conclusion is disputed, but also points to significant evidence in its favor.

4.2.1.4 Date

With the information given above, the date of 2 Peter is obviously as disputed as its authorship. If Simon Peter was alive when the work was written (whether or not he took an active role in writing it), it probably was written before 68 CE, although one could date it later if one rejects the tradition that Simon Peter was martyred by Nero. If it is some type of testament to Peter, drawing on his memory either to give the text authority or to bring authentic Petrine memory into the author's present situation, the date is likely much later. Typically, a date around 90 CE is given.[34]

In deciding on the date, one must consider the literary relationships and general milieu of the work. Epicurean influence is possible at any time during this period, but would be more likely in a more strongly Hellenistic milieu than elsewhere and more likely thirty or more years after the start of the Jesus movement. While it is not impossible for such a movement to have arisen within the Palestinian communities, it is more likely after the Jesus movement reached places like Asia Minor, Greece, and Rome. Clearly 2 Peter knows of a Pauline collection (3:15–16), although we are not informed how many letters are in that collection. If we knew that, we could more easily decide on the date, for the full Pauline corpus, including the Prison Epistles and Pastorals, surely started to circulate after Paul's martyrdom (and tradition puts that at about the same time as Peter's martyrdom). Second Peter also knows Jude, as we will argue below, and that puts the work later than Jude. However, the date of Jude is also debatable.

Bauckham argues that 2 Peter appears to come from a milieu similar to that of *The Shepherd of Hermas*, *1 Clement*, and *2 Clement*. If so, that puts the work at the end of the first century or in a situation similar to that milieu (and probably puts it in Rome as well). He also states that the second-century *Apocalypse of Peter* and *Acts of Peter* know 2 Peter, which pushes 2 Peter before 140 CE and probably toward 110 CE.[35] One can read Bauckham's evidence differently and argue that these works knew and used 2 Peter, rather than that they are contemporaneous.[36] Furthermore, the lack of a concern for church structure and authority, which is very much a part of *1 Clement*, and the lack of a discussion of Christology (2 Peter asserts the honorable exalted status of Jesus—he does not argue for it and certainly does not argue for Jesus' humanity) both set 2 Peter apart from the late first or any time in the second century.

So what we have is a work that shows the Jesus movement thoroughly within the Hellenistic world, able to use the language of that world, and trying to cope with influences from that world that 2 Peter finds objectionable. We are clearly dealing with a second-generation community, for those who evangelized the area are spoken of as absent (3:2, "your official delegates" or "your missionaries," whose words need to be remembered, since they are no longer present). Some believe that the first generation of believers has died (3:4), but this interpretation depends on the identification of "the fathers," who have clearly died, but who are not as clearly

34. Bauckham, *Jude, 2 Peter*, 157–58. Terrance Callan in Duane F. Watson and Terrance Callan, *First and Second Peter* (Paideia; Grand Rapids: Baker Academic, 2012) 136, pushes this to 120 CE.

35. Bauckham, *Jude, 2 Peter*, 149, 157.
36. G. L. Green, *Jude and 2 Peter*, 141–42.

the first generation of that community.[37] The community conditions of 2 Peter would be fulfilled within a few years of the departure of the founding members of the community, which could be anytime after, perhaps 50.

In summary, where one dates the overall picture we have drawn will depend on the decisions one makes about the capabilities of Simon Peter, the freedom he might give to an amanuensis,[38] the number of Pauline letters known to 2 Peter,[39] and how closely 2 Peter fits the milieu of end-of-the-century documents. We do not have clear data for any of these assumptions. The data of 2 Peter allows for a date anywhere between late in the life of Simon Peter (assuming he gave a lot of freedom to his amanuensis) and late in the first century.

4.2.2 Literary Style and Form

We are in much better shape when it comes to describing the literary style of 2 Peter. First, it is clearly written in what is known as the "Asiatic" (as opposed to the "Attic") style. That is, it is showy in its rhetoric and rather florid, even bombastic. In an earlier generation this type of rhetorical flourish, which is evident in 2 Peter's use of rare words, alliteration, and wordplays, was criticized as "poor" Greek, for the standard education that scholars had in Greek was classical (Attic) Greek or, in the period around the first century, Attic revival (there is more of the Attic style in 1 Peter, which, especially in chapter 1, has some lovely periodic sentences). Now, however, scholars recognize that "Asiatic style" was coming into fashion in the first century, a style "which, with its love of high-sounding expressions, florid and verbose language, and elaborate literary effects, was an artificial style which Reicke aptly compares with European baroque."[40]

There are, however, dissenters to this analysis. Duane Watson prefers to call the letter written in the "grand style" rather than "Asiatic style," although he adds to this the caveat that it also contains characteristics of the "swollen" and "frigid" styles (both of which were considered faulty styles in antiquity). That is, 2 Peter does not fit Cicero's definitions of Asianism in that it does have a "weight of thought," which

---

37. Bauckham (*Jude, 2 Peter*, 158) sees this as decisive evidence for a date late in the first century, for by the second century there was little concern about the death of the first generation but the late first century (for him, the 80s) is when this would have to have been processed by those expecting Jesus to return before the death of the last of the apostolic generation. This present author, however, has pointed out (Davids, *2 Peter and Jude*, 265–66) that the term "the fathers" normally refers to the venerable worthies of Hebrew Scriptures; there is no textual indication that this is the only exception to that rule. In fact, the argument for a steady-state universe would have more impact if "the fathers" were the ancestors of long ago than if they were a recent generation.

38. Green, *Jude and 2 Peter*, 140–44, has an admirable discussion of what the church fathers thought about 2 Peter. His most interesting reference is to Jerome, *Letter to Hebidia* (*Epist.* 120.11), "[Paul], therefore, had Titus as an interpreter just as the blessed Peter also had Mark, whose Gospel was composed with Peter narrating and him writing. Further, two epistles also, which are extant as of Peter,

are discrepant among themselves in style and character and structure of the words, from which we understand that he used different interpreters as necessary." One would think that Jerome would know a thing or two about using an amanuensis.

39. It is clear that the author of 2 Peter knew of at least three (2 Pet 3:16), since he says "all," but it is not clear when small collections of Paul's letters began to circulate. For instance, might Phoebe have mentioned when she delivered Romans that Paul had written at least two letters to the Corinthians? Could that have led to the Romans receiving copies? Thessalonica is not that far from Philippi (and is in the same Roman province), so one would not be surprised in their having exchanged letters at an early date. Only if one is somehow sure that 2 Peter is referring to a relatively complete Pauline collection is this reference evidence for a date later than the lifetime of Simon Peter.

40. Bauckham, *Jude, 2 Peter*, 137, citing Bo I. Reicke, *The Epistles of James, Peter, and Jude* (AB; New York: Doubleday, 1964), 146–47.

Cicero believed was absent from the "Asiatic style," even if it is also characterized by "swiftness and impetuosity combined with refined and ornate words."[41]

When it comes to the rhetoric of 2 Peter, Duane Watson has described it in detail.[42] He calls it deliberative rhetoric in that it appears that the overall goal is for the implied readers to choose to follow the author's position over against that of those whom he labels "false teachers." There is an epideictic aspect to the letter, of course, in that in the process of the argument the author seeks to destroy the ethos of the "false teachers" by labeling their behavior as shameful and dishonorable and to underline the honorable status of the course of action he is advising.

Since this is a letter, it begins with an epistolary salutation (Watson labels this an epistolary prescript or quasi-exordium), which, while fitting the epistolary genre, seeks to establish the ethos of the author and the goodwill of the implied readers. We then get the *exordium* (1:3–15), which sets forth the moral stance the author is arguing for (a minisermon), combined with personal data that adds weight to the argument by indicating that the author is old and that this is his testament. This is also the purpose statement of the letter.

Then comes a long *probatio*, which forms the letter body (1:16–3:13) and which, Watson argues, is the refutation of four different charges raised by the "false teachers." It is also clear that at 2:1 (where a counteraccusation is raised followed by the refutation of the third implied charge), we have a major transition where our author starts to follow Jude; then at 3:1 (where Watson sees a *transitio* or secondary *exordium* leading into the refutation of the fourth charge) another major transition takes place, although in this case still following Jude.

Finally, one gets the *peroratio* in 3:14–18, which this present writer labels a "body closing" followed by a "letter closing," and which Watson rhetorically labels *repetitio*, followed by *adfectus*. It is clear that the letter closing is far simpler than in, say, Paul's letters, for the body closing or summary (*repetitio*) is only three verses long, there are no personal greetings, nor is there any health wish; there is only a warning followed by a closing exhortation and doxology, which are Pauline in tone.

Our author, then, is a skilled rhetorician and is using the conventions of the rhetoric of his day—in fact, of the most florid rhetoric of his day (we do not know whether this was his only training or whether he chose to use this style over other possible styles). The letter lacks Semitisms other than those which should be more properly be called Septuagintalisms (i.e., Semitic structures picked up from the Greek translation of the Hebrew Scriptures), much as biblicisms creep into the speech of many Bible readers today.

In summary, the structure of the letter looks like this:

A. Salutation (Epistolary Prescript) (1:1–2)
B. Letter Opening (*Exordium*) (1:3–15)
    1. Opening exhortation (1:3–11)

---

41. Duane F. Watson, *Invention, Arrangement, and Style*, 144–46.
42. Ibid.

What one sees in this outline is a carefully crafted structure that follows the rules of ancient rhetoric and serves the author's purpose of reinforcing a call to moral behavior in the light of the coming return of Jesus and concomitant judgment.

4.2.3 Relationship to Jude

We have been making the assumption all along that 2 Peter is dependent on Jude. There still are some scholars who argue either that both worked independently drawing from a common tradition or that Jude depended on 2 Peter. Either of these theses, of course, makes it easier to date 2 Peter earlier, and the latter of these two theses has seemed to some more in tune with the idea that an apostle wrote 2 Peter, for they think it unlikely that an apostle would draw on the work of another, especially if that other were not himself an apostle. All of these are dogmatic arguments, not arguments based on textual phenomena.

Furthermore, the latter arguments are more drawn from the sensitivities of the later church about apostles than from the sensitivities of the first-century official delegates themselves. First, while Paul wants to make it clear in Gal 1–2 that he neither was nor is dependent on Jerusalem (thus he does not identify any other official delegates of Jesus than those who were identified with Jerusalem), that did not stop him from using preexisting traditional, creedal, or hymnic material and incorporating it into his letters. For example, he cites traditions that he received and passed on in 1 Cor 11:23 and 15:3. Just because one has had direct contact with Jesus does not mean that everything one teaches must come from that direct contact. This would be a strange assumption for those who believed in the body of Christ functioning as a whole.

Second, in antiquity *aemulatio* (i.e., the adaptation and restatement of the words of others, especially of authoritative others) was so accepted that it was part of the rhetorical exercises included in basic education (in the *progymnasmata*).[43] Thus it would be surprising if New Testament authors did not use the material of others in similar ways. We must, as readers of the text, look at the phenomena of the text rather than impose on the text our modern ideas of what ancient authors should have done. Here is the data:

Jude	2 Peter	Comments
[1]Jude, a servant of Jesus Christ and brother of James, To those who are called, who are beloved in God the Father and kept safe for Jesus Christ: [2]May mercy, peace, and love be yours in abundance.	[1:1]Simeon Peter, a servant and apostle of Jesus Christ, To those who have received a faith as precious as ours through the righteousness of our God and Savior Jesus Christ: [2]May grace and peace be yours in abundance in the knowledge of God and of Jesus our Lord.	The form and structure of the letter salutations are conventional. While "servant of Jesus Christ" and "peace … in abundance" are in common, they could be stock phrases.
[3]Beloved, while eagerly preparing to write to you about the salvation we share, I find it necessary to write and appeal to you to contend for the faith that was once for all entrusted to the saints. [4]For certain intruders have stolen in among you, people who long ago were designated for this condemnation as ungodly, who pervert the grace of our God into *licentious*ness and deny our only *Master* and Lord, Jesus Christ.	[2:1]But false prophets also arose among the people, just as there will be false teachers among you, who will secretly bring in destructive opinions. They will even *deny* the *Master* who bought them — bringing swift destruction on themselves. [2]Even so, many will follow their *licentious* ways, and because of these teachers the way of truth will be maligned. [3]And in their greed they will exploit you with deceptive words. Their condemnation, pronounced against them long ago, has not been idle, and their destruction is not asleep.	Here 2 Peter introduces a similar topic to Jude, the presence of "others," whom 2 Peter labels "false teachers." For Jude they come from outside, while for 2 Peter they are internal, but their characteristics are the same. In particular both "deny" the "Master" (*despotēs*, δεσπότης), which is used for Jesus only in these two New Testament passages (and used for God only in Luke 2:29; Acts 4:24; and Rev 6:10).

43. See John S. Kloppenborg, "The Reception of Jesus Traditions in James," in *The Catholic Epistles and the Tradition* (ed. Jacques Schlosser; BETL 176; Leuven: Peeters/Leuven University Press, 2004), 93–141; idem, "The Emulation of the Jesus Tradition in the Letter of James," in *Reading James with New Eyes: Methodological Reassessments of the Letter of James* (ed. Robert L. Webb and John S. Kloppenborg; LNTS 342; London: T&T Clark, 2007), 121–50; idem, "James 1:2–15 and Hellenistic Psychagogy," *NovT* 52 (2010): 37–71. While focused on James, these articles clearly lay out the practice of *aemulatio* and demonstrate its presence in James (see also sec. 2.4.2 on James, where this practice is further explained).

⁵Now I desire to remind you, though you are fully informed, that the Lord, who once for all saved a people out of the land of Egypt, afterward destroyed those who did not believe. ⁶And the *angels* who did not keep their own position, but left their proper dwelling, he has kept in eternal *chains* in *deepest darkness* for the *judgment* of the great day. ⁷Likewise, *Sodom and Gomorrah* and the surrounding cities, which, in the same manner as they, indulged in sexual immorality and pursued unnatural lust, serve as an example by undergoing a punishment of eternal fire.

⁴For if God did not spare the *angels* when they sinned, but cast them into hell and committed them to *chains* of *deepest darkness* to be kept until the *judgment*; ⁵and if he did not spare the ancient world, even though he saved Noah, a herald of righteousness, with seven others, when he brought a flood on a world of the ungodly; ⁶and if by turning the cities of *Sodom and Gomorrah* to ashes he condemned them to extinction and made them an example of what is coming to the ungodly; ⁷and if he rescued Lot, a righteous man greatly distressed by the licentiousness of the lawless ⁸(for that righteous man, living among them day after day, was tormented in his righteous soul by their lawless deeds that he saw and heard), ⁹then the Lord knows how to rescue the godly from trial, and to keep the unrighteous under punishment until the day of judgment

While 2 Peter lacks the first example found in Jude, he has the next two in order, although he puts Noah between them.

The example of the angels has a number of parallels, some of them using synonyms ("chains") and some of them verbally identical ("deepest darkness"); 2 Peter is more Hellenistic (e.g., his term for "hell" [*tartaros*]).

When it comes to Sodom and Gomorrah, 2 Peter adds information about Lot, but otherwise is what one would expect in paraphrasing Jude according to the principle of *aemulatio*.

⁸Yet in the same way these dreamers also defile the *flesh*, *reject authority*, and *slander the glorious ones*. ⁹But when the archangel Michael contended with the devil and disputed about the body of Moses, he did not dare to bring a *condemnation of slander* against him, but said, "The Lord rebuke you!" ¹⁰But these people *slander whatever they do not understand*,

¹⁰—especially those who indulge their *flesh* in depraved lust, and who *despise authority*.

Bold and willful, they are not afraid to *slander the glorious ones*, ¹¹whereas angels, though greater in might and power, do not bring against them a *slanderous judgment* from the Lord. ¹²These people, however, are *like irrational animals*, mere creatures of

While Jude's "reject authority" becomes "despise authority" in 2 Peter, again the ideas are in the same order, with both referring to slandering "the glorious ones," although Jude alone has the example from the *Testament of Moses*.

The accusation of their being like irrational animals has a lot of common vocabulary.

Second Peter lacks the

and they are destroyed by those things that, *like irrational animals*, they know by *instinct*. [11]Woe to them! For they go the way of Cain, and abandon themselves to Balaam's error for the sake of *gain*, and perish in Korah's rebellion. [12]These are blemishes on your love-feasts, while they *feast* with you without fear, feeding themselves.

instinct, born to be caught and killed. They *slander what they do not understand*, and when those creatures are destroyed, they also will be destroyed, [13]suffering the penalty for doing wrong. They count it a pleasure to revel in the daytime. They are blots and blemishes, reveling in their dissipation while they *feast* with you. [14]They have eyes full of adultery, insatiable for sin. They entice unsteady souls. They have hearts trained in greed. Accursed children! [15]They have left the straight road and have gone astray, following the road of Balaam son of Bosor, who loved *the wages of doing wrong*, [16]but was rebuked for his own transgression; a speechless donkey spoke with a human voice and restrained the prophet's madness.

triple examples of Cain, Balaam, and Korah. Both authors discuss the behavior of the "others" at the communal meals.

The Balaam example is brought in and expanded below. The term "wages" or "gain" (in both cases *misthos*, μισθός) is in common, but 2 Peter repeats "wages of doing wrong" from v. 13 ("penalty for doing wrong" there) as if conscious that he has moved the example.

They are *waterless* clouds carried along by the winds; autumn trees without fruit, twice dead, uprooted; [13]wild waves of the sea, casting up the foam of their own shame; wandering stars, for whom *the deepest darkness has been reserved* forever.

[14]It was also about these that Enoch, in the seventh generation from Adam, prophesied, saying, "See, the Lord is coming with ten thousands of his holy ones, [15]to execute judgment on all, and to convict everyone

[17]These are *waterless* springs and mists driven by a storm; for them the *deepest darkness has been reserved*. [18]For they speak *bombastic nonsense*, and with *licentious desires* of the flesh they entice people who have just escaped from those who live in error. [19]They promise them freedom, but they themselves are slaves of corruption; for people are slaves to whatever masters them. [20]For if, after they have escaped the defilements of the world through the

There is a series of similar descriptors of the "others," including the use of a number of verbally identical terms, although sometimes it is the same idea rearranged (instead of waterless clouds carried by the wind, it is waterless springs and then mists driven by a storm).

Second Peter does not have the example from *1 Enoch*, just as he did not have the example from the *Testament of Moses*. This

of all the deeds of ungodliness that they have committed in such an ungodly way, and of all the harsh things that ungodly sinners have spoken against him." [16]These are grumblers and malcontents; they indulge their *own lusts*; they are *bombastic* in speech, flattering people to their own advantage.

knowledge of our Lord and Savior Jesus Christ, they are again entangled in them and overpowered, the last state has become worse for them than the first. [21]For it would have been better for them never to have known the way of righteousness than, after knowing it, to turn back from the holy commandment that was passed on to them. [22]It has happened to them according to the true proverb,

    "The dog turns back to its own vomit,"
and,
    "The sow is washed only to wallow in the mud."

means that Jude 16 needs to be joined with Jude 13 to be compared with 2 Pet 2:17 – 18.

[17]But you, *beloved*, must *remember* the predictions of the *apostles* of our *Lord* Jesus Christ; [18]for they said to you, "*In the last time* there will be *scoffers*, *indulging their* own ungodly *lusts*." [19]It is these worldly people, devoid of the Spirit, who are causing divisions. [20] But you, beloved, build yourselves up on your most holy faith; pray in the Holy Spirit; [21]keep yourselves in the love of God; look forward to the mercy of our Lord Jesus Christ that leads to eternal life. [22]And have mercy on some who are wavering; [23]save others by snatching them out of the fire; and have mercy on still others with fear, hating even the tunic defiled by their bodies.

[3:1]This is now, *beloved*, the second letter I am writing to you; in them I am trying to arouse your sincere intention by *reminding* you [2]that you should remember the words spoken in the past by the holy prophets, and the commandment of the *Lord* and Savior spoken through your *apostles*. [3]First of all you must understand this, that *in the last days scoffers will come, scoffing and indulging their* own *lusts* [4]and saying, "Where is the promise of his coming? For ever since our ancestors died, all things continue as they were from the beginning of creation!"

The first three verses of 2 Peter 3 parallel Jude 17 – 18 with respect to topic, with some common vocabulary. After this, the two letters have different developments and applications of their material.

(Continued on the next page)

²⁴Now to him who is able to keep you from falling, and to make you stand without blemish in the presence of his glory with rejoicing, ²⁵to the only God our *Savior*, through Jesus *Christ* our *Lord*, *be glory*, majesty, power, and authority, before all time and now and forever. Amen.	¹⁷You therefore, beloved, since you are forewarned, beware that you are not carried away with the error of the lawless and lose your own stability. ¹⁸But grow in the grace and knowledge of our *Lord* and *Savior* Jesus *Christ*. To him *be the glory* both now and to the day of eternity. Amen.	It is obvious that Jude has a much more elaborate final prayer, although there is overlap in vocabulary between Jude's doxology and the final exhortation in 2 Peter and overlap in concept between the ends of the two doxologies.

Table 7: A Comparison of 2 Peter and Jude (using NRSV)

In this comparison, one is impressed that the same topics are taken up in the same order (with one exception, but there 2 Peter seems conscious of a dislocation), and there is significant overlapping vocabulary, some of it common words, but some of it rare words. This rules out the two documents being independent compositions.[44] As noted above, one could posit a common source, but the principle of Occam's razor suggests that one should not posit such an unknown third document unless it is necessary to explain the data, which it is not. It is also unlikely that Jude uses 2 Peter, for while there are traces of all of Jude in 2 Peter (with the exception of Jude's application, which would not fit in 2 Peter's context, and of some of Jude's examples, as well as his references to *1 Enoch* and *Testament of Moses*), there are no traces of 2 Peter 1 in Jude, nor of a large segment of 2 Peter 3. It would be difficult to explain why Jude did not need to use any of this material and how he could avoid accidental use of it, but it is not at all difficult to explain 2 Peter's use of Jude.

In fact, once one grasps the rhetorical practice of *aemulatio*, one realizes that here we have exactly what we would expect if one ancient author chose to use the work of another: more or less identical order of topics, some identity in word choices and particularly in the use of unusual words, but rephrasing of much of the document so that it fit the rhetorical style and context of the second author. It is our conclusion, then, that the vast majority of scholarly opinion is correct, namely, that 2 Peter has used Jude and adapted it to its context. Because of this adaptation one cannot simply read Jude and assume that 2 Peter means exactly what Jude does or that he is applying it to the same situation, but because of this use of Jude one does have the original text in Jude that enables one to see more clearly the changes 2 Peter is making.

---

44. If two students were to turn in short papers this similar, an instructor would surely accuse them of colluding in their work or of one borrowing from the other. Or, to put it another way, Turnitin® would flag the high degree of similarity.

4.3 THEMATIC COMMENTARY

Given what has already been said about 2 Peter, it is clear that Jesus' reign and concomitant final judgment are main themes of the work, not because the work is focused on doctrinal correctness, but because the work knows that eschatology determines ethics, and it is precisely the ethics of those whom he addresses about which our author is concerned. We will follow the development of his argument as we observe the rhetorical structure of the letter.

4.3.1 Salutation (Epistolary Prescript) (1:1 – 2)

The letter begins, as noted in the discussion of authorship, by designating the author as "Symeon Peter," a transliteration of an alternative Aramaic given name used here and in Luke–Acts (e.g., Acts 15:14 on the lips of James) for Jonah's eldest son,[45] although normally in the New Testament his given name is the good Greek name Simon (an equivalent name in Greek). Does Acts 15:14 reflect the historical tidbit that Peter's name was originally Symeon, or does it reflect that James used the Aramaic Symeon for this leader rather than the Hellenistic Simon, even though Simon was what his parents had used, reflecting the mixed culture of Galilee? Or did Peter himself use the names interchangeably, perhaps depending on context (as my wife uses Judith in some contexts but Judy in most contexts)? We cannot answer this from that data we have, but it is interesting that this most Hellenistic book uses an Aramaic name. And we lack other examples of a first-century person called by these two names. "Peter," of course, is the nickname, "Rock," which Jesus gave Simeon/Simon when he became Jesus' trainee.

Whatever the case, our author designates himself "a slave" of Jesus the Anointed One and Jesus' "official delegate." A slave was someone without authority or social status in their own right, but who could carry the authority of their master, and a slave sent out as their master's delegate (*apostolos*, ἀπόστολος) would carry the master's authority, regardless of who that master was. Thus our author is both humble about his own importance as a person and at the same time assertive about his authority as Jesus's delegate. In a sense he is indicating that he is not actualizing himself, but actualizing Jesus.

The implied readers are not designated by name or location, but are designated by their commitment: they have received a faith or commitment, like receiving a grant from a ruler, that is "equally honorable" to the commitment that "we" (probably meaning "we delegates [*apostoloi*] of Jesus") have. The reference to "we official delegates" fits the genre of testamental literature, since the work is reminding the readers of the teaching of Peter and the other official delegates before an impending death (1:12 – 15). The addressees have received this faith due to the sovereign's justice, so it is not an inappropriate grant.

---

45. We surmise this birth order from the fact that Peter is normally named before Andrew and appears to fulfill the dominant role of the eldest son.

Then comes the surprise, for the sovereign is named, not as God the Father, but as "our God and Savior Jesus the Anointed One." One can, of course, argue that this is a slip of the stylus, an error in dictation, or too much emphasis on the grammar, and there are some grounds for this in that in 1:11 it is "our Lord [not God] and Savior Jesus the Anointed One" (see also 3:18). We notice that the letter clearly has an emphasis on the role of Jesus with God's role being focused on the events recorded in the Hebrew Scriptures. It is also true that a few manuscripts (most notably Sinaiticus) read "our Lord and Savior" here. But the normal canons of textual criticism[46] demand that we read "God," and the normal rules of Greek grammar (specifically, the Granville-Sharp rule) indicate that we should read this as describing one person. That is, we have two nouns ("God" and "Savior," neither of them a proper name) joined by "and" (*kai*, καί) with an article before the first noun ("God") but without the article being repeated before the second noun ("Savior"). In this case the unity is further underlined by an adjective ("our") that describes both nouns but is positioned after the first noun and before the "and."[47]

Thus 2 Peter starts out with what is arguably the highest expressed Christology in the New Testament, a statement in which Jesus is explicitly called "God" as well as "Savior." In the Hellenistic world this was a political as well as a theological statement in that dead emperors were routinely deified, and some living ones claimed this status (notably Gaius Caligula and Domitian),[48] while all emperors who had won notable battles or protected the empire from a threat were referred to as "Savior" (*sōtēr*, σωτήρ). Now our author, a follower of Jesus, who is identified as God's designated king ("the Anointed One"),[49] is applying those titles to Jesus. There is a king, who is truly God and Savior, and this King (or, as in 1:11, Lord) is Jesus.

It is the readers whom our author addresses to whom he wishes that favor and peace be multiplied "in the knowledge of God and Jesus our Lord." While wishing favor (or grace) and peace was a typical combination of a Greek (*chairein*, "greetings" and in Jas 1:1, which under the influence of the Jesus movement became *charis*, "grace" or "favor") and Jewish greeting ("*šālôm*," translated as "peace"), the focus on the "knowledge" (which is personal knowledge, not abstract knowledge) of God and Jesus our Lord has introduced a major theme of the soteriology of 2 Peter, as we will see below.

---

46. For example: What is the most difficult reading? What reading explains the others? What reading is most widespread in the various streams of manuscript tradition? What reading is the oldest?

47. See Daniel B. Wallace, *Greek Grammar beyond the Basics: An Exegetical Syntax of the Greek New Testament* (Grand Rapids: Zondervan, 1997), 270–73, 276–77. The same rule applies to "Lord and Savior" as one person in 1:11.

48. A coin of Tiberius, such as the coin that Jesus asked to be shown, had the inscription, "Tiberius Caesar, Son of the Divine Augustus, Augustus, High Priest," which, while not explicit, is certainly close to claiming divine status for himself while living. Thus even emperors who were officially deified after death made claims during life that pointed in that direction.

49. *Christos* means "anointed one," which in the Greco-Roman world, which did not anoint rulers, would mean cosmetically or medicinally anointed, but which was in fact a translation of the Aramaic "Messiah," or "Anointed One," which designated God's anointed king in fulfillment of the promises made in the Hebrew Scriptures, and especially the promises to David, as in 2 Sam 7:13. It is our contention that believers in Jesus knew the meaning of this term, so while it might seem like a strange name to an *uninitiated* Greco-Roman reader, it was for initiated believers in Jesus a title of divinely appointed royal status. Thus we have chosen to translate it to bring out its meaning rather than to use the usual transliteration, "Christ."

4.3.2 Letter Opening (*Exordium*) (1:3–15)

The form of the letter opening is typical for New Testament letters built on the Greco-Roman letter format and continues the salutation. The author has already been identified and the recipients have been identified by their faith characteristics, not by name or location. Since there is no reason to believe from the language or content of the letter that they are the same addressees as the recipients of 1 Peter, the form of address of 2 Peter makes it truly a general letter, even if it envisages a particular community or group of communities with a specific problem. As noted, the addressees are identified as "those who have received as a portion an allegiance that is just as valuable as ours," which immediately puts the addressees on the same level as the author, at least in this regard. It also indicates that their allegiance to Jesus and his Father is not entirely a matter of their choice, but a result of a divine grant. This grant was made "in [or 'by'] our God and Savior Jesus the Anointed One's justice." Thus it was not an arbitrary grant, but one justly made.

The grantor is "our God and Savior Jesus the Anointed One." While we recognize "Jesus the Anointed One" or "Jesus the Messiah" as a title identifying Jesus of Nazareth as God's promised ruler, and while "Savior" as a title of a ruler is not only appropriate in the ancient world but also appears 24 times in the New Testament (5 times in 2 Peter) for God or Jesus, the title "our God" applied directly to Jesus is either an early textual corruption[50] or else among the highest Christology of the New Testament (cf. 4.3.1). It presents Jesus in contrast to the ruling emperor. Here, says 2 Peter, is the divinely appointed King to whom such titles really belong. This is the King who has granted them allegiance to his rule and who is the main actor in the opening exhortation that continues the salutation.

4.3.2.1 Opening Exhortation (1:3–11)

The opening exhortation breaks into two parts. The first part describes what Jesus as a divine, royal patron has done for the human beings addressed. There are some significant sovereign benefactions, which are correlated only with the individuals having in some sense repented (i.e., having "fled from the corruption that is in the world"). In this description we discover some interesting theology about the source of this corruption and the character and goals of the divine patron. This exhortation forms a type of *narratio* (to use the rhetorical term) in that it points to what presumably the addressees would agree Jesus has indeed done for them.

The second part is an exhortation to press "further in and higher up" (to use the words of C. S. Lewis) toward this goal, for it is this pursuit of virtue that has benefits,

---

50. Of the major manuscripts, only Sinaiticus has an alternative reading "Lord," which seems to harmonize this passage with the more typical titles for Jesus in 2 Peter (1:8, 11; 2:20; 3:2, 18). Thus if "God" was substituted for "Lord" or an article has dropped out and the "our" is in the wrong place, it must have happened early in the manuscript history. One could argue that the author has made a slip of the pen (more likely, a slip in dictation) and intended something more like 1:2, where God and Jesus are separated, like the other titles for Jesus in the letter, or that he was not aware of the grammar (which would seem strange in a letter with the rhetorical sophistication of this letter). Any of these explanations is possible, but we have chosen to take the text at face value, for it makes sense in both the context of the letter and that of the culture.

while the alternative would be to slip back into corruption. The one action confirms the sovereign divine calling, while the other would, by implication, be something of a "dog returning to its vomit" (2:22) or a denial of "the Master who bought them" (2:1), a failure to confirm the divine calling and so, it seems, disconfirming it.

4.3.2.1.1 Historical Introduction (1:3–4)

While grammatically difficult,[51] the historical introduction's intention is relatively clear. First, God, or "his divine power" (a rather unusual Hellenistic expression, appearing in the New Testament only in 2 Peter and Paul's speech on the Areopagus in Acts), has given followers of Jesus everything needed that leads to life and piety. In other words, there is no excuse for not seeking life or not being pious or godly, since the addressees already have everything necessary.

Second, what is needed came to the followers of Jesus through their coming to know "the one calling" them. This calling was due, not to their virtue, but to the virtue of Jesus: "by his own glory and virtue" (i.e., due to his own honor).[52] In terms of that culture, he is the divine patron, who brought deliverance to his clients because he is an honorable and virtuous person.

Third, it is through his honorable status that Jesus has given his followers "very great, valuable promises," which in the context of 2 Peter probably indicate the renewal of heaven and earth, including the final judgment at which their faithfulness to him will be rewarded, making their following him worthwhile.

Fourth, the goal or purpose of Jesus' action is so that through these promises followers of Jesus might share the divine nature, in other words, that they might share the honor status and virtue that Jesus has. While this is daring Hellenistic language (and probably would be shocking to less Hellenized Jewish groups, not to mention some contemporary religious groups), it does not say more than that redeemed humanity is to be like God (*imitatio Dei*) and fulfill God's plan of human beings fully representing God on earth (*imago Dei*). Moreover, it is clear that this is redeemed humanity that our author is writing about, for those who in the end share in the divine nature are those who have fled the corruption that is in the world due to desire. In other words, they do not flee the world, but the corruption in the world, and this corruption in the world is there because of desire—not particular desires (thus the translation "lust" is misleading, for that seems to separate some desires from other desires), but desire in general.

In other words, human drives (what Freud described with his term *id*), or the human limbic system, the seat of emotional reactivity, is the source of the corruption

---

51. The grammatical focus is on 1:5, where the main verb occurs, but how 1:3–4 relates to this is debated. Is this the continuation of 1:2, or are these verses an anacolouthon? See Peter H. Davids, *2 Peter and Jude: A Handbook to the Greek Text* (Waco, TX: Baylor University Press, 2011), 44. Davids, *2 Peter and Jude*, 170–71, concludes that grammatically there is a dependence on 1:2, but rhetorically a new section begins in 1:3.

52. The terms "glory and virtue," while not identical, are in essence a hendiadys indicating a state of honor. They are datives, and so one could read that the calling was "by" or "for" or "to" his "glory and virtue." Certainly his honor is enhanced by this action ("for") and certainly his followers are to imitate his "glory and virtue" ("to"), as 1:5–7 makes clear, but 1:4 seems to indicate that it was due to or "by" his "glory and virtue" that this calling took place.

in the world. That is a statement that a Stoic could have made, although, unlike 2 Peter, a Stoic would have championed detachment as the remedy. We note, then, that desire within human beings has resulted in corruption in the world; that some individuals have been called, not because of their virtue, but because of the virtue of the divine patron; and that they are equipped by means of knowing him to achieve life and piety, i.e., to become like him. These individuals are those who have actively fled from the corruption in the world, not those still participating in it.

4.3.2.1.2 Call to Virtue (1:5–11)

On the basis of the freedom and privilege that the divine royal patron has granted, the addressees are called to make them effective. While the privileges mentioned in the previous verses are a royal grant, the virtues mentioned in these verses are the result of effort: "make every effort," "do your very best," is the sense of the idiom. What follows is a catalogue of that on which one should focus effort. While the catalogue is given in the form of a chain of adding x to y, the point is that one needs all of these virtues, not that they come in a certain order. The foundation that they are built on is commitment (*pistis*, πίστις) — commitment to the royal person of Jesus, the Anointed One, "our Lord" or "our Lord and Savior" (1:8, 11). But commitment needs to be expressed in imitation and obedience, and that is what we see in this passage, expressed in terms that for the most part were common in Hellenistic philosophy:

Virtue	Meaning	Comment
Virtue (*aretē*, ἀρετή)	Character worthy of praise, excellence of character, exceptional civic virtue[53]	Rare in the New Testament (4 times, twice in 2 Peter), but common in Stoic morality
Knowledge (*gnōsis*, γνῶσις)	Knowledge, can mean knowledge of God, but can also mean moral insight or knowledge of a truth, as in 1 Cor 8	While knowledge of God is not significant in Greco-Roman thought, knowledge used absolutely, as here, is important in several streams of Hellenistic thought
Self-control (*enkrateia*, ἐγκράτεια)	Restraint of one's drives and emotions	Only three times in the New Testament, including Gal 5:23; common theme of Greco-Roman philosophy
Patient endurance (*hypomonē*, ὑπομονή)	Endurance of suffering because of one's faithfulness	Common in New Testament lists (Rom 5:3–5; Jas 1:3–4), but also significant for Stoics

(Continued on the next page)

53. BDAG, *aretē*, ἀρετή, 130.

Virtue	Meaning	Comment
Piety (*eusebeia*, εὐσέβεια)	Piety, devoutness, godliness	15 times in the New Testament, 4 times in 2 Peter, once in Acts, the rest in the Pastoral Epistles. Common in both Greco-Roman thought and Second Temple literature
Familial love (*philadelphia*, φιλαδελφία)	Caring actions toward those within the "family," one's "brothers and sisters"	In five New Testament ethical exhortations. In non-Christian literature only in the sense of loving blood brothers and sisters
Love (*agapē*, ἀγάπη)	Caring, even sacrificial, actions toward others	Common in New Testament lists (Rom 3:3–5; Gal 5:22–23); not common in Hellenistic literature[54]

Table 8: The Virtues of 2 Peter 1:5–7

A quick examination of the table shows that 2 Peter has indeed chosen virtues that have a Hellenistic tone and would be familiar to addressees with a Hellenistic background. In fact, two of the virtues are rare in the New Testament but common in Hellenistic thought. Where 2 Peter shows a morality that belongs to the Jesus movement is in his use of "familial love" (*philadelphia*), not for members of one's blood family (which is rarely a concern for the New Testament), but for members of one's fictive family, that is, the members of the community of the followers of Jesus,[55] toward which the New Testament in general applies the symbols and actions of familial devotion (at times over against love and loyalty toward one's blood family). The community of believers is of central importance to him, as to other New Testament writers.

Our author follows this virtue up with "love," which is also a core New Testament ethical value and, since it by nature must be directed toward others, is especially focused on the community of believers. In other words, for all of his use of Hellenistic virtues, which reveal a person well educated in that culture, our author is also focused on the virtues that build the community of believers.

One needs these virtues in order that one not be "worthless" or "unfruitful" "in the knowledge of our Lord Jesus the Anointed One." James 2:20 uses "worthless" (a term found in three verses in Matthew, twice in the Pastoral Epistles, once in James, and once in 2 Peter) for faith that lacks deeds. A similar thought occurs

---

54. Intrestingly, in the LXX of the Song of Songs this is the only term used for "love." Thus, depending on context, *agapē* can mean erotic concern for the other as well as the type of concern for the other referred to in the New Testament.

55. The followers of Jesus were considered a fictive family. "Fictive" means "not blood," but since "blood" means "by birth," the fictive family trumps the blood family as the new birth trumps the original birth. Thus, family symbols that were not normally used outside the family were used within the Jesus community, such as the kiss. Thus one shared with, loved, and cared for members of the Jesus community, for they were one's true family—one's brothers and sisters.

here, namely, that the person who has come to know Jesus as Lord is "worthless" in relation to that knowledge if they do not follow it up with the pursuit of virtue. Our author underlines this here by saying that such a person is "blind" and "has forgotten the cleansing of their previous sins."

One suspects that our author is already critiquing those he names as "false teachers" in chapter 2, as well as their followers, since they clearly lack virtue. But at this point he does not dwell on the negative; instead, he urges his addressees to "make [their] calling and election firm" (1:10), which implies that those he criticizes are not doing this. He makes his point clear by stating that those "doing these things" (i.e., practicing these virtues, for that is the topic under discussion) will "never stumble"; this can mean "sin" or "go astray" (e.g., Jas 2:10; 3:2), but here likely means experience a disaster, "be ruined, be lost,"[56] that is, ruined with respect to the faith.

Our author becomes even more positive in that he assures the addressees that the pursuit of virtue is not just about avoiding ruin, but also, even primarily, about "providing a rich entrance into the eternal kingdom of our Lord and Savior Jesus the Anointed One." That is, when the kingdom comes in its fullness (the "entrance" is future, so 2 Peter is thinking about the ultimate consummation of the kingdom), the King will naturally reward virtue, as rulers normally did in that culture. If one is moving forward in virtue based on one's commitment to Jesus, one will not need to fear a disaster with respect to that commitment, but instead can look forward to a generous reward from the coming King. The timing of this judgment, of course, fits with what will be discussed in chapter 3.

4.3.2.2 Purpose Statement (1:12–15)

Our author moves on to the purpose of the letter. First, he makes the charitable assumption (which was also rhetorically appropriate) that he has only been discussing what they already know and that they are firmly committed to the truth they already have. But he also believes the truth he has just enunciated is important enough that he intends to keep reminding them of it, refreshing their memory; and since he believes he is going to die soon, he is committing the truth to writing so that they will continue to have a posthumous reminder. This fits with the cultural value that preferred the living voice to the written voice, but in the absence of the living voice, would accept its preservation in writing as second best, that is, the best solution to an undesirable situation (i.e., the death of Simon Peter).

It is not clear how "our Lord, Jesus the Anointed One," had "revealed" or "explained" to our author (the Greek term has both meanings) that he was soon to give up his temporary lodging (i.e., was going to die).[57] There are two passages

---

56. BDAG, *ptaiō*, πταίω, 727 (meaning 2).

57. The term for place of residence is *skēnōma*, σκήνωμα, which comes from *skēnos*, which refers to a tent or temporary place of residence rather than a permanent structure (see BDAG, 929, which has articles on both terms). In Acts 7:46–47, the only other place that *skēnōma* occurs in the New Testament, it is contrasted with "house," a permanent dwelling, just as Paul contrasts his present mortal body, *skēnos*, with the immortal body he will receive in the transformation (his preferred scenario is transformation without death) or resurrection when Jesus returns in 2 Cor 5:1, 4. Thus the emphasis in 2 Peter is on mortality, not with the idea that he wishes to leave earth or live without a body, but with the idea that the author is looking forward to the renewal of the earth and the resurrection, which he will discuss in chapter 3.

in John (13:36; 21:18–19) that could be the words of Jesus that he is referring to, but he just as well could be referring to a postascension revelation by Jesus, since there is nothing in the language of this passage that recalls either of those passages (which use the language of "going," "following," "being led," "stretching out one's hands," none of which occur in 2 Peter), other than the fact that all three passages apparently refer to Peter's death.

This letter, then, is a testament, like other testamental literature of the period, a written reminder to one's family (in this case referred to as "siblings," *adelphoi*, ἀδελφοί) of one or more truths that a dying person wishes to pass on to the coming generation(s).[58]

4.3.3 Letter Body (*Probatio*) (1:16–3:13)

Having "laid his cards on the table" in his opening assertion (1:3–11) and purpose statement (1:12–15), our author now needs to prove that there will be a parousia and that this entails judgment. This is the goal of the bulk of the letter, in which he answers four significant objections to the scenario of a coming rule of Jesus in which virtue will be rewarded. Only the fourth objection is voiced, the other three being implied in his responses.

4.3.3.1 Issue 1: Parousia Is a Fabricated Myth (1:16–18)

The first implied objection is that the parousia is a fabrication, a myth in the sense of something that is not true or real.[59] In response to this implied objection, our author says, No, Jesus' parousia and authority (i.e., his rule) that we proclaimed are no such myth. Rather, we were eyewitnesses of his majesty at his investiture. While the "we" is never defined, the incident is, as in "when we were with him in the holy mountain," a reference to the transfiguration narrative (Matt 17:1–8; Mark 9:2–8; Luke 9:28–36), which Mark describes as seeing that "the kingdom of God has come in power" (Mark 9:1). The point of narrating the event here in 2 Peter is that God the Father invested Jesus with honor and dignity and made the declaration, "This is my loved Son, with whom I am pleased," a formal designation of Jesus as world ruler.[60]

This type of argument is what was termed an "inartificial proof" in that it is not a logical argument, but a presentation of evidence.[61] In presenting it, the author is careful to make a separation between himself and God in that the voice was "borne to Jesus" from "the majestic glory," and that it was this voice that they heard, rather

---

58. We have already noted above that Jas 5:11 refers to the Job of the *Testament of Job*, in which work Job's concern is to pass on to his family the value of patient endurance (*hypomonē*). Other well-known testamental literature of the period was the *Testaments of the Twelve Patriarchs*, which have various lessons to pass on to succeeding generations.

59. The term "myth" (*mythos*, μύθος) originally meant any nar-

rative, but by the first century it had come to mean a fictional narrative, often contrasted with *logos*, used for true history. See BDAG, *mythos*, μύθος, 660. In the present period the English term is sometimes used anthropologically for narratives about deities or prehistory (especially origins), without judgment about their truth value.

60. Davids, *2 Peter and Jude*, 202–6.

61. Watson, *Invention, Arrangement, Style*, 102.

than saying that they had experienced it from God directly.[62] That, of course, does not mean that he plays the experience down; rather, he is trying to detail its exact nature. The point he is making is that in talking about Jesus' coming to rule, they are not inventing some strange idea; they are simply declaring what they had experienced, namely, that in the transfiguration Jesus had *already* been invested with power and dignity by the declaration of God. It is something like saying, "We have been at his coronation, so of course he is king and will return as king."

4.3.3.2 Issue 2: Prophecy Is Equivocal (1:19–21)

The second implied objection is that prophecy is at best equivocal. The experience of the transfiguration has made the prophetic word more reliable in that it has been fulfilled. We are not informed which prophetic word is in question, just that whichever word or words (thinking of "the prophetic word" as a collective term, which it probably is) have to do with the parousia and the reign of the Anointed One are more firm now that the start of the fulfillment has been experienced.[63] Since this prophetic word is something available to the addressees in a way that the experience of Jesus' enthronement is not (it was a past event at which the addressees were not present), they are doing well in that they are paying attention to that word. The assumption is that they are indeed doing this, and that the prophetic word is serving as a light in a dark place.[64]

But the prophetic word is not permanent. When the reality to which it points takes place, it will no longer be needed. So one pays attention to it only until "the day dawns and the morning star rises in your hearts" — that is, until they are aware that the parousia, the fulfillment, has come and thus that the "darkness" of this present age is past.

They are doing well to pay attention to the prophetic word, since they (first of all) know the basis for the reliability of prophecy. This basis is that no prophecy found in Scripture is its own interpretation of the prophetic experience, such as a vision.[65] False prophets might indeed manufacture interpretations of experiences or even induce or make up the experience itself, but that is not true of the prophecies found in Scripture. Rather, the prophet did not speak because he or she wanted to;

---

62. This may show a Jewish sensitivity to avoid speaking of direct experience of the divine. Thus, the law was mediated to Moses through divine messengers (angels); the Lord's messenger (the angel of the Lord) appears to various people in Joshua and Judges; and here the voice is "brought" or "conveyed." That would not necessarily mean that the writer is a Jew; it does mean that he (or the source of the narrative, if not the writer) shared with Jews (and some of other religions) a sense of the majesty of the divine that precluded direct human contact.

63. The author has heard at least the oral argument that 2 Peter means that the prophetic word is "more firm" than the experience, so one would translate, "We have something even firmer than that, the prophetic word." The problem with this interpretation is that there is no "than that" in the text referring backward to the experience. Rather, the text moves from the experience forward (using *kai*) to having (present tense) a firmer prophetic word. It is true that

"the prophetic word" is highlighted by right displacement, but that is because it is the main topic, not that it is now firmer.

64. The term, found only here in the New Testament, normally means "dry" (so a "dry place,"), but, unless 2 Peter is mixing metaphors, it must mean "dark." There is some precedent for its meaning "dark" or "gloomy" (cf. the translation here). See BDAG, *auchmēros*, αὐχμηρός, 154.

65. The text has been understood as indicating that no prophecy found in Scripture should be subject to the *interpreter's* own interpretation, usually understood as opposing 2 Peter's interpretation (and that of the larger group of which he was a part) to that of the false teachers. However, that does not fit the wider context, including cultural understandings of prophecy and the statements that follow in 2 Peter. See further the documentation and discussion in Davids, *2 Peter and Jude*, 210–14.

they spoke through the Holy Spirit and so spoke from God.[66] The ultimate source of prophecy, then, is God, and the proximal source is the Holy Spirit. When prophecies were written down in a form preserved in Scripture, they came to the addressees as "the prophecies found in Scripture," and the addressees are doing well if they allow these to guide them until the parousia that the prophecies point to takes place.

4.3.3.3 Issue 3: Divine Judgment Is "Idle" (2:1–22)

The third implied objection is that divine judgment is "idle," namely, that God does not really judge, regardless of what the prophetic Scriptures may say. This, of course, would fit with Epicurean beliefs that there is no final judgment and that death is the end of personal existence. This objection becomes explicit in chapter 3. The point of the objection is that if there is no final judgment as 2 Peter understands prophecies in Scripture to teach, then there is no sanction for the behaviors that 2 Peter also thinks the Scriptures condemn. To answer this implied objection our author relies on Jude, which he presents to his addressees in modified form using the rhetorical technique of *aemulatio*.[67]

4.3.3.3.1 Transition: Accusation of False Teachers (2:1–3)

The previous paragraph had discussed the situation in ancient Israel when the ancient prophets spoke from God. Our author couples onto this and notes that there were also false prophets back then, just as there "will be" false teachers among his addressees. In that sense, times do not change. Of course, the "will be" is from the perspective taken in the writing of the letter, for the following denunciation makes it clear that these teachers are already active.

Second Peter makes two charges against these teachers: (1) they are introducing destructive ways of thinking (he will make clear later what he means by destruction);[68] and (2) they are in some way denying "the Master who bought them." This

---

66. Sometimes stress is laid on the fact that the verb "carry" is used, and so the prophetic people were "carried along by the Holy Spirit," which indicates a lack of engagement of their own minds. Unfortunately for this interpretation, the same verb is used for prophecy's not "being brought" by "human will." The stress is on the contrast between human will and the Holy Spirit (both are fronted for emphasis) rather than on the means the Spirit uses to inspire. The point is that the prophets were "human beings speaking from God," that is, by the Holy Spirit, not making up stuff that they wanted to say.

67. Even when explicitly quoting, a first-century author felt free to modify the source text, as Jude 14–15 does to *1 En.* 1:9, which Jude considers a written prophecy. The technique of *aemulatio* was the presentation of a source text in one's own words but with enough of that text preserved that hearers will recognize the authority being "cited." This was an exercise that one first did in ancient "elementary school," as found in the *progymnasmata*. Simply quoting the source text would be considered unsophisticated and boring. Thus it is no wonder that 2 Peter follows Jude's topics in order and uses some of his words, but at the same time feels free to modify them and make them his own.

68. In some translations (e.g., ESV, NASV, NIV) the Greek term has been transliterated as "heresies," which is unfortunate, for it introduces a concept that would not develop for another hundred years or so (unless one dates 2 Peter in the second century), namely, that these are deviations from orthodox teaching. The term in its first-century context describes a group, school, or party within the larger community (such as the Sadducees [Acts 5:17], the Pharisees [15:5; 26:5], or the group of the followers of Jesus [24:5] within Judaism) and, secondarily, the distinctive teachings or ideas that demarcate the group. Paul did not like such groups forming within a local community of the Jesus movement (as indicated in his negative use of the term in 1 Cor 11:39 and Gal 5:20), not because their teachings were especially bad, but because they injured the unity of the community, for unity of the one "body of the Anointed King" or those "in the Anointed King" is the central theme of the Pauline letters. The author of 2 Peter *does* think that the teachings of the group he opposes are bad, and to indicate that, he has to describe them as "destructive," something he would *not* need to do if the term itself already meant "heresies" rather than "the distinctive teachings of a party or school."

is slave-owner language, for a slave is purchased by a master and should acknowledge the master as such. The point is that Jesus the Anointed One has purchased these people as his slaves, and they are failing to acknowledge his authority.[69] It is not that they are failing to do this verbally, for if that were the case, they would no longer be part of and would be a danger to the community that defines itself as followers of Jesus. Rather, they are failing to acknowledge Jesus' authority in practice.

The personal result of the actions of the false teachers will be their own quick destruction, as it was assumed in that culture would happen to a recalcitrant slave, but the communal results will be that many will imitate the licentious behavior of these teachers, which will result in slandering of "the way of truth" (i.e., the community following Jesus as Lord and its teaching). For their part, the false teachers are not sincere in their interest in these followers, for they are exploiting them financially by means of their deceptive words.

It is at this point that our author sets the issue that is the real topic of the section, namely, that the condemnation of these people, long ago pronounced by God (perhaps in the same prophetic writings he has already referred to, though 2 Peter does not specify), has not been delayed, nor is this condemnation "sleeping." It may indeed look that way, since they seem to act with impunity, and that is a claim these teachers are making (indeed, in chapter 3 they claim there is no judgment for anyone). But as the following examples show, if one looks at the record in Scripture, this is not the case.

4.3.3.3.2 Lord Able to Judge and Save (2:4 – 10a)

While the targets of 2 Peter's concern differ from Jude's in that Jude's "others" are neither described as teachers nor said to deny final judgment, the rhetorical proofs that 2 Peter advances are largely taken from Jude, although adapted to the different rhetorical context.

The first proof is taken from the material originally found in Gen 6 – 9, but which Jude and 2 Peter take from *1 Enoch* and other Second Temple literature. The divine messengers (angels) who sinned (by having sex with human women, crossing the species barrier) were imprisoned, as *1 Enoch* indicates. Second Peter parallels them to the Titans of Greek mythology by describing them as being held captive in Tartarus.[70] Furthermore, the ancient world, which in Second Temple literature these

---

69. The slave-owner metaphor may be offensive to modern readers, but it was common in the New Testament, for not only does the author of 2 Peter (in 1:1) describe himself as a "slave of Jesus the Anointed One," but Paul does so as well (Rom 1:1; Gal 1:10; Phil 1:1), as do James (Jas 1:1) and Jude (Jude 1). Revelation is a revelation that has been given to God's "slaves" (the believers in the seven churches) by means of God's "slave" John (Rev 1:1). The point is that a slave was or should be entirely subordinate to his or her master's interests and has status (honor) in society only insofar as they represent their master or are doing their master's will.

70. The typical translation of "hell" for Tartarus is misleading in that "hell" (which has no exact Greek equivalent) in Christian theology is the permanent place of punishment (traditionally viewed as eternal torment) for the wicked. In Greek mythology Tartarus is mostly for Titans and other deities who have done evil (thus it is a fitting place for the angels who sinned) and only secondarily for especially evil human beings, particularly those who directly offended against the gods. Roman mythology did increase the number of human beings in Tartarus, making it more of a parallel to hell, but 2 Peter seems to use the term because of the imprisonment of the fallen angels. Both Jude and *1 Enoch* make it clear that this imprisonment is temporary, that something worse awaits them after the final judgment.

angels corrupted with their teaching, also perished in the deluge (which 2 Peter will again use in chapter 3 as evidence of judgment). But our author's point, a point not made by Jude, is that despite the perishing of the ancient world around him (along with the fallen divine messengers), Noah, a proclaimer of righteousness,[71] was protected. Judgment does not preclude deliverance.

The second proof is taken from material originally found in Gen 18:16–19:29 (and anticipated in Gen 13:13), although 2 Peter knows the narrative through some source, written or oral, that has added the idea that Lot was righteous (first found in Wis 10:6). The Lord did judge Sodom, for the city was reduced to ashes; their condemnation went further than that, for the city was "condemned to extinction" in that no new city arose from its ashes.[72] This is not reported because of historical interest, but as an example of what will happen to the impious.

However, again judgment is not the main point; rather, the point is that despite such a complete condemnation, Lot was rescued. That Lot was righteous is seen in that he was distressed by the disgraceful behavior of those among whom he sojourned, behavior characterized by a lack of self-restraint. Second Peter never describes what this behavior was, but it does add an aside to expand on Lot's distress. Drawing on a tradition such as the one Philo uses (*Mos.* 2.58), he notes that Lot had a "righteous soul," and thus as he lived among them as an immigrant could not help but see and hear the Sodomites' "lawless deeds" and so was "tormented day after day." Is 2 Peter perhaps alluding to the distress that he imagines in the "beloved" to whom he is writing as they observe the behavior of those he calls "false teachers"? At the least this aside has served to definitively separate Lot from the Sodomites, for, unlike the situation with Noah, 2 Peter has no tradition that Lot proclaimed righteousness.

Two proofs have been cited, and so 2 Peter now draws its conclusion, indicated by a shift of subject. "The Lord" (is this still God of the examples previously cited, or is our author thinking of Jesus?) knows how to rescue the godly from the trial (or the test)—that is the main point—and, concomitantly, to keep (as in the sense of "keep in a prison") the ungodly under punishment for the day of judgment. We are not talking here about what happens *after* the final judgment, but about the situation of the ungodly similar to the situation of the fallen angels, or those who perished in the deluge, or those destroyed in Sodom and Gomorrah. The Lord can rescue some and put others in a prison of punishment simultaneously. He knows who is who and can distinguish. The narratives show that the Lord's judgment is not indiscriminate.

This leads to a segue transitioning from the examples already noted to the following denunciation of the false teachers: "especially those who go after flesh in

---

71. The tradition that Noah was a preacher is found in Josephus, *Ant.* 1.74 (1.3.1) and *Sib. Or.* 1.125–98. The author of *1 En.* 65.1–67.13 describes Noah as righteous, a term not used for him in Genesis, although the implication is there.

72. While the language is unique in the New Testament, archaeologists note burning levels in many ancient cities, with new cities being built on top of the ashes of the old. Even Rome had experienced a great fire in 64 CE, but it was not permanently burned. Sodom and Gomorrah were never rebuilt, which is the reason that there is debate today about where in the Dead Sea area they were situated.

corrupt desires" (2:10a). This strange construction[73] is difficult, but its overall meaning is clear: the divine messengers (angels) of Gen 6:2, read through *1 Enoch*'s interpretation, crossed the species barrier, as did the Sodomites, although the "day after day" reference in 2 Peter probably indicates a general immorality and abuse of foreigners. This is sexual misbehavior without boundaries. The examples show that it is especially such behavior that "the Lord" knows how to punish while delivering the righteous (perhaps even delivering them from such evil persons, although the examples suggest that it is rather delivering them from the punishment that befalls the wicked). However, there is also a second descriptor of these people that is especially noted: the false teachers despise "lordship," an idea taken from Jude 8 that will be expanded upon in the following digression.[74]

4.3.3.3.3 Digression: Denunciation of False Teachers (2:10b – 22)

The reference to despising "lordship" in 2:10a allows our author to shift to a direct denunciation of those whom he has called false teachers. He now becomes specific again; 2:4 – 10a has been about examples of past judgment, refuting the implied criticism that God does not judge (and if he did, he would judge indiscriminately); now the topic is the behavior of the false teachers in the present, starting with how they despise appropriate authority.

"Audacious! Arrogant! [These false teachers] have no fear of slandering the Glorious Ones!" The Glorious Ones are, as in Jude 8, almost certainly (unfallen) divine messengers, angelic beings. Then, as in Jude 9 – 10, there is a contrast. The angels (in Jude, Michael the archangel in particular), who are greater than these teachers with respect to might and power, do not bring against these teachers a slanderous judgment from or before the Lord.[75] The angels are not willing to usurp the role of the Lord, for, as Jas 4:11 – 12 notes, there is one Lawgiver and Judge. For angels to accuse, even to bring an accusation they heard the Lord make, would be slanderous, something that they do not do.

The teachers, by way of contrast, have no such scruples. Since they are driven by desire, by their drives or emotions, they are like irrational animals, which in the natural order of things are born only to become prey for other animals (a Greco-Roman commonplace also found in Jude). When they slander the Glorious Ones, they have no idea what they are talking about. They, however, seem to be ignorant of their ignorance. "Fools rush in where angels fear to tread," as Alexander Pope put it. The result will be that just as the animals are slaughtered, so these teachers will

---

73. MHT IV: 12 §3 calls this a double Hebraism. However, it draws on the vocabulary of Jude 8 and restructures it to fit this context, perhaps influenced by the LXX's manner of expression.

74. Unlike Eph 1:21 and Col 1:16, this does not refer to the negative ruling powers over which Jesus triumphed, as the expansion will make clear. It is also clear grammatically that the "going after flesh" and "despising lordship" refer to one and the same group.

75. This verse is difficult conceptually and textually. The false teachers slander the "Glorious Ones," whom some take to be fallen angels, but who are probably holy angels, given the normal uses of "glorious." The angels do not "bring a judgment of slander," that is, a slanderous judgment against the false teachers, but is it before the Lord or from the Lord? In the latter case they would be repeating on their own the Lord's condemnation; in the former they could be condemning them before the Lord. For a full discussion see Davids, *2 Peter and Jude*, 234 – 36.

be slaughtered. The expression is difficult, but it seems to parallel the slaughter of animals to the slaughter of the teachers at the end of the age.[76] What is clear is that they are receiving a payback for wrongdoing.[77] Theirs is not just the passive failure to do the good of Matt 25:41–46, bad as the result of that is, but an active wrongdoing, "They consider indulging themselves (or reveling) in daytime pleasure."

What this means is then expanded: "They are spots and blemishes when they indulge themselves (or revel) in their pleasures as they feast with you." These teachers attend the regular gathering of the believers, which at that time was a full meal, a reenactment of the Last Supper as the Lord's Supper or Eucharist. But they are not there imitating Jesus and giving their lives or anything else for others. They are indulging themselves "in their pleasures" at that very meal. Whether 2 Peter is talking about their gluttony, their drunkenness, or their sexual adventures, all of which could take place at a normal Greco-Roman *symposium*, is not clear, nor would he wish to make much of a distinction, since he would have approved of none of it, as we know from Paul's reaction in 1 Cor 11:20–21 in a similar context. What is clear is that 2 Peter uses the expression "in their pleasures," not "in their love feasts" (as in Jude 12). The shift in words is probably deliberate; they have transformed the community meal from a celebration of Jesus' extreme love and the community's self-giving love to one another into a time of overindulgence driven by pleasure.

Our author adds a series of charges related to this overindulgence: "eyes full of adultery" (whether or not they are successful in fulfilling their desires), "unceasingly sinners" (hardly a good habit), "enticing unstable persons" (one feels affirmed if others join, although these "unstable persons" may also be the exploited means of fulfilling the false teachers' desires), "having hearts exercised in greed." Both greed and adultery are mentioned without ranking one as worse than the other. Second Peter ends 2:14 with the exclamation, "accursed children!"

The rhetorical denunciation continues with a series of longer descriptive clauses: they have left the straight road and gone astray (language that may have been suggested by Matt 7:13–14 or Mark 1:3 or perhaps by Num 22:22–35 read in the light of the later ethical passages) like Balaam did literally (as his donkey turned off the road) and metaphorically in that he "loved the wages he received for doing wrong." While the Balaam example is drawn from Jude 11, the narrative is read through later Jewish tradition, for it is the Targums that have the donkey giving the extensive rebuke to Balaam (the Hebrew text of Numbers has an angel rebuking the prophet

---

76. As noted in ibid., 236–37, there are several options, but the one that is most satisfactory is "in their slaughter [that of the animals] they [the teachers] will also be slaughtered." This does not make sense literally, for human beings are rarely slaughtered along with animals, nor does it make sense in 2 Peter if both sides are taken as indicating the final judgment, for as we will see in 3:10, in that judgment the earth is not destroyed, but "discovered" or "revealed," so there is no reason to think about a destruction of the animals at that time. However, if the one slaughter is parabolic for the slaughter of the teachers in the final judgment, one would have a

type of parallel. That appears to be what 2 Peter is expressing, if we assume his view of what happens to the earth is consistent between chapters 2 and 3.

77. One problem in this passage is that English cannot express the wordplays in Greek: "in their slaughter they will also be slaughtered" is one such play on a Greek root, but "receiving" and "wrongdoing" are also from the same root. In the next line "considering," "pleasure," and "day" all start with the same sound. In the bombastic Asiatic style some word choices are surely for rhetorical effect, which may be the reason that they are difficult to deal with analytically.

and the donkey only speaking briefly). This shift heightens the irony of the rebuke, for the normally irrational donkey (speechless would imply mindless in the ancient world, cf. 2:12) speaks in a human voice, while the prophet, who *should* be conveying divine wisdom to humanity, needs to have his madness or insanity restrained. The incident is shaming for the prophet as well as being ironic.

Our author then shifts in 2:17 to rebuking the false teachers (whom, we must remember, he has already compared to false prophets) directly. The images, drawn from Jude 12–13, are piled one upon the other: these teachers promise much but deliver little ("waterless springs," "mists driven by a storm"); the storm metaphor suggests the Tartarus image of 2:4, "deepest darkness," which, our author states, is reserved for them. They speak "inflated words of emptiness" (Jude 16), 2 Peter's estimation of their rationalizations through which they justify their behavior. They entice the followers of Jesus "by means of a licentiousness based in bodily desires" — people who have "barely escaped from those living in error" ("those living in error" is how 2 Peter characterizes the surrounding culture). They do this by promising these folk "freedom" even though they themselves are "slaves of corruption."

Greco-Roman culture in general and Epicureanism in particular encouraged doing "what feels good" and maximizing pleasure. The followers of Jesus, rooted in a Jewish view of life in which desires, although created by God, needed to be kept within bounds, viewed this more or less unbridled pleasure seeking[78] as "corruption" or "error." This lifestyle was far from the true freedom that 2 Peter has described in 1:3–4, an escape from the corruption that is in the world because of desire and a participation in the divine nature.

These teachers, however, promise a pseudo-freedom, since they are themselves slaves to corruption. Referring back to the beginning of the book and his epignostic soteriology (1:3–4), our author notes that these teachers had once "escaped the shameful deeds of the world through the knowledge of our Lord and Savior Jesus the Anointed King." They were, so to speak, "saved," but now they are again entangled in these desire-driven deeds. They are overpowered by desire rather than moving deeper into the freedom of following Jesus, as the virtue list of 1:5–8 advises. As a result, their present situation is worse than their former situation (an idea drawn from Jesus, Matt 12:45/Luke 11:26). In what way is it worse? In that it would have been better for them never to have known "the way of righteousness" (the way of "our Lord and Savior Jesus the Anointed King") than, having come to know it, as they had, to have turned from "the holy commandment" that they had received. Being a rebellious apostate is worse than being an ignorant unbeliever.

Two proverbial sayings, both about animals that were ritually impure to Jews and despised by Greco-Romans (who, even if they ate pigs, did not respect them), round out the denunciation. Neither is original, for the first is drawn from Prov

---

78. Even Epicureans recognized that too much indulgence ultimately did not lead to maximized pleasure but to pain, so there were some naturally imposed limits for them. However, the "golden mean" (where pleasure was maximized without creating negative results, such as indigestion or a hangover) was a practical pursuit, not a moral limit.

26:11 and the second from *Ahikar* 8.18. Both have to do with the irrational animal returning to what it has been freed from, both to disgusting behavior. Common knowledge, 2 Peter implies, supports this denunciation.

4.3.3.4 Issue 4: Parousia Disproved by History (3:1–13)

All along 2 Peter has been making references to the parousia of Jesus and the final judgment either directly or by implication: Jesus already reigns and judges (1:16–18), the Scriptures agree with this (1:19–21), and God can and does punish the unrighteous while delivering the righteous (2:1–10a). Now, having established that the teachers he is condemning are unrighteous (2:10b–22) and noted that they have a reserved place in Tartarus (2:17), our author is ready to meet the teachers' explicit objection head on, namely, to deal with the idea that history disproves there will ever be a parousia.

4.3.3.4.1 Transition: Reminder of Past Teaching (3:1–2)

Our author transitions into his final section by addressing his implied readers. He is transitioning away from Jude and away from denunciation, so he brings the addressees back into the picture. He shifts to the second person (he has spoken about the teachers in the third person), addresses the readers as "beloved," and notes that he has written to them previously (probably not a reference to 1 Peter, since the topics and styles of the two letters are so different). There is a relationship here, unlike the situation between 2 Peter and the teachers.

Furthermore, the "beloved" are not in any way apostate. What they need is a "reminder to stimulate you to wholesome thinking." "Reminder" is rhetorically polite (since it assumes that the person reminded already knows and accepts what is being discussed) and practically necessary (an oral mnemonic culture did not have the ubiquitous books and the ability to read that are present in modern culture, much less vast computer databases). This "wholesome thinking" contrasts with the thinking of the scoffers, who will be mentioned next. Furthermore, this is not just a reminder of 2 Peter's teaching, but, in parallel with Jude 17, it recalls the addressees to the teaching of the "holy prophets" and of "the Lord and Savior."

It is also clear that at least the teaching of Jesus they had not received directly, but through the official delegates of Jesus who had brought the good news to them ("your apostles," which we would today call "missionaries").[79] The community is

---

79. Notice that it is "your apostles" and not "the apostles," nor are these people called directly "apostles of Jesus the Anointed King." We tend to take "apostle" as a technical term and forget that in the first century *apostolos* was the term used for anyone's delegate sent on a mission of some type, whether a businessperson's representative, an emissary of Caesar, or church representatives carrying a financial gift to Jerusalem (2 Cor 8:16–24). What set Paul and Peter and others apart is that they were "apostles of Jesus the Anointed King" (e.g., 2 Pet 1:1); that is, the important point was whose delegates they were, not that they were delegates. In Christian contexts the word often meant "missionary," which is why, decades after the last of the Twelve died, *Did.* 11.4–6 can speak of apostles and instruct that they are to be received, but not be allowed to stay. They are on a mission, and a missionary needs support along the way; but since they are a missionary, they are not going to stay in an established community of the followers of Jesus. Instead, if they are genuine, they will move on to plant a Jesus community elsewhere.

an established community; the founders have moved on, perhaps to found other communities. But they left behind instruction, "the commandment" of "our Lord and Savior." And the community had the writings of the "holy prophets" (which, if Jude is any guide, included *1 Enoch* as well as everything included in the Greek version of the Old Testament). These teachings and documents are what they need to remember.

4.3.3.4.2 Accusation (3:3–4)

Not all of this material referred to above is of equal importance, nor is it all relevant to the present context. Instead, "first of all" the addressees need to know that this teaching (of Jesus and the prophets) indicated that "in the last days" (which for the followers of Jesus had started with the coming of Jesus), scoffers will come "in scoffing" (a superfluous statement that underlines their activity as a contrast to rational teaching). Who these scoffers are is indicated by "living according to their own desires," the very vice (or set of vices) that was condemned in the teachers of the previous chapter.

What are they mocking? It is the return of Jesus to rule openly and therefore the final judgment.[80] "Where is the promise of his coming?" or "Where is the promise of his parousia?" is the basic challenge.[81] If there is no parousia, then there is no resurrection of the dead and final judgment; if the judge is not present, the court does not sit.

Why would anyone doubt the promise of the parousia? Because in the opinion of these teachers, nothing ever changes: "Since the fathers died, everything continues as it has since the beginning, the Creation." This type of issue is not without Jewish precedent: "Where is [Israel's] God?" (Ps 79:10 [LXX 78:10]; Ps 115:2 [LXX 113:10]; Joel 2:17); "Where is YHWH your God?" (Mic 7:10); or "Where is the God of justice?" (Mal 2:17). But in this passage the charge has to do, not with God's deliverance in general, but with a promise specific to the Jesus movement, the parousia, even if the language is Jewish in that the reference to the fathers dying fits Jewish literature.[82]

The idea that the world remains in a more or less steady state until it returns to atoms would, of course, fit an Epicurean worldview or one influenced by the Epicureans. The above statement, then, mocks the idea of the parousia of Jesus as

---

80. Neyrey, *2 Peter, Jude*, 227–29, accurately terms this "the Lord's state visit."

81. Bauckham, *Jude, 2 Peter*, 283–85, is convinced that 2 Peter is following a Jewish apocalypse referred to in *1 Clem.* 23.3 and *2 Clem.* 11.2. While this is attractive, our conclusion, Davids, *2 Peter and Jude*, 264–65, is that there is not enough evidence to prove a common source, especially since the *topos* of unfulfilled prophecy was relatively common.

82. Bauckham, *Jude, 2 Peter*, 290–91, and Vögtle, *Der Judasbrief. Der zweite Petrusbrief*, 216, are typical of commentators who take this to mean the first Christian generation. But if that is the case,

this is the only place in biblical literature that "the fathers" (cf. the Greek *hoi pateres*) has that meaning. It is true that for his followers Jesus was a divine intervention, but unless one accepted his teaching that the ages had changed and that he would return to judge the world, he was hardly much of a blip in the course of history. When it came to final judgment or anything looking like it, nothing had changed since Abraham, or even since creation. Thus, since one can make sense of this passage without giving an unprecedented meaning to "the fathers," there is no reason to refer it to the first Christian generation.

understood by his followers. It was promised, but where is it? Since the beginnings of recorded history, since Abraham and the other patriarchs,[83] the world continues as it always has, with wars and upheavals and natural disasters, for sure, but such things are within the natural order. So when is this parousia going to happen? One can feel the force of this argument as the decades rolled by after the resurrection of Jesus, just as one can feel it even more in the present when decades have turned into centuries.

4.3.3.4.3 Refutation (3:5–13)

Our author refutes this mocking claim, and he will do so by offering three different "proofs" (in the sense the term has in ancient rhetoric).

4.3.3.4.3.1 Proof 1 (3:5–7)

"Not so fast," says 2 Peter. "They are deliberately forgetting something—Noah." The teachers should know that narrative and are purposefully ignoring it, but that does not mean that the event did not take place. To discuss this story, our author goes back to creation, not a creation *ex nihilo* (which is taught in Heb 11 in the New Testament), but to the Genesis narrative in which there is creation from something, from chaos, from everything mixed with water. In that narrative the waters above the heavens were separated from those below by means of an expanse or supporting structure that was then called "heaven" (Gen 1:6–8), in which the sun, moon, and stars were placed (Gen 1:14–16). Likewise, earth in the sense of dry land was created by gathering the waters below the expanse into one place, that is, seas (Gen 1:9–10). All this was done at God's command.[84]

Thus it is neither surprising that 2 Peter agrees with Philo that it is God's word or *logos* that is the creative principle,[85] nor that 2 Peter states that heaven and earth were created "out of water" and "by means of water." Thus we have a brief description of what some have pictured as the ancient model of the world (see next page).[86] Our author's point, however, is not the details of creation, but the fact that (1) God's word was what made it; and (2) that word separated earth and heaven from water.

But the world did not remain more or less steady state until the present: those

---

83. Usually Abraham is referred to as the first of the fathers, and for our purposes this is interesting in that Abraham is in Genesis the start of history as we know it. Namely, he lives in an identifiable place and culture and, starting with him, there is a sustained narrative throughout the Hebrew Scriptures. Before him there is prehistory, short narratives, bits and pieces of tales, that in some cases are generally located in place and culture, but this is always general and we often cannot be sure that the places referred to are the same as those referred to in later parts of the Hebrew Scriptures.

84. While in 2 Peter and Philo, as will be noticed below, the focus is on the speech act itself, the *logos*, the "let there be" of Genesis may well be a statement to the heavenly court, at which wish the divine attendants would have rushed to fulfill the divine desire, for

it is clear in the Hebrew Scriptures that God is often pictured as a great King with an appropriately great court, including courtiers around him.

85. See Neyrey, *2 Peter, Jude*, 233–34, citing Philo, *Mos.* 2.99; *Plant.* 85–89; *Fug.* 101; *Abr.* 121–22. For Philo *logos*, λόγος, was God's first attribute and his executive authority his second.

86. I thank my colleague Edward Gentry for this picturing of the ancient model, which is drawn not just from Genesis, but also from the Psalms and other places where ancient cosmology is described. This pictorial model does show the "waters under the earth," but is not as good at showing the seas surrounding the earth since they seem small compared to the "pillars of the sky." But just as in the verbal model in 2 Peter, so a pictorial model cannot show everything.

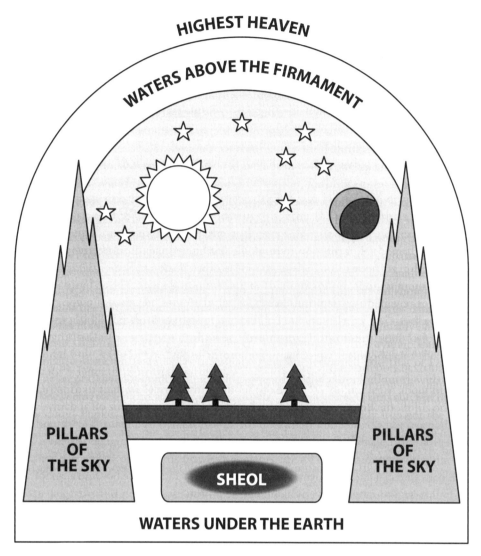

HIGHEST HEAVEN

WATERS ABOVE THE FIRMAMENT

PILLARS OF THE SKY

PILLARS OF THE SKY

SHEOL

WATERS UNDER THE EARTH

same waters[87] out of which and by means of which heaven and earth were constituted destroyed "the order that then existed" (or "the world that then existed," or
"the orderly universe that existed then"—*kosmos*, κόσμος, has multiple meanings).
It was "deluged by water" and "perished." What is unstated, but understood, since
knowledge of the narrative is assumed (cf. 2:4–5), is that this was a divine judgment. "So God has not intervened in judgment, eh? I guess that is what Noah's
contemporaries thought before God sent them swimming." This narrative is what
the mockers or teachers are purposefully forgetting.

---

87. Some manuscripts, most importantly the third century 𝔓69,
have a singular and so could read "on account of which word" or
"on account of which water" (since masculine and neuter genitive
plural pronouns are identical) "the then existing world was deluged
by water." This is an attractive reading, but the manuscript support
is slight and could be caused but the scribe's anticipating what he
thought 2 Peter should have written, so we will accept the more
common reading "through which waters."

The same divine word, the same *logos* that originally created the world, is still at work, but now in its executive function. It is preserving ("reserving" or "saving") the present "heavens and earth" for (or "to" or "by") fire, though not a fire that will destroy them; rather, they are being kept or guarded for the day of judgment and destruction of the ungodly. There will be fire, as our author will later explain, but its purpose is judgment, the destruction of the ungodly, including those who are presently mocking its possibility.

4.3.3.4.3.2 Proof 2 (3:8–9)

There is a second bit of information that the "beloved" need to understand. As Ps 90:4 (or as 2 Peter would have known it, LXX Ps 89:4) says, "For a thousand years in your sight are like a day that has just gone by, or like a watch in the night." Our author does not want to use this to argue for the transience of human life, as the psalmist does, but to argue, in line with some Jewish understandings of this passage, that the divine day is a thousand years. While it is possible that 2 Peter has in mind some particular apocalyptic scenario,[88] it is more likely that the author is simply indicating that a divine "short time" and a human "short time" are two different things; the former is a long time in human terms.

Yet while God's time can be different from human time, it is not as if God is delaying in the sense of failing to act because of sloth or being too busy. That is not his nature. In words recalling Hab 2:3 or, more closely, Sir 35:19 (LXX) — although the theme is found as early as Isa 13:22 — God is not slow in fulfilling his promises (in particular, his promise to judge the wicked), at least not in the way that "some" (perhaps the mockers) would consider being slow. He is not slow, but patient. And the beloved are the object of patience, for "unto you" likely means "to the point of bringing you into his kingdom." The Lord does not want anyone to perish. He wants everyone to arrive at salvation. He is in the rescue business, not in the destruction business. Some will be destroyed, but it will be despite him, not because of him.

Thus the Lord is patiently delaying the parousia so that more can repent and arrive at salvation — and the beloved are some of the fruit of that delay. Yes, his "day" is long, and, yes, his delay is still within the parameters of his understanding of a day, but he is not just waiting out the "day," and he is not just being slow in "getting around to it." He is acting purposefully, patiently putting off the parousia so that as many as possible can arrive at salvation. That is, the Lord is showing the same virtue (patience) that his followers are expected to show (1:6, using a synonym for the term used here).

4.3.3.4.3.3 Proof 3 (3:10)

Although patience may mean a delayed promise, it does not mean an unfulfilled promise, so the beloved need to remember that the end will come. The scoffers have called it "the promise of his state visit (parousia)," and 2 Peter has said "the Lord is

---

88. Various uses of the Psalm 90 passage have been suggested, several of them far from the flow of this passage. Bauckham believes that a specific Jewish apocalypse is in mind. This is possible and attractive, but we do not think that it is proven. However, he has at least shown that the passage could be used apocalyptically in Jewish and early Christian literature. See the detailed discussion in Davids, *2 Peter and Jude*, 275–77.

not slow about his promise," so now we are not surprised when the author asserts, "the Day of the Lord will come as a thief." The comparison to a thief ultimately comes from the Jesus tradition (Matt 24:43–44//Luke 12:39–40), although the image continued to be used by the followers of Jesus (e.g., Rev 3:3; 16:15; *Did.* 16.1) and may have been mediated to 2 Peter via Paul (especially 1 Thess 5:2), since our author admits that he knows several Pauline letters (2 Pet 3:15–16). Whatever the proximate source of the image, its meaning is clear: as a thief comes unannounced and unanticipated, so will the day of the Lord arrive.

But when it arrives, unlike the typical thief, it will be dramatic. The heavens, which in ancient cosmology were between the dwelling of God and the earth, will pass away with a rushing noise or a roar, as one would expect if such a structure were suddenly removed. And the heavenly elements[89] (the sun, moon, and stars), burning up, will be loosed or, more likely, destroyed. But dramatic as it may be, that is just the means to an end, not the end itself. The goal is the final clause: the earth and those things in it will be "found out" or "disclosed." The point of all the "shock and awe" is not destruction — in fact, the text does not assert that the earth will be destroyed — but judgment.[90] With the heavens and heavenly bodies removed, there is no longer any place to hide from the eye of God. Like an anthill with its covering removed, human activities are naked to his sight. The time of judgment has come.

In other words, over against the claims of the scoffers/teachers that the day of the Lord will never come, implying not only delay (which 2 Peter has already addressed) but also that they see no evidence of its coming, our author asserts that it will come unexpectedly, like a thief. But when it comes, it will be dramatic, and there will be no place to hide. The deeds of all will be exposed and, by implication, judged.

4.3.3.4.4 Conclusion (3:11–13)

While 2 Peter has been addressing the assertions of the scoffers, in the larger context he has been addressing the "beloved" (3:1, 8), so now he repeats his direct address, drawing conclusions for their behavior. Since they know that the heavens will not hide them from the Lord or prevent his coming as Ruler and Judge, they should live

---

89. The word for elements (*stoicheia*, στοιχεῖα) has a range of meanings, ranging from Paul's use of the term for angelic or spiritual powers (Gal 4:3; Col 2:8, 20) to something close to the current use of the term for material elements — in the case of the ancients, earth, air, fire, and water — to the heavenly bodies (see Gerhard Delling, *stoicheō*, στοιχέω, *TDNT*, 7:672–82). In our present context with the heavens being mentioned immediately beforehand and the earth afterward, it is fairly certain that the meaning is "heavenly bodies," that is, the sun, moon, and stars, a picture corresponding to Isa 34:4 or Rev 6:12–14.

90. There is a textual issue, for while the text we have translated is attested to in the great fourth-century manuscripts, it was not what the later church, which was increasingly thinking of going to heaven rather than resurrection life on earth, was expecting. Thus the fifth-century Alexandrinus has "burned up," a reading also found in the

Vulgate and the Byzantine traditions, from which it came into the KJV. Several other minor variants also appear, all witnessing to an original "will be discovered" that has been altered (such as by putting a "not" before it). The more difficult reading (in the sense of the less expected), the one found in the earliest codexes, and a reading that was relatively widespread, is the one we have translated. It also fits with the picture of Rev 6:15–17, in which, after the removal of the heavens and the heavenly bodies, the rulers of the earth try to find caves to hide in, for the day has come and they want to hide from the eye of the Judge. Unfortunately Nestle-Aland[28] has compounded the problem by introducing a "not" (*ouk*, οὐκ) into the text with virtually no manuscript evidence, creating the reading "will not be found." The only manuscript evidence is some Coptic and a few Syrian versions.

accordingly. Their way of life should be holy, and they should be pious. This is not a vague description, but rather a summary of the virtues that our author has laid out in 1:5–7, which in turn indicate what it means to live with Jesus the Anointed Ruler as Master and Lord. And if they are living this way, the day of judgment will be welcome, just as anyone who had heard about the parousia of a Roman official knew; such a day was not just the time when vice was punished (to the relief of those suffering from those vices), but also, even especially, a time when virtue was rewarded: civic honors, promotions, and other rewards would be handed out.

For the virtuous, then, the day of the Lord will be a time for celebration. Therefore, as they focus on holy and pious lifestyles, they wait expectantly for that day. In fact, they even speed up its coming—a surprising statement, which probably ties into a Jewish tradition that Israel's repentance would speed up God's day of deliverance.[91]

Furthermore, it is the logical implication of 3:9, where the Lord is said to delay the judgment because he wants all to come to repentance, which is a change of allegiance from the powers of this age to him. The "beloved" demonstrate by their lifestyles that they have done this, and they spread this good news to others, which should shorten his delay. Either way, they are to live in such a way that they are eager for the day of God (we notice that 2 Peter uses several different terms for "the day"), for the fearful events that expose the earth (e.g., the heavens dissolving in fire and the heavenly bodies melting as they burn) are joyful events for them.

Our author then shifts from second person to first: we are expecting, just as he promised, a new heaven and a new earth. That there is a need for a new heaven is clear, since the original one was burned up, but what about earth? It was only "exposed." It seems that the expectation is not for new matter, a new earth in that sense, but for a new order on earth. It is for a world—perhaps, better, a world order—in which righteousness is at home. The decisive difference is not physical but moral. What was dysfunctional in this age will be functional then. No wonder that the renewed earth is something that our author, along with the "beloved," looks forward to expectantly.

4.3.4 Letter Body Closing (*Peroratio*) (3:14–16)

Our author then shifts back to the second person as he closes off the discussion. "You, beloved, are waiting for, or expecting, these things. Therefore 'pedal to the metal' on virtue." They are to "make every effort" (as in 1:10, 15) to be found as they should be. Second Peter uses two cultic images that start with the same Greek letter, "without spot or blemish," for their general virtue (as in Eph 1:4; 1 Tim 6:14; Jas 1:27), but names one specific virtue: "in peace." Especially given the presence of those whom our author terms "false teachers," the community could be prone

---

91. This is most easily seen in *b. Sanh.* 97b–98a, although it is widespread in rabbinic writings and attributed to early rabbis, so it probably reflects discussions going on in the first century (cf. Acts 3:19–20).

to conflict. Of course, since Greco-Roman society was marked by struggle among families and clans (an "agonistic" society), peace was always something that the communities of Jesus' followers had to work at.

Whatever the case, it is virtue in general and in particular peace with one another that the "beloved" are to work at as a result of the discussion in this letter. They are not urged to root out the false teachers. They are not encouraged to roundly condemn them. Perhaps our author thinks that, given the coming judgment, the false teachers are in enough trouble. The "beloved" are urged to have a peaceful, virtuous communal lifestyle.

But when will the Lord come? How long will we have to wait? The answer to this implied question is to consider the delay in the day of the Lord, that is, the Lord's patience, to be salvation or deliverance. Certainly the addressees could reflect on the fact that had Jesus returned earlier, they would not themselves have experienced his deliverance. But likely the emphasis is on deliverance in general or deliverance for others—the longer "our Lord" is patient and delays, the more people will experience deliverance.

Surprisingly, 2 Peter introduces a new thought here: what he has just summarized is something that "our beloved brother Paul" had written about to these addressees. This brings in a second witness, so to speak, a witness that some might have thought was on "the other side." The language used for Paul is not that which one finds in the Apostolic Fathers, for it does not mention his being an apostle, nor does it use any other exalted title; rather, it simply refers to him as "our beloved brother."[92] He is using family terminology,[93] which indicates that Paul was a valued family member and, in such a letter context, coworker. This is the language that Paul himself uses of Tychicus (Eph 6:21; Col 4:7), with either "brother" or "beloved" being used repeatedly elsewhere in New Testament literature.

Why does this language appear here? This is not defending Paul's status, for Paul uses "official delegate (apostle) of Jesus the Anointed King" when he wishes to do this. Could this be intending to indicate that the rift of Gal 2:11–14 has been healed? But there is no reference either to that event or to the topics it was about. More likely our author realizes that the teachers he has condemned have cited Paul, and Paul was an authority in the eyes of those whom Peter is addressing, so he wants to make clear without arguing the point in the detail that Paul is on "his side."

How Paul supports our author's argument is never stated in detail. However, one does not need to look far in Paul before one discovers a call to live in peace (e.g., Philippians) or a call to live a virtuous life (the fruit of the Spirit in Gal 5 being only one example). Paul had written about this general topic in a letter addressed to these same addressees, but since we are neither sure of whom 2 Peter addresses (especially since we have argued that it is rather doubtful that 3:1 refers to 1 Peter)

---

92. Note that our author includes himself with his addressees, as he did when referring to "our Lord" earlier in the verse.

93. Starting with Jesus (e.g., Mark 3:31–35), the followers of

Jesus were considered a fictive family. On the notion of "fictive family," see comments on 2 Pet 1:5–11.

nor of exactly what Paul said, we cannot be sure of the Pauline letter to which our author refers.[94] Suffice it to say that our author indicates at least general knowledge of a Pauline letter written to the same addressees that said similar things about the general subject of 2 Pet 3:14–15. Paul did write using divine wisdom, for the expression "according to the wisdom given to him" is probably a so-called "divine passive," meaning "as God gave him wisdom."

The reference to Paul has been general, and now our author generalizes even more: "speaking of these things as he does in all his letters." Our author knows enough about several Pauline letters ("all" has to mean at least three), perhaps about some form of a Pauline collection, to say that they all call followers of Jesus to virtue and their communities to peace. This, however, does not seem to be his main point. His main point seems to be that Paul does support the message of 2 Peter, but that not everything in Paul's letters is clear. Rather, some things are "hard to understand," and this gives the "untaught and unstable" (again two words starting with the same sound to form a single description) room to distort them. This results in the destruction of those who do the distorting, for they live according to their twisted understanding.

This may refer to the teachers our author has condemned; if so, perhaps because he is close to the end of the letter, it is the kindest thing he has to say about them. Of course, they not only twist difficult passages in Paul's writings, but also things in "the other writings" or "the rest of the writings." Since "the writings" is always used in the New Testament to refer to the Hebrew Scriptures in their broadest sense (although, as in Jas 4:5, we are not always certain to where in that body of literature, which for some could include Second Temple writings), that is probably the sense here. So 2 Peter is at least starting to group Paul's writings with the Jewish Scriptures in general.

But that again is not his point. It is that the "untaught and unstable" twist Paul just as they do the Jewish Scriptures. Both, he believes, back his position, but both, he knows from experience, are capable of being used by those he opposes. Perhaps that is why he refers to Paul toward the end (and only refers to the Scriptures twice, in 1:20 and here in 3:16), for while Paul is a witness to the truth of what 2 Peter is arguing, Paul is a weak witness, for he, like the Jewish Scriptures, can be twisted.

4.3.5 Letter Closing (3:17–18)

Our author is ready to close his letter. He has brought his argument to an end. Now he is ready for a quick double exhortation that sums up all his exhortations and then a doxology.

"You, beloved," again addresses his readers. "Since you know this beforehand, watch out." He does not instruct them to "kick the bums out," nor to withdraw into a form of a pure church, but to make sure that they themselves are not so led astray

---

94. We do not know whether the letter he refers to is still extant, for we know of several Pauline letters that never became part of the Pauline collection.

by the disgraceful error of those teachers he has condemned that they fall from their own "stability." The "unstable" twist Paul in 3:16, and if the addressees do not watch out, they may stop seeing the disgraceful error of the unstable as disgraceful and so be led astray and end up losing their stability and joining the group of the unstable. In other words, they may end up losing their stable grounding in Jesus and so (in our terms) "lose their faith."

But our author started off the letter by arguing that pursuing virtue, going deeper in the knowledge of "our Lord Jesus the Anointed One," will ensure that they will never "stumble," but rather ensure their grand welcome into "the eternal kingdom of our Lord and Savior Jesus the Anointed One" (1:8, 10–11). Now, having delivered his negative admonition, he returns to this positive theme: "Grow in the favor and knowledge of our Lord and Savior Jesus the Anointed One" (3:18, cf. 1:2). "Favor and knowledge" are probably thought of as two sides of a single coin. To know him better is to live in his favor. The one is our seeking him, and the other is his showing favor to us. Indeed, if one is living such an experience, it is, as seen in chapter 1, unlikely that one will need to worry about losing one's stability.

Now that the author has mentioned "our Lord and Savior," a doxology is in order: "To him be honor (glory), not only now, but forever." The "forever" is literally "until the day of the age" or "until the day of eternity." As Bauckham correctly says,[95] we could rephrase this day as "the eschatological age as a day which will dawn at the Parousia." The day will come. Jesus will return. And he will be honored supremely then. Yet even now, "to him be honor," and that appellation brings with it the commitment, so important to 2 Peter, to be part of bringing honor to him in the present by word and deed as we wait for that ultimate day of his honor that is coming.

4.4 IMPORTANT THEOLOGICAL THEMES

Given its bombastic or, more accurately expressed, Asiatic style, one wonders whether 2 Peter might not be all thunder and little substance. However, the work turns out to be far more substantial than one might think. In fact, it is full of original thinking and expression.

4.4.1 Theology

The starting point of New Testament writers is God and their experience of God, including their experience of Jesus and the Holy Spirit.

God himself is only mentioned seven times in 2 Peter, fewer than in one chapter of 1 Peter (1 Peter 4). He can be joined with Jesus (2 Pet 1:2), but mostly he is mentioned independently, as the God active in creation (3:5), in the deluge (2:4, dependent on Jude 6), and in inspiring the prophets of the Hebrew Scriptures (1:21). All of this is what one would expect.

---

95. Bauckham, *Jude, 2 Peter*, 338.

But there are three less conventional references to God. First, he is the one who spoke to Jesus during the transfiguration (1:17); this is the only time that he is called "Father" in 2 Peter, versus three times each for 1 Peter and James. In this 2 Peter is similar to Jude, who only uses "Father" for God in Jude 1.

Second, the day of judgment can be called the "day of God" (3:12), not just the "day of the Lord" or some similar term. That places God at the end of the age as he was the Creator at the beginning.

Finally, in 1:1 we find the phrase "our God and Savior Jesus the Anointed One." There, according to the Granville-Sharp rule (see 4.3.1), we should have one being; that is, Jesus the Anointed One is God-Savior. Did 2 Peter mean this? Or did he mean to say what he says in 1:2, "knowledge of God and of Jesus our Lord," which keeps the two closely joined but separates them as two persons since Jesus is a proper name? Grammatically, 1:1 is one of the few passages in the New Testament that call Jesus God (i.e., divine). However, with a similar expression in the next verse that does not call Jesus "God" and with the whole argument depending on careful, purposeful use of grammar, we will never be sure if 2 Peter *really* means this. Yet, as it stands, that is what he says.

There are, however, some other indicators that that may be what he means. "Lord" is used fourteen times in 2 Peter — obviously a favorite title. In all but six of these it is clearly a title for Jesus as ruler. But it is possible that in all fourteen Jesus is the one indicated. Thus in 2:9, after discussing how God (2:4) acted in judgment and deliverance in the Hebrew Scriptures, our author says, "Then the Lord knows how to rescue the godly from trial, and to keep the unrighteous under punishment until the day of judgment." Is he drawing a conclusion about God the Father, or is he drawing a conclusion about Jesus based on what God the Father did in the Hebrew Scriptures? God did this, so we know that the Lord (Jesus) can also do this.

In 2:11, with the reference to the event in the *Testament of Moses* (found in Jude) dropped, who is the "Lord" whose judgment would be slanderous if brought by a mere angelic being? Is it the same being found in the *Testament of Moses*, God the Father, or is it the Lord Jesus, who presently sits in judgment?

Then in 3:8 it is "the Lord" to whom the timelessness of Ps 90:4 applies, but while in Hebrew the referent of "Lord" (ʾădōnay) is God (ʾēl; see Ps 90:1 – 2), in 2 Peter's Bible, the LXX, Ps 89:1 has *kyrie* (the vocative of *kyrios*), and there is no term for God in Ps 89:2 (just "you are"). So does our author, reading this psalm in the LXX, refracted through Jewish tradition, still understand it as applied to God the Father, or has he now applied to his Lord, Jesus? The latter becomes more likely when the next verse is included, for promises pertaining to the return of Jesus are the stuff of gospel words of Jesus rather than Hebrew prophecy. Thus "the Lord" who is not slow about his promises (3:9) and whose patience should be considered salvation (3:15) should be Jesus rather than God the Father, especially if "day of the Lord" is taken together with "thief in the night," for the latter clearly goes back to the Jesus tradition, even if 2 Peter may have known that Paul also used it (1 Thess 5:2).

Thus, it appears that "Lord" normally applies to Jesus in 2 Peter. Yet we have also noted that "day of the Lord" (3:10) is parallel to "day of God" in 3:12, so there appears to be some porosity between "God" and "Lord"; the one can bleed over into the other, which is what one would expect if 2 Peter viewed Jesus as in some sense divine but has not yet worked out the details, which would be consistent with the grammar of 1:1.[96]

What is clear is that Jesus is never mentioned in 2 Peter without a title. He is either named by his title ("the Lord") or else in the eight places where "Jesus" appears a title is included:

Passage	Name	Title
1:1	Jesus	the Anointed One/Anointed King (Christ)
1:1	Jesus	God and Savior … the Anointed One
1:2	Jesus	our Lord
1:8	Jesus	our Lord … the Anointed One
1:11	Jesus	our Lord and Savior … the Anointed One
1:14	Jesus	our Lord … the Anointed One
1:16	Jesus	our Lord … the Anointed One
1:17	This one	my Son, my beloved one (my beloved son)
2:20	Jesus	our Lord and Savior … the Anointed One
3:18	Jesus	our Lord and Savior … the Anointed One

Table 9: Titles of Jesus in 2 Peter

We can make several observations about Jesus. First, his subordination to the Father as Son is not stressed in 2 Peter; in fact, the transfiguration narrative is idiosyncratic in this respect. Second Peter 1:17 is the only passage in which God is called "Father" and in which Jesus is called "Son," although there "Son" is a title of investiture in that on 2 Peter's reading of the event, it is coupled with Jesus' receiving status ("honor and glory"). Thus, it appears to be a formal declaration of adoption along the lines of 2 Sam 7:12, 14 (as understood in some forms of Jewish messianic expectation).[97] This fits the context, for the issue is whether Jesus is presently vested

96. In other words, we are suggesting that Larry Hurtado is correct in *How on Earth Did Jesus Become a God?* (Grand Rapids: Eerdmans, 2005), that the followers of Jesus more felt their way to calling Jesus "God" (for Hurtado this was through worship) than thought their way. Thus we would not expect the distinctions to have been worked out, although it was natural to attribute the events in the Hebrew Scriptures to God (the Father) unless and until one was applying those Scriptures to Jesus. The philosophical description of the relationship that produced trinitarian language would only be worked out around 200 CE.

97. We are not claiming that 2 Peter has an adoptionist Christology. He does not say enough about the relationship of the Father

to the Son for us to know. What we are arguing is that he expresses Jesus' investiture with the status of a royal son using the adoption language of some strands of Jewish messianic expectation that were built on 2 Sam 7. This adoptive language was also understandable in the Roman world in that ruling "sons" being adopted was part of the history of the Julio-Claudian emperors, even if the Flavian emperors were a single natural family. (The Flavians were followed by the "Five Good Emperors," of whom only the final one was succeeded by a son, natural or adopted.) Thus however one dates 2 Peter, the story of Julius Caesar adopting Octavian (Augustus) and the latter's adopting Tiberius would be known.

with authority and will make a state visit (a parousia). Our author asserts that while he clearly has not seen Jesus' parousia, since it is still future, he has been an eyewitness of Jesus' present authority.

Then comes the description of Jesus' receiving the honorable status of "beloved Son" from God, here designated Father. This investiture with status fits with Jesus having titles of a ruler: the Greco-Roman one "Lord," which fits with Paul's claim (Rom 10:9) that the basic Christian confession was "Jesus is Lord" (note that "Caesar is Lord" was on the lips of all patriotic citizens), and the Jewish "the Anointed One" (translating the Hebrew "Messiah," usually appearing in English Bibles in Greek transliteration as "Christ"). In other words, the accent in 2 Peter is on Jesus as at least world ruler and, to the extent that his exercise of rule appears to have cosmic effects (at least in his parousia), as cosmic ruler.

So in 2 Peter God is still God and is referred to when discussing events such as creation or the deluge, events discussed in the Hebrew Scriptures, even if our author understands those stories through more contemporary literature. But Jesus is God's appointed ruler; he is the Lord who is biding his time, waiting as long as he feels appropriate for as many as possible to be rescued. He is the One whose "day" is coming, who will make a state visit in which he will judge, and whose rule will usher in a world in which "righteousness is at home."

If the emphasis in 2 Peter is on Jesus as Lord and Anointed One, and if God the Father is only mentioned in terms of his classic actions in creation and ancient Hebrew narrative, the Holy Spirit is almost completely omitted. The only reference to the Spirit is in 1:21, in which the Spirit "carried" people who gave the prophecy that one finds in Scripture. This is a distant past action (the ancient character of Scripture is part of its appeal); nothing is said of the Spirit's current activity in the community. That the Spirit can appear so suddenly as the inspirer of prophecy (probably the one inspiring the prophet on how to interpret their visions) indicates, however, that our author thinks that the reference to the Spirit will not be strange to his addressees. That there is only the one reference suggests also that he does not believe that the Spirit is a useful concept for his purposes. His issue is whether there is a final judgment and thus whether one is pursuing a moral lifestyle in the present. For that the ruling Lord, Jesus God's Anointed One, is critical, and his coming parousial judgment is in line with past actions of God. In this context the Spirit is not needed, for the Spirit is not usually connected with judgment.

Before we leave the topic of theology proper, notice that while Jesus will judge (and in that sense take over the role of God from the Hebrew Scriptures), his primary characterization is as Rescuer/Savior. That is a frequent title. When it comes to the "negative" side of judgment, he does not want anyone to "perish." His desire is for 100 percent rescue. There is no implication in 2 Peter that he gets his will, but it is clear that when it comes to his character, he is not a "hanging judge," but a happy rescuer.

4.4.2 Cosmology

God the Father is the Creator of the world. Like Philo, our author believes that God created via his creative word or *logos* (2 Pet 3:5). And like Philo he believes that God's second power is what might be called an executive word or *logos*, by means of which the world is guided toward final judgment. "By the same word the present heavens and earth have been reserved for fire, being kept until the day of judgment and destruction of the godless" (3:7 NRSV).[98] Of course, the idea that creation came about by God's word is already found in Pss 33:6 and 148:5, as well as in Wis 9:1 and Heb 11:3. Hebrews may or may not precede 2 Peter and does seem to breathe some of the atmosphere that Philo did, so it is more a parallel than a precedent. What is striking in 2 Peter is the double function of God's *logos*. There is no doubt that God is the Creator, even if the use of the divine *logos* may separate the cosmos a bit from God.

Second Peter seems to follow the Genesis narrative (although we do not know whether he has read Genesis itself) in that he views the original "stuff" of the cosmos as being watery so that the heavens and earth were existing out of and by means of water.[99] In the Genesis narrative, of course, there is a firmament, expanse, or dome that creates the heavens by separating the waters above from the waters below (Gen 1:6–8). There is no reference here or in Genesis to the "pillars of the sky" or "pillars of heaven" (Job 26:11) that appear to hold the sky up as the "pillars of the earth" appear to keep the earth stable with respect to the "waters under the earth." In that sense 2 Peter is closer to Genesis than to later poetic reflections on creation. The emphasis in 2 Peter is not on the details of creation, but on its having been done by God's *logos* and on the role of water, and that water also destroyed the original creation in the deluge.[100] This is a precedent for God's *logos* preserving the present cosmos (i.e., the heavens and the heavenly bodies) for a fiery judgment.

The cosmos consists not only of the heavens and the earth, but also of a population. That God exists is clear, and that human beings exist is also assumed. Our author also believes in divine messengers ("angels," a transliteration of the Greek word [*angelos*] that means "messenger"). We are not told much about these beings other than that they sinned—2 Peter assumes that his addressees know the *1 Enoch* narrative known by Jude or a similar narrative, for he feels no need to explain either the existence of the divine messengers or the concept that some sinned (2:4). Nor does he expect that his readers need information about the existence of these messengers' present prison in Tartarus, the place in Greek mythology in which the Titans were imprisoned. However, in 2 Peter this imprisonment, unpleasant as it is, is not permanent, but only

---

98. Philo, *Mos.* 2.99; *Plant.* 85–89; *Fug.*101; *Abr.* 121–22. Cf. Neyrey, *2 Peter, Jude,* 233–34.

99. So BDAG, *dia*, διά, A3, 224. On the verb see BDAG, *synistēmi*, συνίστημι, 972 (meaning B3). We have a periphrastic passive construction with the two parts of the verb split, which tends to throw the emphasis on God's word, which is outside the split.

100. One would expect that it was God's *logos* that also caused the deluge, which 𝔓69 and some other manuscripts do indicate, but the majority of the manuscripts have the world perishing through a plural object, which makes best sense if it refers to the dual references to water in the previous verse.

until the final judgment. We are not informed about what will happen at that point, although one can guess from *1 Enoch* and perhaps Revelation 20.

So 2 Peter describes God as the Creator of the world and in control of the cosmos, a cosmos that consists of the heavens, the earth, and Tartarus (subterranean in Greek mythology and perhaps in *1 Enoch*, but located by some Jewish writers and perhaps by 1 Peter in the second of three heavens).[101] This cosmos is populated by God and human beings, of course, but also by divine messengers, some of whom sinned and are presently held in Tartarus. There is no reference to a Satan figure (unlike James and 1 Peter) or to any present activity of the divine messengers, good or evil,[102] for 2 Peter is focused on human responsibility for human evil.

4.4.3 Soteriology

For 2 Peter there is evil in the world, and specifically in the world of human beings. This corruption or depravity is through (by means of) desire. The term "desire" (*epithymia*, ἐπιθυμία) is often translated "lust," but that translation makes the term sound sexually toned and ignores both the connection to the developing Jewish *yēṣer* theology and to Greco-Roman and especially Stoic concerns about desire. For the Greco-Roman world, "desire" (drives, emotions) was problematic, for it diverted one from rationality and equanimity. For the Jewish world, *yēṣer* was problematic in that if left unchecked, it would lead one into evil behavior.

Of course, for Jews the Torah both defined what behaviors were evil and what was the means by which one could control *yēṣer*. While for the Stoic the ideal life is that of *apatheia*, in which one could, through rationality, rise above the vagaries of *epithymia* (or any other term for emotions) and so achieve a life without desire, for the rabbis *yēṣer* was not evil in itself, but a creation of God, which needed control. Indeed, without such drives one would not fulfill divine mandates of sowing and reaping the earth or of procreation. Our author sounds more Greco-Roman in that he does not suggest that desire leads to anything other than corruption, although it would be dangerous to argue that this one line of text contains his full thought on the subject. What is clear is that he is more concerned about the present source of corruption than of the origin about corruption.[103]

There is corruption in the world, but God has provided an escape. Through divine initiative ("who called us," 1:3), for divine honor ("by his own honor and virtue," 1:3), and by divine power, Jesus has enabled humans to escape this corruption by acknowledging him. Through his honor and virtue he has given us fantastic

101. So J. N. D. Kelly, *The Epistles of Peter and of Jude*, 155–56, following *2 Enoch's* location. "And those men took me up to the second heaven. And they set me down on the second heaven. And they showed me prisoners under guard, in measureless judgment. And there I saw the condemned angels, weeping." (*2 En.* 7:1–2).

102. Only much later were the fallen divine messengers described as running hell or afflicting human beings as demons. Such ideas have no basis in the biblical text.

103. For a fuller discussion of *yēṣer* theology and its developments, see Peter H. Davids, *Themes in the Epistle of James That Are Judaistic in Character* (Ph.D. thesis; University of Manchester, 1974), 1–93. While some Jewish literature mentions the "fall" narrative in Genesis 3, that is rare in Jewish literature. Generally, like 2 Peter, Jewish literature simply mentions the existence of *yēṣer* as something that either just is or as something created by God that needs control if it is to lead a person to godly ends.

promises, which include participating in or sharing (becoming *koinōnoi*, κοινωνοί, of) the divine nature. What this means is explained by the two explanations bracketing the discussion: "life and piety (or godliness)" and then, after an expansion of what piety looks like (1:5–7), "an entry into the eternal kingdom of our Lord and Savior Jesus the Anointed One," which appears to explain "life."

The basis of this escape or rescue is in acknowledging "God and Jesus our Lord," "the One calling us," "our Lord Jesus the Anointed One," or "our Lord and Savior Jesus the Anointed One" (1:2, 3, 8; 2:20). This is not knowing *about* Jesus (*gnōsis*, γνῶσις), but recognition or acknowledgment of Jesus as Lord (*epignōsis*, ἐπίγνωσις). A title of rule is always present with Jesus' name; acknowledgment sounds similar to Paul's "confessing Jesus as Lord" (Rom 10:9–10). It appears that allegiance to his Imperial Majesty Jesus is what 2 Peter is getting at.

What is clear is that it does not involve any theory about or knowledge of his crucifixion (even if it is difficult to imagine an early follower of Jesus who did not know about the crucifixion and resurrection). Second Peter does not mention either the crucifixion or any of the various ways of alluding to it (e.g., "tree," "blood," or "ransom")[104] when he mentions that the addressees' Master "bought" them (2:1); the author uses a term for "Master" that means "slave-master" and so paints an image of ownership with only a whiff of some theory of salvation. What he does mention repeatedly is acknowledging (*epignōsis*) the Lord Jesus, and thus we have termed this an epignostic salvation,[105] playing on the word that he uses so frequently.

Second Peter does argue that having been freed from the corruption in the world — that is, having come to epignosis in our terminology — one must live out this freedom through growth in virtue. There is no reason not to do this, since everything needed has been provided. The order of virtues does not seem to be particularly important; rather, it is a means of listing of them, although it may be significant that the list starts with commitment (faith) and ends with love. Commitment appears to mean the same as coming to epignosis, at least a positive epignosis, for 2 Peter never gives a content object of *pistis*, but a personal object, and with a personal object *pistis* means commitment or allegiance.

That is where one starts. There is a King, and that King is Jesus God's Anointed One.[106] Then one adds virtue, knowledge, self-control (all well-known Greek virtues), patient endurance (somewhat better known in Jewish literature, such as the *Testament of Job*), piety, sibling love (in 2 Peter surely self-giving care for the fictive family, the community of the followers of Jesus), and finally love or self-giving care. This idea of love is fundamentally a virtue of the community of the followers of Jesus rather than of the Hellenistic world.

---

104. It is important to include the various circumlocutions as allusions, for even Paul does not use the word "cross" or "crucify" in all his letters. Romans, for example, has no use of "cross" and only has one use of "crucify" and that is metaphorical. In most of his letters, however, he refers to the event that was for him paradigmatic of the life of the followers of Jesus.

105. At this point I will take the Greek term *epignōsis* and coin an English word "epignosis" ("acknowledgment" or "recognition") with the adjectival form "epignostic" (meaning "characterized by recognition or acknowledgment of").

106. Second Peter cannot seem to conceive of a person knowing about this and then deciding to oppose that ruler.

It is not that the virtues are optional, for salvation means freedom from corruption in order to live a life of freedom. One eithers lives the life of freedom (i.e., develops the virtues) and becomes fruitful in terms of the epignosis of Jesus the Lord (to use the metaphor in 1:8), or else one forgets the cleansing of past sin and becomes blind (i.e., like the teachers our author condemns, who by their lifestyle "deny the Master who bought them" [2:1] and who are now in a worse state than before they came to know Jesus the Lord).

Second Peter 2:20–21 puts it clearly: having "escaped the defilements of the world through the knowledge of our Lord and Savior Jesus Christ, they are again entangled in them and overpowered, and the last state has become worse for them than the first. For it would have been better for them never to have known the way of righteousness than, after knowing it, to turn back from the holy commandment that was passed on to them." They had it all—escape from the defilements of the world and its corruption through desire—but rather than pursuing virtue and so becoming sharers of the divine nature, they turned back and got trapped again. They are now in even worse shape (under more severe judgment) because they had epignosis of the right way (recall that epignosis gives the ability to accomplish) and turned back from it. Our author does not believe in eternal security—in fact, he knows of some folk who have "lost their salvation" and for whom it would have been better never to have been "saved" (cf. Heb 6:4–6).

4.4.4 Eschatology

While 2 Peter mentions creation and ancient history (Noah and the deluge, Balaam, etc.) his chief concern is with the present lived in the light of the future. In fact, he views the present period as "the last days," for while 3:3 speaks of scoffers coming in the future, it is clear from chapter 2 that they have already arrived, are already "feasting with" the "Beloved." Thus the future tense of 3:3 is a way of describing the present from the perspective of Peter; it is an epistolary future. Since these are the last days, what is on the cusp of taking place?

The next event is "the day of judgment and of the destruction of impious people" (3:7; cf. 2:9), a day marked by fire as the judgment of the time of Noah was marked by water. This day is also called "the day of the Lord," for it is the Lord Jesus who is the judge (3:10), or the "day of God" (3:12), since the judgment takes place under the authority of God himself or, perhaps, because Jesus and God are merging in 2 Peter, as we saw in 1:1.

On this day the heavens and their *stoicheia*[107] (the sun, moon, and stars) will be set ablaze, pass away, be dissolved, melt with fire. Why? It is certainly not destruction for destruction's sake, but it makes "the earth and the works [done] in it" naked

---

107. We argued in the thematic commentary that *stoicheia* (στοιχεῖα) means, not the elements of the world (i.e., earth, air, fire, and water), but the bodies that are in the heavens (i.e., sun, moon, stars, and planets). Thus translating the term "elements" is mislead-ing, for in this context it does not indicate the elements of this world, much less the elements in the periodic table of elements. Those "elements," to the extent that they are part of the earth, remain unchanged, since the earth is not destroyed.

before the Lord. The fire is not itself the judgment, but the means of "pulling back the bedclothes," so to speak, so that what has been done "under the covers" becomes undeniably evident. The Lord or God is pictured as above the heavens, so their removal "discloses" the earth and everything that takes place there.[108] There is no description, as in Revelation, of Jesus' coming, of ruling seats being set up, or of the detailed negative effects of judgment. "Destruction" is the word that 2 Peter has used more than once, and that suffices.

But judgment in the ancient world always had a positive side, namely, rewarding the faithful. That same event will bring about the renewal of the world. Evil has been purged, so there is a new heaven and earth, a place in which righteousness "lives" (3:13). The earth has not been destroyed, only exposed for judgment,[109] but that purification has made it new, for where evil seemed to dwell, now righteousness does.[110] Another way of describing this positive outcome is that of "being granted a rich entrance into the eternal kingdom of our Lord and Savior Jesus the Anointed One" (1:11); the picture is probably that of entering the presence of a ruler and being welcomed and rewarded for faithful service. This ruler, however, will rule this world forever, and so being granted favor and a reward in his presence has significant consequences.

Thus 2 Peter is arguing that even though virtue (as defined by him, which appears to depend on the teaching of Jesus) has little benefit in this age, this age has no future, and those living for present enjoyment have no future along with it. There is great benefit from present virtue in the coming age, for there will be a judgment, and the King will come and those who have lived according to his definition of virtue will be rewarded. That is what is worth living for, and that is the point. Eschatology is there to support ethics,[111] for Christian ethics only make sense in the light of Christian eschatology.

---

108. Since the purpose of the destruction of heaven and the heavenly bodies is the revelation of what is taking place and has taken place on earth, a revelation that makes sense within the worldview model that 2 Peter is using, it is clear that this fiery action is not destroying the structure that holds up the heavenly bodies and thus the bodies as well. So perhaps if translated into a typical contemporary worldview, this action is metaphorical for the sudden and complete exposure of all human actions, good or evil.

109. See the textual discussion in the thematic commentary on 3:10.

110. The earth is what is renewed in 2 Peter's description, not the heavens, for while there is the uncovering of the earth and its deeds, and their purgation would certainly be renewal, the heavens and heavenly bodies have been destroyed. What does 2 Peter mean by a renewed or new heaven? It is difficult to know for sure, for the language of apocalyptic is pictorial and emotional, and such images do not necessarily have to fit together logically. First, we recognize that 2 Peter is stock language (drawn from Isa 65:17; 66:22, also found in Rev 21:1). Second, "new heaven" does not necessarily imply the re-creation of heaven. In Rev 21 the renewed heaven and earth lacks a sea (21:1, the sea is an image of chaos), a major feature of earth as we know it, as well as a sun and moon (21:23, not needed

with God's presence lighting up the place, nor does eternity need symbols of telling time). The descriptors of the new heaven and earth indicate that it is something other than a purified, idealized re-creation. Rather, the author is describing symbolically the coming rule expressed in terms of the worldview model of the author. So, is our author just leaving out the renewal of heaven, or is he saying that the renewed earth will be totally open to God's heaven, so to speak? Does he even want to describe this in any literal sense? His point is that the earth is full of righteousness under the rule of Jesus the Lord and that the future is worth living for. He does not allow us to pin him down beyond this.

111. While it sounds strange to say that eschatology is there to support ethics, we submit that within the worldview of the New Testament it is unnecessary to know what is coming in the future if one fully trusts him who controls the future. For the one who trusts the King, that is, who is doing the reverse of what happened in Gen 3, eschatology in anything but a general sense serves to identify and reinforce lifestyles that make sense in the present only in the light of the future. There is also a type of apologetic use, but this use is directed toward the wavering believer, and so is in a sense a subspecies of the ethical use.

4.4.5 Minor Themes: Ecclesiology and Scripture

There are several secondary theological themes in 2 Peter. The first is that of ecclesiology. The community to which 2 Peter is addressed is a community whose gatherings are characterized by "feasting together." This is, of course, dependent on Jude 12's reference to the community's gathering as "love feasts." In both Jude and 2 Peter the point is that the others/false teachers are corrupting these community gatherings. This is part of the evidence that the weekly gatherings in the early Jesus movement were around a table, a potluck reenactment of the Last Supper.[112] It was only later (starting about 250 CE and completed by 350 CE) that the meal became symbolic and the feasting together became metaphorical, although the centrality of the reenactment continues verbally in many contemporary liturgies.

This meal character of the central celebration and gathering underlines the familial nature of community, for the Last Supper, assuming that it was a Passover celebration, was a family meal, although in Jesus' case the family was the fictive family of his followers rather than the blood family.[113] But as Mark 3:31 – 35, among other passages, indicates, Jesus privileged the fictive family over the blood family.

This community or fictive family is to remain ethically pure ("without spot or blemish" in 3:14 is a cultic formula applied ethically to the community) and is to be found "at peace." Community unity or peace remains an important value for 2 Peter. The passive "be found" probably indicates that Jesus is the one doing the "finding" at the time of his parousia. This description of the family of believers "at peace" is an important New Testament value. Indeed, one can argue that this is the major theme of such works as Romans and 1 Corinthians.

Yet 2 Peter leaves us with a conundrum: nothing is said about taking action against the false teachers. They are clearly identified. They are threatened with eschatological judgment, but unlike Paul in 1 Cor 5:3 – 5, 6, 13 (and 1 Tim 1:20 is presumably another example), there is no instruction to separate from or drive out the false teachers.[114] At the same time, unlike Jude 22 – 23, there is no instruction to rescue these teachers. Are the "beloved" not in a position to take action? Is the instruction of something like Matt 18:15 – 20 assumed? Or is it assumed that the Lord Jesus will deal with the teachers, perhaps in his parousia?[115] Given the emphasis

---

112. This is imaginatively, but helpfully, described in Robert Banks, *Going to Church in the First Century: An Eyewitness Account* (Chipping Norton, NSW, Australia: Hexagon, 1980).

113. None of the Synoptic Gospels indicates that Jesus' brothers (i.e., his blood family) were believers during Jesus' lifetime. None of them makes Mary his mother a witness of his burial or a witness of the resurrection. Only John places Mary at the cross, but only to be given another son (John 19:25 – 27), and only John indicates that she had some type of insight into him during his life (John 2:1 – 5, the only other place where she appears in the gospel). Acts, of course, indicates that both Mary mother of Jesus and Jesus' brothers were believers after his resurrection (Acts 1:14), which perhaps indicates that the "treasuring" of the events surrounding the birth and early life of Jesus in Luke (where she is the central character, unlike in

Matthew where Joseph is the central character) was a form of faith.

114. Paul, of course, is addressing a situation in 1 Cor 5 that is so flagrant that it violates Gentile ethics, not just those of the community he is addressing. There also does not seem to be a question of even the possibility of repentance. No arguments are given to prove the behavior is evil. The issue is the inaction of the community, not the unethical nature of the behavior. He takes a different approach to those in 1 Cor 6 who are suing one another at law or who are visiting prostitutes, both of which behaviors Paul argues are wrong, but neither of which behaviors is cited as a reason for expulsion.

115. And perhaps, as is stated in Heb 6:5, that it is useless to try to renew them again to repentance, for unlike those in Heb 6, they have abandoned the faith.

on eschatology in this letter, the latter may be the case, but it is clear that the focus of 2 Peter is on enabling the "beloved" to identify the false teachers, to avoid being taken in by their arguments, and to keep themselves in an obedient and virtuous stance. Thus the holiness of the "beloved" is the interest of the letter, not the purification of the community as a whole.

Another secondary theological theme is the nature of Scripture. It is clear that our author and the community addressed value the "holy prophets" (1:19–21). He refers to these as a "prophetic *logos,*" that is, "prophetic word," "prophecy of Scripture," "words spoken previously by the holy prophets" (3:2), or simply "Scriptures" (3:16). It seems obvious that he is referring to written prophecy, and that the chief value of these "writings" is that they are prophetic. These words consist of some visionary experiences (be it auditory or visual, internal or external to the prophet) and prophetic expressions or interpretations, which eventually were written. Our author makes clear that the visionary experiences were not subject to the prophet's own interpretation, but that the Holy Spirit was "carrying" the prophets so that these holy people spoke "from God." It is because of this divine content that one should pay attention to these writings.

That said, our author opens two issues. The first is that the prophetic Scriptures as word or *logos* are an artificial proof, and personal experience (i.e., eyewitness testimony) is an inartificial proof (using the rhetorical categories used in his day); the latter is more sure than the former. Thus for him the experience of the transfiguration proved that Jesus is Lord, God's Anointed King, for Peter has seen the investiture. This makes the prophetic word "more reliable" (1:19), for Peter's experience was that the event to which the prophetic word pointed had actually taken place, at least in part. Thus the rest of the prophetic word can presumably be trusted. In other words, for our author something is more certain than prophetic writings, despite their divine origin: the experience of or testimony to the experience of their partial fulfillment.

The second issue pertaining to the Scriptures is which works our author includes among the prophetic writings that he considers inspired (in the sense that both the prophetic experience and prophetic interpretation are attributed to divine agency). For a work that values prophetic writings, 2 Peter is fascinating in that, unlike 1 Peter, it *never* quotes them. The one place the Hebrew Scriptures are semi-quoted is the use of some version of Prov 26:11 in 2 Pet 2:22,[116] but this is not referred to as Scripture but as a "proverb," and, as if to underline that it is in another category of tradition, it is paired without differentiation with another proverb that is probably derived from *Ahikar* 8:18 (not Scripture at all). It is probable that 2 Peter does not think of either proverb as Scripture; perhaps it is simply an oral proverb. So we have in 2 Peter an author who values writings that he never cites as Scripture.

He does, of course, know at least some of Paul's writings, which he groups with "the other writings" (i.e., "the other Scriptures"), given the normal use of the Greek

116. He is not following the LXX or any other known form of Prov 26:11, so he may know this proverb only from memory.

term *graphē* (γραφή). This probably shows Paul's writings (and he specifically says that Paul had written to the addressees) somewhere on the way to becoming Scripture, although we do not know how far our author would push this association.[117] That is, what other term other than "the other writings" could our author have used to include Paul's writings along with the Scriptures as distortable written entities?[118] He has certainly provided material for the later doctrine of New Testament Scripture, but it is unlikely that, if pushed, he himself would have said, "Yes, Paul's letters are a part of prophetic Scripture." Such a statement would probably have made Paul's writings part of the Hebrew Scriptures, which would hardly make sense.

Our author is aware of a number of narratives found in the Hebrew Scriptures: the creation narrative of Gen 1, the corruption and deluge narrative of Gen 6–8, the Sodom and Gomorrah narrative of Gen 18:16–19:29, and the Balaam narrative of Num 22–25. That he would value these narratives is not surprising in that they are all in the books of Moses, and, as Moses was considered a prophet (as the succession prophecy of Deut 18:15–22 shows), they could be considered "prophetic Scriptures." Furthermore, all first-century Jewish groups that we know about considered the five books of the Torah as sacred Scripture. However, in no case is there evidence that our author has *read* the Hebrew Scriptures themselves, either in Hebrew or in Greek translation.

First, all of these narratives other than the creation narrative (which is only mentioned as the background to the deluge narrative) are included in Jude and mentioned in 2 Peter in the section dependent on Jude, so their use is not original to our author. Second, all of these narratives are being read through the lens of their retelling in Second Temple literature, so our author has read them (assuming he could read) or heard them read or told in something like one of those versions (there was variety in the Second Temple retellings).[119]

Thus, the story of the "sons of God" in Gen 6 is told as the story of the sinning angels found in *1 Enoch*. The story of Noah is told in a form in which Noah is a "proclaimer of righteousness" (not even hinted at in the Genesis text). The Sodom and Gomorrah story is told as the story of the rescue of righteous Lot (whose righteousness is hinted at in the Genesis text, but whose suffering in Sodom is not). The story of Balaam is told in a version in which Balaam did wrong for money (the opposite of the main Numbers narrative in which Balaam refuses to let money sway him from speaking God's word, although perhaps hinted at in Num 31:16), and the donkey, not a divine messenger, rebukes Balaam. These expansions of the

---

117. The association is that both Paul's writings and the Scriptures are being distorted by the "ignorant and unstable"; it is not that they are both being referred to as inspired.

118. The prophetic Scriptures are attributed to God via the Holy Spirit, while Paul's writings are said to emanate from "the wisdom given to him," presumably by God. While one would not wish to push this distinction, this certainly is a far less direct expression of divine involvement than saying "God spoke" and "carried by the Holy Spirit." But note the commonality between what Paul "wrote"

(cf. the verb *graphō*, specifically the aorist *egrapsen*, ἔγραψεν) and the prophetic Scriptures (using the cognate noun *graphē*, γραφή) being "written." Second Peter does not refer to Paul's writings as "letters" (*epistolai*), for that would break the parallel of the false teachers' similar distorting of other writings/Scriptures.

119. We have argued this in some detail in "Use of Second Temple Traditions," in *The Catholic Epistles and the Tradition* (ed. Jacques Schlosser; BETL 176; Leuven: Peeters, 2004), 409–31.

Torah narratives are all the forms in which these narratives circulated in the Second Temple period.

Thus, our author refers to the form of the stories that he knows without any apparent awareness that it is a current version of the stories, not the ancient version.[120] These narratives may be known and traditional because of prophetic Scripture, but our author reveals no need to check or follow that Scripture. The later retellings appear to be all he knows and all he apparently thinks his addressees know. This is not exactly a specific hermeneutic, for a hermeneutic assumes that one knows one is interpreting. This is more a lack of awareness of the original text, despite valuing "prophetic Scripture."

Finally, it is not clear where the boundaries of "prophetic Scripture" are for our author. What is included among "words spoken by the holy prophets" (3:2)? We have suggested that he does not seem to differentiate Proverbs from proverbs from another source (if he thinks that either type of proverb is Scripture), and he does not feel uncomfortable with putting Paul's writings in a loose grouping with apparently sacred writings at least to the extent of their being religious instructional writings, even if he does not attribute the same inspiration to Paul as to the holy prophets. When he draws material from Jude, he drops the citation of *1 Enoch* and the explicit story from the *Testament of Moses*, but he still uses material about the sinning angels that we know comes from *1 Enoch* (i.e., the Gen 6 narrative does not mention any imprisonment of the "sons of God," nor does it use the term "messenger"/"angel" for them) and includes the point Jude makes from the *Testament of Moses* narrative.

We do not know why 2 Peter edits Jude this way. It may be that he does not like this literature, but then why can he still use material or make major points from it? It may be that he is aware that his addressees will not recognize the literature, but he does not indicate this. It may be that as a good practitioner of *aemulatio*, he is trying to rephrase and reapply Jude's material and in the process shorten it.[121] In that case, he may well not be aware that some of what he includes and excludes is part of what later ages will call "Scripture" and some is not.

In short, 2 Peter witnesses to the fluid boundaries of Scripture in the first century. This is both because he lived in an oral-mnemonic culture in which one might be rhetorically trained but not be scribally literate (or not have scrolls available if one were scribally literate), and because canon consciousness was still in a developing form.[122]

Related to the secondary theological theme of the nature of Scripture is the

---

120. This suggests that if one should go back and check the original, ancient version of the OT, our action may well be an anachronism (i.e., insisting that our methodology is that of the first-century).

121. Letters in the ancient world were supposed to be short, and, while 2 Peter is not long by current standards and certainly not long by Paul's standards, it is long for an ancient letter. Given ancient standards, one would expect him to be trying to shorten the letter consistent with what he felt were the demands of appropriate (Asiatic) rhetoric.

122. We follow the general position of Lee M. McDonald, *The Formation of the Christian Biblical Canon* (Peabody, MA: Hendrickson, 1995). If McDonald is correct, true canon consciousness in terms of the Hebrew Scriptures is a product of the second century and later, not the first century or before, although there was general agreement among Jews about the foundational nature of the Torah, even if not about what this meant in terms of interpretation.

theme of the role of the teaching of Jesus. When it comes to Jesus, there is no question but that his words are known in oral form. The phrase in 2 Pet 3:2, "the commandment of the Lord and Savior through your apostles," makes clear that the addressees are expected to know the teaching of Jesus via the missionaries who had evangelized them rather than from writings purporting to quote him.[123] Yet it is clear that that oral tradition is authoritative. It is a "commandment," just as it is a "holy commandment," once received but now rejected, that reveals the shipwreck of the false teachers (2:21). This is what one would expect if Jesus is indeed "Lord," "[God's] Anointed One," "Deliverer (Savior)," "Master," whose "majesty" has been visibly displayed. There is no question but that these titles in the ancient world would have meant, "To hear is to obey."

Ethics, then, is obedience, a listening to the teaching of Jesus and obedience to what one heard. One is to grow in the "favor and knowledge" of Jesus (3:18) and not to be "unfruitful" in one's "knowledge" (1:7 – 8). We argued above that initially knowing Jesus means recognizing the significance of Jesus and giving allegiance to him, but surely the minimal allegiance is obedience to his teaching, following his "commands" (Could a king say anything that is not in some sense a command?). Furthermore, the "knowledge" of 3:18 is *gnōsis*, not *epignōsis* as in 1:7 – 8. It is possible that 3:18 is a traditional expression, "favor and knowledge," taken over by our author; but if he intends the shift, it would indicate a movement from recognition to deeper understanding. What is clear is that for our author the teaching of Jesus is the central authority for life, since Jesus is Lord. Ethics is obeying Jesus. To speak anachronistically, for our author the teaching of Jesus in the Gospels is his "canon within the canon."

4.5 CANONICAL CONTRIBUTION

What is the canonical contribution of 2 Peter? It seems clear (from its conflicted canonical history and its current relegation to the end of courses where it may get little coverage) that many would answer, "Not much." Yet our findings mean we cannot be satisfied with such an answer.

First, 2 Peter joins Jude in underlining the possibility of moral apostasy. If Jesus is not obeyed, Jesus is not Lord. To say he is Lord while not obeying his "holy command" is to deny him. Second Peter follows Jude in making moral apostasy, or its avoidance, the focus of a letter.

Second, our author points out the ethical importance of eschatology, and in particular, final judgment. While the main issue that concerns him is encouraging virtue in his readers and condemning the lack of virtue in those he labels "false teachers," it is clear that the teachers in a sense justified their behavior by denying

---

123. In other words, there is no reference to the written Gospels, which has implications for the dating of the letter, unless one should think that a later author was being deliberately anachronistic.

there will be a final judgment. The direction of the letter, and probably the direction of thought of the teachers, is from behavior to justification ("this behavior does not matter because there will be no judgment"); but that direction of reasoning does not mean that judgment is not important ethically.

This is true for two reasons. On the one hand, since eventually one will be called to task for one's poor behavior, that should hinder one from acting in that manner.[124] More importantly, on the other hand, the awareness that the dysfunction of the current age is not permanent and that a time is coming when one's moral behavior will be rewarded and will fit one for a good existence within that coming age (i.e., the positive side of final judgment) is likely to influence present behavior in a positive direction. Our author puts more stress on this second reason, for he does not dwell on the miseries of those going to destruction, but on the new age that is coming.

When it comes to eschatology, 2 Peter also has a contribution to make, although not the one that many believe it does. He certainly indicates that final judgment is a major doctrine, a basic of the faith. In this he agrees with Heb 6:2. He describes the judgment as taking place within the structure of his own worldview, but he does so with an interesting twist. For the Lord to "see" clearly for judgment, the heavens and that which is in them must be removed, which is the function of the fire. But unlike popular ideas, the earth is simply "discovered," or "laid open to view." Thus, his "new" earth is a judged earth, not a newly created or recreated earth. Its key feature is that "righteousness" is "at home" in it.

This shows at least one view of the continuity as well as the discontinuity of the present and future worlds. Furthermore, it underlines the physicality of the coming age. There may be other views in the New Testament (Hebrews, for example, including chapter 12, seems to present a picture of a heavenly future with the created world being removed), but 2 Peter has one of the voices that need to be heard.

Third, 2 Peter reminds its readers forcefully that Jesus is an imperial ruler. At least grammatically he even goes beyond this and joins a handful of New Testament works (John 1, Hebrews 1, some readings of Philippians 2, etc.) that identify Jesus as divine. But even if one argues that in 2 Pet 1:1 this identification is a grammatical slip or textual error, one still has Jesus as Ruler. Second Peter never mentions him without a title of rule: *kyrios* (Lord), *christos* (the Anointed One = God's Anointed Ruler or Messiah), *despotēs* (Master). Even when he calls him *sōtēr* (Savior, Deliverer), the picture is of someone who deserves submission because he has delivered people and defeated their enemies—a reality that is seen when one considers that this title never occurs without "Lord" and "the Anointed One" along with it. Jesus has given a "commandment" and has a kingdom, a rule present now, but a rule that will be universal in the coming new age.

---

124. "Should" does not mean "is" or "will be," for behavioral studies show that (1) negative reinforcement has little power to change behavior more than temporarily, whether one is a rat or a "rational" human (a fact ignored by advocates of punishment as the chief form of discipline); and (2) distant consequences have less influence over behavior than relatively immediate consequences. Thus the threat of punishment "sometime in the future" is unlikely to have significant effects on current behavior.

Fourth, 2 Peter has a unique picture of salvation, not that the elements cannot be found elsewhere, but that they are put together in a distinctive manner. He never mentions the death of Jesus other than by the allusive "bought them" (2:1), which occurs in a context in which it could mean any type of price or payment; his use of "Savior" is not connected to the cross. Rather, he has what we have termed an "epignostic" salvation in that one comes to know Jesus—that is, to recognize who he is and to behave appropriately with respect to who he is; this means to follow him and to submit to his authority, and it leads to virtue—to getting to know him more and, in the end, to become like him (i.e., participating in the divine nature). It is true that Paul says something similar in 1 Cor 2:16 and Phil 3:7–16, as do other New Testament authors, but no one is as bold and clear as the author of 2 Peter. For him, if one keeps on growing in virtue on the basis of the freedom from corruption that Jesus has granted, one will share in the divine nature.

Fifth, 2 Peter demonstrates a specific hermeneutic of reading the Hebrew Scriptures through the lenses of the Judaism current in his day. He can value the Scriptures, but he never cites them. He can tell stories, but tell them with additions and changes that had accrued in Second Temple literature. He can also speak about Paul's letters in the same breath as the Hebrew Scriptures, demonstrating that he is starting to think about them as at least an adjunct to the Hebrew Scriptures. When it comes to the teaching of Jesus, he appears to refer to it as a "holy commandment" or just "commandment"—it is an authoritative tradition, although he does not refer to it as written. In other words, we get both a hermeneutic demonstration and a lesson in incipient canon formation in 2 Peter. Those who are used to viewing the Scriptures as fixed, final, and firm (although that is not exactly the case in the church)[125] can learn about their nature through such a dynamic view of the canon formation in process.

Hermeneutically, 2 Peter reminds us that no one reads Scripture directly; rather, we read through the lenses provided by our own age, as we see in our author's reading the narratives of the Hebrew Scriptures through the lenses of Second Temple literature. But he also demonstrates a translation of Christian virtue into the language of the Greco-Roman world. Furthermore, he appears to be interacting with a type of Epicurean thought from positions that utilize ideas that are more in the Stoic direction. Thus, he demonstrates translating the message of the community of Jesus into the thought forms of one's age, but he also shows the danger of doing so insensitively (as those he calls "false teachers" apparently did).

---

125. On the macro-level we must remember that the Orthodox church reads the LXX and therefore views the so-called Apocrypha as canonical, and the Anglican churches, as well as others, view them as at least deuterocanonical, that is, to be included in the readings for church services if not used on their own for the establishment of doctrine. On the less macro-level we need to remember that those in the King James only tradition (or any similar tradition that privileges the late Byzantine text type) read the longer ending of Mark (as well as a few other shorter passages) as canonical, while those using other text types and the translations based on them do not. On the practical level, most believing communities function with a "canon within the canon," privileging certain parts of the canon, as Martin Luther did with Galatians and Romans and the Anabaptists did with the Gospels (this was a big reason for their conflicts with Luther).

Chapter 5

JUDE

BIBLIOGRAPHY

Barnes, Thomas. "The Epistle of Jude: A Study in the Marcosian Heresy." *JTS* 6 (1905): 391–411. **Bauckham, Richard J.** "A Note on a Problem in the Greek Version of 1 Enoch i.9." *JTS* 32 (1981): 136–38. Idem. *Jude and the Relatives of Jesus in the Early Church.* Edinburgh: T&T Clark, 1990. Idem. *Jude, 2 Peter.* WBC 50. Waco, TX: Word, 1983. **Berger, Klaus**. "Der Streit des guten und des bösen Engels um die Seele: Beobachtungen zu 4QAmr^b und Judas 9." *JSJ* 4 (1973): 1–18. **Bieder, Werner**. "Judas 22f.: *Hous de eleate en phobōboi*," *TZ* 6 (1950): 75–77. **Birdsall, J. Neville**. "The Text of Jude in P72." *JTS* 14 (1963): 394–99. **Black, Matthew**. "Critical and Exegetical Notes on Three New Testament Texts: Hebrews xi. 11, Jude 5, James 1. 27." Pp. 39–45 in *Apophoreta: Festschrift für Ernst Haenchen*. BZNW 30. Berlin: Alfred Töpelmann, 1964. Idem. "The Maranatha Invocation and Jude 14, 15 (I Enoch I:9)." Pp. 189–96 in *Christ and Spirit in the New Testament: Studies in Honour of Charles Francis Digby Moule*. Ed. Barnabas Lindars and Stephen S. Smalley. Cambridge: Cambridge University Press, 1973. **Boobyer, George H.** "The Verbs in Jude 11." *NTS* 5 (1958): 45–47. **Charles, J. Daryl**. "'Those' and 'These': The Use of the Old Testament in the Epistle of Jude." *JSNT* 38 (1990): 109–24. Idem. "Jude's Use of Pseudepigraphical Source-Material as Part of a Literary Strategy." *NTS* 37 (1991): 130–45. Idem. "Literary Artifice in the Epistle of Jude." *ZNW* 82 (1991): 106–24. Idem. *2 Peter, Jude.* In *1–2 Peter, Jude.* Believers Church Bible Commentary. Scottdale, PA: Herald, 1999. **Chase, Frederic Henry**. "Jude, Epistle of." Pp. 799–806 in vol. 2 of *Dictionary of the Bible.* Ed. James Hastings. New York: Scribner's, 1909. **Daniel, Constantin**. "La mention des Esséniens dans le texte grec de l'épître de S. Jude. *Muséon* 81 (1968): 503–21. **Danker, Frederick W.** "2 Peter." Pp. 84–93 in *The General Letters.* Ed. Gerhard Krodel. Proclamation Commentaries. Minneapolis: Fortress, 1995. **Davids, Peter H.** *The Letters of 2 Peter and Jude.* Pillar New Testament Commentary. Grand Rapids: Eerdmans, 2006. **deSilva, David A.** *The Jewish Teachers of Jesus, James, and Jude: What Earliest Christianity Learned from the Apocrypha and Pseudepigrapha.* Oxford/New York: Oxford University Press, 2012. **Dubarle, André M.** "Le péché des anges dans l'épître de Jude." Pp. 145–48 in *Memorial J. Chaine.* Lyons: Facultés Catholiques, 1950. **du Plessis, O. J.** "The Authorship of the Epistle of Jude." Pp. 191–99 in *Biblical Essays 1966: Proceedings of the Ninth Meeting of "Die Ou-Testamentiese Werkgemeenskap in Suid-Afrika," and Proceedings of the Second Meeting of "Die Nuwe-Testamentiese Werkge-*

meenskam van Suid-Afrika." Potchefstroom, South Africa: Potchefstroom Herlad (Edms.) Beperk, 1966. **Du Toit, Andreas B.** "Vilification as a Pragmatic Device in Early Christian Epistolography." *Bib* 75 (1994): 403–12. **Elliott, John H.** *I–II Peter/Jude.* ACNT. Minneapolis: Augsburg, 1982. **Ellis, E. Earle.** "Prophecy and Hermeneutic in Jude." Pp. 220–36 in *Prophecy and Hermeneutic in Early Christianity.* Grand Rapids: Eerdmans, 1978. **Fossum, Jarl**. "Kurios Jesus as the Angel of the Lord in Jude 5–7." *NTS* 33 (1987): 226–43. **Green, E. M. B. (Michael)**. *The Second Epistle of Peter and the Epistle of Jude.* TNTC. Grand Rapids: Eerdmans, 1968. **Green, Gene L.** *Jude and 2 Peter.* BECNT. Grand Rapids: Baker, 2008. **Grundmann, Walter**. *Der Brief des Judas und der zweite Brief des Petrus.* Berlin: Evangelische Verlagsanstalt, 1974. **Gunther, John J.** "The Alexandrian Epistle of Jude." *NTS* 30 (1984): 549–62. **Hiebert, D. Edmond**. "Selected Studies from Jude. Part 2: An Exposition of Jude 12–16." *BSac* 142 (1985): 245–49. Idem. "Selected Studies from Jude. Part 3: An Exposition of Jude 17–23." *BSac* 142 (1985): 355–66. **James, M. R. (Montague Rhodes)**. *The Second Epistle General of Peter and the Epistle of Jude.* CGTSC. Cambridge: Cambridge University Press, 1912. **Kellett, E. E.** "Note on Jude 5." *ExpTim* 15 (1903–1904): 381. **Klijn, Albertus K. J.** "Jude 5–7." Pp. 237–44 in *The New Testament Age: Essays in Honor of Bo Reicke.* Vol. 1. Ed. William C. Weinrich. Macon, GA: Mercer University Press, 1984. **Kraftchick, Steven J.** *Jude, 2 Peter.* ANTC. Nashville: Abingdon, 2002. **Krodel, Gerhard**. "Jude." Pp. 94–109 in *The General Letters.* Ed. Gerhard Krodel. Proclamation Commentaries. Minneapolis: Fortress, 1995. **Kubo, Sakae.** "Jude 22–23: Two-Division Form or Three?" Pp. 239–53 in *New Testament Text Criticism: Its Significance for Exegesis.* Ed. E. J. Epp and G. D. Fee. Oxford: Clarendon, 1981. **Landon, Charles**. *A Text-Critical Study of the Epistle of Jude.* JSNTSup 135; Sheffield: Sheffield Academic Press, 1996. **Lucas, Dick, and Christopher Green**. *The Message of 2 Peter and Jude: The Promise of His Coming.* TBST. Leicester, UK/Downers Grove, IL: InterVarsity Press, 1995. **Magass, Walter**. "Semiotik eine Ketzerpolemik am Beispiel von Judas 12f." *Linguistica Biblica* 19 (1972): 36–47. **Maier, Freidrich**. "Zur Erklärung des Judasbriefes (Jud 5)." *BZ* 2 (1904): 391–97. **Mayor, Joseph B.** *The Epistles of Jude and II Peter.* Grand Rapids: Baker, (1901) 1979. **Mees, Michael**. "Papyrus Bodmer VII (p^{72}) und die Zitate aus den Judasbrief bei Clemens von Alexandrien." *Ciudad de Dios* 181 (1968): 551–59. **Neyrey, Jerome H.** *2 Peter, Jude.* AB 37C. New York: Doubleday, 1993. **Oleson, John P.** "An Echo of Hesiod's *Theogony* vv 190–2 in Jude 13." *NTS* 25 (1979): 492–503. **Osburn, Carroll D.** "The Christological Use of I Enoch I.9 in Jude 14–15." *NTS* 23 (1977): 334–41. Idem. "The Text of Jude 22–23." *ZNW* 63 (1972): 139–44. Idem. "The Text of Jude 5." *Bib* 62 (1981): 107–15. **Painter, John, and David A. deSilva**. *James and Jude.* Paideia. Grand Rapids: Baker Academic, 2012. **Reese, Ruth Anne**. *2 Peter and Jude.* THNTC. Grand Rapids: Eerdmans, 2007. Idem. *Writing Jude: The Readers, the Text, and the Author in Constructs of Power and Desire.* BIS 51. Leiden: Brill, 2000. **Ross, John M.** "Church Discipline in Jude 22–23." *ExpTim* 100 (1989): 297–98. **Schrage, Wolfgang**. *Der zweite Petrusbrief. Der Judasbrief.* In *Die "Katholische" Briefe: Die Briefe* *des Jakobus, Petrus, Johannes und Judas, übersetzt und erklärt.* Ed. Horst R. Balz and Wolfgang Schrage. NTD 10. Göttingen: Vandenhoeck & Ruprecht, 1973. **Sellin, Gerhard**. "Die Häretiker des Judasbriefes." *ZNW* 77 (1986): 206–25. **Spitta, Friedrich**. *Die zweite Brief des Petrus und der Brief des Judas.* Halle a. S.: Verlag und Buchhandlung des Waisenhauses, 1885. **Vögtle, Anton**. *Der Judasbrief. Der 2. Petrusbrief.* EKKNT 22. Solothurn and Düsseldorf/Neukirchen-Vluyn: Benzinger/ Neukirchener, 1994. **Whallon, William**. "Should We Keep, Omit, or Alter the *hoi* in Jude 12?" *NTS* 34 (1988): 56–59. **Whitaker, G. H.** "Faith's Function in St Jude's Epistle." *ExpTim* 29 (1917–1918): 425. **Wikgren, Allen P.** "Some Problems in Jude 5." Pp. 147–52 in *Studies in the History and Text of the New Testament in Honor of Kenneth Willis Clark.* Ed. B. L. Daniels and M. Jack Suggs. SD 29. Salt Lake City: University of Utah Press, 1967.

Jude is a book that is not so much rejected as neglected. While it is not the short-est letter in the English New Testament, it is right next to them (2 and 3 John), and unlike them Jude does not have a "1 John" to relate to and to give it greater significance. Unlike Philemon, which is about the same length as Jude, Jude is not by a well-known figure (and, of course, Philemon gains a context from the Pauline corpus just as 2 and 3 John do from Johannine literature). Furthermore, Jude's topic is distasteful to many readers. He may start talking about the "shared faith," but quickly shifts to condemning those who have "slipped in." This somewhat bombas-tic condemnation is only relieved in the final section, by which time many readers have had enough. Yet, as we will see, Jude is a significant work for how it portrays the faith, what it criticizes and why, and finally for the response that it counsels. It may be last in the General Epistles, but is hardly least. In fact, it was significant enough that 2 Peter would use it as the basis for over one third of his work. For some that is another reason to neglect Jude and go directly to the "latest version," 2 Peter, but, as we will see, while 2 Peter has adapted Jude, he has not replaced the work. Jude retains his own voice, and that voice needs to be heard.

5.1 Recent Scholarship

While Jude has always had a small but significant place in Catholic scholarship, and while it has been dutifully covered in Protestant commentary series (one thinks, for example, of Charles Bigg's 1902 work in the ICC series, *St. Peter and St. Jude*), it was really Richard Bauckham's 1983 contribution to the Word Biblical Commentary, *Jude, 2 Peter*, that set the stage for modern interpretation.

This is true for several reasons. First, Bauckham was writing for a world that was no longer afraid of apocalyptic and eschatology, as had been the case for much of the twentieth century. Second, Bauckham showed that there was enough material in these works to write a substantial commentary on them without including 1 Peter. Third, Bauckham argued for Jude being late in the first century, but still being the authentic voice of a brother of Jesus; he could maintain this combination because he argued (as Calvin had suspected, but rejected because of his faith in the post-Nicene fathers) that 2 Peter is a later testament of Peter, not a writing by Simon Peter himself. Bauckham was aided in his positioning of Jude by an interest in first-century Jewish or Palestinian Christianity that had peaked by the time he wrote. He followed up his commentary with his *Jude and the Relatives of Jesus in the Early Church,*[1] which showed there was an abiding interest in Jesus' relatives in the first centuries of the church, so the preservation of a work by one of them is not surprising.

Once Bauckham produced his commentary, there were a number of other works written on Jude that increased our knowledge of the work. Duane F. Watson applied rhetorical criticism to the work in his dissertation.[2] Jude was no longer just an addition at the end of the New Testament, but a fascinating rhetorical contribution. This also helped one realize that the bombast of the letter may have been as much rhetorically driven (Asiatic rhetoric rather than Attic rhetoric) as anything else. This contribution was followed by J. Daryl Charles showing in his thesis that Jude in particular (rather than the 2 Peter-Jude pair as a whole) is a fascinating work as a piece of literature, using highly involved structures.[3] Jude was worth reading for its beauty, even if one had issues (which Charles did not) with the content.

There were also those who had issues with the content, or at least with the mirror reading of that content to get an accurate description of those whom Jude opposes. Michael Desjardins argued that Jude is using rhetorical tropes, which should be read as standard criticisms of those whom one opposes rather than as accurate descriptions.[4] This concern that the critiques are more style than content has continued, with many scholars being skeptical that there is anything known about those whom Jude opposes. Ruth Anne Reese took a moderating position on this issue in her published thesis.[5] One seemingly minor contribution of her work that was more important than it looked was her terming those whom Jude opposes the "others" rather than "false teachers"; that latter description is a reading back of 2 Peter into Jude, a failure to recognize that 2 Peter is adapting Jude to a somewhat different situation. She also noted that despite his rhetorical fireworks, Jude actually calls for the rescue of the "others" rather than their consignment to destruction.

Note that Reese's work is a theological reading of 2 Peter and Jude, and it is theological readings that have tended to predominate in recent scholarship. One thinks of Catherine Cunsalus González's theological commentary.[6] This is not a short work like Chester Andrew and Ralph P. Martin's *The Theology of the Letters of*

1. Richard J. Bauckham, *Jude and the Relatives of Jesus in the Early Church* (Edinburgh: T&T Clark, 1990).

2. Duane F. Watson, *Invention, Arrangement and Style: Rhetorical Criticism of Jude and 2 Peter* (SBLDS 104; Scholars, 1988).

3. J. Daryl Charles, *Literary Strategy in the Epistle of Jude* (Scranton, PA: University of Scranton Press, 1993).

4. Michael Desjardins, "The Portrayal of the Dissidents in 2 Peter and Jude: Does It Tell Us More about the 'Godly' Than the 'Ungodly'?" *JSNT* 30 (1987): 89–102.

5. Ruth Anne Reese, *Writing Jude: The Reader, the Text, and the Author in Constructs of Power and Desire* (BIS 51; Leiden: Brill, 2000); she followed this with her commentary, *2 Peter and Jude* (THNTC; Grand Rapids: Eerdmans, 2007).

6. Catherine Cunsalus González, *1 & 2 Peter and Jude: A Theological Commentary on the Bible* (Belief; Louisville: Westminster John Knox, 2010).

James, Peter and Jude, but more like Pheme Perkins's *First and Second Peter, James, and Jude*.[7] Lately there is the masterful commentary by the conservative evangelical scholar Gene L. Green,[8] which in a gracious way brings many of the streams of thought on Jude together.

There have been a number of sociologically informed or social-rhetorical works on Jude. The late Jerome Neyrey did the Anchor Bible commentary on 2 Peter and Jude, which was groundbreaking in this regard.[9] One should not forget Ben Witherington III's *Letters and Homilies for Jewish Christians*.[10] Finally, the more cutting-edge readings of Jude may be found in a book edited by Robert L. Webb and Peter H. Davids.[11]

The text of Jude is also difficult, so we have welcomed the contribution to this field written by Charles Landon.[12] While not the focus of this present work, with fewer early manuscripts than much of the New Testament, Jude presents significant challenges in textual criticism.

5.2 Introductory Issues

5.2.1 Authorship, Date, and Historical Context

5.2.1.1 Authorship

As noted above, Jude has not so much been argued over as ignored, and, with the exception of Richard Bauckham's work, the man himself has been given an undeserved obscurity. The letter attributes itself to "Jude, slave of Jesus the Anointed One, and brother of James." There is a consensus that the "brother of James" part identifies the putative author as the brother of that James who led the community of Jesus-followers in Jerusalem (and thus for many, the whole Jesus movement) from at least 40 CE until his execution in 62 CE. That would make Jude the younger brother of Jesus; in the lists of Jesus' brothers James is always listed first and Jude is listed last (Matt 13:55) or next to last (Mark 6:3). But note that neither Jude nor James mentions a family relationship between them and Jesus[13]

The name itself, Judah (in Hebrew or Aramaic—Jude or Judas is the Greek form), is unremarkable, especially for a Jewish family that claimed Bethlehem in

7. Chester Andrew and Ralph P. Martin, *The Theology of the Letters of James, Peter and Jude* (Cambridge: Cambridge University Press, 1994; Pheme Perkins, *First and Second Peter, James, and Jude* (Interpretation; Louisville: John Knox, 1995).

8. Gene L. Green, *Jude and 2 Peter* (BECNT; Grand Rapids: Baker Academic, 2008).

9. Jerome Neyrey, *2 Peter, Jude* (AB 37C; New York: Doubleday, 1993).

10. Ben Witherington III, *Letters and Homilies for Jewish Christians: A Socio-Rhetorical Commentary on Hebrews, James and Jude* (Downers Grove, IL: InterVarsity Press, 2007).

11. Robert L. Webb and Peter H. Davids, ed., *Reading Jude with New Eyes: Methodological Reassessments of the Letter of Jude* (London: T&T Clark/Continuum, 2008).

12. Charles Landon, *A Text-Critical Study of the Epistle of Jude* (JSNTSup 135; Sheffield: Sheffield Academic, 1996).

13. The Catholic tradition since Jerome, of course, understands the term *adelphos* (ἀδελφός) as indicating a cousin, the men being sons of Mary wife of/daughter of Clopas, who was a relative of the Virgin Mary (some have said "sister," but while two cousins named Mary would not be surprising, two sisters would be). While this is not the first choice of a gloss for *adelphos*, it is possible (as is "relative") and has in its favor that neither implied author mentions a filial relationship to Jesus.

Judah as its ancestral home. Jude differentiates himself from other leaders in the Jesus movement of the same name — Judah son of James (Luke 6:16; Acts 1:13) and of course Judah son of Simon Iscariot (John 6:71) — in that he never claims to have been sent on a mission by Jesus (before or after Jesus' resurrection) and thus does not call himself an official delegate (apostle). In fact, like James (Jas 1:1) and like Paul in his less controversial letters (Rom 1:1; Phil 1:1; Titus 1:1 and by implication in Gal 1:10), Jude calls himself Jesus' slave, but this is a statement of authority, especially since in all of these contexts Jesus is coupled with a title of royal authority, [God's] "Anointed One" [or Anointed King, i.e., Messiah, Christos].

A slave had no status in society, but if one were a slave of an exalted personage, one had the status of that person insofar as he represented him or her. Neither James of the letter of James nor Jude of the letter of Jude uses the title that would later be given to them, "brother of the Lord,"[14] nor is there evidence that Jesus' family ever themselves made use of their relationship to Jesus, although there is clear evidence that others did recognize and revere it.[15] Instead, they use a title of personal self-deprecation ("slave"), which free people generally avoided, but couple it with "of Jesus the Anointed One," that turns it into a title of authority insofar as they are operating within Jesus' rescript. Any follower of Jesus might use such a title if Jesus gave him a job to carry out, but in doing so one makes it clear that one is not operating under the authority of the emperor or other high official, Roman or Jewish, but is serving an alternative kingdom. This is the language of the first-century Jesus movement, for by the second century we find more exalted language used for the family of Jesus. Jude's simple "brother of James" lets everyone know that the putative author is in Jesus' family, nuclear or extended, for there was only one James who was that well known in the Jesus movement. That much is clear.

But did this brother of Jesus actually write this letter? Naturally, one could simply take a fideistic approach and say, "Jude 1:1 says Jude, the brother of James, wrote it, and I will believe that that is accurate," or a church tradition approach and say, "The leaders of the church had decided by the end of the fourth century that Jude had written this, and I accept their decision." Given the paucity of information about Jude, neither of these is a bad approach, but assuming that we do not choose simply to take the ascription to Jude at face value and want *evidence* that Jude is the one who wrote the letter, we have a much more difficult question.

Jesus was born in or before 4 BCE, the death of Herod the Great. We do not know when his siblings (or cousins) were born, but if we allow that Mary (whichever Mary it may be) had a child approximately every two years (not unusual spacing for a woman who is breastfeeding each child for two or three years), that if the Mary was Mary of Cleopas she started childbearing about the same time as

---

14. Paul uses the title "brother" or "relative" (in the Catholic view) "of the Lord" for James in Gal 1:19, so it does appear relatively early, depending on one's view of the date of Galatians. It becomes a common designation later, for it helps separate him from the others in the New Testament with the name James. Paul, of course, was never a part of the Jerusalem or even the Palestinian community of the followers of Jesus, so his usage may not reflect local usage.

15. See Bauckham, *Jude and the Relatives of Jesus in the Early Church*, for a book-length discussion of the role that Jesus' relatives played in the Jesus movement.

the Virgin Mary, and that mixed in among Jesus' brothers were at least two sisters, Jude was probably born between 7 and 10 CE.[16] If there were more sisters or if the time between births was longer, Jude could have been born several years later. If the 7 to 10 CE birth is accurate, then Jude, about whom there is no tradition of martyrdom, could have lived to 90 CE and still only have been eighty—old for those days, but not an unknown age.[17] This is not to say that Jude did live this long, but only that one could date the work in the 80s and still reasonably attribute it to Jude. Any earlier date for the work would make the attribution to Jude that much easier.

The real issue with Jude, then, in terms of authorship, is not the date of Jude's life or the self-designation of the author, but the style of the work. Jesus is presented in our literature as the son of a Galilean peasant, a landless artisan. We would expect this family to speak Greek, not least because the major building project near Nazareth during the period in which Jesus was growing up was the Gentile town of Sepphoris/Zippori, where interaction with the foremen would have been in Greek. Furthermore, in Galilee in general the trade language was Greek. Thus there is little question but that Jude and the rest of Jesus' brothers could function in Greek. Yet, as anyone knows who has lived where there is a dominant group speaking one language and a nondominant group that has another language, but has learned to function in the language of the dominant group, being able to function practically in a second language does not mean literary skill in that language, even in a country with universal public education.[18]

In the case of Jude we are talking about a time period in which perhaps 10 or at most 20 percent of the population were educated, and even fewer were scribally literate. Jude was a younger, perhaps the youngest son of a peasant family, so it is unlikely that he received any education other than a practical education.[19] It may not be a coincidence that Hegesippus presents Jude's grandsons as simple peasant farmers, even if the account is more legendary than historical. Naturally, one cannot know for certain that Jude did not receive any education, but that is certainly what

---

16. In primary focus of this sentence and what follows we are obviously assuming the Helvidian theory of Jesus' siblings, that is, that they were actual children of Joseph and Mary, not the Epiphanian, namely that they were Joseph's children from a previous marriage and thus older than Jesus, which idea informs the *Protevangelium of James.* The Hieronymian theory makes them cousins of Jesus, children of the mother of Jesus' sister, Mary daughter of Clopas and Alphaeus. These theories are discussed in some detail by Pierre-Antoine Bernheim, *James, Brother of Jesus* (London: SCM, 1997), 14–29. In our view the easiest reading of the data of the text makes them Jesus' siblings, while church-traditional views about the Mary's perpetual virginity (and, in the case of the Hieronymian theory, Joseph's virginity as well) create the other views, which are possible, if not as easy readings of the text. There would be little change to the basic argument on authorship if one were to opt for the Hieronymian theory.

17. Hegesippus mentions grandsons of Jude living in Domitian's

reign (81–96 CE), according to Eusebius (*Eccl. hist.* 3.19–20). No mention is made of either Jude's being alive or his presumed sons. But admittedly, the whole narrative sounds legendary in that it connects the event to the cessation of Domitian's persecution and presents Domitian as not being concerned with the grandsons' claims of an eschatological kingdom. It does, interestingly enough, present these grandsons as Palestinian peasant farmers.

18. Thus we agree with Witherington, *Letters and Homilies for Jewish Christians,* 565, that Galilee was bilingual, but not that this would mean that the typical peasant had any literary skill or spoke Greek without a strong accent.

19. J. Daryl Charles ("Literary Artifice in the Epistle of Jude," *ZNW* 82 [1991]: 118) points out that Galilee produced a number of well-educated individuals, not least the historian Josephus, but this begs the point, for there is no claim that Galilee lacked educational resources, just that literary education was not widespread and that it was the upper classes who received it.

we would expect.[20] So we have the situation of a work that is full of wordplays, alliteration, and other skillful rhetorical devices, all in Greek and none of which would work in Hebrew or Aramaic,[21] yet the book is attributed to a person whom we would not expect to be educated.[22] How could the man Jude write the Greek of Jude?

If one says, "An amanuensis helped him," then one has at least an unknown ghostwriter and perhaps the real literary author of the work, with Jude's giving a bit of basic direction, depending on how much freedom one thinks that the amanuensis had (which in turns depends on how well educated one thinks that Jude was). Thus we may well be discussing a work whose essential author is unknown even if Jude were the author in a technical sense. Yet, let us be clear, this whole discussion is based on probabilities: we know the author was skilled in Greek, and we know something about what level of education the average Galilean peasant would have. We know how amanuenses were used. We know nothing about Jude's biography. Decent Greek education was available in Galilee, but we do not know whether Jude was the exceptional peasant who somehow gained access to it. Probabilities do not equal realities.

Yet is it likely that the work is pseudonymous? We do not think so. Jude appears to speak to a specific situation, so it is hardly the work of someone wanting to influence the whole Jesus movement. And while the person Jude may have been known within the Palestinian Jesus movement, he was certainly not known outside of the area. Even within that area there were bigger names, such as that of James. If one wanted to have influence using a pseudonymous letter, why not use a name that carried real authority—James, perhaps, or Peter, or (in the right circles) Paul? Jude? "Who's he?" "He's the brother of James." "That's nice; I will speak respectfully about him, but I'd rather hear from James." The improbability of the implied author is probably the strongest historical argument that this work actually has Jude son of Joseph (or Alphaeus) behind it. There seems to be no good reason for someone writ-

---

20. There are situations in which someone whom one would not expect to have any education has by some fluke of fate received an education, for example, by having helped a wealthy or educated individual who then paid for their education or personally tutored them. There are also situations in which a person of a lower class taught themselves to read (e.g., Absalom Jones, an African-American slave in the USA). But these situations are rare, so not something that one can give a probability to, and they can only be known by having a detailed biography of the individual or, perhaps, of their benefactor. We do not have these in the case of Jude, so we realize that we are talking in terms of probabilities, not known actualities. Also, Jude differs from Absalom Jones in that books were not as available in the first century as in the eighteenth century.

21. Richard J. Bauckham, *Jude, 2 Peter* (WBC 50; Waco, TX: Word, 1983), does believe that Jude shows evidence that he knows the Hebrew form of some passages from the Hebrew Scriptures and the Aramaic form of parts of *1 Enoch*; however, our evaluation is that while this is possible, it is far from proved. See Peter H. Davids, *The Letters of 2 Peter and Jude* (PNTC; Grand Rapids: Eerdmans, 2006), 26. And given that it is possible, it would show exposure

to Hebrew, such as one might get by hearing it in the synagogue, which leaves open the question of whether one were able to read it oneself. Thus this says more about the provenance of the work than the authorship.

22. It is also true that the Jesus movement was centered in Jerusalem for the first period of its existence, that Jerusalem had Greek educational facilities to match its many residents and visitors who were Greek-speaking, and that the students of rabbis like Gamaliel (e.g., Paul) studied Greek thought as well as Torah. But, as anyone knows who has tried to pick up literary skill in a second language as an adult, gaining literary skill is a different task than basic communication in the language. Furthermore, the sense that Jesus might return soon, the need to evangelize as widely as possible, and the needs of a growing community of believers would hardly have given any of the early leaders time for extensive study. Significantly, Jude is only said by tradition to have been a missionary in Galilee rather than further afield, where he would have had to speak Greek exclusively and where people were not used to Greek being spoken with a Galilean accent.

ing under a pseudonym to choose Jude; there would be good reasons not to choose Jude, for the author of such a letter in any area where Jude was known as uneducated (assuming he was uneducated), and also good reasons for choosing a better known leader (even a deceased leader, such as James).

5.2.1.2 Date

Having seen that it is questionable that a pseudepigraphic author would pick the name "Jude" out of the air, there is the further question of when the work was written. The fact is that we have precious little information to go on. The problem that is being addressed could have arisen relatively early in the history of the Jesus movement or decades later. No historical clues are given. There is no reference to any ruler, to any war, to any Jewish leader, to any Christian leader (except James, and in that case there is no information as to whether he is alive or deceased), to the temple, or to the temple's having been destroyed. Our informed guesses to the date of this work are just that, informed guesses, built on inferences that we make from what information we possess.

First, we note that Jude refers to "the faith" in vv. 3 and 20. While this expression can be found in the late 40s and 50s, especially in contexts of opposition and defense (1 Cor 16:13; 2 Cor 13:5; Gal 1:23; Phil 1:27), most references are in later New Testament works: Acts 13:8; 14:22, Heb 4:14 ("the confession"), and thirteen times in the Pastoral Letters. Of course, the date of the Pastoral Letters is also debated, but at the earliest they are late in Paul's life (i.e., the mid-60s CE). Given that Hebrews and Acts are probably from the 70s (or later), this linguistic evidence should make us guess at a later date for Jude, perhaps around the time of the Pastoral Letters, rather than an earlier one, although it does not make an early date impossible.

Second, there is also the evidence that those originally evangelizing the community being addressed are no longer present. In Jude 17 our author refers to what "the official delegates (apostles) of our Lord Jesus the Anointed One predicted." That says a lot less than we might wish. It indicates that they had heard certain predictions from people commissioned by Jesus to carry his message. This group included the Twelve, but it also included Paul, Barnabas, James, and numerous others who believed that Jesus had commissioned them to carry his message. In Rom 16:7 Paul can refer to a group of such people who know, respect, and include Andronicus and Junia—thus a group certainly far wider than the Twelve.

In *Did.* 11.3–6 we find that such individuals are common enough in the second-century community that the addressees need to know how to discern the true from the false claimants to this title. Given that no honorific title is used with "official delegates," such as "holy [apostles]," we are probably not talking about the later period (i.e., the second century and later) when the earlier delegates of Jesus had started to be specially revered. And given that the addressees are to remember what these missionaries, probably the founders of this particular community of the faithful, had predicted, it is likely that these church planters are no longer around.

But this does not mean that they are dead, nor does it say much about the community. For example, Paul rarely stayed long in the communities he founded, and in no case does he spend longer than three years in residence. By the end of the 50s he had made his farewell predictions to all of his believing communities (see, e.g., Acts 14:22; 20:29 – 30), intending to leave the eastern half of the Mediterranean and to travel on through Rome to the western half, specifically Spain. The fact that he instead spent some years in prison, arriving in Rome in chains, does not negate the fact that in his mind he was past tense with respect to those communities that we know he had founded.

Now we do not know whether all missionaries traveled as quickly as Paul did, and we know nothing about who those were who founded the particular community addressed in Jude. But that means that we can draw little information from the clause calling the community to remember other than that their community is not newly founded; it is old enough that the missionaries Jesus sent to evangelize them have said their farewells and left,[23] either as part of the evangelistic plan ("This community is mature enough; time to move on to a fresh area") or as part of necessity ("We are getting out of town before they come for us"). Paul shows us that that could be relatively quick at an early stage of the Jesus movement (Acts 14:22 is at the end of his first missions journey), yet since everyone probably did not plant and release communities as quickly as Paul did, it could also be significantly later.

Third, we do know that our author does not seem to have any problem citing Second Temple literature such as *1 Enoch* and the *Testament of Moses*, which indicates he has not lost touch with the Jewish roots of the movement (about which we will have more to say later). That again would place him in the first century. This is consistent with the fact that he also does not seem to have a problem with those he opposes over Christology, which is assumed rather than discussed, nor does he discuss church structure. Both of these are more second-century concerns.

So we can root Jude relatively firmly in the second half of the first century, but there is nothing in this letter that would prevent us from dating it earlier or later within this period. This whole period is also well within the possible lifetime of the putative author. Beyond that we cannot be any more specific other than to say that, since we have argued that 2 Peter uses Jude, Jude must have been written before 2 Peter, without specifying whether that "before" means two years or twenty years.

5.2.1.3 Addressees

Can we gain any more specificity by looking at the addressees? They seem to be a community known to the author, and to the degree that this is true, Jude is not really a "General" or "Catholic" letter, just a letter whose addressees are not identifiable. We say this because, while the address itself is general enough, the

---

23. Luke places the types of warnings that Jude 17 refers to in farewell discourses (Acts 14:22; 20:29 – 30); if he is accurate (and at the least he is telling us when such things *should* ideally be said), he may be reflecting a widespread perception that such warnings were the appropriate things to say upon leaving.

situation the letter speaks to is specific: "certain intruders have stolen in among you" (Jude 4, NRSV). The faithful members, whom Jude presents as the majority, apparently including the leadership, are frequently termed "beloved" (vv. 3, 17, 20). This term "beloved" is language that Jude shares with the other Catholic Epistles, including the Johannine ones, for, while the term occurs in the main Pauline letters (other than Galatians) and also occurs in Hebrews, it is rarer in that literature even before considering the massive size differences. For example, Romans has two similar usages of "beloved" as a noun of address; to match Jude's relative frequency it would need forty-eight. In this work we will use Jude's terminology and refer to these addressees as the "beloved."

The "beloved" are, at least in the mind of the author, familiar with Second Temple literature, for Jude can refer to such narratives without identifying the literature and expect the "beloved" to have at least a vague familiarity. In fact, as we will discuss below, all of the references to narratives found in the Hebrew Scriptures are probably from Second Temple literature, since, where checkable, they contain details not found in the Hebrew Scriptures themselves. But there is no indication of whether the "beloved" are ethnically Jews or Gentiles. They are Greek-speaking and show no indication of knowing Aramaic or Hebrew. Jude appears to think that they will appreciate or at least be influenced by his rhetoric, which relies on, among other things, wordplays and repeated sounds, so he must think of them as verbally sophisticated. They meet around meals, which Jude refers to as "love meals" (Jude 12), although this is probably no different from the rest of the early Jesus movement, which seems to have met in the context of a reenactment of the Last Supper.

We do not know where these people are located. Given the association of Jesus' family with Palestine, we might guess that that territory (or the surrounding countries) was also the location of the community. That would be no problem if Jude were written in the 50s or early 60s. However, after 66 CE there was significant disruption in Palestine, including the reported withdrawal of the bulk of the Jesus movement from Jerusalem and Judea to Pella in what is now Jordan. Thus, if one thinks of Jude as later than 66, one could argue for Antioch in Syria or Alexandria in Egypt (to name larger centers—the addressees seem urban, but they are not necessarily in the largest urban centers), for one would expect that the authority of James, Jude, and possibly other members of Jesus' family extended over the whole eastern end of the Mediterranean. Antioch in Syria makes a bit more sense than Alexandria, for that makes it easier to explain how the work came to the attention of a Petrine circle, since we know that Peter had influence there.[24] But these are educated guesses at best. The climatic and other geographic references in the letter probably come from the LXX. Even if these references are from the experience of

---

24. We will say "Petrine circle" since the authorship and dating of 2 Peter is so controversial. If 2 Peter is in some sense by Simon Peter himself, then Jude has to have been recognized as significant and sent on to Peter or Peter's ghostwriter, since by 60 CE Peter was in Rome, if the tradition connecting him to Rome is correct. If 2 Peter is a testament of Peter written by someone in the name of Peter, then one has more time, but still someone for whom "Peter" was their inspiration needed to have come across Jude. What is clear is that stylistically 2 Peter and Jude are similar; they have more than just content in common.

the author, they would at any rate fit the whole eastern end of the Mediterranean except Egypt.

Jude does not seem to have circulated widely. The earliest references to it come in the fathers from the southeastern Mediterranean. The earliest manuscripts with it included come from the same area. This may also suggest the area in which the original addressees lived.

5.2.1.4 The "Others" and the Historical Context

It is clear that Jude is written to oppose the influence of a group or movement within the larger community of the followers of Jesus. Often these have been termed "false teachers," but that is to import 2 Pet 2:1 into Jude. Jude never refers to those he critiques as teachers; in fact, the few references to their speech (Jude 8, 10, 16 and in quotations that may or may not be intended to indicate their assertions, vv. 15, 18) do not indicate any teaching role. It is their behavior, including verbal grumbling and the like, that is the issue, not their teaching. Second Peter does use Jude, but he adapts the critique in Jude to his own situation.

Because we do not know whether those Jude critiques are teachers, we will follow Ruth Anne Reese in terming these people the "others."[25] Within modern New Testament scholarship these "others" have often been called Gnostics.[26] However, in order to be even gnosticizing, let alone full-blown Gnostics, one would expect some reference to their claims of knowledge and some mention of body-spirit dualism. The only reference to knowledge or wisdom in Jude is Jude 10, which does not indicate any claims to knowledge by the "others." And while their licentiousness has been taken as evidence of antinomianism, there is no indication that this was based on a rejection of the body as evil or insignificant. We are not reading 1 John, where there are some of these indications, but Jude.

There are descriptions of the behavior of the "others," but we must ask how accurate these descriptions are. It was common in the ancient world to attribute evil behavior of various types to those you criticized. If their heads were in the wrong place, they must also be licentious, lazy, and larcenous. Are we not dealing with such negative *topoi* in Jude, *topoi* that give no real information about the "others?" One should not rule out the possibility that this is partially the case, that the criticisms would be recognized as the rhetoric of condemnation; yet we immediately note that in Jude these *topoi* are *not* used to show that people holding certain ideas or positions are also immoral. Rather, these people "pervert God's favor into *permission for* licentious behavior" and "*by their behavior* [since that is all that is mentioned] deny our only Master and Lord, Jesus the Anointed One" (Jude 4).

Given that it would not fit the teaching of Jesus to denounce someone without

---

25. Ruth Anne Reese, *2 Peter and Jude* (THNTC; Grand Rapids: Eerdmans, 2007), 24.

26. See Charles Bigg, *A Critical and Exegetical Commentary on the Epistles of St. Peter and St. Jude* (ICC; Edinburgh: T&T Clark,

1902), 312–20, where he refers to a number of scholars who hold Jude to be opposing Gnosticism (and also gives his reasons for not accepting the Gnostic background).

some basis, it appears that something about their behavior gave rise to the charge that these "others" were licentious. Of course, whether a charge is accurate depends on the standards by which one judges; what may be a horrific murder to one culture may be honorable behavior in another—indeed the only way to restore the honor of the clan or family. Some of King David's exploits in 2 Samuel would be considered war crimes today.[27] Furthermore, perceptions of behavior and especially the rumors that one hears about the behavior of those one rejects for one reason or another are to some degree subjective.

What we know about these "others" is that Jude considers them outsiders. They have "crept into" the community (Jude 4), so they are from the outside. This description hardly means that the "others" thought of themselves as coming into the community under false pretenses, but that Jude sees them as coming into the community without really being a part of it—specifically without their being part of it in terms of behavior that Jude identifies with Jesus' functioning as Lord and Master. These behavioral standards are not necessarily ones that the community Jude addresses found strange even before their commitment to Jesus as Lord. We do not know, since we do not know their background. What we know is that there is no need on Jude's part to defend the standards to the "beloved."

In other words, we have a type of culture clash. The "beloved" generally live within (or at least affirm) certain behavioral standards that they identify with Jesus. These "others" have entered their community, either as new converts or as those coming from another type of community in the Jesus movement. They have not conformed to the behavioral standards of the community of the "beloved" and have apparently defended their behavior by criticizing the angelic mediators of the Torah. Some of the noncore original members of the community (whom Jude describes as less stable) are attracted to the "others'" way of life. We do not know the details. Jude describes it in generalities. But at least one possible scenario would be a group of individuals (i.e., the "others") who were very much at home in the Greco-Roman world becoming part of a believing community that was comfortable with Jewish ethical standards.

The community does not necessarily consist of ethnic Jews, nor was it necessarily Torah observant—there were Gentiles attracted to Judaism because of its ethic, Gentiles who never became proselytes and who later became followers of Jesus because he did not demand that they become Jewish proselytes. But the community does know Jewish stories and the "beloved" do affirm the basically Jewish ethic of Jesus. The "others" are not accepting that ethic that they view as the imposition of Torah. Their definition of living in divine favor allows for them to continue certain Greco-Roman behaviors that Jude finds scandalous. We cannot say that such a scenario is the reality that Jude is experiencing, but we can say that it fits the behavior that he describes and that similar types of culture clashes have recurred down

---

27. E.g., 2 Sam 8:2; also 2 Samuel 21's report of the execution of Saul's grandsons for the evil Saul had done.

through the ages right up to the present, as a type of culture clash that Paul was deal-ing with in 1 Corinthians 6 and also 8 – 10 (which means as early as the mid-50s).

5.2.2 Literary Style

Jude is a letter in that it has a typical letter salutation ("Jude ... to x ... mercy, peace, and love"), a letter body, and a two-verse doxology as an ending. Furthermore, it is short, which is what letters were supposed to be in the ancient world. However, the recipients are not specifically named and the body of the letter is short on details about either the "beloved" or the "others." Also, while doxologies are found in the final verse of some Pauline letters (Rom 16:27; Phil 4:20; 2 Tim 4:18; cf. Heb 13:20 – 21; 2 Pet 3:18), Jude has none of the other elements of a letter ending, such as a summary, a purpose statement, greetings, or a health wish (or prayer). Because of this Richard Bauckham has suggested that Jude's body is "more like a homily than a letter" in that it is more like a midrash on certain texts followed by a paraenetic section.[28]

While we will argue that Jude is more of a midrash on Jewish narratives than on Scripture texts in that in most cases the author does not seem dependent on either the Greek translation or the Hebrew text of the Hebrew Scriptures, and while we have shown above that ending with a doxology is well known in other first-century Christian letters, Bauckham does have a point. The rhetoric of Jude is more like a homily than a letter in that it leaves out specifics and seems more to address the individuals than to dialogue with them. There is a sort of a text-and-application style to it. But we must remember that there was no fixed rhetorical form for the body of a letter in the first century. Thus it was appropriate for someone writing a letter to use a homiletic style in the body so long as they had a proper letter opening and closing. This is what Jude seems to do.

Within the basic structure, which he punctuates by addressing the "beloved," Jude's rhetoric is that of deliberative rhetoric, as Watson has shown; that is, Jude is calling his readers to a decision. The outline looks like this:[29]

A. Letter Opening: Salutation/Epistolary Prescript (vv. 1 – 2)
B. Letter Body (vv. 3 – 23)
    1. Body opening (vv. 3 – 4)
        a. *Exordium* (purpose) (v. 3)
        b. *Narratio* (shared assumptions) (v. 4)
    2. Body Proper/*Probatio* (arguments) (vv. 5 – 16)
        a. First proof (vv. 5 – 10)
        b. Second proof (vv. 11 – 13)
        c. Third proof (vv. 14 – 16)
    3. Body Closing/*Peroratio* (Concluding Exhortation) (vv. 17 – 23)
C. Letter Closing: Doxology (vv. 24 – 25)

---

28. Bauckham, *Jude, 2 Peter*, 3.
29. In order to bring out both the letter structure and the rhetori-cal structure, we have merged the outlines of Davids and Watson from Davids, *2 Peter and Jude*, 23 – 24. Watson's outline is found in its original context in Watson, *Invention, Arrangement, and Style*, 77 – 78.

Within this structure Jude loves rhetorical repetition. His most prominent features are the two triplets: (1) exodus–divine messengers who abandoned their position–Sodom/Gomorrah (vv. 5–7); and (2) Cain–Balaam–Korah (v. 11). But there are also triplets of nouns or verbs in vv. 1, 2, 8, 15, 19, 22–23, and a four-part series in vv. 12–13. We should think of these series as building up a composite picture of what is being discussed, not of discussing discrete elements.

Jude's vivid imagery brings eighteen new words into New Testament vocabulary. Most of these are not rare in Greek literature as a whole; they just indicate that Jude had a good Greek vocabulary. At the same time his literary expression is influenced by "Bible Greek"; that is, he has Semitisms that come from his familiarity with the Hebrew Scriptures in Greek. Yet there is no place where Jude actually quotes either the Greek or the Hebrew forms of the Scriptures.[30]

On the linguistic level Jude is similar to 2 Peter (and both are dissimilar to 1 Peter). Paul (and 1 Peter as well) uses many relative clauses and tends to have long sentences with clause chained on to clause. Jude uses few relative clauses, but he does use a lot of participles. His sentences are shorter than Paul's. In other words, Jude's style is more rhetorical, more oral. His is not the restrained Attic style, though, but more the bombastic Asiatic style, a style that is much in evidence in 2 Peter.

What we have in Jude, then, is a writer with a decent basic Hellenistic education (unlike 80 to 90 percent of his contemporaries). He likely does not have advanced education, but he has mastered the basics and probably the *progymnasmata* (think of it as his having primary and at least some secondary education, but not having attended university). But this education has been combined with life in the community of Jesus' postresurrection followers. He has heard the Scriptures read; their reading has influenced the language of his community. As a result, Semitisms creep into his style. He is probably unaware of it. Conscious quotation would mean that he would have to be aware, but linguistic influence often operates on the unconscious level.

5.2.3 Use of 1 Enoch and Other Second Temple Literature

While Jude does not quote the Hebrew Scriptures in either their Hebrew or Greek form, he does quote a written source; that is, in Jude 14–15 he quotes *1 En.* 1.9. What form of the text Jude knew is debated, for in Jude 14 he appears closer to the Aramaic version (which is, unfortunately, fragmentary), while in Jude 15 he appears closer to the Greek version.[31] As was not uncommon in Christian writers quoting

---

30. Bauckham, *Jude, 2 Peter*, 7, thinks that there are some places Jude betrays knowledge of the Hebrew text: Jude 12/Ezek 34:2 and Prov 25:14 and Jude 13/Isa 57:20. Our analysis, however, shows that while it is clear that Jude is not referring to the LXX, it is not clear that he is referring to the Hebrew text. These are expressions that may have been proverbial or that are not really that close to the Hebrew text. Bauckham may be correct, but we do not believe that he has proved his case. See Davids, *2 Peter and Jude*, 26.

31. Bauckham (*Jude, 2 Peter*, 77–78) argues that Jude knew the Aramaic version, making it certain that he knew Aramaic and thus more likely (although not definite) that he also knew Hebrew. However, while Bauckham's argument is attractive, we do not believe it is proved because (1) Jude 15 is definitely closer to the Greek version; (2) the Aramaic text is fragmentary and so we lack the full quotation; and (3) Jude definitely alters the *1 Enoch* quotation in some places, so we cannot be sure that he has not done so in others, producing an artificial similarity in Jude 14. See the full discussion in Davids, *2 Peter and Jude*, 77–79.

texts, Jude alters the text so that it reads in relation to Jesus the Lord rather than in relation to God, as in *1 Enoch*. He also shortens it slightly, which has the effect of focusing it on the evildoers and their words rather than the "all flesh" of *1 Enoch* and both their words and deeds. Now it is true that Jude does not call this text a "writing" (often translated "Scripture," Greek *graphē*, γραφή), but he does call it a prophecy by saying that Enoch "prophesied." It is anachronistic to ask whether this was, then, part of his "Bible," for that assumes that he had a closed canon of Scripture, which we do not believe was true until the second or third century CE for Jews or the fourth century for Christians.

There is a consciousness of Law and Prophets in the New Testament and a realization that the Psalms did not fit into either section (e.g., Luke 24:27, 44), but that does not mean that the prophets were necessarily a closed entity or that there were not other works that should be venerated alongside the Psalms. We are left with some of that fuzziness, for since there is no evidence of a version of the LXX that did not include the Deuterocanonical books, we assume that those first-century believers who used the LXX (basically all of them that have left written records) also read these Deuterocanonical works without asking any questions. Jews would later reject them, but among Christians the Orthodox have always fully accepted them, while the Roman Catholic position only firmed up once some Reformation churches rejected them (for dogmatic reasons). But even then Luther thought they should be read, if not used to establish doctrine, and Anglicans included them in their liturgical readings.

In Jude's period such issues had yet to arise. While it was clear that the Torah was Scripture, the borders of the rest of Scripture were fuzzy (unless one was a Sadducee or a Samaritan who thought that only the Torah was Scripture). For Jude *1 Enoch* is inspired prophecy (e.g., Jude 14; v. 15 may pick up elements from *1 En.* 5.4 or 27.2). It is also clear that the narrative in Jude 6 is probably from *1 Enoch* in that we know that Jude knew *1 Enoch* and that *1 Enoch* has the material about the divine messengers that is not in Gen 6.

Jude also uses other Second Temple works. The best-known example is the narrative of Michael and the devil in Jude 9, which is clearly not from the Hebrew Scriptures as we know them, but which the church fathers tell us comes from the *Testament of Moses*, a work that we have discovered, but without its ending that would include this story, so we cannot check if the church fathers were correct. There are also details in the other five narratives mentioned in Jude that are in the Hebrew Scriptures that indicate that Jude is at least reading those narratives through the lenses of Second Temple literature, such as *Jubilees*, or traditions, such as those found in Josephus's writings.[32]

There is no evidence that Jude actually looked at the text of Scripture while writing his letter. This should not be surprising. First, a person in the first century

---

32. This is discussed in some detail in Peter H. Davids, "The Use of Second Temple Traditions in 1 and 2 Peter and Jude," in *The Catholic Epistles and the Tradition* (ed. Jacques Schlosser; BETL 176; Leuven: Peeters/Leuven University Press, 2004), 409–31

could be rhetorically skillful without being scribally literate. In other words, we do not know whether Jude could read.

Second, a person could also be able to read but not have scrolls of the Hebrew Scriptures available. Scrolls were expensive, so it is unlikely that they would be personally owned unless one were rich. Even whole communities of believers might not own all or even most scrolls of the Hebrew Scriptures (in either Greek or Hebrew). And even if one were writing in a place where the scrolls were available, finding the right one, unrolling it, and finding the right place would be a process that would interrupt the flow of thought with respect to writing.

Third, a person then, as now, often did not realize that the form of a narrative that was in their memory was the form it took in Second Temple literature (in our period, the equivalent would be the form in popular literature of various types). Contemporary literature, often more vivid or more fitting to the contemporary situation, colored the memory of the ancient text. Given that the ancient culture was an oral mnemonic culture, one would not be as likely to feel it necessary to "check out" one's memory by referring to the original text — or one might not have cared.[33] Whatever the case with Jude (we obviously cannot ask him about his state of mind as he wrote), it is clear that narratives he reports could have come entirely from Second Temple literature, either because those are the "glasses" through which he "sees" or remembers the narratives of Scripture or because those are the texts he has been reading or hearing.[34]

5.3 THEMATIC COMMENTARY

5.3.1 Letter Opening: Salutation/Epistolary Prescript (vv. 1–2)

Jude begins with the implied author identifying himself: Judas (Greek form of the Hebrew Judah; we traditionally use Jude to avoid confusion with other Judases in the New Testament). Since this was a common name among Jews, the author needs to identify himself further and so adds "slave of Jesus the Anointed One," indicating his standing in the Jesus community. While "slave" is often thought of as a humble title, it is to some degree anything but self-deprecating. That is, it indicated that one had no status in oneself, for a slave in Greco-Roman society was a zero on the

---

33. Memory is often viewed as a fixed entity, a physical encoding in neuronal structures, but recent memory studies have shown that even in the case of vivid eyewitness memories, memory is dynamic. Later retellings by the person slowly shift and shape it; differing versions that one hears also shape it (e.g., a different person telling the story, especially if the person is from one's group, or a person asking one questions about the story). We in our contemporary age are as concerned as we are about being right because we can often easily go back to written documents or photographic evidence. That concern was not totally absent in the ancient world, but it is much less in evidence. And often one is not conscious that there is an issue

that one needs to check out, especially if no one is challenging one's memory of a given story or event.

34. Jude appears to have been accepted by the church at first, as Jean Cantinat, *Les épitres de Saint Jacques et de Saint Jude* (Paris: Gabalda, 1973), 276–82, shows, but during this period *1 Enoch* was also valued. Later there were issues with Jude, sometimes because of his use of *1 Enoch*, but they were not enough to stop his eventual acceptance, even if objections were occasionally raised through the ages. See Gerald L. Bray, ed., *James, 1–2 Peter, 1–3 John, Jude* (ACCS; Downers Grove, IL: InterVarsity Press, 2000), 254–55, cf. 245.

honor scale, not really a person. But if one were an imperial slave or a slave of some other high official on the business of that person, one took on an authority derived from the one whose slave one was. This was also true in the Hebrew Scriptures, where Abraham's slave negotiates a wife for Isaac in Abraham's name (Gen 24), or Moses is called the "slave of Yahweh" (Deut 34:5; Josh 1:1). So Jude is indicating that he is an official in the service of a particular royal personage, Jesus. This is the promised divine ruler, or Messiah, that is, God's Anointed One (i.e., Christ, which is a transliteration of *christos*, Χριστός). Paul also introduces himself in this way in Rom 1:1; Phil 1:1; and Titus 1:1.

But there was at least one Judas among the Twelve besides Judas Iscariot (e.g., John 14:22; Acts 1:13), as well as certainly other leaders in the Jesus movement with that name. Thus Jude adds, "brother of James." There was only one James (or Jacob) that could be named so simply, and that was Jesus' younger brother, the leader of the mother community and thus to a large extent of the whole first-century Jesus movement.[35] So Jude is claiming to be not just any leader in the Jesus movement, but the younger brother of James himself, and thus a younger brother of Jesus, although within the New Testament neither James nor Jude mentions this relationship, perhaps because Jesus himself said his real family was that of his followers, not his blood family (Mark 3:13–35).

The recipients are not identified here by where they live, as is common in New Testament letters, but by their relationship to God. They are those who "are called"; that is, they are a chosen people even if they are ethnically Gentiles.[36] But who has called them? Two further descriptions relate them to the Father and to Jesus. First, they are "loved in God-Father"; second, they are "kept (or guarded) for Jesus the Anointed One."[37] Who is the agent of the calling, the loving, and the keeping? It is surely God himself: God calls, God loves them because they are in him, God guards or keeps them for Jesus his Anointed One. These virtues bracket the letter, for the "beloved" are to keep themselves in the love of God in Jude 21 (where the same verb for keeping and the noun form of loving are used), and God keeps them in the doxology in Jude 24 (although a synonym for the word here is used). We see, then, that these are those who are fully believers, and to be a believer is to be part of God's chosen or called people, to be "beloved" in God, and to be kept for one's sovereign, Jesus. This consciousness informs the whole letter.

Having identified author and recipients, Jude gives the third part of a proper letter opening, the greeting. It is more than the typical "[divine] favor" or "[divine]

---

35. While Paul has a big place in the New Testament, the evidence of his letters and the rest of the New Testament is that his influence outside the circle of churches he had founded was limited, even controversial, while leaders like James, Peter, and John—and certainly the first two of these three—had influence and were recognized as leaders in all segments of the first-century Jesus movement.

36. This is made explicit in the Syriac text and a few Greek manuscripts, which read, "To those called Gentiles," but it is implicit

in Jude's description in that one would not normally need to tell Jews that they were a called or chosen people and in that there is nothing in the text to indicate that the "beloved" have an ethnic Jewish origin.

37. Some translations have "loved by God the Father" and "guarded by Jesus." Those are possible meanings, and we find them attractive, but normal Greek grammar has another way of expressing "by," so it is our conclusion that "in" and "for" respectively are what Jude intended. See Davids, *2 Peter and Jude*, 37–38.

favor and peace (or well-being)"; it is tripartite, for Jude loves triplets: "mercy, peace, and love." Mercy suggests some type of neediness being met, for one showed it when giving to those in need as well as when not giving someone a punishment they deserved; peace, especially if our author is informed by the Jewish concept of shalom, suggests well-being; and love is the virtue that results in actions such as the granting of mercy or peace. Like most of Jude's triplets, this one forms a composite picture: Jude prays upon them the multiplication of God's divine favor.

5.3.2 Letter Body (vv. 3–23)

Having identified himself and greeted his recipients, Jude gets down to the "stuff" of the letter, that is, the letter body. As is frequent in ancient letters, there is an opening section, then a long discussion that forms the bulk of the body, and finally a closing exhortation that functions as a body closing. Each of these also serves a rhetorical purpose, for Jude is designed to be read aloud, as was typical for ancient letters, and so is designed for rhetorical performance more than silent reading.

5.3.2.1 Body Opening (vv. 3–4)

The body opening sets the stage for the rest of the letter, letting the recipients know what the letter is about (via a purpose statement) and then laying out assumptions that will inform the rest of the letter and that are shared with the addressees.

5.3.2.1.1 *Exordium* (Purpose) (v. 3)

Our author knows those to whom he writes and had intended to write to them concerning their "shared salvation (or shared deliverance)." We do not know what he intended to write about it or how he would describe it, but only that he was preparing to do so with eagerness or zeal. Does that mean that he was gathering his thoughts? Or does it mean that he was making arrangements for an amanuensis to come with his writing materials and perhaps also gathering the necessary funds to pay him? While it is likely that he was at least doing the latter, it is clear that especially in the ancient world letter-writing was a process, a process that took enough time that it could be interrupted.

This time the plan was indeed interrupted. "I had the necessity," writes Jude, "to write to you, appealing to you to exert intense effort on behalf of the commitment (or faith), that one which was handed over to God's holy ones once (for all)." On the one hand, Jude is demonstrating virtue (*aretē*), "the Greco-Roman ideal of dedication to the welfare of the larger group."[38] On the other hand, he indicates that in some way their faith is under attack and they must struggle (the verb "exert intense effort" suggests an athletic metaphor) to preserve their commitment. What the letter does not say is who or what one must struggle with. The addressees are never told

---

38. BDAG, 356, *epagōnizomai*, ἐπαγωνίζομαι. The demonstration of virtue is significant in that that is one of the things that 2 Peter believes is part of progress in one's commitment to Jesus (2 Pet 1:5).

to defeat or cast out someone, although they are told in the end to rescue someone. The focus seems to be on them, the "beloved" — *they* need to recognize compromise and its effects and *they* need to remain firm. So perhaps the main struggle is with themselves, with their own desires, as they are tempted to compromise their own behavior.

In other words, when one is committed to a particular dietary regime and someone offers something clearly out of bounds, the point is not to rebuke the other person and convict them of their dietary ignorance and perhaps their evil intentions, but rather to refuse to obey one's appetite, calm one's watering mouth, and hold true to one's commitment. That is the type of struggle with respect to the commitment to Jesus that Jude is addressing here.

5.3.2.1.2 *Narratio* (Shared Assumptions) (v. 4)

The reason this struggle is needed is that there are "others" in the group who were once not part of the group and who are living a lifestyle that denies the authority of Jesus over their lives. We are not told who these people are, only that they have snuck in, a term of rhetorical vituperation[39] that probably indicates that the "beloved" were unaware of their differences from these "others." This verse also perhaps indicates their gradual coming into the group, but that does not in its rhetorical usage mean that they consciously infiltrated. The "sneaking in" is the result, not the plan. But now the "beloved" have in their group these "others."

We are told precious little about these "others." Jude sees them, or at least their condemnation, predicted "long ago," probably in the Hebrew Scriptures or Second Temple literature, for he will cite such literature against them in the next paragraph. But this says little about the "others" except that he can find precedents of some type in this literature. He also notes that they are "impious," that is, "violating the norms for a proper relation to the deity."[40] What norms are they violating? No doctrinal issue is mentioned, but rather that the "others" are transforming God's favor into licentiousness — that is, "lack of self-constraint which involves one in conduct that violates all bounds of what is socially acceptable,"[41] although that raises the issue of which society is defining what is acceptable. This charge sounds at least like these "others" are saying that since God accepts them just as they are because of their belief in Jesus, their behavior does not matter.[42]

The second charge is in some ways implied in the first, namely, their denial of "our only Master and Lord Jesus the Anointed One." Since there is no indication in the rest of the letter that the "others" denied that Jesus is Lord, that he truly died on

---

39. Andreas B. du Toit, "Vilification as a Pragmatic Device in Early Christian Epistolography," *Bib* 75 (1994): 408–9.

40. BDAG, 141, *asebēs*, ἀσεβῆς.

41. BDAG, 141, *aselgeia*, ἀσέλγεια.

42. They might be under Pauline influence and saying that because they are rescued as a result of God's favor and not because of their following the Torah, they are free to live according to their desires. Paul finds it necessary to refute just such a warping of his teaching (Rom 3:8; 6:1, 15). However, we cannot be sure that Paul's is the teaching they are distorting, for there is no reference in Jude to the Torah or other critical terms in this debate. The only term in common here is divine favor (grace), and that is not an exclusively Pauline term.

the cross, that he rose from the dead, or that he is in fact God's promised Messiah (Anointed One), the issue does not seem be a doctrinal denial. Indeed, it is difficult to imagine how they could in any way be part of a community in the first-century Jesus movement without confessing verbally that Jesus is Lord, since that was the basic confession that defined the whole movement. But the term "Master" is typically used of a slave's master, whom the slave was expected to obey. Likewise "Lord" indicates a sovereign, one whom in Greco-Roman society one was also expected to obey. If one ignored the teaching of Jesus as the standard for life, one would be denying in practice that Jesus was "Master" and "Lord." And since Jesus certainly did not teach licentious behavior (if anything, a stricter standard of morality, at least in some respects, than the Pharisees), the "licentious" behavior of the "others" would indeed be a practical denial of Jesus. In our author's eyes, one does not gain God's favor through allegiance to Jesus without Jesus being in reality one's Master and Lord.[43]

Those are the two charges, and, given the place they have in the rhetoric of the letter (in the *narratio*), Jude assumes that the "beloved" agree with him that these "others" exist and that the community has a problem because of their behavior. Have the leaders of the community he is addressing informed him about these "others"? Or has someone "spilled the beans," as Cloe's people apparently did in the case of Corinth (1 Cor 1:11)? We do not know how Jude knows about the presence of these "others" or why he makes the assumption that his diagnosis of the problem is shared by the "beloved." We do know that Jude seems confident about his knowledge and that he puts this into the rhetorical place that assumes his view is shared by those he is addressing.

5.3.2.2 Body Proper/Probatio (Arguments) (vv. 5–16)

Having laid out the situation, Jude goes on to refute the idea that one can transform God's favor in Jesus into permission to transgress social norms, that is, that one does not need to follow Jesus' ethical teaching. These are arguments that the "beloved" can use, but which, realistically speaking, are aimed directly at the "others," in that a letter was read aloud to the community. These refutations or condemnations fall into three groups.

5.3.2.2.1 First Proof (vv. 5–10)

Jude makes the polite assumption that those hearing his letter are already familiar with the narratives of Israel, narratives that he derives from versions circulating in the Second Temple period. Thus he says, "I want to remind you, although you know everything. . . ." It may well be that the leaders of the community or even the whole community did know all the stories the author is about to cite, but it may also be that while knowing them, they were not reading them in the way he will now read

---

43. Could it be that the "others" argued that Jesus' teaching belonged to the old dispensation of the law? After all, it took place before his death and resurrection. We do not know, for we are never given the reasoning of the "others," but somehow they could be part of a group characterized by its confession of Jesus as Lord and justify their practical ignoring of his teaching.

them. He will point to three negative stories from the larger narrative of Israel and then one positive story. The "others," of course, are behaving more like the negative stories and are doing the opposite of the positive one.

First, the Lord (i.e., Jesus, the Lord mentioned in Jude 4 — some ancient manuscripts have even substituted "Jesus" for "Lord") saved or rescued a people from Egypt.[44] The language is probably deliberate: "saved" or "rescued" (Greek *sōzō*) is the verb that followers of Jesus used for their own rescue by Jesus; "a people" reminds the readers that they are also "a people," a people who are "called" or "chosen," as Jude says in v. 1. Furthermore, Jesus is made the agent, just as in the case of the addressees' deliverance. Only the "out of the land of Egypt" makes it clear that the story of Israel is being referred to.

But that story, now being read as the addressees' story, does not end on the edge of the Sea of Reeds. It is not clear which incident Jude is referring to — in fact, he may be referring to a number of incidents rolled together — but it is clear that those who rebelled against Yahweh, whether in the golden calf incident (which involved feasting and likely immoral behavior), or in the complaining about the manna, or in the refusal to follow Moses into the land after hearing the reports of the spies, or in a number of other incidents, all died. "Those who did not believe" (or, if the object of belief or commitment is personal, either Moses or Yahweh) — i.e., those who rebelled — the Lord destroyed. Read as a parallel to the history of the addressees, this historical precedent is a warning that "the Lord," who has saved them, will destroy those who fail to follow through on their commitment to him, just as Jude has charged that the "others" have done.

Second, "the divine messengers (angels) who did not protect or guard the domain or sphere of influence that belonged to them, but left their proper dwelling" is a reference to the Gen 6 narrative as reflected in *1 Enoch* 6 and 7. *First Enoch* 6:2 reads, "And the angels, the children of heaven, saw them and desired them; and they said to one another, 'Come, let us choose wives for ourselves from among the daughters of man and beget us children.'" What we have in that passage is the crossing of the species barrier, doing what is not appropriate for divine messengers. This transgression (and the text goes on to make it clear that the messengers knew that it was a transgression) is motivated by desire. So the text continues in *1 En.* 7:1, "And they took wives unto themselves, and everyone (respectively) chose one woman for himself, and they began to go unto them. And they taught them magical medicine, incantations, the cutting of roots, and taught them (about) plants."

The resulting offspring, whether because of their parentage or because of the incantations, were huge (450 feet high), like the Greek Titans. They consumed the produce of the earth and then turned against people, consuming them and oppress-

---

44. There is a "once for all" in the text, but it is unclear where it fits. Some manuscripts have it with their knowing, "you were once for all fully informed" or "you know everything once for all," while others have it with the rescue from Egypt, "the Lord once/once for all rescued a people from Egypt." The manuscript evidence is so evenly divided that the main evidence for where the "once" fits is not the manuscript evidence, but the "then" or "afterward" of the next clause, which makes it fit better with the rescue from Egypt.

ing the natural world: "And then the earth brought an accusation against the oppressors" (*1 En.* 7:6). Thus, the crossing of the species barrier in transgression of God's ordinance leads to fantastic beings, but it also leads to violence, overconsumption, and (as the next chapter in *1 Enoch* states) sexual evil. In a sense all of these are charges made against the "others," although their violence is that of slander rather than physical violence.

So far Jude is not too dissimilar to the Genesis text, although he is clear that the "children/sons of God" in Gen 6:2 (both in Hebrew and in the Greek translation) are (divine) messengers (angels). However, Jude continues, "[The Lord] has kept them in eternal chains under gloom (i.e., the darkness of the underworld) for the judgment of the great day." So in *1 En.* 10:4–6 God says to an archangel, "Bind Azaz'el hand and foot (and) throw him into the darkness! . . . And he covered his face in order that he may not see light; and in order that he may be sent into the fire on the great day of judgment." Then in *1 En.* 10:12–14, "Bind [the angels who sinned] for seventy generations underneath the rocks of the ground until the day of their judgment and of their consummation, until the eternal judgment is concluded. In those days they will lead them into the bottom of the fire — and in torment — in the prison (where) they will be locked up forever."[45]

This part is not in Genesis at all. It includes the binding of the angels who sinned (whose sin is said to be fornication) in darkness. However, this prison is not their final punishment, for there is a coming "great day of judgment" when they will go to their ultimate fate, all of which elements are in Jude. The implication is that the "others" may have been among the rescued and so have had a place of divine favor and privilege, but their forsaking that for their desire-driven adventures will result in a destruction parallel to that of the divine messengers who defected on that same "day" that the messengers are condemned.

The third negative example is that of Sodom and Gomorrah, which is joined to the second example with an "as" (*hōs*), so it is almost a part two of the divine messenger narrative, a human example that shows that the punishment of the angels was not peculiar to them. In Genesis Sodom is identified as evil: "The citizens of Sodom were evil, great sinners against Yahweh" (Gen 13:13). As a result, we are surprised when in Gen 14 God enables Abram to rescue them, although there is some foreshadowing of their end in that Abram undertakes this rescue for the sake of Lot, not for the sake of the other Sodomites. Then in 18:20 we hear about "the outcry against Sodom and Gomorrah, for it is great, and their sin, for it is exceedingly heavy." In neither place is their sin described. The one sin that gets described is that which occurs when the divine messengers come to Lot: the people of Sodom violate hospitality and also try (perhaps unwittingly — there is no indication that the Sodomites knew that the "men" who came to Lot were divine messengers) to

45. The narrative in the first part of *1 Enoch* goes on to discuss how Enoch went down to the prison where these beings were held, and they requested him to take their appeal to God. He does this, but God sends him back to the imprisoned beings to inform them that they will never be forgiven, but are headed for something worse than their present prison.

cross the species barrier by sexually assaulting the messengers, in essence a reversal of what the angels did in the previous incident (perhaps compounding the offense because as human beings they were inferiors).

This certainly fits Jude's "departing after flesh of a different type," that is, angelic rather than human.[46] But Jude also goes on to say that Sodom indulged in illicit sexual relations (the same verb is used in the LXX to describe Tamar's actions in Gen 38:24). That understanding of the Sodom story is found in *Jub.* 16.5–6; 20.5; *T. Levi* 14.6; *T. Benj.* 9.1. In other words, Jude reads the Sodom narrative according to the widespread understanding in Second Temple literature that the Sodomites were sexually promiscuous, including indulging in adultery. This, not the problem of the Genesis narrative, is what Jude thinks that the "others" also indulge in. The "others" should remember that the Sodomites serve as an example of suffering in a sentence of eternal fire, a type of double entendre since Sodom suffered eternal fire by being burned up never to be rebuilt, while the fire of the final judgment that the angels who sinned endure is eternal in the other sense, namely, that it lasts forever.

Jude now draws some threads of comparison together as he transitions to his final example, one different than the trilogy that he has already discussed. Just as those in the three examples cited did, these "dreamers" (1) stain the flesh, (2) despise the majestic power or authority that the Lord wields, and (3) slander the Glorious Ones. In calling them "dreamers" Jude may be alluding to the authority that they claim for their behavior, namely, that it was sanctioned by their dreams or visions—presumably, according to them, from God. Or this may simply be a way of putting them down, dreaming versus reflecting on the logic of the narratives, dreaming versus *logos* or reason.

When it comes to the comparisons, the "staining of the flesh" is clear, since the author accuses the "others" of sexual immorality more than once, and that parallels two of the three examples. The despising of lordship is more complicated because the term is a rare word found in the New Testament only here and in 2 Pet 2:10, which probably picks it up from this passage. Here it functions as a reference back to the "others'" rejection in practice of "our only Master and Lord, Jesus the Anointed One" (Jude 4).[47] In failing to submit to his ways, they are despising his authority. Jude mentions no verbal attacks on the authority of Jesus, although the "others" surely gave some justification to their rejection of Jesus' teaching.

There is, however, verbal abuse in the third charge, the slandering of the "Glori-

---

46. The Sodom narrative in the Hebrew Scriptures and in Jude is thus *not* about homosexuality, for that would be flesh of the same type. That interpretation of the Sodom narrative is found in Philo, *Abr.* 135–36. A different interpretation of the Sodom story from both that in Genesis and that in Jude is found in Ezek 16:49–50. "This was the guilt of your sister Sodom: she and her daughters had pride, excess of food, and prosperous ease, but did not aid the poor and needy. They were haughty, and did abominable things before me; therefore I removed them when I saw it." In Ezekiel, of course, Sodom is viewed as more righteous than Judah, as the passage cited goes on to point out.

47. There is a textual problem in that some manuscripts have the plural form, "lordships," which would mean denying the majestic authority of a collective group of lords or the authority that any lord wields. In that case this would merge with the next charge of slandering the Glorious Ones. However, followers of Jesus, while they may refer to many people as "my lord" in everyday discourse, only recognize One as Lord in the sense the term must have in this context; thus it would not fit angelic beings. Furthermore, the textual evidence seems stronger on the side of the singular. Thus it is likely that Jude views the "others" as despising the authority of Jesus.

ous Ones." This charge points forward to the next paragraph, the fourth example in this series, so it is clear that the "Glorious Ones" are divine messengers. But are they the so-called "holy" angels or are they the imprisoned angels mentioned previously? Since the other uses of "glory" or "glorious" in the New Testament are for good or holy or righteous beings, especially God, it is clear that Jude is talking about the "others" slandering God's messengers, not slandering the "fallen" beings. This is serious, not just because of their high honor status (indicated by "glorious"), but also because they represent God, and as an attack on Caesar's slave was considered an attack on Caesar, and an attack on Jesus' slave is an attack on Jesus, so an attack on the "Glorious Ones," even if the abuse is only verbal, is an attack on God. That, at least, is how the ancient world would read it.

Jude contrasts the behavior of the archangel Michael with that of these "others." While Michael is a personal name in Num 13:13 and then in several later works of the Hebrew Scriptures, the angelic figure only appears in late parts of the third section of the Hebrew "Bible" (Dan 10:13, 21; 12:1). In the New Testament he also appears in the central passage of Revelation (Rev 12:7). But while his relationship to Israel in Daniel may be behind this use in Jude, the incident referred to is not found in the Hebrew Scriptures. In Deut 34:5–6 Moses dies and is buried—period. There is no reference to the "Slanderer" ("devil" means a "slanderer") at all, neither in that passage nor anywhere else in the Pentateuch. So where does Jude get this narrative from that includes the devil?

Clement of Alexandria (*Fragments on the Epistle of Jude*) claimed that the narrative comes from the *Assumption of Moses*, a work that most scholars today identify with the *Testament of Moses* from the so-called Milan manuscript. Unfortunately, the ending of this work, which would contain this story, is lost, but from the testimony of various church fathers we understand that it ran this way: Moses dies; Michael comes at God's behest to bury the body; the devil comes and argues that the body should be given to him instead, since Moses was a murderer (due to his killing the Egyptian in Egypt) and thus should not receive an honorable burial. Michael does not so much argue as appeal to the judgment of God with, "The Lord rebuke you." The devil withdraws, knowing that God would decide in favor of Moses' honor and against the devil's slander.[48]

Jude expects that his addressees will recognize and accept the narrative, that they are familiar with the contents of the *Testament of Moses*. The point is that even so great a being as Michael does not accuse the devil of slander, neither slander of Moses nor slander of God (since God has sent Michael to bury Moses). Rather than judge on his own, Michael refers the matter to God: "May the Lord rebuke you." We are not informed when he expected the Lord to rebuke the devil, just that he refers

48. See further Bauckham, *Jude and the Relatives of Jesus*, 235–80. We do not agree that 4QAmram is the original form of this story, although it does show that arguments between the devil and an angel were known in first-century Judaism, but we do agree with Bauckham's reconstruction of the content of the ending of the *Testament of Moses*. On the *Assumption of Moses/Testament of Moses* in general, see R. H. Charles, *The Assumption of Moses* (London: A&C Black, 1897); *APOT*, 2:407–34, which abbreviates the earlier work.

the matter to God. In the *Testament of Moses* the devil withdraws, knowing that he cannot face up to God. In Jude the point is the appropriate behavior of Michael, not whether the Lord would rebuke the devil immediately or in the final judgment. It is this behavior of Michael that stands in contrast to that of the "others."

The "others" do not submit judgment to the Lord; rather, they slander "whatever they do not understand." That includes, apparently, the "Glorious Ones," whom they surely do not understand! Why would they criticize or slander them? It may be because these beings were associated with the Torah (e.g., in Gal 3:19), a morality that the "others" apparently reject.[49] However, since there is no explicit reference to the Torah in Jude, we cannot be sure of this. What we know for sure is that Jude describes the "others" as slandering divine messengers, beings whom they do not understand, although they surely *claimed* sufficient understanding. There is, however, something that they *do* understand, and that is their natural drives, those that they share with the animals. But their behavior in this regard is as if they were animals without reason (which is how any Greco-Roman would describe the thought processes of animals). They understand such bodily pleasures very well, at least on an animal level, and because they follow and seek such pleasures, they are corrupted by them. The ironic contrast is intentional: they claim rational knowledge beyond what they have and so tread boldly where they should not tread in terms of slandering the Glorious Ones, but what they do really know they know irrationally, like animals, and this corrupts them.

5.3.2.2.2 Second Proof (vv. 11 – 13)

The previous discussion based on the *Testament of Moses* has been a segue into the second argument against the "others," namely, that they care only about themselves and do not benefit the community, despite their claims to the contrary.

Like Hosea (7:13; 9:12) and some other Hebrew prophets, Judith (16:17) and several other Deuterocanonical works, and Jesus (Luke 6:24 – 26, among other places), Jude pronounces a woe oracle on the "others," a woe oracle supported by another trilogy. "Woe to them!" Why? "Because they have gone Cain's way." Is Jude accusing them of murder, the only explicit charge against Cain in Genesis 4? Not at all. Rather, he is at least following the tradition that made Cain's murder metaphorical, turning it into anger or hatred of one's fellow (1 John 3:12; *T. Benj.* 7:5; *1 Clem.* 4:6 – 7) and probably following the Jewish interpretation that viewed Cain as a practitioner and teacher of all sorts of wickedness, including pleasure-seeking (Josephus, *Ant.* 1.52 – 62; Philo, *Post.* 38 – 39).

They have also given themselves over to Balaam's error for pay. Again Jude differs from the Hebrew Scriptures, for while these Scriptures do say that Balaam was killed

---

49. Bauckham, *Jude, 2 Peter*, 58 – 59, discusses this at some length and advances the idea that these teachers were influenced by Paul and his rejection of the Torah. This is possible, for, as 2 Pet 3:16 testifies, Paul was often misunderstood or misused. In fact, at least part of 1 Corinthians is certainly related to a misunderstanding of a letter that Paul himself is correcting, (1 Cor 5:9 – 11). But we look in vain in Jude for characteristic Pauline terms that would prove that the "others" derived their ideas from Paul. Likewise, as Bauckham also points out, we cannot find in Jude any Gnostic ontological terminology indicating that they are (later) Gnostics.

by the Israelites (Num 31:8) and while they do bring a variety of charges against him (advising the women who induced Israel to worship the Baal of Peor [Num 31:16] and practicing divination [Josh 13:22]), he is specifically said to have *refused* to prophesy for pay and, when he followed through on this threat and blessed rather than cursed Israel, lost any pay he might have received (Num 22:18, 38; 24:10–13). However, Second Temple Judaism, picking up on the comment in Num 31:16–18 (the focus of which is a command to kill every female Moabite captive who is not a virgin and every male child, the adult males having already been killed), amplified the "word" of Balaam into long speeches in which Balaam, apparently motivated by a desire to gain the money he lost, advised the Moabites and Midianites on just how to seduce Israel (Josephus, *Ant.* 4.126–30; Philo, *Mos.* 1.292–99; *b. Sanh.* 106a). In other words, Balaam's error was suggesting moral entrapment and doing so in order to profit himself. Both of these are issues for Jude. Moral entrapment is clearly evil, but the profit motive is also spoken against elsewhere in the New Testament (e.g., 1 Tim 6:5–10).

They have also "perished in Korah's rebellion." Of the various Korahs in the Hebrew Scriptures, Jude is clearly referring to the Levite from the same Kohathite clan as Moses and Aaron (although from a different branch of the clan), who was a leader of a rebellion against Moses and Aaron in Num 16, specifically challenging Aaron's exclusive right to the priesthood on the basis of the priesthood of all Israelites. The end result was that he and those who joined with him were burned up by divine fire/swallowed by the earth.[50] Korah naturally became proverbial for a schismatic person in Jewish tradition (Josephus, *Ant.* 4.14–21; *L.A.B.* 16). The point that Jude is making is not that Korah raised an actual sedition (which is in fact the clear issue in the LXX and Josephus, which use the Greek term *stasis* or *episystasis*), but that he challenged Moses' authority; he spoke against or argued with him (*antilogia*, ἀντιλογία), which is like the somewhat later rabbinic tradition found in *m. ʾAbot* 5:17. Again the lens of tradition shapes how Jude reads the text. Jude also chooses to arrange the three examples for rhetorical effect, starting with the milder "they have gone in the way of," moving to "given themselves over to," and ending with "perished,"[51] even though this means putting Korah after Balaam, which is neither the chronological order nor the order of Numbers. Rhetoric trumps chronology.

---

50. There are two traditions about Korah. In Num 16:19 Korah is placed with those offering incense and therefore presumably died in the fire from God (16:35), as 26:10–11 says, making clear that his children did not die. But in Num 16:23–34 Korah is grouped with Dathan and Abiram, indeed as their leader, and the earth splits and swallows them: "The earth opened its mouth and swallowed them up, along with their households—everyone who belonged to Korah and all their goods. So they with all that belonged to them went down alive into Sheol; the earth closed over them, and they perished from the midst of the assembly" (Num 16:32–33, NRSV). Since it specifically says his dwelling was included ("Get away from the dwellings of Korah, Dathan, and Abiram.... So they got away from

the dwellings of Korah, Dathan, and Abiram," 16:24, 27, NRSV), it is difficult to avoid the implication that his children were included in the destruction as Dathan and Abiram's explicitly were. We do not know which version of destruction Jude is thinking about, but either fire or falling into a crack in the earth would fit his terminology, and neither is desirable.

51. We do not know if he expects his addressees to remember that Cain was exiled, Balaam died in battle (an honorable way to die, assuming that he was resisting), and Korah dies in a gruesome, public manner, dishonored by God. He does not mention the results of their activities for either Cain or Balaam.

However, Jude does not want his addressees to get too focused on the examples, for they are just that, examples. Instead, he moves us back to the "others" with the word "these." They are "those feasting fearlessly with you, reefs in your love-feasts." The worship of the church in the first century (and probably up to 250 CE) was a meal, the Greco-Roman *symposium*. It was the Lord's Supper, the Eucharist, the reenactment of the Last Supper.[52] Jesus was present in the Spirit. Here were those who feasted fearlessly in the presence of Jesus and of his community despite their problematic behavior previously noted. They are like reefs to a ship, but they are reefs at the Lord's Supper itself.[53] They are, of course, no danger to Jesus, but they are a danger to the rest of the community. They are shepherds who do not care for the flock, but only for themselves (perhaps recalling Ezek 34:2–3).

Then, moving away from human images to the natural world (perhaps influenced by *1 En.* 80.2–6), they are in fact like (1) clouds that bring hope in areas largely dependent on agriculture, for they hold the promise of rain, but these "others" are waterless clouds, promising but not producing (cf. Prov 25:14). They are just carried along by the winds. They are like (2) trees in the autumn, without any fruit to harvest. Like trees in the autumn they are seemingly "dead," their leaves falling—but these are doubly dead, not just because they are leafless, but because they are doomed to be uprooted because of it (like the cutting down of a tree in Matt 7:19). They are worse than that, for they are like (3) wild waves of the sea, water that is dangerous, on the one hand, and water that is polluted, on the other, as it stirs up the seabed and creates froth—but this is a foam of their shame, for the deeds they may boast about and certainly do not hide are in reality shameful.[54]

Jude completes his series of examples from land, air, sea, and heaven, by noting that the "others" are (4) "wandering stars," that is, planets, which do not keep their proper place. Stars, of course, were often identified with angels, so stars that left their places and wandered would be like the angels of Jude 6. This identification is clear in *1 En.* 18.15; 21.6 and elsewhere, but is also suggested in Rev 9:1. As a result of this deviation from their proper place, for such "stars," including the "others" to

---

52. I. Howard Marshall, *Last Supper and Lord's Supper* (Grand Rapids: Eerdmans, 1980), 127, argues that the meal and the "breaking of bread" were separate parts of the service in Acts 2, although on pp. 144–45 he argues that by 1 Corinthians 11 the meal and the "breaking of bread" were integrated (cf. pp. 130–31, where he cites a variety of theories held by various scholars). However, Larry W. Hurtado, *At the Origins of Christian Worship* (Grand Rapids: Eerdmans, 1999), 84–85, convincingly argues that the whole meal was cultic from the beginning. For instance, Hippolytus, *Apostolic Tradition* 26 and *Epistle of the Apostles* 15, discusses which foods were appropriate for the cultic meal. See also M. J. Townsend, "Exit the Agape?" *ExpTim* 90 (1978–1979): 356–71; Marshall, *Last Supper and Lord's Supper*, 110–11. See also R. J. Banks, *Going to Church in the First Century* (Chipping Norton, NSW, Australia: Hexagon, 1980), which reconstructs such a meeting in narrative form. By Justin Martyr's time (130–165 CE, probably toward the end of this period) there is some evidence that the meal and the Eucha-

rist, which had by now become a ritual, were separating, at least in some locations. This seems to be clearly the case when the altar has become the center of the church in 250 CE.

53. Jude clearly wrote "reefs" (*spilas*, σπιλάς), as a unified textual tradition asserts, but some commentators and translators (NIV, NRSV) read "blemishes" (*spilos*, σπιλός). Jude may well intend the wordplay, but he writes "reefs" since he is worried that the "others" will be copied by the "beloved," the irony being that the danger of the reef is present at the most sacred time of all.

54. If this image is drawn from Isa 57:20, it shows a dependence of Jude on the Hebrew text, since the last phrase of this verse, "whose waves cast up mire and mud," is not in the Greek text. However, (1) there is no assurance that Jude is dependent on Isa 57:20; and (2) other Jewish writers also use the image, e.g., 1QH 2:12–13 (10:12–13), so it may have been a culturally current image. In other words, Jude may have known the Hebrew Scriptures in Hebrew, but he also may well not have known Hebrew at all.

the extent that they are like them, "the deepest darkness is reserved forever." We are full circle, back to Jude 6.

5.3.2.2.3 Third Proof (vv. 14–16)

The Enochian images in the examples from nature lead to a third proof of the bad state of the "others," a proof from a Scripture, an ancient writing, which, rhetorically speaking, is an "inartificial proof" to the extent that it is about the "others." Jude cites *1 En.* 1.9 as a "prophecy," that is, a prophetic work. The person Enoch is ancient, the seventh generation from Adam (Gen 5, if one counts Adam as the first generation; the fact that Enoch was seventh is repeatedly mentioned in Second Temple literature, e.g., *1 En.* 60.8; 93.3; *Jub.* 7.39). He is the one who was said to have "walked with God" and to have disappeared for "God took him," so he was a righteous ancient authority, with whom Jude expects his addressees to be familiar.

The quotation from *1 En.* 1.9 has been modified,[55] for instead of the "he" (God) of *1 Enoch*, Jude has "the Lord," probably meaning Jesus. It was, of course, a common practice among followers of Jesus to take texts from the Scriptures and apply them to Jesus (Isa 63:1–6 in Rev 19:13, 15; Isa 66:15 in 2 Thess 1:7; Zech 14:5 in 1 Thess 3:13). Second, instead of "all flesh," Jude has "every person" or just "all." Third, Jude leaves out the judgment prophecy from *1 Enoch*, for Jude has enough of that elsewhere. Finally, Jude leaves out "deeds" and so focuses on the words that the unrighteous have spoken, which will also be the next point he makes about the "others." So we have, "See, the Lord is coming with ten thousands of his holy ones, to execute judgment on all, and to convict everyone of all the deeds of ungodliness that they have committed in such an ungodly way, and of all the harsh things that ungodly sinners have spoken against him" (NRSV).

God is often pictured as coming from his dwelling (e.g., Deut 33:2) to take action, and when he comes, like any great king, he comes with an appropriate military escort and dignitaries. Moreover, also like any great king, he will set up court to reward the righteous (which in *1 Enoch* is mentioned before the passage quoted) and to bring about justice by convicting and punishing the unjust, especially his enemies. It was a fearful thing to be on the wrong side of a king's (or emperor's, since a Roman *parousia* was the same sort of event) justice when the ruler came.

These "others" are on the wrong side of the "Lord," in three ways (v. 16). First, they "grumble about their fate," as Israel did in the wilderness, picking up Jude 5 and 11. Paul agrees that copying ancient Israel in this way is not a good idea (1 Cor 10:10).

---

55. It is debated as to whether Jude knew the Greek or the Aramaic version of *1 Enoch* (or the parts of *1 Enoch* that he knew). See Davids, *2 Peter and Jude*, 76–79. The Ethiopic and Greek versions read, "Behold, he [= God] will arrive with ten million of the holy ones in order to execute judgment upon all. He will destroy the wicked ones and censure [or rebuke] all flesh on account of everything that they have done, that which sinners and the wicked ones committed against him" (trans. E. Isaac, *APOT, 1 En.* 1.13–14). The Aramaic reads, "[16][when he comes with] the myriads of his holy ones [to carry out the sentence against everyone; and he will destroy all the wicked] [17][and he will accuse all] flesh for all their [wicked deeds which they have committed by word and deed] [18][and for all their] arrogant and wicked [words which wicked sinners have directed against him]" (trans. Florentino García Martínez, *Dead Sea Scrolls Translated: The Qumran Texts in English* [trans. W. G. E. Watson; Leiden: Brill, 1994], 250). The [ ] indicate where there are missing or obscure letters in the text and editors have interpolated.

One may be grumbling about leaders or directly about God, but in either way God, or in this case, the Lord (who appointed the leaders), takes it personally.

Second, they are desire-driven (many translations have "evil desires" but the Greek only has "desires"—when one's drives and emotions are in control, one has a problem in the view of Jude, James, and most other New Testament writers). With desire in control, they surely transgress the boundaries of acceptable behavior.

Third, they speak boastfully, surely about themselves (and in the light of the use of this image in Dan 11:36 [Theodotion] and Rev 13:5, surely over against "the Lord"), but certainly about others, although they do not speak about others sincerely, for they "flatter others for personal profit." Are they boasting that they know better or are more enlightened or more updated than Jesus? Their language in any case is not the language of one who is submitted to Jesus as their Lord. And their language about others may be quite nice, but it is hypocritical, flattery with the hope to exploit the person. Neither hypocrisy nor flattery, let alone trying to manipulate others for one's personal gain, gets positive reviews in the New Testament. This is the type of thing that Jas 2:1–4 talks about, as well as *T. Mos.* 5.5 (which work Jude probably uses in Jude 9), and which both works condemn.

5.3.2.3 Body Closing/Peroratio (Concluding Exhortation) (vv. 17–23)

The proofs of the condemnation of the "others" have ended, and it is time to draw the conclusions for the addressees, for it is the "beloved," not the "others," to whom the work is addressed, as Jude shows in indicating that the "you" being addressed are "beloved."

First, they are to "remember." This whole situation should not take them by surprise. The official delegates (apostles) of our Lord, Jesus the Anointed One, had warned them about this previously. This warning is in the past, and it is attributed generally to the official delegates, not specifically to a single official delegate, much as the traditions about Jesus, including his resurrection, are not traced to individuals among the Twelve. Since the term *apostolos* (ἀπόστολος) is often used for the missionaries evangelizing a community, this warning to be remembered appears to be a prophetic word that was passed on to the community by their founders, perhaps in the name of the generalized group of such leaders, which included the Twelve, of course, but also the Seventy (Luke 10:1—the noun *apostolos* does not appear, but the verbal form does, along with a verb for appointing or commissioning), Paul and Barnabas, and various others.

Jude does not group himself with these who were sent out, perhaps because he saw himself more as a nontraveling leader than as one "sent out," similar to how James does not describe himself as an official delegate of Jesus (although Paul does in Gal 1:19—self-perception and others' perception can differ). From this group arose a prophetic word, similar to what Luke says happened to a group of prophets and teachers in Antioch in Acts 13:1–2. Note that prophecy is a characteristic phenomenon of the Jesus movement, something that Acts claims is a predicted mark of the Spirit (Acts 2:17–18, where "and they will prophesy" is added to the Joel text to make this point clear).

The prophecy Jude refers to was a warning: "In the last days there will be scoffers, who will live in accordance with their desires—their impious ones!" The "last days" for the followers of Jesus began with his resurrection and ascension, that is, with their awaiting his return to reign openly. The old age was still around, but was passing away, and the new age had begun. Thus for Jesus' delegates to say this was in essence to say, "Now, in this age, not in some future age." The characteristics of those who are coming, and whom Jude sees as now present, are those of the "others," that is, improper speech (mockers, which 2 Peter picks up on in 2 Pet 3:3) and improper behavior (desire-motivated, and by desires that come from a distorted view of God).[56] These point in summary form to the behavior of the "others," which Jude has just finished describing.

Jude makes the application clear: "these are those." The "those" are those who are making divisions in the community (while the term is unique to Jude, the horror of division is well known in the New Testament, as 1 Cor 1–3 demonstrates). Because they are desire-driven, they are "soulish" or "merely natural" (cf. 1 Cor 15:44), and it therefore goes without saying, though Jude makes it clear, that they "do not have the Spirit" (1 Cor 2:12 and Jas 3:15 make it clear that to be *psychikos* or "soulish" is to lack the Spirit). If one is desire-driven, one is not Spirit-driven. However, the "beloved" are not to be surprised, for the Lord Jesus was not surprised—he predicted the "others" beforehand. He is Lord; he is in control. He not only knows about the situation, but he knew about it before it happened. Remembering helps the community contemplate it calmly.

Second, the "beloved," rather than focusing on the "others," who do not have the Spirit, "by building [them]selves up with respect to [their] most holy commitment, by praying in the Holy Spirit," are to "keep [them]selves in God's love." The main thing they are to do is to make sure they stay in the sphere of God's love. This is not love in the sense of God's loving the world, but love in the sense of love versus hatred or love versus wrath, that is, judgment. The "beloved" are presently in God's love, which is why they are the "beloved," but Jude has indicated that there are "reefs" about, even in their very love feasts/Eucharistic celebrations (Jude 12). They need to stay the course, for Jude has given ample examples that those who wander away are anything but "in God's love"; rather, they are under his condemnation.

How do the "beloved" do this? There are two ways: (1) strengthening ("building themselves up in") their "most holy commitment" to Jesus as Lord, God's Anointed One, which, of course, means obeying him as the "others" do not; and (2) praying inspired or empowered by the Holy Spirit. The Lord's Prayer surely models the submission and dependence that such prayer entails. Together these steer them from a life dominated by their drives and toward one dominated by wholehearted commitment to Jesus, to God's kingdom.

This commitment is not just a commitment aimed at avoiding condemnation. As they keep themselves in God's love, they are to be "looking forward to" or "waiting

---

56. BDAG, *asebeia*, ἀσέβεια, 141. The point in using this word is that the deeds stemming from the desires are not just morally wrong in some general sense of morality, but they are impious; they are an affront to God. God is the standard, not a societal or philosophical sense of morality.

for" something, namely, the "kindness" or "compassion" of "our Lord, Jesus, God's Anointed One," a kindness that leads to "eternal life." There may be much kindness they receive from the Lord, Jesus, along the way, but this is a specific one, something that they are waiting for, namely, his coming and sitting in judgment and awarding them the life of the coming age. Yet this is not spoken of in terms of what they deserve. It is spoken of as Jesus' kindness shown to someone in need.[57] It is again the picture of a king sitting in judgment, before whom someone comes who has a need that he cannot meet but which the king fulfills out of sheer compassion or kindness. The result in this case is that they enter the life of the coming age (perhaps better than "eternal life" in that it is not the length of life that is stressed but its quality as belonging to the coming age). They may have kept themselves in God's love by building their commitment and praying in the Spirit, but in the end when Jesus returns in judgment, they are expecting to meet, not his justice, but his kindness, his compassion. Jude apparently does not believe that eternal life can ever be earned.

Third, the "others" are still there in the community. What are the "beloved" to do about them? Should they not be cast out as totally reprobate? But how can this be right if the "beloved" are not looking for or expecting the strict justice of Jesus? They are expecting kindness, compassion, and mercy. If that is the case, they should themselves be like their king in showing that quality right now.[58]

Some in the community are caught between two opinions; they doubt.[59] The point of view of the "others" seems reasonable and perhaps goes with the flow of the surrounding culture, but they are aware of the pull of the teaching of Jesus as they have received it through those evangelizing them. They are caught in the middle. Treat them with kindness or compassion, says Jude. The loving, accepting call to follow Jesus is more in line with how Jesus treated the "beloved" than a strict "line-in-the-sand," "you-are-with-us-or-you-are-with-them" attitude.

Some in the community are committed, but to the wrong side. They are the "others." Mercy or kindness in this situation means a rescue mission. Jude has already spoken of fiery destruction (e.g., the Sodom and Gomorrah analogy of Jude 7 or in the Hebrew Scriptures Korah's rebellion of Jude 11), so we are not surprised that he sees these "others" as slipping into a "fire." Calling them back to obedience to Jesus in a compassionate or merciful manner will save them. As Jas 5:20 says,

57. BDAG, *eleos*, ἔλεος, 316.

58. We recognize that the textual evidence is so evenly divided here that we cannot be sure of the exact reading. All versions of the text support the general outline of what we are arguing, but whether two or three groups are envisaged is difficult to say. Bauckham, *Jude, 2 Peter*, 108–11 (as well as several other commentators), follows 𝔓[72], the most ancient witness, and so reads two lines, "Snatch some from the fire, but on those who dispute have mercy with fear, hating even the clothing that has been soiled by the flesh." Given Jude's predilection for triplets, however, the text accepted by Anton Vögtle, *Der Judasbrief. Der 2. Petrusbrief* (EKKNT 22; Solothurn and Düsseldorf/Neukirchen-Vluyn: Benzinger/Neukirchener, 1994), 102–5, has intrinsic probability. It is supported by ℵ and comes close to the text in A and B, both of which latter readings probably

arose from it. The Byzantine textual tradition and the Vulgate follow it, as do the latest editions of the United Bible Societies and Nestle-Aland texts. This reads, "Be merciful to those who doubt; save others by snatching them from the fire; to others show mercy, mixed with fear—hating even the clothing stained by corrupted flesh" (NIV; also NLT, NRSV, CEB).

59. We recognize that *diakrino* (διακρίνω) can mean "dispute" or "doubt," and that in Jude 9 it does mean "dispute." But in Jude 9 it has a topic that the dispute is about, the body of Moses, and here there is no such topic. Where this verb is used with an object, it usually means "doubt." This is the nearly universal translation in the major translations (except the KJV's "making a difference," which really does not fit the grammar of the passage.

"Whoever turns a sinner back from their wandering way will save a person from death and will cover a multitude of sins." It will be like a firefighter snatching a person from a fire, an image perhaps suggested by Zech 3:2 (which, like Jude, has a dispute with Satan) or less likely by Amos 4:11 (which also refers to Sodom and Gomorrah). However, both of these passages speak of a "brand" snatched from the fire, a key term missing here, and both of them use a different verb in the LXX than the verb used here. The image of neighbors or firefighters snatching someone from a burning building is sufficient to make Jude's point. Save them, or else they will die.

But Jude is not naïve. "But be merciful to them (or be compassionate toward them) in fear." But what type of fear? Since in five of the six times this expression occurs in the New Testament (including 1 Pet 1:17; 3:2) it indicates the fear of or reverence for God, that is most likely the meaning here, resulting in the CEB translation, "Fearing God, have mercy on some, hating even the clothing contaminated by their sinful urges." It is the proper fear of God that will keep the "beloved" from getting sucked into the behavior of the "others." With this fear, the type of reverential fear in which one knows one is safe so long as one lives within the appropriate parameters (such as we observe all the time in an impersonal situation in repair and maintenance people working confidently in potentially dangerous situations because they know they are following the appropriate policies and safety standards), one will show the kindness or mercy that is needed, but will still hate the practices of the "others."

Jude stays with the image of saving the person from the fire, but this time putting in the caveat, "hating even the 'flesh-stained' *chitōn* (χιτών)." Of the two pieces of clothing that a person wore, the *chitōn* was the full-length undergarment, whereas the *himation* (cloak, although also the generic word for clothing; a single piece of cloth with a hole and a seam around it in the center for the head) was what one used as a blanket at night and when one went outside the house. The *chitōn* was, therefore, next to the skin, the garment that would get stained by sweat and other bodily fluids ("the flesh" in our image). The "flesh" became a metaphor for the natural drives, which are indeed rooted in our physiology. So they are to rescue the person, but because of their fear of God, they are to hate, not the fire or the *chitōn* singed by the fire, but the *chitōn* stained by the flesh, uncontrolled by divine teaching or the power of the Spirit. One is to hate this, even though by implication it would mean rescuing the person stark naked. That is mercy. One must save the person, one must show mercy, for that is the way of the Lord, but one must hate what he hates and separate the person from their shameful behavior. It is in this way that one can appropriate the mercy of the Lord in the fear of the Lord.[60]

---

60. As noted above, this image is often thought to draw on Zech 3:1–5, for Joshua is not just a "brand plucked from the fire" but he is also clothed in filthy clothes, which are removed, and he is reclothed in festal clothes. Furthermore, there is the image of Satan accusing him with a "the Lord rebuke you" spoken to Satan. However, there are both similarities and differences between this passage and Jude. We have already noted the differences in Greek terminology and the absence of any word for "brand" in Jude. There is also a difference in that the metaphor in Jude is about the individual transgressive urges and behaviors in the "others," while in Zechariah one can question whether Joshua's personal guilt is the issue at all, or "did Joshua's filthy garments (3:3, 4) represent the contamination of all the people? The latter seems to be the proper meaning" (Ralph L. Smith, *Micah-Malachi* [WBC 32; Dallas: Word, 1984], 199). So while it is possible that Jude is drawing images in a general way from this passage, there is less indication that Jude is directly alluding to this passage. If he is, he is individualizing it or, perhaps, has not understood it as referring to collective guilt that the high priest carried as representative of the people.

5.3.3 Letter Closing: Doxology (vv. 24–25)

Jude's message is finished. What remains is a final doxology. Romans ends this way (16:27), as do Philippians (4:20), 2 Timothy (4:18), Hebrews (13:21), and 2 Peter (3:18); Ephesians has an intermediate doxology (3:21), as do 1 Timothy (1:17) and 1 Peter (4:11); and Revelation has several (1:6; 5:13; 7:12; 19:1). Jude has talked about their guarding or keeping themselves in God's love in Jude 21. Now he gives honor to the One "who is able to guard/keep [different verb, but similar meaning] you free from stumbling and to stand you rejoicing unblemished before his glory." The metaphors merge, for the "beloved" do not stumble but rather stand; they are unblemished (as one might become blemished if one stumbled), and so they rejoice rather than experience shame in the presence of the One's glory or honor.

Who is this One? It is the only God (as any Jew would say), our Savior (he is the one who rescues). Glory or honor is given to him "through Jesus the Anointed One, our Lord," for he is the leader and it is in relationship with him that one has relationship with God. Then the words pile up: "to him be glory, majesty (i.e., greatness or preeminence), might, and authority (the one being power and the other the right to exercise the power)." These are rightfully his over the whole span of time, "before all the ages and now and unto all the ages." There is one King, one Governor, one Ruler, and he did not need to gain total authority, power, majesty, and honor, but has always had and will always have them. We, says Jude, simply recognize that fact. And to that statement the only appropriate response is, "Amen," "So be it."[61]

5.4 IMPORTANT THEOLOGICAL THEMES

What type of significant theology does one get in a work so short? The answer is clearly, "More than one might expect." There will, of course, be significant overlap with 2 Peter, since 2 Peter used Jude, but where there is overlap, Jude has pride of place, for it is the original (even if the other author may have chosen to use Jude because that work was theologically compatible with his thought). The obvious starting point for theology is also the starting point of this overlap, namely, God.

5.4.1 God

For Jude the determining factor of life and thought from first verse to last is the one God (Jude 25). This God is the one whom Jude refers to as "God the Father" or "Father-God" (v. 1), which pictures him as a *paterfamilias*, the head of a family. We are not informed whether this is his relationship to the world outside the community of Jesus-followers (the outside world is hardly referred to in Jude, and when it is, it is by way of illustration), but it is clear that this is indeed his relationship to that community.

---

61. This was, perhaps, the expected response of the auditors to the reading of Jude, or at least to the reading of this final doxology.

How would someone in Jude's world understand this relationship? First, the *paterfamilias* was the source of authority in the extended family. His word was law. Second, he was the source of provision in the family and beyond, for he would see to it that the needs of everyone in the family and beyond the family (i.e., all his clients) were supplied, although often others did the hands-on managing of the supplies. Third, he was the source of status for the family, for his honor status was the status of the family, and each family member had honor in their respective relationships to him.

When it comes to relationship, this Father-God is always depicted as being in a positive, caring relationship to those in his family (again, we are not informed about his relationship to those outside of the community). They are the "called" or "chosen" "in Father-God's love" (vv. 1, 21); love is not a feeling but a willing of good for the other, a caring for the other. They are those who have experienced God's "favor" or "grace" (v. 4, i.e., the favorable disposition of a patron or ruler, often expressed in concrete ways). They are the ones who have experienced his rescue or deliverance (he is "God our Savior," v. 25). He is also the one who protects those he has delivered, for he can "guard you from stumbling" and can "stand you unblemished and rejoicing in the presence of his glory" (v. 24). Every time God is mentioned, he is in a positive relationship to those in his community: loving, being gracious or favorable, rescuing/saving, guarding. This is Jude's God-image, an image he uses consistently. Surely he could have told us something about God as creator as well as something about God as sovereign over the world outside his community, but he has chosen not to do so. His focus is on God in relationship to his own "family," and that relationship is a positive, gracious, favorable one.

Jude also knows about "Jesus [God's] Anointed One," who is also mentioned in the first and last verses of Jude (vv. 1, 25) and three times in between (vv. 4, 17, 21). Since "Anointed One" or "Messiah" is a Jewish term for God's human agent through whom he expresses his rule (as in a first-century reading of Psalm 2), we are not surprised to discover that it is through this One that God is Savior or that praise comes to God.[62] Unlike 2 Peter, Jude never uses language that explicitly identifies Jesus as anything more that God's agent in expressing his rule, God's Anointed One, but he does suggest this "more" indirectly in his applying the title "Lord" to Jesus. This term is, of course, a political term in that "Caesar is Lord" was the patriotic acclamation and "Jesus is Lord" was the counter acclamation and basic confession of the Jesus movement (Rom 10:9). It is not totally foreign to the family metaphor in that Hellenistic family members could refer to the *paterfamilias* as "lord" or "my lord," as we see in such works as the *Testament of Abraham*, which tradition influences 1 Pet 3:6. In Jude the narratives in the Hebrew Scriptures attributed to YHWH are read as actions of "the Lord," which almost certainly in v. 5 and then

---

62. The phrase "through Jesus the Anointed One" in Jude 25 could be read with the immediately preceding word, "Savior," or with the following attributions of honor to God. One doubts that Jude would have wanted to clarify this ambiguity, since however the verse is read, Jesus is the agent through whom God saves and through whom God receives honor.

probably in vv. 9 and 14 are being read as Jesus' actions.[63] So Jesus is read as God's agent, as world-ruler or Lord, but so identified with God that he can be seen as his agent throughout world history (not forgetting that the actions of vv. 6 and 7 are attributed to the subject of v. 5) and into the eschaton (v. 14).

This identification was facilitated by Jude's "Bible," the Greek translation of the Hebrew Scriptures (which we know as the Septuagint), since that regularly translates YHWH as well as *'ādôn* ("lord") with *kyrios* (κύριος, "lord"). So we know that Jude views Jesus as God's executive agent, that he attributes to Jesus a number of the actions of God in the Hebrew Scriptures. We also know that Jude never says grammatically that Jesus is divine as 2 Pet 1:1 (or John 1:1 or Heb 1:3) does. He is, perhaps, at an early, less self-conscious stage in the development of this doctrine. But it is clear that Jesus is God's fully empowered agent and has been since at least early in the history of creation.[64]

Jesus is specifically presented as a ruler. Whether one looks at *Christos* (Χριστός, "Anointed One"), *kyrios* (κύριος, "lord"), or *despotēs* (δεσπότης, "master"), all of which appear together in Jude 4, one has a title of authority. Thus Jude is his "slave" (v. 1), even if a slave of such a master was someone with significant authority, at least while doing his master's business. This One sends out official delegates (v. 17) who speak on his behalf. Even more significantly, this One saves and destroys (v. 5), keeps in eternal chains (v. 6), is coming in judgment (vv. 14–15), and will show mercy/kindness to the "beloved" in that judgment (v. 21). In fact, all judgment in Jude is attributed to Jesus (cf. John 5:22). Thus in Jude we have the gracious, favorable Father and the Lord Jesus who has executed and will execute judgment, which certainly throws a monkey wrench in the works of the popular picture current in our culture of a judging Father and a caring Son (Jude, of course, never uses Father-Son language for Jesus and God, as John does, but rather Father/empowered, authorized Agent).

So Jude has at least an incipient description of the first two members of the Trinity, but what does he think about the third, the Holy Spirit? He does not have much to say, for his focus has been on the lordship of Jesus under the caring oversight of the Father. But what he does have to say is significant. First, the "others" lack the Spirit, as is evident in their causing divisions (v. 19). That is, they are merely natural people, driven by their own desires, not inspired by the Spirit (who they may have claimed inspired them). The Spirit, then, is found in those submitted to the rule of Jesus. We do not learn in Jude that he controls one's drives or desires, but it is clear

---

63. Every time the referent of "Lord" is explicitly identified in Jude, it is Jesus (vv. 4, 17, 21, 25). With respect to "Lord" in v. 5, it is "our Lord Jesus the Anointed One" that comes in the last phrase of v. 4 that is the nearest antecedent. One would have to jump over this explicit "Lord" to claim that "Lord" in v. 5 refers to the more distant "God" of v. 4. The other two references to "Lord" in Jude (vv. 9, 14) would then be applied to the same "Lord" as v. 5, since there is no other "Lord" mentioned in Jude.

64. This can be read two ways, either as God being so present in Jesus that "the Lord" of the LXX is identified with "the Lord"

Jesus, or as Jesus being in some sense preexistent to his embodied form and so being "the Lord" of the LXX. One doubts that Jude was this reflective, but rather he appears to simply read the LXX unreflectively through a Jesus-is-God's-executive-agent lens. Such worship of Jesus, as we see in Jude, will be reflected upon as teachings about Jesus' nature develop. We say "since at least early in the creation" because the earliest event that Jude mentions is found in Gen 6, which is placed after the creation narrative and human multiplication on earth.

that, as in the case of wisdom in Jas 3:14–17, the Spirit in Jude is not someone who lives in "soulish" or "natural" people and is not someone who is compatible with creating divisions in the community. The Spirit unifies the community under the rule of Jesus.

Second, the Spirit is associated with prayer. One should pray "in the Holy Spirit" (v. 20). While this exact terminology does not occur elsewhere in the New Testament,[65] it appears to mean Spirit-inspired prayer, which Paul suggests using a related expression in 1 Cor 14:15 could be glossolalic prayer, but which in our more general context need not necessarily be limited to that (Paul's teaching in Rom 8:26–27 is less parallel, because there the Spirit prays *for* people rather than people praying "in the Spirit"). Presumably Jude believes that those whom he addresses know the difference between prayer "in the Holy Spirit" and other forms of prayer (which are not necessarily inappropriate, but are not what Jude believes to be helpful in his addressees' circumstances). Thus the Spirit in Jude is associated with the community, with its unity and submission to the rule of Jesus, and with its prayer. He is clearly the least developed member of the Trinity, either because he is not important to Jude's purposes or because Jude has not reflected on him further.

5.4.2 Humanity

In our discussion of God/Jesus/the Spirit, human beings have frequently cropped up, since the former are normally mentioned in relationship to the latter. Humanity is presumably divided into two groups, those within the community and those without. Nothing is said about those without, since neither they nor their state is addressed in Jude, but in the language that designates God as a rescuer, the "beloved" share a rescue or salvation with the author. Moreover, the analogous reference to "the Lord" as the one who rescued a people from Egypt suggests that the community is a community of those who have been rescued. However, not all who are in the community of the rescued are presently safe, for Jude divides the rescued into two parts: the "beloved" and the "others."

The "beloved" are beloved "in Father-God," whose favor (certainly including acceptance) they (along with the "others") have experienced. They are the called; that is, they are God's (or perhaps God's and Jesus' — the word has no clear subject) chosen people. They have a destiny in that they are kept for Jesus the Anointed One. They have a commitment (or faith) to Jesus as Lord and Master (in which case they see themselves in relation to him as slaves). Associated with their community are leaders, such as Jude, who designates himself a "slave of Jesus the Anointed One," presumably a slave who represents his Master on official business. The community was founded by official delegates (*apostoloi*), who have left them instruction and

---

65. It appears five times in relationship to baptism "in the Holy Spirit" and six times in the Pauline letters, mostly Romans, but never in relationship to prayer "in the Holy Spirit." In 1 Pet 1:12 it appears in connection to evangelism. The closest parallel is 1 Cor 12:3, where one says "in the Holy Spirit" that "Jesus is Lord." The more general expression "in [the] Spirit" is more associated with revelation than with anything else.

committed to them as holy ones the commitment to Jesus that they share (see vv. 1–4, 17).

Yet it is not as if the "beloved" are therefore totally safe, their fate decided, their destiny secure. There are decisions they can make that can affect them for good or for ill. They need to keep themselves in God's love (v. 21). They have a holy commitment, but they must build themselves up in relation to that commitment, which, along with praying in the Holy Spirit, are the ways they will keep themselves in God's love (v. 20). Their motivation for this is eschatological expectation, namely, an expectation of experiencing the Lord Jesus' kindness/mercy at the final judgment, a kindness that will result in life of the coming age (v. 21). They may already have faith, and God is able to keep them from falling and to present them unblemished and rejoicing before himself (v. 24); but their decision and effort are still called for, since the whole letter assumes that the "others" are a potential danger to the "beloved."

There are those in the community who, apparently bit by bit, have abandoned this commitment to Jesus as Lord and Master. We hear nothing about their doctrinal rejection of Jesus, but a lot about their practical ignoring of his teaching and authority. We are not told how they manage to justify this behavior. Since there are many parts of their behavior that may indicate that they were importing standard Greco-Roman mores into the community, they may have attributed Jesus' teaching to Judaism, which, they may have believed, was not binding on them. What we do know is that they were in one way or another trading on God's favor or grace, transforming this gracious favor into permission to violate normal ethical standards, or at least what Jude views as normal ethical standards (v. 4). They have made the type of decision that Jude does not want the "beloved" to make.

Jude argues by analogy. There was another "saved" people (i.e., Israel), and after they were "saved" from Egypt, those who broke faith, who were not committed, were destroyed (v. 5). That is his closest analogy, so it is first. Furthermore, there were divine messengers or angels who had a position, a dwelling, but they did not "keep" it; their decision was to abandon it (a decision that *1 Enoch* describes in detail). So now they live in a dark prison, and their future is eternal condemnation.

The "others," then, have not kept themselves in the "love of God." They have exercised their freedom in the wrong way. It is true that their condemnation was "written about in advance," indeed "long ago" (v. 4), but we see the nature of this "writing in advance" in the examples presented starting in v. 5, in the *1 Enoch* passage cited later, and perhaps in the author's mind in other pronouncements of the Hebrew Scriptures. God has said that those who do x will receive y. The "others'" impiety is seen in that they still do x.[66]

The freedom that Jude assumes, the freedom to "keep" oneself in God's love and the freedom to deny "our only Master and Lord," is a choice for or against another

---

66. Reese, *2 Peter and Jude*, 80–82, although one must quibble with her in that when she says, "judgment is an action that only God performs," she is correct only if "the Lord" is God. However, we have noted that in Jude God is never said to judge and "the Lord" is probably Jesus, so it would be more correct to say, "judgment is an action that only the Lord performs" or "only Jesus performs."

force in the human life, which the Jews would call *yēṣer* and the Greeks *epithymia* (desire). The "others" have rejected Jesus as Lord and are under this influence; they therefore understand "by instinct" (v. 10), for desire or drives are instinctual. However, there is no hint in Jude that their submission to this force is not a choice on their part. There is a type of "predestination" in Jude, but it is that those doing the practices that the "others" do will face eventual condemnation in the final judgment — the Lord is planning this and will carry it out. But their individual fate is far from sure, since Jude can talk about having mercy on them and saving them. They are going down a road past a sign that says, "Bridge out!" But they have not yet dropped into the river. They may be willfully ignoring the sign, yet there is still hope of getting them to change their course.

The contemporary tendency is to try to place Jude onto the spectrum of Reformed–Arminian or Augustinian–semi-Pelagian–Pelagian thought. However, we must remember that Jude comes several centuries too early even on the latest datings for the letter. He is blithely unaware that there will ever be such a controversy. We also need to remember that the key discussion point in all of those controversies is the ability of those outside any commitment to Jesus to turn to Jesus, but such an outside group is off Jude's radar. He is talking about two groups within the believing community and gives no indication of how they got there.

So, finally, we must remember that the issue in Jude is that some are morally apostate. They have accepted God's favor, but have transformed it into permission to live according to their desires. They have pledged themselves to Jesus as Lord, but now they deny his authority in their lives. We are not told in what ways God did or did not hinder this process, but we do know something about their choices; they are now lacking the Spirit and are headed for a negative outcome in the final judgment. This is Jude's issue: that there is freedom after Christian initiation, not whether there is freedom beforehand.

5.4.3 Ethics

It is clear that for Jude ethics is not something indifferent, but rather is an integral part of what it means to be committed to Jesus as Lord and through him to be under the rule of Father-God. Jude regularly refers to Jesus as "Lord," as a ruler, and he also refers to Jesus as "Master" and to himself as a "slave" of this master. This means that what one does is not indifferent to the extent that Jesus has made his will known. Jude does not discuss ethics in detail, although he does note certain types of transgressions, such as crossing sexual boundaries, slander (especially of divine messengers), selfishness/greed, and rebellion — all community-destroying vices. He normally sums up the behavior of those the critiques under such headings as "impiety" and desire-driven license.[67]

---

67. We recognize that there probably is in Jude a certain degree of using "stock charges" as a rhetorical strategy. It certainly would not do to attempt to read the contemporary ethical meanings of such charges back into Jude. At the same time, it is interesting to observe the pattern of charges, for Jude does not accuse the "others" of everything that was possible. Thus the pattern is probably more important than the specific charges.

Jude does know that when one is in the Jesus-community, one lives under God's favor. Divine favor has already been shown to people through their commitment to Jesus as Lord; it is apparently not something that one needs to earn. However, it is possible to take this divine favor and transform it into permission to transgress social norms—whether those norms are the norms of the believing community or the norms of the wider society is not said (v. 4). Such a misuse of the divine favor places one outside of God's love; that is, one has not kept oneself in God's love (which means being God's positive care for the individual or group).

One wonders, then, if Jude is not dealing with a type of ethical dissonance that comes from differing social norms. Other than his repeated references to Jesus as Lord, Jude does not let us know the source of his ethical reasoning. But it is clear that the source of all of his examples of ethical transgression and eventual condemnation are from the Hebrew Scriptures. These Scriptures are being read through Second Temple literature, but that Second Temple literature itself is an expression of various first-century (and before) Judaisms. The foundation narrative for all Judaisms, however interpreted, was the Torah, the ultimate source for all of Jude's examples. Furthermore, there was a strong tradition within many first-century Judaisms that divine messengers/angels were responsible for mediating the Torah to Moses and were in one way or another responsible for its enforcement. Jude tells us that the "others" slander angels in particular, which would not be a strange charge if they felt that such beings were foisting the Torah onto the community of Jesus-followers.

It is not that in Jude we see a replaying of the Pauline controversy over the role of the Torah. Paul normally draws his examples from the boundary markers of Judaism, such as circumcision, the rules of kashruth, and the keeping of festivals, especially the Sabbath, but Jude never mentions these things. But we do have behavior such as that mentioned in 1 Cor 6 and 11,[68] where Paul addressed the issue of bringing Greco-Roman sexual and meal mores into the community. Indeed, sexual looseness—in Jewish eyes—was very much a part of the *symposium* of a Greco-Roman communal meal, as also was focusing on one's own honor and advantage; note that there are references to divisions in Jude 19, which would be a general description of what Paul faced in Corinth and elsewhere.

This data makes one suspect that in Jude, one sees in the "others" Greco-Romans who have come into the community on the basis that their pledge of allegiance to Jesus as Lord placed them within the sphere of God's favor, but they did not realize that this pledge also placed them under obligation to serve Jesus. They may have

---

68. We note that the behavior described as lawsuits and the use of prostitutes in 1 Cor 6 and meal practices in 1 Cor 11 were normal, unexceptional Greco-Roman behavior. Paul argues against them vigorously, but never tries to excommunicate or otherwise separate the offenders (although he does suggest some of the behavior has led to sickness and premature death). In 1 Cor 5 we have behavior that Paul describes as outside of Greco-Roman norms, transgressive in both believers' and nonbelievers' ethical codes. This is not a clash of ethical codes, but a living outside of all ethical codes. This person Paul summarily instructs the community to "hand over to Satan" or to "expel." So while Paul may not ultimately tolerate those living morally according to Greco-Roman standards, what we observe him doing is arguing with them (perhaps similar to Jude's "rescuing" of the "others"); when it comes to the person violating even Greco-Roman ethics, Paul does not argue but pronounces a sentence.

argued that God's favor or grace meant that Jewish social norms were optional at best, and that what they were being told Jesus taught was in fact an extension of the moral code of the Torah, from which they were free. To Jude their Greco-Roman behavior is transgressive, shameful, and rebellious against Jesus, while they may have felt that it was socially acceptable (within Greco-Roman society) and that they were living within God's favor anyway and were not obligated to live in fear of Jesus.

Obviously this scenario is hypothetical, although it is a hypothesis that explains the data in Jude. What it makes clear is that for Jude submission to the ethical norms that flow from the Torah through Jesus to the community is part of what it means to call Jesus Lord, while for the "others" another norm is at work, perhaps a Greco-Roman one that Jews and those influenced by Judaism would view as licentious, shameful, and impious.

5.4.4 Divine Messengers

For Jude the universe is populated by far more than human beings. There is God, of course, and Jesus, God's designated ruler. But there are also the "holy ten thousands" (v. 14), which a number of manuscripts probably rightly understand as myriads of divine messengers, namely, angels. Any king should have an appropriately honorable retinue, and this is the greatest of kings ("the Lord"), so the largest number is used.[69] We should note that if Jude has the same concept that John of Revelation does, the retinue adds splendor, gravity, and honor to the situation, but it is not, strictly speaking, needed, for in the parallel scene in Revelation Jesus is the only one who acts and he acts by speaking (Rev 19:21). Jude believes that this holy retinue is organized, perhaps hierarchically, for Michael is designated a chief angel or ruling angel (i.e., archangel), a term only found in Jewish and Christian literature (v. 9). This passage also informs us that at least some of these beings have names. Given Jude's familiarity with *1 Enoch*, he probably could name a number of other archangels as well. Collectively these beings are referred to as "the Glorious Ones" (v. 8), as we have argued in the thematic commentary.

The unseen realms are not just sweetness and light. Jude knows about "the Devil" or "the Accuser"; *diabolos* (διάβολος) is the way the Hebrew *śāṭān* ("Accuser") is often translated. This being is pictured as being in a dispute with Michael; if those patristic writers who expand the story are correct, Satan is accusing the deceased Moses of murder and thus trying to prevent his honorable burial. From Jude alone we would not know where in the development of the Satan figure we are, since the activity could be that of the overzealous "heavenly prosecutor" of Job and other literature of that period, or it could be that of a more malevolent figure, such as that of Matt 4:1–11//Luke 4:1–13.[70]

---

69. "Ten thousand" (*myrias*, μυριάς) is the largest number term in Greek. Beyond this one would have to say something like "thousands of ten thousands" or "ten thousands of ten thousands," i.e., pile up terms.

70. On the development of Satan/the Devil, see Stephen F. Noll,

Angels of Light, Powers of Darkness: Thinking Biblically about Angels, Satan and Principalities (Downers Grove, IL: InterVarsity Press, 1998); and Sydney H. T. Page, *The Powers of Evil: A Biblical Study of Satan and Demons* (Grand Rapids: Baker, 1994).

While the role of "the Devil" is brief enough that we cannot be sure exactly what Jude believed about him, the same is not true for the "divine messengers who did not keep/protect their own authority/proper place in the order of the universe" (v. 6). We know that Jude knows *1 Enoch* and the story that is presented there, that these beings, knowing it was wrong in God's eyes, chose to depart their proper sphere and mate with human women—crossing the species barrier, so to speak. So they "left their dwelling" in the divine sphere. They are now in a prison in "deepest darkness" (often, but not always located in the underworld in Second Temple literature—*1 Enoch* describes which angels were sent to imprison them). This is not their ultimate fate, for this is just a prefinal judgment prison; they await that final judgment.

Thus Jude knows of "fallen angels," but we need to be careful in using that term, for often there is an idea of a precreational fall of angels (often including Satan), which it is doubtful that any biblical writer knows anything about. The events of Jude 6 are not precreational, but rather the events of Gen 6, as 2 Peter rightly understands in connecting them to Noah's deluge (2 Pet 2:4 and 5, respectively). This deluge comes more than seven generations after Adam, that is, after Enoch and thus long after creation.[71] What we can conclude from Jude is that for him the universe is populated with divine agents, with a devil who at least at times opposes a divine agent, and with divine agents who abandoned their positions. The latter, however, are not dangerous (and thus not to be identified with demons, whom Jude does not mention), for they are imprisoned. The remaining divine agents, whether angels or archangels or other beings, are to be respected, for human beings are largely ignorant about them, and these divine beings are themselves of high honor in the universe ("the Glorious Ones").

5.4.5 Eschatology

Jude does have something to say about eschatology. If we understand Jude correctly, the Lord Jesus is "coming," that is, coming to this world or sphere of being, with a grand retinue. The purpose of this "coming" is, as anyone familiar with the visits of rulers in the ancient world would know, judgment (v. 15). That means he will reward his faithful ones and punish the unfaithful. This day of judgment is probably viewed as imminent by Jude, for he uses the expression "the last of time" with respect to the "others" who are already present (v. 18).

When this judgment happens, Jude suggests, it will not go well with the "others," unless they repent. The Israelites who abandoned trusting YHWH were destroyed; Cain, Balaam, and Korah (to use Jude's order) did not meet good ends. The most concrete thing that Jude says is that they will be "convicted" about their evil (v. 15). Jude is a bit more pointed about the "fallen angels," for while in v. 6 he only says that

---

71. Rev 12:7–9 knows of a war in heaven in which angelic beings were cast down, but this also is not precreational; in fact, if one reads the chapter as having any chronology (and in Revelation that is a big "if"), John places this "fall" after the ascension of Jesus.

they are now in prison awaiting final judgment, in v. 13 he states that "the deepest darkness has been reserved until the ages [i.e., forever]" for the "wandering stars."[72]

Meanwhile, the "beloved" have a better expectation. They can look forward to the final judgment as a time when they experience "the kindness/compassion/mercy of our Lord, Jesus the Anointed One," for this kindness results in "the life of the ages" (v. 21). For Jude "the life of the ages" (i.e., "eternal life") is not something that believers have now, but something that they are granted in the final judgment. In this Jude takes a somewhat different stance than Paul, perhaps because it fits his purposes, perhaps because he is unaware of Paul's teaching. Another way Jude has of putting this future event pictures the judgment scene with confidence, for it pictures the "beloved" standing "with joy unblemished in the presence of his glory" (v. 24). The "beloved" rejoice, for they will receive something positive since they are unblemished. Of course, lest we think that this is done by unaided human effort, we must remember that God is the One causing them to so stand before his glory. They keep themselves and God keeps them (vv. 21, 24).

5.4.6 Community

A final theological theme in Jude is that of community. Virtually nothing is said in Jude about individuals. People always appear in groups. The community that Jude addresses is that of the "beloved," which more or less says it all in that they are not only those Jude presumably loves, but, in the context of the work, they are primarily those whom God loves. They are "beloved in God" (v. 1); they are the "holy ones" to whom "the faith" was committed (v. 3). They are ones who may well remember the predictions of Jesus' official delegates (v. 17). They can keep themselves in God's love (v. 21) and can expect to stand confidently in God's presence in the end (v. 24), facing judgment without anxiety. For them Jesus is indeed Master and Lord.

There is another group in the same community. These are never described as outsiders, that is, external to the community, for they are those who have "slipped in" (v. 4), whether in the sense that they entered the community with problematic ideas that no one recognized or in the sense that they gradually developed these ideas. At any rate, they apparently know God's favor, perhaps it is even their slogan (a sort of early misuse of *sola gratia*), but for them it is permissible to break the community's moral boundaries. As part of the community they surely confessed Jesus as Lord, but their behavior denies that he is Lord and Master—perhaps they deny that his teaching has any authority in their lives. They are in utmost danger of condemnation in the final judgment, yet they are still part of the community, enjoying the Lord's Supper together with the community, although they are a danger to the others there.

Jude appears ready to leave the sorting out of this mixed community to "the Lord." While Jude has strong things to say in general, he also notes that Michael the archangel would not condemn even the devil, but rather said, "The Lord rebuke you," leaving judgment to God. That, however, is not the whole picture, for Jude wants the "beloved"

---

72. While he compares the "others" to these and a number of other objects in the earth, the seas, and the air, the "wandering star" image fits the divine messengers that did not keep their place, as we argued in the commentary section above.

to recognize the danger that the "others" pose, to realize that God will ultimately condemn them; thus, God calls the "beloved" to rescue them, not just those who are "doubting," but also those who need to be, so to speak, "snatched out of the fire" (v. 23).

Yet such rescue is not for the fainthearted. A rescuer could, at least in theory, be pulled into the fire himself or herself. This same mercy or kindness that God has shown to them needs to be shown to the "others" "in a state of reverence toward God" in which they (again metaphorically) "hate even the *chitōn* stained by the body"; that is, rescue the person, but avoid anything "soiled" that is associated with him or her. Rescue is what God did, for he is "God our Savior" (v. 25), so rescue is what his "beloved" will do. But every rescuer knows that it does no good if the rescuer ends up in the same dire straits as the rescued person. In such a situation the community ends up with two members in danger, not just one.

Jude notes that the "others" display community-destroying vices. The "beloved," by their solidarity with one another, their submission to Jesus as Lord, and their care for their erring brothers and sisters, display community-building virtues. They are thus indeed keeping themselves in the love of God as they pray in the Holy Spirit. Jude does not use the word "church," but the community he describes is the church as it should be.

5.5 CANONICAL CONTRIBUTION

We have read through Jude and looked at its various theological themes. Is there anything unique in this work? Is there anything in it that it contributes to the wider canon of the New Testament, recognizing that the concept of canon is one that developed much later than Jude's time? And just how does it fit into the larger story that is narrated, what we now call canonical literature?

5.5.1 Reading the Story

First of all, it is clear that Jude is an example of a way of reading and appropriating the foundation narrative of Israel, the Torah (or Pentateuch), within the community of the followers of Jesus. It is a tradition that the addressees should know and therefore be able to remember (v. 5). In this sense the Torah fits alongside the "predictions of the official delegates of our Lord Jesus the Anointed One" (v. 17) as the two narratives in which the addressees are rooted. "Remembering" may be a rhetorical device making the charitable assumption that they do know and can remember, but it also points to what they should know and should remember.

With Jude it is the narratives that should be remembered, unlike 1 Peter or Paul, who often cite didactic passages from the Hebrew Scriptures. And with Jude the narratives all originally come from the Torah, in particular Genesis, Exodus, and Numbers.[73] There is no reference to Joshua, none to the prophets, none to David

---

73. Unless the reference to the dispute in the *Testament of Moses* in v. 9 is taken as a reference to Deut 34:6, there is no reference in Jude to either Deuteronomy or Leviticus. Of course, neither is particularly full of narrative.

or Solomon, except in a derivative way through the use of the "the Anointed One" (Messiah) as a title for Jesus. That focus on the Torah means that this story, the story of Israel, is also the story of Jesus' followers.

In fact, the story of Israel is read as the story of Jesus, for while "the Lord," in translations of the Hebrew Scriptures themselves, refers to Yahweh, in Jude, by means of the use of *kyrios* ("Lord") for YHWH in the LXX,[74] this Lord becomes "the Lord Jesus the Anointed One." Jesus as the actor in the ancient history joins that ancient history to the contemporary history of God's people for whom Jesus is Lord. This is not unique to Jude; to name three examples: 1 Cor 10:4 views Jesus as "the Rock" in the wilderness; Ps 110 is frequently read in terms of Jesus, perhaps going back to Jesus himself (Mark 12:36);[75] and Heb 7:3 uses Melchizedek typologically as one "like" Jesus. But Jude reads the narrative consistently in terms of Jesus and does so without either saying "like" or identifying Jesus with any element of the story other than Yahweh himself. In Jude's reading Yahweh's action is Jesus' action; the divine person and the divine agent are interchangeable. This reading strategy allows Jude both to appropriate the narrative and to underline the exaltation of Jesus, setting up the support for the more explicit declaration about Jesus that we find in 2 Pet 1:1.

Jude also appropriates the narratives in the form that he knew, that is, from the literature of his day. In fact, his first triplet is also found in more than one piece of Second Temple literature,[76] although Jude moves the rescue from Egypt to the first position in the series so that salvation and then the later condemnation of a part of the people of God takes pride of place. When it comes to reading the narrative about the "sons of God" who "took [human] wives" in Gen 6, Jude knows the form in *1 Enoch* or possibly the *Testament of Naphtali*, which puts the emphasis on the angelic beings and their departure from their "place" rather than on the later deluge. That, of course, is the point Jude wants to make, namely, the danger of leaving a secure and blessed "place," for that is what the "others" have done.

Turning to the Sodom narrative of Gen 19, Jude's reading focuses on crossing the species barrier and sexual immorality rather than the hospitality focus of Gen 19 or the focus on a failure to care for the poor in Ezek 16:49. Jude's "others" may not be trying to have sex with angels, but they are attacking them verbally and are violating the sexual mores Jude represents.

The same can be said about Jude's use of the burial of Moses narrative from the

---

74. That, of course, is probably because Jews had already stopped pronouncing Yahweh (out of reverence, not wanting to misuse the name), and instead read the letters YHWH as 'ādôn ("lord") or 'ădōnāy (a variant spelling when referring to God), which resulted in the Masoretic convention of writing the vowels for 'ădōnāyy under the consonants YHWH as a reminder. This would eventuate in the hybrid word "Jehovah," a type of "neither fish nor fowl" term, in English, since it transliterates the consonants YHWH and inserts a version of the vowels the Masoretes used.

75. This is also probably dependent on the Greek translation of Ps 110 in that if one is reading the Hebrew one would naturally read it as a "Declaration of Yahweh to my lord" (i.e., the minstrel addressing the king as "my lord"), "Sit at my right hand until I make your enemies a footstool for your feet." In Greek, both "Yahweh" and "lord" are translated by the same word *kyrios*, and the psalm is viewed as sung by David rather than to David.

76. See Davids, "Use of Second Temple Traditions," 415–18.

Testament of Moses, or the Cain, Balaam, and Korah stories. The first is an apparent haggadic exposition based on a single verse in Deuteronomy, while the others show later reflection on narratives in the Hebrew Scriptures; and at least in the case of Balaam there is quite a different emphasis. So Jude shows us how to read narratives in the way that they are being told in his contemporary age and how to read them in the light of what is going on in one's own community. He is part of a nexus of writers of what will become the New Testament who read the ancient narrative in a new way, a way that enables them to appropriate it. In other words, he was part of the hermeneutic process then, and he informs our hermeneutic processes now.

Likewise, Jude shows that the boundaries of ancient narrative are not yet fixed. It is not just that he reads the Torah narratives through Second Temple glasses, nor that he can read a later haggadic exposition (on the death of Moses) as if it were part of the original narrative, but that for him *1 Enoch* is a prophetic work that is also part of the ancient story. Enoch, of course, appears in Gen 5:21–24, which is within Jude's favored body of literature, even if Jude never cites that brief story. However, when it comes to *1 Enoch*, not only is it the version in which Jude knows the Genesis 6 narrative, but the only prophetic word that he cites is also a word from *1 En.* 1.9, cited in Jude 14–15. While he does not call *1 Enoch* "scripture," choosing instead to focus on it as prophecy, it is the only text he cites verbally, the only prophetic work that he cites at all, and it is a text that he handles in the same way as he does narratives that originally stemmed from the Hebrew Scriptures; that is, he identifies "the Lord" of *1 Enoch* with Jesus and reads the objects of the prophetic denunciation in *1 Enoch* as the "others," those whom he opposes in his own day. Such a use of *1 Enoch* would be impossible later in church history, once canonical boundaries were firmly drawn. Jude lets us know that something that may not ultimately end up as part of the rule of faith may still be inspired writing.

5.5.2 The Roles of God and of Jesus

The popular picture of God is that of his being the "Judge of all the earth" (Gen 18:25; cf. 1 Sam 2:10), and usually he is a judge before whom one comes as an accused criminal, perhaps as a guilty one. Likewise, the popular notion of Jesus, if he is not thought of simply as a teacher who was unjustly executed, is summed up in the phrase the "grace of our Lord Jesus Christ" (1 Cor 16:23; 2 Cor 13:13; Gal 6:18). Jude lets us know that these roles are not fixed and exclusive ones, that the Father is full of grace and love and the Son is indeed the coming Judge.

It is not that Jude is unique in this. God's grace is referred to in Acts 20:24 and Rom 5:15, among other places, and God and Jesus are linked in grace in Rom 1:7; 1 Cor 1:3–4; 2 Cor 1:2; Gal 1:3; Eph 1:2; and Phil 1:2 (it was part of the standard Pauline greeting). Furthermore, 2 Cor 13:13 (among other passages) refers to God's love. Jude's contribution is his consistency that does not allow one to overlook the realities he portrays.

Jude *always* refers to the Father in relationship to love, favor (grace), or salvation. So the addressees are loved "in God" (or, perhaps "by God," v. 1). It is God's favor (or grace, v. 4) that the "others" pervert. The "beloved" are to keep themselves "in the love of God" (v. 21). God is our Savior who will keep us from falling (v. 25). Every time we read of God in Jude, we get a picture of a patron whose favor is on the addressees, in whose love they live and need to keep living, and whose saving action is the source of their past rescue and present security. The pieces of this picture are all there elsewhere in the canon, but in Jude they are put together to reveal a consistent picture, a picture similar to that of James of a good God who gives only good gifts and therefore grants further favor when his followers fail.

Turning to Jesus, the picture is always that of a ruler who will bring justice to his people. He is "the Lord," a Greco-Roman ruler's title, and "the Anointed One," the Jewish hoped-for one who is God's appointed ruler. He is the Master (v. 4). He is "the Lord," who not only saved a people but also "destroyed those who did not trust" (v. 5). He has imprisoned the angels who did not keep their place (v. 6). He is the only judge, who has the right to rebuke (v. 9). He is the one who is coming to execute judgment (vv. 14–15), and he is the one who will show kindness or mercy in that judgment, a kindness that will lead to the life of the coming age (v. 21).

We get a more conventional picture of Jesus in his sending out official delegates (v. 17) and in his subordination to the Father (v. 25), but in Jude these are also pictures of authority, like that of the Roman commander bringing honor to the emperor. Again Jude's picture is similar to James, in that in James also Jesus appears with the titles of rule (especially Jas 2:1); Jesus is the one who promises a good outcome in judgment (Jas 1:12, since it is only Jesus elsewhere in the New Testament who is related to a "crown of life"); it is Jesus who is the giver of the "royal law" (2:8), who is the coming Lord who is near, who is the Judge at the door (5:7, 8, 9). But James is not as consistent in his use of "Lord" as Jude is, nor is he as consistent in separating the judging function from God. His tendency goes in the same direction as Jude, but Jude puts things in starker relief. He lets us know that Jesus may be a "friend," in the words of other writers of the New Testament, even if never in Jude's words, but Jesus is a superior friend, a ruling friend, a friend who will not show us partiality. He is "friend" in the same way as the Roman emperor had friends: they enjoyed his patronage; they were consulted or at least talked with him as he worked out his plans, but in the end they had better know who was emperor.

This portrayal of the Father and of Jesus fits, of course, with Jude's wider picture of God and Jesus and with the purpose of the letter. If what is attributed to God in the Hebrew Scriptures can be attributed to Jesus, if they are that closely identified, then it is not at all problematic to attribute judgment to Jesus. If the problem with the "others" is that they are not following the teaching of Jesus, it is his function as coming judge that both they and the "beloved" must understand as being of utmost importance. The "others" need to understand this to help them turn from their ways, and the "beloved" so that they will not be tempted into the ways of the "others." At the same time, saying that a particular portrayal is in some ways rhetorically determined does not mean that it is insignificant. Jude throws into relief aspects of the Father and Jesus that are present elsewhere within the canon, but which may be missed without Jude's clear contrast.

5.5.3 The Tension of Standing and Falling

If Jesus is the Lord and is coming in judgment, then it is important that people know where they stand in relation to him. It is here that Jude walks a fine line. On the one hand, he is not anxious about "the beloved." They are "kept" for Jesus the Anointed One (v. 1). They are within the tradition, for they can be exhorted to "remember." There is a commitment (faith) that has been passed on to God's holy ones, and the "beloved" are surely among them (v. 3). And God is capable of "making them stand" in the presence of Jesus rejoicing, for the unspoken assumption is that they will receive reward rather than condemnation in the judgment (v. 24). All of this indicates that Jude is not anxious about them, which fits with the wider canonical tradition of the believer being protected; one reflects, for instance, on the protective nature of the good shepherd in John 10, to name but one passage.

On the other hand, the "keeping" is not one-sided. They may be the "called" of God (v. 1), but so was Israel called and saved in being brought out of Egypt, yet those who did not trust "the Lord" ("trust" or "commit" is a better translation than "believe" when there is an implied or explicit personal object) were destroyed. The "saved" can be destroyed, just as the divine messengers who were in a good place are now in prison because they departed from that good place. They were indeed secure as long as they did not leave their security. Thus the "others" are part of the community, but the divine favor that they enjoyed they have twisted, and they are being false to the Lord to whom they have pledged themselves. They are still members of the community, participating in the communal meal. But Jude implies that they are in great danger of the "fire" side of judgment. So it is possible to be "in" and end up being "out."

Thus, one must exert effort: it is by strengthening their commitment and praying "in the Spirit" that the "beloved" keep themselves in God's love (vv. 20 – 21). Then they will be able to look expectantly for Jesus' kindness in the final judgment, the kind word that will designate them for the life of the coming age. Surely Luther would not have liked this, for it smacks of "works," but then it was James, whom Luther also did not like, who said, "Faith without works is dead ... useless" (Jas 2:17, 20, 26). Likewise, in 2 Peter 1 we saw that while the author can talk warmly about the "epignostic" salvation that his addressees enjoy, he can also admonish them to move on in virtue if they do not wish to become reprobate. The same Paul who talks about God's favor being the way to deliverance can also say that those practicing certain evils (probably sample lists rather than exhaustive lists) will not inherit God's kingdom (1 Cor 6:9 – 11; Gal 5:16 – 21). And of course there is Hebrews with its confidence in the present status of the addressees (Heb 6:9 – 12) coming right after a warning about what will happen if the fully initiate apostatize (6:1 – 8).

Likewise, in Jude there is no nail-biting anxiety, but there is also sober realism. The "beloved" are kept, but they must keep themselves. They are to rescue the "others," but those very "others" they are to rescue from the fire are part of the community. They are to rescue, but they are to do it carefully, for it is dangerous work. The angels were safe, but only as long as they kept their proper place. Wandering stars end up in deepest darkness. Again, these are not unique themes to Jude, but themes that Jude makes to stand out more clearly since they come together in so short a letter. Jude will not let us deny either side of the balance or resolve the antinomy, and as such he corrects any doctrinal formulation that reads only one set of texts in the New Testament and minimizes the other set.

5.5.4 The Struggle of Differentiation

A final significant canonical contribution of Jude is his underlining the struggle behind the differentiation of the Jesus movement within the Greco-Roman world. He is an example of dealing with those who follow Greco-Roman mores rather than those of the Jesus movement. One could call this "ethics," but that would only be one part of the issue. Jude is hardly alone in the New Testament in condemning licentious behavior, although he and 2 Peter (which draws from him) are unique in rejecting the human critique of angels. His description of virtues and vices is interesting and adds to the wider picture of ethics in the New Testament, but it is hardly unique. Rather in Jude the real contribution is in how one *deals* with those who differ.

Dealing with groups whose behavior one believes to be wrong is a perpetual issue in the Jewish and Christian worlds. One might assume that Jews would have had unified assumptions on lifestyle, but that is not so. Examples of lifestyle conflict are numerous: the prophets of the Hebrew Scriptures excoriating their fellow citizens; the conflicts noted in Ezra-Nehemiah between the Jews who returned from exile and the Jews who remained in Palestine during the exile; the conflicts with Hellenism and other influences recorded in 1 and 2 Maccabees (i.e., the conflict among Jewish groups). And, of course, the New Testament era witnesses the Qumran group rejecting both the Pharisees and the temple establishment, and the Pharisees trying to define Torah obedience over against the laxity of much of the people of the land. This also includes their conflict with the understanding of Torah exhibited by Jesus of Nazareth. At least in the Synoptic Gospels the initial hostility toward Jesus by the Pharisees had more to do with his understanding of what submitting to the Torah looked like than with claims regarding himself.

As the community of Jesus' followers developed after Easter, they too had to find their identity and express it in their lifestyle. They appear to have started off as a relatively unified group, largely (but not exclusively) Galilean Jews who had absorbed Jesus' teaching in terms of lifestyle. A general perspective on Torah obedience was assumed, with Jesus viewed as the promised Messiah and his teaching modifying their previous understandings of Torah. There was surely a variety of understandings within the movement, but at least the leaders appear to have been a relatively homogenous group.

While there were several stages in development as the group expanded (Acts points to the absorption of Hellenistic Jews and of Samaritans as two of the stages), the first major issue came in the expansion of the Jesus movement among non-Jews.

Both Acts and much of Paul's corpus deal with the differences within the community in their understanding of the relevance of Jewish ethnicity to obedience to Jesus as Lord. The one group argued that one must become a Jew, that is, be circumcised if a male, observe the laws of kashruth, and observe Jewish festivals, especially the Sabbath. This in Greco-Roman eyes meant that one had abandoned their former nationality and become part of another national and ethnic group, Jews. This would be true even if one were part of a particular sect of Judaism, that is, those who followed Jesus as Messiah.

Acts and Paul, of course, championed another position: Greco-Romans did not need to become Jews but rather to commit to Jesus as Lord. Thus circumcision, dietary rules, and Jewish festivals were irrelevant. Even within this position there were differences. In Col 2:11–12 Paul argues that one reason a person does not need to be circumcised is that he is *already* circumcised in the circumcision of Jesus (variously interpreted by biblical scholars). Yet in Acts 15:19–20 a type of compromise is suggested by which former pagans could fully share with Jews by avoiding certain evils which in Jewish eyes would make them unable to share a meal with a Jew without polluting the Jew—a type of compromise that Paul puts differently in, say, Rom 14.

As one sees in the Acts passage, the issue was not only whether the new followers of Jesus needed to become Jews—eventually answered in the negative—but also whether they needed to give up parts of their former culture (e.g., eating foods containing blood). This culture clash would continue to be clarified. For example, Paul makes it clear in 1 Cor 10 that participation in sacrificial meals in the temples of Greco-Roman gods was not appropriate for a follower of Jesus, even if that meal were, say, a birthday party held in temple precincts and the sacrifice itself a minor part of the celebration.

But there were other issues with Greco-Roman culture that also needed to be addressed. While 1 Cor 5 deals strongly with a person who has violated not just Jewish, but also Greco-Roman moral values, 1 Cor 6 argues in some detail about accepted Greco-Roman values that were not acceptable within the Jesus movement, namely, lawsuits and visiting prostitutes. While Paul makes it clear that neither of these activities is acceptable, he does not announce any sanctions but seeks to persuade rather than condemn. He also does not present these issues as behaviors condemned by the Torah, for that might make it seem as if Paul is trying to get the former pagans to become Jews. Instead, he seeks to persuade—sometimes by using the teaching of Jesus (1 Cor 6:7 is probably a Jesus saying present via the rhetorical method of *aemulatio*), sometimes by using logic.

It is here that Jude makes his contribution, for the "others" in Jude are likely "normal" Greco-Romans who do not believe that becoming part of the Jesus movement requires a change in certain behaviors. If this reconstruction is correct, they reject Jesus as an authority to be followed (perhaps thinking that his preresurrection teaching was in essence Jewish), and they also reject the Torah (if that is what their slandering angels refers to, i.e., the angels mediating the law). Or perhaps they reject the arguments of Jude and the "beloved" because, in the "others'" view, those arguments are thinly disguised Torah. The "others" claim that their behavior is sanctioned by God's favor. It is also clear that the types of behavior the "others" are accused of would fall within the spectrum of normal Greco-Roman behavior.

But Jude believes that this relatively normal Greco-Roman behavior is a twisting of the divine favor and a rebellion against Jesus. Unlike the pattern we see in Paul, we do not know from Jude where Jude is drawing the line. His condemnations are relatively general. But we do know that he is drawing a line. Some behaviors and attitudes are not compatible with following Jesus. Jude, then, is another aspect of the Jesus movement's dealing with its differences from Greco-Roman culture and drawing the line between divine favor (grace) and license. In Jude's case the teaching is addressed to those for whom he has no criticism, the "beloved," who appear to be the majority. However, surely he knows that his rhetoric will be "overheard" by the "others," since a letter such as this would be read aloud in the community gathering.

What is interesting is that like Paul, Jude does not propose strongly sanction-ing these individuals. Like Paul (e.g., 1 Cor 6:9–10) he suggests that there will be divine sanctions if the behavior continues (e.g., Jude 23), but, also like Paul, he does not order any immediate sanctions. Rather, Jude argues that the "beloved" must strengthen their own commitment and should then seek to rescue the "others," whether these persons are those who doubt as to which side is right or those who already, so to speak, are in "the fire." This activity must be done carefully and with discernment, but it is still a rescue activity, not a cut-off. Thus Jude's canonical contribution in this respect is to give one more example of a community discussing where the boundaries of Christian behavior are to be found, and doing so in the light of its eschatology, that Jesus is the coming judge, so the believers are not the collective judge or individual judges. Yet grace is not license, submission to Jesus as Lord does mean obedience, and kindness if not love dictates that those outside the boundaries be denounced (in the case of Jude, using bombastic Asiatic rhetoric) and called back to their allegiance to the Lord Jesus the Anointed One.

Conclusion

In the first century, as we have pointed out in a number of places, there were a number of well-known theological voices. First among these was that of Peter son of Jonah, privileged follower of Jesus of Nazareth, designated leader of the resulting movement. He was "Rock," even if 1 Peter says that Jesus is the only cornerstone. Second only to Peter was James son of Joseph, whose influence became greater than Peter's (if Acts 15 is an accurate guide) as Peter began to travel. The Jude of our literature was James's younger brother in a world where being a relative of the right person meant something. In that first-century world there was also Paul of Tarsus, a controversial and perhaps irascible leader, who planted Jesus communities all around the northeast quarter of the Mediterranean, but whose status in the "mother" community and the movement as a whole was not entirely secure.

All of these people along with others have contributed works (whether by writing personally or lending their names; see the introduction to each of the letters covered in this book) eventually gathered into our New Testament. All of these saw themselves as interpreters of Jesus, propagators of his movement, or defenders of what it meant to be loyal to him. While they were theological voices, they were theological voices by default rather than as a primary vocation, because one needed to "do" theology in order to lead a movement under the rule of Jesus, God's Anointed One. Theology was, so to speak, done on the fly as need arose. Much theology developed unconsciously in the context of worship and obedience and was only later brought to consciousness. What they wrote was written largely in response to problems in the communities. The letters we have are occasional letters, incorporating the teaching of or traditions from these leaders.

The problem is that especially since the Reformation, Paul has dominated in Western Christianity, and especially viewed through a particular set of lenses. In some circles Paul has dominated at the expense of Jesus, for the Gospels were largely reduced to favorite verses and Sunday School stories, with the exception of the birth and passion-resurrection narratives, which must surely be believed. We might call this a type of "Apostles' Creed Christianity," for it leaves out most of the works and words of Jesus, namely, those that should form our lifestyle (although the Apostles' Creed does make an excellent "pledge of allegiance," detailing who it is whom we follow).

Paul would have been appalled. Yet, if he has at times dominated more than Jesus, he has virtually obscured the writers of the General Epistles, who were major leaders in his day. Either he wrote more, or more of his writings were preserved since the areas of his ministry were spared the upheavals of 66–70 CE and then again those of 132–135. He wrote to solve problems in the communities he founded. That problem-solving focus by necessity created a one-sided picture, with Paul's dealing with his particular concerns at the expense of other concerns and his speaking into a context that he at least hoped would understand him (although 1 Cor 5:9–11 shows that his hopes were sometimes not realized). Without the voices of the other leaders whose concerns differed from Paul's, Paul himself would surely recognize that one had an unbalanced picture.

The collection of the Catholic (or General) Epistles balances this picture, whether it was done intentionally (as Nienhuis, *Not by Paul Alone*, argues) or unintentionally (as a means of preserving these letters by putting them together in a single codex). If Paul has often been read (somewhat unfairly) as giving a dark, judgmental view of God, these letters remind us that the Father is good, always giving good gifts, showing human beings his favor, and entering into a relationship of care (i.e., love) in which human beings can live. If Jesus has often been portrayed as a sacrifice, albeit one who rose from the dead, with the cross being the dominant picture (and this also is not fair to Paul, for he wrote Romans without once using "cross" or "crucify" to refer to the death of Jesus), these letters remind us that Jesus is the exalted Lord, not just of his community but of the world, who is returning as openly declared world Ruler and thus as Judge. They can do this without referring to the death of Jesus (in the case of James, 2 Peter, and Jude) or with only a few references that call for our identifying our experience with that death or dedicating ourselves anew because of that death (in the case of 1 Peter).

Also, if John has been read as giving us a "friend in Jesus," who is our buddy (a misreading of John, but a common one), these works remind us that we may be Jesus' people and even his extended family, but we are not his equals. We should say "sir" when we address him, or, even better, "your Majesty." He is always spoken of with one of his titles of rule: "the Anointed One" or "the Lord." These were well understood in his day. He is "the Judge" and "glorious." We are his "slaves" and his "sheep." There is a vast status difference between us, and yet he does care, does show kindness, and does give us reason to rejoice in his presence.

If Paul has been read as teaching "faith alone," so that it is enough if we are committed to the right things as true and have "asked Jesus into our heart," and if we have received "grace alone" so that "Jesus loves me no matter what I do," these letters remind us that we will face him in the final judgment and there will be no favoritism. Any "faith" that does not result in obedience to Jesus (i.e., "works") is useless, a dead corpse. Any idea of "grace" or "favor" that ignores submission to Jesus as Lord is "perverted" (in the words of Jude). For these writers it is possible to depart from God's love. Yet these writers do not give us a sense of anxiety. The world is a hostile and dangerous place, it is true, but there is a Father who keeps us.

If Paul has sometimes been read in ways that play down his apocalyptic eschatology, for example, by those who wish to ignore 2 Thessalonians, these letters remind us that such imagery was widespread, whether one looks at the scenario in Jas 5:1–6, the frequent references to the last judgment in 1 Peter, or 2 Peter's hope of eventually being in a world that has been apocalyptically exposed and judged and so is fit for those who will walk in God's righteous ways. In some ways these General Letters are hopeful, for they are full of expectation of the coming Lord. It is not that this theme is absent in Paul, but more that Paul has enough other axes to grind that this one often gets overlooked.

Finally, if Paul has been viewed as giving a carte blanche to the rulers of this world (we think of some interpretations of Rom 13),[1] 1 Peter reminds us that we are members of a new people of God and so foreigners in the lands of our birth; James reminds us that we do not live by the values of this age and that the elites ("rich") of this age stand under Jesus' judgment; and 2 Peter reminds us that our hope is in a coming age. All of these do so without saying that "heaven is our home," for their hope is not in heaven after death (they do not speak about this), but in a transformed world ruled by Jesus himself. Their future world is not human democracy, but divine monarchy (2 Peter in particular, but also Jude, and in another way 1 Peter, are clear that Jesus is a divine monarch).

We could go on to other aspects of the believer's relationship to culture, to a number of aspects of ethics. All of these are places where "the rubber meets the road" and where the cultures we were born into seek to pull us into their way of thinking. These letters remind us of a God who has chosen the poor, not the rich; who has called us out of Egypt; who has rescued us from Sodom; whose motto is not "if it feels good, do it," or "self-fulfillment." Instead, we are called to live under Jesus as Lord, in the kingdom or rule of God, and for his honor, not ours (even if he will honor us in the end for living this way).

These letters call us to Jesus and in one way or another to the teaching of Jesus. They balance Paul, perhaps, but in their own minds they are completing and defending the Gospels. They want to show what it looks like to live under the authority of Jesus in the second half of the first century in the eastern half of the Roman Empire.[2] We may live in a different world today. However, we are the heirs of that Roman Empire and live among people who are, well, people, and so behave with analogous values to those living in that empire. Jesus has not changed over the years, nor has his teaching altered. Thus these letters are also guides to twenty-first-century followers of Jesus who grasp what they teach and apply it to the world in which they live.

---

1. This became clear to this writer when he realized in his first teaching post that his dean and also the leader of the whole missions and educational organization at which he taught, both good evangelicals, had fought in World War II as German soldiers, in one case as an officer, out of their obedience to God because of their inter-pretation of Rom 13, while there were Americans, Canadians, and British at whom they were shooting and who were shooting at them who were motivated by the same interpretation of the same passage.

2. First Peter may have been written in Rome, but it is addressed to Asia Minor, which is part of the eastern half of the empire.

BIBLIOGRAPHY

Abrahams, Israel. *Hebrew Ethical Wills*. Philadelphia: Jewish Publication Society, 1926.

———. *Studies in Pharisaism and the Gospels*. 2nd series. Cambridge: Cambridge University Press, 1924.

Achtemeier, Paul J. *1 Peter*. Hermeneia. Minneapolis: Fortress, 1996.

Adams, Edward. "Where Is the Promise of His Coming? The Complaint of the Scoffers in 2 Peter 3.4." *NTS* 51 (2005): 106–22.

Allison, Dale C., Jr. *James: A Critical and Exegetical Commentary*. ICC. London/New York: Bloomsbury T&T Clark, 2013.

———. *Testament of Abraham*. CEJL. Berlin/New York: Walter de Gruyter, 2003.

Andersen, Francis I. "Yahweh, the Kind and Sensitive God." Pp. 41–88 in *God Who Is Rich in Mercy: Essays Presented to Dr. D. B. Knox*. Ed. Peter T. O'Brien and David G. Peterson. Homebush West, NSW: Lancer / Grand Rapids: Baker, 1986.

Aune, David E. *Prophecy in Early Christianity and the Ancient Mediterranean World*. Grand Rapids: Eerdmans, 1983.

Bailey, Robert Edson. "Is 'Sleep' the Proper Biblical Term for the Intermediate State?" *ZNW* 55 (1964): 161–67.

Balch, D. L. *Let Wives Be Submissive: The Domestic Code in 1 Peter*. SBLMS 26. Ed. J. Crenshaw. Chico, CA: Scholars Press, 1981.

Baltzer, Klaus. *The Covenant Formulary*. Oxford: Basil Blackwell, 1971.

Banks, Robert J. *Going to Church in the First Century: An Eyewitness Account*. Chipping Norton, NSW: Hexagon, 1980.

Barnes, Thomas. "The Epistle of Jude: A Study in the Marcosian Heresy." *JTS* 6 (1905): 391–411.

Barr, James. "'Abba, Father' and the Familiarity of Jesus' speech." *Theol* 91 (1988): 173–79.

———. "Abba Isn't 'Daddy.'" *JTS* ns 39 (1988): 28–47.

Barrett, C. K. "Myth and the New Testament: The Greek Word *mythos*." *ExpTim* 68 (1957): 345–48.

———. "Things Sacrificed to Idols." *NTS* 11 (1964–1965): 138–53.

Bauckham, Richard J. "The Delay of the Parousia." *TynBul* 31 (1980): 3–36.

———. "James, 1 and 2 Peter, Jude." Pp. 303–17 in *It Is Written: Scripture Citing Scripture; Essays in Honour of Barnabas Lindars*. Ed. D. A. Carson and H. G. M. Williamson. Cambridge: Cambridge University Press, 1988.

———. *James: Wisdom of James, Disciple of Jesus the Sage*. New Testament Readings. London and New York: Routledge, 1999.

———. *Jude and the Relatives of Jesus in the Early Church*. Edinburgh: T&T Clark, 1990.

———. *Jude, 2 Peter*. WBC 50. Waco, TX: Word, 1983.

———. "A Note on a Problem in the Greek Version of 1 Enoch i.9." *JTS* 32 (1981): 136–38.

Bauer, J. B. "Der erste Petrusbrief und die Verfolgung unter Domitian." Pp. 513–27 in *Die Kirche des Anfangs: Festschrift für H. Schürmann*. Ed. R. Schnackenburg. ErfTSt 38. Leipzig: St. Benno, 1978.

Beare, Francis Wright. *The First Epistle of Peter*. Oxford: Basil Blackwell, 1970.

Belleville, Linda. "Ἰουνιᾶν … ἐπίσημοι ἐν τοῖς ἀποστόλοις: A Re-examination of Romans 16.7 in Light of Primary Source Materials." *NTS* 51 (2005): 231–49.

Berger, Klaus. "Der Streit des guten und des bösen Engels um die Seele: Beobachtungen zu 4QAmr^b und Judas 9. " *JSJ* 4 (1973): 1–18.

Bernheim, Pierre-Antoine. *James, Brother of Jesus*. London: SCM, 1997.

Best, Ernst. *1 Peter*. NCB. Grand Rapids: Eerdmans, 1971, 1982.

Bieder, Werner. "Judas 22f.: *Hous de eleate en phobō*." *TZ* 6 (1950): 75–77.

Bigg, Charles. *A Critical and Exegentical Commentary on the Epistles of St. Peter and St. Jude*. ICC. Edinburgh: T&T Clark, 1901, 1902².

Birdsall, J. Neville. "The Text of Jude in P72." *JTS* 14 (1963): 394–99.

Black, Matthew. "Critical and Exegetical Notes on Three New Testament Texts: Hebrews xi. 11, Jude 5, James 1. 27." Pp. 39–45 in *Apophoreta: Festschrift für Ernst Haenchen*. BZNW 30. Berlin: Alfred Töpelmann, 1964.

———. "The Doxology to the *Pater Noster* with a Note on Matthew 6:13b." Pp. 327–32 in *A Tribute to Geza Vermes*. Ed. Philip Davies and Richard White. Sheffield: JSOT, 1991.

———. "The Maranatha Invocation and Jude 14, 15 (I Enoch I:9)." Pp. 189–96 in *Christ and Spirit in the New Testament: Studies in Honour of Charles Francis Digby Moule*. Ed. Barnabas Lindars and Stephen S. Smalley. Cambridge: Cambridge University Press, 1973.

Blass, F., and A. Debrunner. *A Greek Grammar of the New Testament and Other Early Christian Literature*. Trans. and rev. by Robert W. Funk. Chicago: University of Chicago Press, 1961.

Blazen, I. T. "Suffering and Cessation from Sin according to 1 Peter 4:1." *AUSS* 21 (1983): 27–50.

Blomberg, Craig L., and Mariam J. Kamell. *James*. ZECNT. Grand Rapids: Zondervan, 2008.

Bloomquist, Gregory. "The Epicurean Tag in Plutarch: Implications for New Testament Study." http://www.bloomquist.ca/publications/articles/Epicurean%20Tag%20in%20 Plutarch.htm.

Blue, Ken. *Authority to Heal*. Downers Grove, IL: InterVarsity Press, 1987.

Boismard, M.-É. *Quatres hymnes baptismales dans la première épître de Pierre*. Lectio Divina 30. Paris: Editions du Cerf, 1961.

Bonus, A. "2 Peter III. 10." *ExpTim* 32 (1920–1921): 280–81.

Boobyer, George. H. "The Indebtedness of 2 Peter to 1 Peter." Pp. 34–53 in *New Testament Essays: Studies in Memory of T. W. Manson*. Ed. A. J. B. Higgins. Manchester: University of Manchester Press, 1959.

———. "The Verbs in Jude 11." *NTS* 5 (1958): 45–47.

Borgen, Peder. *Bread from Heaven: An Exegetical Study of the Concept of Manna in the Gospel of John and the Writings of Philo*. NovTSup 10. Leiden: Brill, 1965.

Bornemann, W. "Der erste Petrusbrief: Eine Taufrede des Silvanus?" *ZNW* 19 (1919/1920): 143–65.

Bowker, John. *The Targums and Rabbinic Literature*. Cambridge: Cambridge University Press, 1969.

Boyd, Gregory A. *Repenting of Religion: Turning from Judgment to the Love of God*. Grand Rapids: Baker, 2004.

Bray, Gerald, ed. *James, 1–2 Peter, 1–3 John, Jude*. ACCS, New Testament 11. Downers Grove, IL: InterVarsity Press, 2000.

Brown, J. P. "Synoptic Parallels in the Epistles and Form-History." *NTS* 10 (1963–1964): 27–48.

Brown, R. E., K. P. Donfried, and J. Reumann, eds. *Peter in the New Testament.* Minneapolis: Augsburg, 1973.

Brown, Raymond E. "Does the New Testament Call Jesus God?" Pp. 1–38 in Raymond E. Brown, *Jesus, God and Man.* Milwaukee: Bruce, 1967.

Brox, N. *Der erste Petrusbrief.* 2nd ed. EKKNT 21. Zürich: Benziger, 1986.

———. *Zeuge und Märtyrer: Untersuchungen zur frühchristlichen Zeugnis-Terminologie.* Munich: Kösel, 1961.

Bruce, F. F. *The Canon of Scripture.* Downers Grove, IL: InterVarsity Press, 1988.

———. *Peter, Stephen, James, and John: Studies in Non-Pauline Christianity.* Grand Rapids: Eerdmans, 1979.

Buchanan, George W. "Eschatology and the 'End of Days.'" *JNES* 20 (1961): 188–93.

Bultmann, Rudolph. *Theology of the New Testament.* New York: Charles Scribner's, 1955.

Burer, Michael H., and Daniel B. Wallace. "Was Junia Really an Apostle? A Re-examination of Rom 16.7." *NTS* 47 (2001): 76–91.

Burkitt, F. C. *Christian Beginnings.* London: London University Press, 1924.

Burridge, Richard A. "The Gospels and Acts." Pp. 512–13 in *Handbook of Classical Rhetoric in the Hellenistic Period, 330 B.C.–A.D. 400.* Ed. Stanley E. Porter. Boston/Leiden: Brill, 2001.

Burtness, J. H. "Sharing the Suffering of God in the Life of the World." *Int* 23 (1969): 277–88.

Calvin, John. *Commentaries on the Catholic Epistles.* Ed. and trans. J. Owen. Calvin's Commentaries 22. Grand Rapids: Baker, (1551) 1979. Some citations are from the electronic edition, Bellingham, WA: Logos Bible Software, 2010, although the page numbers in the print edition are preserved.

Campbell, Barth L. *Honor, Shame, and the Rhetoric of 1 Peter.* SBLDS 160. Atlanta: Scholars Press, 1998.

Campbell, J. B. "Domitian." Pp. 237–38 in *The Oxford Companion to Classical Civilization.* Ed. Simone Hornblower and Anthony Spawforth. Oxford/New York: Oxford University Press, 2004.

Cantinat, Jean. *Les épîtres de Saint Jacques et de Saint Jude.* SB. Paris: J. Gabalda, 1973.

Chaine, Joseph. *Les épîtres catholiques; la seconde épître de saint Pierre, les épîtres de saint Jean, l'épître de saint Jude.* Études bibliques. Paris: Gabalda, 1939.

Charles, J. Daryl. *2 Peter, Jude.* In *1–2 Peter, Jude.* BCBC. Scottdale, PA: Herald, 1999.

———. "Jude's Use of Pseudepigraphical Source-Material as Part of a Literary Strategy." *NTS* 37 (1991): 130–45.

———. "Literary Artifice in the Epistle of Jude." *ZNW* 82 (1991): 106–24.

———. *Literary Strategy in the Epistle of Jude.* Scranton, PA: University of Scranton Press / London: Associated University Press, 1993.

———. "'Those' and 'These': The Use of the Old Testament in the Epistle of Jude." *JSNT* 38 (1990): 109–24.

———. "The Use of Tradition-Material in the Epistle of Jude." Undated paper read at a SBL annual meeting.

Charles, R. H. *The Apocrypha and Pseudepigrapha of the Old Testament.* Oxford: Clarendon, 1913.

———. *The Assumption of Moses.* London: A & C Black, 1897.

Charlesworth, James H. *The Old Testament Pseudepigrapha*. Garden City, NY: Doubleday, 1983.

Chase, Frederic Henry. "Jude, Epistle of." Pp. 799–806 in *Dictionary of the Bible*. Ed. James Hastings, vol. 2. New York: Scribner's, 1909.

Chester, Andrew, and Ralph P. Martin. *The Theology of the Letters of James, Peter, and Jude*. New Testament Theology. Cambridge: Cambridge University Press, 1994.

Chevallier, M. A. "Condition et vocation des chrétiens en diaspora: remarques exégétiques sur la 1re Épître de Pierre." *RSR* 48 (1974): 387–400.

Chilton, Bruce D. "The Transfiguration: Dominical Assurance and Apostolic Vision." *NTS* 27 (1980–1981): 120–21.

Chilton, Bruce, and Craig A. Evans, eds. *James the Just and Christian Origins*. NovTSup 98. Leiden, Brill, 1999.

———, eds. *The Missions of James, Peter, and Paul: Tensions in Early Christianity*. NovTSup 115. Leiden, Brill, 2005.

Chilton, Bruce, and Jacob Neusner, eds. *The Brother of Jesus: James the Just and His Mission*. Louisville: Westminster John Knox, 2001.

Clemen, C. "The First Epistle of St. Peter and the Book of Enoch." *Exp* 6/4 (1902): 316–20.

Collins, John N. *Diakonia: Reinterpreting the Ancient Sources*. Oxford: Oxford University Press, 1990.

Conti, Martino. "La Sophia di 2 Petr. 3.15." *RivB* 17 (1969) : 121–38.

Cross, F. L. *1 Peter: A Paschal Liturgy*. London: Mowbray, 1954.

Cullmann, O. *Petrus: Jünger-Apostel-Märtyrer*. 2nd ed. Zürich: Zwingli, 1960. ET: Trans. F. V. Filson. *Peter: Disciple, Apostle, Martyr*. Philadelphia: Westminster, 1962.

Dalton, W. J. *Christ's Proclamation to the Spirits: A Study of 1 Peter 3:18–4:6*. AnBib 23. Rome: Pontifical Biblical Institute, 1965.

Danby, Herbert. *The Mishnah*. Oxford: Clarendon, 1933.

Daniel, Constantin. "La mention des Esséniens dans le texte grec de l'épître de S. Jude." *Muséon* 81 (1968): 503–21.

Danker, Frederick W. "1 Peter 1:24–2:17: A Consolatory Pericope." *ZNW* 58 (1967): 93–102.

———. "2 Peter: A Solemn Decree." *CBQ* 40 (1978): 64–82.

———. "2 Peter." Pp. 84–93 in *The General Letters*. Ed. Gerhard Krodel. Proclamation. Minneapolis: Fortress, 1995.

Davids, Peter H. "Are the Others Too Other? The Issue of Others in Jude and 2 Peter." Pp. 201–14 in *Reading 1–2 Peter and Jude*. Ed. Eric F. Mason and Troy W. Martin. Resources for Biblical Study 77. Atlanta: Society of Biblical Literature, 2014.

———. *The Epistle of 1 Peter*. NICNT. Grand Rapids: Eerdmans, 1990.

———. *The Epistle of James*. NIGTC. Grand Rapids: Eerdmans, 1982.

———. *The Letters of 2 Peter and Jude*. Pillar. Grand Rapids: Eerdmans, 2006.

———. "The Meaning of Ἀπείραστος in James i.13." *NTS* 24 (1978): 386–92.

———. "The Meaning of Ἀπείραστος Revisited." Pp. 225–40 in *New Testament Greek and Exegesis: Essays in Honor of Gerald F. Hawthorne*. Ed. Timothy Sailors and Amy Donaldson. Grand Rapids: Eerdmans, 2003.

———. "A Silent Witness in Marriage: 1 Pet 3:1–7." Pp. 224–38 in *Discovering Biblical Equality: Complementarity without Hierarchy*. Ed. Ronald W. Pierce and Rebecca Merrill Groothuis. Downers Grove, IL: InterVarsity Press, 2004.

————. "Themes in the Epistle of James That Are Judaistic in Character." Unpublished PhD thesis, University of Manchester, 1974.

————. "The Use of Second Temple Traditions in 1 and 2 Peter and Jude." Pp. 409–31 in *The Catholic Epistles and the Tradition*. Ed. Jacques Schlosser. BETL 176. Leuven: Peeters/Leuven University Press, 2004.

————. "What Glasses Are You Wearing? Reading Hebrew Narratives through Second Temple Lenses." *JETS* 55 (2012): 763–71.

Deichgräber, Reinhard. *Gotteshymnus und Christushymnus in der frühen Christenheit*. Göttingen: Vandenhoeck & Ruprecht, 1967.

Deissmann, Gustav Adolf. *Bible Studies: Contributions Chiefly from Papyri and Inscriptions to the History of the Language, the Literature, and the Religion and Hellenistic Judaism and Primitive Christianity*. Trans. Alexander Grieve. Edinburgh: T&T Clark, 1901, 1903.

Delling, Gerhard. "MONOS ΘEOS. " Pp. 396–400 in *Studien zum neuen Testament und hellenistischen Judentum: Gesammelte Aufsätze, 1950–1968*. Göttingen: Vandenhoeck & Ruprecht, 1970. Previously in *TLZ* 77 (1952) : 469–76.

Deppe, Dean B. *The Sayings of Jesus in the Epistle of James*. Chelsea, MI: Bookcrafters, 1989.

deSilva, David A. *Honor, Patronage, Kinship and Purity: Unlocking New Testament Culture*. Downers Grove, IL: InterVarsity Press, 2000.

————. *The Jewish Teachers of Jesus, James, and Jude: What Earliest Christianity Learned from the Apocrypha and Pseudepigrapha*. Oxford/New York: Oxford University Press, 2012.

Dibelius, Martin. *Der Brief des Jakobus*. KEK. Göttingen: Vandenhoeck & Ruprecht, 1921, 1964[11]. Trans. Martin Dibelius and Heinrich Greeven as *James: A Commentary on the Epistle of James*. Hermeneia. Philadelphia: Fortress, 1976.

Donfried, Karl P. *The Setting of Second Clement in Early Christianity*. NovTSup 38. Leiden: Brill, 1974.

Dubarle, André M. "Le péché des anges dans l'épître de Jude." Pp. 145–48 in *Memorial J. Chaine*. Lyons: Facultés Catholiques, 1950.

Duke, Rodney K. "Priests, Priesthood." Pp. 646–55 in *Dictionary of the Old Testament: Pentateuch*. Ed. T. Desmond Alexander and David W. Baker. Downers Grove, IL: InterVarsity Press, 2003.

Dunn, James D. G. *Jesus and the Spirit*. London: SCM, 1975.

Dunstan, William E. *Ancient Greece.* Fort Worth, TX: Harcourt College Publishers, 2000.

du Plessis, O. J. "The Authorship of the Epistle of Jude." Pp. 191–99 in *Biblical Essays 1966: Proceedings of the Ninth Meeting of "Die Ou-Testamentiese Werkgemeenskap in Suid-Afrika," and Proceedings of the Second Meeting of "Die Nuwe-Testamentiese Werkgemeen-skam van Suid-Afrika."* Potchefstroom, South Africa: Potchefstroom Herlad (Edms.) Beperk, 1966.

Dupont, Jacques. *Gnosis: La connaissance religieuse dans les épîtres de Saint Paul*. Louvain/Paris: Nauwelaerts/Gabalda, 1949.

Du Toit, Andreas B. "Vilification as a Pragmatic Device in Early Christian Epistolography." *Bib* 75 (1994): 403–12.

Edgar, Thomas R. "Robert H. Gundry and Revelation 3:10." *GTJ* 3 (1982): 19–49.

Elliott, J. H. *1 Peter: Estrangement and Community*. Chicago: Franciscan Herald, 1979.

————. *1 Peter: A New Translation with Introduction and Commentary*. AB 37. New York: Doubleday, 2000.

————. *I–II Peter/Jude*. ACNT. Minneapolis: Augsburg, 1982.

———. *The Elect and the Holy: An Exegetical Examination of 1 Peter 2:4–10 and the Phrase* βασίλειον ἱεράτευμα. NovTSup 12. Leiden: Brill, 1966.

———. *A Home for the Homeless: A Sociological Exegesis of 1 Peter, Its Situation and Strategy.* Philadelphia: Fortress, 1981.

———. "The Rehabilitation of an Exegetical Stepchild: 1 Peter in Recent Research." *JBL* 95 (1976): 243–54. Reprinted pp. 3–16 in *Perspectives on First Peter.* Ed. C. H. Talbert. Macon, GA: Mercer University Press, 1986.

Ellis, E. Earle. *Paul and His Recent Interpreters.* Grand Rapids: Eerdmans, 1961.

———. *Pauline Theology: Ministry and Society.* Grand Rapids: Eerdmans, 1989.

———. "Prophecy and Hermeneutic in Jude." Pp. 220–36 in *Prophecy and Hermeneutic in Early Christianity.* Grand Rapids: Eerdmans, 1978.

The Episcopal Church. *The Book of Common Prayer.* New York: Seabury, 1979.

Erickson, Millard J. *Christian Theology.* Grand Rapids: Baker, 1985.

Feldmeier, Reinhard. *Der erste Brief des Petrus.* THICNT 15. Leipzig: Evangelische Verlagsanstalt, 2005.

———. *The First Letter of Peter.* Waco, TX: Baylor University Press, 2008.

Ferguson, Everett. *Backgrounds of Early Christianity.* Grand Rapids: Eerdmans, 1993².

Filson, F. V. "Partakers with Christ: Suffering in First Peter." *Int* 9 (1955): 400–412.

Finegan, Jack. "The Original Form of the Pauline Collection." *HTR* 49 (1956): 85–104.

Fitzmyer, Joseph A. "The Name Simon." Pp. 105–12 in *Essays on the Semitic Background of the New Testament.* London: Geoffrey Chapman, 1971.

Fossum, Jarl. "Kurios Jesus as the Angel of the Lord in Jude 5–7." *NTS* 33 (1987): 226–43.

Frankemölle, Hubert. *Der Brief des Jakobus.* Kapitel 1/Kapitel 2–5. Ökumenischer Taschenbuch-Kommentar zum Neuen Testament 17/1–2. Gütersloh: Gütersloher Verlaghauser, 1994.

Friedrich, Gerhard. "Lohmeyers These über das paulinische Briefpräscript kritisch beleuchtet." *TLZ* 81 (1956): 158–64.

Furnish, V. P. "Elect Sojourners in Christ: An Approach to the Theology of 1 Peter." *PSTJ* 28 (1975): 1–11.

Gamble, Harry. "The Redaction of the Pauline Letters and the Formation of the Pauline Corpus." *JBL* 94 (1971): 403–18.

Gerhardsson, Birger. *The Testing of God's Son (Matt 4:1–11 & Par): An Analysis of an Early Christian Midrash.* ConBNT 2/1. Lund: Gleerup, 1966.

Gibson, Craig A., trans. and ed. *Libanius's "Progymnasmata": Model Exercises in Greek Prose Composition and Rhetoric.* Writings from the Greco-Roman World 27. Atlanta: Society of Biblical Literature, 2008.

Gilmour, Michael J. *The Significance of Parallels between 2 Peter and Other Early Christian Literature.* Academica Biblica 10. Atlanta: Society of Biblical Literature, 2002.

Goldstein, H. "Die politischen Paraenesen in 1 Petr. 2 und Röm. 13." *BibLeb* 14 (1973): 88–104.

Goppelt, L. *Der erste Petrusbrief.* KEK 12. Ed. F. Hahn. Göttingen: Vandenhoeck & Ruprecht, 1978.

Green, E. M. B. *2 Peter Reconsidered.* London: Tyndale, 1960.

———. *The Second Epistle of Peter and the Epistle of Jude.* TNTC. Grand Rapids: Eerdmans, 1968.

Green, Gene L. *Jude and 2 Peter.* BECNT. Grand Rapids: Baker, 2008.

Green, Joel B. *1 Peter.* THNTC. Grand Rapids: Eerdmans, 2007.

Gross, Carl D. "Are the Wives of 1 Pet 3:7 Christian?" *JSNT* 35 (1989): 89–96.

Gross, J. *La divinisation du chrétien d'après les pères grecs.* Paris: Gabalda, 1938.

Grudem, Wayne. *1 Peter.* TNTC. Grand Rapids: Eerdmans, 1988.

Grundmann, Walter. *Der Brief des Judas und der zweite Brief des Petrus.* Berlin: Evangelische Verlagsanstalt, 1974.

Guelich, Robert A. *The Sermon on the Mount: A Foundation for Understanding.* Waco, TX: Word, 1982.

Gundry, R. H. "Further 'Verba' on 'Verba Christi' in First Peter." *Bib* 55 (1974): 211–32.

———. "'Verba Christi' in I Peter: Their Implications Concerning the Authorship of I Peter and the Authenticity of the Gospel Tradition." *NTS* 13 (1966–1967): 336–50.

Gunther, John J. "The Alexandrian Epistle of Jude." *NTS* 30 (1984): 549–62.

Haaker, Klaus. "Justification, salut et foi: Étude sur les rapports entre Paul, Jacques et Pierre." *ETR* 73 (1998): 177–88.

Haaker, Klaus, and P. Schäfer. "Nachbiblische Traditionen vom Tod des Mose." Pp. 147–74 in *Josephus-Studien: Untersuchungen zu Josephus, dem antiken Judentum und dem Neuen Testament; Otto Michel zum 70. Geburtstag gewidmet.* Ed. O. Betz, K. Haaker, and M. Hengel. Götteningen: Vandenhoeck & Ruprecht, 1974.

Hamilton, Edith. *Mythology.* New York: New American Library, 1942.

Harris, Murray J. *Slave of Christ: A New Testament Metaphor for Total Devotion to Christ.* NSBT 8. Downers Grove, IL/Leicester, UK: InterVarsity/Apollos, 2001.

Harris, William V. *Restraining Rage: The Ideology of Anger Control in Classical Antiquity.* Cambridge, MA: Harvard University Press, 2001.

Hartin, Patrick J. *James of Jerusalem: Heir to Jesus of Nazareth.* Interfaces. Collegeville, MN: Liturgical, 2004.

———. *James and the Q Sayings of Jesus.* JSNTSup 47. Sheffield: JSOT, 1991.

Helyer, Larry R. *The Life and Witness of Peter.* Downers Grove, IL: InterVarsity Press, 2012.

Hengel, Martin. *Der unterschätzte Petrus: Zwei Studien.* Tübingen: Mohr-Siebeck, 2006.

Hennecke, Edgar. *New Testament Apocrypha.* Ed. Wilhelm Schneemelcher. Trans. R. McL. Wilson. 2 vols. London: Lutherworth/SCM, 1963, 1965.

Hiebert, D. Edmond. "Selected Studies from Jude. Part 2: An Exposition of Jude 12–16." *BSac* 142 (1985): 245–49.

———. "Selected Studies from Jude. Part 3: An Exposition of Jude 17–23." *BSac* 142 (1985): 355–66.

Hill, D. "On Suffering and Baptism in 1 Peter." *NovT* 18 (1976): 181–89.

Hillyer, Norman. *1 and 2 Peter, Jude.* NIBC. Peabody, MA: Hendrickson, 1992.

Holdsworth, J. "The Sufferings in 1 Peter and 'Missionary Apocalyptic.'" Pp. 225–32 in *Studia Biblica* 3. Ed. E. A. Livingstone. Sheffield: JSOT, 1980.

Holladay, Carl R. *Theios Aner in Hellenistic Judaism.* SBLDS 40. Missoula, MT: Scholars Press, 1977.

Holtzmann, O. "Die Petrusbriefe." In *Das Neue Testament nach dem Stuttgarter griechischen Text übersetzt und erklärt.* Vol. 2. Giessen: Töpelmann, 1926.

Hornblower, Simon, and Antony Spawforth. *The Oxford Companion to Classical Civilization.* Oxford: Oxford University Press, 1998.

Horrell, David G. *1 Peter.* New Testament Guides. London/New York: T&T Clark, 2008.

———. "'Race,' 'Nation,' 'People': Ethnic Identity-Construction in 1 Peter 2.9." *NTS* 58 (2012): 123–43.

Hort, F. J. A. *The Epistle of St. James.* London: Macmillan, 1909.

Hunter, Archibald M. *Paul and His Predecessors*. London: SCM, 1961.

Hurtado, Larry W. *At the Origins of Christian Worship*. Grand Rapids: Eerdmans, 1999.

———. *How on Earth Did Jesus Become a God?* Grand Rapids: Eerdmans, 2005.

Huther, J. E. *Kritisch-exegetisches Handbuch über den 1. Brief des Petrus, den Brief des Judas und den 2. Brief des Petrus*. 4th ed. KEK 12. Göttingen: Vandenhoeck & Ruprecht, 1877. Trans. D. B. Croom and P. J. Gloab. *Critical and Exegetical Handbook to the General Epistles of Peter and Jude*. ICC. Edinburgh: T&T Clark, 1881.

Isenberg, Sheldon R. "Anti-Sadducee Polemic in the Palestinian Targum Tradition." *HTR* 63 (1970): 433–44.

Jackson, Howard M. "Ancient Self-Referential Conventions and Their Implications for the Authorship and Integrity of the Gospel of John." *JTS*, ns 8 (1999): 1–34.

James, M. R. *The Second Epistle General of Peter and the Epistle of Jude*. CGTSC. Cambridge: Cambridge University Press, 1912.

Jastrow, Marcus. *A Dictionary of the Targumim, The Talmud Babli and Yerushalami, and the Midreashic Literature*. New York: Judaica Press, 1975.

Jeffers, James S. *The Greco-Roman World of the New Testament*. Downers Grove, IL: InterVarsity Press, 1999.

Jeremias, Joachim. "Abba." Pp. 11–65 in *The Prayers of Jesus*. SBT 2/6. London: SCM, 1967.

———. "Isolated Sayings of the Lord." Pp. 85–90 in Hennecke, *NT Apocrypha*, vol. 1.

———. *Unknown Sayings of Jesus*. Trans. R. H. Fuller. London: SPCK, 1957.

Jobes, Karen H. *1 Peter*. BECNT. Grand Rapids: Baker Academic, 2005.

———. "The Syntax of 1 Peter: Just How Good Is the Greek?" *BBR* 13 (2003): 159–73.

Johnson, Luke Timothy. *Brother of Jesus, Friend of God: Studies in the Letter of James*. Grand Rapids: Eerdmans, 2004.

———. *The Letter of James*. AB 37A. New York: Doubleday, 1995.

Jonsen, A. R. "The Moral Teaching of the First Epistle of St. Peter." *ScEccl* 16 (1964): 93–105.

Josephus, Flavius. *The Works of Josephus*. Oak Harbor, WA: Logos Research Systems, Inc., 1997.

Kamlah, E. *Die Form der katalogischen Paräenese im Neuen Testament*. Tübingen: Mohr, 1964.

Käsemann, Ernst. "An Apologia for Primitive Christian Eschatology." Pp. 169–95 in *Essays on New Testament Themes*. Trans. W. J. Montague. SBT 41. London: SCM, 1964. = "Apologie der urchristlichen Eschatologie." Pp. 135–57 in *Exegetische Versuche und Besinnungen I*. Göttingen: Vandenhoeck & Ruprecht, 1960.

Kee, Howard Clark. "The Terminology of Mark's Exorcism Stories." *NTS* 14 (1968): 232–46.

———. "The Transfiguration in Mark: Epiphany or Apocalyptic Vision?" Pp. 137–52 in *Understanding the Sacred Text*: *Festschrift for M. S. Enslin*. Ed. John Reumann. Valley Forge, PA: Judson, 1972.

Kellett, E. E. "Note on Jude 5." *ExpTim* 15 (1903–1904): 381.

Kelly, J. N. D. *The Epistles of Peter and of Jude*. BNTC. London: Adam & Charles Black, 1969.

Kennedy, George A., trans. and ed. *"Progymnasmata": Greek Textbooks of Prose Composition and Rhetoric*. Writings from the Greco-Roman World 10. Atlanta: Society of Biblical Literature, 2003.

Kirk, J. A. "The Meaning of Wisdom in James." *NTS* 16 (1969): 24–38.

Klijn, Albertus K. J. "Jude 5–7." Pp. 237–44 in *The New Testament Age: Essays in Honor of Bo Reicke*. Ed. William C. Weinrich. Vol. 1. Macon, GA: Mercer University Press, 1984.

Kloppenborg. John S. "Reception and Emulation of the Jesus Tradition in James." Pp. 121–50 in *Reading James with New Eyes: Methodological Reassessments of the Letter of James*. Ed. Robert L. Webb and John S. Kloppenborg. LNTS 342. New York: T&T Clark, 2007.

Knox, W. L. "The Epistle of St. James." *JTS* 46 (1945): 10–17.

Koester, Helmut. *Introduction to the New Testament*. Vol. 2: *History and Literature of Early Christianity*. Philadelphia: Fortress, 1982.

Kraftchick, Steven J. *Jude, 2 Peter*. ANTC. Nashville: Abingdon, 2002.

Kraus, Thomas J. *Sprache, Stil und historischer Ort des zweiten Petrusbriefes*. WUNT 2/136. Tübingen: Mohr Siebeck, 2001.

Krodel, Gerhard. "Jude." Pp. 94–109 in *The General Letters*. Ed. Gerhard Krodel. Proclamation. Minneapolis: Fortress, 1995.

Kubo, Sakae. "Jude 22–23: Two-Division Form or Three?" Pp. 239–53 in *New Testament Text Criticism: Its Significance for Exegesis*. Ed. E. J. Epp and G. D. Fee. Oxford: Clarendon, 1981.

Ladd, George Eldon. *A Theology of the New Testament*. Grand Rapids: Eerdmans, 1993².

Landon, Charles. *A Text-Critical Study of the Epistle of Jude*. JSNTSup 135. Sheffield: Sheffield Academic, 1996.

Lapham, F. *Peter: The Myth, the Man and the Writings; A Study of Early Petrine Text and Tradition*. JSNTSup 239. Sheffield: Sheffield Academic, 2003.

Laws, Sophie. *The Epistle of James*. HNTC. New York: Harper & Row, 1980.

Lightfoot, Joseph B. *The Apostolic Fathers*. London: Macmillan, 1890.

Loewenstamm, Samuel E. "The Death of Moses." Pp. 185–217 in *Studies on the Testament of Abraham*. Ed. G. W. E. Nickelsburg. SBLSCS 6. Missoula, MT: Scholars Press, 1976.

Lohmeyer, Ernst. "Probleme paulinischer Theologie: I. Briefliche Grussüberschriften." *ZNW* 26 (1927): 158–73.

Louw, Johannes P., and Eugene A. Nida. *Greek-English Lexicon of the New Testament Based on Semantic Domains*. New York: United Bible Societies, 1988, 1989.

Lövestam, Evald. *Son and Saviour: A Study of Acts 13, 32–37*. ConBNT 18. Lund: Gleerup / Copenhagen: E. Munksgaard, 1961.

Lucas, Dick, and Christopher Green. *The Message of 2 Peter and Jude: The Promise of His Coming*. TBST. Leicester, UK/Downers Grove, IL: Inter-Varsity, 1995.

Magass, Walter. "Semiotik eine Ketzerpolemik am Beispiel von Judas 12f." *Linguistica Biblica* 19 (1972): 36–47.

Maher, Michael, trans. and ed. *Targum Pseudo-Jonathan: Genesi*. In *The Aramaic Bible*, vol. 1B. Collegeville, MN: Liturgical, 1992.

Maier, Friedrich. "Zur Erklärung des Judasbriefes (Jud 5)." *BZ* 2 (1904): 391–97.

Malina, Bruce J. "Christ and Time: Swiss or Mediterranean?" *CBQ* 51 (1989): 1–31.

Marín, F. "Apostolícidad de los escritos neotestamentarios." *EstEcl* 50 (1975): 226.

Marshall, I. Howard. *Last Supper and Lord's Supper*. Exeter: Paternoster, 1980.

Martin, Ralph P. *James*. WBC 48. Waco, TX: Word, 1988.

Martin, Ralph P., and Peter H. Davids, eds. *Dictionary of the Later New Testament and Its Developments*. Downers Grove, IL: InterVarsity Press, 1997. = *DLNT*

Martin, Troy W. *Metaphor and Composition in 1 Peter*. SBLDS 131. Atlanta: Scholars Press, 1992.

———. "The *TestAbr* and the Background of 1 Pet 3:6." *ZAW* 90 (1999): 139–46.

Martínez, Florentino García. *The Dead Sea Scrolls Translated: The Qumran Texts in English*. Trans. Wilfred G. E. Watson. Leiden: Brill, 1994.

Mason, Eric F., and Troy W. Martin, eds. *Reading 1–2 Peter and Jude: A Resource for Students*. Resources for Biblical Study 77. Atlanta: Society of Biblical Literature, 2014.

Mayor, Joseph B. *The Epistles of Jude and II Peter*. Grand Rapids: Baker, (1901) 1979.

———. *The Epistle of St. James: The Greek Text with Introduction, Notes and Comments, and Further Studies in the Epistle of St. James*. London: Macmillan, 1913.

McCartney, Dan G. *James*. BECNT. Grand Rapids: Baker Academic, 2009.

McKnight, Scot. *The Letter of James*. NICNT. Grand Rapids: Eerdmans, 2011.

McNamara, Martin. *The New Testament and the Palestinian Targum to the Pentateuch*. AnBib 27. Rome: Pontifical Biblical Institute, 1966.

———. "The Unity of Second Peter: A Reconsideration." *Scr* 12 (1960): 13–19.

———, trans. and ed. *Targum Neofiti 1: Genesis*. In *The Aramaic Bible*, vol. 1A. Collegeville, MN: Liturgical, 1992.

McRae, G. W. "Why the Church Rejected Gnosticism." Pp. 128–30 in *Jewish and Christian Self-Definition*. Ed. E. P. Sanders. Vol. 1. London: SCM, 1980.

Mees, Michael. "Papyrus Bodmer VII ($\mathfrak{P}^{72}$) und die Zitate aus den Judasbrief bei Clemens von Alexandrien." *Ciudad de Dios* 181 (1968): 551–59.

Meier, Sam. "2 Peter 3:3–7: An Early Jewish and Christian Response to Eschatological Scepticism." *BZ* 32 (1988): 255–57.

Metzger, Bruce M. *A Textual Commentary on the Greek New Testament*. New York: United Bible Societies, 1971.

Metzner, Rainer. *Die Rezeption des Matthäusevangeliums im 1. Petrusbrief*. Vol. 74. Tübingen: Mohr, 1995.

Meyer, Arnold. *Das Rätsel des Jakobusbriefes*. Giessen: Töpelmann, 1930.

Michaels, J. Ramsay. *1 Peter*. WBC 49. Waco, TX: Word, 1988.

———. "1 Peter." *DLNT*, 914–23.

———. "Eschatology in I Peter III.17." *NTS* 13 (1966–1967): 394–401.

———. "Jewish and Christian Apocalyptic Letters: 1 Peter, Revelation, and 2 Baruch 78–87." *SBL Seminar Papers* 26 (Atlanta: Scholars Press, 1987): 268–75.

Millard, Alan Ralph. *Reading and Writing in the Time of Jesus*. Biblical Seminar 69. Sheffield: Sheffield Academic, 2000.

Millauer, H. *Leiden als Gnade: Eine traditionsgeschichtliche Untersuchung zur Leidenstheologie des ersten Petrusbriefes*. Bern: H. Lang, 1976.

Milligan, G. "2 Peter III. 10." *ExpTim* 32 (1920–1921): 331.

Moffatt, James. *The General Epistles: James, Peter and Judas*. MNTC. London: Hodder & Stoughton, 1928.

Molland, Einar. "La thèse 'La prophétie n'est jamais venue de la volonté de l'homme' (2 Pierre I, 21) et les Pseudo-Clémentines." Pp. 64–77 in *Opuscula Patristiuca*. BTN 2. Oslo: Universitetsforlaget, 1970. = *ST* 9 (1955): 67–85.

Moulton, James H., Wilbert F. Howard, and Nigel Turner. *A Grammar of New Testament Greek*. Edinburgh: T&T Clark, 1919–1976.

Mowry, Mary Lucetta. "The Early Circulation of Paul's Letters." *JBL* 63 (1944): 73–86.

Mussner, Franz. *Der Jakobusbrief*. HTKNT. Freiberg: Herder, 1964, 1967.

Nauck, W. "Freude im Leiden: Zum Problem einer urchristlichen Verfolgungstradition." *ZNW* 46 (1955): 68–80.

Neusner, Jacob. *The Mishnah: A New Translation*. New Haven, CT: Yale University Press, 1988.

Neyrey, Jerome H. *2 Peter, Jude: A New Translation with Introduction and Commentary*. AB 37C. New York: Doubleday, 1993.

———. "The Apologetic Use of the Transfiguration in 2 Peter 1:16–21." *CBQ* 42 (1980): 504–19.

———. "The Form and Background of the Polemic in 2 Peter." Unpublished PhD dissertation, Yale University, 1977.

———. "The Form and Background of the Polemic in 2 Peter." *JBL* 99 (1980): 407–31.

Niebuhr, Karl-Wilhelm. "Der jakobusbrief im Licht frühjüdischer Diasporabriefe." *NTS* 44 (1998): 420–24.

Niebuhr, Karl-Wilhelm, and Robert W. Wall, eds. *The Catholic Epistles and Apostolic Tradition: A New Perspective on James to Jude.* Waco, TX: Baylor University Press, 2009.

Nienhuis, David R. *Not by Paul Alone: The Formation of the Catholic Epistle Collection and the Christian Canon.* Waco, TX: Baylor University Press, 2007.

Oleson, John P. "An Echo of Hesiod's *Theogony* vv. 190–92 in Jude 13." *NTS* 25 (1979): 492–503.

Osburn, Carroll D. "The Christological Use of I Enoch I.9 in Jude 14–15." *NTS* 23 (1977): 334–41.

———. "The Text of Jude 22–23." *ZNW* 63 (1972): 139–44.

———. "The Text of Jude 5." *Bib* 62 (1981): 107–15.

Osiek, Carolyn. *The Shepherd of Hermas: A Commentary.* Hermeneia. Ed. Helmut Koester. Minneapolis: Fortress, 1999.

Pagels, Elaine H. *The Gnostic Paul: Gnostic Exegesis of the Pauline Letters.* Philadelphia: Fortress, 1975.

Painter, John. *Just James: The Brother of Jesus in History and Tradition.* Minneapolis: Fortress, 1999.

Painter, John, and David A. deSilva. *James and Jude.* Paideia. Grand Rapids: Baker Academic, 2012.

Pearson, B. A. *The Pneumatikos-Psychikos Terminology in 1 Corinthians.* SBLDS 12. Missoula, MT: Scholars Press, 1973.

Perkins, Pheme. *First and Second Peter, James, and Jude.* Interpretation. Louisville: Westminster John Knox, 1995.

———. *Peter: Apostle for the Whole Church.* Minneapolis: Fortress, 2000.

Pfitzner, Victor C. *Paul and the Agōn Motif: Traditional Imagery in the Pauline Literature.* NovTSup 16. Leiden: Brill, 1967.

Philo Judaeus. *The Works of Philo.* Oak Harbor, WA: Logos Research Systems, 1997.

Picirelli, Robert E. "The Meaning of 'Epignosis.'" *EvQ* 47 (1975): 85–93.

Pilch, John J., and Bruce J. Malina, eds. *Biblical Social Values and Their Meaning.* Peabody, MA: Hendrickson, 1993.

Piper, John. "Hope as the Motivation of Love: 1 Peter 3:9–12." *NTS* 26 (1980): 212–31.

Plumptre, Edward Hayes. *The General Epistles of St. Peter and St. Jude.* CBSC. Cambridge: Cambridge University Press, 1892.

Popkes, Wiard. *Der Brief des Jakobus.* THKNT 14. Leipzig: Evangelische Verlagsanstalt, 2001.

Raphael, Lawrence W. "The Teaching of Writing an Ethical Will." *Judaism* 48 (1999): 174–80.

Reese, Ruth Anne. *2 Peter and Jude.* THNTC. Grand Rapids: Eerdmans, 2007.

———. *Writing Jude: The Reader, the Text and the Author in Constructs of Power and Desire.* BIS 51. Leiden: Brill, 2000.

Reicke, Bo Ivar. *Diakonie, Festfreude und Zelos.* UUÅ. Uppsala: Lundequistska, 1951.

————. *The Epistles of James, Peter, and Jude*. AB 37. Garden City, NY: Doubleday, 1964.

Reimer, Andy M. "In the Beginning . . . Lessons Learned in Teaching Genesis 1 to Evangelical College Students." *Canadian Evangelical Review* 29 (2005): 32–44.

Richards, E. Randolph. *Paul and First-Century Letter Writing: Secretaries, Composition and Collection*. Downers Grove, IL: InterVarsity Press, 2004.

————. "Silvanus Was Not Peter's Secretary: Theological Bias in Interpreting διὰ Σιλουανοῦ ἔγραψα in 1 Pet 5:12." *JETS* 43 (2000): 417–32.

Richardson, R. L., Jr. "From 'Subjection to Authority' to 'Mutual Submission': The Ethic of Subordination in 1 Peter." *Faith & Mission* 4 (1987): 70–80.

Ridderbos, Herman. *Paul: An Outline of His Theology*. Grand Rapids: Eerdmans, 1975.

Riemer, Jack, and Nathaniel Stampfer. *Ethical Wills: A Modern Jewish Treasury*. New York: Schocken, 1983.

Riesner, Rainer. "Der zweite Petrus-Brief und die Eschatologie." Pp. 124–43 in *Zukunftserwartung in biblischer Sicht: Beitrage zur Eschatologie*. Ed. Gerhard Maier. Wuppertal: Brockhaus, 1984.

Roberts, J. W. "A Note on the Meaning of II Peter 3:10d." *ResQ* 6 (1962): 32–33.

Robinson, James M., Paul Hoffmann, and John S. Kloppenborg, eds. *The Critical Edition of Q*. Leuven: Peeters, 2000.

Ropes, James Hardy. *A Critical and Exegetical Commentary on the Epistle of St. James*. ICC. New York: C. Scribner's Sons, 1916.

Ross, John M. "Church Discipline in Jude 22–23." *ExpTim* 100 (1989): 297–98.

Sanders, Jack T. *Ethics in the New Testament*. Philadelphia: Fortress, 1975.

Scaggs, Rebecca. *The Pentecostal Commentary on 1 Peter, 2 Peter, Jude*. Cleveland, TN: Pilgrim, 2004.

Schaff, Philip. *The Ante-Nicene Fathers*. Electronic ed. Garland, TX: Galaxie Software, 2000.

Schattenmann, J. "The Little Apocalypse of the Synoptics and the First Epistle of Peter." *ThTo* 11 (1954–1955): 193–98.

Schelkle, Karl Hermann. "Das Leiden des Gottesknechtes als Form christlichen Lebens (nach dem 1. Petrusbrief)." *Bib* 16 (1961): 14–16.

————. *Die Petrusbriefe, der Judasbrief*. HTKNT 12/2. Freiburg: Herder, 1980[5].

Schlatter, Adolf. *Der Brief des Jakobus*. Stuttgart: Calwer, 1932.

Schlosser, Jacques. "Les jours de Noé et de Lot: A propos de Luc, XVII, 26–30." *RB* 80 (1973) : 13–36.

Schmitals, Walter. "Zur Abfassung und ältesten Sammlung der paulinischen Hauptbriefe." *ZNW* 51 (1960): 225–45.

Schnabel, Eckhard J. "Paul, Timothy, and Titus: The Assumption of a Pseudonymous Author and of Pseudonymous Recipients in the Light of Literary, Theological, and Historical Evidence." Pp. 383–403 in *Do Historical Matters Matter to Faith? A Critical Appraisal of Modern and Postmodern Approaches to Scripture*. Ed. James K. Hoffmeier and Dennis R. Magary. Wheaton, IL: Crossway, 2012.

Schrage, Wolfgang. "Zur Ethik der neutestamentlichen Haustafeln." *NTS* 21 (1974–75): 1–22.

————. *Der zweite Petrusbrief. Der Judasbrief*. In *Die "Katholische" Briefe: Die Briefe des Jakobus, Petrus, Johannes und Judas, übersetzt und erklärt*. Ed. Host R. Balz and Wolfgang Schrage. NTD 10; Göttingen: Vandenhoeck & Ruprecht, 1973[11].

Schreiner, Thomas R. *1, 2 Peter, Jude*. NAC 37. Nashville: Broadman & Holman, 2003.

Schultheiss, Tanja. *Das Petrusbild im Johannesevangelium.* WUNT 2/329. Tübingen: Mohr-Siebeck, 2012.

Schutter, W. L. *Hermeneutic and Composition in First Peter.* WUNT 2/30. Tübingen: Mohr-Siebeck, 1989.

Schwank, B. "Wir Freie—aber als Sklaven Gottes (1 Petr. 2:16): Das Verhältnis der Christen zur Staatsmacht nach dem ersten Petrusbrief." *ErbAuf* 36 (1960): 5–12.

Seitz, O. J. F. "Two Spirits in Man: An Essay in Biblical Exegesis." *NTS* 6 (1959): 82–95.

Sellin, Gerhard. "Die Häretiker des Judasbriefes." *ZNW* 77 (1986): 206–25.

Selwyn, Edward Gordon. *The First Epistle of St. Peter.* New York: Macmillan, 1946², 1969.

———. "The Persecutions in I Peter." *Bulletin of the Society for New Testament Studies* 1 (1950): 39–50.

Senior, D. "The Conduct of Christians in the World (1 Pet. 2:11–3:12)." *RevExp* 79 (1982): 427–38.

Sevenster, J. N. *Do You Know Greek?* NovTSup 19. Leiden: Brill, 1968.

Sibinga, J. Smit. "Une citation du Cantique dans la Secunda Petri." *RB* 73 (1966): 107–18.

Sickenberger, Joseph. "Engels- oder Teufelslästerer im Judasbrief (8–10) und im 2. Petrus-briefe (2, 10–12)?" Pp. 621–39 in *Festschrift zu Jahrhundertfeier der Universität zu Breslau.* Ed. T. Siebs. MSGVK 13–14 (1911–1912).

Sidebottom, E. M. *James, Jude and 2 Peter.* NCB. London: Nelson, 1967.

Sleeper, C. F. "Political Responsibility according to 1 Peter." *NovT* 10 (1968): 270–86.

Sly, Dorothy I. "I Peter 3:6b in the Light of Philo and Josephus." *JBL* 110 (1991): 126–29.

Smit, Peter-Ben. "A Symposiastic Background to James?" *NTS* 58 (2012): 105–22.

Smith, Ralph L. *Micah-Malachi.* WBC 32. Dallas: Word, 1984.

Smith, Terence V. *Petrine Controversies in Early Christianity: Attitudes towards Peter in Christian Writings of the First Two Centuries.* WUNT 2/15. Tübingen: J. C. B. Mohr, 1985.

Snyder, Graydon F. "The *Tobspruch* in the New Testament." *NTS* 23 (1976–1977): 117–20.

Snyder, John I. *The Promise of His Coming: The Eschatology of 2 Peter.* San Mateo, CA: Western, 1986.

Spicq, Ceslas. *Les Épîtres de Saint Pierre.* SB. Paris: Gabalda, 1966.

Spitta, Friedrich. *Der Brief des Jakobus untersucht.* Göttingen: Vandenhoeck & Ruprecht, 1896.

———. "Das Testaments Hiobs und das Neue Testament." Pp. 139–206 in *Zur Geschichte und Literatur des Urchristentums,* III/2 Göttingen: Vandenhoeck & Ruprecht, 1907.

———. *Die zweite Brief des Petrus und der Brief des Judas.* Halle a. S.: Waisenhauses, 1885.

Stein, Hans Joachim. *Frühchristliche Mahlfeiern.* WUNT 2/255. Tübingen: Mohr Siebeck, 2008.

Stendahl, Krister. *Paul among Jews and Gentiles.* Philadelphia: Fortress, 1976.

Steuernagel, V. "An Exiled Community as a Mission Community: A Study Based on 1 Peter 2:9, 10." *Evangelical Review of Theology* 10 (1986): 8–18.

Strobel, August. *Untersuchungen zum eschatologischen Verzögerungsproblem auf Grund der spätjüdisch-urchristlichen Geschichte von Habakuk 2,2 ff.* NovTSup 2. Leiden: Brill, 1961.

Sylva, D. "The Critical Exploration of 1 Peter." Pp. 17–36 in *Perspectives on First Peter.* Ed. C. H. Talbert. Macon, GA: Mercer University Press, 1986.

Talbert, C. H., ed. *Perspectives on First Peter.* Macon, GA: Mercer University Press, 1986.

Taylor, Vincent. "Does the New Testament Call Jesus 'God'?" Pp. 83–89 in *New Testament Essays.* London: Epworth, 1970.

Thiede, Carson Peter. "A Pagan Reader of 2 Peter: Cosmic Conflagration in 2 Peter 3 and the *Octavius* of Minucius Felix." *JSNT* 26 (1986): 79–96.

Thomas, J. J. "Anfechtung und Vorfreude: Ein biblisches Thema nach Jakobus 1:2–18, im Zusammenhang mit Ps 126, Röm 5:3–5 und 1 Petr 1:5–7, formkritisch untersucht und parakletisch ausgelegt." *KD* 14 (1968): 183–206.

Thompson, J. W. " 'Be Submissive to your Masters': A Study of 1 Pt 2:18–25." *ResQ* 9 (1966): 66–78.

Thurén, Lauri. *Argument and Theology in 1 Peter: The Origins of Christian Paraenesis.* SBLDS 114. Atlanta: Scholars Press, 1995.

———. "The General New Testament Writings." Pp. 587–607 in *Handbook of Classical Rhetoric in the Hellenistic Period, 330 B.C.–A.D. 400.* Ed Stanley E. Porter. Leiden: Brill, 2001.

———. "The Relationship between 2 Peter and Jude: A Classical Problem Resolved?" Pp. 451–60 in *The Catholic Epistles and the Tradition.* Ed. Jacques Schlosser. BETL 176. Leuven: Peeters, 2004.

———. *The Rhetorical Strategy of 1 Peter.* Åbo: Åbo Academy Press, 1990.

Townsend, Michael J. "Exit the Agape?" *ExpTim* 90 (1978–1979): 356–71.

Utley, Bob. *The Gospel according to Peter: Mark and I and II Peter.* Study Guide Commentary Series, NT 2. Marshall, TX: Bible Lessons International, 2000.

van der Horst, Pieter W. *The Sentences of Pseudo-Phocylides.* SVTP 4. Leiden: Brill, 1978.

van Unnik, W. C. "The Teaching of Good Works in I Peter." *NTS* 1 (1954–1955): 92–110.

Vermes, Geza. "The Targumic Versions of Gen 4:3–16." Pp. 96–100 in *Post-Biblical Jewish Studies.* Leiden: Brill, 1975.

Villiers, J. L. de. "Joy in Suffering in 1 Peter." *Neot* 9 (1975): 64–86.

Vögtle, Anton. *Der Judasbrief. Der 2. Petrusbrief.* EKKNT 22. Neukirchen-Vluyn: Neukirchener, 1994.

———. *Das Neue Testament und die Zukunft des Kosmos.* Düsseldorf: Patmos, 1970.

Volkmar, G. "Über die katholischen Briefe und Henoch." *ZWT* 4 (1961): 422–36.

von Allmen, Daniel. "L'apocalyptique juive et le retard de la parousie en II Pierre 3:1–13." *RTP* 16 (1966): 255–74.

Wall, Robert W. "The Canonical Function of 2 Peter." *BibInt* 9.1 (2001) 64–81.

———. *Community of the Wise: The Letter of James.* The New Testament in Context. Valley Forge, PA: Trinity Press International, 1997.

Wall, Robert W., and David R. Nienhuis. *Reading the Epistles of James, Peter, John, and Jude as Scripture.* Grand Rapids: Eerdmans, 2013.

Wallace, Daniel B. *Greek Grammar beyond the Basics: An Exegetical Syntax of the Greek New Testament.* Grand Rapids: Zondervan, 1996. Electronic ed. Garland, TX: Galaxie Software, 1999.

Ward, Roy Bowen. "Partiality in the Assembly: James 2:2–4." *HTR* 62 (1969): 87–97.

———. "The Works of Abraham: James 2:14–26." *HTR* 61 (1968): 283–90.

Watson, Duane Frederick. *Invention, Arrangement, and Style: Rhetorical Criticism of Jude and 2 Peter.* SBLDS 104. Atlanta: Scholars Press, 1988.

Watson, Duane Frederick, and Terrance Callan. *First and Second Peter.* Paideia. Grand Rapids: Baker Academic, 2012.

Webb, R. L. "The Apocalyptic Perspective of First Peter." Unpublished ThM thesis. Regent College, Vancouver, BC, 1986.

Webb, Robert L., and Betsy Bauman-Martin, eds. *Reading First Peter with New Eyes: Meth-*

odological Reassessments of the Letter of First Peter. LNTS 364. London/New York: T&T Clark, 2007.

Webb, Robert L., and John S. Kloppenborg, eds. *Reading James with New Eyes: Methodological Reassessments of the Letter of James.* LNTS. London/New York: T&T Clark International, 2007.

Wenham, David. "Being 'Found' on the Last Day: New Light on 2 Peter 3.10 and 2 Corinthians 5.3." *NTS* 33 (1989): 477–79.

Werdermann, Hermann. *Die Irrlehrer des Judas- und 2. Petrusbriefes.* BFCT 17/6. Gütersloh: Bertelsmann, 1913.

Wessel, W. W. "An Inquiry into the Origin, Literary Character, Historical and Religious Significance of the Epistle of James." Unpublished PhD dissertation, Edinburgh, 1953.

Whallon, William. "Should We Keep, Omit, or Alter the *hoi* in Jude 12?" *NTS* 34 (1988): 56–59.

Whitaker, G. H. "Faith's Function in St Jude's Epistle." *ExpTim* 29 (1917–1918): 425.

White, John L. *The Form and Function of the Body of the Greek Letter.* Missoula, MT: Scholars Press, 1972[2].

Wibbing, S. *Die Tugend- und Lästerkataloge im Neuen Testament.* BZNW 25. Berlin: Töpelmann, 1959.

Wikgren, Allen P. "Some Problems in Jude 5." Pp. 147–52 in *Studies in the History and Text of the New Testament in honor of Kenneth Willis Clark.* Ed. B. L. Daniels and M. Jack Suggs. Studies and Documents 29. Salt Lake City: University of Utah Press, 1967.

Wilson, W. E. "*Heurethēsetai* in 2 Pet. iii. 10." *ExpTim* 32 (1920–1921): 44–45.

Windisch, Hans. *Die katholischen Briefe.* HNT 15. Tübingen: Mohr Siebeck, 1930.

Witherington, Ben, III. *Letters and Homilies for Hellenized Christians II: A Socio-Rhetorical Commentary on 1–2 Peter.* Downers Grove, IL: InterVarsity Press, 2007.

———. *Letters and Homilies for Jewish Christians: A Socio-Rhetorical Commentary on Hebrews, James, and Jude.* Downers Grove, IL: InterVarsity Press, 2007.

———. "Not So Idle Thoughts about *eidōlothyton*." *TynBul* 44 (1993): 237–54.

Wolters, Al. "'Partners of the Deity': A Covenantal Reading of 2 Peter 1:4." *CTJ* 25 (1990): 28–44.

———. "Postscript to 'Partners of the Deity.'" *CTJ* 26 (1991): 418–20.

———. "Worldview and Textual Criticism in 2 Peter 3:10." *WTJ* 49 (1987): 405–13.

Workman, Herbert B. *Persecution in the Early Church.* Oxford/New York: Oxford University Press, 1980.

Wright, N. T. *Justification: God's Plan and Paul's Vision.* Downers Grove, IL: InterVarsity Press 2009.

———. *Simply Christian: Why Christianity Makes Sense.* New York: HarperOne, 2006.

Zahn, Theodor. *Introduction to the New Testament.* New York: Scribners, 1909.

Scripture and Apocrypha Index

INDEX OF CLASSICAL AND JEWISH SOURCES

SUBJECT INDEX

Author Index